Harold H. Alexander

UNIVERSITY OF ILLINOIS

Design

Criteria for Decisions

Macmillan Publishing Co., Inc.
New York

Collier Macmillan Publishers
London

Macmillan Publishing Co., Inc.
866 Third Avenue, New York, New York 10022

Collier Macmillan Canada, Ltd.

Library of Congress Cataloging in Publication Data

Alexander, Harold H
    Design: criteria for decisions.

    Includes index.
    1. Design.   I. Title.
NK1510.A57   745.4   75-9697
ISBN 0-02-301660-4

Printing: 1 2 3 4 5 6 7 8   Year: 6 7 8 9 0 1 2

To Marge and our children

Preface

My primary concern in the development of this book has been to identify and investigate the information and criteria used when making environmental decisions—decisions relating the planning and selection of the spaces, structures, and objects that intimately surround our bodies to the larger considerations of the environment. My intention, however, is not to give simple answers, as there are no *simple* answers in environmental design, but rather to offer pertinent information to aid in the process of forming valid decisions.

The premise that a decision is the sum of *all* of its components is undoubtedly true and a decision concerned with the environment is no exception. Since it is also evident that there continually exists a myriad of components for consideration, it is necessary to select the most important factors and to adjust, increase, or decrease their significance until a satisfactory balance is achieved.

I too had to judge and establish priorities for the kind of information to include in this book which would best serve the reader. Consequently the fundamentals of design (form, space, line, texture, color, balance, continuity, and emphasis) are discussed first. These aesthetic, but often functional, fundamentals are the basis of most decisions concerning our environment, even though they may be consciously or subconsciously utilized by the individual. The concept of the *total* environment is investigated—from large regional spaces to smaller interior spaces. In addition to functional and physical considerations, there is also a discussion of the historical development of urban planning and house plans. The history of architecture and furniture is comprehensively covered in the later sections of this book. These chapters provide the stylistic background that, when coupled with the design fundamentals, is the base for contemporary environmental decisions. For, without the knowledge of design, or of basic spatial planning, or of historical precedents, how can an individual make choices today with any validity? I contend he or she cannot.

As with many of the concepts and ideas we each prescribe, the underlying premise of this book also began as a nebulous thought that matured through time, and is, of course, the product of all experience. Looking back, however, certain individuals and events stand out as being especially significant to the development of this book.

One of the first persons to help me perceive the importance of the totality of design was Theodora Pottle, an art teacher with spirit, verve, and uncompromising principles. A second and much later influence was Burgoyne Diller, a painter and teacher of unsurpassed skill. And I am particularly indebted to my wife, Marjorie. In addition to being a wonderful companion, she has been my most astute critic and discussant. Because of her never-tiring enthusiasm for new knowledge, many of the ideas in this book were first introduced to me by Marge.

I must also give credit to all of my past and current students. Through the years their questions, enthusiasm, and, yes, often eagerness to learn stimulated me further to investigate and define my thoughts.

My thanks, too, go to my friends and associates who were more directly concerned with the development of this book; they include Curt Sherman, Richard Montena, Margaret Goodyear, Barbara Sergent, Ronald Raetzman, Anthony Monaco, Barbara Kostelnicek, my editors John Beck and David Novack, and the book's designer, Andy Zutis. Each has contributed ideas, photographs, references, advice, and encouragement.

Lastly, I am aware of the experiences of physical and geographic changes. Regardless of time, place, or circumstance, the stability of design criteria repeatedly and constantly manifests itself wherever I look.

My hope is that I have offered to you, the reader, whether you are a student in an interior design or other environmental design program or a layman in search of more environmental knowledge, a source of information which will stimulate and develop within you an ever-increasing awareness and appreciation of natural and man-made design, and serve as your own *criteria for decisions.*

H. H. A.

Contents

Design

Foreword

There is a useful and crucial difference between being in an environment and doing things in it.

Constance Perin

Never before in the history of mankind have people had such freedom of choice or encountered the extensive array of products that exists today in the United States. There are few restraints and the available alternatives and variations of any single product are continually increasing in number, material, price, and quality.

Ironically, the more alternative products presented, the harder it is for the consumer to make decisions and this is cause for concern. It is particularly essential, therefore, that the criteria and methods of decision that will affect our near environment be examined, clarified, and evaluated. Too often choices are based on impulse, hazy impressions, or false monetary values, with complete disregard for the basic elements of design, historical heritage, and general aesthetic character.

F-1 *Standing derelict on the Illinois prairie, this once proud Gothic revival house quiety awaits its fate. Its forlorn and somewhat spectral appearance causes passing motorists to slow down; the author hopes to question, "Why?"*

Our technological and mechanical proficiencies have far exceeded our design capacities. We live in a strange era; there exists a dichotomy of style concepts that clearly indicate our inability to conceive a humane technology, one that lends dignity and grace to contemporary life. The latest, the newest, is held in high esteem. The most recent is the most admired; yet, as new forms, techniques, materials, and ideas are presented, they are continually being forced into pseudohistorical molds, seldom being allowed to develop naturally and truthfully. For example, glaringly fake eighteenth and nineteenth-century interiors (styrofoam "hand-hewn" beams, fiberglass "used" bricks, and plastic lampshades) are installed in glass-sheathed skyscrapers, and the excellent new synthetic materials are shaped and colored to imitate traditional moldings or furniture forms.

Sadly, however, despite the seeming reverence for historical design, what *is* old, regardless of merit (structural or design) is dismissed or destroyed with scarcely a wave of the hand. During and after World War II man has almost destroyed his past, man-made and natural—either piecemeal or by the bulldozer and wrecking ball, or with greater speed and efficiency by the bomb. The validity of such actions has always been open to question; nevertheless, the general tendency of urban redevelopment planners, highway engineers, and other decision makers is to dismiss efforts to protect historical monuments and artifacts as sentimental and romantic, secondary to their ideas of "progress." On the contrary, the awareness and familiarity with the past is of central importance to our cultural future.

The average individual also does not often concern himself with the "arrangement of the parts" whether these parts join to become a single object, a house, a city block, or a complete community. He is unaware of his place in this arrangement; he makes no visual judgments for he is usually insufficiently equipped and generally exists in a perceptual vacuum. He is shaken from his apathy only when he finally becomes aware of some gross infringement on his own personal being or when his "natural" right as an

F-2 *A scene too often repeated today. These two private mansions, still structurally sound, were torn down to make way for a parking lot.*

individual is threatened, and then he will resist and take an impulsive stand. Unfortunately, it is often too late and the irrevocable damage has been done. It is the responsibility of each individual to constantly seek out the best designed, the most functional, and the most aesthetically pleasing solutions for his needs. It is his responsibility to know the *reasons* for these selections.

Design is a natural growth; therefore, every human being has the capacity to develop an appreciation for design. It is a continuing process that expands and contracts with experimentation and experience. Serious social consequences are often the result of distorted growth and frequency of ugly, poorly designed, and dehumanized environments. Benjamin Thompson, professor of architecture at Harvard, states,

Ugliness does matter immensely . . . because every sensory experience, beautiful or ugly, affects people deeply. It changes them as much as a blow on the head. . . . Man is an *adjustable* animal and one way he adjusts is to *insensitize himself.* When physical or emotional conditions are severe, his very survival hangs on his ability to *"turn off"* part of his circuitry so that destructive messages don't tear his system apart. But when he does this, he shuts down half his potential, indeed, he is only half-alive.

The seriousness of such an insensitized individual in contemporary society cannot be underestimated. The greatest danger exists because this person is not aware that he is "turned off" yet must still make decisions—decisions that will considerably affect his, and man's environment.

I am here concerned with this environment of man—in other words, I care what surrounds him whether it is a chair, a room, a home, a neighborhood, or a city. Does it work for him physically, socially, and emotionally; does it please him visually; does it have the best quality of design that is obtainable with the materials, techniques, and funds available? And, does it satisfy the *human* in him? Difficult as these questions may be, their answers can and must be realized.

F-3 *Our aesthetic environment has often been reduced to the lowest levels as a result of decisions made by those who are ignorant of matters of aesthetics and design.*

It is specifically the responsibility of the designers of environment, that is, urban planners, landscape architects, architects, and interior designers (and yes, politicians) to develop plans and designs that will enhance human lives. They must understand in depth the scope and ramifications of the present conditions *and* those that are possible and probable. It is also their responsibility to guard the layman against, and alert him to conditions that may ultimately do him harm. This is not a flag-waving, fanatical attempt to increase dissension or the disruption of urban or rural tranquility, but rather a pointed reminder that our homes, and to a lesser extent our places of work and neighborhoods, are the last refuges of individualism and must at all costs be preserved.

It is also my aim to expand the reader's awareness of how design can and does affect human life. I want him to be alert to the order or disorder in his surroundings. I want him to see, to *perceive,* which forms, colors, textures, and spaces comprise his environment. I want him to *react* to them! Too often we become isolated from our world and close our minds and eyes to what is around us. We ignore it. We travel from one place to another in an isolation box; we only *look at* the view, almost like looking through the viewfinder of a camera, we do not inspect it or become part of it. All of us must become aware of the design that surrounds us, and then *judge* it.

Our world is almost totally designed, not by nature, but by man. There is little left that does not show the hand of someone; our countrysides are divided into fields, reshaped (bulldozed level or into hills), and planted; our rivers are straightened, deepened, and widned; and our seashores and harbors are constantly being controlled. Attempts, frequently successful, have been made to seed clouds to produce rain, to disperse fog, and to dissipate storms and hurricanes, and certainly within our buildings we are air conditioned, humidified, dehumidified, and heated to perfection.

Both designers and average citizens must always be cognizant of such environmental changes, controls, and conditions and must constantly question their effect upon human life. I recognize that each one of us can never know about all aspects of our lives and that we must have experts and resource persons who can aid us in many of our decisions, but we must remember that when each individual takes the initiative to question, examine, and respond to the environmental decision makers, political or professional, he becomes involved, and when a person is part of a decision, *it is his decision.* As the ideas of individuals mingle with those of professionals, the outcomes will, in every way, be more satisfactory and rewarding for the total population.

Here, then, is why this book is written.

It is dedicated to the *human,* the sensitive, appreciative total man, aware of his heritage, his past, and cognizant of his future, and to his designing of an environment for a better life for himself *and* for others. It is because someone long ago, in a different land and in a different time, said, "If you have two loaves, sell one and buy hyacinths."

Part One
Aesthetic Design

Aesthetic values everywhere precede
and accompany rational activity,
and life is, in one aspect, always
a fine art; not by introducing
inaptly aesthetic vetoes or aesthetic
flourishes, but by giving to everything a form which, implying a
structure, implies also an ideal
and a possible perfection.

George Santayana

1 Organization Through Form, Line, Space, Texture

All forms that exist in the natural world are imbued with a specific structure; they are ordered, regulated, and predictable. Each plant, each organism is composed of elements and parts that are arranged with precision and balance. These arrangements can be found in so simple a union as one and one or in combinations and structures more complex than the human mind can yet possibly imagine.

Within man also lies a natural desire for orderly arrangements. He has been created with an intuitive and innate ability to attempt to find order and regularity in an otherwise chaotic environment. Chaotic because, despite the fact that there is order in nature, there is also disorder, distortion, disease, pollution, overpopulation, and other disrupting elements. Most of these disturbances are caused by man; but the laws of nature accommodate both the good and the bad, beautiful and ugly, or rich, plentiful, poor, and sparse. These are the laws of contrast—they are necessary to existence.

The Gestalt psychologists[1] found that intuition, the innate cognitive function of man, is the faculty that most frequently permits the recognition of a Gestalt configuration. The Gestalt configuration is, of course, the pattern that carries the message of identity. Intuition allows selectivity to occur; an individual, considering a vast range of possibilities, can glean out the relevant, make connections, and generally aim for a satisfying, appealing, and aesthetically unifying perception. The question also arises: If man has this innate ability to find order and regularity, why doesn't he use it more often?

Children of preschool age (one to five years) in their early drawings show a remarkable feeling for symmetry, form, line, mass, and movement. This inherent tendency to *arrange* the elements in their drawings almost always results in satisfying compositions. An examination of the crafts, structures,

---

[1] One premise of Gestalt psychology is that the whole is greater than the sum of its parts.

and art of primitive peoples further corroborates this inborn sense of order and structured design. Buckminster Fuller has described basic human powers of visualization: "I am astonished at how accurately and quickly the eye can see balance between mass and verticality. Most men's eyes can read what engineers call slenderness ratio in construction; the ratio of cross section to length in, for example, a column . . . this ability is built into the eye; it isn't something taught to humans by other humans" (1967). Florence Cane in her book *The Artist in Each of Us* (1951) states categorically, "In my many years of work with children of all ages, I have become firmly convinced that the sense of design as well as the sense of form are innate."

It is very perplexing; what influences come to bear upon man that all but obliterate this innate sense? What occurs within the development of most children that causes their aesthetic and innate ability for order and structure to wither instead of developing, when they enter school or reach the age of five, atrophying in many cases to a final death?

Rhoda Kellogg in her book *Analyzing Children's Art* (1969) points out how parents advertently or inadvertently influence their children through the use of bad models of "how to draw," prohibiting the use of art materials because of their fear of messiness and their negative or apathetic responses to the child's scribblings (of prime importance to the child's normal development). The child's natural innate Gestalt is constantly being infringed upon the adult-devised formulas for representing objects that he sees in the home, the school, picture books, magazines, newspapers, comics, and television animated creations. The child, not knowing how to accommodate everyone, frequently just turns off; a very human trait.

What sensitivity for design that does survive childhood is further attacked by the individual's seldom having to work with raw materials as is necessary in less developed societies, the complicated and involved process of modern life, the lack of understanding by others, and the unusual emphasis upon monetary values. The knowledge of design—that combination of parts and

1-1 *A rock painting by early inhabitants of Colorado. The seeming disorder of the simplified and abstract linear designs, when carefully analyzed, shows an apparent arranging and modifying of some of the designs to fit the space. The areas between individual paintings sometimes seem as important as the paintings themselves.*

1-2 *Few areas in the United States have escaped the hand of man. There is no evidence in this aerial photograph that even a small portion of this area has not been reshaped—the earth has been leveled, marked into geometric areas, and trees and plants have been planted in rows.*

elements that creates a useful and aesthetic whole, ultimately becomes cognitively minimal for most adults.

The surroundings of most people are almost totally man-made. There are few places in the world, and especially in the United States, where man has not been and has not reshaped nature. One only has to drive across the country and see mile after mile of cities, towns, highways, and fields that are the results of the efforts of human beings.

Each day everyone, not just the interior designer, architect, or artist, but *everyone*, must make many decisions concerning his near environment (rooms, house, places of work) and with the native ability of good design selection all but forgotten, these decisions are often based merely upon whim or some vague idea of what is "right or wrong." Unfortunately, the majority of those who are responsible for the selection of elements that make up our larger environments, neighborhoods, apartment complexes, and communities, are also unaware of what constitutes design, the direct affect design can have upon the human being, and the importance of design elements in consumer choices. Further, the criticality of the consumer is lower now than ever before as evidenced by his acceptance of the appalling non-planned urban sprawls engulfing the once verdant countryside, of the visually blighted structures —commercial buildings, community buildings, and houses—which are constantly being built under the guise of progress, and of the objects that stuff these structures and flaunt the selector's "taste."

Design criticality is, for the most part, an intangible consideration. The color of an object seldom affects its function, whether a design is "good or bad" does not necessarily change its cost or can it be said that only outstanding designs perform tasks. But, well-designed objects often *do* function better, *can* be more valuable, and *can* positively enhance our lives. With so many variables and alternatives possible in every design solution, there is no one "correct" answer. However, design criteria is not a bit of extraneous froth that one need not have. On the contrary, the person with an aesthetic appreciation and knowledge of design is without doubt better equipped to make decisions, and, being able to judge competently from many viewpoints, he possesses one of the most meaningful and vital qualities an individual might have. When he is aware of this, he will find it to be one of his most rewarding and vital assets.

Although everyone should be appreciative of good design, it is the designer who must know *why* he chooses the objects or elements that make up the whole (whether he designs the interior or exterior components of where individuals live is not important here). He must be able to defend his choice and often he must further influence someone else to agree with his decision. He must also be able to understand and use a vocabularly that is familiar to other designers, thereby assuring for himself the ability to professionally communicate with his clients. He must, in other words, *learn* the basics of design. He must, in a sense, regain, revive, and redevelop his original sense of design. He must be so competent and confident in his ability to effectively manipulate design that he is constantly able to conceptualize about the new as well as the old.

The inclusive idea of design is so basic to all objects, natural and man-made, yet so complex, that to separate these concepts into fundamental comprehensible components is difficult. Although this separation is being attempted in this investigation of design, it must be remembered that each part, each device, element, or detail incorporated into a design has a direct relationship to all of the parts. There is no limit to the flexibility of design.

Traditionally, the considerations grouped together under the generic term of *basic design* are divided into two areas—the *elements* and the *principles*. These two areas are related and intertwined but each has very distinct qualities that can be isolated and discussed. These two areas, in turn, are further divided into five elements and three principles. The *Elements of Design* are *form, space, line, texture,* and *color*. The *Principles of Design* are *balance, continuity, and emphasis.* As so frequently happens when one is involved with intangible subjects,

1-3 *The strong drama of light and shade seen in this building is achieved by the large rectangular forms surfaced with different textures.*

nomenclature and semantics can become problems, and for reasons of clarity, the commonest terms are used in this book; however, other similar terms are noted. Regardless of the nomenclature, these elements and principles are vital tools with which the designer works. It is his knowledge of design, basic design, that will enable him to *create* (and it is create if he is to do his job) a satisfactory solution.

The Visual Elements of Design

FORM

The importance of *form* is primary when discussing architecture and interiors. Almost every object, device, or element used in building is three-dimensional and exhibits form.[2] However, the external shape of an object is but one part of this visual design element. Form is more than the mere "outsides" of an object; consideration must also include the inner structure and the apparent weight. To be unaware of these three considerations, one could not completely understand form.

The very young child first perceives the shape of objects. As he grows and develops, details, colors, and ornament become increasingly important. Frequently, he, as an adult, partially loses his ability to see the basic forms and becomes too aware of the superficial elements. It is far better that he retain the ability to observe the general forms or shapes of objects and by so

[2] The main emphasis in this book is upon the three-dimensional components that make up the environment—furniture, interiors, houses, architecture, and urban planning. However, a form does not need to be actually three-dimensional. For example, all types of painting—abstract, non-objective, and representational—contain forms, and whether these forms depict recognizable objects or are "smears of paint," they often have the visual feeling of depth or thickness as well as of height and width. Without this spatial quality they become mere shapes and do not have the substance and weight required in most successful compositions.

1-4 *Right-angled forms and surfaces dominate this multilevel view of Habitat in Montreal.*

1-5 *The introduction of an ornate sofa and ruffled, truncated cone lamp shade destroys the quiet unity of the rectangular forms.*

doing he can visually classify objects as being straight, curved, irregular, or some other category. As each category is capable of generating a specific emotional response, the simple geometric shape or combination of shapes that gives an object its distinct form must be carefully analyzed. The basic forms can often tie an arrangement together. For example, a group of objects, that is, a boxy sofa, a parson's table, and lamp with a rectangular base and shade will appear harmonious because of the unifying rectangularity of their basic forms, whereas the substitution of a multicurved sofa and an ornate, irregular based lamp would destroy this unity and visual chaos would result. An interior with different periods of furniture can appear as a total arrangement by the careful handling of the basic furniture and accessory forms.

STRAIGHT FORMS. There is a regularity about rectangular forms. Each side of these forms is straight and flat and the sides all meet at 90-degree angles. Although not based upon nature,[3] rectangular forms are the most numerous and common of man-made forms. With few exceptions the floor plans, furniture, rooms, doors and windows, buildings, and street layouts found in the near and far environments are all straight sided, and usually there is a dominance of 90-degree angles. The universal use of these right-angled (90-degree) forms is the result of: 1) the ease with which such forms fit together with no wasted space, 2) the convenience with which designers and carpenters can work with these forms and angles both in the shops and on the site, and 3) the clear, stable appearance of each 90-degree angled form.

The square and the three-dimensional cube, being equal on all sides,

[3] Interesting questions arise when thinking about purely geometric forms and nature. Because there are rarely, if ever, true rectangles, squares, circles, or even straight surfaces or edges found in nature, should man continue to use geometric solids in designs as he has for centuries? Should forms be more nature-like? Should *only* natural forms be used? What effect should the answers to these questions have upon housing and architecture in general?

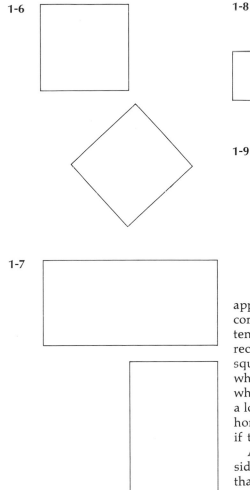

1-6

1-8

1-9

1-7

appear to be the most stable[4] in the rectangular group, but if placed upon a corner this stability is affected. They also are quite formal and there is a tendency toward monotony when these forms are used indiscriminately. The rectangle or rectangular solid also appears stable but is not as formal as the square and cube. There is a degree of movement with rectangular forms when one dimension is longer than the others, and this movement increases when this dimension increases in relation to the other dimensions. Thus, if a long, thin rectangle is placed in a horizontal position there is considerable horizontal visual movement (placed vertically the movement is vertical) but if the rectangle is more square, less movement will be observed.

Angular forms, with sides not meeting at right angles, include the three-sided triangles and pyramids. These forms suggest even more movement than squares and rectangles; their nonperpendicular sides create diagonals that always imply motion. These forms are considered the most stable forms because, structurally, they cannot be changed without bending or breaking one of their sides (a rectangular solid can be crushed without changing any of the dimensions of the sides; only the angles are changed). With the broad base of a triangle or pyramid at the bottom, this great stability is quite apparent. However, despite the structural sturdiness of the actual forms, when the apex is at the bottom they appear to be the least stable of forms. There is great flexibility possible when using these triangular and pyramidal forms (the angles can be varied and are not fixed at certain degrees in comparison with rectangles), and exciting and dynamic designs can be made with them.

Forms with more than four sides also do not use right angles but instead of being as vigorous and distinct as the triangle and pyramid, they begin to assume the characteristics of circular forms as the number of their sides

[4]The ancient Greeks used the cube as an earth symbol undoubtedly because of its stability of form.

1-10

1-11

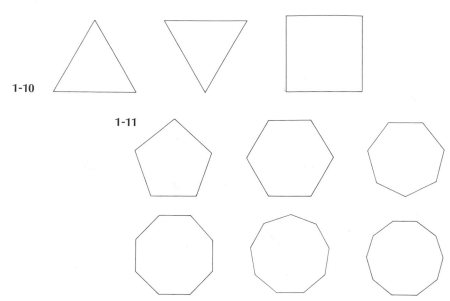

increase: an octagon, for example, relates more to the circle than does the pentagon.

CURVED FORMS.   Curved forms suggest nature and natural objects; flowers, trees, rocks, and hills are curved. A curved form used in conjunction with straight forms can also imply movement; without angles to impede this movement, the curved form is a powerful design consideration.

The two-dimensional circle and the three-dimensional sphere are the most economical forms that can be used. As evidenced in domes, the circle and sphere enclose more space with less surface than any other form. They are self-contained and complete. Because no point on their surface is further from the center than any other point, they express unity. When surrounded with other forms, the circle or sphere can easily dominate the arrangement.

Cones and cylinders are three-dimensional curved forms, which, when viewed in drawings or real life, can appear two-dimensional and straight sided. They convey a surface movement that is not found in squares, circles, or spheres. Being three-dimensional with at least one flat surface, they do not seem as easily moved as a sphere, yet the curved surface does indicate more directional motion; in cones, this motion continues until it spins off at the apex.

IRREGULAR FORMS.   Up to now, most of the geometric two- and three-dimensional forms have been regular in their arrangements; angles have been fairly constant and the sides have distinct relationships to the other sides of the form. Irregular forms, combining both straight and curved surfaces with various angles, offer unlimited variety. Often these forms can be separated into components of smaller and more simple forms and analyzed, but the irregularity of some forms defy such division. There is danger of instability and lack of strength when using complicated irregular forms. Often, however, if a design has too many irregular, non-related forms, the addition of a few square or rectangular forms can enhance this arrangement and improve it aesthetically.

1-12   *The combination of curved and straight surfaces and forms in this sculpture creates a strong visual statement.*

1-13

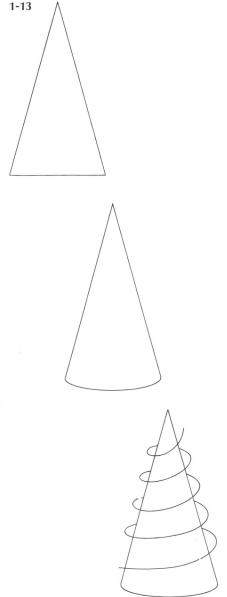

1-14 *Regardless of the complexity of a structure, it is almost always a combination of simple geometric forms.*

The geometric forms just described can be found throughout the homes, offices, schools, and factories that are familiar to all individuals. They are not abstract, unfamiliar forms, but objects that are seen and used each day. Frequently, they have been combined into such complex arrangements that it may be difficult to discern the basic geometric forms within an object or building, but underlying the ornament, details, and extraneous additions, the forms are there. Actually, the typical house is but one or more rectangular forms topped with a roof composed of one or more triangular solids. The chimney is another rectangular form, thin and vertical. Porches, bay windows, and other projections can also be analyzed as rectangular or curved forms. Inside, the flat surfaces (the walls, floor, and ceiling of each room) customarily meet at right angles, like a box, and enclose smaller, more complicated forms (tables, chairs, beds, refrigerators, and so forth).

Form is closely allied to inner structure. The external surface is important but *what* causes the outside form is equally of value. If the structure, the framework, of an object is known and understood then the exterior becomes more easily comprehended. The method of constructing a wall governs to a great extent the form of that wall for example.

The arrangement of living areas or rooms within a house should determine the exterior forms of a house. Frequently someone states that they want "a center-hall colonial" or "a square house" or some similar exterior. How can the rooms within this rigid exterior be arranged? Does the hall *have* to be in the center? Will all the interior space requirements fit within a square floor plan? Ofttimes, no. Yet, this is but one example of the need to be aware of the inner structure of form.

Weight is the third consideration when discussing form. It is, however, not actual weight that is so important but the *apparent weight.* How much an object *appears* to weigh is what concerns the designer. The familiar story of the two boxes is a case in point. Black boxes were thought to be extremely heavy and those persons who had to move them continuously complained about the

weight of the boxes. When the boxes were painted a pastel color, there was
general agreement among those responsible for moving the boxes that the
"new" boxes were lighter and more easily moved. The actual weight remained the same, only the apparent weight changed. The form was affected.

Another example of apparent weight: A large sofa, upholstered in a dark
fabric, sits against a wall that is painted white. The sofa seems to dominate
the room. The owner slipcovered the sofa in a fabric that blended with the
wall and the sofa lost its importance. Again, form was affected.

Another aspect of form is the difference between *mass form* and *skeletal form*.
A mass form usually suggests weight, is opaque, and is a dominant element
in any scheme; a skeletal form is, as the name implies, a framework. The
form is defined but appears less heavy, does not obstruct vision entirely, and
often almost disappears. An illustration: a refrigerator and a wardrobe are
both large, closed box-like forms. They enclose space and are easily seen. A
set of open shelves and a room divider of similar dimensions may also
require as much space but these do not visually occupy space as completely
and do not appear to weigh as much as the refrigerator or the wardrobe.

The size of a form in relation to the forms surrounding it is an additional
consideration. Everyone has probably experienced selecting an object in one
set of surroundings, and after placing the object in another environment, the
size of the object appears differently. Again, the familiar illustration. The
pyramids rise high above the almost level desert of Egypt, but if it were
possible to move them to the Rocky Mountain area of the United States, the
Pyramids would undoubtedly lose much of their dominance and appear
almost small.

A common experience occurs when a house is planned and the foundation
is seen for the first time. With no other elements by which to compare, the
dimensions of the foundations seem small. As the house is erected, relationships are invariably established and the house seems to increase in size. The

1-15 *The apparent weight and importance of an object in its environment can
be affected greatly by the relationships of
the values and patterns. The first illustration is an English engraving c. 1840.
The three illustrations that follow have
been altered to show how the appearance
of the figure and the surrounding objects
can be changed by manipulating the value
contrasts and textures of the dress, chair,
fabrics, and background.*

1-16 *A skeletal form suggests less weight
than one that is more solid in appearance.*

1-18 *The surroundings of an object can affect its
form as seen here. The Pyramids appear much smaller
when surrounded by mountains.*

1-17 *The open shelves separating the kitchen from the
dining area, although occupy-
ing the same space, have less
visual weight than the solid
brick wall.*

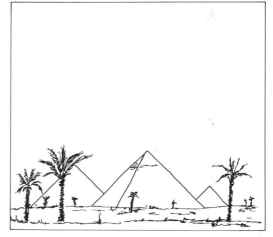

house appears largest when the framework is up but before the wall surfaces have been applied. It then loses some of its inner size with the closing of the house surfaces, but the exterior continues to retain and indeed may increase its visual size. The interior spaces are judged first by the skeletal form concept before the wall surfaces are installed and the observer sees *through* the forms, whereas the surfaced exterior and interior are judged by the massed form alone.

Direction, color, and texture, which also affect form, are discussed under succeeding headings.

SPACE

The definition of form is broad enough to include the tangible concepts of rational shape and structure, as well as an intangible entity capable of evoking aesthetic responses that may be less than rational. Everything has form, tangible or intangible; however, form cannot exist without space and time. Together, form and space describe a profound duality of existence. In a sense, the reality of each is mutually dependent upon the other. As elements of design, space and form constitute the very basis from which to begin any analysis.

Seldom has there been a period in history that man has not been involved with the relationships of his forms and his spaces. As tangible forms change, man's form of living changes and with this his emphasis on space usage will also change. There have been and will continue to occur new methods of describing space, new techniques of enclosing space, coping with a lack of space, vast space, horizontal and vertical space, all of which become prime considerations of design.

The incredible achievements of the latter half of the twentieth century have expanded man's horizon to include a spatial environment that was once merely a figment of science fiction. Amazingly, these new frontiers have been won not only with the fearless vigor of a few highly skilled individuals, but

1-19 *The rigid frontalism of the IV Dynasty sculpture of King Mycerinus and his queen reflects the two-dimensionality of Egyptian art.* Courtesy, Museum of Fine Arts, Boston.

despite a public banality that is indicative of man's inability to conceive of space that has heretofore not been articulated by man-made forms.

Although the interior designer is most immediately confronted with three-dimensional spatial problems, the two-dimensional space manipulated in the design of rugs and carpets, wallpaper and fabric, as well as some simulated surface textures and patterns will present a special challenge to his training and skill. Traditionally, the painter has been occupied with a limited two-dimensional space that offers only an illusional third dimension. However, painters of the 1960s and 1970s are broadening their concepts to include a greater use of three-dimensional forms—the division between painter and sculptor becomes less discernible. The emphasis has centered upon an environmental art, that includes a broadened concept of space and time. The significance for the designer is that a thorough knowledge of both the three-dimensional space that we occupy and manipulate is no more important than the two-dimensional space that has its basis in the history of man and his art.

Man may first *perceive* objects in a flat, two-dimensional way. This is not to say he *sees* objects in this manner but that he thinks of objects two-dimensionally. A cursory look at man's depiction and involvement with space through history may better illustrate this. The paintings, sculpture, and architecture of early man, primitive man, the Egyptians, the Mesopotamians, the Archaic Greeks (to c. 480 B.C.), Orientals, and even children are all very flat and show little depth. It is not a matter of "not knowing." Certainly, the Chinese, Japanese, and Egyptians were all capable of showing depth in their work (and occasionally they did), but they *chose* not to. The objects in their paintings are arranged so that what would be behind is shown above. The Egyptians, for example, evolved a complicated scheme to illustrate objects in a very two-dimensional manner, for example, the human figure was painted to show the most representational view of the individual parts of the body —profile head with a front view eye, front view shoulders, and profile hips

1-20 *The two-dimensionality common in Egyptian design is apparent in this wall painting from the Tomb of Nakht, from the XVII Dynasty, Thebes. The figures are flattened; no foreshortening, modeling, or shadows are employed; objects and figures are arranged on base lines; and there is little evidence of a setting.* Photograph by Egyptian Expedition, The Metropolitan Museum of Art.

and legs. The hands and feet were usually the same regardless to which arm or leg they were attached and showed the under palm and arch. (The total figure looks almost natural but is impossible anatomically.) Egyptian sculpture is rigid, straight, and was expected to be viewed from only one side, customarily the front. One facade of each building—the front—was emphasized although the appearance of the others were scarcely considered.[5]

By approximately 400 B.C., a major change in spatial concept had occurred in Greece. Sculpture became less rigid, figures twisted in movement that required more space, and were to be viewed from all sides. Architecture also became more three-dimensional with each facade of a building being important. Paintings gained the illusion of depth. This three-dimensional (sometimes called Western or Occidental) concept of space developed and continued for about eight hundred years. (The Romans had very spatial frescoes and mosaics.)

With the coming of Christianity (an Eastern religion, by the way), there was a reversal of thought and a period of two-dimensional (Eastern or Oriental) design began that lasted about one thousand years. Images flattened, decorative design became two-dimensional, little sculpture was done, and buildings were given only one important facade.[6]

One of the earliest developments of the Renaissance was the invention of

[5]An emphasis upon the front of a building is not foreign to America of the nineteenth and twentieth centuries. Buildings in the gold rush towns of the West are noted for their high false fronts, but almost any city or town in the United States has buildings with ornate facades hiding lesser structures behind. Uncounted numbers of houses that have been erected more recently have stone, brick, or a better siding on the front elevations than on the other three sides. "Frontalism" is an old idea but it is in use.

[6]During the last four hundred years of these Early Christian and medieval periods an effort to enclose large spaces developed producing Romanesque and especially Gothic churches and cathedrals of great size and height. Sculpture began to be done but remained architectural.

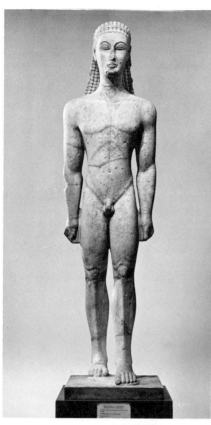

1-21 *The complete shift from two-dimensional to three-dimensional spatial concepts in Greek sculpture can be seen in these two statues. The photograph (left) of a kuros or youth (c. 615–600 B.C.) with its rigid frontal pose is remarkably similar to that favored by the Egyptians but is released from the architectural setting. Venus de Milo on the right (second century B.C.) the most famous statue of the Greek goddess Aphrodite twists in space, spiraling upward, and is completely free of any "best side," all views being interesting and surely considered by the sculptor.* (Left) The Metropolitan Museum of Art, Fletcher Fund, 1932. (Right) Caisse Nationale des Monuments Historiques.

linear perspective by the architect Filippo Brunelleschi (1377–1446). A renewed interest in the depiction of three-dimensional space quickly caused murals, easel paintings, and decorative elements and details to loose their flatness, and illusionary space was again dominant. Walls and ceilings virtually disappeared with space-filled murals. The lavish use of mirrors, reflecting and refracting images, further destroyed the space-limiting walls and created illusions of additional space. Sculpture again became an important art form and was very three-dimensional, twisting and spiraling in space. Gardens became exercises in perspective and illusionary spatial deception.

It was not until the latter half of the nineteenth century when an interest in Japanese prints and African sculpture renewed two-dimensional concepts of spatial depiction. Since that time both concepts have been used by designers, artists, and architects. The realization that these two philosophies of space are used and are equally accepted answers many of the questions concerning the arts today. A quick inspection of almost any exhibition of painting, display of silverware, drapery fabric, or wall coverings, or the decorative details found on architecture and furniture will reveal both kinds of spatial concepts, and how well each serves its particular purpose.

Regardless of which manner of space is depicted, just how is space preceived? Actually, without forms to define it, space cannot be easily calculated. Indeed, it is relationships and proportions of forms that indicate space to the observer.

1. The phenomenon (called the *constancy phenomenon* by psychologists) of identical figures or objects casting different sized images on the retina of the human eye, the closer the figure the larger the image, is one indication of depth. (Architects often include a human figure or other familiar object to give a sense of "scale" to their renderings.)
2. Parallel lines extending away from the observer will appear to come closer

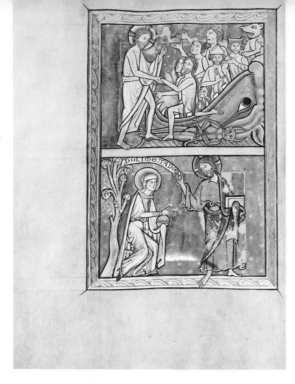

1-23 David *by Michelangelo illustrates the full return to the three-dimensional concept of design that occurred during the Italian Renaissance. The figure twists in three-dimensional space, free of spatial limitations.*

1-24 *The constancy phenomenon, converging of parallel lines, overlapping forms, and blurring of details, all indications of distance, are readily apparent in these photographs of the Arc de Triomphe in Paris.*

1-25 *The positive space occupied by the strong forms of the stonework in the side entrance of the famous Chicago landmark Glessner House is matched in importance by the negative space of the opening. The quiet, dark space balances the texturally interesting stone.* Courtesy of Glessner House.

together in the distance, and if extended to infinity will appear to converge on the horizon or eye level. (This is the basis of linear perspective.)

3. The overlapping of forms immediately gives the illusion of space. The form that is partially hidden is perceived as being behind. There usually seems to be space *between* these forms, too.

4. As objects recede in the distance their details become less distinct and only the basic and simple forms are reflected upon the retina; thus more complicated and detailed forms seem closer.

5. There are several significant changes in color as objects are removed in space. These phenomena are discussed under the color section.

Individuals may regard space two-dimensionally or three-dimensionally as they see space in several ways, but they live in a three-dimensional environment. There is width and height, and there is depth in their surroundings. When plans, drawings, elevations, and details are drawn, they indicate on a two-dimensional surface three-dimensional objects in space.

The terms *positive space* and *negative space* are often encountered. Positive space refers to the area defined (filled or occupied) by an object or form. Negative space is that space surrounded by or surrounding positive space. This is a simple division, but it is of major significance when judging design and structure. Frequently, only positive space is considered, whereas, in truth, the negative space is equally important.

Since the dawn of history man has sought to enclose space. Early man attempted to create a shelter for himself, his family, and his belongings by covering or surrounding an area with materials that were immediately available. As he became more adept and efficient, more complicated methods and better materials were used to enclose large and more flexible areas. The history of architecture is the history of enclosing space. Lao-tzu, the sixth-century Chinese philosopher wrote, "The reality of architecture resides in the space rather than its mass." And so it is.

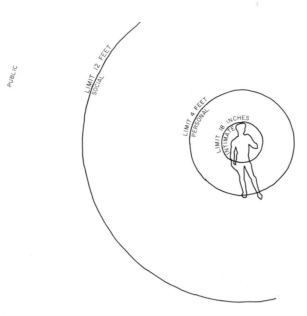

1-26

The psychological and emotional qualities of space are of major importance. Frequently, the fixed dimensions of a room's interior or the arrangement of furniture is not compatible with an individual's personal or informal sense of space. Each person has a "space bubble," a sphere of space with which he surrounds himself. This *territoriality* is a natural behavior of man and animals. Specific distances govern activity and the relations formed during that activity.

Edward T. Hall in his book *The Hidden Dimension,* while discussing *proxemics* or the interrelated observations and theories of man's use of space, divided this informal space into four zones. The closest to the individual, which Hall calls the *intimate zone,* allows physical contact or the high possibility of physical involvement. It normally exists from skin surface to a distance of about eighteen inches. Actual discomfort can be experienced if someone unknowingly penetrates an individual's intimate zone. The angry expression, "He shook his fist *in* my face," although physically impossible, illustrates man's personal identity with the intimate zone.

Personal distance, from one and a half to four feet, is the limit of the normal sphere of space maintained by an individual. Friends may come close to this zone but seldom penetrate it, and, if so, only briefly—a handshake or similar brief contact. There is less difficulty with eye contact at this distance than in the intimate zone; details can be seen without difficulty but the overall object or figure cannot be seen at once. Conversation is somewhat below normal voice level. The phrase, "I kept him at arm's length" illustrates this strong personal spatial zone.

The spatial zone in which informal social and business affairs are conducted is called *social distance,* four to twelve feet. Most of any figure and all but the finest details can be seen. Voice levels are normal within the social distance but tend to be slightly raised near the outer limits (twelve feet). Within this distance, business is usually conducted and that conducted at the farthest distance is more formal than that which occurs when individuals are somewhat closer. The placement of office furniture is an indication of proxemic preference and easily affects relationships.[7] The chair opposite the desk can often place the visitor from eight to nine feet from the person behind the desk. If, however, the visitor's chair is at the side of the desk the distance is almost reduced by half. Without additional information, the placement of the visitor's chair at the side of the desk would indicate the possibility of a more informal meeting.

There can be a certain amount of insulation or privacy provided by a distance above ten feet. Even though a person can be easily seen, he can continue with his work without feeling compelled to acknowledge and participate verbally with another individual; however, normal verbal communication is possible if desired.

Public distance extends beyond the twelve foot limit of social distance. Formal behavior becomes evident at this distance. The eye can encompass more and the voice becomes louder automatically, and what is spoken is more formal in style and enunciated more clearly. The individual at this distance has a spatial wall that can be penetrated only by his closest associates. Interestingly, an important figure almost automatically has about thirty feet around him.

Hall cautions that his stated proxemic classifications are only approximate and apply only to the group of individuals examined. They cannot be applied to Americans in general. Negroes, Spanish Americans, and persons from other areas of the world and ethnic backgrounds would have different proxemic patterns. What *is* important, however, is that such patterns do exist. The designer, and indeed, all individuals, should be cognizant that personal space requirements differ but are essential, vital, and life-supporting.

The dimensions of space limit the world in which man moves and lives. An

[7] An extreme example was Mussolini's thirty-meter-long office. What visitor could retain his composure during the hike to Mussolini's desk?

1-27 *The serene beauty inherent in a Japanese "dry" garden is enhanced by the carefully executed linear pattern in the gravel.*

infant experiences the limit of his world when he touches the walls of his crib. As he grows the space in his room becomes known to him. Often spatial limits can be gauged with one's eyes closed or even asleep—not falling out of bed but sensing the nearness of the edge is a case in point.

Space of unusual proportions can also affect emotions. Rooms with unusually high or low ceilings cause a feeling of discomfort to many. (Claustrophobia is frequently experienced when one is caught between floors in an elevator, for example.) Yet limiting of space in some degree is essential. The desire for a "roof over our heads" often makes rooms with glass roofs undesirable for some people. The openess of window walls and "picture" windows is repeatedly filled with screens, shutters, curtains, draperies, and lamps; yet rooms with no windows can be a cause for anxiety interfering with work and social activities.

The speed and increased ease of transportation and communication now possible have lessened the feeling of space and distance. Distances that once took months, then weeks, or days, now take only hours to cover. The development of supersonic jet airplanes and passenger rockets hold the promise of further time-space reduction. Concepts of distance and space once held change and become less clear; yet, even today, physical discomfort can be produced by too rapid transportation from one time zone to another.

Finally, space is fast becoming a precious commodity. The costs to enclose space in homes, factories, or office buildings are continually rising; available space to construct buildings, to build highways and airports, and to develop recreational areas becomes increasingly difficult to procure; and space for individual privacy is diminishing.

LINE

Line, the path traced by a moving point, is a device natural to man but not found in nature. Of all the elements of design, line does not occur in the natural world; what man *sees* as line is in reality an edge of a surface, a division between forms, or the change in direction of a plane. Yet line is an important adjunct to design.

Man and some animals are able to make lines, a stick marking in the sand, a swipe of a stained finger on a rock. As a baby develops into the small child, the earliest graphic device he uses to express himself is a line. He continues to use lines in scribbling and later in more meaningful (to the adult) arrangements until his lines can express many ideas and forms.

The letters on this page are composed of lines of different direction, length, and combination, but nevertheless lines express ideas. Lines can also indicate form. The linear techniques of drawing—schematic, orthographic, and perspective as well as etchings and engravings—can give the impression of form on a surface. Laszlo Maholy-Nagy, in his book *Vision in Motion* (1947), states that drawing is a motion study, the lines are the paths of motion recorded by graphic means. Lines can guide the eye, and as the eye travels and shapes are enclosed, the forms and space of a design begin to be established in the mind.

Lines can also be symbols. A curved line combined with a vertical line becomes ¢, the symbol for cent. \$, →, ♭, =, ×, ♂, ♀, *, †, ♪ are also well known symbols composed entirely of lines.

The expressiveness of line is varied, yet universal. If a line is drawn while one is angry, the line clearly reveals this anger just as when one is calm, the "doodle" drawn expresses this calmness. In few places on earth could one find the drawing of an elongated ∫ in the air with the hands not understood as something feminine. In fact the "S" curve is indeed also called the feminine curve and was especially dominant during the mideighteenth century in France.

Direction can give additional meaning to a simple line. The horizontal line is the most restful and nonmoving line. Almost all animals and human beings rest and sleep in a horizontal position. The quiet lake, the rolling meadow, and the far horizon suggest calmness and tranquility. Any composition,

1-28 *Visual movement through the direction of lines is clearly evident in this photograph of some of the newer buildings in San Francisco. The quiet horizontal movement seen in the second building on the right and the smaller structures in the foreground is opposed by the stronger vertical movement observed in the building on the left. However, the active diagonals discerned on both the tall pyramid and the rectangular dark building produce even more visual movement.*

design, or arrangement of forms having a dominant horizontality will tend to appear serene and quiet. A vertical line is also stable, but appears to be more capable of movement than the horizontal. Objects and the human figure can stand vertically without moving, but there is the suggestion of more effort and alertness necessary to oppose the pull of gravity. Tall trees and the soaring majesty of Gothic cathedrals trying to pierce the heavens are excellent examples of vertical lines expressing awe, inspiration, and dignity. The diagonal line expresses movement and excitement. Almost without exception, compositions that have a dominance of diagonal lines, sloping forms, or tilted objects appear active. There is also a suggestion of impending disaster or chaos as in the zigzag of lightning or the crashing of trees. When the human figure walks or runs, it normally leans toward the direction of movement and the more rapid the movement the greater is the angle from the vertical. (The comic antics of several familiar cartoon characters and the Keystone Cops are intensified by the abnormal vertical positions of their swiftly moving figures). However, if one diagonal is opposed by another diagonal line; that is /\, the arrangement, like the triangular form that it resembles, becomes very stable and nonmoving.

Line can express emotion. A simple curved line might denote happiness ∪, but invert the same line and sorrow is suggested ∩. A line can be a laugh, a wave, a conflict.

A line need not be only one dimension as opposed to the line in mathematics; it can have thickness, width, and texture, and this is referred to as the *quality* of line. A line can be open or closed, hard or soft, passive or active, controlled or uncontrolled, continuous or broken. The limitless variety of line can express limitless meanings and emotions.

Line can affect as well as indicate form. A room, for example, can be heightened by strong vertical lines such as might be found on striped wallpaper. It is an old idea—verticals heighten and horizontals widen—and a true one, *but*, if the designer is knowledgeable about illusion, a series of

1-29

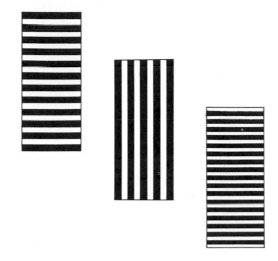

1-30 *The variety of natural and man-made textures found in this farm courtyard in Germany seem almost limitless.*

narrow vertical lines can create just the opposite effect—*width* instead of *height.*

The term *line* can also refer to the dominant directions or forms found in objects. "The lines of a chair are pleasing," "the house has good lines," or "the curved lines of this sofa are too ornate," are heard in this context. It is in this connotation that line can exist in nature but the words *form, flow, relationship,* or *rhythm* would work equally as well.

TEXTURE

Texture refers to the quality of the surface of natural and man-made objects and materials found in the environment, and allows man to explore his environment through his sense of touch. Rubbing or stroking the fingers across a variety of textures can produce sensory responses and if the texture is only *seen,* not touched, man, accustomed to actual textures, transmits through his eyes these sensory responses. Therefore, texture is the surface. Texture is the tactile sensation. Texture is the "feel."

There is a strong interrelationship between the visual sense—seeing—and the tactile sense—touching. Relationships exist between all of the senses, for example, the smell of a skunk will produce a mental image of a skunk, or the rattle of a rattlesnake, the snake, but the relationship is probably stronger between sight and touch and each, in turn, stimulates and enhances the other. The desire to touch and feel an object, fabric, or other material is a basic and primary response to seeing it. Invariably the customer fingers and touches the clothes on the rack in the store, "seeing" the fabric by the sense of touch as much as the sense of sight. Furthermore, the terms used to describe textural qualities or attributes are also allied to both touch and sight. A surface might be characterized as hard or soft, rough or smooth (touch), and/or a surface might be dull or shiny, dark or light (sight).

Expected (or unexpected) relationships of texture and form or texture and function of objects can also arouse strong aesthetic responses. Such com-

1-31 *Peachtree Center in Atlanta, Georgia, affords the observer a textural visual feast. The smooth, shiny surface of the Regency Hyatt Hotel Annex (center) acts as a foil to the different patterns and surfaces of the precast concrete exteriors of the other buildings and, yet, all are composed of rectangular forms.*

binations can enhance or detract from a design. A smooth, moist, water-worn stone half covered with a rich, soft growth of moss can attract; yet a firm, smooth, shiny apple with a wet, rotten, moldy side can repulse; the beauty of a soft, silky fur against the pale skin of a young woman is almost sensual in its attraction, but the same fur lining a milk-filled cup is highly repulsive. The architect, the sculptor, and designer have long been aware of the significance of textural contrast and the correlation of sight and touch.

When considering texture, the designer is soon aware that there are two "faces" of texture occurring in nature as well as on man-made objects. 1) *Actual* or *tactile* texture can be felt when touched; there are tactile sensations. For example, the surfaces of a wall made of crude bricks and mortar and painted white or of highly polished black plate glass would exhibit tactile textures. The surface textures are what give interest. 2) *Simulated* or *visual* texture cannot be felt when touched; it is seen. If the wall had been smooth, but covered with wallpaper printed to look like bricks, or if the glass had been marbleized with black, white and gray lines and patterns[8], they would have exhibited visual texture. All surfaces have both visual and tactile textures. Sometimes, they are nearly the same as a salt-and-pepper, hand-woven fabric might have. However, frequently they are not. Almost all of the illustrations in this book show surface textures but, if the fingers are placed upon the page with the eyes closed, little variation of texture can be discerned as the fingers are moved back and forth regardless of what the subject matter in the photograph or drawing is.

The significance of any one texture is greatly affected by the textures

1-32 *The exquisite selection and placement of different textural materials beside a seventeenth-century Japanese palace intensify each surface. In addition, there is a beautiful transition from small to large and from irregular forms to more precise geometry.*

[8]The visual texture found on some materials and objects is frequently referred to as *pattern.* The term is often applied to a printed or painted surface design that repeats, that is, a motif is duplicated in an orderly placement.

1-33 *Although some of the forms in this visually cluttered living room are partially obscured by the strong pattern of the brick fireplace wall, there is little textural unity.*

surrounding it; contrast is the cause. A rough texture will appear much rougher when it is near smooth surfaces than if it is combined with surfaces that are also rough.

The source, direction, and quality of light that will illuminate the surfaces being investigated are of major importance. A surface with light falling from one direction and parallel to that surface will cause a texture to appear rougher because the highlights and shadows are strongly contrasted. The more perpendicular to the surface the light source, the less are the shadows cast and the less textural emphasis results. Light that is diffused will also lessen the textural feeling or appearance of a surface.

The lightness or darkness of a surface is also a determining factor when manipulating texture. A dark surface will appear less textural than a light one—simply a matter of light and shade or contrast. (Dark surfaces will absorb more light waves and have fewer noticeable shadows, thus minimizing the variation of surface.)

Frequently in the past, the more smooth and fine the surface, the better and more well-made the product was considered. Poorly or crudely made objects almost always had rough surfaces. Today, this is not always the case. Modern technology and machines can polish a surface to maximum smoothness without difficulty of workmanship. A new appreciation of rough or "textured" surfaces has developed in recent years. Today, a "hand-made" object may have a textured surface or it may not. Many objects made by machine have surfaces that are not smooth. The variety within every price range and the level of quality in construction is very broad. This variety permits the designer flexibility in his choices of texture and enables him to create designs of wide and stimulating textural interest.

The surface of a form affects its inherent qualities of weight and density. The contrasting of a form's surface to background texture or pattern will increase the importance of that form. In fact, the form may even appear larger. But, if similar textures or patterns are used the form will be minimized. It is the old camouflaging trick. A large form can even be visually broken into smaller forms, completely destroying the original total form, by using bold, contrasting patterns.

There have been few references to "practical" considerations, but here one should be made. It is generally agreed that the more textured the surface, the harder it is to keep clean. The irregular surface collects and holds dust, dirt, and debris. For example, carpeting with an unusually deep, dense pile may appear to look quite rich and luxurious; however, if it is being used in an area that has to accommodate a heavy flow of human traffic, it may become impossible to maintain and clean. (The carpet's fiber content would, of course, affect its wear and maintenance, but here texture is the only consideration.) A hard-surfaced floor covering could offer an answer, but then other disadvantages such as noise and unsafe footing might result. (The previous illustration is not intended to indicate that a texture that is neither rough or smooth is ideal. It is used only to clarify one functional aspect of surface and that care must be exercised when selecting textures.)

One further aspect of texture is its ability to control and condition the quality of sound. In general, extremely rough, soft surfaces tend to diffuse sound by trapping and dissipating the vibrations between the varying heights of projections of the surface. Surfaces that are smooth and hard will tend to produce the opposite condition—they will reflect the vibrations almost totally. The accoustical quality of an interior, for example, can be considerably changed by manipulating the textures of the surfaces.

2 Organization Through Color

COLOR

It is estimated that up to 90 per cent of all information about man's environment is received through his eyes. Although the human eye is not as complicated as the eyes of some insects, the visual perception of man is unique because his brain is capable of combining and explicating several hundred million visual fragments into a common image. The experience of visual perception is thus one of the most precious senses in the complex makeup of the human being and the added phenomenon of color vision is an incredible dimension of sight. John Ruskin, the nineteenth-century English author and critic, stated: "Color is the most sacred element of all visible things." Paul Shepard in his essay *Man in the Landscape* surmises, "Color vision probably appeared among early primates to help them find red durian fruits in the green canopies of tropical forests." No mammals below the primates possess man's color vision; however, many lower animals such as insects, fishes, reptiles, and birds have excellent color vision.

Man finds color in his surroundings wherever he turns. Color occurs in every natural object and has been incorporated in man-made objects as well; today color is found in more places and in more shades and intensities than ever before. The shifting of light and atmospheric conditions further produces color variations. The emotional and psychological influences of color upon man are indicated by his using such common phrases as "gray day," "yellow coward," "white lie," "in the pink," "blue mood," "green with envy," and "red-blooded." Each color term conveys an idea or feeling easily recognized.

For many individuals, color selection has developed intuitively, by habit or training that is either currently fashionable, or dismissed as unimportant. However, the way of design is to retrain the eye to demand color relationships that are always effective. Artists, craftsmen, designers, and architects have long depended upon color not only to enrich the objects that they create

35

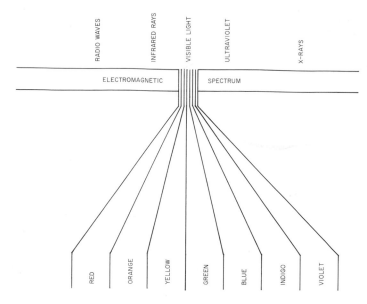

2-1 *A portion of the electromagnetic spectrum. Visible light is only a small part of the total spectrum.*

but also to establish the moods or emotions they wish to emphasize. It is very important to accept the notion that color makes significant demands upon the eye. The ambiguities and interplay of color dynamics can and must be cognitively presented, practiced, and understood by all individuals. Why is it that when a selection of colors is necessary the average individual is timid and apprehensive? With the wealth of admired color combinations available in nature, for example, why do colors selected often seem ill-chosen? Is it, perhaps, that color is so accepted and natural that it is taken for granted, and only when forced to decide does one then realize how little he knows about color? Unfortunately, the decision is frequently to use little color hoping that the palid no-color effect will suggest subtlety of taste. In truth, the so-called pastel colors are so light discordant that they lack character and vigor, not relating internally to any other hue in their environment. Later in this chapter there is a more thorough discussion of the relationships and importance of hue, value, and intensity. Nevertheless, the emphasis here is clear: light, tinted color choices should not be mistaken as subtle color discrimination, and knowledge of color usage is one of the most important skills the designer must possess. Interestingly, the use of color cannot only indicate cognitive knowledge but emotional tendencies as well. Psychologists working with Rorschach tests have found that emotionally inhibited persons are embarrassed by color, emotionally rigid persons are insensible to it, and emotionally responsive persons react to it freely.

There is an affinity between light and color because color is not an essential of objects but is dependent upon the absorption and reflection of light waves. Without light there can be no color and all light is color; indeed, white light contains all the visible colors and only when there is the complete lack of light (black) is there no color. However, it is by no means rare that architects and designers frequently discuss forms, structures, and objects as if they were colorless, relegating color considerations to minor importance. In truth, nothing that can be seen is completely without color.

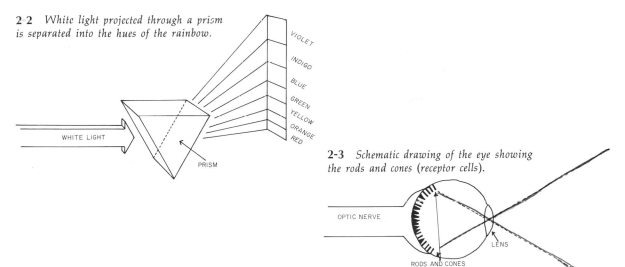

2-2 *White light projected through a prism is separated into the hues of the rainbow.*

VIOLET
INDIGO
BLUE
GREEN
YELLOW
ORANGE
RED

WHITE LIGHT

PRISM

2-3 *Schematic drawing of the eye showing the rods and cones (receptor cells).*

OPTIC NERVE

RODS AND CONES

LENS

Light is the visible form of radiant energy. It consists of electromagnetic radiation traveling through space in straight lines at the speed of 186,000 miles per secons. These radiations travel in wavelengths that are measured in millimicrons (millionths of a millimeter). The wavelenghts differ and the human eye is sensitive to those ranging between 400 and 800 milimicrons.

Light energy is available from both natural and man-made sources. "White light" or the radiant energy from the sun contains almost equal amounts of all the visible colors, and with the aid of a prism these color components can be separated into the familiar rainbow, that is, *spectrum.* The spectrum consists of red, orange, yellow, green, blue, indigo, and violet rays, with the red rays larger and stronger. The violet end is often referred to as the shorter end with rays of least length. Beyond the visible spectrum extend the invisible infrared rays on the red end and the ultraviolet rays on the opposite end.

Often the color components are not balanced and the light source emits light that has a dominance of one or more rays resulting in what is called "colored" light. Therefore, the light may appear to be red, blue, green, or yellow, for example.[1] The source of light frequently determines the color. Direct sunlight, as stated, is the purest white light; if, however, this light is reflected, filtered, or otherwise affected the pureness will be altered. Reflected light, especially from water or foliage, takes on a bluish or greenish cast. Light from artificial sources is also not as pure as sunlight. The most common source, the incandescent light bulb, produces an abundance of rays in the red-yellow range and a deficiency in the blue range. Ordinary fluorescent

---

[1] Yellow light is considered to be the best for visibility (automobile fog lights) whereas deep red, blue, or violet afford the poorest visibility. For example, with blue light, the human eye has difficulty focusing and objects appear blurred and surrounded by halos—a fact known in the burlesque theater of yesterday.

tubes have more emitted energy toward the blue region and a deficiency of red-yellow color components. Special incandescent and flourescent bulbs are available that produce a more favorable balance of light rays and are being used more frequently but have not replaced the more common types of light bulbs. There are other sources, fire and candlelight, mercury lamps, neon tubes, and the like each with distinct combinations of emitted rays.

Within the eye, attached to the back of the retina, are rods and cones that are the receptor cells sensitive to light. These sensitive cells transform light energy into the electrochemical vernacular of the brain. (The retina is actually part of the brain, the only part that receives impulses directly from outside the body.) The rods are sensitive only to the amount of light cast upon the retina but the thicker cones can distinguish color. There is an uneven distribution of the rods and cones (some 120 million rods and seven million cones in each retina): the cones are concentrated near the central foveal region with the more primitive rods on the periphery. The red rays are focused normally at a point behind the retina causing the lens of the eye to become convex. The blue focus is slightly in front of the retina causing the lens to flatten out. This accounts for the illusion of some colors seeming to advance or recede.

How then does an object appear to be colored? The simple answer is: the surface reflects the rays of a particular color within the light falling on that surface and these rays in turn fall upon the rods and cones of the eye.

Three important factors determine the apparent color of an object: 1) the ability of a surface to reflect light; 2) the color components present in the light source; and 3) the intensity of the illumination.

The surface is of primary concern. Its texture is important, whether it is smooth and highly reflective or slightly rough and markedly textured will affect the reflected light quality and strength. Further, colored substances or

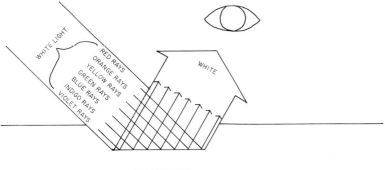

WHITE LIGHT

RED RAYS
ORANGE RAYS
YELLOW RAYS
GREEN RAYS
BLUE RAYS
INDIGO RAYS
VIOLET RAYS

WHITE

WHITE PIGMNENT

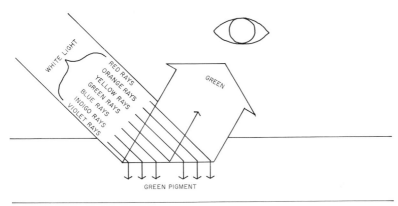

WHITE LIGHT

RED RAYS
ORANGE RAYS
YELLOW RAYS
GREEN RAYS
BLUE RAYS
INDIGO RAYS
VIOLET RAYS

GREEN

GREEN PIGMENT

2-4 *The pigment in the surface of an object reflects only the colored light rays that are identical to the color embodied in the pigment; all other colored rays are absorbed.*

2-5 *If a light source is deficient in the rays of a particular color, a color identical to the pigment of an object, then no light rays can be reflected; all are absorbed.*

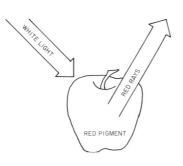

WHITE LIGHT

RED RAYS

RED PIGMENT

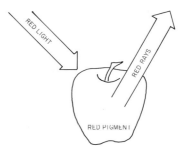

RED LIGHT

RED RAYS

RED PIGMENT

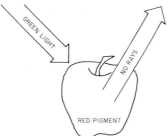

GREEN LIGHT

NO RAYS

RED PIGMENT

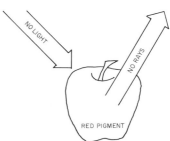

NO LIGHT

NO RAYS

RED PIGMENT

pigments[2] that have been applied to the surface or embedded into the surface have the ability to absorb and reflect certain colored light rays thus allowing the color to be seen. For example, an apple is seen as red because the "red" pigment in the skin of the apple reflects the light rays within the red range and absorbs all other light rays. This means that the apple is not seen as blue, green, orange, yellow, or violet because these colors are absorbed and are not reflected to the retina. However, if the light source was deficient in red rays, the so-called red apple would appear less red, for example, a light composed of only green rays cast upon the same apple would be absorbed and the red pigment could not reflect any rays and the apple would appear gray. Perhaps such extreme conditions are rarely encountered except upon the stage or other locations where light can be easily controlled. But, how often has a color seemed to change when seen under one kind of illumination and then under another? The matching of colors can be difficult unless the same source of light is used. For example, a clear red seen in daylight will appear slightly orange under the yellowish light of an ordinary incandescent bulb, but seen

---

[2]The pigments used to produce paints and dyes today are vastly different and have, by and large, more brilliance than those used in the past. The majority of the pigment sources came from nature—walnut hulls, onion skins, beach plum leaves, Saint-John's-wort, madder, insects, indigo, and from the earth itself; ochers, siennas, and umbers. All had a subtle, "earthy" quality that is still admired. However, in 1856, a young English research assistant William Henry Perkins, searching for a substitute for quinine, discovered the first permanent synthetic dye, a coal tar product. A brilliant purple, the new dye was named *mauvine* and became extraordinarily popular, so much so that the latter years of the nineteenth century were called "The Mauve Decade." soon a rainbow of synthetic colors was flowing from the chemist's test tubes and colors undreamed of in intensity, permanence, and variety a few years before became commonplace. Continued research has produced even more colors in recent years. Perkin's discovery was also the keystone to many related scientific developments—synthetic drugs (aspirin), plastics and fibers (celluloid and rayon), and even explosives.

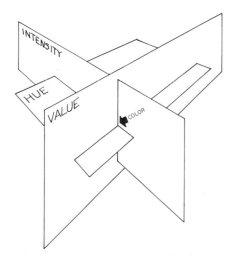

2-6 *The three dimensions of color: hue, value, and intensity.*

in a reflected "north" light or under an ordinary fluorescent light the red will be dulled somewhat and seem slightly violet.

The appearance of a color is affected not only by the quality of the light falling upon it but also by the quantity of light. A brilliant source of illumination may make a color combination appear garish and raw, but with less intense light the colors may make a handsome combination. Frequently, the entire character of a color will change when the amount of light is altered. Green, for example, can change from a "fresh" color to one quite "dead" when the illumination is lowered.

Although the investigation of colored light is fascinating and holds much interest and warrants study, the color in light has distinctive qualities and behaves differently than color in pigment and the initial concern of this discussion is the latter. When describing or classifying a colored pigment it is necessary to consider three dimensions, characteristics, or attributes. They are:

1. *Hue,* commonly the name of a color. It is the characteristic resulting from stimulation by light of different wavelengths.
2. *Value,* the lightness or darkness of a color. This second characteristic is determined by the physical result of the amplitude of the light wave.
3. *Intensity,* saturation, or the brightness or dullness. It is the composition of the light wave; if composed of only one or a few related light waves, the color will be brighter than if many different wavelengths are combined.

To better understand the qualities of each of the dimensions of color they are discussed separately; however, their close interrelationships should constantly be kept in mind.

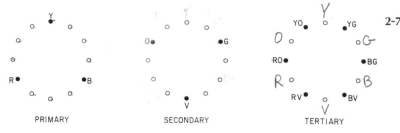

PRIMARY   SECONDARY   TERTIARY

2-7

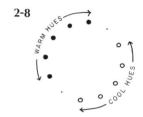

2-8

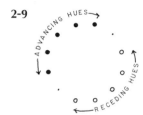

2-9

H U E. The color wheel illustrated has each of the hues arranged in the same order as the spectrum.[3] Between each of the six spectrum hues (indigo is omitted) additional hues have been added, making a total of twelve. These twelve hues are divided into three groups or categories:

The *primary hues,* labeled 1) are red, yellow, and blue. They cannot be obtained by mixing other hues together, but if combined in varying amounts will produce a great many other hues.

The *secondary hues,* labeled 2) are orange, green, and violet. Each secondary hue is located midway between the two primaries that produce it when they are combined in equal amounts. Thus, orange is the mixture of red and yellow, green is blue and yellow, and violet is red and blue.

The *tertiary hues,* labeled 3), are red-orange, yellow-orange, yellow-green, blue-green, blue-violet, and red-violet. These six hues are obtained by mixing equal amounts of a primary and an adjacent secondary hue, and are placed equidistant between the two "parent" hues. It should be noted that the name of each tertiary hue is a compound hyphenated name and the primary's name is first, for example, red-orange *not* orange-red. Of course, many more hues could be obtained and do exist and the designer should not limit himself to just these twelve arbitrary gradations. (Probably up to 10,000 different hues, values, and intensities can be discerned by the human eye, but only under the most ideal lighting and seeing conditions.)

[3]Sir Isaac Newton, in about 1666, made a circular chart in which he placed the seven colors of the rainbow (spectrum) side by side thus creating the first color wheel. Since then, many experts have devised other theories and wheels, eliminating and adding hues but always arranging them in the same sequence as the spectrum. The system used in this book was devised by Sir David Brewster and is the simplest and most frequently used of the well-known theories. The color systems of Albert Munsell and Wilhelm Ostwald, although being precisely color notated and used in industry, are based upon slightly different primary hues. However, the Brewster system is less complicated and easier to understand, and except in the most precise usage, serves well as a basis for color selection.

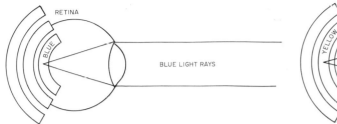
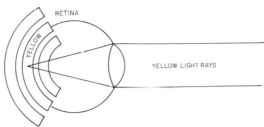

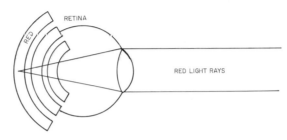

2-10 *Advancing hues focus slightly behind the retina; receding hues focus in front of the retina*

An examination of the completed color wheel reveals that the hues fall into specific relationships, that is the yellows, oranges, and reds are on one side of the wheel and the remaining greens, blues, and violets are on the other. Almost immediately there is a difference of visual temperature discerned, the yellow-red group appears warmer than the green-violet group. Indeed, the hues yellow through red are considered the *warm hues* and the hues green through violet are considered the *cool hues.* There are exceptions in nature such as blue flames, but almost all warmth producing factors (sunshine and fire) are generally in the yellow-red range whereas those seeming cold or cool (water, leaves, shadows on snow) are green to violet. Frequently, and especially before air conditioning, statements such as "never use a warm color on the sunny side of the house," were heard. Although this can be disregarded to some degree today, it is true that the *apparent* temperature of a room can be raised or lowered by the use of color alone.

Hues that are warm also tend to excite and cause more physical energy to be exerted. Action will often be speeded up and a spirit of restlessness will prevail in an environment that is predominantly warm in hue. On the other hand, cool hues tend to be more relaxing and actions are more slow (to some, cool hues are even depressing).[4]

The same hues, the warm group and the cool group, exhibit another pair of characteristics. Based somewhat upon the placement of focus on the retina, the warm hues, having longer and stronger wavelengths, seem to *advance* or come nearer the observer. Conversely, the cool hues, being shorter and

[4]There is evidence that color can even affect the pulse, blood pressure, and the nervous and respiratory systems. In Europe, a hospital has used blue in rooms with patients with high blood pressure to relax them and red in rooms with patients suffering from low blood pressure for stimulation. Yellow has also been used with mental patients to give them a sense of well-being.

weaker, seem to *recede*.[5] Thus, a form (object, interior, building) can be visually moved. For example, a blue room (a receding hue) will appear larger than a red room (an advancing hue) although the dimensions of both rooms are identical. A square room can be made to appear rectangular by having one wall a receding hue and the other three walls an advancing hue, or vice-versa. The hues do not have to be strong as even the palest pastels produce this spatial phenomenon.

The warm-advancing hues and the cool-receding hues together include ten hues. The remaining two, yellow-green and red-violet, are considered neutral and can take on the characteristics of either groups depending upon which hues are adjacent to them.

The selection of hues to be combined is one of the most exciting aspects of designing. Individual preferences, the designer's knowledge of the effects that one color has upon others, and the visual consequences of different light sources and qualities upon color all come into play.

Certain formalized combinations of hues produce color harmonies that throughout history have been considered to be better than others, but the contemporary use of such rigid and fixed schemes is frequently minimized. However, without any criteria of color judgment, how are decisions made? Can only intuition serve as valid determinants? The answer is a positive no! It must be strongly iterated, however, that the following traditional color schemes should only serve as *aids* for color selection and *not* be considered as the only acceptable color combinations. Just as the foregoing color wheel included only twelve of the large number of hues available, there are also almost unlimited combinations of these hues that can be exciting, calm,

---

[5] In nature as objects are removed from the observer they take on a bluish cast. This visual phenomenon is caused by the refraction of light rays by the dust particles in the air. Just as the sky appears blue, so do objects in the distance.

2-11

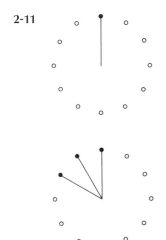

stimulating, or quiet, *and* acceptable. And frequently, it is the unexpected combination of hues that is the most satisfactory.

The color schemes are divided into two basic groups, the first group, consisting of schemes having one or more hues in common, are called the *related color schemes*. Two schemes or combinations are within this group, the *monochromatic* and *analogous* color schemes. Combinations that have no hues in common are called the *contrasting color schemes* and include the *complementary, double complementary, split complementary,* and *triad* color schemes.

Each of the following color schemes may include the use of black, white, or an unlimited number of grays as these are considered *neutrals* and are not colors in the strictest sense. The hues used in each color scheme may also be any value or any intensity. Hue is the only consideration at this time.

A *monochromatic color scheme* is based upon one hue. A monochromatic color scheme can be sophisticated and elegant, calm and soothing, or monotonous and dull. The sucess or failure of such a color scheme is dependent upon the skill of the designer. No pat formula can assure success but frequently variations in value and intensity and the addition of considerable amounts of white or black can enhance a monochromatic scheme. Such variety, although the hue does not change, provides interest for the eye.

An *analogous color scheme* is composed of three hues that are adjacent on the color wheel. These three related hues are pleasing, soothing, and generally easy to use. There is greater variety with which to work and the danger of monotony is not as strong as with a monochromatic scheme, yet it remains a quiet and soothing combination. Generally, however, analogous color schemes are kept either warm or cool.

A *complementary color scheme* is an exciting combination. Consisting of two hues that are directly opposite each other on the color wheel, there is no common

2-12

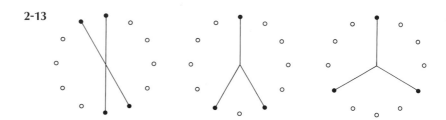

2-13

color in its composition. A more difficult scheme than either monochromatic or analogous, this exciting and lively combination offers many possibilities for personal expression.

Complementary hues generate strong visual stimulation; yet, paradoxically, when placed side by side, in small quantities they cancel each other out visually. The close relationship between complements is shown by the occurrence of colored *after-images.* A simple experiment can illustrate this in the easiest manner: if a spot of color, any color, is placed upon a white background and stared at in bright sunlight, a "halo" will soon appear. If the eyes are then shifted to the white surface, the identical shape of the spot will appear, but will be the complement of the original color. True complements can be ascertained in this way. It is a physical reaction; the cones on the retina of the eye that are receptive to the original color become fatigued, a temporary physical breakdown of a photochemical substance occurs, and the cones receptive to the complement are stimulated. Another occurrence in nature also concerns complements. The color of a shadow is not just darker or grayer; it is also the complement of the color of the light causing the shadow. This is the reason shadows on snow appear blue or blue-violet, sunlit grass is yellow-green but grass in the shade is blue-green, and mountains frequently are purple (violet) at sunset.

A *double complementary color scheme* retains the chromatic qualities of complements but they are tempered by those of analogous hues. Here, two sets of complementary colors are used, but they are adjacent on the color wheel. The two sets or related hues provide a stronger sense of harmony and unity and, therefore, are slightly easier to work with.

A *split complementary color scheme* is based upon one hue and the two hues on each side of its complement, but not the complement itself. Slightly less stimulating than a simple complementary scheme, it digresses just enough from the obvious to afford some unexpected hues, yet is relatively simple to use.

A *triad color scheme* has three hues equidistant on the color wheel. The nonrelated hues are always exciting and difficult to use, yet the triad color scheme is a favorite with many designers.

Two other color schemes are sometimes included in a listing of color schemes. A *tetrad scheme* is composed of four hues equidistant on the color wheel and a *near complementary scheme* uses one hue and another hue on one side of the complement but not the complement. It is believed however, that the six major color schemes are enough and that the tetrad and near comple-, ment schemes are extraneous. The experienced designer or color consultant seldom considers any of these combinations, working instead directly with each color. Actually, all colors can be combined successfully with all other colors if the three dimensions, value and intensity as well as hue, are carefully considered; and it is often the unusual combination that wins the plaudits.

   VALUE. The value, lightness or darkness, of a color is determined by the ability of the pigment to reflect light. When a color reflects a large amount of light, it is said to be a *high value,* and when a small amount of light is reflected (or most of the light is absorbed) it has a *low value.* Each hue has a "normal" value[6] and that value can be both actually or visually

---

   [6]The normal value of the different hues varies from light to dark. Yellow is the lightest hue; if placed at the top of the color wheel it will be found that as the colors descend on either side they become darker in equal steps to the darkest—violet. Thus there are seven steps or gradations of value 1) yellow, 2) yellow-orange and yellow-green, 3) orange and green, 4) red-orange and blue-green (which is middle value, equivalent to equal amount of black and white mixed together), 5) red and blue, 6) red-violet and blue-violet, and 7) violet. (These values correspond to the gradations found on a value scale divided into seven equal steps between black and white.)

2-14 *The forms of the two white swans are clearly defined against the dark water; however, it is difficult to discern the exact outline of the black swan in the second picture.*

altered. The *actual value* of a color can be changed by mixing the color with varying amounts of white or black pigments. If white is added to the normal value, thus raising the value, a *tint* is produced. If black is added, lowering the value, the resultant color is called a *shade*. For example, white added to red makes a tint of "pink" and a darkened red becomes a shade of "maroon." It is technically incorrect to say "a shade of pink." Brown is dark orange and olive green is dark yellow—both are obtained by adding black to the original color.

The value of a color can be visually altered by manipulating the adjacent values.[7] If the values are strongly contrasted each will strengthen the other and the forms will be clearly defined and increased in importance. However, forms having similar values are less distinct and tend to disappear. This principle can be applied to all objects, furniture, accessories, and even clothing. For example, it is not uncommon to find a large dark couch dominating and perhaps visually filling a light-walled room or space. Recovering the couch with a fabric of similar value to the background will make it appear less massive and heavy.

The apparent value of a hue can also be raised or lowered by varying the intensity of the light falling on the surface. As the illumination is dimmed, less light will be present to be reflected and the apparent value of the hue will be slightly lowered. Increase the lights and the value will appear to be raised. For this reason, a dark red wall will often appear to be almost black under very dim illumination. It should be remembered that a large area such as a wall will also look six to ten degrees darker than a small sample; and it is often wise to select paint, carpeting, and fabrics accordingly.

---

[7] In the 1830s, Chevreul, the French colorist, observed that an area of a particular value will appear to be lighter on the edge next to a darker value giving the effect of shading. He termed this phenomenon "simultaneous contrast."

2-15 *As forms recede they become middle value. The darkest and the lightest forms are both observed at a close range.*

2-16 *By controlling the values of the individual tile components of the floor, an entirely different design seems to appear; note especially the near and far areas.*

The visual effects of value are as diverse and important as they are with hue. Spatially, for example, a light color will seem to recede and a dark one will seem to advance. A small bedroom having very pale tints of blue will appear much larger than the same room painted dark shades of blue. It is possible to cancel out the spatial attributes of a hue with that of value. A dark color also has more visual weight than a light one. This may account for most heavy household equipment such as vacuum cleaners and sewing machines being available in light colors and thus giving the impression of easy movability, whereas small products, such as clocks and radios, are often made in dark colors that give them a heavier and more substantial appearance.

Distance also has an effect on visual value. Objects near the observer will have the most contrast in value and will often range from very light to very dark. As objects recede these contrasts blend visually, and objects are often seen in the distance as middle value. This is very apparent when viewing clumps of trees or similar groupings of objects; those close by will have very light areas or highlights and very dark shadows but in the distance the mass will be quite even and have little value variation. Thus, if strongly contrasting values are used, that surface or object will advance. For instance, a foyer that has been floored with contrasting black and white squares will not appear as spacious as one with a plain floor.

Of particular interest to the designer is the manipulation of values that can often accent or minimize a form. Perhaps the most familiar example is the painting of woodwork to match the walls: the woodwork all but disappears. An interesting architectural detail can be emphasized and given more importance by having it contrast with the value of its environment. Yet, several hues can often be combined, each with the *same value,* and the resulting color combination is generally quite sophisticated.

INTENSITY. The brightness or dullness of a color (also called *saturation*) is the third dimension. With the side range of colors now available from the most brilliant hue to the dullest neutral, *intensity* is even more important than it was in the past. Frequently, a color is correct in hue and value but the intensity seems to be wrong. Attempts to change its intensity sometimes prove frustrating because it is impossible to increase or raise the intensity of a color by mixing other pigments with it. Any addition to a color will tend to dull it. However, there are several ways to make the color *appear* brighter.

1. Surround the color with its complement. Each color will intensify the other and both will appear brighter. This can be seen at meat counters where the red meat is frequently surrounded by green ferns or parsley (real or imitation). A blue form will "sing" when placed next to an orange or brown background. However, these colors should be of sufficient size so that from a distance they do not visually blend together and appear dull.

   Often when two complementary colors are both of high intensity and similar value they will appear to vibrate. Although this is sometimes used with great success as an attention-getting device, it can be most distracting in an interior and it is perhaps best not to allow this to happen. Lowering the value of the intensity of one of the colors will correct the problem.

2. Surround the color with black. Although this does seem to make a color a little brighter, it really is only value contrast. (White works almost equally well around darker colors.) Frequently, the use of a very dark complementary color other than pure black is used combining these first two methods of visually raising the intensity.

3. By using small "patches" of closely spaced analogous colors instead of just one flat color, a surface can take on added strength. This is the "broken color" that was developed so successfully by the Impressionist painters of the latter half of the nineteenth century. What happens, of course, is that the eye mixes these analogous spots into richer color with more depth.

4. Any color will appear brighter if there are more rays of that color available that can be reflected. Consequently, if a light source has an abundance of

rays of a particular color, objects of that same color will appear brighter. This method is repeatedly used in supermarkets. For example, the light source above the meat counters often emits a maximum of red rays and the meat, in turn, appears redder (and fresher). Above the green vegetables an abundance of green rays is also found. The use of "pink" incandescent light bulbs will flatter the skin tones of those in that light.

The need to dull or lower the intensity of a color without appreciably changing the value of a hue is also frequently necessary and can be accomplished with much less difficulty. As was previously stated, the addition of any pigment will dull a color, but adding the complement will do this more quickly and with less effort. The slightest amount of the complement added to a color will markedly dull it. If two complements are mixed in equal amounts, the result should be a middle value gray—a gray not unlike an equal mixture of black and white. This is true when any set of complements are mixed. However, because of the natural variety of colors, a marvelous range of grays can be quickly produced that are far superior and more interesting than any grays mixed with just black and white. Black and white can, of course, be added if the value must be changed after the neutralized colors have been achieved.

The intensity of a color can also affect the visual spatiality. A bright or high-intensity color will advance whereas a duller color will recede. Thus, each of the dimensions of color can alter the spatial quality of forms.

HARMONY. Most of the literature relating to color touches one way or another upon the condition referred to as harmony. Paintings, interiors, rugs, fabrics, and the like are all frequently described as having harmonious color. Unfortunately, the term is applied in such a way as to imply that harmony is the only real aim of color combinations. Just as in music, the form of the composition is dependent upon the tones and how they are combined; harmony is one of the combinations that can occur. Likewise, the *dissonance*, or opposite of harmony, is also used by the composer to complete the form of the composition. It is wrong, both in music and color, to assume that harmony is the only true aim of the form. Some form of contrast must exist to establish a continuing vitality; whether it be counterpoint, dissonance, spacing, proportion, clash, discord, or whatever, it should be there. In a sense, harmony can exist when there is evidence of contrast to articulate it.

In the discussion of the analogous and monochromatic color schemes, it was pointed out that although either of these two color schemes is pleasant and soothing, there is a danger of the total effect becoming monotonous and dull. Three adjacent colors used together are harmonious and a monochromatic arrangement is inevitably so, but a large expanse of either of these choices in an interior would be much more effective if a small amount of a hue from the other side of the color wheel were introduced into the setting. The contrast would be the spark that ignites the viability of the harmonious arrangement. Of course, the position as well as the proportion of the accent is of utmost importance.

Significant also is the fact that contrast and harmony cannot refer only to hue but to value, intensity, temperature, or proportion as well, and are just as important as that of hue. Indeed, by using hues of the same value or intensity—a harmony can be achieved, as can a dominance of warm or cool hues.

Harmony is a condition or design component that can also apply to the other design elements: form, line, space, and texture. It is simply a general similarity or order that produces an accord among several parts and in many ways is synonymous with the principle of continuity discussed in the next chapter, but the term is more frequently applied to color because many people make the mistake of assuming that harmony is the only true consideration when making color combinations.

EMOTIONAL TENDENCIES. Throughout history, colors have stimulated emotional responses, and today's individual color preferences are

The subtle yet rich contrasting textures, colors, and forms admired in this detail from the great center doors of the Cathedral at Gerona, Spain, are the result of an excellent design and expert craftsmanship combined with the abrasion of weather and time. Covered in iron and copper, the heavy wooden doors lead the way to the widest Gothic vault in Europe (73 feet wide).

The jeweled brilliance that fills the walls of Gothic cathedrals can only be hinted in a colored photograph. The large rose window in the south transcept in the Cathedral of Notre Dame, Paris, almost "sings" when strong sunlight strikes the colored glass.

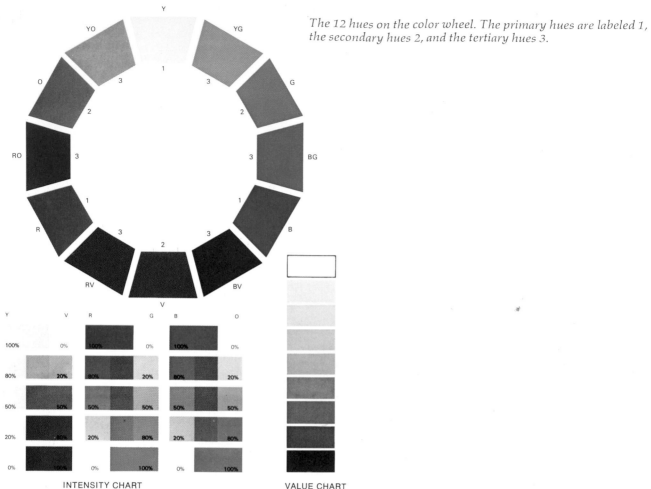

The 12 hues on the color wheel. The primary hues are labeled 1, the secondary hues 2, and the tertiary hues 3.

INTENSITY CHART

VALUE CHART

The colors used in this dining room emphasize the warmth of the sunlight filtering through the woven window blind. Although the design of the rug and color scheme reflect late Twentieth Century casual trends, the furniture, of Eighteenth Century French inspiration, adds a note of formality to the room. Photograph courtesy of Roz Mallin Interiors.

frequently based, albeit often subconsciously, upon color usage and symbolic interpretations stretching back to man's beginning. Prehistoric drawings have depicted evil spirits in red that are not unlike the image of the devil now, for example. The ancient world was a colorful place and archaeological research has revealed remnants of color of surprising brilliance and variety on Egyptian, Greek, and Roman buildings. Color had great significance in the past and even now it is a rare person who does not consider white as the color for brides, yellow as a "sunny" color, and purple (violet) as a color worn by royalty, or who has not used terms such as "red as fire, yellow streak, blue Monday, or green with jealousy." Some of these responses and expressions are rooted in antiquity, and some are of more recent origin, but all are related to the heritage of Western man.

Traditionally each color has had a wide range of recognized meanings, both positive and negative, and this color symbolism is, of course, reflective of ethnic background, tradition, and national heritage. Many of the rigid requirements of color symbolism that were prevalent in the past have fallen into disuse, and it would be impossible to list comprehensively the many nuances and customs of every hue; however, the following are some of the more common symbolic and mystical significances of color.

Red is the most emotion-stimulating color. Preferred in early childhood more than any other color and perhaps seen first, it denotes heat, bravery, earthly love, cheerfulness, and fervor. In a negative sense, red can also be interpreted as sin, danger, passion, hatred, and fire.

Yellow, the lightest hue, stands next to white in its purity. In the ancient world, yellow was more golden than now and orange is regarded symbolically as a modified yellow. Warmth, luminosity, wealth, and divine love are all qualities of yellow. Negatively, yellow signifies treason, deceit, cowardice, and sickness. Yellow has traditionally been the imperial color of China.

Green is closely allied to blue and indicates peace, hope, innocence, and fertility; yet it can also be interpreted as signifying jealousy; ghastliness, and inexperience.

Blue has long been identified with the sky and the heavens. Truth, wisdom, divine love, and immortality are expressed by this color. It is emblematic of a love less ardent than red and more celestial than yellow. Blue has a strong negative symbolism: coolness, despondency, and reserve.

Violet (purple) has traditionally been associated with royalty and the ancient purple was probably more like the crimson of today. In its sinister sense, purple is the emblem of mourning—but of a grief that is not as recent as one indicated by black, for example, the current use of purple veils over crosses in some churches during Lent.

Black, although not in the strictest sense a color, has long been important symbolically. Seeming to lack color and light, black is used to express gloom, death, fear, and defilement. However, in a positive sense, black is also used to show dignity and strength as in judicial and academic robes.

White symbolizes light, triumph, innocence, purity, and joy. White was worn by the vestal virgins of ancient Rome. The Romans also marked auspicious days with white chalk and less favorable days with charcoal. White, in it negative concept, signifies pallor, blankness, and ghostliness.

Value and intensity, as well as hue, express emotional tendencies. A *high value* can suggest daintiness and youth or instability and weakness, whereas a *low value* suggests strength and stateliness or mystery, wickedness, and depression. A *bright* color is associated with adventure, forcefulness, emotion, and elation and negatively expresses escitement, passion, violence, arrogance, and ostentation. A *dull* color can be subtle, refined, quiet, and peaceful or it can be depressive, morose, gloomy, and melancholy.

Clean, clear colors, the best antidote to the grayness of our industrialized environment, have an added worth beyond their aesthetic importance and psychological implications. Color can be functional too. Faber Birren, the noted color consultant, has stated: "It is commonly admitted today by many psychologists that color has one simple and clear effect: its emotional impact tends to lead to outwardly directed attention" (1967). Increasing numbers of designers are using color to indicate and to inform. Red is usually reserved to warn of danger—"stop" lights, firefighting equipment, "on" buttons, and emergency equipment. Green, on the other hand, is for permissiveness —"go" lights, first-aid kits, and directional information. Yellow has been found to be visible farther than any other color and is thus often used as a warning—low ceiling beams and projecting machinery in factories, school buses, "caution" signs, and yellow lines on a highway mean "do not pass." Brown, the color of the earth is frequently used for "outdoor" information such as parks, recreational areas, forests, and campsites. The National Safety Color Code is a standarized designation of specific colors for use in various utility systems. To aid in locating trouble and to minimize the possibility of error when servicing, electrical conduits are labeled red, gas pipes are yellow, water pipes are green, steam pipes are orange, and air ducts are blue.

The investigation of color to this point has been rather factual. The "human" aspect of color is also important and certainly must be considered by designers and others responsible for color selection. What colors do people prefer? Research findings are inconclusive, but, in general, people tend to prefer cool to warm colors, although red is second (after blue) in popularity. Young children prefer warm colors but as they mature their preferences gradually shift to cooler hues. Also, with increasing education, age, income, and experience in color selection, preferred colors become increasingly subtle and in combinations with little contrast.

Human eyes, minds, and palates are sensitive to any change from accepted color norms—milk is expected to be white; lettuce, green; coffee, brown; and so on. Studies have also been made in which the color of objects and food has been changed to nonfamiliar hues. An experiment was conducted by S. G. Hibben in which the steak was colored whitish-gray, the celery was pink, the salad was blue, the peas were black, the milk was red, and the coffee was yellow. Most of those who were served this meal lost their appetites and some became violently ill.

In summary, each basic element of design can be manipulated and made to change as desired by the knowledgeable designer. Just as form and space can be modified by the selective use of color, direction, and texture, color can be changed by playing hue, value, and intensity against the other. Architectural and furniture faults can all but be erased with color alone. The lively and bold use of color can "furnish" a room or "wipe out" necessary furniture to achieve a sparse look. The number of choices are limited only by the designer's experience and familiarity with the qualities of form, space, line, texture, and color.

3 Organization Through Balance, Continuity, Emphasis, Form Follows Function

The Elements of Design encompass the components used by man and found in nature, which, together, make up the near environment. Yet, these elements are only elements. An order must be established. According to Rudolf Arnheim, "Without order our senses could not function: the visible shape of an object must be clearly organized if we are to recognize, remember, and compare it with others. . . . If the world were not orderly, and the mind unable to perceive and create order, man could not survive. Therefore, man strives for order (1966)." To arrange these elements or components in a way that is agreeable with this natural desire for order and organization inherent in the composition of human beings, further considerations must be investigated. These are the *Principles of Design*, or *balance, continuity,* and *emphasis,* the organizational tools needed to construct a design.

BALANCE

When two or more design components or objects are combined, a degree of balance or equilibrium is established, each interacting with the other. Equilibrium is a basic force in everyone. From the moment a child attempts to become vertical, it is imperative that he maintain equilibrium; if he does not, shocks or even injuries can result. The maintenance of the horizontal and vertical directions, equilibrium, is dependent upon the small balance organs in the inner ears, the semicircular canals. If these are ever impaired, either through injury, age, or other cause, one's sense of well-being and orientation is seriously hindered. (A fear of falling and of loud noises seems to be fundamental with each person from birth.)

Aside from this *physical balance*, which is concerned primarily with actual weights and gravitational pull, *visual balance* is also of consequence. How important or heavy a form *looks* rather than *is* is the concern of the designer. It has been noted that a form can be changed by altering its color of value, for example, a sofa slipcovered to match the walls becomes less important and "weighty" than one that contrasts with the walls. Therefore, objects do not

57

3-1

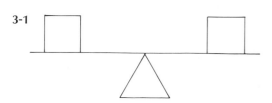

3-2 *A quiet symmetry is found in this Italian cloister.*

always have to be the same size to establish visual equilibrium, it is, in fact, possible to have a large form balance a small one just as a large area of dull color can equalize a small spot of brilliant color. The possible variations are limited only by the sensitivity of the person combining the component forms.

There are three basic forms of balance.[1] The first and the most simple, familiar, and probably the one that is most used is called *symmetrical, formal, static, or passive balance.* Symmetrical balance consists of an arrangement of forms with one half the mirror image of the other with an imaginary central axis bisecting this arrangement. Thus, two identical candlesticks with a bowl of roses centrally placed between them, all on a mantel, or two small boys on a seesaw—each the same distance from the fulcrum—would be simple symmetrical arrangements. Symmetrical balance occurs frequently in nature, including many leaves, plants, and animals—the human skeleton when viewed from the front or back is so arranged. No doubt because of man's symmetry many of his objects, chairs, tables, buildings, and his clothing are also formally arranged.

Symmetrically balanced forms often connote a feeling of impressiveness, stateliness, dignity, and formality (as one name implies). Such arrangements are also rigid and nonmoving with little or no variation possible, and there is a tendency toward design inertia, static effect, and lack of interest.

Throughout history, most buildings have been symmetrically designed. It is especially evident during the classical periods and those periods influenced by classical periods. (In fact, if the designer is desirous of creating a formal, classical feeling, it perhaps is almost mandatory to use such balance.) Frequently, not only the facades of both the interior and exterior were

[1] The variety of terms used to describe the relationships of visual and actual weights are more diverse than with almost any other aspect of design. It is the purpose here to discuss the concept, and the most familiar terms are used in the discussion.

3-3 *The elaborate embroidered decoration on the back of a peasant vest is symmetrical in its basic design.*

3-4 *The almost rigid formal arrangement of the large forms of this house is completely disregarded in the window, door, garage door, and chimney placement resulting in a poorly balanced facade. One wishes that the garage door had not been painted white, but ruther a value that gave it some visual weight, and that the entrance door had been centered.*

3-5

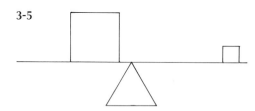

symmetrical but often even the floor plans had axes that divided one half from the other (sometimes both front to back *and* side to side). Interestingly, it is not uncommon to find during some periods (the seventeenth and early eighteenth centuries, for example) that nonfunctional architectural elements (false doors and windows) have been incorporated into buildings to achieve the "correct" and desired formal arrangements.

Symmetrical balance is simple and easy—often too easy. All that is required are two identical forms or objects, and since it is so simple it is often that which is first considered and used. Although it can be a handsome and beautiful answer to an arrangement problem and certainly should not be discounted entirely, symmetrical balance has been so misused that care and discretion should govern its use today.

The second kind of balance is called *asymmetrical, informal, occult, or active balance.* Again, using the seesaw as an illustration: a small boy is now balanced by his grandfather who must sit close to the fulcrum to make the seesaw work. Equilibrium is attained, yet duplication of figures is not necessary; one side is not the mirror image of the other. Simply by adjusting distances from the fulcrum the small boy can easily be balanced by an older brother, his sister, or even a smaller cousin.

The standing human figure also displays asymmetrical balance. A vertical line dropped from the base of the skull will reveal that in the side view of a skeleton individual forms shift direction from one side of that line to another. In fact, any physical activity will cause relationships in the human figure to be asymmetrical, if balance is maintained.

The possibilities are infinite. Not only can size relationships be adjusted to create informal balance but it is also possible for a dull object to balance a bright object, one of considerable interest to balance one of little distinction, or an object of small contrast in color or value to one of great contrast. A grouping (constellation) of small objects can even balance a large object. In essence, it is the apparent weight that is important. There is a feeling of

3-6 *Originating to the right of center, the linear direction of this small architectural detail flows down, to the left, and then slightly up again creating a remarkable sense of equilibrium.*

movement, often of spontaneous placement and of a more casual and informal mien.

This dynamic and tenuous type of equilibrium is also much more personal. There are no rules for asymmetrical balance; the balance must be "felt." The individual who is arranging the various elements or parts must employ his sensitive judgment, and each part is dependent upon all the other parts. One consideration that does come into play is the orientation of the design—the shifting of an arrangement from vertical to horizontal may, for example, change the feeling of balance drastically. It is the rare asymmetrical design that maintains its equilibrium in all attitudes.

Asymmetrical designs are often identified with the rustic and the Oriental. Most Oriental design, both Japanese and Chinese, are not formally balanced, yet have a remarkable sense of equilibrium. Japanese floral arrangements are excellent examples of this. The informality of rustic design, however, is often the result of missing parts rather than by design (medieval buildings were originally quite formally balanced in plan and facade but time, war, and later additions have often altered their appearance giving the impression of a more active equilibrium). Historically the asymmetrical was dominant in only a few periods of Western culture. However, during the Rococo period of the mideighteenth century, as a reaction to the stiff formality of the seventeenth century and the early years of the eighteenth, there was a decided preference for informally balanced design. Wall and door panels, arrangements of interior architectural parts, and even furniture design often reflected this preference. During the nineteenth century there were also marked preferences for informal design as seen in the Gothic revival, and its informally arranged interior and exterior spaces, and during the latter part of the century when a greater freedon of design existed. Today, it is generally accepted that asymmetrical balance is preferred, a reflection of the informal and active life of most people.

The third type of balance is called *radial.* Not encountered as frequently as

3-7

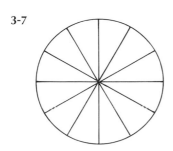

3-8 *The delicate sphere of bronze wire seeming to float above the water is an example of three-dimensional radial balance. If one were to view the fountain from above, the water jets, the circular form of the pool, and the spherical sculpture would combine to make a radial balanced design.*

symmetrical or asymmetrical balance, it is, nevertheless, of importance in design. Equilibrium is established around a central point and the design elements extend out from this point rather than from an axis. A feeling of movement is also sustained. Radial balance thus differs from a design that is symmetrically arranged on both vertical and horizontal axes.

Examples of radial balance can be seen in a wagon wheel, a rose window in a church or cathedral, in a daisy, and in the decorative patterns seen on many plates, bowls, and similar round objects.

However, if the wheel, for example, should lose a spoke or two and a piece of the rim, the wheel would no longer be radially balanced but would become symmetrically balanced only. The wheel would revolve until the broken section would be at the top and the left half would be the mirror image of the right.

CONTINUITY

So often when analyzing interiors, buildings, and objects, the successful design solutions are those in which the individual elements seem to "fit" together forming total units. This is frequently the result of continuity, sometimes called *rhythm* or *organized movement*. As fundamental in nature as it is in the designs of man, continuity is the "glue" that holds disparate elements together. It is also the perceptual quality that causes the eye to "flow" from one unit to another with a certain regularity.

There are several ways to achieve continuity. One way is to repeat elements, motifs, or parts throughout the design rather than each part's being entirely different. *Repetition* creates a simple rhythm in the design—1,1,1,1,1,1,1,—and helps hold it together just as a repeated beating of a drum can tie together different sounds into a musical composition.

The repeating of the same forms, colors, lines, and the like in a design easily brings regularity to the composition, but it can also just as easily achieve monotony and dullness. As the ticking of a clock retreats quickly into

3-9 *The delightful variety of canned fruits and vegetables gain continuity by the repetition of the glass jar form in this photograph of "fancy packs" entered at the Century of Progress World's Fair in Chicago in 1933. (Note the jar on the left, top shelf.)*

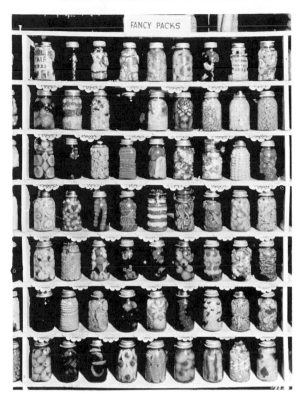

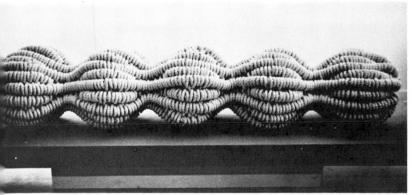

3-10 *The repetition of the large forms, the ribs, and the rope thickness produce a strong feeling of a total composition in this macrame sculpture by Nancy Fisher.*

3-11 *Despite the seeming complexity of this carved stone relief from Thailand, only two basic motifs are alternated.*

the background and is not consciously heard, so can the constant repetition of design elements become unimportant. Repetition can, if sensitively handled, produce successful solutions to design problems, the repeating of columns across the facade of the Parthenon, for example.

A slightly more varied and interesting way of achieving continuity is by alternating design elements. *Alternation,* instead of the even beating of a drum, is a rhythm of 1,2,1,2,1,2,1,2, or left, right, left, right, left, right, or black, white, black, white. A checkerboard is a good example of alternation with its light and dark squares. The reference to the Parthenon to illustrate repetition can also be used to illustrate alternation. One is now made additionally aware of not only the columns but also of the spaces between. The alternation of the sunlit columns and shadowed negative spaces achieve some variety, yet disruption of the design does not occur.

A third and even more varied method of continuity is *progression.* Here it is 1,2,3,4,5,6,7,8, and so on—a gradual change from one element to another. Forms changing from large to small, square to round, or bright to dull in a regular manner illustrate the concept of progression. Nature provides excellent examples of progression. Small streams flowing together form larger tributaries and in turn join into rivers, and the central trunk of trees leading to the smallest twigs above the ground *or* the roots below are but two examples.

Progression is the most dynamic and flexible method of achieving continuity. It is not necessary that the elements be juxtaposed, because as the eye moves from one part to the next there is a visual tying of the whole together.

There have been repeated comparisons made between music and architecture and interior design; *frozen music* is an often heard term. There are, of course, many similarities between all the arts and like terms and concepts are used. Motifs and elements are duplicated in each, for example. However, they are each distinct. Painting is painting, music is music, and architecture is architecture. Painting uses sight, music uses hearing—and time. Understand-

3-12 *The roof forms of this Thai temple progress upward, culminating in the layered spire.*

3-13 *The dramatic white form slashing across the facade of this building attracts the eye, but it is the "hole" in it that dominates the composition. The angularity of the painted design is further heightened by the clustering of the circular openings at the top.*

ing architecture, and especially interior design, requires sight, touch, hearing, plus time *and* motion.

As one progresses from one place to another he experiences the various types of continuity. Buildings and decorative elements come into view that are similar to those just observed. The flicker of highlight and shadow is seen everywhere. The freedom of movement within and without a sheltering environment is a continuing and difficult challenge to the interior designer and architect. Each turn, each view, each opening of space should be exciting and rewarding. An imposing facade or interior is too often followed by spaces of lesser importance and interest, and the visual and spatial experiences that could be afforded the observer are cut short if not stopped entirely.

EMPHASIS

Every successful design solution has a visual interplay of varying strengths that has been established among the components making up the whole. It is this consideration of importance that comprises the third principle of design —*emphasis*. The term *center of interest* is sometimes used in place of emphasis. Actually, most knowledgeable designers consider emphasis as being the more comprehensive concept of design in which all the parts are evaluated, whereas center of interest usually refers only to the main "focal point" of a design, that part which the observer sees first and to which the eye continuously returns. If the designer had a checklist against which he could evaluate his designs, listed under emphasis would be three terms—*dominant, subdominant,* and *subordinant.* These are the essentials to the understanding of emphasis.

In the effective design the eyes are invariably drawn to different components, components that seem to dominate and have greater visual importance. Furthermore, other components are found to be of somewhat lesser importance and still others may seem almost negligible. Success in the use of

3-14 *The lack of emphasis in the facade of this apartment building gives it a sterile look. One wonders if the inhabitants are affected by its prison-like appearance. This building is also an example of how simple repetition can sometimes diminish the effectiveness of a design rather than enhance it.*

emphasis is determined by the appropriate selection and distribution of these parts. It is not a matter of marked contrast between a few selected areas but rather it is this successful use of graded degrees of visual dominance and subordination that are distributed throughout the total composition. The use of many gradations of visual importance will result in a design that is both pleasing and inviting in its variety and intricacy.

Emphasis takes into consideration the arrangements, qualities, and quantities of all the forms, shapes, spaces, lines, colors, and textures in all areas of a design and can be applied to each of the elements of design individually as well as totally. Size is one way to gain dominance; intensity and contrast are other ways. In fact, much that has been written about the elements of design dealt with the consideration of emphasis.

When investigating and analyzing an interior or even a complete home, it is sometimes found that even though there is a functional furniture arrangement, good use of space, easy flow of traffic from one space to another, and the proper elementary selection of textures and colors, the total effect is one of uninviting monotony, confusion, or restlessness. All the pieces of furniture may be the same basic size, proportion, line, and shape; the spaces between each piece may be almost identical; or the color used may have too little value contrast, intensity, or variety. Whatever the cause, the total does not work effectively.[2] It is here that the "checklist" can be used. Does the room or rooms have a dominant theme, a dominant color, a dominant form and so on, for example, is it a "French" room, a blue room, does it have many curves? If it does, then it can be said that there is dominance. Does it *also* have a lesser theme, color, form, and the like,—subdominant considerations. There should be a lesser theme because these subdominant components,

---

[2] A design with sharp unrelieved contrast of the elements of design can be as disconcerting as one with little contrast. In either case, the elements cancel out each other and no emphasis is attained.

3-15 *The harmony of many patterns, materials, and forms seen in this low-cost apartment is reinforced by the dominance of the smooth, rounded form of the chair in the foreground. The chair, being red and without pattern, also contrasts with the smaller rounded forms of the pillows covered in small patterns of red, white, and blue.*

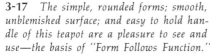

3-17 *The simple, rounded forms; smooth, unblemished surface; and easy to hold handle of this teapot are a pleasure to see and use—the basis of "Form Follows Function."*

3-16 *What could be nicer than a cup of hot tea in a little vine-covered cottage? This teapot despite its symbolism does not adhere to the dictum of "Form Follows Function."*

although not as important as the dominant ones, serve as buttresses and support. Further, are there small accents, small details, motifs, parts that add spice to the design? These are the subordinate elements. These can be changed, moved, or added to without altering the total design to any appreciable extent but they are contributors to the total effect and are often a "delight to the eye" upon discovery.

FORM FOLLOWS FUNCTION

An additional design consideration that falls both within and without the circumscription of the elements and the principles of design is what is most commonly called *Form Follows Function*. Although Louis Sullivan, the important late nineteenth and early twentieth-century American architect, is credited with coining the phrase, Form Follows Function is not a recent idea. Designer-craftsmen of the world have always followed its precepts. But with the increasing influence of the industrial revolution and the accompanying remoteness of the designer from the finished product, the concept of Form Follows Function had been all but forgotten.

It is a very simple concept, but one that is frequently disregarded. Of course, every period in history has had poorly designed products as well as well-designed ones, but fortunately the better ones have survived in greater numbers. Today, however, most design critics would agree that the percentage of poorly designed objects is far larger than in the past. This is no doubt the result of the variety of objects available, the ability of a machine to spew out thousands of objects instead of the craftsman's tens and in all probability the lower design criticality and ready acceptance by today's more affluent consumer. One only has to go to the nearest shop and look at the articles on display to discover that many of the products now available were designed as if the idea of Form Follows Function never existed. One of the worst groups of objects are those that are commonly called "accessories." Rarely does the average consumer question a lamp base shaped like a head

3-18 *Many of the accessories available in retail stores flagrantly disregard the axiom of Form Follows Function. Note the mailbox hanging above the couch to be used as a planter, the lamp base on the side table in the form of a sailor at the helm of a ship, and the bottle in the shape of a duck (the head unscrews), the covered bowl on the coffee table molded to look like a pile of fruit, the floor lamp with fake candles, and, of course, the overblown couch and chair.*

with a light socket protruding from the top; a clown cookie jar—lift the hat and get a cookie out of the brain cavity; a statue of Venus de Milo with a clock cleverly stuck into her navel, a cow cream pitcher, a candle with a light bulb sticking out of the end, a toby mug, a sugar scoop switch plate, a plant container in the shape of an animal—the plant forming the tail of a dog or cat, for example; a beer mug with a handle in the form of a shapely female nude—the list is endless. These are extreme cases to be sure, and if they were rare they could be considered amusing transgressions of design, but when confronted with identical dozens of such designs on the shelves it is an affront to the sensibilities of everyone.

In the total concept of one's environment, more is included than the "cute and decorative" articles found in the interiors of many stores and homes. Form Follows Function applies just as much to the larger objects as well as to the smaller ones. No less appalling are the television sets or refrigerators "hidden" in French armoires or Spanish chests; electric heating elements in the top of new cast iron "coal or wood-butning" kitchen ranges; fake bricks, stone and shingle surfaces; plastic nonfunctional beams; dovecotes applied to the gables of houses; and yes, split-level houses on flat land and ranch houses on hills.

What then should be included as acceptable? Some designers and critics believe that a strict interpretation of Form Follows Function means that everything must be extremely functional and that a complete avoidance of any ornamentation is mandatory. The resulting designs are stripped to the minimum, to the simplest form. However, when considering Sullivan's own architectural triumphs, such a rationale must be questioned. He did not design buildings that were devoid of ornamentation. On the contrary, his buildings are often heavily ornamented, but only at important and structural points and here the eye finds great pleasure and variety. Therefore, Form Follows Function does not just mean the bare minimum; it means, too, that

3-19 *Louis Sullivan's Northwestern Bank, in Owatonna, Minnesota, has considerable ornament on the exterior and the ornament itself is elaborately designed. However, its judicious placement enhances and enriches the building rather than detracts from it.*

whatever the form, it should express its function, but that form might also be a delight to the eye.

Curiously, almost every discussion of Form Follows Function centers upon form rather than upon function; however, in practice it is the function that determines the success of an object, interior, structure, or urban plan. It should always be remembered that it is how it is used and not just the appearance that, in the final analysis, is important; the elements of human use and time must be included in every analysis. Perhaps nothing should be judged until time and use have been allowed to "mellow" the design. Yet, how often are the interiors in the latest magazines and books shown with occupants? In these most proximate spaces, all the accessories and artifacts are there but the inhabitants are missing. The written descriptions accompanying the illustrations refer only to the forms, colors, and layouts, seldom to how they relate to the occupants, and one can only imagine how they truly function.

Further, it should also be remembered that many articles and objects often function just as efficiently today as they did in the past and that it is not always just the "new" that is best. It is a matter of careful selection not just age (or rather, the lack of it) that is a criteria of Form Follows Function.

Part Two

Enviromental Design

Knowledge about man's immediate environment, the hollows within his shelters that he calls offices, classrooms, corridors, and hospital wards, is as important as knowledge about outer space and undersea life.

Robert Sommers

4 Historical Development of City Plans

Only a few short years ago the term *environmental planning* to most people would have meant the design of a garden or perhaps the planning of a street or a park. It might even have been a completely unknown term to them. The environment was everywhere; it was just there and there was plenty of it to go around. However, that viewpoint has given way to broader and more serious considerations. Truly, the environment does include everything—the earth, plants, rivers, structures, roads, furniture, rooms, and people—but the increasing insistence of urban blight and renewal, the unprecedented and unplanned sprawl of suburban housing, the proliferation of superhighways, the lack of rural and urban open spaces, and the growing bleakness of working and living areas all indicate the lack of environmental planning.

Piecemeal, "cookie cutter"[1] developments are not valid or desirable; whole regions must be considered at one time and as a single entity because each part, whether it is urban or rural, is dependent upon the others. The rapid technological developments, man's ability to travel and communicate greater distances in shorter times, the mechanical equipment capable of moving and reshaping huge tracts of land and materials, and the population explosion have necessitated a quickened awareness of environmental design.

Never before has there been so great a need for careful evaluation of the natural and man-made physical resources and the planning of the development. It has been estimated that urban space equivalent to the size of Hartford, Connecticut, must be constructed *each* week of *every* year until the year 2000 to house and serve the 100 million additional Americans expected to be born during this period. Invariably the question, "Where to build?" is

---

[1]"Cookie cutter" developments are those in which everything is the same: the same house structures and street layouts inhabited by the same kinds of families with the same ages, incomes, racial backgrounds, and having the same time payments. Frequently, these developments are cut out of the countryside with little regard or respect for the surrounding areas, as a cookie is cut from the dough.

4-1 *Can human be-
ings living in identical
houses in featureless
surroundings escape
not being desensitized?
Urbanites are no less
immune to this danger
than are those living
beyond city centers.*

asked. Yet, the geographical size of the United States *could* accommodate five
times its present population, or 1 *billion* people, and still not be as densely
populated as Switzerland, which is considered to be a pastoral country.

What then is the solution? Careful and thoughtful environmental planning.
Each housing area, each city, town, and hamlet, each acre of land must be
carefully planned for the present *and* for the future. These plans must be
prudently considered and have built-in flexibility for later adaptions. There
must also be strengthened rules of enforcement, because after the plans have
been completed they must not be sabotaged for shortsighted monetary gains,
changes in political destinies, or individual whims. They must encompass not
only the functional but the geographic, visual, and humanistic considerations
as well. This may be authoritative, but it is absolutely necessary.

Only by careful evaluation and expanded knowledge can positive, far-
reaching planning be developed. The people, the users, must be included in
environmental decisions; if they are ignorant or unaware of the criteria for
such decisions they must be educated, for "it is for want of education and
discipline that a man so often insists petulantly on his random tastes. . . ."
(George Santayana). The pedagogical techniques that are necessary are those
that include not only scientific methodology, replication of cognitive material,
and behavioral objectives but also those of an affective domain that include
interpretation, analysis, and value judgment.

There is a clear need to increase environmental awareness and to combat
the traditional enemies of that awareness—adaptation, habituation, con-
formity, and adjustment. Man is an adaptive animal; he can adjust his life to
accommodate the stresses that conflict with it. All too often the admirable
qualities of the environment are subtracted by bulldozer, disease, and human
error and we, human beings, notice and are aware of what has gone, but
soon, apparently, do not notice the loss. The process is repeated *ad infinitum.*
The adaptation becomes a habit and is a subtle and insidious deceiver. For
example, if a person can adapt or turn off *10* per cent of some disturbing

4-2 *Without doubt, the absurd combination of structural and decorative materials and forms of this diner is seldom noticed by individuals who pass it.*

condition, why not *12* per cent? A slight raise means little. If 12 per cent is accepted what about *15* per cent—*20* per cent? At what point is it not acceptable? What is so insidious about this process is that the amount of stimulus necessary to be noticed as a change is proportionate to the *existing* level of stimulation. Thus, acceptance begets greater acceptance until eventually the environment becomes unbearable and the individual must move, succumb, or perhaps, become less of a human being, a half-person.

Psychiatrist Matt Dumont has stated, "The extent to which a person can influence his environment will determine his ability to perceive himself as a human being." The interior of an individual's home or apartment is one of the few areas where he can freely choose components, but even there, if others are involved, the decisions must be shared. Elsewhere, the anomaly of contemporary society has now thrust upon each person environments he did not choose. Yet, Americans have always valued their freedom of choice and assumed their "right" to determine the direction of their lives. Notwithstanding, rare is the person whose "environmental freedom" is more than a mere illusion; he is already controlled by external influences. All to frequently the design consideration—and the functionability—of his place of work, his school, his neighborhood have been made by someone or some agency far removed from him, perhaps an absentee landlord, government agency, or corporate head—or the architect, planner, or builder. Although often well intended and sincere, these nonuser decision-makers frequently fail to adequately comprehend and satisfy the needs and desires of the users. Therefore, it is the responsibility of everyone to become aware, and knowledgeable and to participate in his environmental planning; only through a melding of opinions can the goal of a satisfactory environment be achieved (being simply aware of a situation does not change or improve it).

The criteria and background of environmental decisions are here more important; the processes, not the final products. There can be no absolute scientific standards as the complexity of modern life and the adaptability of

4-3 *The visual punishment inflicted upon the individual is seldom considered when many design decisions are made. It is hard to imagine that in this photograph each form—sign, building, letter, car, post—is the result of a separate design decision made by some person or persons, even though this is undoubtedly what happened.*

man precludes rigid norms. Environmental awareness is not an either/or process, nor is it the effect of the environment upon human potential; there are many variables, levels, and degrees. Different decisions are requisite for each area or region; there are no single answers, but like all design problems there are precedents and similar underlying considerations.

The city is a dynamic, living organism. Its structure is determined by the combination and interactions of the many smaller individual components (neighborhoods, factories, business centers, families, and the like), which merge and blend to produce the character and flavor of the larger unit. Any major change in one or more components ultimately influences the arrangement and interactions between all of them. The uses of land space, the methods of transportation, the location and types of industry, and the population shifts and changes also affect the total balance of priorities within the city. Never static, this constantly expanding system of life is a multifaceted arrangement of individual units that attract, alter, and, in turn, create new and different patterns of interaction.

Throughout history, nothing has been more complex or has so disclosed the spirit of the people than the structure of their urban environment. The city has regularly been developed around the organization of usable spaces that enhanced and accommodated the needs and wants of its occupants. The city provided protection from enemies, a place to live and work, the material necessities of life, a place for socialization, and a center of education, but the design of a city is successful only when it adequately fulfills these needs and can still accommodate the changing patterns of growth and development.

Early man did not enjoy the benefits and protection that are provided by the well-developed city. Instead, he lived, hunted, and socialized as a mem-

The Historical Development of the City

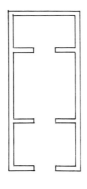

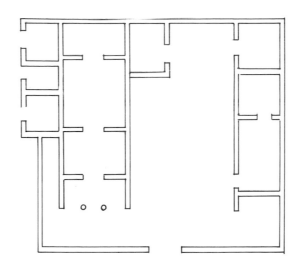

4-4 *In the eighth and seventh century B.C., ordinary people lived in small huts, often of rectangular plan (left). Later these huts were often expanded to include a courtyard with surrounding structures for other members of the clan.*

ber of a small nomadic clan. Each member of the clan was dependent on the success of all the other members for his food, his protection from enemies, his education, and his social interaction.

When man began to enjoy the benefits of food provided by agriculture in addition to food obtained from the hunt, the clan became less nomadic and remained longer in one location. Such a change in living habits led to the formation of the small village. Each clan soon realized that less mobile living conditions made them more vulnerable to attacks from their enemies. As agriculture increased in importance, more land was needed for cultivation and the division of labor within the clan developed into those who hunted, those who farmed, and those who maintained the homesite; therefore, greater attention had to be paid to the defense of these activities. The territory needed soon became too large for one clan to defend by itself. With this development in social living man gradually realized that greater protection could be gained by banding together isolated clans into adjacent clusters or small villages. These walled cluster villages afforded their occupants better protection from the attacks of wandering tribes and migrating invaders. The original plans of such cities as Nineveh in Assyria, Persepolis in Persia, early Athens, and the small village that would eventually grow to become the city of Rome were based upon the concept of the walled and fortified village cluster pattern.

Almost without exception these small villages developed in fertile valleys (the Indus and Nile, for example) where more grain could be produced and navigable waterways provided easy and cheap transportation. Rome was the first city (and civilization) that did not rely almost solely upon water transportation although it was situated on water. Early in the development of Rome a vast system of paved roads was expanded, some of which are still used today.

With the collapse of the Roman Empire and the advent of the "Dark Ages"

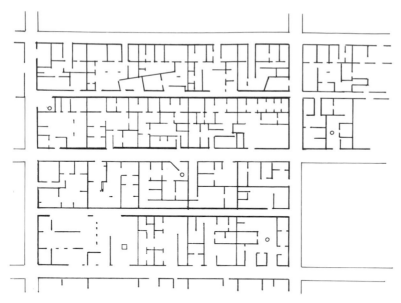

4-5 *Hippodamus of Miletus laid out rules for town-planning in the fifth century B.C. Throughout Greece and Asia Minor houses were laid out in large geometric blocks.*

4-6 *Typical of castles throughout medieval Europe, this fortified castle in Germany guards the valley below.*

of medieval Europe, the walled cluster villages were replaced by the heavily fortified castle surrounded by a thick wall. Although some villagers lived within the walls, most lived without on small farms surrounding the castle. The lord of the castle gave these exposed farmers refuge from attack in return for their services as producers of food for the castle and as members of a supporting army for his military activities. As trade began to increase between these fortified castle "cities," shops of merchants and small industries were set up within the walls, if space was available, but more often outside their protection. Eventually, another wall was built to shield these new commercial additions and with further expansion additional encircling walls were built. Often these early fortified cities had the appearance of being surrounded by concentric rings.[2]

Natural fortifications also provided protection from attack. Medieval towns made inaccessible by very hilly terrain or isolated by water were often well protected without the inclusion of the heavy walled castle. Even as late as the seventeenth century, the city of Quebec, Canada, originally an outpost for French trading, was sited for the protection afforded by the natural palisades rising from the Saint Lawrence River.

Water has proved to be as effective for protection as did rugged terrain. Early examples are the prehistoric Swiss lake dwellers with their small settlements consisting of homes raised several feet above the water on closely spaced poles. These individual structures were interlinked by small wooden walkways. Although these settlements were usually located near the shoreline of the lake and connected to the bank by a wooden ramp, some were placed farther away and boats were used.

[2] A similar development of concentric growth rings can be seen in the evolution of many of the larger cities of the present day. A more detailed discussion of this growth pattern is given in Chapter 5.

4-7 *Viewed from the castle wall, the present town of Epstein, Germany, reflects the* civitas *of the Middle Ages.*

The inhabitants of Venice, Italy[3], who were originally from the mainland, were afforded protection from warring tribes when they settled on mud islands on the shore of the Adriatic. Eventually the importance of their move increased as trade was developed with the eastern part of the known world and Venice became the significant crossroads of commerce between the Orient and western Europe.

The plans of river or seacoast cities were largely dependent upon the shape and function of their waterfronts. Most of the trading areas and the storage and manufacturing establishments were located near the docks. Spreading away from these areas were the more quiet residential sections and clusters of small shops that served the immediate community. Consequently such river, lake, or seashore cities had plans that offered a wide range of possible inland contours, but generally they stretched out in a fan shape from the water's edge.[4]

Except for the few cities that survived from the Roman Empire (there were less than a dozen in all of Europe), most medieval cities and towns did not develop until after the year 1000, when only about 10 per cent of the total population of Europe lived in towns. The rest were peasants who lived on manorial farms. Tilling a small area of ground, the average peasant frequently knew only his village, the manor house, and the surrounding woods and fields—perhaps no more than two square miles. However, the steady

[3] Natural islands were also utilized as the sites for Stockholm, Sweden, and Paris, France. Originally a settlement on the small island of Lutetia in the Seine River, Paris was used by the Romans as a well-fortified military outpost during the colonization of Europe. Its strategic location in the center of the Seine allowed the Romans to control and trade along that important artery.

[4] The original plan of Rome spread away from the docks on the Tiber River and was contained by the seven hills surrounding it. Cincinnati, Ohio, the sister city of Rome, grew, and developed in a similar way along the Ohio River.

4-8 *Narrow, twisting streets lined with closely packed houses characterized the medieval town, and even today, despite different architectural styles and construction dates, there is a sense of unity in many of the older sections of European towns.*

development of towns and cities after the year 1000 marked a change in a way of life. Travel became increasingly safer and commerce prospered. Trade fairs were held annually and merchants from Scotland to Egypt and beyond exhibited their wares. The merchants, needing bases of operation and places to spend the winter months, selected sites at the crossroads of trade routes and near strong fortifications and were soon joined by the butchers, bakers, and tavernkeepers; and new towns developed. As the importance and size of these towns increased (there was also a noticeable increase in the population of Europe during this time), the autonomy of the cities also increased, often becoming completely independent. Here a new class developed, the *urban* class.

The medieval town, the *civitas*, differed from its later counterparts in the visualization and utilization of space. The town evolved in a very organic way, and by today's standards, time moved very slowly, populations expanded and declined with an almost stately pace. Dramatic shifts in population were practically nonexistent (with the exception of a few local wars and the plague). Consequently, the medieval town grew and changed when and where it needed to expand. Preconceived, fixed two-dimensional plans on paper were not used; instead, the town developed three-dimensionally as its function and the needs of its small collection of inhabitants changed.[5]

The medieval town was characterized and influenced by a most important factor: the enclosing fortified wall. This wall limited the outward expansion of the town and made space within a decided luxury. Houses were packed together, separated by narrow, twisting streets only six to ten feet in width, and made even narrower by overhanging upper stories. Sewers were non-

[5] During the twelfth century an ordinary town might have only 2,500 inhabitants with larger centers up to 20,000. Paris, the largest city in central and northern Europe, had, perhaps, 100,000.

existent and pigs and other livestock roamed the dank and filthy streets. Diseases yearly took a heavy toll of the inhabitants.

The whole town expressed a strong verticality and regulations were often pronounced governing the height of all structures.[6] Nevertheless, the masses of different buildings were considered when new or existing ones were changed, and because of the slow progression of time, each building was gently fitted into the existing plan of its neighborhood. Although the architectural style of a new building might not be the same as the structures surrounding it, attention was paid to its scale and mass in an attempt to integrate it with its environment. Individual independence was highly valued in the design of architectural details that would both complement adjacent structures and also set a definite stamp on the structure under construction.

The cramped, tightly packed homes within the walls were almost totally of wood and devastating fires were frequent. London had four fires during the twelfth century, for example. Yet, each time the cities were rebuilt, or when they expanded, about every 50 to 100 years, larger, higher, and thicker walls were built (when the old walls were taken down, streets and new structures quickly filled the space). The walls were, however, highly prized because they not only afforded protection but, even more importantly, they distinguished the more independent town from the open and smaller villages.

The encircling wall also served another purpose; it created a sharp division between the interior configuration of the town and its surrounding countryside. Not only was the town protected from outside attack but, conversely, the unspoiled quality of the countryside was protected from the pollution of the town's inhabitants and from the random, ill-planned expansion of the town.

---

[6]In Rheims, for example, the height of the eaves of the cathedral governed all building height and the archdeacon was directed to look out of the eave windows each day to check for violations.

During the twelfth and thirteenth centuries, the plan of the town underwent a change as the church began to control (even more strongly than before) the spiritual and social lives of the inhabitants. The sheer size and complex architecture of the building dominated the visual appearance of the town[7] and the flow of traffic through it.

The center of town life began to move away from the waterfront or manufacturing district and toward the area surrounding the church. Frequently, the space in front of the church was left or made clear providing a better view of the impressive facade of the church and the eventual development of the town square. It was soon the custom to hold the fairs and markets here, often in the church itself. With increasing interest in more contemporary architecture, the whole architectural character of the town began to emulate the Gothic style.

Frequently, as the cities grew larger the main church became a cathedral of great size and smaller churches were then built throughout the city. These parish churches (perhaps as many as one for each one hundred families) also had small squares near them and each became a center of activity. The resulting decentralization of the city caused the development of neighborhoods with distinct characteristics and a "sense of place" was established. Areas were also developed outside the walls, called *faubourgs*, which were the equivalent of today's suburbs. They were eventually enclosed by new defense walls just at twentieth-century city limits are enlarged annexing new housing areas.

By the fourteenth and fifteenth centuries, Europe had begun to enjoy a higher level of prosperity and peace than it had seen since the Roman

[7] Religious structures have almost always been built on the highest ground available and the medieval period was no exception. With the high elevation and towering Romanesque and especially Gothic church architecture, the most visually dominant element in the medieval town could only be its religious structure.

Empire; trade increased and there was a demand for new goods and services. Each city and town was no longer relatively self-sufficient. The appreciation of articles of richer and more skilled craftsmanship caused the development of a tradition that was to strongly influence and shape the plan and appearance of the town. This was the establishment of *guilds*.

There were originally two types of guilds, the merchants in general and those of specific crafts, but in time the craft guilds became the more dominant. The guilds controlled practically all economic transactions, regulated the quality, price, and design of the goods produced, and had the final authority in the selection of new members, and the training of apprentices (up to ten years).

Each guild was housed in its own building, or guildhall, and its size and complexity reflected the needs and wealth of the guild. The more important guilds competed for space around the open area or square in front of the church. Consequenty, the square that had been originally dominated by the imposing structure of the Gothic church became even more impressive in appearance with the structural grandeur of each competing guildhall. The Golden Square in Brussels, Belgium, is a good example of such a square. Thus, city plans began to be opened up and controlled vistas were created.

The civitas of the medieval period provides three clues to contemporary environmental design: 1) As a town or city grows it develops centers and subcenters that automatically become the focus of community life. 2) The visual unity of a city can be retained even though the changes occur. 3) The ranking of component priorities of urban design is common and desirable.

The population of Europe increased by almost 17 million or almost one third between 1450 and 1600, yet few new urban centers were developed. It was a period, however, of reorganization and redevelopment of the existing cities. The Renaissance inherited the medieval civitas and expanded, opened, and fundamentally changed them. Perhaps one of the most powerful stimuli was the development of linear perspective. The predilection to develop three-dimensional volumes of public space, extended vistas, and theatrically conceived stages for the dramas of life soon changed the cramped and vertical city to one that was more open and spread out.

Although environmental design often is the product of continuous change rather than singular and isolated events, it is from the Renaissance that most of the concepts of visual order come. The Renaissance love of symmetrical design resulted in repeated attempts to create plans for neighborhoods and even entire cities in a regular and balanced arrangement. Canals, the use of water and fountains, and the distribution of open spaces were also introduced. But, many of the most artful Renaissance city plans remained on paper. However, one should not dismiss the Renaissance conception of urban design. Its strength lies in the grand design of open public spaces, especially the design of walls, pavements, and fountains and the movement from one space to another. Rome, Florence, and Siena are but three illustrations of the Renaissance planner's desire for grand and monumental squares and *piazzas.* Marketplaces that once had been virtually inaccessible were opened, connected by wide streets, and filled with fountains and monuments. They became significant adjuncts to the lives of the city's inhabitants. Important shrines and churches were also connected by thoroughfares in much the same way. Where the medieval town was an almost impenetrable maze of narrow streets, the Renaissance city could be easily traversed.

Transportation has always played an important role in any environmental planning and the Renaissance and Baroque cities were no exceptions. The narrow streets and alleyways of medieval towns forbade much more than horseback or possibly the sedan chair. The new, broad streets that had opened the Renaissance city permitted the use of the coach and carriage. The inhabitants were able to move more freely and for greater distances, and their "sense of place" enlarged.

It should be noted that the open areas in Renaissance urban design contained little if any plant material. It was a "hard" landscape. The beauty

Inspired by the dramatic design of the draperies, the spirited complementary color scheme of blue and orange used in this interior is not oppressive or offensive. On the contrary, the room has an attractive strength and controlled vitality difficult to achieve with such strong, brilliant hues. Note how the physical limits of the space have been manipulated by extending the pattern of the draperies around the corner. Photograph courtesy of Roz Mallin Interiors.

The smooth expanse of white acts as a foil for the strong, rich colors used in the super-graphics and furniture in these rooms by Roz Mallin Interiors. Chrome and glass furniture of Bauhaus origin add sparkle and crispness. Photograph courtesy of Roz Mallin Interiors

The Palais de Versailles, the most admired palace in the world, was the inspiration for new palaces in almost every country in the Western world. In the 1860s, Ludwig II of Bavaria had the central unit, called Herren Chiemsee, reproduced on an island in the middle of a small lake in southern Germany. The main stairway duplicates one at Versailles and evokes the ostentatious richness of French Baroque. Unlike the original, the gleaming, colorful surfaces are largely fake; except for the marble steps and handrail, all else is painted plaster.

4-9 *The magnitude of Versailles is only hinted in this aerial view. The size of the palace may be grasped when one realizes that the small specks are human beings. The boulevards radiating from the entrance gate can also be seen. However, only a small portion of the extensive gardens are seen in the photograph.* Courtesy of Caisse Nationale des Monuments Historiques.

and perfection of design is gained through the carefully controlled proportions of the architectural surfaces surrounding the space and incorporation of sculpture, fountains, stairs, and pavement patterns. Apparently because the countryside was never far from the city center there was no need for trees, bushes, and flowers. The only exceptions were the private gardens of the ruling and wealthy classes. Exotic and rare plants were mixed with sculpture and architectural details to create the formal arrangements that are so much admired.

The broad plans of the Renaissance stimulated further environmental designs. A larger concept of urban or man-controlled space evolved, and although not necessarily a conscious enlargement, it nevertheless occurred. Elizabeth I of England is credited as being the first to decree the establishment of what has been called a *greenbelt*. In order to provide inexpensive food for the increased population of London[8] she directed "all manners of Persons . . . to desist and forfeare from any new buildings of any house or tenement within three miles of said citte of London." Her successor James I extended the belt to ten miles in width. Unfortunately, these controls were largely ignored and it was not until the 1920s that serious attempts were made to further the greenbelt concept.

With the shifting of political, cultural, and artistic leadership from Italy to France in the seventeenth century, the Baroque attitude of *les grands plans* has no more complete illustration than Versailles. The total subjugation of nature to the will of man is nowhere better seen. The dusty plain a few miles outside of Paris was converted into a totally planned, man-made, and controlled environment. At a cost estimated to be the equivalent of almost $500 million, vast and extensive vistas, miles of promenades, fountains by the score, and countless identical trees and bushes stretch as far as the eye can see. The

[8] During the reign of Elizabeth I (1558–1603) the population of London increased from about 100,000 to nearly 250,000.

whole surrounds and enhances the Palais de Versailles. Today it stands as a reminder that civic extravagance may spawn a revolution if human values are disregarded. From the palace stretches a boulevard, straight as an arrow, to Paris, several miles away.

Paris itself was also transformed. By the seventeenth century all of Paris looked like a garden. The châteaux of France had been noted for their gardens for over a century and with a relaxing of social behavior, especially recreation, garden design was incorporated into the urban environment. Promenades and *allées* (tree-lined avenues) were introduced where the new bourgeoisie and royalty mingled and played cricket and other games.

Soon other cities in France and throughout Europe were imitating the urban environment of Paris and Versailles. Huge, open spaces lined with facades of identical design were built in an attempt to be French. These were linked by broad, tree-lined avenues arranged in formal plan in a rigid pattern that seldom considered the topography of the land or the activities of the cities' inhabitants. (Often behind the facades and between the major streets the maze of medieval streets and structures still existed.) Saint Petersburg (Leningrad), Russia, was described as "more French than Paris itself."

The medieval spirit lingered in England; London remained a medieval town far longer than did Paris. The Great Fire of 1666 in London in which 13,000 houses were destroyed could have provided the opportunity for a comprehensive and far more functional plan. Sir Christopher Wren proposed a plan for the entire destroyed area. It was, however, rejected by the citizens and London again rose amid the ashes with a street pattern that was not too different from its original medieval design. (The same opportunity arose in London during and after World War II, but again, now because of existing water, gas, and electrical facilities buried under the former streets, the destroyed sections remained essentially the same plan as before.) Regulations formulated in part by Wren did demand more fireproof construction that altered the appearance of the structures and helped usher in the Georgian

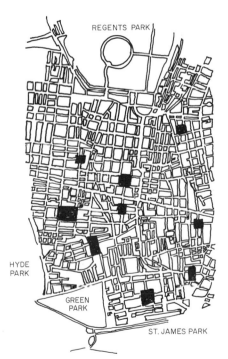

4-10 *The plan of central London showing
some of the many eighteenth-century urban
squares.*

architectural style. However, because of the increased affluence of some of
the inhabitants, the urban square surrounded by Georgian style mansions
and connected houses became popular. Scattered throughout London, such
squares as Grosvenor and Belgravia became models for later developments in
American cities.

Until about 1730, farming practices in England and the rest of Europe were
little changed from what had been done during the medieval period. Interest
in "improved" farming methods increased causing a sudden shift in population. Tenant farmers and farm workers soon found themselves "freed" from
the farm. The need for farmhands lessened with the more efficient methods
of crop production and the consolidation of farmlands. The lack of work
forced the farmhands to travel to the cities.

A substantial increase in population also put an additional burden upon
the cities.[9] The city as it was known in the eighteenth century might have
survived the increase and shift of population but for a development that
started in England and was of even more magnitude: the industrial revolution.

The first twenty years of the nineteenth century were a period of great
change; seldom, if ever, in history were so many people obliged to so rapidly
change their way of living. Before this time there were basically only two
classes, the aristocracy and the peasants—or the landowners and those who
worked on the land. Although this may not have been the most desirable
arrangement, the peasants did have certain rights, were fed, and their place
was secure in that arrangement. When released from the farm the peasants
were frequently left to starve. The new industrialist, on the other hand, did
not assume any responsibility for the welfare of the workers as did the

[9] The population of England and Wales rose from about 6.5 million to 9 million in the last
half of the eighteenth century, or five times the increase that had occurred during the first
half.

former agrarian aristocrats. The wages of the workers could be kept low because of the constant flow of new workers from the country. There were no longer any labor shortages and no demands for increased wages. Urban housing, always in short supply, deteriorated rapidly and slums came into being as cities expanded and bulged to overflowing with displaced farm families. Living conditions in the cities became abominable, the crime rate increased at a phenomenal rate, and the structure of the family all but dissolved.[10] The disruption of established morals was decisive. An agrarian society became an industrialized society.

Although city plans providing better living conditions for factory workers were proposed even in the earliest years of the nineteenth century, reform measures were slow in coming. The impact of the industrial revolution on the English nation could not be abated. The pastoral landscape was quickly inundated with factory grime and industrial waste, and cities soon became huge—unplanned, undesirable, and unloved.

The sinister image of the early nineteenth-century industrialist as one who dispassionately destroyed the countryside and subjected the workers to living and working conditions of the most base level while amassing fantastic fortunes is not too far wrong. The landowner and the peasant had lived in close proximity and saw each other frequently, but the rich industrialist had little or no contact with his workers. He lived in another part of town, even miles away, and rarely visited his mines and mills. The disparity of their lives

[10] By 1851, the number of people in England living in cities was more than those living in the country. Crowded together in jerry-built tenements or former mansions (one house in London had 63 people in nine rooms, each room having but one bed), they had few sanitary conditions, and pure water was a luxury. Frequently, their only release was drugs or liquor. Children were often drugged with opium compounds to keep them quiet. In Manchester, England, population 400,000, there were 1,600 saloons and it was not uncommon to see "drunken women by the hundreds lay(ing) about . . . in the mud."

4-11 *The plight of the workers in the factories and sweatshops continued throughout the nineteenth century. This dramatic 1888 engraving illustrates a story about the working conditions in the garment industry in New York City.*

also affected their life expectancy; the wealthy industrialist could expect to live to be at least 38 years but the worker's average life expectancy was only 17 years.

The industrial revolution ushered in a new pattern of demands on the use of available land space. Industry tended to concentrate in areas where power and raw materials were easily obtainable, and the increase in manufacturing establishments demanded a like increase in the labor force. Thus, the population of the city became highly concentrated in these manufacturing areas for several reasons. The workers needed to live very close to their source of employment because of the lack of public transportation. Land values rapidly rose and speculators crowded as many tenements and the small shops and stores to provide the necessities of life into the surrounding areas as was possible. The need to include the humanizing factors, such as public parks and playgrounds, were seldom, if ever, considered; besides the children as well as the adults worked the long tortuous hours.[11]

With the evolvement and growth of the slums surrounding the increasing industrialized city center, the more affluent urban dwellers began to move to the outer fringes of the city to avoid the overloaded streets and the deplorable environment. Soon, shops and stores catering to the rich were also opened there. Thus, the pattern of growth for most of the cities of Europe and the United States of the nineteenth and twentieth centuries was established.

Not every factory owner disregarded the well-being of his workers, although they were far outnumbered by those who did. Early in the nineteenth century, Robert Owen, whose textile mills in Scotland were some of

---

[11] In 1819 the first effective Factory Act was passed in England. It limited the hours of labor for children over nine years old and forbid children under nine to work.

the finest in Great Britain, was writing and planning new communities. Others built industrial towns in England; of these two are particularly worth noting, Sir Titus Salt and W. H. Lever. Salt (the owner of a textile mill) built Saltaire (1853–1856) with a planned population of over 4,000. The houses had parlors, kitchens, and backyards and there were separate bedrooms for the parents and the children. Lever, the founder of Lever Brothers, built Port Sunlight (1888), which had the same basic amenities as Saltaire. Port Sunlight also had more green space within the community and was less densely populated. Both cities flourished and are still functioning but have not remained company towns because not all the inhabitants are workers in the mills or plants.

In the United States, only the largest cities approached the conditions found in England and other European cities. However, industry, especially mills and mines, were often built in the country on sites where power or natural resources were plentiful. Isolated from more populous centers, company towns were also built to house the workers. Owned, managed, and maintained by the company, they varied in plan and comfort as their counterparts did in England. Some of the earliest mill towns in New England exhibited a considerable amount of planning and thought for the well-being of their workers. However, some of the mining towns of Pennsylvania and other coal-producing areas were not so considerate. The poorest provided no more than what could be expected in the meanest city factory district, small, cheaply built houses crowded on muddy, treeless streets with a single store, a "company" store, providing the daily essential materials, food, and clothing, at increased prices.

To establish a company or factory town with facilities that provided more than the barest minimum of social and physical benefits was tantamount to planning the entire community, housing, factories or mills, and community services at one time. Since most factory towns were privately owned by one company, continuity of design and intent were more easily controlled, but

4-12 *Four views of Pullman, Illinois, as illustrated in Frank Leslie's Illustrated Newspaper in 1888. View A shows Florence Boulevard leading into the city with the Florence Hotel behind the trees on the right. View B is the 100-room Florence Hotel. Views C and D show the exterior and interior of the Arcade.*

frequently the lack of money restricted the best laid plans. However, some outstanding company, or "model towns" as they were called by critics of the nineteenth century, were built. These included Vandergrift, Pennsylvania; Sparrowpoint, Maryland; Hopedale and Waltham, Massachusetts; Pelzer, South Carolina; and Leclaire and Pullman, Illinois.

The creation of public parks was a nineteenth-century idea. The great parks found in the cities of Western Europe, St. James's Park and Hyde Park in London and the Tuileries in Paris, for example, were at first the private grounds of kings. Even in the Georgian squares in London, the small park had a high iron fence and only the residents of that square had access to the park area within. During the Victorian age the renewed interest in open spaces and the countryside were, in part, the result of a rekindling of romantic attitudes. This wistful looking back toward times before the industrial revolution caused medieval-looking products, buildings, and surrounding to be produced. Cemeteries were the first to reflect the return to romantic environments with their naturalistic landscaping, walks, and sculpture.

Also responsible for the establishment of urban parks was the realization that the social and environmental problems of the industrial city were caused primarily by the overcrowded and tragic surroundings of the factory worker. Open spaces, facilities for recreation and entertainment, were found to reduce liquor consumption, ease social tension, and enhance human values.

In 1853, plans were formed to create a large park in New York City.[12] By 1857, 840 acres had been consolidated and Frederick Law Olmsted and

[12] The first master plan for New York City, prepared on April 22, 1625, in Holland by an engineer, Cryn Fredericxsz, was abandoned a year later. Since that time several other plans for the city have been proposed, adopted, and abandoned, but perhaps the most unique idea was the incorporation of a large public park within the city proper.

4-13 *One of the first indications of a return to naturalistic landscaping was in the cemeteries of the first quarter of the nineteenth century. Although the tombstones and monuments are derived from classical and Egyptian designs, this print of a cemetery in Philadelphia shows paths and walkways following the contours of the land and informally placed trees and bushes. Apparently, it was considered a pleasant place to take a leisurely stroll.*

Calvert Vaux[13] were chosen to plan it. Rather than shape the area to the formal designs that were so admired by the seventeenth- and eighteenth-century planners, Olmsted and Vaux carefully controlled nature, leaving half of the area virtually untouched and adding to or redefining the rest with such features as walks and drives, ball and game areas, ponds and lakes, picnic areas, a casino, and restaurants. Vaux is credited with the lowering of the necessary cross-traffic streets so that they do not intrude upon the rural setting. Finished, Central Park was acclaimed immediately; the designers had succeeded in enhancing the beauty of nature while planning a place of infinite surprises and a joy to all city inhabitants. Within ten years, every major city in America had large urban spaces of a similar rural character. The direction of subsequent landscape and environmental planning in America was established, and to this day, most of the parks, playgrounds, college campuses, and other recreational and civic areas are "naturalized."

The methods and speed of transportation affect the inhabitants of any area or city, as well as the plan of those cities. In 1829, George Stephenson, an Englishman, developed the first successful "traveling engine." The impact upon time and space was tremendous. At last man and materials could travel faster and farther than ever before. The inhabitants of the world became

[13] Frederick Law Olmsted (1822–1903) became the recognized authority on parks and community planning of his time. He is credited with the design of more than 80 public parks including Central, Riverside, and Morningside Parks in New York City, Prospect Park in Brooklyn, the site plan of the Columbia Exposition (1893) and the accompaning Jackson Park in Chicago, and parks in Boston, Detroit, Louisville, Buffalo, Milwaukee, and Montreal. He also designed the grounds around the Capitol in Washington, D.C. His city plans include those of Riverside, Illinois, and Vandergrift, Pennsylvania. Calvert Vaux (1824–1895) collaborated with Olmsted on several of these parks and was the architect of a number of important buildings including the Museum of Natural History and the 1874 Metropolitan Museum of Art building in New York. His book, *Villas and Cottages* (1857), helped set the style of many homes in the 1860s and 1870s.

4-14 *The New York Central and Hudson River Railroad Station at 138th Street in New York City was described in 1887 as "without doubt the finest, most complete way station in the country." Made of red brick and terra-cotta, it was based upon the Romanesque style of architecture.*

instantly more mobile. By 1851 there were over 6,000 miles of track in Great Britain. Produce from distant farms could be quickly brought to the city and the historical reliance upon the slower water transportation was lessened. The railroad and its terminals influenced environmental planning considerably.

The railroad station became, almost overnight, one of the most important and architecturally rich buildings in the city; sometimes even rivaling in size, materials, and cost the cathedrals and major civic buildings. Frequently situated in the center of the city, the railroad station became the hub of radiating streets and markets. Bridges, docks, and warehouses were made larger to accommodate the increased handling and disposition of goods carried by the railroad. Despite the smoke-belching engine showering cinders and sparks on everything and everyone, the railroad permitted inhabitants of one city to travel to another with greater ease and speed. In the United States, by 1860, railroads had linked the cities of the eastern seaboard and had pushed westward beyond the Mississippi River. After the Civil War, gigantic efforts of railroad building were put forth, and by 1869 the railroad spanned the continent. What had been a grueling trip lasting up to six months, traversing the country by train, now took only six days. Cities and towns sprang up along the railroad right-of-way and where two lines crossed or joined. By the time of World War I, over 160,000 miles of track had been laid in the United States. (At the same time, all the hard surfaced roads in the United States, if laid end to end, would not reach from Boston to New York.)

The railroad often bisected the towns and frequently caused a separation of social and economic areas. There became a right—and a wrong—side of the tracks. Better housing, business establishments, and community services were concentrated on one side in contrast to the factories and poorer sections of the town located on the other.

The impact of the railroad upon the city plan is equaled by the development of the trolley. First developed in Richmond, Virginia, in 1887, within

4-15 *After the Civil War the increased rail traffic required numerous tracks coming into a city that caused a physical separation of one side of the urban area from another. This engraving depicts Atlanta, Georgia, in 1887.*

one year, 25 cities had started electric trolley systems and within ten years, 100 million people were being transported by trolleys annually.

Workers who had been forced to live in the congested city center because of inadequate transportation could now live on the outskirts of the city. There was revolution in mass housing because wherever the trolley lines extended to the city limits inexpensive houses were clustered. The exclusive right of the wealthy to live on the perimeter of the cities had been broken. The American dream of the rose-covered cottage with a plot of ground could be realized. The type of recreation and places of entertainment also changed. It became fashionable to ride the trolley not only to work but on holidays as well. Families would go on outings to the end of the lines to newly developed parks and picnic grounds.[14] Even those who lived in the inner city were not restricted there. The city became as a wheel, with the spokes radiating from the industrial and business hub, the trolley lines; and the rim, the ring of houses, and parks all set in the green countryside.

The interurban trolley further extended the area in which workers could live and still commute to work. Eventually intercity lines connected most of the cities of the eastern part of the United States. Around the perimeter of the cities small communities developed and became the "bedrooms" of the commuters.

The automobile, at first a plaything of the rich, has caused even more changes in the city. In addition to extending evermore the distance one can live from his work, it also provides flexibility of location. No longer does the trolley line or railroad control the place of residence or the time of departure or arrival. However, one of the prime causes of urban problems is the automobile. The number of automobiles has almost doubled in the last

[14] Powered by electricity provided by the trolley line, the first major addition to a new park was often the merry-go-round. These ornate, wonderful creations of fanciful animals, flashing mirrors and lights, and color and sound soon became the nucleus of the amusement park.

4-16 *The provision of facilities to park automobiles often requires more space than is devoted to structures or recreational activities.* Courtesy of Miami-Metro Department of Publicity and Tourism.

twenty-five years and in some communities the area devoted to hard-surfaced parking lots and roads exceeds that given to buildings and parks. Transportation systems, storage facilities, and air and sound pollution levels caused by the automobile alone are rapidly compounding problems that must be solved or the city may become completely paralyzed as it has never been before.

To some critics and urban planners, the unlimited growth of cities is cause for alarm. They believe that if a city becomes too large, its function and environmental qualities are adversely affected. In 1898, Ebenezer Howard published his book, *Tomorrow: A Peaceful Path to Real Reform.* In it, Howard proposed the establishment of self-sufficient towns of 32,000, surrounded by an agricultural belt (greenbelt). His ideas were not original or new, but the influence his book had upon subsequent planning was considerable.

Howard's proposed *Garden City* was circular in form, about one and a half miles in diameter. The center was an open plaza surrounded by the community buildings (town hall, hospital, theater, museum, and concert hall). Encircling this were concentric rings containing shopping and business, residential, and industrial areas. Cutting through the rings were six radiating roads, as spokes of a wheel, separating the city into six neighborhoods or wards. Midway between the outer greenbelt limits of the town and the inner plaza was a broad band of park area, 420 feet wide, so that no one would live more than 240 yards from a park. Schools were placed in each ward in this band of green. (No pupil had to walk more than one quarter mile to school). The first Garden City to be built was Letchworth, England (1903), and is a prospering city today.

In the 1930s, the federal government developed several greenbelt towns in the United States to relieve the congestion in the cities. Greenbelt, Maryland, outside of Washington, D.C., Greenhills, Ohio, near Cincinnati, and Greendale, Wisconsin, near Milwaukee were constructed. Each town varies to some extent but each has a central civic and commercial section with residential

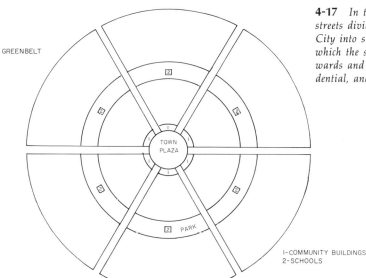

GREENBELT

TOWN
PLAZA

PARK

1-COMMUNITY BUILDINGS
2-SCHOOLS

4-17 *In this schematic plan, the six major streets divided Ebenezer Howard's Garden City into six wards. The circular park in which the schools were located bisected these wards and each contained shopping, residential, and industrial areas.*

areas radiating out from it. (No provisions for industry were made because these were to be "bedroom" communities.) The towns were planned in their entirety with urban planners, architects, landscape architects, engineers, sociologists, educators, interior and furniture designers, artists, and sculptors working on the project. Provisions were made so that children need not cross thoroughfares to get to school nor was it difficult to walk to parks and shopping areas. Housing was clustered and attached (modified row houses) to conserve land space.

Since the greenbelt towns were never to increase in size, in the event more housing and facilities were needed, additional greenbelt cities would be built rather than expanding the existing ones. The greenbelt areas surrounding the towns were to be the site of farms producing food for the towns. The resulting plan combines the convenience and advantages of both the life in the city and the life on the land. However, the greenbelt concept never became universally accepted.

Since World War II, there has been an increased demand for new housing throughout the world. In the United States, this demand has been partially satisfied by a proliferation of housing areas filled with individual houses on individual lots, the "American Dream." These residential areas often are developed around small villages and hamlets located within commuting distance of the larger cities and have developed little or no thought to regional planning (planning has always been considered a threat to free enterprise and the American way of life). The rapid rise in population of these communities has brought many problems that have proved difficult to solve—need for more schools, disposal of garbage and sewage, increased traffic, and the lack of entertainment and recreation facilities.

The expansion of the physical size of cities with their satellite suburbs spawned a decentralization of the city. Services and facilities became duplicated and industry is scattered throughout. As the cities grew the intervening spaces between became smaller. The connecting routes of transportation and especially the highways have carried urbanization even further into the countryside until now it is possible to travel great distances and still not be totally free of the urban environment. Critics and futurists foresee the formation of the *megalopolis*—a huge, multicity complex covering thousands of square miles.

The northeastern and central eastern seacoast of the United States is particularly prone to this development. It is now possible to drive from north of New York City to beyond Philadelphia and not be entirely rid of city or urban scenery. It has been forecast that one huge megalopolis will reach from south of Richmond, Virginia, to north of Boston, Massachusetts, in the foreseeable future if immediate steps to thwart such a trend are not taken. Other threatened areas are Cleveland-Toledo-Detroit, Gary-Chicago-Milwaukee (some propose that these two megalopolises may join to form a mega-megalopolis), Los Angeles-San Diego, and Houston-New Orleans-Mobile.

5 Urban Land Use, Contemporary City Plans

Urban Land Use

The historic development and growth of the city has shown the shifting of land use. An area that was once residential may become one devoted to stores and businesses, and quiet, bucolic, sparsely settled surroundings can give way to a congested industrial complex. It is the unceasing change and constant pressures exerted by the diminishing of one land use for another, more vigorous one that is one cause for the life of a city. However, if these changes are unchecked and not carefully considered, the quality of the city, the fitness for human habitation and industry, is diminished.

The freedom so cherished by most Americans is often threatened by uncontrolled growth and change in their living environments. Zoning, which does limit freedom of choice, is, however, more protection than threat. Many gradations, definitions, and elaborations are found in zoning ordinances. Each community, town, city, country, and state has laws and regulations that govern where and what can be built or developed, and the degree of adherence and enforcement of existing laws varies perhaps even more than the laws themselves. The pros and cons of individual regulations are not discussed here, but rather the need for fair, carefully considered, *and* enforced zoning laws that preserve and protect the environment of the inhabitants within a given area must be emphasized.

Within the urban geographical limits are four distinct land uses or zones that should be constantly considered whenever change and developments within the city are requested or planned. These zones are *residential, community, commercial,* and *industrial.*

RESIDENTIAL. The areas within a city where people live[1] should occupy land that is the most desirable, the most free from air, water, soil, and sound pollution, and the most conducive to human awareness. The first consideration of any planner, city or government administrator, or citizen

---

[1]Single family dwellings, duplexes, and multiple family dwellings all fall within this category and often have different regulations but all house people.

99

should be for the placement and quality of residential areas. This does not mean the land must always be the largest single area, the most level, free of vegetation, or the most fertile, but rather, it could be hilly or rolling, tree covered, and, perhaps, even rocky. Large size is also not too important as the residential areas should be divided into pleasant neighborhoods that allow the inhabitants to feel a "sense of place" and identity, and if too large, this is often lost. Views, scenic beauty, and natural attributes should always be considered when selecting residential areas. The basis for selection should always be the potential quality of the environment.

COMMUNITY. The community areas are usually scattered within the residential areas. Comprising those areas devoted to schools, parks, playgrounds, libraries, churches, concert halls, and other public buildings, community uses vie for the same type of land as residential, and it *is* most desirable that these two zones most involved in the daily lives of the city's inhabitants be proximate. Frequently, the schools and the adjacent playgrounds are determinants of the neighborhood definition. Churches can also affect the identity of a group's "sense of place." Structures and land uses of a more wide interest and application, such as city halls, courthouses, concert halls, museums, and theaters, do not necessarily require the closeness to housing as the more intimately used areas and often are placed in a general location to many residential areas rather than within a specific neighborhood or housing complex.

COMMERCIAL. The commercial category of land use applies to stores and businesses. Again within this definition there are variations. The small, family owned "corner grocery" is often found, especially in the larger urban areas, located within or very near the residential zones. Larger establishments such as department stores are found in "downtown" sections along with other businesses of a similar nature. In the past, these establishments were grouped in a concentrated zone and were served by the various methods of public transportation. They formed the *city center* together with the city hall, courthouse, and the like.

The development of automobile transportation has changed this arrangement to a considerable degree, and, in turn, the lives and habits of the city dweller have been altered. The city center often deteriorates because of the increased difficulty in getting to it. As cities have grown in size and people have moved farther away from the commercial center of the city, many people have refrained from coming "downtown," preferring instead to use commercial centers nearer their homes. Two developments in the placement of commercial zones have, therefore, occurred.

Without sensitive zoning regulations, major access highways and streets have become lined with large and small businesses, pennant-encrusted service stations, garish food-dispensing establishments, small jerry-built cut-rate merchandizers, and potholed parking areas. These "strip" developments invariably contribute to the visual blight of our cities and are often responsible for numerous traffic accidents as a result of higher speed limits on highways and the large number of automobiles that enter and exit from the many parking areas.

The development of the larger "shopping centers" have further contributed to the deterioration of the city center commercial areas.[2] Generally considered to be more desirable in both visual appeal and services and merchandise offered, they are frequently branch stores of those in the city center. Shopping centers are usually located on the perimeter of urban areas and occupy large tracts of land with their encircling parking lots, which must

[2]Conversely, the shopping center causes suburban growth. Outlying shopping centers have frequently spawned housing developments. The shopping center consequently becomes the community center of the area with the necessary municipal buildings and services often incorporated within the shopping center complex.

5-1 *Heavy industry creates pollution and environmental problems, in general. However, if properly controlled and placed, the negative aspects can be tolerated because industry does offer many employment opportunities and taxation benefits.*

be relatively flat. These lots often absorb the most productive and fertile land and can cause considerable damage to watersheds and drainage because of their inherent waterproof surface. What often results is that instead of a greenbelt surrounding a city, it is a blackbelt of treeless asphalt parking lots and highways.

The buying habits of today's citizen are far different from what were common only a few years ago. Instead of making daily trips to several scattered, but not distant, individual stores to obtain the day's food or other necessities, the urban dweller of today usually drives a considerable distance to a shopping center and purchases enough food for a week or longer at one time. During the same visit, purchases of clothes, equipment, and other necessary and nonnecessary items are also made. Frequently all of these purchases are made under the same roof and, if not in closely spaced stores, identified as related because of their location in a specific "shopping center."

INDUSTRIAL. The fourth major category includes land occupied by industry. It is a very necessary and vital part of any community. The loss of a major industrial concern can often threaten the economy of an entire city. The closing down of a single factory has caused entire towns to wither and die. Further, the importance of industry is shown by the tax base it provides to the cities. However, extra care in the placement and type of industry must always be exerted. Industry, too, falls into more than one type.

Light industry, such as electronic equipment, drug supplies, and small manufacturing plants are often in medium-size structures and do not emit fumes, noise, or other contaminants. Since the number of employees in these industries is usually relatively small, there is little need for large parking lots and few traffic problems develop. Frequently, in older cities, some light industrial facilities may even be located within dominantly residential areas and cause little disruption to the daily lives of those living adjacent to them.

On the other hand, heavy industry—railroad yards, foundries, chemical plants, oil refineries, and the like—do cause pollution and contamination.

5-2

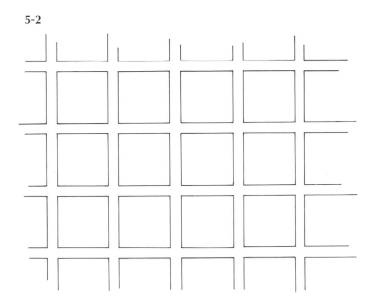

Although often providing many opportunities for employment and contributing substantial monies to local governments through taxes, their inclusion in any urban plan must be carefully considered. Ideally they should be placed beyond and away from the residential environment. In addition to distance, the direction of prevailing winds is another determinant in the location of factories emitting smoke and noxious fumes. Such industry, if placed on the windward side of residential areas, could still cause less desirable conditions without actually being visible from those areas.

Carefully planned methods of easy access and egress, both for those employed and the raw and manufactured materials, must be provided, but this is a small obligation when judged against the possible positive benefits reaped by the community at large.

STREET PLANS

Cities have dimensions, history, texture. They also must move. Within each clustering of dwellings, schools, stores, factories, and warehouses there are roads and streets that permit individuals and machines to move from one location to another. The manner or layout of these "channels of movement" often determine the quality of the area or city. Movement can be speeded or slowed, made safer or more hazardous, or become a pleasant or unpleasant experience depending upon how the streets are arranged. Sometimes it is the width and surface material that affects movement but more often it is the physical plan.

By far, the most common street plan in America is one that is composed of streets running parallel and at right angles to each other. This rigid plan, called *gridiron*, is easily drawn on maps and creates orderly blocks from which orderly building lots can be divided. The streets are often numbered or lettered, and with each block designated numerically, finding an address is accomplished without difficulty.

Traditionally, Hippodamus, a native of the Greek island of Melos and

5-3 A typical residential street as laid out in 1912 (left) and a similar street widened in 1970 to accommodate traffic.

described by Aristotle as "having long hair and . . . interesting political views," is credited with inventing the gridiron plan. However, the Egyptians and Romans, as well as the Greeks, used the plan extensively. It was seldom used during the Middle Ages and the Renaissance and was only revived during the nineteenth century. The ancients "adjusted it to the land." Not so the nineteenth- and early twentieth-century planners, whose rigid plans were often forced upon the land as evidenced by the illogical street patterns found in the hilly cities of Duluth, San Francisco, and Seattle. Natural aberrations from a flat, tabletop terrain such as hills and cliffs, rivers and streams, and shorelines produce ludicrous but frequently costly and dangerous results.

There are other disadvantages. With today's swift and heavy traffic, each street intersection is the genesis of accidents. Even with some streets designated as "through" streets and others "side" streets, the danger still exists.

The typical gridiron plan uses more land for streets, more than 28 per cent than most other street plans, and streets are continually being widened to facilitate more traffic and the parking of more automobiles.[3]

Variations of the gridiron plan have been suggested. The width and length of the spaces between streets and of the streets themselves can be adjusted to avoid the monotony and help reduce some of the hazards associated with the gridiron plan. However, a variation that seems to offer even more possibilities is one suggested by Colin D. Buchanan, an English traffic engineer. He proposes that instead of an orthogonal pattern (traditional gridiron) the streets should be laid out in a hexagonal plan. The resulting three-way intersections would cost less and are estimated to be 14 times safer than the usual four-way intersections.

[3] During the past fifty years highways have more than tripled in width to provide more safety and to permit increased speed and number of automobiles.

5-4

5-5

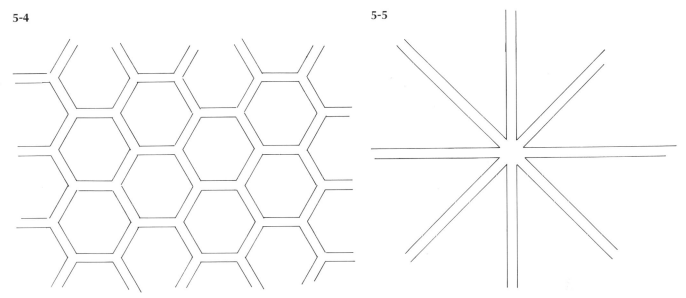

5-6

Not all cities of the past had gridiron plans. A second type, developing from the natural growth of the *civitas*, medieval town, is usually divided into two parts for purposes of explanation, but in practice forms a plan not unlike a spider web.

The *centric* plan consists of streets radiating from a central point, as the spokes of a wheel. The centric layout of streets provides emphasis to important structures and points in the city by allowing longer vistas and rapid inward and outward movement. However, there is traffic congestion because of the convergence of the major streets. The areas between the "spokes" are often divided by either irregular street layouts or the gridiron plan.

Historically, this type of plan permitted a more efficient military defense of important objectives. For example, in a city with a typical gridiron plan the enemy could easily penetrate to within a block or two of its objective without being seen if the defense forces were not deployed around the perimeter of the entire town. A large number of soldiers were thus required to defend the town. With a centric plan, the town's defense forces could be smaller and concentrated around the military objective. As the approaching enemy could easily be observed, the defense forces could then engage them at a distance and with greater speed and numbers, not being scattered around the city. Such defense considerations are no longer necessary as in the past but the street patterns of Paris and Washington, D.C., were so designed because of this reason.

Evolved from the destruction of city walls (as cities grew and new walls were built), the *ring* plan consists of concentric wide streets encircling the city center. Vienna, Austria, and Frankfurt, Germany, are but two European cities with such street plans.

With a combination of the centric and ring plans, urban inhabitants can rapidly and easily go from within to the outer limits or from one side to

5-7

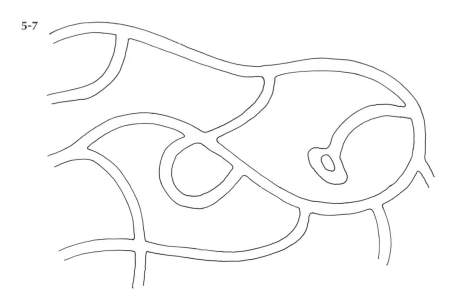

another of the city on the major dividing streets. Modern cities often have such plans but without any of the historical reasons, that is Ebenezer Howard's Garden City.[4]

The third street plan, one frequently favored by developers today, is not rigidly and geometircally conceived. It is *organic and functional* (or should be). Irregular in plan, based upon use and topography, this type of plan can produce an informal and relaxed feeling but is not conducive to mass movement. It is more often found within neighborhoods or areas defined by more efficient traffic patterns. One can experience some difficulty when attempting to find a particular address and lot sizes are frequently irregular in shape, but these are minor negations. Unfortunately, the uncontrolled convoluted meanderings of some streets found in residential areas cause residents and visitors alike to question the validity of such plans.

A fourth street or urban arrangement is called *linear* or *ribbon*. This plan is one that frequently evolves rather than being planned. As the name implies, it is based on a line, that is, a main road or transportation artery, with small areas developing along its length. These areas may be small residential, manufacturing, or commercial areas, each more or less isolated from the other and with possible different street patterns. This type of urban plan has developed along the major highways of America. Rare is the highway that is not girded by scattered housing developments, commercial centers, and manufacturing plants which are often inadequately zoned and regulated. Yet this type of plan can, with careful attention to topography, prevailing winds, and land use, produce excellent environments for all concerned.

---

[4] There is an increasing use of an adaptation of this web idea. Multilane highways, part of the Interstate Highway System, are being built that encircle cities and from these other multilane limited access roads penetrate to the city center. The highway patterns of Indianapolis, Indiana; Atlanta, Georgia; and Columbus, Ohio, are examples.

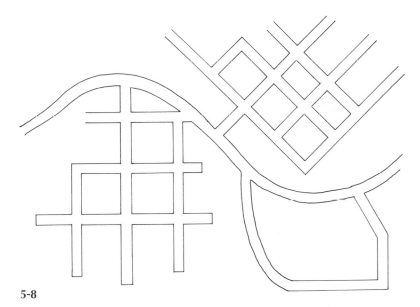

5-8

URBAN SCHEMES

Designs for cities are being projected with increasing frequency. Some are imaginative, exciting, and almost beyond the realm of practicability, whereas others are repetitions of old methods of planning. Not all of the proposals will be built but most will have some effect upon the development of cities, existing ones as well as those of the future.

Two visionary concepts for cities, proposed in the 1920s and 1930s that have influenced present city planning, although neither were built, were Frank Lloyd Wright's Broadacre City and Le Corbusier's Voisin Scheme.

Briefly, Wright proposed a plan (1935) in which cities would be decentralized. Families would live in architecturally compatible single houses on leased land, large enough (at least an acre)[5] to grow some fruits, vegetables, and flowers. Apartment houses would also be built. Industry would be widely spaced and carefully separated from residential districts. Isolated, high-rise buildings would provide office and commercial space where needed. Major, elevated traffic arteries with both public transportation and surfaces for high-speed individual automobiles would connect these urban elements. Beneath the elevated roadways, facilities for storage and community services would be located.

Wright believed that with such close contact with the earth, the inhabitants of Broadacre City would regain the natural birthright of sun, air, and land, and by raising some of their food would regain a degree of independence. To develop a city as proposed by Wright would necessitate the reshaping a redeveloping of large areas of the countryside. Vast numbers of people would have to be relocated and trained for the return to semiagrarian ways.

[5]The density of one family per acre is far different than that found in New York City today. It is not uncommon to find 1,100 persons per acre in the more congested areas, and densities of 800 or 900 are routine.

5-9 *Urban renewal projects such as the
ill-fated Pruitt-Igoe complex in St. Louis
have rapidly developed into vertical slums
when the needs of the human inhabitants
have not been fully considered.*

Although criticized by some as rural rather than an urban proposal,
Wright's idyllic concept has influenced many. The suburbanite who culti-
vates his property and delights in his freedom and his "rural" surroundings
is experiencing some of what Wright felt was natural to all men.[6] The
Interstate Highway System and the high-speed trains now being developed
are certainly akin to some of Wright's suggested transportation methods.

Le Corbusier developed his Voisin Scheme in 1925. He proposed that 600
acres located in the congested center of Paris be cleared and replaced by 16
widely spaced, glass walled, 60-story, cruciform towers. These buildings
would provide housing, office facilities, and store space for 20,000 to 40,000
people. The street pattern would be an enormous gridiron of wide streets
about 1,200 feet apart. Between the large skyscrapers and the streets would
be tree-filled park-like areas with low shops and restaurants to provide
human scale to the entire area. Le Corbusier's proposal is in effect a garden
city that is both horizontal and vertical.

His Voisin Scheme was not realized but Le Corbusier did build, following
World War II, a structure in Marseilles, France, which is a complete community and is similar in concept if not in design to his proposed skyscrapers.

Both his Voisin Scheme and Marseilles building have influenced architects
around the world. The image of giant towers, like large minimal sculpture in
a park, has dominated the proposals of urban planners ever since even
though the concept does not naturally fit with how people actually live. The
United States has been particularly prone to building large, slab-like towers,
pockmarked with small windows, and isolated in barren "parks" to provide
"adequate" housing. Most have become vertical slums soon after their
completion.

Perhaps the most remarkable example of Le Corbusier's Voisin influence is

[6]The average lot size in 1920 was $\frac{1}{10}$ of an acre, today the average size lot is more than
twice that.

seen in Brasília, Brazil. Planned by Lúcio Costa with the buildings designed by Oscar Niemeyer, the high-rise residential buildings, broad avenues, and open spaces are certainly outgrowths of the Voisin Scheme.

The unprecedented growth of cities and the demand for more housing following World War II have caused the proliferation of suburbs and the establishment of new towns. In Europe, especially in Great Britain and Scandinavia, housing has been provided with considerable success through the development of new towns rather than through the expansion of the suburbs of an older city.

In Britain, as a result of the New Towns Act[7] enacted after World War II, 27 New Towns[8] have so far been created. These are, for the most part, within a radius of forty miles from London and were originally planned to have populations of about 45,000 (later enlarged to 80,000), and in plan can be traced to the Garden City proposals of Ebenezer Howard 50 years earlier.

These New Towns at first did not have populations with a blend of ages but were made up of young families with young children. In some, one-fifth of the population was under five years old, but as the New Towns have matured so have their inhabitants and a better spread of population ages has developed.[9] Outstanding examples are Harlow, Hatfield, Stevenage, and Crawley in England, and Livingston and Cumbernauld in Scotland.

---

[7] The New Towns Act of 1946 provided for the establishment of developing corporations, the Town and Country Planning Act of 1947 set national controls on land use, and the Distribution of Industry Act of 1945 gives the national government the jurisdiction over the location of any new industry.

[8] The British designation, New Town, is just that, a new town; it is not a suburb. Each New Town is an entirely self-contained community with residential, community, commercial, industrial, and recreational facilities.

[9] Also contributing to the success of British New Towns is the fact that they are not considered to be alternatives to the poorhouse and that inhabitants are not forced to leave when their income passes a maximum figure—a policy often followed in the United States.

5-10 *An apartment tower near one of the lakes in Reston, Virginia. Across the water, town houses and individual homes are clustered.*

In the Scandinavian countries the most successful new town has been Tapiola, six miles from Helsinki, Finland. Developed in 1953, the town incorporates a varied landscape with different building sizes and types; in addition, families of different ages, sizes, and incomes have been encouraged to give a cultural breadth to the town. Tapiola's planning director, Heikki von Herzen, sums up the successful planning philosophy thus: "Create environment, not housing. Start from man. That's the only thing important—the individuality of man and the nearness of nature. . . ."

America is not without recently planned communities. There are at least 100 towns currently on the drawing boards or being developed in the United States. Tragically, many are being built with little or no consideration of a total regional plan, concern for the visual quality of the structures and landscape, or adequate regard for the quality of life provided the town's future inhabitants. Tragically, because if these cities are built they will no doubt remain with basically the same plan and with the same negative qualities for years to come, adversely affecting the lives of those who live there.

Reston, Virginia, located 17 miles from Washington, D.C., is by far the most famous community developed in the United States in recent years. Located on a 10-square-mile tract of undeveloped land, Reston was planned to provide living and working space for 75,000 people, and its sensitive planning required little large-scale bulldozing or removal of trees. Reston, started in 1962 and scheduled to be completed in 20 years, was originally to be composed of seven "villages" separated by open land.[10] To preserve as much land as possible, housing was to be clustered—about 70 per cent town

---

[10] About 1,500 acres of land were earmarked for recreational and open space, that is, golf courses, playgrounds, parks, an outdoor theater, and facilities for swimming, boating, and horseback riding.

houses and 15 per cent apartments, whereas only the remaining 15 per cent were to be detached houses. The automobile, while considered, is almost an intruder into town life; separated walkways provide circulation to the community and commercial locations. The architecture is varied, yet compatible; sculpture, lookouts, views, graphics, street furniture, and lighting have all been planned and provide visual excitement to the town center.

Reston is like a medieval walled town; it is a self-sufficient community, not a "satellite" or "bedroom" community. Industry has been considered (500 acres were provided as industrial sites) and at least 50 per cent of the population could be employed there. Entertainment and cultural facilities are also provided. Reston has shown that a planned community does not have to be dull, cut with the same "cookie cutter," and that the T-square and triangle need not be the only tools of an environmental planner.

A change in management in the late 1960s, coupled with some adjustments of basic plans, has somewhat altered the original concept of Reston. Nevertheless, the flexibility of the original plans and the already established physical structures will no doubt serve well as determinants for future development. Reston has already proved a landmark in urban development and illustrates what *can* be done with foresight, planning, dedication, and sensitivity.

The question of control arises when considering any carefully planned community. For example, a point repeatedly raised is, "Can a developer dictate a way of life and public taste?" As with any "designed" object, the designer must make certain assumptions and establish criteria that *do* influence choices and *may* limit and restrict the consumer or user, so it is with the development of any community, new or old. Zoning regulations, cost and size of dwellings, schools, churches, recreational facilities, and types of commercial establishments indirectly control the lives and tastes of the inhabitants. The difference in a planned community is that the developer or

planner instead of "fate" or nameless decision-makers determines the level
of environmental quality, and if the planner is skilled and creative and
sensitive to human qualities, a better environment in which to live should
result.

Reston with all of its admirable and noteworthy attributes has not been
without its critics. In the areas completed, the carefully planned environment
is so structured that any changes or developments that might be desirable in
the future cannot be easily made. A town is a living organism, as history has
shown, and must not remain static. Perhaps a more realistic approach to
urban planning would be to provide a less rigid system, one that allows space
for later structures and has built-in adaptability. Thus, instead of the need to
develop another village or shopping center, limited expansion and adjustment of space and structure use can be permitted. Limits and regulations are
necessary, but should not be so rigid that no changes are possible.

Recent significant innovations in urban development have not been confined to the establishment of new towns. Across the nation large areas of
inner cities have been cleared and new housing complexes have been
errected. Where there was once a varied mix of housing, stores, friendships,
and a "sense of place"—admittedly often in crowded substandard buildings
only a few stories high and with little or no open space except the streets
themselves—high-rise, poorly conceived adaptations of the vertical towers
once proposed by Le Corbusier have been built. Increased crime, loneliness,
and loss of "belonging" often result from the disruption of established family
ties and neighborhood friendships causing one to question, "Is new housing
always an improvement over the old?"

One project that offers considerable possibilities for urban renewal is the
mass-produced community developed in Montreal as part of Expo 67. Called
Habitat, this city within the city was designed by a young Israeli-born
Canadian architect Moshe Safdie and was built on a peninsula projecting

5-11 *Stacked like children's blocks, pre-fabricated concrete units form the multiple housing structure called Habitat in Montreal.*

into the Saint Lawrence River. What makes this structure, it is a single structure, so unique is its method of construction, flexible arrangement of component parts, and, perhaps even more important, its concern for those who live there. It has been designed to give a "sense of place."

Habitat was conceived three-dimensionally. It is neither horizontal or vertical, but both. It is truly a three-dimensional, densely populated urban environment, yet considerable privacy, freedom from noise, and more than adequate space is afforded.

Stretching about 950 feet, Habitat is a masterpiece of prefabrication and was constructed of hundreds of precast concrete boxes, $38\frac{1}{2}$ feet long, 17 feet wide, and 10 feet high, made on the site. These were fitted with wiring, plumbing, additional interior walls, windows, and kitchen and bathroom facilities, then lifted by crane and stacked one upon another, bolted together, and topped with concrete slabs. Each dwelling unit consists of one, two, or three boxes. These units or houses, which indeed they are rather than apartments,[11] may have from three to seven rooms and be one or two stories high. Each has at least one large terrace with much space for plantings; the surrounding walls have built-in planting boxes, for example. An almost limitless variety of floor plans exist, emphasizing the flexibility of the total design concept.

Located beneath the whole complex of 158 dwellings[12] are individual

[11] In an apartment building the ceiling of one apartment is the floor of the one above. In Habitat, each house has its own walls, ceiling, and floor of concrete (the terrace floor is an exception as it is the roof of the house below). Unlike in most apartments, there is no sound transmission from one Habitat house to another.

[12] Originally the plans called for 1,000 dwellings but cost considerations required the reduction to 158. However, this does not reduce the importance of Habitat and with an increased use of the building materials and special equipment the costs would be drastically lowered.

automobile parking facilities next to a private, good-sized storage or work room for each house (corresponding to a basement in a suburban dwelling). Three elevators located along the length of Habitat take the resident to his "street level." He walks to his house. These pedestrian streets are outside, partially covered, and have heated surfaces to melt snow; they turn, twist, go up and down, and vary in width—sometimes becoming spacious playground-parks.

The importance of Habitat is not in its singularity but rather in its flexibility. By the introduction of the fourth dimension—time—Habitat can be a design and structural basis for urban-renewal projects. It would not be necessary to wipe out acres of substandard housing and disrupt neighborhoods for long periods of time, but rather, attractive, functional and, above all, human housing could be quickly built, unit by unit, and individual families could be transferred feet rather than miles from their old homes, and thereby retaining social contact with their neighbors. The design flexibility would allow desirable buildings to remain if needed, buildings scheduled for demolition left standing until the occupants can move into new construction, and streets could be bridged as the structures meandered from one place to another as condemned buildings were removed. The final development would include stores, offices, schools, playgrounds, theaters—all the elements that a true community requires, yet all would be accomplished without destroying the vital "sense of place" for those who live there.

The idea of a complete urban community in a single structure has taken many forms. Le Corbusier's Unité d'Habitation is a horizontal slab resting on stilts and Habitat is a cluster of stacked blocks. The quest for space in the center of cities has given rise to tall buildings and many have incorporated several uses within the single structure. The John Hancock Center in Chicago (1965) is a notable example of such a building. Designed by the firm of Skidmore, Owings, and Merrill, it rises 1,105 feet above the ground (1,449

5-12 *A forthright solution to the problem of walking in an intemperate climate was admirably conceived in the transparent, enclosed walkways.*

5-13 *The John Hancock Center in Chicago is a complete city in itself. It is possible to live, work, shop, and be entertained, yet never leave the building.*

feet with its twin television towers) and was the second tallest building in the world when it was built.[13]

Aside from its height, distinctive sloping sides and great "X" braces, the John Hancock Center is unique in that it is in essence several buildings stacked vertically—a commercial building, a garage, an office building, and an apartment building. Starting at ground level, the first five floors are occupied by a department store and banking facilities. Floors 6 through 12 are a parking garage for tenants entered from a spiral ramp at the sixth-floor level. Office space occupies the next 28 floors—13 through 41. On the forty-fourth and forty-fifth floors is a lobby for the apartments above, a restaurant, a post office, shops, and recreational facilities. Apartments are on the forty-fifth through the ninety-second floors (smaller apartments are on the lower levels with those larger and more expensive ones on the upper floors). An observatory is on the ninety-fourth floor and a restaurant occupies the ninety-fifth and ninety-sixth floors. The other floors are used for mechanical equipment.

Although the Hancock is certainly not an urban-renewal project and does not meet all the requirements of a true city or town, it does have a variety of uses and it would be possible to live, work, and relax there without leaving the structure, even though it is not possible to get from the apartment floors of the Hancock Building to the office floors without first descending to ground level and taking different elevators. The two areas are not connected.

The rapidly increasing world population, the concern for the environment,

---

[13] The 102-story Empire State Building, New York (1930), is 1,250 feet high (1,472 feet to top of the television antenna) and for a long time was the world's tallest structure. That record was challenged by the 110-story twin towers of the World Trade Center, New York (1968, both 1,350 feet high). The Sears Roebuck Building, Chicago (1971), towers above them all at 1,450 feet. These are all commercial buildings and do not incorporate housing in their design.

and the seeming lack of available land for future urban development have
prompted many suggestions to satisfy the demand for housing and for
commercial and industrial sites. They have included designs for floating
cities with space below and above the water line and anchored close to shore
or at sea; cities suspended above existing areas such as rail yards, docks, and
industrial complexes; domed cities with their own purified atmosphere; and
cities constructed in space and on distant heavenly bodies. But few visionary
architects or urban planners have captured the imagination as has Paolo
Soleri.

Environmental design is often conceived two-dimensionally; regional
maps, street layouts, and floor plans are drawn on paper and seldom does
anyone develop the three-dimensional concept during initial planning. The
tendency is to spread out the various urban land uses so that "adequate"
space can be made available. The results are often huge, sprawling mega-
lopolitan monsters that constantly engulf the countryside. Paolo Soleri
champions urban planning by implosion rather than explosion. His concept
of *archology* (a blend of architecture and ecology) is based upon the use of
concentrated space. Soleri believes that man should live in a confined area to
better experience the rhythm and pulse of the city because the city is an
extension of man himself. It is the city where man is humanized by the
cultural and institutional advantages inherent in concentrations of parti-
cipants. He proposes cities of up to 550,000 inhabitants contained in one
huge megastructure. The concept is as staggering as are the dimensions of
the architectural framework. For example, one of his archologies is designed
to be about 6,000 feet high and 9,000 feet in diameter.

Soleri has designed several archologies for cities of different sizes and
terrains. They vary in appearance and form considerably, but all are similar
in basic arrangement. Tne outermost layer would contain spaces to house the
inhabitants. Each individual or family unit would be allotted space sufficient
for its needs and, in turn, could adjust, divide, or change this block of space

as it preferred. The basic size of an apartment is planned to be approximately 60 feet long, 35 feet wide, and 20 feet high. Being on the perimeter of the city, the residents would be able to enjoy the natural environment surrounding them. Fresh, clean air and light would not be at a premium.

The interior of the gigantic structure would contain the civic, commercial, and industrial facilities. Offices, theaters, museums, universities and schools, and department stores are to be located near the residential areas, and deep within the structure are power plants, warehouses, and heavy industrial units. Jet and heliports would be at the top of the city.

Many analogies can be perceived between the medieval city and Soleri's proposals. Both the civitas and the archologies are primarily vertical; there is a concentration of population, industry, and civic activities; and perhaps most important, there is a complete separation between the man-made urban environment and the natural surrounding space. There is no filtering of city into country; beyond the archology is an unspoiled landscape.

Soleri is currently building a small archology planned for 1,500 people. Called Arcostanti, it is located near Phoenix, Arizona, and will test many of his theories of urban planning. As Soleri's visionary concept slowly takes tangible form, the question that hovers like a specter over any "planned" city and certainly over such concentrated and man-made conditions as has Soleri's archologies must be asked. Is this concentrated, man-made, isolated, urban environment the catalyst for human collectivization? Would living in an archology provide a suitable location for a psychocivilized society as proposed by B. F. Skinner?[14] Would it be any different than the old "company towns" where everything was controlled by one authority? Could an

---

[14] Burrhus Frederick Skinner (1904–), psychologist and author of *Walden II* (1948) and *Beyond Freedom and Dignity* (1972), proposes that mankind cannot afford unlimited freedom anymore, but must live in a controlled culture and environment if he is to retain any of the qualities now considered desirable.

archology simply be a vertical "cookie-cutter" community? Can an individual develop imaginatively and aesthetically in an environment such as an archology? Time and observation can only answer such intriguing questions and Arcostanti in the Arizona desert may provide answers that will affect urban design consideration for years to come.

6 Interior Environmental Considerations

6-1 *The spaces where we live, work, and relax are of utmost importance. The stark, rectangular surfaces and spaces in this photograph convey a sense of power and drama, but at the same time may not be ideal for human habitation.*

The interior spaces within the structures where people work, relax, eat, sleep, that is, live, are as much a part of the environment as the exterior spaces that surround these structures. Americans, perhaps more than citizens of any other nation, spend the greater part of their lives under roofs; yet, the majority of those voicing concern for the environment seemingly omit or disregard interior spaces (and the objects that define those spaces), which are, with the exception of clothing, the *nearest* environment of the human being.

It is known that man responds both psychologically and physiologically to his environment. A room that may be admired and considered pleasant could be made most uncomfortable by merely raising or lowering the temperature 20 or 30 degrees, for example. Furthermore, it has been shown that apparent space can be enlarged or diminished by the manipulation of color or visual barriers. So simple a change as the walls being painted a light "cool" color instead of middle value "warm" one can both visually enlarge a space and decrease the apparent temperature.

The complexity of contemporary society has thrust upon each person near environments that he did not choose but must exist in—his offices, factories, school, and shops. The interior of his own home or apartment is about the only place where he has any chance of feeling like an individual and can choose the components, but even there if others are concerned, the decisions must be shared. Those sharing the decisions may be other members of the household or persons who may be unknown to the individual. This is not as strange as it may seem. Seldom can a person independently design and make the structure, furniture, and accessories he lives with as he almost always accepts some previously designed objects, uses a specified location, finds that monetary considerations are prohibitive, or discovers his lack of an adequate design background. It is then necessary for him to adapt to the housing space that exists rather than adapt spatial arrangements to his particular needs. This adaptation is also true of furnishings. However, selections can be made and changes accomplished. Rarely, if ever, can "nothing" be done to make a

119

6-2

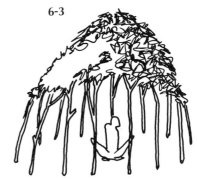

6-3

dwelling more functional and fit the requirements of those living there.

In this chapter the interior or near environment of dwellings is examined. Many of the considerations apply to other interiors as well, but for simplification the interior spaces of houses is the primary concern.

The need for shelter is one of the most basic requirements of man. This requirement has been translated into a variety of structural forms and materials and each culture has developed floor plans for its shelters that were best suited to the living patterns of the people.

Early man probably first sought shelter in the natural earth formations such as under outcroppings of rocks or in water-carved caves. As his ability to manipulate the natural environment developed, man may have created his first artifical shelter by lashing down the branches of a living tree to form a semicircular roof over his head. It is believed that from this advancement in protection came the idea of using vertical poles in a circular arrangement with a roof made of woven branches and vines.

Whatever the materials man used, the plan of his structure was the most simple plan of all, the circle. The round tent and the early domed or peaked roof hut had such a floor plan and repeatedly was one room with a door but no windows. This single room served as the focus for such activities as sleeping, eating, and socializing, with most of the cooking and domestic work being done outside the "home."

In time, the circular single-room plan gave way to the one-room square or rectangular plan as better systems of building construction and joinery were learned. This new plan, dominated by four right-angled corners, is the basis for most of the interior floor plans that later evolved—new rooms can be more easily fitted when and where needed with no wasted or strange shaped leftover spaces. A cursory look at the historic development of interior spaces shows how the 90-degree angle has dominated floor plans.

The Historical Development of Interior Spaces

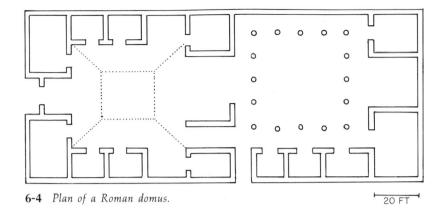

6-4 *Plan of a Roman domus.*

20 FT

The most simple design used for the creation of residential floor plans during the Egyptian, Greek, and Roman periods consisted of the single room with a square or rectangular configuration. The small Egyptian one-room house, called the *serekh* house, was multipurpose, but as the order of life in Egypt became more complex, more rooms were added to the perimeter of the main room, which, enlarged, became the central receiving area. The evolution of the Greek house followed that of the Egyptian. The rectangular room became a centrally located receiving chamber flanked by adjacent minor rooms and was fronted by a courtyard. The plan for the Roman *domus,* or city residence, was, in turn, based on this Greek multiroom rectangular plan.

Throughout the entire Middle Ages there is little regularity in the floor plans of the castles. Primarily a structure for defense, the castle was dominated by the *donjon,* the large central structure that enclosed the major interior space, the *great hall.* In this large rectangular room occurred most of the activities of the court—meals were eaten (and often prepared), entertainment was performed, trials and audiences were conducted, and usually the lord or king slept in a large curtained bed in the corner.

Other rooms were arranged around the great hall and were used for a variety of purposes, generally not distinct or fixed. Much of the daily activities were performed outside as the interior of the castles were usually damp, dark, and cold.

With the coming of the Renaissance in Italy and the renewed interest in the classical architecture of ancient Rome, a more ordered arrangement of rooms within the dwellings of the wealthy began to be used. (The poor usually lived in one-room structures until comparatively recent times.) The large palaces of the early Renaissance merchant princes were generally square in plan with square or rectangular rooms arranged, one room deep, around an inner courtyard, with more than one floor used for living space. Rooms began to be used for specific purposes and varied in size with the larger ones serving many of the functions of the medieval great hall. However, special rooms for sleeping, studying, and even dining began to be developed. There were no halls as are known today, and to get from one room to another might necessitate going through several other rooms. Doors were usually near the corners of the rooms so that the area along one wall functioned somewhat as a passageway. As the Renaissance developed, doors were placed in the center of the walls and took on added architectural importance. Halls were eventually introduced into the plans in the early eighteenth century.

The basic square or rectangular shape of the Italian Renaissance palace influenced the plan of almost every European and American dwelling, large and small, until the nineteenth century. Depending upon the size and elaborateness of the structure, the plan might be more than one rectangle or may or may not include an inner court, but seldom were curved floor plans used. For example, Versailles, the seventeenth-century masterpiece, was originally "U"-shaped, built around a rectangular courtyard on three sides. Long rectangular wings were later extended from the two opposite sides. The problem of successfully integrating interior spaces with different sizes and functions within a fixed exterior shape was often difficult. In many cases, the use of space did not always lead to logical divisions as the exterior appearance of the building was often designed first and the interior rooms were then adjusted in shape and location so they would fit into the exterior facade.

The eighteenth- and early nineteenth-century Georgian and Greek revival houses in America were often designed in this manner. Their basic overall plan was rectangular, with the longest dimension forming the front and rear of the structure. The plan was divided in half by a centrally placed main hall that bisected the house, horizontally and vertically. The requisite formal balance was achieved in the design of the facade by an equal number of evenly spaced windows, arranged on either side of the centrally positioned door. The interior spaces (rooms) were formed by walls, governed by the central hall and the even spacing of the windows.

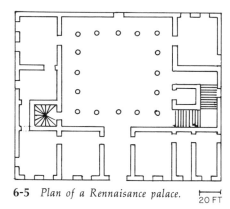

6-5 *Plan of a Rennaisance palace.* 20 FT

6-6 *Plan of a Greek Revival house.*

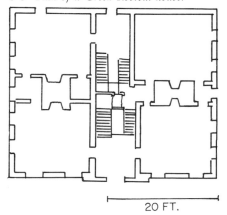

20 FT.

Shortly after the beginning of the nineteenth century the formal and rigid arrangement of rooms within buildings began to be replaced by a more informal type of plan, especially evident in Gothic revival houses. Functionally arranged rooms, circular features, and irregularities such as protruding, multisided bay windows and rooms with curved ends and alcoves contributed to the informality.

By the midnineteenth century, most of the room-use designations that are currently employed were established. Kitchens, long relegated to the lower levels or completely banished from the main house structures as in the houses in Williamsburg were again being incorporated into the plans (they were never completely removed from *northern* American homes but often were in a lean-to at the rear).

The first municipal water system was completed in Philadelphia in 1801. The city dweller could, at last, have an adequate supply of good water for cooking, drinking, and, for a few, bathing. Except in the most eccentric houses in Europe there were no bathtubs; what bathing that was done took place in portable basins. Bathrooms and indoor toilets were first installed in the developing luxury hotels[1] and it was not until after 1830 that bathing and toilet facilities began to be incorporated into house plans. The primitive structure behind the house began to be replaced by indoor plumbing.[2]

One bathroom was considered adequate in most homes until after the 1940s and since then it is not uncommon to find two, three, and even four bathrooms in moderately sized homes. Some of these are not always com-

---

[1] Tremont House (1828) in Boston, Massachusetts, was one of the first "modern" hotels built in the United States. It had numerous water closets and in the basement bathtubs with running water.

[2] Catherine E. Beecher and Harriet Beecher Stowe proposed in their book *The American Woman's Home* (1869) the use of "earth-closets," best described as "somewhat like . . . a water-closet, except that in place of water is used dried earth." Needless to say the proposal did not catch on.

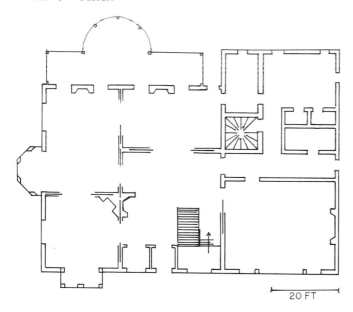

6-7

6-8 *The large opening between the back "living room" (foreground) and the front parlor allowed family activities to flow between the two rooms. The draperies could be closed to separate the spaces if desired.*

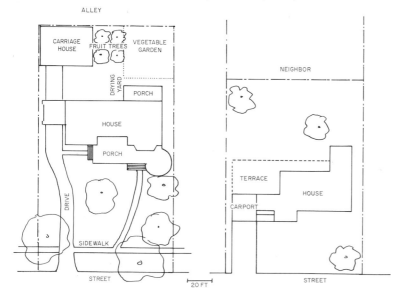

6-9 *The typical house of 75 years ago (left) sat back from the street, was surrounded by porches, and was oriented toward the street. Today, the average house is nearer the street, has an attached garage or carport, and the majority of outdoor space is in the rear. Lots are seldom as deep now as they were in the past.*

plete bathrooms but are "half-baths"—without a bathtub—and are located near the entrances and the family room. The number of bathrooms is a frequently cited status symbol by many builders and developers of medium priced homes.

By the 1860s, the informal arrangement of rooms found in the Gothic revival style combined with the increased tendency toward picturesque architecture culminated in the variety of styles and configurations loosely termed Queen Anne. The floor plan of a Queen Anne house was designed functionally; in fact, this was a primary consideration. The exterior was the natural outgrowth of the interior plan. The first floor of the house became almost one room; the entrance hall was enlarged into usable living space and with large archways and sliding panels the whole space was opened up. The development of central heating made this openness practical in any climate and for the first time in history, houses where the winters were cold were heated throughout. The new arrangements caused the once almost sacred area of the house, the parlor, to disappear. The parlor, where the best furniture was found and where the most important functions such as weddings, funerals, and formal receptions were held, was supplanted by the "living room." The large first floor space of the Queen Anne house became the living area and the entire household began to use it daily.

Sleeping porches became popular in the 1880s and continued until after World War I. These were usually located on the the second floor, opening off the bedrooms, and screened to protect the sleepers from insects.

The increased use of the automobile affected the interior plan of houses just as it affected the plans of the city. The front porch, that social center for friendliness and relaxation, was discarded and a garage was built on the back of the lot instead. The once quiet, pleasant street became filled with cars, fumes, and noise. Friends and neighbors rode rather than walked past and the porch on the front of the house became, more and more, an unpleasant place to relax.

Additionally, the automobile influenced changes in the orientation of the house plan as well. The major entrance to the house moved from the street side to a door nearest the driveway or garage and the need to further escape the noise of the street frequently caused the living room to be moved to the rear of the house, shifting the service areas, kitchen, and baths to the street side. Houses have also moved toward the front of the lot with the larger space behind rather than in front. The backyard is now filled with living spaces, terraces, patios, barbeques, and the like, instead of gardens, clotheslines, and a chicken or two.

The popularity of television has also influenced house plans. The "family room," or "rec room," has become almost a necessity in many homes, and is often the most frequently used room. It is interesting that along with the development of the family room, the kitchen, which during the 1920s and 1930s was almost a sterile laboratory, has increased in size and like the family room has become again a warm, livable, and inviting area, easily compared in spirit, feeling, and function with the "keeping" room or "hall" found in the homes of the early settlers of New England.

The informality and complexity of contemporary life have caused great variety in the floor plans and the locations in which people live. There is really no typical floor plan today, nor do people live in one or two types of shelter. Single family, duplexes, garden apartments, studio apartments, split-level, tri-level, ranch, center-hall colonial, contemporary, mobile home, high-rise, and town house are only some of the terms used today to describe housing. However, floor plans *can* be divided into two distinct types: *closed plans* and *open plans*.

CLOSED PLAN. Floor plans that have living spaces designated for specific uses, which are enclosed by walls, and where movement from one

Interior Enviroment Considerations

space to another is usually through doors are considered to be closed plans. Terms such as dining *room,* bed*room,* living *room,* and bath*room* usually indicate a closed plan orientation. This type of plan was almost universally used in the past when rooms were individually heated and could be shut off if not needed by merely closing a door. The division of the interior space with solid walls inherently provides greater privacy for the occupants as well as easier sound control.

OPEN PLAN. During the past 25 years closed plans have been frequently replaced by the open plan. An open plan house does not have walls that separate the functional spaces; one space flows visually and actually from one area to another, and terms such as living *area,* dining *area,* and study *alcove* (but not room) are used. The open plan is not a new idea since it has been used for centuries in warm climates and the Queen Anne houses and the early houses of Frank Lloyd Wright at the turn of the century had open plans. One reason for the recent popularity of the use of open plans is that houses now being built are often smaller and the available space is *apparently* increased when spaces designated for two functions, for example, dining and entertaining or living, are combined. The eye is not blocked by solid walls and is allowed to continue into another space.

Visually, the open plan has much in its favor; small spaces invariable do seem larger. However, sight lines are frequently inadequately explored. It is not uncommon to find that it is possible to be seated in the living area and see directly into a bathroom or bedroom, or to have a direct view from the street through a large expanse of glass into a dressing or bathing area. The need for privacy should not be ignored and often it is only necessary to shift a screen, storage wall, or panel to achieve the desired visual isolation.

Houses frequently have plans that combine both the closed and open concept; the more quiet and private areas (bedrooms and bathrooms) are more closed whereas the living and entertainment areas are more open. It is not uncommon to find, however, that although there may be walls, the only door that can be shut is the bathroom door; all others either do not exist or are blocked by furniture. Perhaps the most famous house with a very open plan is the Philip C. Johnson House in New Canaan, Connecticut, built in 1949, in which there are no interior walls except a cylinder enclosing the bathroom and all of the exterior walls are transparent.

FUNCTIONAL DIVISIONS

Regardless of the kind of structure, location, size, or plan, to evaluate any dwelling—house or apartment—it is necessary to judge it against user requirements. The home user is not just a consumer but a *participant* in this environment, as he is in all environments. Only when a house or interior space "fits" a person or family, that is, when it effectively protects, warms, and cools, their bodies and possessions, functions efficiently for their uses, and satisfies their aesthetic wants can that house be considered successful or even adequate. What may be an excellent and preferred residence for one person or family may be inadequate for another.

A house should be flexible.[3] Western man often attaches labels to interior

6-10 *The inside and the outside fuse into one when the exterior walls are slid back in the traditional Japanese house. The tatami mats on the floor serve as the modular unit—all room sizes are governed by their size.*

---

[3]Much could be learned from the Oriental house. In both traditional Chinese and Japanese architecture the "space" is more dominant than is the "mass." Walls are but sliding panels and screens—flexible, lightweight partitions—and can be arranged and rearranged in many combinations to divide and define the space in various ways as needed. The resulting functional modular system provides a decorative grid pattern that is readily apparent to those unfamiliar with the more subtle building devices. Japanese houses have a quality of unity and organic wholeness that is the result of this relationship between all parts.

Several different panels and screens are used, but the Japanese *shoji* is the best known. The shoji consists of a light wooden framework divided into small panels or panes covered with translucent paper. Technically shoji screens are translucent, allowing the light to filter through the paper, but American adaptations have been made using opaque materials. (Opaque sliding wall panels are called *fusuma* in Japan.)

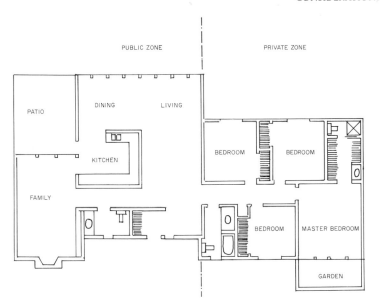

PUBLIC ZONE   PRIVATE ZONE

PATIO   DINING   LIVING

KITCHEN

FAMILY

BEDROOM   BEDROOM

BEDROOM   MASTER BEDROOM

GARDEN

6-11 *The public zone in this plan is open—one area flows into the next without doors and with few dividing walls. The private zone is a closed plan. Each space is separated from the others by solid walls and doors.*

spaces.[4] Whether defined by walls or merely suggested by furniture arrangements, these labeled areas do not always indicate the aggregate uses of the space. A dining room, for example, frequently is used for activities other than dining and conversely not all food is consumed there. The house should not be so constructed that a space cannot be adapted to different activities or that different arrangements or types of equipment or furniture are not possible within a space. The changing interests of the occupants over time must also be accommodated as well as the change from one owner to another.

Houses have two basic activity zones: the *public zone* and the *private zone.* The public zone consists of the entrance, living-social, cooking and eating, and outdoor activity spaces, and the spaces where sleeping, bathing and laundering, and storage activities dominate constitute the private zone. The success of a house plan, and its eventual use, is often determined by how well these activity spaces comprising the public and private zones are grouped and by their mutual accessibility. Each activity taking place in each space often tends to complement and reinforce activities found in adjacent spaces. Very quiet areas for sleeping are usually bordered by bathing areas, dressing areas, and storage areas for clothing, for example. The following functional and spatial divisions should be carefully considered when evaluating a house relative to the needs of those who now or shall live there.

ENTRANCE SPACES. Although frequently disregarded, how and where one enters a dwelling is very important. The transition from the exterior to interior is accomplished here and beginning traffic patterns are immediately established. Entry into a dwelling may be through a single door or through several doors, placed at different locations. Each door may have a distinct function and be used by different people or at different times. The "front

[4] These labels—bedroom, living room, kitchen, and the like—have only been employed for the past 200 years. Prior to the eighteenth century rooms were almost always multi-purpose.

6-12

door" may be the prime entrance for visitors yet may be seldom used by the inhabitants of the house. Convenience, methods of transportation and movement, and nearness to the kitchen, bathroom, laundry or "my room" may be the determining factors in choosing a particular entrance door.

Ideally, storage should be provided at each entrance where people might remove their outer garments. Further, it is preferred that a visual barrier be established to give some privacy to those within the house when strangers are at the door.[5] It is frequently found that the size of the entry or the direction the door opens can prevent more than one or two people to be at the door at one time, which may cause confusion and embarrassment. Importantly, a visitor's initial impression of the character and quality of the occupant's life-style is first established by the visual and functional qualities of the exterior and interior entrance spaces of a house.

6-13

LIVING-SOCIAL SPACES. Upon entering a dwelling the spaces used for entertainment and relaxation are usually first encountered and are almost without exception the largest in the house and the most richly furnished. These activities are frequently combined and at times use the same spaces, but there is a marked difference between entertaining and relaxing. The term *entertain* usually implies that more than one person is involved and that some physical or verbal energy is being expended. However, to *relax* indicates a lessening of tension, quiet, and perhaps introspection—a solitary activity. Further, where one entertains is frequently more "formal" than where one relaxes, just as "living room, parlor, or front room" bring to mind a far different impression and imagined use than does "family room or recreation room." Therefore, a careful analysis of the daily life *and* the life-style of the occupants of a dwelling must be made to determine the spatial requirements of the household.

[5] One particularly questionable but recurring spatial arrangement found in many plans is to have the dining area serve also as the entrance space.

Where do the occupants of the dwelling entertain their friends and acquaintances? How formal is their entertaining and how many are entertained at a time? There are those who consider a weekly cocktail party for 150 people "simple" entertaining, whereas to others just having another person over for a "couple of beers" might be a great undertaking. Is all entertaining done in the "living room" or are other areas used, that is, a teen-ager's room, the kitchen, the patio, or the terrace?

Similar questions must also be asked concerning relaxation and recreation space. What does the household do when the members relax? Is reading a major activity, or is watching television? Do family members engage in hobbies and games? Does one designated space function best or should various areas in a house be conducive to relaxation?

One further consideration concerning major "public" interior spaces must be discussed. It is not uncommon to find a sizable amount of space allotted to a room that is filled with choice furniture and accessories, yet is seldom used. Many homes have one or more rooms that are almost "off limits" to the members of the household. Measured by space utilization standards such rooms would seem very wasteful, especially if interior space is at a premium. However, to some people a room of this type may be very important —psychologically. It may mean that this room is "how it should be," not "how it is." It is the author's opinion that with today's fabrics, surfaces, and materials no room need be so "sacred." It is far better to live with *and use* prized and beautiful objects than to just look at them. To isolate and rarefy beauty is as bad as to destroy it. Objects are to be enjoyed rather than worshipped from afar.

Cooking and Eating Spaces. The spaces where members of the household cook and eat are more varied today than they were in the past. Just as methods of cooking and types of food have changed, so have the places in which it is cooked. Until a few years ago, the question, "Where is your food cooked?" would have invariably been answered, "in the kitchen."

6-14

Yet, it is possible, and indeed probable, that now must be added, "in the dining room, the terrace, the bedroom, and the family room." With today's appliances (electric skillets, coffee makers, corn poppers, toasters, and small freezers and refrigerators), the popularity of open-fire cooking, and the availability of frozen and precooked foods, the preparation and cooking of food is no longer limited to one space.

The type of food and time needed to prepare food should also be considered. Today's premixed, frozen, and precooked foods require far less time in the kitchen than previously, yet, kitchens have become larger and more elaborate in the last 20 years—almost in reverse ratio to the ease of food preparation. The increased popularity of the "family kitchen" with its invitingly warm, homey, and nostalgic decoration (often fake) indicates that most people consider the kitchen to be the center of the home, the nucleus around which all activities revolve even though food preparation time is less and "mother" is no longer constantly in the kitchen.

The food storage and preparation areas should be convenient to the places where the cooking and eating are done. Often it is difficult to get to the outdoor cooking area from the kitchen, for example. Conceivably today's living practices demand more than one area of food storage and preparation, but proper planning could adequately satisfy this requirement.

The household should make a careful study of who eats where and when. Many families when asked will immediately say they all eat together, practically every meal, yet upon further reflection discover that perhaps at only one meal a day does the family eat together. Breakfast has become a grab-and-run affair; lunches are eaten at school, place of work, or not at all; and the evening meal is the only one at which the family might all be together.

Similarly, food is no longer eaten only in the dining room or in the kitchen. Meals are eaten throughout the house—in front of the fireplace, in the family room, on the terrace, or even in one's bedroom. Moreover, eating is often an

6-15

adjunct to entertaining and frequently the places where guests are served food are those in which the household normally does not eat.

The preparation and consumption of food must necessarily be coupled with the disposal of food wastes or garbage. The proliferation of packaging materials in addition to the usual food preparation wastes have caused increased problems for the homeowner. It is not simply just the increased amount of garbage that must be dealt with (a major problem for many urban communities, however) but problems of ecology and recycling of resources are also involved. The continual consumption of materials without regard to their reuse is considered by many to be of primary concern. Consequently, there is an increased need for convenient storage and disposal of waste products originating in the kitchen.

OUTDOOR SPACES. One of the most remarkable phenomena of twentieth-century culture is the desire to be outdoors. Throughout history man has endeavored to create shelters that protected him from the elements and to find better methods with which to cook his food. However, now that sturdy, air-conditioned and centrally heated structures are common and cooking facilities are efficient, man increasingly turns toward the outdoors to spend his time and to cook his food over open fires.

Furthermore, homes, as well as public buildings, have become less inward oriented; large windows and even transparent walls have replaced opaque facades that previously separated the interior from the exterior. Large sliding glass doors permit freedom of movement from the inside to the outside and the visual space afforded by this transparency, of course, is much greater. House plans are frequently found to incorporate atriums and enclosed open spaces around which the rest of the house is oriented.

It is important to consider the outdoor activities of a family when evaluating a dwelling. The terrace or patio with its accompanying cooking facilities is common and the private swimming pool is no longer restricted to the very wealthy. Gardening is a task enjoyed by many and has become in many

6-16

cases, a suburbanite's obligation. So simple an activity as sunbathing also requires consideration. Easy entrance and egress, closeness of dressing and bathroom facilities, and ease in storage of equipment are all prime requisites. Frequently, the elimination of a flight of stairs by the construction of a deck or an exterior grade change might markedly increase the efficiency of a house.

Above all, however, is the fact that most people *do* live outdoors at least part of the year, airconditioning notwithstanding, and the house and surrounding space must be so judged.

SLEEPING SPACES. What is needed in the space allotted for sleeping? Does it hold a bed (or beds) and little else? Is the bed the dominant piece of furniture or is it almost nonexistent visually? How big does this space have to be? Must it be physically isolated from the rest of the house? Are there activities other than sleeping performed in this space? How many people must have sleeping facilities and must they be grouped together? What are the ages, sex, and relationships within the household? These questions are but a few that should be raised when considering the largest of private spaces in the house.

Sleeping space requirements change over time. The small child needs little space; as he grows his sleeping space is combined with a place to play quietly. By the time the child becomes a teen-ager the room will be the meetingplace of his friends, where he can pursue his hobbies and listen to records, as well as where he sleeps. In the young adult's first apartment the only sleeping facility may be a couch or a mattress, or it may be the major piece of furniture. The newly married couple will put much emphasis on the sleeping arrangements. The parents of school-age children frequently incorporate space for sitting and relaxing in their sleeping area—a retreat from the rest of the house. The sleeping arrangements of the older person may again be minimal and exposed, as might be those of someone living in a one-room apartment.

6-17

In addition to basic sleeping requirements are those most closely associated with sleeping areas, for example, facilities for study, dressing, even entertaining (in the case of the teen-ager or the elderly person, for example), and the storage of clothes. It is well to consider the sleeping space requirements of a household as carefully as those in the more public areas of the house.

BATHING AND LAUNDERING SPACES. Perhaps the most private areas in a house are those given to bathing and other toilet needs. The inclusion of a specific space within the house for the bath is a relatively recent addition to the plan. First seen in modern times[6] about 150 years ago, the bathroom has only become universal during this century.

A tendency in recent years has been to develop large and elaborate bathrooms. Again it is a question of what activities are to be done there. Frequently these large spaces have facilities for exercising, relaxing, dressing, and sunbathing (by both natural and artificial light), and perhaps even a sauna.

The bathroom is one of the most expensive rooms for its size in a house, yet the cost can be considerably reduced if plumbing can be clustered, that is, if bathrooms can be placed back to back and not dispersed. Costs can be further reduced if not every bathroom has a bathtub but is a "half-bath" (just the lavatory and toilet).

It has become increasingly common to have at least one half-bath on each level of the house. The convenience of this arrangement is without question; however, placement of this room should be carefully considered. Often one finds a little "powder room" near the front entrance of the house that is seldom used except when there are guests. Yet, if the family includes young children a more functional approach might be to have a "mud room" near the

[6]The Romans were noted for their baths but even these were not always within the private house but were community structures.

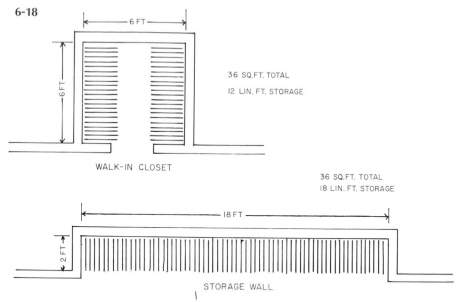

6-18

6 FT

6 FT

36 SQ. FT. TOTAL

12 LIN. FT. STORAGE

WALK-IN CLOSET

36 SQ. FT. TOTAL

18 LIN. FT. STORAGE

18 FT

2 FT

STORAGE WALL

door they most frequently use. (The mud room usually consists of not only toilet and bathing facilities but also laundry equipment.)

Recent changes in the laundering of clothing and linen have made possible a shift of position of laundering facilities that is long overdue. Researchers have found that the most efficient placement of the laundering equipment is near the sleeping and bathing areas in the house. Most of the clothes and linens that must be washed originate there and the clean clothes are stored there, and importantly, the necessary plumbing is near. In the past, because of the necessity to heat water, the use of several tubs of water, the need for outside drying, and finally, the long hours of ironing, the task of getting clothes clean was a complicated process that was relegated to the basement or near the kitchen and back door. This is not so today. Automatic washers (coupled with water heaters) and dryers, and noniron fabrics have replaced this laborious, time-consuming process.

STORAGE SPACES. The problem of storage has become acute in recent years. Houses are being built increasingly smaller and space is often at a premium, yet in today's society the accumulation of objects is not difficult. Where does one store his "needs?"[7] No longer do houses have large storerooms, attics, basements, or a convenient barn with a commodious haymow. Where do the cars, bikes, recreational equipment, gardening tools, clothes (both winter and summer), cooking appliances, unfinished projects, and the like go? Unless a person is almost ruthless and completely dedicated to a Spartan life, the accumulation of objects requiring storage increases daily.

Even in the smallest dwelling, a great deal of unused space could be used for storage, the spaces over kitchen cabinets, behind doors, or under stairs,

[7] Some architects and designers believe that approximately 25 percent of a house should or must be devoted to storage.

6-19 *Released from the conventional regularity of right angles, the spaces in this small house allow for flexibility of activities and movement.*

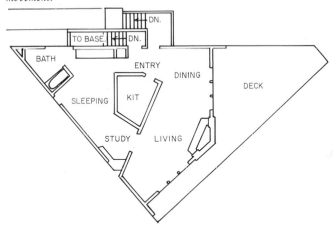

for example. Closets are noted for their waste space unless they are carefully arranged.[8]

The use of built-in storage has been extolled for years and with good reason. It is efficient and inexpensive if properly planned when the house is built. However, built-in storage has not always been accepted by the average person; perhaps because it is often inflexible and necessarily must be left when the family moves. An alternative solution would be the use of free-standing components that can be combined to give functional storage space. The advantage of built-in storage would be possible yet the flexibility needed for people in a mobile society would be there.

MOVEMENT BETWEEN INTERIOR SPACES

Since personal privacy, the control of unwanted noise, and the channeling of human traffic are vital considerations in the palnning of the interior, the establishment of effective traffic patterns is of primary concern. The effectiveness of a proposed floor plan or an actual structure can be tested by trying to figure out how well one can travel through it. Imagine living and carrying on daily activities within the confining patterns of the plan. For example, try to figure out how a meal would be cooked and served. Is the cooking area convenient to the eating area? Is it possible to go from the kitchen to the eating area without going through a third space that is used for a conflicting activity? While cooking, will a steady flow of traffic through the kitchen be disturbing?

Determine how easily one could enter carrying bags of heavy groceries, or taking out the garbage. Is the kitchen conveniently located near a door that serves the parking area? Or, is it necessary to walk through the main entrance

---

[8]The walk-in closet wastes at least one-third of its potential storage space when compared to a storage wall with the same square footage. *maybe so, but a walk-in closet is easier to use + doesn't waste wall space!*

hall, living room, dining room, or den to reach the kitchen? If someone is entertaining in the living area, is it possible to move from each bedroom to the kitchen for a snack without entering the living area and creating a disturbance?

The most common way of channeling the flow of human traffic between spaces is through halls. Strategically located, a well-placed hallway allows freedom of personal movement without seriously disturbing activities in other spaces and it often forms the axis or backbone of the traffic flow for the entire dwelling. However, because of poor planning, many houses have too much space devoted to halls and the occupants of these dwellings frequently feel as if they were living in a maze of narrow spaces pierced by a myriad of doors.

Although the major function of the hall is the channeling of traffic, its placement and design can serve other uses. The hall can be designed to create additional spaces for living. A major hallway that is wide enough can often serve as additional seating, conversational, or reading areas, if these activities do not seriously interfere with movement through the hall. Storage units can be located within the walls where needed, thereby considerably increasing the utilitarian function of the hall. Halls should be well lighted, naturally or artificially, and well ventilated. A dark, stuffy, narrow hall, deep within a house, contributes little to the quality of an interior environment.

NOISE CONTROL

One of the major problems that affects contemporary living is the control of noise. Noise is unwanted sound and is an intensely personal irritant (one person's music may be another's cacophony). As more and more people are crowded together in closely packed living and working arrangements, their activity sounds overlap. Seldom does one find himself free of the exterior sounds of automobile traffic, power mowers, overhead jet planes, neighbors, and architectural construction (or destruction); the interior sounds of vacuum cleaners, dishwashers, clothes washers and dryers, plumbing, mixers, garbage disposals, typewriters and air conditioners, and the incessant howl of radios and television sets everywhere.

Most sources of noise are man-made and have been allowed to invade the urban (and rural) man's life in the name of democracy and progress—toward what end no one seems to ask. People have, however, become recently aware of sound pollution and that irritating noise levels may be what has been bothering them. Researchers have found that noise can play havoc with the nervous system, cause headaches, and reduce the level of sleep accounting for fatigue, irritability, anxiety, tension, and reduced efficiency.

Everyone has a sound level above which irritation is caused, and this level changes with the time of day, the mood of the individual, and the background sounds; a dripping faucet may not be noticed during the day, but at night it may be very distracting. Sound is not like light or warmth. If too much light comes through a window, curtains can be drawn or the eyes shut; or if it is too cold, a sweater or a thermostat change can alleviate the discomfort. It is not so with sound. The ear remains constantly open and sounds are heard whether one is inside, outside, awake, or asleep.

Modern construction methods are frequently not as sound absorbing as those that were used previously. This is especially true in newer apartment buildings, and to a lesser degree in single family houses. Solid masonry walls are rarely built and walls seldom have lath and plaster surfaces. Walls are now usually surfaced with Sheetrock (plasterboard) nailed to 2 inch by 4 inch studs. Sound waves originating on one side of the wall have little difficulty vibrating through to the other side. Further, many walls often have numerous openings, back-to-back electrical outlets and medicine cabinets, or shared heating and air-conditioning ducts, which allow conversation, music, or other noises to pass freely from one space to another.

Proper sound-retardant construction should be used. Staggered studs, where each surface is nailed to a separate set of 2 by 4s permitting each side of wall or floor-ceiling to vibrate freely but does not transmit the vibration to the other side, are one alternative. Separate heater and air-conditioning units, solid masonry walls, electrical outlets that are not back-to-back (at least 3 feet apart), and the spaces between the wall surfaces filled with sound-absorbing materials are other methods that combat the transmission of noise.

Noises originating *within* a structure can be minimized by using soft, sound-absorbing materials such as carpeting, draperies, upholstered furniture, and acoustical ceilings. Soft textured surfaces are more sound absorbing than are hard, slick ones as the more dense the air or material is the more the sound will travel through or be reflected. Architecturally, sound waves can be dissipated by reducing the number of parallel surfaces. Sound waves bounce back and forth intensifying themselves if surfaces are parallel, but if angled or curved surfaces are found in an interior the sound waves are diffused and their intensity[9] is lowered (a sound wave looses some of its energy if it must bend 45 degrees or more).

Noises originating outside the structure will also be lessened by these methods. In addition, double doors and windows, and weatherstripping[10] reduce the noise from the outside. Windows are the weakest barriers against unwanted sound, especially if they must be opened or are one thickness of glass. Ideally they should be placed away from the source of exterior sound. Natural noise barriers such as knolls or manmade berms, bushes, and trees will also reduce the noise level near a house. If a proposed house is to have a

[9]The intensity of sound is measured in *decibels* (dB). Measurements of some common noise-producing objects and activities are leaves rustling, 20dB; auto traffic, 64 dB; vacuum cleaner, 70 dB; power mower, 95 dB; and rock band, 114 dB. The Occupational Safety and Health Act (April, 1971) has stated that no one should be subjected to 115 dB for more than 15 minutes or to 90 dB for more than 8 hours.

[10]A crack of $\frac{1}{64}$ inch is enough to allow sound to pass that can negate other sound stoppage procedures.

plan that is "U" shaped, it would be advisable to orient the house so that the inner part of the "U" is away from the primary noise sources as the two parallel walls can catch and amplify the unwanted sounds.

The irritation of an unwanted sound can be reduced by adding "white noise," which is often used to mask other noises. This method can be experienced when soft music is played in offices, clinics, and stores (canned music with canned food); it is difficult to hear other sounds distinctly but the total noise level is raised somewhat.

It is far better to reduce or prevent noise than to mask it. Better sound-control construction and more efficient sound-abatement legislation and enforcement are needed. Individuals must also become convinced that sound does not necessarily mean power. Does the average housewife believe that a quiet vacuum cleaner does as good a job as one that is more noisy, *or* does the motorcycle or sports car enthusiast think that a quiet engine has the power of one that emits a loud roar on takeoff? Generally not, but until the public demands quieter products *and* a quieter environment, manufacturers or the courts and local governments will probably do little to bring about an abatement of noise.

PRIVACY

Throughout this book the importance of the individual has been championed. Nowhere is this attribute challenged more than in the lives of all people today because the boundaries within which the private self may not be intruded upon are continually being attacked and weakened.

More and more people are being treated as objects, as statistics. For example, each taxpayer now has a number that identifies him, names are no longer important. Street after street is lined with identical houses and uncounted apartments are undistinguishable regardless of occupant needs, numbers, or interests. Moreover, the slightest deviation in any thing from the "normal" is suspect. It is as though there was an attempt to homogenize

6-20 *Frequently, individuals and families live in converted single-family dwellings. If the original interior design—one space flowing into another—as many homes 50 to 75 years old are, the noise and privacy problems can be particularly acute. A visually disastrous attempt at privacy was made here by giving each apartment a separate entrance, but the structure now appears to be in the death grip of skeletal outside stairways.*

everyone into one level, one norm, although without individualism, without identity, the impersonalized being becomes a cog in a machine to be manipulated, managed, and moved.

Privacy is not a luxury; it restores psychic balance for without privacy there can be no individuality. Attitudes toward privacy are culturally shaped[11] and are complex and varied; however, to most Americans privacy means visual protection from other people. Ranging from the seldom seen recluse to the always visible gregarious extrovert, it is the rare person who does not value some private moments.

Present population density has lessened the availability of space for most individuals. Seldom can a person be so physically isolated that he has as much privacy as he might want; therefore, he must, within a confined space, find ways to maintain a sense of personal privacy.

Many housing areas, denuded of vegetation during construction, offer little natural visual protection, and rare is the activity, interior as well as exterior, which is not soon observed by the neighbors and the passersby in such areas. To relieve this "goldfish syndrome," fences, hedges, and other visual barriers are soon utilized.

Orientation should be carefully considered when planning a new house or remodeling an older one because the placement of doors, windows, and outside living areas can frequently be so arranged as to give considerable privacy. Everyone is familiar with houses having large expanses of glass (facetiously called "picture windows") that are covered with layers of fabric and usually filled with an ornate lamp and shade. One wonders why these windows exist when no view but a much-used street, the neighbor's garage, or an identical window is to be seen through them. Little light penetrates the curtains and lamp shade, indicating that they are not needed for interior illumination. The validity of such architectural embellishments (if they

[11]Nonliteral societies seem to need less privacy than more developed societies.

warrant such a term) is open to question, especially when away from the street in more private areas enlarged wall openings might be more enjoyable and require less shielding.

For years some architects and designers who thought that the American idea of an urban house sitting in the center of a lot, visually vulnerable from all sides, was wasteful and poorly conceived. Could not more livable exterior space be utilized if the basic structure was moved to the lot edge and the remaining land be walled for privacy? The ancient Roman *domus*, and twentieth-century houses in India, Iran, and Latin America are oriented inwardly, and although using less land area afford considerably more privacy to the inhabitants of the house. The marked increase in land costs and population density may force a rethinking of "livable" urban and suburban house design.

Within the house, the individual's right to some measure of privacy should not be ignored. The "private zone" of the house, sleeping and bathing areas predominantly, should be indeed private and within these areas, if members of the household so desire, further means of visual isolation should be available. The popularity of the open plan has resulted in houses with few private places. However, even in the most open plan, if sight lines and traffic patterns are carefully considered, a modicum of privacy can be had.

Part Three

Architectural Design

I believe that out of the past comes the best of the present and out of the present comes the future.

Frank Lloyd Wright

7 Architecture: Prehistoric Through Roman

Man has tried to enclose space, to create a better shelter for himself and his sacred objects, since the beginning of time. His early attempts were often futile and unsophisticated, but his continuing search for better methods and designs have produced solutions of great variety and merit. The climate, availability of materials, socioeconomic conditions, and architectural heritage have all been important factors that influenced the builder's decisions. The intended use was also important to the design of the buildings.

The chronological study of architecture and building is the familar, traditional approach, but is the one that rationally follows the development of the subject as if stone were placed upon stone until the fabric of the structure is formed. It is through the historic study of architecture that buildings today are understood and evaluated. As Cicero wrote in the first century B.C., "Not to know what happened before we were born is to remain perpetually a child. For what is the worth of a human life unless it is woven into the life of our ancestors by the records of history?"

Man undoubtedly did not construct shelters in the early dawn of history, but sought protection from the elements under the outcroppings of rocks or branches of trees. His first attempts to create a shelter probably used materials that were at hand, an uprooted bush, broken limbs, or branches from a tree, and with these partially enclosed a space, perhaps only a depression in a cliff. Over time (time is figured in tens of thousands of years when measuring the development of man's culture) he accepted less conditions as he found them. He changed his shelters, enlarging or narrowing openings to caves, making the caves deeper or even digging new ones, blocking fissures in the walls, and raising the level of the floors with dirt.

It is not certain if early man even lived in fixed dwellings. There is evidence, however, that in addition to living in caves he also constructed shelters using slender saplings as flexible frameworks and covered them with leaves, rushes, plaited twigs, hides, or bark. These at first were no more than

7-1

147

7-2

flimsy huts or windbreaks, but eventually they became more substantial. Almost without exception round in plan, these early shelters were constructed by inserting long, slender, flexible poles in the ground in a circular configuration and tying the tops together to form a cone-shaped structure, not unlike the tepee of the American Indian. Later the poles used were thicker and remained vertical with flexible branches woven between them to form a cylinder (the walls). The roof was still cone shaped. It was later in the development of shelter construction that the rectangular floor plan evolved. Using similar construction methods but implanting *both* ends of the poles in the ground, a series of parallel arches formed the framework of a half-cylindrical shelter. These two shelter construction techniques have been used by primitive peoples throughout the world and are still in evidence today, differing only in types of covering materials, size, and location. Where little wood existed, stone was the material used. But again, the circular plan seems to have evolved first followed later by the rectangular plan.

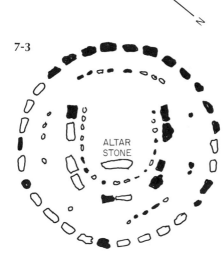

7-3

■ STILL STANDING

The post and lintel method of building thus developed in the earliest periods and was used by men of the Mesolithic and Neolithic periods (about 20000 to 2000 B.C.). By the third millennium substantial structures were being built. The civilizations of Egypt and the Near East were producing buildings of large size and accomplishment. However, cultures and their accompanying technical skills do not mature at the same rate in all areas, and in northern and central Europe the structures were less complicated and far less imposing. Little remains of the structures of the period but scattered throughout northern France and England are *dolmens* (*dol*, "table" and *men*, "stone") consisting of several stones set on end with a covering slab. *Megaliths*, single stones, some 70 feet high, are found singly or arranged in rows as at Carnac in Brittany. Circles of stones, *cromlech*, are also found. The most notable is *Stonehenge* on the Salisbury Plain in the south of England.

The general plan of Stonehenge is composed of two concentric circles

7-4 *The basic quality of post and lintel construction is seldom as forcefully displayed as at Stonehenge in England.* Courtesy of The British Tourist Authority.

enclosing two horseshoe shapes. The outer circle, 97 feet in diameter, originally consisted of 30 vertical stones (13½ feet above the ground) topped by 30 lintels. Each stone has been shaped and surfaced and on the top of each vertical stone is a projection (*tenon*) that fits into a depression (*mortise*) in the bottom of each lintel. The lintels are curved to follow the curve of the circle. The second circle is 76 feet in diameter and had 60 smaller vertical stones. The larger horseshoe originally had five *trilithons* (three stones, that is, two uprights and one lintel) varying from 20 to 30 feet high and weighing up to 40 tons. In front of the trilithons stood 19 tall slender stones, the inner horeshoe ranging from 6 to 8 feet high. These stand on a circle of 39 feet in diameter. In the center is the "altar stone," 16 feet long, 3 feet 4 inches wide, and 1 foot 9 inches thick.

The precision and methods of construction are of more interest here than simply the arrangement. Using no wheels, some of the stones (the "bluestones" used in the inner circle and the inner horeshoe) are believed to have been transported overland about 180 to 200 miles to their present location. The surface of the stones was not dressed with hammer and chisel but was pounded to dust with a round stone (some have been found during excavations and weigh up to 60 pounds each). Each tenon, mortise, and groove was so shaped. The large vertical members were laid into place, raised to their upright position, allowed to settle, and then were dressed to their proper height, thus accounting for the difference in depth, 4½ to 6 feet, but regularity in height.

Much has been written concerning the reason for the construction of Stonehenge, the date it was built, and who conceived the idea of carrying out such a mighty work with such exactness. No one can yet say what man or tribe is responsible for Stonehenge but through modern computation it is now agreed that it was used as an almanac of the sun and moon and as an ancient computer for predicting of eclipses. Stonehenge which was built about 1800–1400 B.C.[1], represents the building of Stone Age man rather than being comtemporary with the builders of Egypt and the Near East.

The Egyptian civilization developed along the Nile River over 4,700 years ago. Here was an ideal climate, an area of rich soil protected from invaders and an easy route for transportation and communication. Flowing more than 4,000 miles from sources deep in Africa northward to its mouth in the Mediterranean, the 750 mile stretch of the Nile from the First Cataract to the sea was the site of ancient Egypt. The valley of the Nile cut a green slash through the desert, an elongated oasis in a sterile land. Almost without rain, the warm land provided man a place to live and crops to grow only by using water from the Nile, first by natural flooding and later through extensive irrigating systems. Each year the Nile flooded, swollen by the rains in Ethiopia, and brought a layer of fertile silt—"black land" as the Egyptians called it to distinguish it from the sterile "red land" of the desert. "When the Nile inundates the land," the Greek historian Herodotus wrote in the fifth century B.C., "all of Egypt becomes a sea, and only the towns remain above water, looking like islands of the Aegean." The Nile also determined the seasons. There were three: "inundation," the time of flood, approximately from June through September, "Emergence of the Fields from the Water," October to February, and "Drought," the remainder of the time. Out of this cycle came the first practicable calendar and the one from which the modern Western calendar is derived. These seasonal divisions also determined behavior. During the "Emergence" the waters were trapped and hoarded in ponds and behind dikes and the seeds were planted in the mud of the receding waters. The time of "Drought" was the period of harvesting. During the "Inundation," when the river and fields were under water, the Egyptians hauled stones for the Pharaoh's building projects.

[1]Construction continued intermittently for several hundred years; however, a stump found at the base of one of the stones has, by its carbon content, been dated about 1800 B.C.

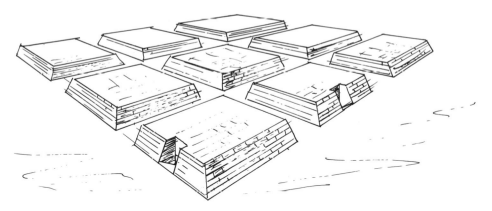

7-5 *Mastabas.*

With the protection of the desert on the west and east, the cataracts to the south, and the Mediterranean on the north, Egypt developed aloof and secure—free from foreigners and their influence. The Nile provided a swift route of communication binding the country together.

The Egyptian resistance to change is particularly evident. Although variations of detail, have been noted, the art and architecture of the Egyptians remain virtually the same for over 2,500 years. Three factors contributed to this: 1) The art and architecture was primarily religious and religion by its nature clings to tradition. 2) The Pharaoh was the chief patron of the arts. The artist worked as an artisan not an an innovative person. 3) The Egyptians were conservative by temperament.

To the Egyptian, life after death was a real existence, not just a substitute for life on earth. The Egyptians believed the soul left the body at the time of death but it would return to it through eternity. Therefore, the body must be preserved. Elaborate preservation methods were used, in some cases taking 70 days to complete, and many precautions were taken to protect the mummified body. Prehistoric graves were covered with mounds of sand or stones, but the constant winds blew away the sand or the jackals dug among the stones. (Anubis, the god of the dead and the guardian of tombs, was represented as a recumbent jackal.) Later graves were made safer and by the beginning of the dynastic era (3100–2686 B.C.) mastabas, flat-topped platforms with slanting sides and made of mud brick, were built over the burial chambers.

Sun-dried bricks were ancient Egypt's most common building material and until about 2700 B.C. were used for all buildings. Then, with spectacular suddenness, stone buildings developed and within 100 years after the first Pharaoh of the Old Kingdom (2686–2181 B.C.), Egyptian builders were producing a highly sophisticated stone construction, the first stone buildings in man's history. Considered to be the first major structure built entirely of stone, the Step Pyramid at Sakkarah was constructed for the Pharaoh Djoser

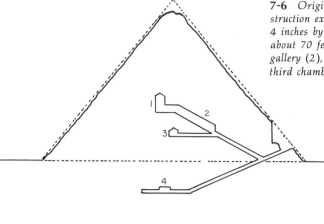

7-6 *Originally 480 feet high, the Great Pyramid of Khufu is solid masonry construction except for three small chambers. The largest, the king's chamber (1), is 34 feet 4 inches by 17 feet 2 inches and is topped by 5 massive horizontal stones in a space about 70 feet high, the lowest stone is 19 feet from the chamber floor. Below the grand gallery (2), which leads to the king's chamber is the smaller queen's chamber (3). The third chamber, the subterranean chamber (4), is below ground level.*

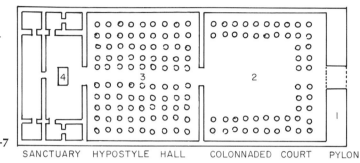

7-7

SANCTUARY   HYPOSTYLE   HALL   COLONNADED   COURT   PYLON

by Imhotep, an architect. This monumental structure, 413 feet by 344 feet at the base, stands about 200 feet high. Built of small blocks of stone laid together like bricks, it developed from the *mastabas* of earlier times and is really a series of six mastabas, one on top of the other.

In less than two centuries after Imhotep's success the first true pyramids were built. The Great Pyramid of Khufu at Gizeh was the wonder of the ancient world and is the mightiest royal tomb ever built. Constructed of more than 2 million limestone blocks, most weighing about $2\frac{1}{2}$ tons each, the pyramid, amazingly, was completed within the Pharaoh's reign of 23 years by men who had only the simplest implements and were without draft animals or even the wheel. The burial chamber, deep within the pyramid, is lined with smoothly fitted granite stones. The base of the Great Pyramid covers 13 acres and is about 775 feet square. Originally, the apex was 480 feet above the ground but the top 30 feet have been removed as has most of the smooth exterior surface. Using modern instruments, experts have found that the base at the southeast corner is only $\frac{1}{2}$ inch higher than the northwest corner. The Egyptians used a series of connecting trenches filled with water to find the true levels when constructing the pyramids.

More elaborate than the tombs, Egyptian temples of great size were also built of stone. Using a plan that changed in proportion and size but retained the four basic features, the Egyptian temple consisted of 1) the bastion-like *pylon,* 2) the colonnaded *court,* 3) the *hypostyle hall,* and 4) the *sanctuary,* all girdled by a wall. The pylon was the monumental gateway with smooth sloping walls, not unlike two truncated pyramids, and broken only by the doorway and large vertical grooves that held great flagstaffs.

Behind the pylon was the roofless court with colonnades on three sides. Here the public was sometimes permitted to enter, but could go no further. Beyond the court and opposite the pylon was the hypostyle hall. The hypostyle hall was filled with columns supporting the roof—a giant forest of stone tree trunks all carved with scenes and topped by huge capitals derived

7-8 *The basic form of an entrance pylon to an Egyptian temple. The flat battered (sloping) walls were usually ornamented with large incised reliefs.*

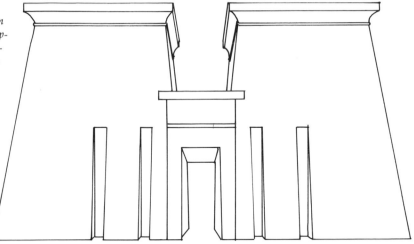

7-9 *The Egyptian style has influenced architecture several times throughout history. The entrance to the Grove Street Cemetery in New Haven, Connecticut, was built between 1845 and 1848 and is obviously based upon the entrance pylon before an Egyptian temple. The two supporting columns are similar to the lotus bud column.* Photograph by Wayne Andrews.

THE DEAD SHALL BE RAISED.

7-10 *Hypostyle hall.*

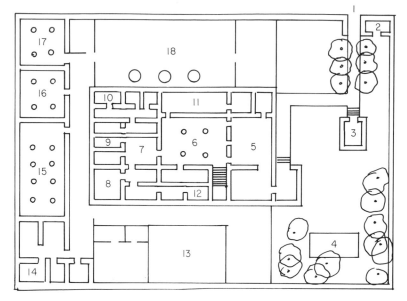

7-11 *A typical plan for a house of a wealthy Egyptian of the Middle Kingdom: 1) Main entrance, 2) gatekeeper, 3) chapel, 4) pool and garden, 5) entrance hall, 6) main reception room, 7) harem, 8) main bedroom, 9) guest rooms, 10) bedrooms, 11) loggia, 12) lavatories, 13) animal pens, 14) kitchen, 15) servants' quarters, 16) workshops, 17) stables, 18) granaries.*

from plants, either closed bud, of open flower of the papyrus or lotus. To light the interior, the central part of the roof was raised above the sides. This formed a *clerestory*, a form ultimately reaching its most dramatic form in the medieval cathedrals of Europe. Coming from the brilliantly sunlit court into the twilight interior of the hypostyle hall and then into the dimness of the sanctuary would certainly enhance the mystery of the god and the power of the priests, who alone were admitted to the sanctuary.

Little is known about the homes of the Egyptians because they were made primarily of sun-dried bricks and were often flooded. Although evidence has been found of homesites, his grave, in the Egyptian's mind a more permanent abode, provides by mural and inscription a better idea of what kind of houses the Egyptians constructed. The earliest houses (*serekh*) consisted of only one room, but by the Middle Kingdom (2445–1580 B.C.) this single-room, multi-purpose plan had enlarged in size and complexity as the Egyptian society stratified and became more sophisticated. And although the homes of those of lesser station remained primitive, the nobles lived in considerable luxury. Their houses were surrounded by high walls and within were landscaped gardens, lofty reception rooms, balconies where available breezes might be enjoyed, sleeping porches, bedrooms, kitchens, guest rooms, and bathrooms with lavatories and basins with running water. Even the most humble house had sanitary facilities. The contrast between this wall-enclosed, carefully tended, and controlled environment in which the Egyptians lived and the hot, arid landscape that stretched to the horizon must have been considerable.

The central reception room deep within the building complex had a ceiling several feet higher than the surrounding rooms, and light and ventilation were gained by clerestory openings just below the ceiling. The large space within the room was broken, both physically and visually, by a row of four or more brightly painted columns that bisected the room and supported the roof. Further enlarged, the central reception room became the palace au-

7-12 *A relief (721–705 B.C.) from the
Palace of Sargon II in Khorsabad, Iraq,
showing two courtiers carrying a stool and
a city model.* Courtesy of the Oriental
Institute, University of Chicago.

dience hall which, in turn, was surrounded by individual multiroom structures, each with its own reception hall.

Brightly colored furniture was used in the interiors, which were equally
intense in color having ceilings, floors, and the supporting columns ornamented with bright patterns of brilliant hues. The total visual appearance of
such an interior and its furnishings must have been both breathtaking and
highly invigorating as one moved from the stark brilliance of Egyptian
sunlight into the cool, vividly colored interior. The furniture that the Egyptians used in their homes has been found in tombs and many examples of
extremely sophisticated and well-constructed furniture of that time is in
existence today.

Far to the east of the Nile a contemporary civilization had developed. Some
5,000 years ago in what is now an aird, unprepossessing region, in the valley
between the Tigris and Euphrates rivers, and even before Egyptian civilization had evolved, a people known as the Sumerians developed the world's
earliest true civilization based upon foundations in prehistory. It was here in
Mesopotamia that man first lived in cities, used the arch, wrote epic poetry,
studied the stars, compiled a legal code, and invented the wheeled machine.
It was not a welcoming land to which farmers from the north emigrated early
in the fifth millennium B.C., but nevertheless, families settled here and
hamlets consisting of several flimsy reed and mud huts gradually grew into
villages of adobe with houses of up to six or seven rooms around a courtyard—not unlike the homes of Iraqi peasants today.

Why then did not these people, who were the first to be civilized, continue
to be known and exert a strong influence on later civilizations? The main
reason is that they did not build with enduring materials. The only material
that could be easily obtained was mud, as little stone or even timber was
available. The structures were made primarily of sun-dried brick, but rain,
floods, and shifting sands have slowly eroded the brick, and what had been
palaces and towers became again shapeless mounds of dried mud.

Because of this lack of stone and wood, the use of the true arch was forced upon the Mesopotamian builders. As early as 2400 B.C., the arch and simple vaults were being used. Sun-dried brick is not especially strong and the sizes of the arches and vaults were necessarily limited and supporting walls had to be extremely thick.

Though concurrent with the Egyptian civilization, the inhabitants and civilizations of Mesopotamia differ from that of Egypt. The Mesopotamian land itself was far from hospitable, and not being isolated as was Egypt, marauding peoples were more able to invade the valley. The various cultures—Sumerian, Babylonian, and Assyrian—were developed by different peoples, each absorbing and rejecting what had been before. The dominance of religion and the preoccupation with life after death influenced the Egyptians far greater than it did the people of Mesopotamia. The latter were a vigorous people, interested in the present and not so concerned with the future. It is more appropriate to discuss first their houses rather than their tombs and temples. Their religious structures were impressive, however.

Behind the defense walls that enclosed the Mesopotamian city were narrow, unpaved streets without plan. Most of the houses were small, closely packed, and of one story, but scattered among such houses were those of the well-to-do. These were often two-story structures of kiln-fired and sun-dried brick. The walls were very thick, as much as 6 feet, to help insulate the interiors from the intense summer heat that is known to go up as high as 130 degrees. A small vestibule served as the entrance and from here the visitor stepped down into an open court, with rooms opening off of it. Although the plan varied from house to house, there was usually a fairly large room where guests could be received, guest room, bathroom, kitchen, servant quarters, storeroom, and a small chapel where household gods were worshipped. Under some houses, tombs for the burial of family members were found. Stairs led to the second floor, which had a balcony around the court, and this led to the private quarters of the family. Access to the flat or slightly sloped

7-13 *A typical plan for a house of a wealthy Mesopotamian family: 1) entrance hall, 2) open court, 3) stairs to upper rooms, 4) guests, 5) workroom, 6) storeroom, 7) slave quarters, 8) kitchen, 9) lavatory.*

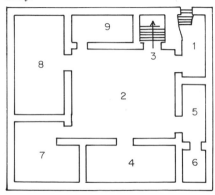

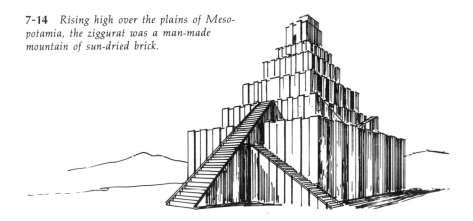

7-14 *Rising high over the plains of Mesopotamia, the ziggurat was a man-made
mountain of sun-dried brick.*

roof, which often served as a place to sleep on warm summer nights, was by
a ladder.

The largest structure found in any Mesopotamian city and certainly
dominating the plain was the *ziggurat;* more than 30 have been found
scattered all over Mesopotamia. The ziggurat is often compared to the Step
Pyramid. Physically the two are quite similar but spiritually they are oppo-
sites. The Step Pyramid is a tomb; the ziggurat is a ladder to god. These solid
brick towers rose as high as 290 feet and were customarily surmounted by a
temple. They were of almost any plan; square, rectangular, circular, or oval,
but most often they were square or rectangular with the corners oriented to
the points of the compass rather than having their sides parallel to the
directions as in Egyptian pyramids. They were composed of terraced stages
sometimes numbering to seven, and decreased in size and height upward. On
three sides the walls were smooth and on the fourth a series of stairs
connected the terraces and led to the summit.

As the period developed, the temples lost some of their significance and
became part of the ever-enlarging palaces. Built during the eighth century
B.C., the Palace of Sargon II measured 1,050 feet by 1,140 feet and contained
a multitude of narrow rooms probably covered with brick vaults. These
rooms were grouped around courts that provided light and air. A few larger
rooms are thought to have had skylights. The lower part of the interior walls
were decorated with friezes of low relief and were often brightly colored.

A third civilization of the ancient world was centered around the Aegean
Sea. Lost except in legend, it was not until the twentieth century that the
ruins of the ancient Aegean world were discovered. Before 1900 nothing had
been discovered to prove the existence of the legendary heroes from which
the Greeks believed themselves to be descended. In 1870, Heinrich
Schliemann found the ruins of Troy on the coast of Asia Minor, and later
excavated at Mycenae on the Greek mainland. But it was not until Sir Arthur
Evans began to work on the island of Crete that the legends of King Minos

and the labyrinthine prison of the Minotaur were proven to be based on fact.

Sir Arthur had hardly begun his excavations when he uncovered the palace at Knossus. This was the palace of kings not fearful of invasion; it was a palace without fortified walls, protected by the sea.

The Minoans, named after their most famous king, were a lively, sensuous, and pleasure-loving people. Their homes, often as high as five stories, had broad stairways, gaily decorated living rooms, audience halls, workshops, and even bathrooms with flush toilets (unmatched until Victorian times). The well-lit interiors, by means of inner courts, light wells, and set-back terraces, were comfortable and gay, and everything spoke of luxury, wealth, and splendor.

The structure was formed of huge, finely cut blocks of stone and wooden columns. The columns had a small circular base, a smooth shaft that tapered toward the bottom[2], and at the top a rather large cushion-like form and a square block that composed the capital upon which rested the lintel. The walls and columns were brightly painted with flowers, fish and sea life, animals, bullfights, and other scenes of Cretan life.

The Mycenaeans, from the Greek mainland, conquered the Minoans about 1400 B.C. and were worthy successors of the Minoans. They too were spectacular builders, but being from the mainland and subject to attack, built formidable citadels with walls of 10 to 20 feet in thickness. The open palaces of the Minoeans became more compact, somber, and massive. At *Tiryns* the walls are built of unhewn or roughly dressed stone with corbelled galleries. The openings in the walls are formed by two huge pillars topped with a huge stone lintel (the Lion Gate at Mycenae). The area above the lintel is covered

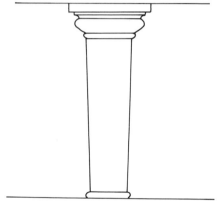

7-15 *The distinct tapered columns of the Palace at Knossus are the acknowledged prototypes of the later Doric columns of the Greeks.*

---

[2] It has been suggested that the taper was derived from tree trunks that once supported the buildings and which were placed upside down so that rooting or sprouting would not take place.

by a corbelled arch relieving the weight of the walls from the lintel. The triangular space is filled with a slab which in the Lion Gate is covered with a high relief.

About 1599 B.C., Indo-European nomads, the Dorians, began to infiltrate the Greek peninsula from the north. Originally more militant and crude than the native inhabitants, the newcomers eventually overwhelmed and mixed with the Mediterranean stock and by the seventh century B.C. had become the peoples now called the Greeks, although they called themselves "Hellenes" and their country "Hellas." It was this combination of the Indo-European, the Mycenaean, and the Cretan cultures that produced the Greek culture.

The Greek mainland is a 300-mile-long peninsula, mountainous, barren, rocky, with isolated fertile valleys, always penetrated by the sea. No part is more than 60 miles from the water. The mountains provided some of the finest marble in the world; in the valleys grew the Mediterranean "triad": grain, grapes for wine, and olives whose oil was the butter, soap, and lamp fuel of antiquity; and the sea gave the Greeks salt and seafood. The noted brilliant, clear Greek light adds a touch of beauty to what is really a harsh landscape. The climate is extreme, bitter winters and hot, dusty summers, yet the love of the outdoors caused the Greeks to spend as much time as possible outside. Their homes were usually unpretentious places in which to eat and sleep.

The basic Greek house consisted of one rectangular room with either a simple pitched, thatched roof or a flat, sod-covered roof. If occupied by a leader of the tribe or group, it was known as a *megaron* or "room of the chief." A front porch was often created by extending the side walls and roof forward and adding several wooden posts for additional support. Smaller structures were frequently built near the main building to serve as living quarters for the women of the house and servants, and for storage, cooking, and workshops. The whole was surrounded by a wall. Later a colonnade within the wall was added for more outdoor living space.

7-16 *Towering over the surrounding buildings, this bank sits with classical dignity on a city corner. The exterior, a combination of Greek and Roman architectural details, clearly expresses the "correct" bank image of the past 150 years.*

The Greeks remained divided into small city-states and were never unified except in language and common beliefs. This pattern of independence may have come from the natural separation caused by the mountain ranges, jagged coastline, and isolated valleys, or from old tribal loyalties, but the resulting intense military, political, and commercial, rivalry of the city-states must surely have stimulated the growth of ideas.

The Greeks early became a seafaring people who engaged in trade and contacted the older civilizations—Egypt, Mesopotamia, and Phoenicia, and from each they acquired ideas, motifs, and processes.

A closer kinship exists between the Greeks and modern cultures than with the other civilizations previously discussed; they are almost as close as old friends. Is not the bank downtown similar to one of the Greek temples, are not most modern coins like theirs, and do not our statues and monuments often resemble theirs? Many words in the English language are of Greek origin. Most people look upon the Greek civilization as the beginning of Western ideas and culture.

The Archaic period of the Greek civilization, or before 480 B.C., is of no concern here except that it was the period of the artistic development of crafts—pottery and coins, when sculpture became more representational, and when the development of the Doric and Ionic orders began.

The Golden Age, 480–400 B.C., saw the greatest developments in architecture, the building of the Parthenon and the Erechtheum on the Acropolis in Athens, and refinement of the Doric and Ionic orders.[3] The classical orders of architecture consist of the *column* (post) and *entablature* (lintel).

The Doric order of architecture may have been derived from the Cretan column and, although the shaft tapers upward and is fluted, the capital does have similar forms. It is believed to be the oldest of the classical orders and

---

[3] The architecture of the Greeks developed from wooden prototypes but by the fifth century B.C. had been translated into stone.

7-17

was developed on the Greek mainland. The Doric column has no base, rising directly from the platform (stylobate) with vertical, concave, touching grooves called *flutes* and it tapers slightly toward the capital. The capital consists of a cushion-like form called the *echinus*, which is topped by a square flat form called the *abacus*. Resting on the abacus is the entablature, which is divided into three horizontal divisions. The lowest is the *architrave* with a plain surface, next is the *frieze*, which is divided into alternating sections, the *triglyphs* and the *metopes*. The rectangular triglyphs project slightly and have vertical grooves dividing the surface into three areas. (Some authorities believe these are derived from the ends of wooden beams of earlier wooden temples.) The metopes are often covered with relief sculpture and correspond to the panels used to fill the spaces between the beams. The third division projects beyond the others and is called the *cornice*. On the long side of the building the cornice is horizontal but on the ends the cornice splits and the upper section, following the line of the slanting roof, becomes the *raking cornice* and the resulting triangular area is known as the pediment. In the Doric order this is filled with sculpture.

The Ionic order is named after the Ionians, an Indo-European people who settled on the Aegean Islands and on the nearby coast of Asia Minor where the order is thought to have developed. The Ionic column has an ornately profiled base, is more slender with less taper, and is fluted, but with a narrow flat surface (*fillet*) between each flute, which is unlike Doric fluting. The capital consists of a smaller echinus that is almost always carved with a decorative surface and a thinner abacus. Inserted between the echinus and abacus is a large *volute* or double scroll, which is the dominant form of the capital. The entablature is again divided into three horizontal layers. The architrave is now divided into three horizontal faces each projecting slightly over the lower. The frieze is usually covered with low relief. The cornice is basically the same whereas the pediment normally does not have sculpture in it. The Ionic order has greater elegance and grace and is richer in embellish-

7-18 *Doric*

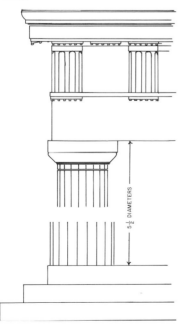

7-19 *Ionic*

7-20 *Miles from the Acropolis and far from true Ionic capitals, these rather primitive decorative additions to turned porch posts in Illinois owe their design to the volutes of Ionic capitals.*

7-21 *The "Glory that was Greece" is no better expressed than in the matchless Parthenon.*

7-22 *Plan of the Parthenon*

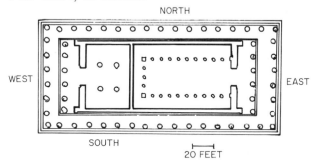

NORTH

WEST | | EAST

SOUTH

20 FEET

ment. It becomes the feminine counterpart to the more masculine Doric order.

The Golden Age, which produced some of the purest examples of artistic expression and clarity of form the world has ever known, is approximately between the end of the Persian Wars (479 B.C.) and the beginning of the Peloponnesian War (431 B.C.). In 480 B.C., one year before the final Greek victory, the Persians completely destroyed all that was atop the Acropolis in Athens.

Under the political leadership of Pericles, the rebuilding of the spiritual center of Athens was begun and Parthenon was started in 477 B.C., dedicated in 438 B.C., and finished in 432 B.C. It was built on the site of an older temple to Athena. Ictinus and Callicrates were the architects and the sculpture was under the direction of Phidias. It is one of the largest Greek temples, 101 feet by 228 feet, and is also one of the most perfect examples of the Doric order.

The Greek temple is a distinct form in the history of architecture. Based upon the megaron, it is very simple but served its purpose well. The temple housed a single large religious statue and had no other function. There was no need to enclose a large space as in a Christian church because the worshippers stood outside the building. The one room called the *cella* or *naos* displaying the cult statue was often the only room within the temple, although the most elaborate and expensive temples traditionally added another room called the *treasury* in which the religious trappings and paraphernalia were stored. Always rectangular, the Greek temples varied from rather long and narrow shapes to the more compact oblong of the Parthenon with dimensions in a ratio of approximately four to nine.

The Parthenon, made of Pentelic marble and constructed without mortar, sits upon a platform of three steps, the *stylobate*. Rising directly from the surface of the stylobate are 46 Doric columns, each 33 feet high, which form a colonnade known as the *peristyle* (*peri*, "around" and *stylos*, "a column"). Within the peristyle is an open passageway or *ambulatory*. Vertical smooth

7-23 *Despite the green park setting, the full-scale reproduction of the Parthenon in Nashville, Tennessee, offers the visitor a remarkable opportunity to experience what the original Parthenon once was.*

stone walls on each of the long sides, separated by the ambulatory but parallel to the columns, enclose the rooms—the larger cella on the east and the treasury on the west. (The longitudinal axis of the Parthenon is approximately east and west.) At each end is a *pronaos* (*pro*, "before" and *naos*, "room"), another row of columns on a raised platform suggesting a porch within the peristyle. The rooms were entered through large bronze doors, the only source of natural light within the Parthenon. The cella of the Parthenon contained the monumental statue of Athena by Phidias. This wooden statue was 40 feet high with clothing of gold, skin of ivory, and precious stones for the eyes. We can only imagine its magnificence. It was carried to Constantinople in the fifth century A.D. and sometime between the sixth and tenth century A.D. was destroyed by fire.

The building was measured with great accuracy by F. C. Penrose in 1851. His findings confirmed what had intrigued earlier architectural writers and critics for centuries, as much had been written concerning the subtle refinements found in the architecture of the Parthenon. Recent arguments have modified the theory that the design of the Parthenon was intended only to correct optical illusions, and the assumption that a deeply felt aesthetic necessity motivated the Greek builders has also been proposed. Nevertheless, these refinements are remarkable: The platform upon which the Parthenon rests is not a level plane but is bowed up in the center. The rise amounts to almost $2\frac{1}{2}$ inches on the ends and to $4\frac{1}{4}$ inches along the sides. The entablature also is bowed up but slightly less than the stylobate. The columns are not vertical but incline inward making the entablature slightly smaller than the stylobate. The shafts of the columns are not straight but, in addition to their taper, are also curved. This curve (*entasis*) starts about one-third of the way up from the bottom, and more subtle than the simple arc of a circle, continues to the bottom of the capital. Each flute on the shaft also has a slight entasis. The columns are slightly heavier at the corners and are also closer together there, a little over 6 feet apart compared with just over 8 feet along the front and sides. The triglyphs and metopes of the frieze are also adjusted to permit the triglyphs to meet at the corners.

The sculpture of the Parthenon is of exceptional caliber. The east pediment had the *Birth of Athena*, destroyed early in the Christian era and its appearance can only be conjectured. The west pediment had the *Contest Between Athena and Poseidon for the Land of Attica*,[4] which also has been removed and the major portion lost. What has survived, mostly as the Elgin Marbles, is now in the British Museum in London; it is in battered and fragmentary condition but still conveys a spatial freedom and mastery of technique seldom found in the best classical sculpture. The 92 metopes, alternating with the triglyphs on the frieze of the entablature, were carved in high relief and were all different with subjects drawn from mythological combat.

A most important sculptural feature of the Parthenon was the inner frieze in low relief that encircled the top of the exterior wall of the cella, next to the ceiling of the ambulatory. It is 525 feet long and depicts a procession of youths, horsemen, chariots, maidens, and sacrificial animals moving along both sides of the temple and coming together at the center of the east side above the major entrance where some of the gods are seated. This procession was the culminating ceremony of the Greater Panathenaea, a festival held in honor of Athena every four years. The Parthenon was first opened to the public during the festival held in 438 B.C.

The perfection of the building technique employed when the Parthenon was erected is shown in its subsequent history. For nearly 900 years it was a temple dedicated to Athena. In the fifth century A.D., with only minor changes—the wall separating the cella and treasury was removed, the central sculptural unit on the east pediment was taken down, and the east door was sealed—the Parthenon became a Christian church for almost 1,000 years. The Turks captured Athens in 1458 and by adding a minaret at the southwest

---

[4] Poseidon was the god of the sea and brother of Zeus.

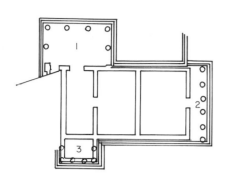

7-24 *The plan of the Erectheum:*
1) North porch, 2) east porch, 3) porch
of the maidens.

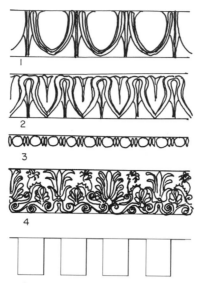

7-25 *Greek Moldings: 1) Egg and dart,*
2) leaf and dart, 3) bead and reel, 4) hon-
eysuckle, 5) dentils.

corner, the Parthenon became a Muslim mosque. About seven o'clock on the evening of Friday, September 26, 1687, over 2,100 years after it was built and still almost complete, the Parthenon was destroyed. While the Venetians were attempting to capture Athens from the Turks a Venetian shell fell in the center of the building and exploded a cache of gunpowder. The entire central portion was blown to pieces. Remarkably, part of the Parthenon remained standing.

The importance of the architecture of ancient Greece cannot be under-estimated when considering the architecture of later centuries. Therefore, one more temple built upon the Acropolis in Athens, the Erectheum, should be considered.

The Erectheum (421–405 B.C.) is the complement to the Parthenon about 150 feet to the south. The daintiness and asymmetry of the Erectheum is a welcome foil for the strength and symmetry of the Parthenon. The Erec-theum is not rectangular, but irregular, and is believed to have once enclosed four rooms on two different levels. There seems to be religious as well as physical reasons for such an arrangement. Here, as legend explains, was the very site where Poseidon struck the rock with his trident and a salt spring gushed forth, and here, too, was where the first olive tree, Athena's gift, grew and later won the contest between the two gods. Legend also says that this tree, destroyed by the Persians, miraculously sprang to life and grew to its original size in three days. Here, also, was the ancient image of Athena, which is said to have fallen from heaven and during each Panathenaic Festival the maidens of Athens presented a robe that they had woven. The name comes from Erechtheus, a legendary king of Athens.

The order of architecture is Ionic. The carving on the columns and mold-ings and around the doors and windows is exceptionally fine and, according to accounts inscribed on the building, was more expensive than that of figure sculpture. The continuous relief, originally on the frieze, has been lost, but the pediments were plain.

7-26

7-27 *Corinthian*

9 DIAMETERS

The side facing the Parthenon is blank except for the famous *Porch of the Maidens*. The supports for the entablature are not columns but maidens. These female figures, *caryatids*, stand on a high parapet and are relaxed in pose. The almost parallel lines of their drapery suggest fluting. The careful adjusting of thickness and pose does not remind the viewer of any discomfort (the necks are reinforced by large club-like arrangements of hair in the back). The use of caryatids was not originated on the Erectheum and similar maidens are seen throughout history on both architecture and furniture.

The delicate and feminine quality of the Erectheum along with the Porch of the Maidens certainly must have influenced a Turkish governor 2,000 years after its construction to use the temple for his harem.

The late fifth century B.C. saw an increasing emphasis on detail and ornament. The severity that had been so admired earlier gradually gave way to more complicated designs. The third order of classical architecture began to appear at this time. The Corinthian order is very similar to the Ionic but with a different and more complex capital. The Corinthian capital is taller than the others and makes the column appear even more delicate than does the Ionic. The capital consists of two parts. The larger and lower part is an inverted bell shape surmounted by a thin abacus with concave edges. The bell shape is covered with foliage in high relief. The leaves are generally arranged in two vertical rows with the ends curving slightly outward at the top. Although many kinds of leaves have been used, the most common leaf is that of the *acanthus* plant, a prickly plant found throughout the Mediterranean area. Its large, deeply cut, scalloped leaves are circinate in form and the curling ends add a strong three-dimensional quality to the capital. Of the three orders, the Corinthian capital provides a smoother transition from the vertical movement of the shaft of the column to the horizontal of the entablature. The Corinthian order was originally used only in the interior of buildings but after 300 B.C. was replacing the Ionic order. The Romans used the Corinthian order extensively and it became almost the standard on Roman buildings of every description.

Critics and writers when discussing classical architecture have often implied that architecture began to decline after the buildings on the Acropolis. This concept has been challenged in recent years with increasing frequency. Although the Romans did not adhere to the fixed standards of Greek architecture, they, nevertheless, created structures of great size, beauty, and technical achievement. Indeed, often it has been the Roman prototype rather than the Greek that has inspired later designers.

The Latins, of Indo-European origin as were the Dorians, arrived around 1000 B.C. at the top of the Italian boot, moved southward conquering the native peoples as they went, and finally settled on the volcanic plain of Latium south of the Tiber River. About 800 B.C., a mysterious people, the Etruscans, landed north of the Tiber and moved inland. Within 200 years the Etruscans dominated a large part of northern Italy. Thought to have come from Asia Minor, the Etruscans' influence upon the Roman architecture and civilization is considerable, although they were later absorbed by the Romans. It is known that the Roman temple form has Etruscan components (the high podium, the wide cella, and the deep porch) as it has the familiar Greek elements.

Before Roman architecture can be discussed, several considerations should be acknowledged. 1) Notable is the Roman's love for monumental and colossal dimensions. Although not altogether foreign to the Greek builder, the magnitude of Roman structures far surpasses those built previously elsewhere, often overshadowing those of Egypt. The Colosseum is 620 feet long, 500 feet wide, and over 157 feet high. It could seat at least 40,000, and the Circus Maximus was capable of holding about 260,000 spectators. In the Baths of Caracalla, one room was 226 feet long, 82 feet wide, and the vaults were 114 feet above the floor. The whole bathing complex sat upon a raised platform that was *1,080 feet on each side.*

7-28 *The versatility and technical achievements exhibited in Roman architecture were first exploited in utilitarian structures. This Roman aqueduct in Segovia, Spain (c. A.D. 100) is only one example of such engineering and construction triumphs.*

7-29 *Roman temples were frequently of brick or concrete, but covered with a stone surface. The vestiges of arches are seen beneath the remains of the entablature moldings and frieze. Easily recognized are dentil, egg and dart, and bead and reel moldings.*

7-30 *The most perfectly preserved Roman temple, the Maison Carrée in Nimes, France, inspired Thomas Jefferson by its purity of line and proportion. The half round Corinthian columns attached to the cella walls make it a pseudoperistyle type temple.* Courtesy of French Government Tourist Office.

7-31 *Thomas Jefferson's interpretation of the Maison Carrée has been the Capitol of Virginia since 1785. The side structures were added in the twentieth century. Although the proportions of the Capitol are similar to those of the Maison Carrée, the architectural order is not. Jefferson used the Ionic rather than the Corinthian order.* Courtesy of Greater Richmond Chamber of Commerce.

2) The Romans developed the potentialities of concrete, a mixture of mortar, gravel and rubble (small pieces of building stone, brick, and the like), which is thought to have been the vital element that made possible such monumental structures. Although used for foundations and inner structures that were seldom left exposed, it is the fact that such a monolithic mass could be and was made that is important—so important that it is classed as a major event in the history of architecture.

3) A third characteristic of Roman architecture is the use of the arch and vault combined with the post and lintel of the classical orders. Long considered to be inferior to the post and lintel, when the prejudices against the arch weakened, Roman designers began to work with both systems and produced dramatic and much admired solutions.

A consideration of all the important buildings of Roman origin is far beyond the scope of this book. A brief discussion of a few that have been most influential to later architecture will thus have to suffice.

One of the most perfectly preserved Roman temples is the Maison Carrée in Nimes, France (A.D. 14). An important feature of this structure that is observed on Roman temples and different from the typical Greek temple is the replacement of the stylobate with a *pedestal* or *podium*. With vertical walls, the podium raises the whole temple a half-story above the ground and provides storage space beneath the temple while also increasing the visual importance of the structure. The cella is not as rectangular as found in the Greek temple but more square. It is made wider, to the edge of the podium, and shorter, providing space for the deep porch or *portico*. The cella thus becomes larger and better able to serve its function; that is, not only hold the cult statue but also display the trophies (weapons, statues, and the like) of the conquering legions. Access to the portico is gained by a broad flight of stairs that extends across the entire end of the structure. The Greek temple often had a peristyle of freestanding columns separated by an ambulatory from the cella walls. The cella walls of the Roman temple, extending to the edge of the

7-32 *The Capitol of Virginia is not the only structure that has been inspired by the Maison Carrée. This church near the campus of the University of Illinois also resembles the Roman temple; however, the broad flight of steps has withered to a narrow band of five and the order has been changed to a Renaissance version of the Doric.*

podium, did not permit this but, instead, the columns are "engaged" or half round and form a pseudoperistyle. The columns are almost always Corinthian.

The Roman sequence of architectural elements are podium, columns, entablature, and pediment. This is the *"temple front"* that has been repeatedly attached to exteriors, interiors, and furniture of later date and use, and in all sizes and proportions throughout the world to give a "classic appearance." The Maison Carrée, itself, was the inspiration for Thomas Jefferson when he designed the Virginia State Capitol in Richmond, Virginia (1785–1789).

The Colosseum, dedicated in A.D. 80, remains one of the largest single buildings ever built and continues to be the major prototype of sports arena design. It is a masterpiece of efficiency and engineering; utilizing the arch, barrel vault, and groin vault; the inner passageways, ramps, and 80 entrances could easily handle the throngs, and beneath the arena vaulted spaces contained the gladiators, animals, and equipment needed for the spectacles and *venationes* (animal contests). (At the dedication 5,000 animals were slain.) It is the exterior that is of major interest, however. The surface of the exterior is divided by superimposed classical orders, each arranged by its "weight." Doric is on the lower level, Ionic on the next, and Corinthian on the third. Each order is complete with podium, engaged column, and entablature. The horizontals of the entablatures are sensitively balanced by the verticals of the columination. Almost filling the space between each of the 80 evenly spaced columns is an arched opening stating the actual method of construction. (The use of arched openings with an overlaid classical order and the superimposition of one order over another with the Doric-Ionic-Corinthian arrangement as standard, again, is repeatedly found on architecture and furniture.) The fourth level of the exterior of the Colosseum was not arched, but solid, and had pilasters instead of engaged columns.

The Romans, as they developed the use of concrete, soon realized the advantages of this material. Unskilled workman could construct buildings

7-33 *The familiar exterior seen today of the Colosseum in Rome gives a somewhat false impression. Originally the arched wall overlayed with columns, and entablatures encircled the entire structure rather than ending in the distinctive diagonal seen here. Medieval and Renaissance builders found it a handy "stone quarry." Today it is threatened again by the constant vibration of automobile traffic. Courtesy of Italian Government Travel Office.*

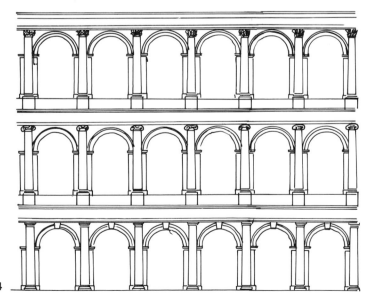

7-34

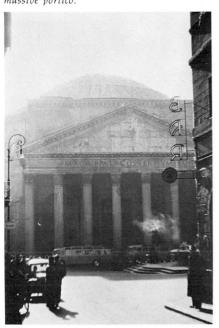

7-35   *Although surrounded by buildings of later date and accessible only through narrow, twisting streets, the grandeur of the Pantheon is undiminished. Modern paving covers the flight of steps leading to the massive portico.*

with materials that were easily obtainable throughout the empire and only a few skilled architects were needed to supervise the construction. The concrete building, although not beautiful, was structurally very strong, and with the addition of thin slabs of stone to cover the inner concrete structure the building could easily have the "proper" appearance. Concrete was also fast; a structure could be built in less time and put to use almost immediately.

The combination of concrete and the use of arches and vaults permitted the Romans to enclose large spaces. This was the first time in history that man could construct a building with vast open space with the interior not encumbered by pillars, columns, or posts. The Romans' love of large structures could be satisfied. The Roman architects began working with enclosed space rather than with mass and they became the first to do so. It was not until the thirteenth century in France when the great Gothic cathedrals were built that space would again be so considered.

Possibly the most remarkable Roman building illustrating this concept of space is the Pantheon (A.D. 118–125). A round temple, the exterior of the Pantheon can be best described as a large windowless cylinder topped by a rather shallow dome with a typical Roman portico indicating the entrance. The curve of the cylinder and the rectangular form of the portico are a strange combination, but the Pantheon has influenced architects and designers since its erection. Originally a broad flight of steps led up to the porch, but the surrounding streets are higher than they were in antiquity so a somewhat submerged temple is now seen. The masonry construction of brick and concrete was originally covered with marble slabs that have been lost but the gray and red granite Corinthian columns still rest on their marble bases. Sculpture was in the pediment and gilt-bronze plates were on the roof.

Entrance to the Pantheon is through the original great bronze doors and the visitor is immediately struck by the drama of the interior space. The great dome is a true hemisphere with a diameter of 142 feet, the same as the total height of the building. It is one of the largest masonry domes in the world,

7-36 *The original campus of the University of Virginia was designed by Thomas Jefferson in 1817–1826. The Library is remarkably like the Pantheon in Rome.*

and to help control the thrust the supporting 20 foot-thick cylinder extends higher on the exterior than the interior, and the thickness of the dome varies from 6 feet near the center to 20 feet at the outer rim accounting for the shallow profile of the exterior. In the center is a great *oculus*, a 30-foot aperture, which floods the interior with natural light. With no screen, glass, or closing device covering the hole, the ever-changing sky and clouds and the golden shaft of sunlight glittering with tiny motes of dust are dazzling. The interior walls and pavement, much as they were, are covered with marble. The cylinder wall is not of the same thickness. There are seven large niches partially penetrating the masonry. Corinthian columns are in front of these niches giving the illusion of far greater space or even adjoining rooms than what actually exists. The dome, in fact, does not rest on a solid cylinder but upon eight great piers.

This survey of architecture has not often touched upon the type of structure in which the people lived. It is, however, possible to discuss the homes of the ancient Romans from considerable evidence. The ancient cities of Pompeii and Herculaneum, covered by the eruption of Mount Vesuvius in A.D. 79, and the ruins in Rome and Ostia, the ancient port near the mouth of the Tiber, are but a few of the sites where Roman domestic architecture has been researched. A vast amount of references and descriptions of domestic architecture has also survived in the writings of ancient Romans. The Romans had three basic kinds of domestic structures: The *insula*, the *domus*, and the *villa*.

The insula can best be compared to an urban block or an apartment complex. It was a large structure built of concrete and brick and often with wooden floors, up to five or six stories high, and with balconies above the first floor. The ground floor held shops that were usually shaded by a long portico and within the structure was an enclosed court. With vines and flowers growing about and on the exterior, the insula could be quite beautiful. Inside was another matter. The lower floors could contain private

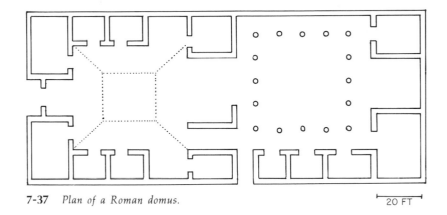

7-37   *Plan of a Roman domus.*

20 FT

quarters similar to the domus and frequently were quite elegant. But the higher the living quarters the more wretched they became, with the poorest families crowded together at the top. No plumbing facilities of any kind were in these buildings, on any floor. They were poorly lighted, and the only heat for warmth or cooking was provided by braziers and movable stoves. It was common for buildings to burn, thus trapping all of the inhabitants at the top. Numerous incidents of collapsing insulae because of faulty construction are also recorded.

The domus or private town house of the wealthy was far less numerous than the insula. The exterior of the house presented a blank wall to the street or was lined with shops that had no access to the house itself. The rooms of the domus were evenly arranged with a main axis running from the entrance to the back of the house. The narrow entrance opened into a vestibule that led into the major room of the house, the *atrium*. This large room had a ceiling that was open to the sky. The roof slanted toward this opening and rain was collected in the pool below. Small rooms were on either side except at the far side where the atrium widened forming two extensions (*alae*). Behind the atrium, on the axis, was the *tablinum* where the important family records and artifacts were kept. This could be closed off or left open to permit the occupants to proceed into the *peristyle*, an inner garden with plants, flowers, fountain, and sculpture, surrounded by columns (as the name suggests) and an ambulatory. On either side of the peristyle were the private rooms of the family. Beyond the peristyle were other rooms for various purposes and sometimes another garden. The interior walls of the domus were brightly painted with scenes, figures, and architectural details that destroyed any confined feeling. The family life was turned within the house for privacy. The plan of the domus has considerable merit, and, although over 2,000 years old, is still applicable to the housing needs of the congested twentieth century. An increasing number of modern houses are turning inward. The exteriors and surrounding area are of less concern than what is enclosed, and the in-

7-38 *Twentieth-century tourists can readily appreciate the peristyle of the Roman domus. It provided private exterior space in a crowded urban setting, precious in today's world of little privacy.*

7-39 *The classical division of exterior surfaces has seldom been adapted to large twentieth-century structures. The County Courthouse in Milwaukee, Wisconsin, has a very high Roman pedestal topped by a band of columns and pilasters that is surmounted by high attic structures. The horizontality of Greek and Roman architecture has been "grandized" almost beyond the limits of acceptability. To "humanize" the monumentality of the building, the facade has a pedimented doorway and windows in the large, ground-level arches.*

corporation of open space (still called an atrium) within the walls of the structure makes possible a controlled and possibly more functional environment that would not otherwise be possible or practical. The "atrium house" frequently requires less land area for the same activities and permits a more dense population without sacrificing privacy.

The villa or country house had many variations and sizes. It was a sprawling complex of structures that permitted the wealthy to enjoy the pleasant countryside far from the masses of Rome.

8 Architecture: Early Christian, Byzantine, Romanesque, Gothic

As in an epic poem, the narrative of architectural history does not always flow smoothly. The characters change, new emphases are brought forth, and new directions are taken. The beginning of the new era of Christianity is a time of such change.

Early in the fourth century A.D., during the reign of Constantine I (306–337), decisions were made that drastically changed the course of history. In 313, the Edict of Milan declared Christianity an official religion, recognized by the Roman state and accorded all the rights and privileges of other state religions. At last the Christians could erect houses of worship and display holy artifacts. The second decision, coming about ten years later, was the resolution to move the capital of the Roman Empire from Rome to the Greek town at the mouth of the Bosporus, Byzantium. The court moved officially to the new capital, renamed Constantinople (now Istanbul, Turkey) in 330, after six years of frenetic building. This move precipitated the splitting of the empire although the Eastern emperors did not surrender control to Western rulers for a hundred years.

An attempt was made during the rule of Justinian (527–565) to unite again the East and the West. The conquest met with considerable success and for a brief period the whole Mediterranean area flourished with peace and prosperity. Churches were built in both Constantinople and Ravenna, the main Byzantine outpost in the West on the Adriatic coast of Italy. Unfortunately, this period of peace was short-lived and by the end of the sixth century, all centralized government had disintegrated and the West had become the prey of the Visigoths, Vandals, Ostrogoths, and Lombards. The east withstood the aggression and, although reduced considerably in size, the Eastern Roman Empire or the Byzantine Empire survived until 1453 when Constantinople finally fell to the Turks.

The political division of East and West was in part the result of the widening divergence of thought evidenced as early as the third century in religious dogmatic arguments. The manner of depicting man and his universe

178

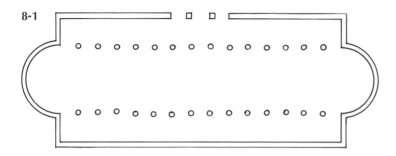

8-1

became a matter of extreme importance. Two different, yet often inter-mingled, ways vied for supremacy: the abstract, two-dimensional, and symbolic representation of ideas versus the naturalistic, three-dimensional concept of space and form.

The separation between East and West also allows our discussion of architecture to divide into two periods or stylistic groupings: Early Christian and Byzantine. Although the demarcation is often not clear, it is usually understood that Early Christian refers to that which has been accomplished in the West and during the first 700 years of the Christian era. A more direct linkage with the remaining structures and art of Rome is also apparent. The term Byzantine is applied to the culture associated with the Eastern empire, and is more directly influenced by the Greek and Oriental elements of design, *not* the Roman. The span of the Byzantine period is much longer, lasting until 1453, the fall of Constantinople and the Empire.

The most significant architectural achievement of the Early Christian builders was the development of the *basilica*. Until Constantine decreed that Christianity was the state religion, no buildings of consequence for Christian religious services existed. Immediately there was a need for imposing religious structures and under the patronage of Constantine a number of churches were built. The architectural design of these churches was new, different, and admirably suited to the liturgical needs of the Christian religion. This plan, so quickly conceived, and with only small changes, has withstood the test of time and an overwhelming majority of twentieth-century churches are of a similar if not exact plan.

The Early Christian basilica is a rectangular structure with design origins in Egyptian and classical temples, the Roman domus, and the public meeting halls or basilicas found in the Roman fora.

The Roman basilica was also rectangular and was entered on the long side, with a curved projection or *apse* at each end. The interior was divided by two rows of columns into three longitudinal sections, the larger center or *nave* and

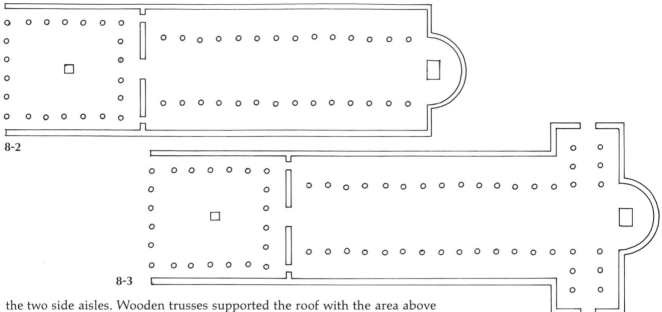

8-2

8-3

the two side aisles. Wooden trusses supported the roof with the area above
the nave higher than the roofs of the side aisles permitting clerestory
windows to illuminate the interior. (This is almost identical to the arrangement observed in the hypostyle hall of the Egyptians (see Chapter 7, p. 152).

The basic Roman basilica plan was adjusted by closing the side entrance
and moving the entrance to the end from which the apse was removed. An
altar was placed in the remaining apse. By the fifth century the orientation of
the Early Christian basilica was to have the entrance on the west and the altar
on the east. A colonnaded courtyard, similar to the Egyptian temple courtyard and the peristyle of the Roman domus, was added to the entrance end.
This enclosed area was named the *atrium* and a baptismal font frequently was
placed in the center. The east side, touching the basilica, became the *narthex,*
or vestibule. The atrium is a desirable transition from the outer, worldly
environment to the more secluded and reverent interior of the church.

Upon entering the church the rhythm of the double row of columns on the
sides of the nave directs the eye to the altar in the apse, which is the only
vaulted (half dome) area in the building. The vast wall spaces demanding
decoration were adorned with frescoes, marble, and glittering mosaics, which
provided the rich and colorful background for the religious services.

Soon, an additional architectural unit was added to the plan, the *transept,*
which was a rectangular area "slipped" between the apse and the nave. The
transept was usually longer than the width of the building, and, therefore,
extended beyond the outer walls of the basilica. This, at last, becomes the
Latin cross floor plan of Christian churches. The central axis of the building
extends through the atrium, narthex, nave, the crossing of the transept, the
altar, and the apse, whereas a minor axis passes through the transept. The
nave, transept, and apse arrangement is also very similar to the grouping of
the atrium, alae, and tablinum of a Roman domus (before 313 religious
worship was held in the homes of wealthy Christians).

The brick and stone exterior of the Early Christian basilica is bare and

8-4 1) *Exterior elevation.*
     2) *Interior elevation.*

1

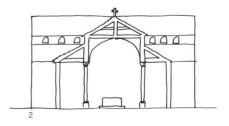

2

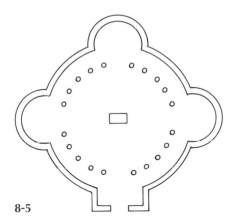

8-5

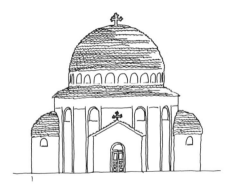

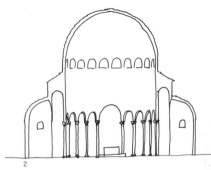

8-6   1) *Exterior elevation.*
      2) *Interior elevation.*

devoid of ornamentation, presenting somewhat the appearance of a warehouse or other utilitarian structure. The contrast between the plain exterior and the shimmering and resplendent interior is phenomenal.

Although the longitudinal-type basilica has exerted great influence upon modern church building patterns, another concept of Christian religious structure was also introduced at this time, the *central type*. Probably developing from the baths and round temples of Rome, the central type building has a ground plan in the form of a Greek cross—the arms are of equal length. The central section is cylindrical with the surrounding wall raised upon columns, and the whole is generally topped by a dome. Around the circle of columns runs an ambulatory with side chapels that form the arms of the cross. With the altar placed, logically, at the center under the dome, the plan does not lend itself easily to most Christian ceremonies; therefore, this type became the pattern for tombs and baptistries. Many churches use this plan and during the Baroque period it was the preferred plan. An increasing number of churches are being built with a central plan today.

Many architectural historians have debated the intriguing question, "What might the Early Christians have built had there not been the availability of pagan temples?" Almost without exception, columns, lintels, and other parts of Roman temples are found in the fabric of the Early Christian churches. It is not uncommon to find components obviously originating in different buildings used in a Christian structure. Fine building materials, already crafted, could be obtained from the now despised Roman pagan temple. Thus, the pagan temple was destroyed *and* Christian churches were simultaneously built with minimal effort. Historically, it is regrettable that soundly structured Roman architecture was eliminated to clear space or provide components for latter buildings, but the latter half of the twentieth century has evidenced the same, and even more senseless destruction.

In our time, the continuing wasteful demolition of buildings, solidly constructed and often of architectural merit, is appalling. Today, there are no

8-7 *The exterior of Hagia Sophia does not indicate the magnificent space within. The large rectangular masonry masses projecting from the central architectural block help control the weight of the dome. The four slender minarets were added after the structure became a mosque.* Courtesy of Turkish Tourism and Information Office.

plans to reuse the materials and there are no strong religious causes. The reasons for tearing down perfectly sound buildings are usually potential monetary gain, lack of discrimination, and insensitiveness to perceptual values. The Early Christians should not be harshly condemned for their destruction of Roman temples. History cannot be changed. Our wrath must be directed toward those who are *now* responsible for the thoughtless obliteration of America's architectural past.

The most important architectural triumph of the Byzantine Empire is Hagia Sophia. Built 532–537 for Justinian by the architects Anthemius of Tralles and Isidorus of Miletus (both from Asia Minor), it is the fourth church of the same name on this site (the first was sponsored by Constantine I). Hagia Sophia (The Church of the Holy Wisdom) combines the architectural ideals of the East and the West. Its design suggests the central plan church, split crosswise with the great dome resting lightly on a circle of 40 windows and supported on a square of masonry inserted between the halves. The longitudinal axis of the structure forms a rectangular or rather oval nave, and with the original atrium (now destroyed) attached to the west, the rectangularity of the synthesis was completed.

The intent here is not to examine at great length this magnificent building but to identify some of the structural elements and concepts used in Hagia Sophia that have been employed in later buildings.

It is in Hagia Sophia that the pendentive method of supporting a circular dome on a square base was fully realized, and it is the prototype for Saint Peter's Basilica in Rome and Saint Paul's Cathedral in London as well as a great many buildings of lesser size and importance. The massive dome, surmounting the whole structure, gives an importance to the exterior that the exterior of the basilica could not achieve. The use of a dome over the crossing of the transept and nave can be found in many churches, that is, the dome by Brunelleschi on the Cathedral of Florence.

Hagia Sophia is composed of about 40 per cent brick and 60 per cent

8-8 *The great Byzantine cathedral dedicated to Saint Mark in Venice is a central plan religious structure. The shimmering mosaics and colorful frescoes decorating the dimly lit interior are some of the finest in Western Europe.* Courtesy of Italian Government Travel Office.

8-9 *Italy, never far from the classical tradition, incorporated Roman detailing in its medieval architecture. This portion of the facade of the notable cathedral in Pisa reveals many Roman and Byzantine decorative elements. Round arched arcading, in this example open (with the columns freestanding), is typical of the architectural style.*

concrete with stone used for the four great piers supporting the dome. The dome is made as light as possible by using hollow tile so that the thrust problem would be lessened. (It collapsed at least two or three times during construction and shortly afterward.) The system of buttressing is illogical, and it is believed that the architects hoped that by making the building as monolithic as possible there would be no problem of thrust. Apparently this is the reason that the dome stands today, as many architectural engineers believe it to be incontestably the boldest and perhaps most reckless structure ever built.

Hagia Sophia remained a Christian structure until the fall of Constantinople when it was converted to a mosque. A minaret was added to each of the corners of the building and the magnificent mosaics of the interior were covered with whitewash. It remained so until the 1930s when it was converted into a museum. The whitewash has been partially removed revealing again the Byzantine mosaics. The Turks were so filled with wonder by Hagia Sophia that they used it as the archetype for later mosques and buildings, notably the famous sixteenth-century Blue Mosque built only a few hundred yards away. In fact, the domed architecture of the Muslim world did not come into being until after the Turks had seen Hagia Sophia; for example, the exquisite Taj Mahal at Agra, India (1632–1653).

No discussion of Early Christian and Byzantine architecture and design can disregard the mosaics of these periods. Designs using small pieces of colored stones or similar materials embedded in plaster had been produced in the Near East as early as 3000 B.C. The Greeks and Romans had become so adept at using small cubes of marble (*tesserae*) that whole scenes as well as abstract designs were created, but not for walls. The designs were almost always on the floor. These mosaics, using only the natural gradations of intensity, value, and hue found in natural stone, were muted in color but rich in variation. Chromatically, it was the work of the mosaic masters of the Early Christian and Byzantine periods that released this art form into a shimmering, glittering, brilliant, and intense color medium. Mosaics were moved from the floor to the walls and ceilings, and glass tesserae of a broader and more intense spectrum, which included gold, were used. The shining irregular surfaces reflected the light with a dazzling splendor comparable to the stained-glass windows of the later Gothic period.

At the same time, Western Europe was encountering a period of change and a shifting of aesthetic and political leadership. The Roman Empire had crumbled and the migrations of Germanic tribes, settling down within the remnants of the late Roman-Christian civilization, founded kingdoms of their own—the Franks in Gaul, the Visigoths in Spain, and the Ostrogoths and Lombards in Italy. For the first time in history, the region north of the Alps would achieve a dominance of architectural and artistic activity usurping the Mediterranean leadership.

The term *Dark Ages* was used a hundred years ago to denote the period between the fall of the Roman Empire and the beginning of the Renaissance. Classically oriented historians labeled this period of almost 1,000 years as one of little civilization with no advances in art, architecture, or literature. True, the civilization of the Romans had become almost nonexistent and the crafts of the ancient world were all but forgotten; however, continuing research of this millenium has dispelled the bleak and negative attitude prescribed by former critics. Today the term *Middle Ages* is perferred, although it too inadequately describes this complex and critical period. In fact, as in no other period, ideas and concepts were developing with exciting variety and originality everywhere and a new, viable civilization was emerging. Each district, each kingdom and province, seemed to discover its own individual answers to problems peculiar to its region. This autonomy encouraged imaginative, empirical directions that were destined to serve as models for future improvisation. For example, it was at this time that laws were enacted that would directly influence twentieth-century courts and governments, that monumental sculpture was revived after almost 500 years,

8-10 *The steep roof and the exposed "half-timbered" wood construction of this thousand-year-old Rathaus (municipal building) in Michelstadt, Germany have nothing in common with the classical structures of the Greeks and Romans.*

8-11 *The Church was dominant. Not only did the church structure usually tower over the whole countryside but the forces of Christianity were practically the only link with the past.*

8-12 *A typical Romanesque window. The extremely slender, engaged columns are not structural but are merely decorative; they divide the walls vertically. Note the similarity to photograph 8-14 (top).*

that builders rediscovered how to vault buildings (lost in the West since the Romans), and that solid cut-stone masonry techniques were re-established. This period also saw the salvaging of Roman manuscripts and their preservation at the monastery at Monte Cassino. It was not a time of inactivity, bereft of any consequential occurrences or developments but, rather, it was a period ripe with potential and productive results.

On Christmas Day, 800, Charles the Great, or Charlemagne (Carolus Magnus), was crowned emperor of the Roman Empire by the Pope in Rome. The Roman Empire had not existed in the West for 300 years but, nevertheless, this event marks a turning point. The Carolingian Empire lasted for only 150 years and then the central political power it once held quickly reverted back to the local and lesser nobility. However, the period of Charlemagne has culturally influenced Western civilization continuously since that time. Charlemagne, although only able to write his name, championed learning and the arts. It was he who encouraged the Benedictines in their preservation and copying of extant Roman literature.[1] And it was he who established schools and monasteries and encouraged building using the technology of the Roman structures.

The architectural style that grew out of these experiments is known today as Romanesque, that is "from the Roman." The Romans used the engaged column, round arch, vaulting, and heavy proportions as did the Romanesque builders, but the two forms of architecture are not otherwise similar. The diversity of Romanesque structures is almost as varied as the number of buildings classified as being of this period. The modifications are endless.

Almost all major architecture of this period is religious. The homes of the people offered little comfort—primitive hovels made of wood, mud, and twigs, with dirt floors and little light and warmth. The nobility had little

---

[1] Charlemagne encouraged the standardization of handwriting, and the printed letters on this page owe much of their design to Carolingian manuscripts.

8-13 *The design exuberance of these early twelfth-century cloister columns partially indicate the diversity and originality that are characteristic of Romanesque architecture.*

8-14 *The architects of the latter half of the nineteenth century were often infatuated with medieval architecture. These two photographs are not details of a true Romanesque building, but rather from an 1895 structure, the Yerkes Observatory in Wisconsin. Nevertheless, their variety and almost playful design detail delight the eye.*

better. Their castles of stone were drafty, wet, and dark and the center fire in the great hall only slightly relieved the chill.

Immediately prior to the year A.D. 1000, little architecture was built. The enormity of the fear that the world would be consumed by fire—the millennium of the Apocalypse—should not be underestimated. The date of the holocaust passed and a time of religious fervor commenced. The renewed faith stimulated pilgrimages to Christian shrines, the first of the Crusades was begun in 1097, and Europe caught *morbus aedificandi*, a disease of building. It has been estimated that in France alone at least 1,587 churches were built between 1000 and 1100. The eleventh-century monk-historian Raoul Glaber wrote, "it was as though the very world had shaken herself and cast off her old age, and were clothing herself everywhere in a white garmet of churches."

The plans for these churches were developed from the Early Christian basilica. The nave, transept, and apse were modified for better space and circulation, the structures were covered with vaulting, and means of providing better illumination of the interiors were investigated.

The Latin cross plan of the basilica had proven to be adaptable to the liturgy and ceremony of the church. The churches were enlarged to accommodate greater numbers of worshippers. The size change not only affected the total church dimensions but also the number and size of individual parts. To illustrate these changes a composite of northern Romanesque churches might be described in the following manner.

The nave is larger and wider than that in the basilica. The inner side aisles (there are at least two on each side) continue around the arms of the transept and encompass the apse. The apse itself is now moved away from the transept and inserted between is a rectangular area, the *choir*, which is the width of the nave. The surrounding aisle, or *ambulatory*, permits processions to move freely from one section of the church to another. Radiating from the

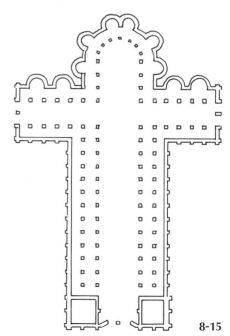

8-15

8-16

8-17 *The great triumphal arches of Rome have stylistically declined and have been reproportioned and attached to the facades of buildings serving as entrance porches. Despite the shift of function, the podium, column, entablature, and pediment elements still are recognizable. This porch on St. Trophîme in Arles, France (c. 1150), was reproduced on the architectural triumph of H. H. Richardson, Trinity Church in Boston (1872–1877). (See photo 12-18.)* Courtesy of French Government Tourist Office.

apse and extending from the eastern side of the transept arms are side chapels. The roof is no longer of wood but masonry. (Neglected except in the apse for 500 years, the churches at last had a fireproof stone covering.) Combinations of barrel vaults and groin vaults are used over the bays of the nave, aisles, and chapels. The use of the round arch and engaged column of all sizes is seen everywhere and windows open the clerestory and aisle walls to illuminate the interior. The dimly lit interior of our composite Romanesque church is now faded but was once bright with color. The walls, vaulting, and piers were painted rich greens, blues, and purples with touches of gold everywhere. Rich tapestries were much in evidence and most of the sculpture was gilded. The Bibles, chalices, candlesticks, and other accoutrements used during the religious ceremonies were of gold, silver, and ivory, set with rubies, emeralds, sapphires, and pearls, or ornamented with glowing enamels.

The facade on the west is composed of a large central door set deeply in the surface with concentric round arches expanding away from the door itself. The half circle above the door, the *tympanum,* is covered with shallow relief sculpture. On either side of the central portal are two smaller doors that open into side aisles. Over the center door is a round window that floods the nave with the light of the afternoon sun. Above the two side entrances rise large, solid towers, almost like watchtowers, which indeed they sometimes were. These towers, from which come the spires and steeples of later churches, were incorporated into the structure of the church for the first time and were not freestanding *campaniles,* bell towers, as were used in Italy. The rhythm provided by the vaulted bays inside and echoed by the buttresses and windows on the exterior with the differing heights of the nave, aisles, transept, choir, and apsidal chapels suffuse the structure with a meter as rich as the Gregorian chants that reverberated within.

The loveliness of the Romanesque is but a prelude to the regal elegance of

8-18 *The county courthouse, an American institution, has been built in all architectural styles. The Champaign County Courthouse in Urbana, Illinois (c. 1900), is Romanesque with the prescribed blind arcading, massive proportions, and a clocktower reproducing a German church tower.*

8-19 *The Cathedral of Notre Dame in Paris, although appearing more massive, less vertical, and not as linear as the Cathedral at Rheims (see 8-25), is nevertheless one of the great Gothic cathedrals. Courtesy of French Government Tourist Office.*

the *Gothic* church.[2] The most famous cathedrals in Europe are Gothic and almost without exception, the major churches in America were inspired by or modified because of this style. The design of domestic architecture and furniture of the midnineteenth century was also strongly influenced by it.

Until now each period has been dated in a very general way, and placed in an indefinite geographical area. Not so with the Gothic style, whose origin can be traced to the reconstruction of the choir of the Abbey Church of Saint-Denis $2\frac{1}{2}$ miles outside the northern walls of Paris. Started in 1137 by Abbot Suger, seven years later, on June 11, 1144, it was dedicated with King Louis VII, Eleanor of Aquitaine, his queen, five archbishops, 14 bishops, and a vast throng in attendance.

The choir with its seven wedge-shaped, rib-vaulted chapels radiating out from the center of the apse in geometric order and the large stained-glass windows in the exterior walls soon became the prototype for the buildings not only in France but throughout Europe. As the Gothic style spread so did the customs of France along with its books, clothes, and manners. France, and especially Paris, became the center of the Gothic world.

The number and diversity of Gothic structures is astounding—more than 500 great churches were built in France alone between 1170 and 1270. It is necessary to investigate the Gothic style, the Gothic method of construction. "Why is it unusual? Did not it develop from the Romanesque?" are questions frequently asked. It *is* true that the basic floor plan of the Gothic church is very similar to the Romanesque. It is also true that every component that makes the Gothic structure unique can also be found in a Romanesque

[2]The Italian Renaissance architect, painter, and writer Giorgio Vasari (1511–1574) is believed to have first used the term *Gothic* when referring to buildings of this style. Not being based upon Greek or Roman ideas, he considered them Gothic or "barbarian." When this style was in ascendance, it was known as *opus modernum* or *francigenum* (modern or French work).

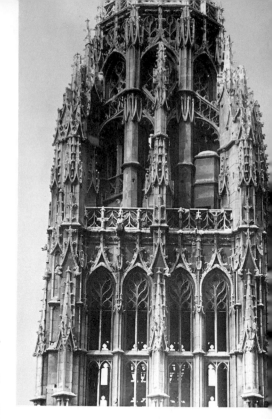

8-20 *The Butter Tower of Rouen Cathedral (top) was the inspiration for the Tribune Tower in Chicago (1922). The Gothic style of architecture unfortunately adapted easily to the skeletal, vertical forms of skyscrapers and many high structures were built in that style during the last 100 years.* (Top) Courtesy of Caisse Nationale des Monuments Historiques.

building, but these elements were never *all* combined in just the manner that is peculiar to Gothic.

The plastic mass of the Romanesque church is dominant, but Gothic is linear. Lines seem to be everywhere, a web of filaments stretching to and unfolding across the vaults high above the floor. The Gothic structure is a *stone skeleton* that stands in equilibrium, each thrust countered by another thrust. This delicate combination of stone lines, mainly vertical, always balanced, is a frame, a structural concept that predicts the construction of the steel skyscrapers of the twentieth century.

The lightness of this skeleton construction, including the rib vault solved two problems that perplexed earlier builders. First, the walls no longer were needed to support the structure; they could now be opened to permit windows. Walls changed to translucent curtains of stained glass filling the churches with glorious light. The quality and beauty of stained glass developed during the Gothic period has seldom been surpassed. Second, during the Romanesque period efforts were repeatedly made to raise vaults higher and higher. The light, balanced construction of the Gothic skeleton permitted even higher vaulting. Towns everywhere competed for the honor of building the tallest churchs. Notre Dame in Paris, begun in 1163, raised a vault 114 feet. Chartres, begun 30 years later, surpassed it with a vault of 123 feet, and Amiens, begun 1220, reached a height of 138 feet. Beauvais, trying to exceed these heights, had two vaults collapse before successfully covering the choir with vaults 157 feet high. (The church was never completed; the transepts were finally finished in 1500 and the nave was never constructed. Nevertheless, Beauvais still holds the record for the highest Gothic vaulting.)

To achieve such heights, innovations were necessary. The skeleton construction of rib vaulting was vital, of course. The adoption of the pointed arch instead of the customary round arch was also of importance. Not only is the width-height ratio of the pointed arch more flexible but also of greater

8-21 *Walls of glass supported by ribs of stone, braced by thicker buttresses, and seemingly guarded by gargoyles from another world, the exteriors of Gothic churches have few horizontal lines.*

8-22 *Terminated by the functionally essential, but decorative, pinnacles, the flying buttresses diagonally brace the upper walls of the chevet and add even more skeletal forms to the main structure of the Cathedral of Notre Dame in Paris.* Courtesy of French Government Tourist Office.

8-23 *The soaring pointed-arch entrance porch of the Cathedral at Rheims dwarfs the entrance doors to the church. Each sculptured figure, detail, and decorative element tells a story. Note the extensive damage produced during World War II in the upper left-hand corner.*

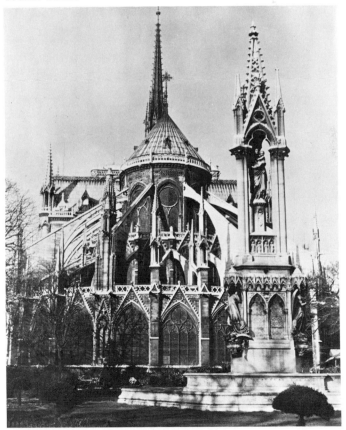

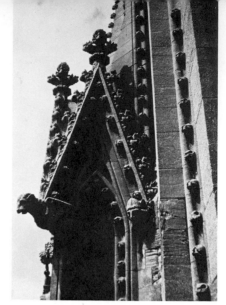

8-24 *Pinnacles adorned with crockets and enlivened with heads of beasts and humans alike are everywhere.*

significance is the angle of the thrust. The thrust of the pointed arch is at a steeper angle toward the ground and is more easily contained.

Because of the height of the vaulting and the larger glass areas in the clerestory level of the nave and choir, it was necessary to devise a method of abutment that could counter the thrust yet not block the windows and not interfere with the side aisles below. The use of the *flying buttress*, a stone half arch, impinging from approximately the haunch of the vaulting and sweeping down in about the same direction as the thrust to lower pier buttresses on the perimeter of the side aisles and chapels of the church, fulfilled these requirements. The pier buttresses are topped with ornamental pinnacles of stone that look very decorative but are structurally important as their weight forces the thrust to an even more vertical direction.

This analysis of Gothic structure has only been concerned with changes and innovations that were peculiar to the period; therefore, to convey a more complete concept, a cursory examination of a typical Gothic cathedral[3] is required.

The Gothic cathedral is a city building, a product of the skills and crafts of an urban population. The cathedral sits on the highest ground and its towers rise high above the houses, shops, and surrounding countryside. It is the center of city life. The markets and fairs of the town are held in the square outside the church, often overflowing within its walls.

Ascending above the pavement of the square, the towers seem to reach toward the heavens and everywhere the dominant lines of the facades are vertical. Upon examining the western end of the cathedral, a careful order is discovered, even more so than is found in a Romanesque church. This facade is divided into three parts vertically and three parts horizontally. The vertical divisions separated by the tower buttresses are more dominant than the

[3]The characteristics of Gothic churches varied from country to country causing quite distinct national types; this composite cathedral is based upon those found in France.

8-25 *Lively, linear, vertical, the facade of Rheims Cathedral soars heavenward as if it were almost weightless. The beauty of its proportions and delicate, lace-like surface is the epitome of Gothic religious architecture.* Courtesy of French Government Tourist Office.

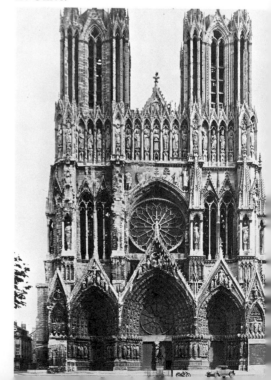

8-27　*The basic structure of this simple "A" frame contemporary church seems appropriately Gothic with the side "flying buttresses," steep roof, and linear cross on the front.*

8-26　*Few churches built in the nineteenth and early twentieth century did not exhibit Gothic architectural elements. The design of this wooden church in southern Wisconsin stresses the vertical by the steeply angled roof almost touching the delicately arched steeple, pointed arches, and board and batten siding. The stringcourse marking the line of the second floor is the only horizontal component.*

horizontal, which are only divided by stringcourses but the facade is definitely separated into nine rectangles. Three sets of double doors are recessed into the fabric of the facade by large pointed arches. These openings are splayed or slant outward and the splayed surfaces are covered with sculpture and carvings of saints and apostles and small columns and other architectural details. Each door is surmounted by a *tympanum*, which is covered with a high relief; over the center door the relief depicts the Last Judgement. The doorway opens directly into the nave. The two other doors are similar but smaller and also have reliefs on their tympana. They open into the side aisles. Above the central doorway, on the second level, is a large round window, or *rose window*, which almost fills the space. The design made by the supporting stonework (*tracery*) imparts a complicated fullblown flower form. Above the two side doors and between the tower buttresses is a *compound arched*[4] opening that also occupies most of the rectangular space. Above each of these compound arches rises a tower. These towers are not the same and as on many other cathedrals, they were built at different times and reflect the current concept of Gothic design. The space between the towers and above the central rose window is empty. The strong contrast of the lighted and shaded details and the seeming multitude of sculptured saints and figures that are placed in almost every conceivable spot contribute to the lacy look pervading the entire facade.

The southern elevation clearly shows the lower side aisles with the exterior pier buttresses and pinnacles, the flying buttress stretching to and holding the clerestory of the nave. the large windows and adjacent walls are covered with a web of tracery. The south transept extends just beyond the line of side aisles but being as high as the nave it is clearly identified. Three doors, smaller, but similar to the western portals, open into the transept. The large

[4] A large arch filled by two smaller arches placed side by side and supported where they meet in the center by a column. Filling the space above and between the two smaller arches and under the crown of the larger arch is a small rose window.

8-28 *The ribs of the stone vaulting are elegantly ornamented with gilded rosettes where the ribs join.*

rose window above dominates the upper part of the exterior. There are no large towers on the transept. Beyond the transept is the *chevet*, which includes the choir and apse. The exterior is very similar to that of the nave but being rounded on the eastern end, the flying buttresses and pinnacles are more clearly seen. Several small curved-plan structures (chapels) are tucked between the pier buttresses encircling the apse. These give an almost scalloped outline to the eastern end of the cathedral. Above the *crossing* of the nave and transept a slender, delicate tower or *flèche* points upward. The north facade is similar to what has been described on the south. The lacy, sculptured surface dominates the entire exterior.

Returning to the western portals and entering the central doorway, the visitor is immediately struck by the soaring space. The rib vaults seem much higher than could be imagined from the exterior. The solid walls and piers rising with such regularity down the length of the nave almost disappear between the stained-glass walls. The gloriously colored light filtering through the clerestory windows stains the stone of the north walls with a thousand rainbows. Seldom have interiors ever been so charged with the feeling of light, space, and air.

Walking slowly upon the patterned stone floor toward the altar, one's eyes are drawn to the sculptured ornament and detail accenting the skeletal structure. The altar is under the crossing and backed by a large altarpiece and choir screen of carved and painted wood. The altarpiece is a *triptych*, which is now closed revealing only the *grisaille*[5] surface, but on feast days when the wings of the triptych are opened and the colorful paintings in the interior are displayed, the effect is indeed splendid.

Behind the altar, elaborately carved choir stalls or seats line the choir and separate it from the ambulatory. The walls above seem even more trans-

[5] Painting rendered in monochromatic gray tones and often used to give the effect of relief sculpture.

8-29 *Appearing to be only decorative, the ribs in the vaulting are the structure itself.*

8-30 *Overhanging second floors, gables, dormers, chimneys, half-timbered construction, all in a jumbled arrangement, observed in these late medieval houses in Warwick, England (left), have often been interpreted in more recent times. This large hotel building in the Midwest built in the early 1920s attempts to present the same image.*

parent and luminous than those of the nave. Radiating out from the ambulatory and divided by the piers are side chapels, each dedicated to a saint and equipped with an altar. Even here the walls are stained glass.

The total effect of the Gothic cathedral is overwhelming and it is not hard, even now, to accept literally the words spoken in 1260 when the Cathedral of Notre Dame at Chartres was consecrated: "This is a place of awe. Here is the court of God and the gate of Heaven."

The unsettled conditions that pervaded most of the medieval period allowed little luxury or even comfort in domestic architecture. In this period as today, the innovations and advances developed in other forms of architecture were not used in the homes, although Gothic ornamentation was often applied. The ruling class lived in cold and damp castles that were little more than fortifications of stone.[6] Daylight was filtered through narrow openings in the walls that were often covered with wooden shutters to keep out the weather and when closed only small holes filled with mica or horn permitted any light at all. (It was not until the fifteenth century that glass began to be used in dwellings.) Heat was provided by open fires on the stone or brick floors; the smoke escaped through the door and window openings or dissipated among the rafters and through the roof. During the fourteenth century the fire was moved from the center of the room to a wall below a hole so that the smoke could escape more easily. A hood was then put over the fire and eventually the fireplace was developed.

[6] The *motte and bailey* castle was the most primitive. The *motte* was the mound of earth taken from the encircling defense ditch. A thick-walled stone tower (*keep or donjon*) rose several stories above the motte and each floor had but one room. The first level was usually windowless, provided storage, and had a well. The next level was used for the garrison, over that was the floor for cooking and eating, then came the lord and his family's quarters, and on top there might be a chapel. Surrounding the tower and motte was a walled courtyard or *bailey*. The entire castle was enclosed by a ditch or moat. From this crude defense structure grew the great fortresses that dominated the countrysides of Western Europe and Britain until modern warfare made them obsolete.

8-31 *Built in the 1830s, this small stone Gothic revival church in northern Illinois clearly follows the architectural tradition established 500 years before in Europe.*

The main room of the castle was the *great hall*. Here most of the activities of the court were held. The walls were bare stone or sometimes covered with paneling part way up the wall. This *wainscot*[7] was about 12 feet high and was made of oak and consisted of small panels no wider than one board. Above the wainscot were hung trophies, armor, and banners. Frequently the floors were covered with rushes. The ceilings were either beamed or trussed and were often colorfully painted.

The nobility fared better than the mass of the population, however. Small houses of stone, wood, or a combination of both with thatched roofs, dirt floors, and even less comfort were the homes of the ordinary people.

The influence of Gothic architectural design, construction, and details upon more recent work has been considerable. In later chapters, references to Gothic are found in the architecture, furniture, and interiors of the eighteenth through the twentieth centuries. The nineteenth century was especially receptive to Gothic design and the terms neo-Gothic and Gothic revival were used throughout most of the century.

[7]The derivation of the word *wainscot* is not known with certainty. Originally used with reference only to the type of wood rather than the paneling itself, there is evidence that wainscot comes from *wagenschot,* a hard close-grained oak used for wagon shafts.

9 Architecture: Italian Renaissance, Spanish

Throughout the centuries, until the discovery of the New World, Italy had the enviable geographical position of center. So too had she once held the intellectual and stylistic focus of the world. With the shifting of the capital of the Roman Empire to the east and the subsequent barbarian invasions from the north, Italy did not regain this supremacy for a thousand years. However, throughout the medieval period, northern Italy developed into a trade center. Supplies for the Crusades were obtained here and from here they set forth to wrest the infidel from the Holy Lands. It was here that shipments of goods from distant lands, especially from the Orient, were inspected and purchased by buyers from other parts of the Western world. Italy became the trade and banking center of Europe.[1]

Venice, Florence, Milan, Siena, and other northern Italian cities became powerful city-states ruled by trade guilds or *communes*. The rivalries between these city-states were intense and even within the city walls, intrigue and competition for supremacy was tantamount. Guilds, families, and even individuals tried to take control of their community, with political tides shifting constantly. Individuality, almost nonexistent during the Middle Ages, became an incessant and assertive force. The drive for personal achievement brought both new ideas and physical changes. With each power shift new decrees were issued, new buildings commissioned, and embellishments added to the city to the honor and glory of the ruler or rulers.

By 1400 most of the forces we now identify with the Renaissance[2] were

[1] The papal desire that Christians become involved with banking instead of the Jews and Levantines caused the establishment of branches of Florentine and Sienese banks in the Low Countries as early as the thirteenth century.

[2] The term comes from the Latin *renascī*: *re* ("again") and *nascī* ("to be born") or "rebirth." The men of the Renaissance were aware of the importance of their time and of their debt to antiquity. In fact, when reference was made to their age, they used the term *rennovatio*, which translates approximately the same as Renaissance. For purposes of simplification no division is made between Early Renaissance (1400–1500), High Renaissance (1500–1525), Mannerist (1525–1600), and Baroque (1600–1750) architecture.

199

developing. A period of investigation and exploration, of intellectual, scientific, and artistic curiosity was at hand. This is the period that brought the exploration of the globe, the beginnings of modern science, the reintroduction of classical artistic ideals, the development of printing, and a questioning of accepted religious practices. The Renaissance was not a synthesis or a bringing together of ideas and principles and of building techniques that had existed for some time as almost 300 years before with the development of the Gothic, but rather it was a fundamental change in human nature.

The individual became important. Man's rights as a human being began to be asserted and it was now that people began to demand more than simple protection from the elements in housing and clothing and more than minimal diets. The individual wanted comfort and health. He wanted to live with beauty; he wanted a better life and he wanted to *better* his life on earth. The uncounted Roman ruins that were everywhere began to take on added quality, and what had been simply accepted were now questioned and, indeed, provided the impetus for investigating the ancient world, which, in turn, provided stimulus for further changes in the contemporary life.

The first flutterings of Renaissance thought can be seen in the literature of Dante (1265–1321), Petrarch (1304–1374), and Boccaccio (1313–1375). Sculpture also early reflected the new spirit but it is architectural design that interests us most. With but a cursory glance, the architecture of the Renaissance seems to be quite "classical." This is partially true, especially in the details, but the basic structures and certainly the use to which the buildings are put are not Roman or Greek.

One of the purposes of this discussion of architecture is to acquaint the reader with the structures of the past; not to give simple knowledge of architectural history but rather to aid in the appreciation and consideration of choice that is required in today's world. By far, the greater majority of the buildings discussed in the preceding chapters were nonresidential, not by

9-1

choice, but by necessity. Where evidence of homes and housing of significant design is available such information was included. But, for the most part, nonresidential structures were foremost stylistically during the preceding periods and have through the ages been the primary sources for later architectural designs used in residential, religious, public, and other major buildings. It is only now, the Renaissance, that major attention can finally be turned toward where people lived rather than where they worshipped, played, or were buried. This is not to say that no outstanding nonresidential architecture was built; on the contrary, many buildings of great significance and lasting influence were built. However, the emphasis here is where people live with little reference to structures that are other than residential.

The person considered the first truly Italian Renaissance architect was Filippo Brunelleschi (1377–1446). Trained as a goldsmith and sculptor, he nevertheless is credited with creating the new architectural style of the Renaissance. When he failed to win the competition of 1401–1402 for bronze doors for the Baptistery of the Cathedral of Florence, he went to Rome where he became an enthusiastic student of the ruins of the ancient city and in turn became an architect. He pledged himself to the restoration of the architectural principles of the Romans and Greeks. Upon his return to Florence he was successful in a competition sponsored by the Wool Guild and was commissioned to design and build the huge dome that was to cover the crossing of the still unfinished Gothic cathedral.

Begun in 1420, this dome, spanning 150 feet, was the first dome of such size since Hagia Sophia 800 years before. Based upon the pointed arch and constructed with ribs, it consists of two interlocking shells, and weighing considerably less and having a thrust more easily contained than the traditional dome, it was possible for Brunelleschi to construct this dome without the usual heavy and complicated trusswork and scaffolding. Because of this construction and the more vertical and thus more distinct exterior form,

Brunelleschi's dome has become the prototype of the majority of domes built in the last 500 years, especially those designed in the Renaissance and post-Renaissance styles.

Brunelleschi also designed the facade of the Hospital of the Innocents (c. 1418)[3] and the Pazzi Chapel (begun 1430). These three structures are considered to be the first Italian Renaissance buildings and established the norm for succeeding Renaissance buildings. Using classical columns and pilasters, round arches, domes, pedestals, and podiums, Brunelleschi did not base his buildings upon Roman or Greek models but rather developed a statement of his own. He is also credited with being the first truly *modern* architect because it was he who first used scale drawings. During his analytical investigations he also invented the system of linear perspective, which, unlike the empirical methods of depicting space of the past, was objective, precise, and rational. This alone would have placed him as one of the most influential innovators in the arts.

It was not, however, Brunelleschi who was chosen by the Medici family[4] to design a magnificent residence in Florence. The Palazzo Medici-Riccardi, begun in 1444, was designed by Michelozzo Michelozzi (1396–1472). The plan submitted to Cosimo de Medici by Brunelleschi was rejected because it was of such imperial magnificence, fit for a prince, and not thought appro-

[3] The Hospital of the Innocents is the first major building that expresses the consuming interest in the past that extended well into the twentieth century.

[4] During the Renaissance if one lacked princely ancestors and yet wielded power, one would simply adopt princely virtues and live in a style that would likely convince the people that their ruler or ruling family was, indeed, the one to decide their destinies. The Medici, Pitti, Strozzi, Pazzi, and Riccardi families of Florence; the Sforza and Visconti of Milan; the Colonna, Este, Borgia, Orsini, and Borghese families of Rome; and others in Venice, Genoa, Verona, Siena, and Ferrara all exerted great power and were rivals for influence. Much of their great wealth was spent patronizing the arts and providing themselves with luxurious palaces filled with rich furnishings that, surrounded by equally elaborate formal gardens, rivaled the size and beauty of those built for the ancient Roman emperors.

9-2

priate for the first citizen of the republic. The commission went to the younger Michelozzo whose plan was considered more suitable.

Typical of many palaces, the Medici-Riccardi Palace is based upon the medieval Italian palace with its characteristic square plan and interior courtyard. The structure turns its back to the city presenting a handsome, but closed, facade and the life of the palace literally centered around the court. The fortress-like appearance was not entirely inappropriate as this residence was also the center of the family banking business. The original facade had ten windows across the second and third levels and the interior court (*cortile*) was centered within the square plan. The building was acquired by the Riccardi family in 1659 and in 1680 an addition was built on the north side increasing the number of windows to 17 on the main (east) front. The plan is now asymmetrical with the additional rooms on the north and a large open court on the west.

The exterior is divided into three horizontal divisions by stringcourses indicating the interior floors and each division graduating in height. The widest at the lower or street level is surfaced with rough-hewn, "rustic" stone and the upper divisions are progressively smoother, the second or *plino nobile* ("noble floor") with smoothly dressed stone with rusticated joints and the very smooth top floor with regular ashlar having hardly noticeable joints. On the second and third levels, regularly spaced round arched openings penetrate the fabric of the wall. These arched openings are in turn divided by paired narrow arched windows with a slender column between and above this divider and, under the crown of the larger arch, a circular window. The medieval compound arched opening has been translated into the Renaissance idiom. The rectangular block of the structure is topped by a massive Roman cornice one-tenth the height of the building. This cornice is decorated with classic dentils, egg and dart moldings, and acanthus leaves.[5] Originally the

[5] These three devices, stringcourse, compound window, and heavy projecting cornice, become much used design elements as the Renaissance spirit moves beyond northern Italy.

ground level had large arches, entrances to a loggia where the family banking business was conducted, but 75 years after the palace was constructed Michelangelo filled them with rectangular windows sitting on brackets and topped by projecting triangular pediments in the High Renaissance style.

Within this imposing facade the family lived on the second and third floors. With the central courtyard and garden providing light and air and the house turned inward, the concept is not unlike the ancient Roman domus. The luxurious rooms encircle the courtyard in single file; there are no halls and consequently there also was little privacy.

As the Renaissance developed so did the interior comfort and luxuriousness of the palatial residences being constructed. Smaller and more personal as well as the customarily larger rooms became common, and more public rooms and rooms used for purposes similar to today; that is, as bedrooms, studies, and the like. These rooms were decorated and furnished by some of the foremost artists and designers of the times.[6]

These interiors are rich and varied and it would seem that the owner of each palace was trying for the "honor" of having the most lavish home, which was often the case. The interiors were constantly being remodeled and redecorated. Fortunately, the Palazzo Davanzati (c. 1428) in Florence has been restored to its very late medieval–early Renaissance appearance and with

9-3 *The fully developed Renaissance palace facade, as shown on the Farnese Palace in Rome, is a carefully composed arrangement of classically inspired architectural detail. Often used to illustrate the Principles of Design, note especially the subtle use of repetition, alternation, and progression in the window forms.*

[6]The versatility of the artist during the Renaissance is the result of the apprentice system that flourished. Each master artist had a shop (*bottega*) in which apprentices worked, often beginning at the age of 10 or 12. Here the apprentice learned several crafts and eventually was able to leave, join the guild, and set up his own bottega. The masters and their apprentices could provide architectural designs, paintings and sculpture, furnishings, and decorative accessories for churches and palaces; costumes and equipment for the frequent pageants; and, as often as not, were also able to furnish utilitarian and defense designs. For example, Leonardo da Vinci, when writing to the king of France, described his abilities as a designer of fortresses—adding as a postscript that he could paint as well.

204

9-4 *The facade of this house (c. 1890) in the Renaissance revival style in Milwaukee, Wisconsin, is divided by pilasters and entablatures with windows filling the spaces between. The window designs are loosely based on the types seen on the Medici-Riccardi and the Farnese palaces. The "temple front" porch, however, appears to be extraneous and is a continuation of the Greek revival style popular earlier in the nineteenth century.*

later rooms preserved in other palaces in Florence, Rome, and elsewhere in Italy, is is possible to get the essence of typical Italian Renaissance interiors.

When viewing these noble rooms one is immediately struck by how much more comfortable they are compared to contemporary rooms north of the Alps. The number of pieces of furniture, although not great, is far larger than in the still medieval courts of France, England, and Germany. The rooms are of a much more human scale and although considered large by today's standards, are definitely more in keeping with the "human" concept than the medieval great halls. The furniture of the Renaissance is discussed in Chapter 15 but it is sufficient to say that the comfort and variety was considerable compared to that of the Gothic.

The ceilings of the Italian palaces are high-beamed, coffered, or vaulted. Beamed ceilings were a continuation of medieval design and are found in the earlier palaces. Large timbers, of walnut, oak, cypress, or cedar, were placed several feet apart across the narrow dimension of the room. These supported smaller, more closely spaced beams running lengthwise to the room and the floor above rested on them. Such beamed ceilings are frequently painted with stripes and medallions in brilliant colors and are often the dominant feature of the room. The vaulted ceilings are plastered, decorated with bas-reliefs, and painted. The groins are accented by ornament, either painted or molded, and a favorite device was to combine molded, three-dimensional designs with those painted to appear three-dimensional. As the period progressed, flat ceilings without the pattern of the supporting beams became the dominant form. The surface was then enriched with freer ornament combining coffering, painting, and architectural detail.

Floors in major rooms are made of tile, brick, or marble. The tile, usually 6- or 8-inch hexagons or squares, is plain or patterned, natural terra-cotta, or glazed in colors. Brick floors are often laid in a herringbone pattern and marble floors are repeatedly checkerboard in highly contrasting colors and values. As the Renaissance moved toward the sixteenth century, wood floors became increasingly popular. During the early period, simple walnut and oak plank floors were used in upper rooms but later elaborate *parquetry* floors in rare and colorful woods competed with ornate marble and stone floors. Few rugs or other floor coverings were used, but occasionally small Oriental rugs were placed upon the floor.

The walls are always furnished with a paneled wainscot, traditionally of wood, but occasionally of marble. This wainscot is sometimes designed in the form of an order with classical pilasters and entablature. Above the wainscot the walls are customarily smoothly plastered. This surface, now often found plain and even textured, was almost always painted with geometric patterns with a frieze above or in small panels and small pictures. Some walls were painted in imitation of patterned tapestry. Later large, elaborate paintings and murals were in favor with the wall divided by architectural details —either painted or molded. The feeling of "surface" was not considered to be important, and the more "spatial" the painted wall the more it was admired.

Walls are pierced with doors, windows, and *niches*. For the first time doors became part of the design of the room rather than just openings. Their moldings and frames were designed to complement the architecture of the room and were based upon Roman models; frequently these consisted of pilasters with a frieze above topped by a pediment. The early Renaissance doors were traditionally located near the corners of the room, perhaps because of convenience, but, as the Renaissance progressed doors took on added importance by being moved to the center of the wall. The doors themselves were simply paneled around 1400 but within 75 years had become quite ornate with painted and carved decorations and moldings. Windows, like the doors, began to be treated with architectural detailing but remained less ornamented. Frequently shuttered, windows did not have

9-5

9-6 *The broad sweep of the facade of Saint Peter's Basilica is accented by the shadowed entablature supported by the Corinthian columns and pilasters. Michelangelo's dome, set back over the crossing, rises majestically above the church.* Courtesy of Italian Government Travel Office.

draperies. Niches, recessed wall spaces, were with and without doors. Used to display sculpture or ceramics, those without doors were frequently decorated with pilasters and other architectural details. Niches with doors were simpler and were less decorative and served more utilitarian purposes.

Fireplaces, which had only recently been developed by moving the open fire to the wall and surmounting it with a hood to control the smoke, were now further embedded into the wall and the hoods flattened. Eventually only the support for the hood remained (the wall above is flat) and became a mantel, carved and decorated with pilasters, scrolls, and friezes of shields, garlands, and *putti* (small nude boys, usually winged; if they carry bows and arrows they are called cupids and are the personification of love.)

The Italian Renaissance interior is one of color, pattern, and form combined to give the most luxurious appearance. The strongest and most varied colors were used, and when viewed as a whole it is immediately apparent that these interiors have a "total" look about them, a balance of design. Where individual pieces or a single device stood out in the medieval interior, here each part is but a segment of the collective whole. Almost within the span of a man's adult life the interiors of the medieval world disappeared and the new interiors of the Renaissance with their exquisite craftsmanship, rich materials, interpreted classical architectural ornament and detail, luxurious comfort, and human considerations have taken their place.

The largest Christian church ever built, the mighty Basilica of Saint Peter in the Vatican, is the work of many men. Originally an Early Christian basilica built in 330, it stood for almost 1,200 years, but in 1505 Pope Julius II decided, while planing for a tomb for himself, to rebuild the venerable church. Plans were submitted and Donato Bramante (1444–1514) was charged with the construction of the new Saint Peter's Basilica. The traditional Latin cross plan was discarded for the Greek cross with arms of equal length. Construction had barely started when Bramante died. A succession of

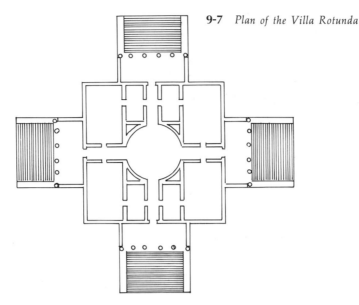

9-7 *Plan of the Villa Rotunda*

architects were placed in charge, but little construction was done until Pope Paul III appointed Michelangelo Buonarroti (1475–1564) as architect.[7]

Few men at age 72 are faced with such a task, and it is to the genius of Michelangelo that the present structure stands. Using Bramante's basic plan but strengthening, adapting, and enlarging it, the construction of Saint Peter's progressed and the drum of the mighty dome was underway when he died. Models were left and the dome and lantern were finished according to his plans in 1590. Later the nave was lengthened and the gigantic facade was built across the front. Finally, Giovanni Bernini (1598–1680) built the enclosing colonnades on each side of the piazza (1655–1667).

Grandiose, ornate, and immense, the present Saint Peter's is so vast that it is almost impossible to feel a sense of human scale. Measurements, although often difficult to relate to, do give some idea of the colossal size. The interior length is 600 feet (exterior, 700 feet) and across the transept is 450 feet. The interior barrel vault of the nave is 150 feet high and 84 feet across. The dome is $137\frac{1}{2}$ feet wide and the cross surmounting the lantern on the dome is 452 feet above the pavement below, three times as high as the highest Gothic vault (Beauvais). The facade of Saint Peter's (167 feet high) has columns 90 feet, 9 inches high, 9 feet in diameter, and standing on pedestals 18 feet high. This massive grandeur is the result, to a large extent, however, not of sheer size but placement. If it were not for Bernini's magnificent piazza (650 feet wide) with its glorious sweep of colonnade on either side, all would be lost.

---

[7] Michelangelo, born into the distinguished Buonarroti family of Florence, is an impressive example of the versatility of the artist of the Renaissance. While still a very young man he first won fame as a sculptor with the *Pietà* (c. 1498) as one of his first significant works. Also renowned as a painter, he is best known for his *Sistine Chapel Ceiling* (1508–1512) and the *Last Judgment* (1536–1541), both in the Vatican. He is no less distinguished as an architect with the major portion of Saint Peter's as his most monumental building. When he died at the advanced age of 89, he was recognized as one of the world's leading citizens and was mourned "like an emperor."

9-8 *The Villa Rotunda by Andrea Palladio has inspired residential and public architecture for 400 years.* Photograph by Wayne Andrews.

No other cathedral, or even public building, has such a noble approach. Sir Banister Fletcher, former president of the Royal Institute of British Architects, has called it, "the greatest of all atriums before the greatest of all churches in Christendom."

Before completion of this cursory study of the architecture of the Italian Renaissance, the work of one more Italian architect must be examined. Andrea Palladio (1518–1580) has been called "the most influential architect of the whole Renaissance." These are strong words, considering that Michelangelo, Brunelleschi, and Michelozzo were just discussed, but with all respect to these three great masters it *is* Palladio who influenced the architecture of England, France, and America as did no other architect.

Palladio was born in Padua but moved to Vicenza when still in his teens and it is here and in Venice that most of his buildings were built. Two buildings of major interest are in Vicenza, the Villa Capra (c. 1567) and the Basilica (1549). The Villa Capra, more popularly known as the Villa Rotunda, is a square building with a low, tiled hip roof topped by a low dome. Each facade of the square has an almost identical classical temple front consisting of a broad flight of stairs, six columns, entablature and pediment, the Roman portico. Each portico leads into the central circular hall, below the dome, and rooms are arranged symmetrically around the dome, within the square. The plan of the Villa Rotunda was a departure from the usual Renaissance residential design but it became a favorite and was copied both in England and in other parts of Europe.

The Basilica, or Town Hall, was a medieval structure to which Palladio added Renaissance arcades. It is the design of these two-storied arcades that is of especial interest. Palladio superimposed two classical orders, Doric on the bottom and Ionic on the top, to cover the piers. The width-height ratio of the bays, the area between the piers, was determined by the old building and Palladio considered this too wide for the height. To reduce the apparent width he designed what has become known as the Palladian motif; that is, a

9-9

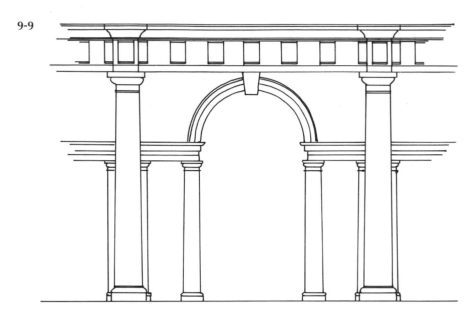

round arch supported by columns with narrow rectangular openings, the height of the columns only, on each side. This motif has been adapted, adopted, used and misused on buildings ever since. It was extemely popular in England and America during the eighteenth century and translated into a window, known as a Palladian window, it can be found on many eighteenth century-style homes.

It is doubtful if Palladio's influence would have been so great if it were not for the publication of his book, I quattro libri dell' Architettura (*Four Books on Architecture*) in 1573, which contained designs of buildings, both completed and proposed. Distributed throughout Europe, Palladio's designs had a profound influence upon architects and designers. In England, where Inigo Jones, a most influential seventeenth-century architect, was an ardent disciple, Palladianism developed into a style of architecture of restrained classicism and dominated English (and Colonial American) architecture until the mideighteenth century.

The "flow" of architectural design progresses smoothly from Italy to France. However, because of the Spanish influence on residential architecture during the twentieth century, the architecture of Spain must be considered before continuing north of the Alps.

Spain and Portugal occupy the Iberian Peninsula at the southwest corner of Europe. It is a harsh and frequently uncompromising land cut off from the rest of Europe by the rugged Pyrenees mountains. Even within this geographical barrier, mountain ranges isolate one area from another. Consequently, the cultures, languages, and temperaments of these people developed separately. The original inhabitants of the peninsula, the Iberians, were early mixed with the Celts. Later the Phoenicians, Greeks, Berbers, and Romans made settlements and, although each left an imprint, it was the Romans who left an impressive architectural heritage. With the collapse of the Roman Empire, the Visigoths occupied the Roman settlements and feudal states developed with only Christianity as a common bond.

9-10 *On the upper floor of an early twentieth-century Georgian-style building, this Palladian window is typical of the many that can be found in older neighborhoods.*

9-11 *What could be more appropriate for an Italian restaurant than a High Renaissance facade! This restaurant in Minneapolis, Minnesota, is housed in a former private club.*

9-12 *This small church in southern Spain typically has flat, plain walls but rich, complicated ornamentation based upon Moorish, Renaissance, and Baroque designs is above and around the entrance.*

Early in the eighth century, the Moors[8] crossed the narrow Straits of Gibraltar and invaded the Iberian Peninsula with great military success. The Moors overpowered the disorganized feudal states and in 732 crossed the Pyrenees where they were driven back by Charles Martel, the grandfather of Charlemagne. One can only conjecture the course of history if Martel had not been successful in stemming the Islamic tide in Europe. The next five centuries saw the struggle for the domination of the Iberian Peninsula and by the thirteenth century the Christian forces had reduced the Moorish holdings to the Kingdom of Granada, which was held until 1492 when the armies of King Ferdinand of Aragon and his wife, Queen Isabella of Castile, forced the last Moorish king Boabdil to flee to North Africa.

Although the important date of 1492 is considered the year when Spain was free of the Moors, it cannot be said that after that date Spain was free of Moorish influence. Imperishable traces of Islamic customs, arts, and intellect can still be found. It is this blend of East and West, of Islamic and Renaissance Christian, that has produced what is now called Spanish.

Spanish architecture is a combination of Gothic, Renaissance, and Moorish traditions set in an austere land. The divisions of the various periods found in Spain's architectural history will be disregarded so that a synthesis of the traditions and forms can be identified. No specific example, either imaginary or real, is described; but rather only the characteristics of this architecture are discussed.

[8] In 622, Mohammed, the Prophet of Allah, was forced to flee Mecca because of his religious preaching based upon one God (Allah). Within a few years he returned and by 632 his was the religion of all Arabia. It was known as Islam ("to surrender") and his followers were called Moslems or, in Arabic, Muslims. The rapid spread of Islam was both a social and religious revolution and within a century the empire stretched from western Africa to the Indus River in India. The intellectual and economic climate of the Muslim Empire was far superior to anything found in the Middle Ages of Western Europe and not until the Renaissance did Europe approach this level. The name Moor is used when referring to the Muslim-Berber peoples of northwest Africa.

9-13 *The brilliant sun reflected from the floor of a courtyard magically lights the delicate yesería surfaces in the cool, dim interior of the Alhambra in Granada, Spain.*

9-14 *An admiration of Moorish architectural detail, the heritage of encircling porches, and the versatility of wood were combined to produce this example of lively Victorian architecture in Galveston, Texas.*

Spanish architecture has been described as rugged, virile, masculine, austere, and even brutal. This is not to say that it cannot have great beauty, for it can. It is marked by individualism as each building, each interior, has its own identity, but certain generalities can be discerned. There is 1) a general largeness of scale; 2) a lack of windows in the lower exterior walls echoing the desire for seclusion (a Moorish trait); 3) a universal use of large, elaborate doorways; 4) a frequent use of flat or low-pitched, tiled roofs with wide eaves; 5) a top story repeatedly encircled by arcades; and 6) a recurring use of exquisite wrought-iron grills and screens. As in most southern and warm climates the Spanish buildings invariably turn inward and secluded courts (*patios*), fountains, and gardens of great charm and beauty are found within. The use of pierced stone tracery, the horseshoe arch, ceramic tile, and excessive ornament—often quite two-dimensional—and set off by expanses of flat surfaces are all Moorish features. The pointed arch and tracery of the Gothic, the classical details of the Italian Renaissance, and the robust three-dimensional qualities of the Italian Baroque are often found mixed freely with the Moorish. The term *Mudéjar* is given to this blending, although it once referred only to Christianized Moors and their work.

The interior of the Spanish house is positive in tone. Each detail, each material, and each piece of furniture stands out and the architectural character is always evident. There is a sense of spaciousness about the interior produced, to some extent, by the height of the ceiling (10 feet or more) as well as by the sparseness of the furnishings. At no time is the dominance of the walls, floor, and ceiling forgotten.

Floors are paved with tile, stone, or brick; on the upper levels wood is used. The tile used on the floor is generally devoid of pattern and is the color of fired clay. Sometimes small brightly colored and patterned tiles are sparingly used to relieve the expanse of dull red. Stone and brick are laid in regular and simple patterns.

The walls, however, are not without color. Brightly colored and patterned tiles form the *dado* (the lower portion of a wall, a low wainscot about three or four feet high), make the trim around doors and windows, cover window seats, line niches and cupboards, and decorate fountains. The effect is frequently dazzling. Above the dado the wall is ordinarily plain, a visual relief from the pattern of the tile. Near the ceiling a richly modeled frieze encircles the room. This frieze frequently is decorated with a type of work known as *yesería* (shallow lace-like plaster relief).

Ceilings are usually made of wood and fall into two types—one is quite similar to the beamed ceilings found in Italy at the beginning of the Renaissance and the other is of Muslim origin. The second type consists of small wooden panels of different geometric[9] shapes surrounded by complicated moldings. These unique geometric designs, which are also found on paneled doors and chests, attest to the original skill of Moorish craftsmen and are a particular characteristic of Spanish interiors.

[9]The representation of human or animal forms was forbidden by Islamic law and, being excellent mathematicians, the Muslims devised a wealth of abstract pattern and nonrepresentational design along with the use of the beautiful Arabic script. Some animals and humans are, however, depicted in Islamic art as some Muslims were less orthodox than others and allowed such representations.

10 Architecture: French, English

By the middle of the fifteenth century, medieval mysticism and the concepts of spiritual man in France were being replaced with a more worldly philosophy; the Middle Ages were on the wane and a new era was beginning. A growing taste for Italian ideas could be found among the royal houses, but not until Charles VIII (r. 1483–1498) marched through Italy to claim the Kingdom of Naples did the still basically medieval world of France encounter the full spirit of the Italian Renaissance. The French passed through the cultural centers of Florence[1], Lucca, Pisa, and Rome, and entered Naples on February 22, 1495. This contact with the literature, art, science, luxury, and refinement of the Italians, so completely unknown in the Gothic world, impressed Charles tremendously and he envisioned such a world at Amboise. Upon his return he brought back not only the riches gleaned from the conquest (one shipment alone had 87,000 pounds of paintings, sculpture, tapestries, and books) but 22 craftsmen—architects, sculptors, gardeners, and woodworkers. The Renaissance was to become fact, not just an idea.

The French contact with Italy did not end; in 1508 Louis XII, with Florence now an ally, attacked Venice, and in 1525 Francois I (1515–1547) invaded Italy to enforce his claim to the duchy of Milan. He was defeated and held prisoner for a period of time at Pavia. Returning to France upon his release from prison, Francois invited many of the finest Italian artists to his court to design, construct, and instruct in the new fashion. Among those who came was the great Leonardo da Vinci who spent the last three years of his life at Amboise. Andrea del Sarto, Cellini, Primaticcio, Vignola, and Il Rosso were also at the court of Francois. And, it is *Francois I* who is considered the first

---

[1]The French, as invaders, had the right to ransack and plunder as they progressed down Italy's boot. The Italians were reluctant to open their doors but had no choice, and in 1494 Charles lived for some time in the Medici-Riccardi Palace.

truly French Renaissance king. A succession of French monarchs[2] followed, each of whom built even more luxurious and increasingly Italianate palaces and châteaux.

The special character of French Renaissance is the melding of both Gothic and Renaissance, a combining of totally different architectural concepts, yet a distinct and picturesque style. The more familiar horizontality of classical and Renaissance architecture is rejected in favor of the vertical tendency of Gothic. The spires, pinnacles, and buttresses of Gothic are transformed with columns, pilasters, pediments, and entablatures. Renaissance moldings, cornices, and panels of classical derivation are applied to the surface of structures of still Gothic form and construction. Roofs are steeply sloped and studded with dormer windows and numerous chimney stacks. All add a new vocabulary to Renaissance architecture.

Other distinctions can be made between French Renaissance architecture and Italian Renaissance architecture. 1) There was no need for new religious structures in France as in Italy because of the numerous churches built during the medieval period; therefore, almost every French Renaissance building is secular—palaces and châteaux. 2) With very few exceptions the major buildings of the Italian Renaissance are urban structures that are seen from streets and generally with only one or at the most two major facades. In France the buildings are found outside Paris and in the Loire Valley, and are often situated in park-like surroundings where all exteriors are important. 3) The irregular plans that are so often found in Gothic architecture and the freedom from limiting spatial requirements are reflected in the sprawling plans of French Renaissance châteaux. 4) The climate of France, which is less

---

[2]Two French kings married members of the Medici family of Florence: Henry II (r. 1547-1559) married Catherine de' Medici who was the mother of three kings—Francois II (reigned 1559-1560), Charles IX (r. 1560-1574), and Henri III (r. 1574-1589); Henri IV (r. 1589-1610) married Marie de' Medici. Both women were very influential, politically and artistically, and brought additional Italian craftsmen and artists to France.

10-1 *The rectangular formality of the still medieval plan of the Château de Chambord can be discerned in this aerial view. However, dominating everything is the veritable forest of chimneys, dormers, towers, and cupolas, all encrusted with Renaissance detail. Courtesy of the Caisse Nationale des Monuments Historiques.*

mild than in Italy, affected the architecture, that is, steep roofs, many chimneys, and more numerous and larger windows with mullions and transoms (a carry-over from Gothic tracery).

During the sixteenth century many important French Renaissance structures were built, and as is so often the case, they were remodeled, added to, and changed so that one palace or château might now have wings of different styles and periods. The interiors are quite often not the same style as the exterior. However, some of the most famous and best examples of sixteenth-century French structures are the Château de Blois (1508–), the Château de Chenonceaux (1515–), the Château d'Azay-le-Rideau (1518–1527), the Château de Chambord (1519–1547) (all in the Loire Valley), and the Palais de Fontainebleau (1528–) outside of Paris.

The most famous of the Loire châteaux, Chambord with 440 rooms, has a plan very similar to that of a medieval fortress. A rectangular block or *donjon* with conical towers on each corner is set in a court and is enclosed on three sides by a larger rectangle (a line of rooms acting as a wall) which, in turn, was surrounded by a moat. The stiff formality of the plan, however, is in keeping with Renaissance ideals. The walls are "clothed" with three restrained, superimposed classical orders in the accepted Italian manner. The medieval heritage is very apparent in the roof, which is steeply pitched with dormers, turrets, cupolas, pinnacles, and more than 360 ornamental chimneys, but they are all covered with every classical and Renaissance decorative device imaginable. The dignified and formal lower levels are in decided contrast with the elaborate, restless, and definitely picturesque skyline.

French interiors of the sixteenth century became increasingly Italian as the century progressed. At first, Italian details, pilasters, capitals, and moldings were applied to what could only be called Gothic walls. Not until the *Gallery of Francois I* was built at Fontainebleau between 1534 and 1539 by Il Rosso and Primaticcio was there an interior in the complete Renaissance idiom. The traditional oak used for the wainscot was about all that was traditional. The

panels were large and carved with classical moldings, motifs of trophies and cartouches, the letter *F* in monogram form, and the salamander (the symbol selected by Francois). Above the wainscot the wall was decorated with boldly modeled white and gold stucco reliefs alternating with colorful frescoes of allegories and myths. The wood ceiling was beamed and deeply coffered. French interiors would never again reflect the traditional medieval great hall.

Succeeding interiors are increasingly architectural, have larger wall paintings, and show more restraint when contrasted with the vigor of the interiors of Francois I. The human figure became a more important decorative element and exotic and natural creatures such as sphinxes, chimerae, griffins, eagles, lions, and rams are found. The foundations are laid for the burgeoning of the Baroque of the seventeenth century.

Italian and Flemish influences permeate the architecture of the early seventeenth century. Henri IV, before he was assassinated in 1610, had set up workshops in the *Louvre*[3] where craftsmen could work under royal protection in an effort to develop the decorative arts. Henri's heir, Louis XIII, was only nine years old when he became king, and his mother, Marie de' Medici, was named regent; it was she who was responsible for much of the artistic development of the period. The workshops were soon filled with Italian and Flemish craftsmen at her invitation. She was a powerful and energetic woman, and the resources of the crown were often used to create luxurious

[3] The Palais du Louvre (1546–1878) is now the national art museum of France and is said to be the world's most important museum. The building covers more than 45 acres in Paris on the right bank of the Seine River. There has been a royal residence on this site since the beginning of the thirteenth century when a medieval fortress was built by Philip Augustus. Declared the official residence of the king by Charles V in the fourteenth century, it continued to be so until the French Revolution, when on November 8, 1793, the Louvre was opened to the public. The original Gothic building was partially rebuilt in 1546–59 for Francois I in the "new (Renaissance) style" and has since been enlarged and remodeled by almost every ruler of France until 1878. The exterior facades and the interiors exhibit a complete history of French architecture from the time of Francois I to that of Napoleon III.

10-2 *The Gallery of Francois I reflects the immediate assimilation of Italian Renaissance decorative details by the French after the French had been exposed to them. The medieval great hall has been transformed.* Courtesy of the Caisse Nationale des Monuments Historiques.

palaces for her. Being Florentine, she favored Italian architectural design as seen by her *Palais du Luxembourg* (1615–1624) in Paris, which has as exterior based upon the garden facade (1550–1570) of the *Palazzo Pitti* in Florence, but she turned to the Flemish painter Rubens[4] to decorate the interior.

At first dominated by his mother, Louis XIII was never a strong or brilliant ruler. Although she was later banished, it was his mother's influence that brought Cardinal Rishelieu to the fore. Richelieu was made a member of the king's council in 1624 and was the virtual ruler of France until his death 18 years later. It was Richelieu who is credited with the "rediscovery of the national soul," and it was he who continued the development of the arts and gathered around himself pictures, sculpture, rare furniture, and *objets d'art*. And, it was also he who formulated the policy that made possible the absolute power of the French monarchs of the next 150 years.

Louis XIII died a few months after Richelieu, leaving a five-year-old son[5] who would become Louis XIV, *Le Roi Soleil* ("the Sun King"), the lover of

[4] Peter Paul Rubens (1577-1640) is considered one of the greatest and most prolific Baroque painters. Born in Antwerp, he was trained by local painters and went to Italy in 1600 where he was court painter for the Duke of Mantua for eight years. Returning to Flanders Rubens was appointed court painter to the Spanish regent and later was a confidential advisor and courier. With entrance to the royal households of Europe he obtained many important commissions and with the aid of many assistants was able to accomplish a vast amount of work. Probably the most famous series of large decorative paintings that Rubens did in the 1620s is that which glorifies the career of Marie de' Medici. Those paintings are in the Palais de Luxembourg.

[5] Louis XIII lived a wandering life inherited from feudal times, and during one of his travels, passing through Paris on his way to Fontainebleau, a violent storm prevented him from reaching his destination. It was necessary for him and his retinue to sleep at the Louvre. Taxing the capacity of the palace, the king found no bed available except that of his wife, the queen, whom he had left several years before. Nine months later, to the day, the queen gave birth to a son. An intriguing question is: "What would the artistic, cultural, and political heritage of France and the world have been without the storm on that fateful evening?"

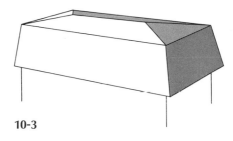

10-3

10-4 *The frivolous architectural extrava-
ganzas of the latter half of the nineteenth
century frequently were topped with complicated mansard roofs.*

10-5 *The mansard roof, developed during
the seventeenth century and re-established
with distinction in the nineteenth century,
has been ignobly resurrected during the
twentieth century.*

pomp and splendor, the creator of *Versailles*, the ruler of France for 72 years (1643–1715).

The mother of the young king was named regent as was done when his father had become king. Anne of Austria, so ignored by her husband, became, at last, the center of the court and with her favorite, Cardinal de Mazarin, ruled France. Mazarin, an Italian by birth, was a man of great subtely, cunning, and an extreme fondness for money. He inherited the tradition of Richelieu and through intrigue maintained it. When he died in 1661 he left Louis XIV a stable government, a successful foreign policy, and the unquestioned right to say, "L'Etat c'est moi." Mazarin was also a patron of the arts, the Italian arts, and during his tenure was very instrumental when decisions pertaining to architectural design and decoration for the Louvre and other royal residences were concerned.

The architectural character of the exterior facades of major buildings were quite Italian with the exception of the roofs, which were still steeply pitched, often with two slopes[6], but with fewer dormers, chimneys, and other distracting elements; by the end of the seventeenth century, even those had almost disappeared. The influence of classical architecture was most apparent as French exterior design now followed the conservative pattern set by Palladio as opposed to the more flamboyant concepts found in Italy and in French Renaissance architecture of a century earlier. This is no doubt the result of the seventeenth-century predilection to rational authority and system in all things. The symmetrically arranged facades are broken by

[6]The *mansard* roof with a nearly vertical lower section and an upper part, which usually had a slight slope but was sometimes flat, is named after François Mansart (1598–1666), a distinguished French Baroque architect. It was again a common roof type of the "Second Empire" (1848–1870) in France and is found repeatedly in late nineteenth-century English and American architecture. Surprisingly, it has recently gained great popularity with builders often with disastrous results, for example, mobile homes with pseudomansard roofs covered with split shakes.

10-6 *The precursor of Versailles, Vaux-le-Vicomte, reflects the exterior architecture of French Renaissance, but its magnificent gardens and interiors, achieved by the collaboration of Le Vau, Le Brun, and Le Nôtre induced the jealous wrath of Louis XIV and motivated the creation of Versailles—the epitome of French Baroque.* Courtesy of the Caisse Nationale des Monuments Historiques.

strong horizontal elements such as stringcourses and entablatures with orders superimposed one above the other. There is a tendency toward rusticated elements such as quoins and *chaînes* (vertical strips of slightly projected masonry between the horizontal string-moldings that divide the surface of the building into areas or panels), and although stone continues to be the predominantly used material, brick combined with stone details is an early favorite. Thus, French Baroque, universally identified with Louis XIV, was already a mature style in 1661, the year the 23-year-old-king had freedom to rule.

The Baroque style had been developed in Italy to glorify a triumphant papacy, was brought to France by Richelieu and Mazarin, and was considered to be the only adequate style for a *grand monarque.* Indeed, the expansion of French Baroque and consequently its synonymity with Louis XIV is in no small way due to the irritation and envy experienced when the king saw the new château of his Surintendant des Finances, Nicolas Fouquet. (1615–1680).

From 1655–1661, Fouquet had built for himself, halfway between Paris and Fontainebleau, a magnificent home, Vaux-le-Vicomte—105 lavishly decorated rooms with chairs of Chinese plush, Persian carpets, crystal chandeliers, gold clocks, and silver vases—set in 170 acres of formal gardens. Costs spiraled as the work progressed, and yet no expense was spared. The king, hearing of the elaborateness and costliness of his finance minister's new home, suspected irregularities in the minister's books and ordered them investigated.

Fouquet, disregarding the king's displeasure, planned an elaborate banquet to celebrate the completion of his château. At six o'clock on the evening of August 17, 1661, the king and queen mother and their attendants arrived at Vaux-le-Vicomte. Fouquet showed the king through his home and gardens, then the banquet for 6,000 guests was served on plates of gold, silver, and lacquer. A play by Molière was presented as was a ballet in the garden, and, finally, fireworks ended the evening. The young king was furious, as he

10-7 *Although not all of Versailles as known today was built during the reign of Louis XIV, he achieved his wish—to create the most monumental palace in the world.* Courtesy of Caisse Nationale des Monuments Historiques.

knew that the money to pay for most of this splendor had come from the royal treasury.

Nineteen days later Fouquet was arrested, charged with treason and corrupt conduct, and sentenced to life imprisonment. (He died nineteen years later.) Vaux-le-Vicomte was closed and the furniture was sold to pay off the creditors. Interestingly, the best furnishings were purchased by the king.

How had Fouquet been able to create such a spectacular and enviable home, one in which the exterior, interior and furnishings, and the setting all blended into one grand design? He had comissioned Louis Le Vau (1612–1670), the leading architect of the time, to design the house; he had discovered an exceptional young painter, Charles Le Brun, (1619–1690) and put him in charge of the interiors; and he had André Le Nôtre (1613–1700) design the elaborate formal gardens. But it was Fouquet's development of a special workshop in Maincy that was the catalyst that brought all this to its ultimate and extraordinary fruition. This workshop under the direction of Le Brun was filled with Flemish craftsmen and it was here that the tapestries and other furnishings were created for Vaux-le-Vicomte.

Louis XIV decided that *he* should have the palace that no one could surpass, a palace in a world worthy of his royal dignity. He commissioned Fouquet's Le Vau, Le Brun, and Le Nôtre to transform his father's small hunting lodge at Versailles into the most grand, most elaborate, and most monumental palace in the world, an Olympian residence, an enchanted château. His wish was fulfilled and it has influenced, almost without exception, every palace, manor house, or mansion constructed ever since.

The construction of the Palais de Versailles was started in 1668 and continued for almost a century. The complex structure today stretches almost a half mile and at one time housed 10,000 people. Le Vau designed the central block around the original Louis XIII building intending the Garden Front, over 400 feet long and bearing the inscription *A toutes les Gloires de la France* ("To all the glories of France"), to be the principal facade. This elevation is

10-8 *The garden side of Versailles is the most distinctive. This facade, rather than the entrance-courtyard elevation, has inspired most later architects.* Courtesy of the Caisse Nationale des Monuments Historiques.

broken into advancing and receding planes, symmetrically arranged, with the larger center section projecting more than those on the ends. The resulting deep pattern of light and shade gives a slight feeling of the Baroque to an otherwise classical French Renaissance exterior. The facade is also divided horizontally in the traditional manner with the inner floor levels visible on the exterior. The lower ground floor is of rusticated stone with regularly spaced large round-arched windows. The *piano nobile* (second level) has a clearly defined order of pilasters and columns laid over the arched windowed surface and above this is an *attic*[7] similar to those found in Roman architecture and with rectangular windows and decorative pilasters. Encircling the top is a balustrade with sculptured figures, both singular and groups, which gives an unbroken skyline. Le Vau died shortly after the construction of Versailles, and in 1679 Jules-Hardouin Mansart[8] was the architect in charge. He built the large extensions on the north and south but did not alter the scale or architectural details. Thus, the whole facade tends to be monotonous and repetitious, and from the garden the building becomes almost a wall with little mass or weight.

The exterior architectural style found at Versailles did not change appreciable during the long reign of Louis XIV nor did it during the reigns of the next two monarchs. It always retained its classic French character and only well into the nineteenth century did it fall from favor.

No historical building is better "tied" to its surroundings than the Palace of Versailles is to its gardens and parks. The masterful planning of Le Nôtre produced a prototype to be repeatedly copied by other European sovereigns. Based upon Italian models, which were attempts to re-create the gardens of

[7] A low wall or story extending above a cornice or entablature and usually treated with inscriptions, sculpture, or with pilasters aligned with the order below.

[8] Jules Mansart was the grandnephew of François Mansart. He is noted particularly for his Church of the Invalides (1680–1691) (where Napoleon is buried) in Paris as well as his work at Versailles.

the ancient Roman villas, the Gardens of Versailles are a combination of carpets of grass, boxwood, mazes, promenades, vistas, arbored walks, flowers, potted trees, sculpture and ornamental vases, lakes, canals, and fountains. Water is an important part of the design, and the reflecting pools catch the images of the buildings. Masses of trees and the fountains with their statues of river gods provide sound and movement. The carefully designed whole, treated as a palace of greenery, is to be viewed and enjoyed both from within the gardens themselves and from the rooms of the Palace. Indeed, the views from the Galérie des Glaces are "truly worthy of a royal glance" and stretch from the Palace to the horizon.

Now almost empty of furniture, the interiors designed by Le Brun for Louis XIV at Versailles are unequaled; they are classic architecture and decoration forced to the utmost in dignity and splendor. The forms used in French Baroque interiors are predominantly rectangular, but simple, geometric curves are also found. The motifs of a *salon* are always clear and the effect can be seen at a glance, but there is always detail that can require longer scrutiny. Decorative devices are almost all classical, derived from the Roman, usually correctly used with the classic orders in purer forms but on a larger scale. The proportions of the rooms are regal—ceiling heights might be 15 feet and the design of a door could be 11 feet. Normal widths of doors and windows are maintained to amplify the heights. The architectural forms in the rooms are large but the ornament on them is skillfully crafted and finer than was done in Italian Baroque. The principle of symmetry was absolute. Formal arrangements of parts were considered mandatory and often a real door is matched by a false door, windows on one wall are balanced by mirrored panels of the same form and treatment, and even in the royal monogram the "L"[9] is always

---

[9] This monogram of interlocking script "L's" is often found incorporated in the decorative ornament. Another symbol, a sun with spreading rays, is also repeatedly used as Louis XIV, called Le Roi Soleil or the Sun King, was frequently compared to Apollo, the classical god of light, music, poetry, prophecy, and manly beauty.

10-9 *The Galerie des Glaces (Hall of Mirrors) of Versailles, although now stripped of its luxurious furnishings, is nevertheless still overwhelming in its richness. The interior architecture is a masterful blend of mirrors, marbles, bronze, gold-leaf, and painted surfaces.* Courtesy of French Government Tourist Office.

doubled. Color is not emphasized but is used to reinforce the lines of the architecture such as colored marble pilaster shafts and panel frames. Paneling is usually painted white, off-white, or gray with the moldings and carved ornament gilded. The brighter colors are found in the paintings, tapestries, hangings, and rugs.

Important public rooms are large and dignified, perhaps none more renowned than the Galérie des Glaces or "Hall of Mirrors," which is 240 feet long, 34 feet wide, and 43 feet high. The entire room is covered by a simple barrel vault upon which Le Brun painted the largest allegorical painting in the world. The ornate and richly decorated entablature is supported by Corinthian pilasters of green marble with gilded capitals. The windows between the pilasters are on one long wall and are matched by mirrors on the opposite wall, hence the name. It is this use of mirrors that transforms a lavish gallery into a fantastic Baroque interior. Mirrors, favored by the Italians, pierce walls so that rooms are enlarged, multiply light—from a window or chandelier, and break off all contact with reality. So it is in the Hall of Mirrors, all the wealth of architectural detail, marble paneling, gilt stucco, bronze ornament, paintings, and even the vistas through the windows are reflected and multiplied. One can only imagine the sumptuous splendor of this room filled with furniture. And what furniture! A contemporary account (c. 1682) tells us that the king's throne and almost all the other furniture was *solid* silver. Also of silver were tubs for bejeweled orange trees, ewers, braziers, chandeliers, candelabras, and sconces hung with cut-glass prisms. Although only an absolute monarch as Louis XIV could afford such luxury, even he was not immune to financial obligations, and by 1689 the melting pot had claimed most of these grandiose pieces.

Before the reign of Louis XIV ended a shift in the life-style began to occur. The court remained at Versailles with all the rigid formality required by the king and he continued to determine the political future of France. But the aristocracy now lived in Paris and the dictates of fashion were now being

10-10 *Adapted from a design in the* Oeuvre *of Juste Aurele Meissonnier published in Paris about 1750, this drawing of shells, rocks, water, and plant life symbolizes the Rococo style.*

decided in the salons of Parisian society. The impressive and oppressive grandeur of the Baroque was discarded; the demand was now for more intimacy, and interior architecture became more frivolous and "smart."

The period from 1700 to 1720 is called the Régence, although, in truth, it was only from 1715–1723 that an actual regency existed.[10] These were years of transition when the pompous formality of the court was being exchanged for a sophisticated atmosphere where wit, intrigue, and enthusiasm for life would be supreme. Although more important when furniture is under consideration, Regency interiors are less formal, smaller, and more intimate; the decorative elements are less massive and less classical; curves are more noticeable and freer; and a lightness permeates everything. When Louis XV began to rule, the trends started earlier in the century were continued and the mature style (c. 1730) became known as Rococo.[11]

Not every interior needs the presence of people as does the Rococo. The rooms should be filled with men and women in lustrous satins, lace, and rich brocades, talking and laughing—playing with all the clever wit, manners, and daring demanded of the day. The interior architecture matches such cleverness, daring, and zest and when the room is studied it is found to be very different from the interiors of the French Baroque.

Significant changes occurred in building plans. First, this is a period of city mansions and townhouses (*hôtels*) rather than châteaux and palaces. Because

[10] The successor of Louis XIV was his great-grandson, a child of five. The new king, Louis XV, had as regent Philippe, II, duc d'Orlèans, a courageous and generous man, who was also a libertine. Although the morals of d'Orlèans are not to be judged here, it is perhaps he and his influence that amplified the increasing sensuality and exuberance that is evidenced in the architecture and furniture of this period. He died after serving eight years as regent and Louis XV began to reign in 1723.

[11] The word Rococo is derived from the French words for rockwork, *rocaille,* and cockleshell, *coquille,* two motifs frequently found in the ornament of the mideighteenth century, but it was not used as the style or period name until the nineteenth century.

of the limited and irregular sites of the buildings of this period, their exteriors and gardens are of much less importance than are interior considerations. Secondly, there is a change toward comfortable and private living with the rooms connected by halls and corridors rather than being in sequence. There are also rooms for both public and private[12] use: drawing rooms, sitting rooms, libraries, boudoirs, dining rooms—every type of room prevalent today except one, the bathroom.

The portions of the rooms are smaller and the rooms are better heated. The ceilings are lower, dimensions are less, and paneling is more narrow and more vertical. (There are almost no horizontal lines.) It is a style of curves. Corners are hidden by ornament or curved in the paneling, room corners are rounded, and there are even rooms where the plan is totally curved. The angle where the wall meets the ceiling is eliminated by a painted and decorated plaster cove. The curves are free and irregular, however, and not geometric. There is a daintiness, a gracefulness in everything. The whole is very linear with moldings reduced almost to lines and every line seems curved, slight deliciously sensuous, and willowy. It is as if a draftsman with a pencil instead of a woodcarver has been responsible for the ornament. Ornament is delicate and tucked a bit here and a bit there—as lightly placed as a touch of laughter or a raised eyebrow. The searching eye can never be still as each minute detail of carving or painting delights and amuses.

The classical details and orders that have remained on the exterior have disappeared; within there are no columns, pilasters, entablatures, or pediments. There is a whole new set of motifs and devices that are French, Rococo French. These include scallop and cockleshells, asymmetrical scrolls

---

[12] Secret rooms, *cabinets particulièrs,* were popular. Entered through hidden openings in the paneling or through the back of wardrobes, these small intimate rooms were used for trysts and confidential meetings.

10-11 *The illusionistic use of mirrors and the dominance of curving, undulating lines are both clearly shown in this engraving, a design by Juste Aurele Meissonnier, c. 1750.*

that suggest waves, strange animals, masks, flowers (roses and daisies), curling foliage, volutes, and symbols of love (Cupid with his bows and arrows in quivers).

Symmetry, so strong and demanding a few years before, is still evident and considered as essential as good manners, but a slight twist here or a change there gives the sparkle of life.

Walls are paneled in carved wood (*boiserie*), and wide panels were often alternated with quite narrow ones. The vertical was always emphasized and any forms approximating a square were shunned. Within the panel moldings delicate floral arrangements or fanciful scenes were sometimes painted. These scenes occasionally were Oriental in feeling (*chinoiserie*) or with playful monkeys engaged in human activities (*singeries*). Some interiors have panels covered with fabric, such as silks or printed cottons, instead of painting. Windows had complicated draperies of fabric matching the wall panels and upholstery. Floors are wood in parquetry designs and with large Rococo patterned rugs in delicate colors.

Colors are no longer dark nor are there heavy masses of color or gold. Colors are like the people who lived in the rooms; light, clear, and fresh. Now somewhat faded, the paneling was painted blue, rose, sea green, putty, lilac, jonquil, or white just touched with gold. With the delicate, colored furniture quite often with flower-strewn carving and upholstery, the entire ensemble took on the appearance of a charming bouquet.

Fireplaces have also undergone a change. The mantle is a low marble frame of fanciful curves and within this is a decorative inner iron frame that protects the marble from the smoke. Almost universally, a mirror is placed above the mantle. In fact, mirrors are even more numerous than before and often take the place of paintings. Although disapproving of such substitution, Lafont de Sainte-Yenne wrote in 1746 in his *Réflexions sur l'état de la peinture en France,*

I admit that these mirrors have advantages that are almost miraculous, in many ways deserving the favor bestowed on them by fashion . . . how could man, the enemy of darkness and of everything that can cause sadness, have helped loving such a device, such an embellishment, which both gives him light and leads him astray and which, in the act of deceiving his eyes, gives him a pleasure that is no deception.

The influence of the style of Louis XV, so charming and feminine, so gay and amusing, extended far beyond the salons of Paris. Every monarch in Europe tried to create a facsimile of Versailles and its newly redecorated apartments in Rococo style. France exported architects, plans, furniture, accessories, and ideas and became the absolute center of the artistic world. In France, the middle class, both in Paris and in the provinces, wholeheartedly accepted the style and continued to do so long after the styles of Louis XVI and the Empire had replaced it in Paris. The Rococo of the court and hôtels of Paris was adapted and simplified, coarsened somewhat, and darkened with more natural wood being used, but still retained the character of Rococo, especially the scale, comfort, and the use of curved lines. It is not unusual to find interiors throughout France that echo the interiors of the mideighteenth century; today this adaptation is called *French provincial*.

The Rococo style, which did not fully develop until after Louis XV became king, reached its apogee about 1760. Although the king continued to prefer this style, it was to be replaced before he died in 1774 by more restrained and classical designs. As early as midcentury the murmur of a reaction to the voluptuous curves of Rococo was beginning to be heard. It was not the king (or even men) who now set the style and mode of the court and society, but women. Women of both royal and lesser rank were the pacesetters, and it was two of the king's favorites who turned the Rococo tide toward classicism.

Madame de Pompadour (1721–1764), a woman of culture and a patroness of learning, was much concerned with the development of the arts and architecture of France. She had sponsored the ceramics works at Sèvres, invested in the Compagnie des Indes, the French equivalent of the British East India Company, and led the vogue in using silks, porcelain, and other Eastern products. It was also she who was interested, financially and intellectually, in the excavations being made at Herculaneum (discovered 1719) and Pompeii (discovered 1748). Between 1749 and 1751 her brother, the future Marquis de Marigny, traveled in Italy in company with a group of classically disposed artists inspecting the newly discovered Roman cities. They returned to France steeped in classical culture. This was not an isolated trip but it does illustrate the renewed interest in antiquity that was stirring throughout Europe.

The other favorite of the king, Madame Du Barry (1746–1793) ordered large quantities of furniture *à la grecque.* By 1771 the style had evolved into the distinct design form called neoclassic or Louis XVI[13], although he was not to be king for three more years.

It is ironical that the neo-classical style, which is perhaps more elegant and restrained than any historical style of furniture and interiors, would also carry the name of Louis XVI. As a young man he was reserved and considered by many as not being too intelligent. More interested in things mechanical, such as lock-making and printing, he took little interest in the intrigues and amorous affairs of the court. As king, his taciturnity and weak will did not help the rapidly worsening political and financial situation in France that had been intensified by the old king's ill-advised decisions and the excessive spending on his mistresses (for example, the 500 diamond necklace ordered for Madame Du Barry and valued at between $300,000 and $400,000, which later was the center of a scandalous and fraudulent incident involving the queen), as well as the youthful frivolities and extravagances of Marie Antoinette. His own decision to help the American colonies in their struggle for independence was fortuitous for the colonies but was disastrous

[13]Louis XVI (1754–1793), was the grandson of Louis XV and was married to Marie Antoinette, the youngest daughter of the queen of Austria, Maria Theresa, when he was 16 and his bride was 15.

10-12 *The monumentality of Versailles is countered by the more humanistic architectural scale of the Petit Trianon; at once one is aware of the intimacy of size. Classical and Renaissance architectural devices are used in new and unrestricted sizes and arrangements. The stringcourse and the strict arrangement of layered orders are no longer employed.* Courtesy of Caisse Nationale des Monuments Historiques.

for France because it was a major factor in hastening the financial plunge toward national bankruptcy. And it was the American Revolution that quickened and roused the enthusiasm for republicanism that eventually toppled the monarchy. Nevertheless, the names of this feeble but well-meaning ruler and final style of eighteenth-century France are both Louis XVI.

The classical movement stimulated a growing respect for "purer" architecture and stripped the exteriors of any Baroque or Rococo tendencies and returned them to more Roman forms. The way was opened for further classicising during the early part of the nineteenth century when, prompted by Napoleon's military campaigns, Greek, Roman, and Egyptian motifs were combined.

One structure noted for its purity of Neoclassic style is the Petit Trianon. Located in the park at Versailles, it has been called the "most superb piece of domestic architecture of the century." The building was designed by J. A. Gabriel in 1762 and took six years to build. As the seasons change so do destinies. The Petit Trianon was suggested by Madame de Pompadour but by the time it was completed she had died and Madame Du Barry received it as a gift from the aging Louis XV. However, it is Marie Antoinette who is most closely associated with it.

The building is approximately a square block with simple proportions and clarity of design. Each facade is almost identical with the others and has a ground floor of smooth faced rusticated stone and the two upper floors are smooth with flat Corinthian pilasters[14] rising both floors to a complete entablature topped by a balustrade. The two floors are not indicated by stringcourses but the "piano nobile" is accented by higher windows than those on the top level. The interiors are perfect examples of the Neoclassical style.

[14] The east facade has no pilasters and the west has columns instead of pilasters.

It is the interior architecture and furniture that more clearly reflect the shift from Rococo to the neoclassic. Favorite rooms in Versailles and other royal residences were remodeled to conform to the new ideal just as rooms had also been changed to reflect the Rococo spirit. It is a style of much beautiful decoration. The charm, intimacy, and delicate qualities so admired in Rococo interiors are retained, but the curvilinear attributes are discarded and straight, unbroken lines are *de rigueur*. If curves are found they are no longer free and irregular, but are instead semicircular or segmental. Lines and proportions are even more slender than in the style of Louis XV, and the decorative elements and moldings are slimmer and more elongated.

Walls are, almost without exception, paneled and painted, and the outer moldings surrounding the rectangular panels are raised and decorated with a classical ornament such as egg and dart. The panel corners frequently have square rosettes in them. Panels are arranged in symmetrical groups of wide and narrow dimensions, and elongated and subtle classical arabesques are found in the narrow panels. Classical orders and details are once again used with taste and discrimination.

Colors are pale, and white or off-white perhaps a delicate touch of gold were favored. Grisaille paintings imitating bas-relief scuptured panels are frequently used above doors and mantels.

Ornament and motifs include all those found in Roman and Greek architecture; egg and dart, leaf and dart, and bead and reel moldings; dentils, honeysuckle, frets, guilloches, arabesques and *rinceaux,* rosettes, masks, trophies, garlands, swags and wreaths of roses, and daisies and chrysanthemums tied with ribbons and bows are but some of the motifs used. All are treated with utmost delicacy and sophistication.

The adverse political situation in France continued to deepen and after several feeble attempts to stop the rush toward insurrection, the seemingly inevitable happened. Versailles was attacked by a mob and the king and his family were taken prisoners on October 5–6, 1789. The period of Louis XVI came abruptly to an end. The next decade was a period of turmoil and discord that did not encourage fresh ideas or the need for the refinements of civilization. The government was unstable and human destinies rose and fell as did the guillotine.[15]

It was not until the ascendancy of Napoleon Bonaparte to power following his campaigns in Italy and his brilliant victory in Egypt at the Battle of the Pyramids that the political atmosphere became conducive to the re-establishment of culture. Napoleon was crowned emperor at Notre Dame Cathedral in Paris on December 2, 1804, and the Empire period officially began.

As with every period after violent change, those in power require the accoutrements denoting their prestige. And so it was at the beginning of the nineteenth century. Fortunately some of the architects, cabinetmakers, and artisans who were responsible for the masterful designs of the neoclassic architecture and furniture were still alive and opened their workshops to fill the new rush of orders.

The democratic aspirations of the times were easily associated with the democratic city-states of ancient Greece and Roman independence, and the classical trends were thus reinforced. Exterior architecture became even more dry in the interpretations of Roman architecture and no one thought it strange to use strict classical architectural schemes for buildings whose uses did not exist in ancient times, for example, hospitals, government offices, and, later, even railroad stations.

Interiors continued the traditions started during the reign of Louis XVI because columns and classical details did not refer directly to the king, but the rooms became more Roman, copied from the recent discoveries at Pompeii. Columns without flutes or reduced to pilasters were frequently

[15] Considered a humane method of execution, the guillotine claimed over 2,500 victims during the Reign of Terror from January, 1793, to July, 1794. The king and queen were both executed during this period, Louis XVI on January 21, 1793, and Marie Antoinette, October 16, 1793.

10-13 *In the Château de la Malmaison, the fabric-hung bedroom of
the Empress Josephine is based upon
a Roman campaign tent. The elaborate gilded bed (c. 1810) is supported by cornucopiae and swans,
and rests on a raised platform.*

used around the walls in place of panels and the favorite capital was Doric.
Walls were painted, often to imitate marble, and although off-white was the
more popular wall color, dark greens and reds (again influenced by Pompeii)
were occasionally found, first as upholstery colors and later as the color of
wall hangings or wallpaper. The effect is masculine and in sharp contrast to
the femininity of both the Rococo and neoclassic styles of Ancien Régime.

Ornament and decorative details continued to be influenced by the ancient
civilizations, including Egypt, plus the military symbols of Roman and the
Napoleonic armies. The use of bronze and gold colored ornament contributed to the heaviness of the style.

A major achievement in the interior design of the Empire period was the
transformation of the Château de la Malmaison. Madame Bonaparte, later to
become Empress Josephine, acquired the building in 1799 and the architects
Percier and Fontaine designed the interiors and furniture for the music room
and library. The result, with columns and paneling of mahogany, was a new
elegance and contributed greatly to the development and acceptance of the
Empire style.

Most of the royal residences had been stripped of furniture during the
tumultuous days of the Revolution and, consequently, the demand for
furniture was far greater than it was for buildings. It is the furniture of the
first years of the nineteenth century that attains a distinct style more than
does the architecture. This furniture is discussed in Chapter 14.

Concurrent with the development in one country is that in another and the
interrelations and influential forces exerted by one to the other are so
intertwined that it is often difficult to divide them in a reasonable and
comprehensible way. This is the problem now. The significant architecture,
both exterior and interior, of France has just been discussed from about 1500
to 1800, a period of 300 years. Very little has been said about what was
happening architecturally in other countries. Did France so overshadow the
rest of the world with such developments as the châteaux of the Loire Valley

and the superb palaces of the Louvre and Versailles that nothing else is of consequence? Not at all. Although French influence was certainly manifest in Europe, the developments elsewhere were significant, especially in England.

It is now time to cross the English Channel to Great Britain and see what architecture had been developing there. The clock must also be turned back to the period when the spirit of the Renaissance penetrated the Gothic "mantle" that clothed England for so long. England was the last to fall under the influence of the Renaissance, and as was the case everywhere, the first indication of a change in style is in ornament—then in form.

English architecture has a tradition unlike that of continental building. Being isolated from the rest of Europe, its forms have developed somewhat by themselves. Climate and materials have also influenced English architecture. For example, the western portals of the great Gothic cathedrals and churches in England have porches that shelter the nave and side aisles from the blasts of wind, whereas in France the doors open directly into the church. Windows are also much larger in England to admit more light and warmth from the sun. Some of the stone, such as the granites of Cornwall and Devonshire and the sandstone of Yorkshire, are very hard and have made sculptured ornament almost impossible. Brick as a building material has also been used since the time of the Romans, and, as will be seen, is of architectural importance during the sixteenth, seventeenth, and eighteenth centuries. No place can claim timbered roofs as varied and intricate as in England. The notable accomplishments in wood construction are to a large extent the result of the magnificent oak forests that covered large parts of England. And since no part of England is far from the sea, in almost every town there was someone familiar with boatbuilding and its requisite woodworking skills.

The ceilings of late Gothic buildings, whether they were wood or stone, are far more elaborate than their French counterparts. One that is a culminating success of the English builders in the medieval tradition is the *fan vaulted* ceiling of the Henry VII Chapel, which extends from the east end of West-

10-14 *The elaborate half-timbered construction of this inn in Warwick, England, is a gaudy display of the woodworkers skill.*

minster Abbey. The ceiling is covered with lace-like tracery and pendants that hang down seemingly defying gravity. The date of this Gothic marvel is of interest. This chapel, the final resting place for Henry VII and his queen, was built between 1503–1519 (100 years *after* the Dome of the Cathedral of Florence, and contemporary with the beginning of the Château de Chambord). A bronze screen of Gothic tracery encloses the tomb. The tomb itself is *not* Gothic, but is a choice example of early Renaissance design. The black marble tomb (1512) has Corinthian pilasters and winged cherubs, and is the first example of English Renaissance design extant.

The coronation site of English kings through the centuries, Westminster Abbey is a triumph of English Gothic architecture. Said to be built on the site of an A.D. 616 church, it has been continuously built, torn down, and rebuilt, and stands today with all the architectural styles from Early English and Norman (Romanesque) to Gothic, and the monuments and tombs within reflect succeeding styles and periods. Originally the church was but one part of a triple group—monastery, church, and royal palace. The church stands alone today; the others are gone—torn down or burned; the last, the palace, occupied the site of the present Houses of Parliament.

Henry VIII came to the throne in 1509 upon the death of his father Henry VII. Certainly aware of the Renaissance and having brought Italian craftsmen to England, Henry VIII, nevertheless, did not recognize the true extent of the Renaissance until 1520. In that year under the influence of his lord chancellor, Thomas Cardinal Wolsey, he amiably met Francois I of France in unsurpassable splendor on the "Field of the Cloth of Gold."[16] The seeds of the Renaissance were now sown and in the fertile soil of England began to bear fruit immediately.

---

[16] The two monarchs met near Calais for three weeks to discuss an alliance and during that time the elaborate and magnificent tournaments, feasts, and masses gave the meeting place its name.

Hampton Court Palace stands today as a remarkable example of this early architecture (Tudor). Started by Cardinal Wolsey about 1520, it was filled with beautiful and rich furniture and tapestries. Its magnificence apparently caused the king to be envious as it was given to him in 1526 and he subsequently increased its size considerably but in the same architectural style. The original brick sections (on the west and north) are basically medieval in form with turrets, towers, and battlements, but the Renaissance exerts itself with the formal layout of both the plan and the facade and the use of stringcourses on the exterior. The brickwork is justly famous, a mellow red with thick mortar joints and laid in a diaper pattern formed by darker headers. Details, ornaments, and the center *oriel window* are picked out in white stone.[17]

The conflict between Henry VIII and the Pope in Rome was responsible for a sharp increase in the number of houses constructed. With the passing of the Act of Supremacy by Parliament in 1534, which made the king the supreme head of the Church of England, and the passing of subsequent laws in 1536 and 1539, which suppressed monasteries and confiscated all monastic properties, land was available to favorites of the king and to the rapidly expanding and new class of wealthy merchants and traders who were eager to build homes in keeping with their wealth and newly elevated stations in life. The new style with its grand proportions and noble design was exactly what they demanded. To supply the technical force needed, foreign artists versed in Renaissance forms began to emigrate to England and continued to do so through the seventeenth century. It was also fashionable for the young men of wealthy families to travel on the Continent and especially in Italy, and so again the Renaissance spirit was reinforced.

During the long and prosperous reign of Elizabeth I (1558–1603) and

10-15 *The west facade of Hampton Court Palace, built in the early sixteenth century combines medieval and Renaissance architectural and decorative elements. The battlements along the upper edge of the building, the verticality of the towers, the Tudor arches, the oriel window, and the multiple, decorated chimneys reflect the middle ages, yet the formality of the overall design and the stringcourses indicate a rudimentary awareness of Renaissance architectural style.* Courtesy of British Tourist Authority.

---

[17] The structure had an extensive addition by Sir Christopher Wren attached to the east and south in the late seventeenth century, which is Renaissance in style.

10-16 *Red brick with white stone trim, Tudor arches, and towers guarding the entrance, this high school facade is typical of many built in the 1920s based upon the entrance to Hampton Court Palace.*

10-17 *Reflecting the gradual shift to Renaissance forms, Hardwick Hall (1590–1597) appears to be virtually all windows divided horizontally by stringcourses, prompting the saying "Hardwick Hall, more glass than wall." The bay window towers are topped by scrollwork and the initials "ES" for Elizabeth, Countess of Shrewsbury.*

continuing through the reign of James I (1603–1625) many manor and country houses were built in England. These mansions were designed outwardly with plans in the shapes of E's, C's, or H's instead of the inward oriented hollow square that was common before. More elaborate settings were thus required with forecourts, gateways, and drives on the entrance side and with formal gardens, terraces, and parks on the other sides.

The two-or three-story exteriors, brick or stone, have a formal regularity about them with projecting bays, strong stringcourses, and walls pierced with large, mullioned windows. It was common to have an elaborate balustrade at the roof line that often partially hid the low sloping roof and many chimneys.

Plans invariably consisted of a great hall, a grand staircase, and a long gallery with smaller rooms such as bedrooms, chapel, kitchen, and service rooms arranged around them. The great hall, a holdover from medieval times, retained its central position in both plan and use. Two stories high, the walls are covered with oak paneling to a height of 8 or 10 feet with the walls above decorated with armour, portraits, or trophies. The ceiling was either of elaborate open timber construction or of molded plaster. At the entrance end a carved oak screen separated the hall from the entrance and the kitchen. The grand staircase with its carved[18] newel posts and balustrades was located near the great hall in an open stairwell and changed direction at a landing about halfway to the top. This was a recent development in England (the design originated in Spain); stairways were previously small and between walls.

The long gallery is unique to the late sixteenth-century English manor house. Long, low, and narrow, it is lavishly decorated with elaborate fire-

[18]The carved and molded ornament is a strange blend of Gothic and Renaissance forms and appears in all materials and on panels, pilasters, ceilings, friezes, fireplaces, and furniture. A favorite was *strapwork*, which resembles leather straps that interlace forming geometric patterns and appears to be fastened to the background surface with nails or rivets.

places and ornamental plaster ceilings and the walls between the large windows are paneled or covered with tapestries. Each room is filled with light and air and it is this, perhaps more than anything, that distinguishes Elizabethan or almost any later English home from those in other countries.

Houses of less pretentious plan also began to appear in England. As the population increased[19] and it was no longer possible or necessary to live within the walls of the castle, smaller homes were built outside this protection. The simplest home consisted of but one room and with an exterior form faintly like that of a Greek temple—a rectangular block with a sloping roof and two gable ends. As the family's resources increased, additional rooms were added where they were considered most desirable with reference to need, site, weather and view orientation. The resulting structure with its chimney pots, roof angles, and pinnacles is picturesque and varied. The development of the fireplace[20] in Tudor times permitted a second floor that often extended beyond the lower walls. These overhangs were frequently decorated with pendants similar in basic form to those found in the fan vaulting of the Henry VII Chapel. Made of local materials, the houses could be of stone or *half-timbered*, an exposed framework of wooden posts, beams, and braces with the spaces between filled with various materials and then stuccoed. Roofs were either of split slate, or tile or were thatched with straw.

These mansions and smaller homes are the ancestors of most of the houses today—not the urban palaces of Italy or the châteaux of France—and most Americans immediately feel completely familiar with them. The whole gives the effect of a comfortable, cheerful, and informal life within.

During the first half of the seventeenth century the developing English Renaissance architecture continued to be domestic rather than religious, but

[19] The population of London alone increased from 100,000 to nearly 250,000 during the reign of Elizabeth I.

[20] Many English houses lacked chimneys as late as 1500.

10-18 *The Long Gallery of Haddon Hall (1567–1584) is 109 feet by 18 feet with the side wall broken by room-like bays. The molded plaster ceiling, large windows, ornamental chimney pieces, and paneling are all unique to late sixteenth-century English architecture.*

10-19 *One of the most famous Tudor cottages, Anne Hathaway's Cottage near Stratford-on-Avon, has a roof thatched with straw. Beside the house is an excellent example of an informal, "natural" English garden, which, if properly designed, is really a tour-de-force in careful garden planning.*

10-20 *English architecture was admired in the 1920s and early 1930s in the United States. The "small Tudor cottage" with simulated thatched roof is in Illinois.*

10-21 *The formality of Palladian architecture marks the facade of Inigo Jones' Banqueting House in London.*

the buildings were more likely to be designed by one person rather than by several as in the previous century. The designs were still a mixture of medieval and Renaissance forms and ornament, freely mixed and neither appreciably dominant. Inigo Jones (1573–1652) is primarily responsible for the eventual whole-hearted acceptance of Italian Renaissance architecture in England.

Inigo Jones, born of an obscure family in London, first visited Italy in about 1601 and returned to England four years later as a designer of costumes and scenery for court festivals. He visited Paris in 1609 and returned to Italy in 1613 for a year and a half. He was then named surveyor of the king's world and began to design the buildings that have secured his fame. Jones introduced Palladian Renaissance architecture to England with his Banqueting House in Whitehall, London.

Built between 1619 and 1622, the facade is what interests us most. About 120 feet long and 70 feet high, it is a thoroughly considered example of the correct classical proportions as stated by Palladio. It is not based upon previous structures but is an original interpretation by Jones. The Banqueting House exterior is divided into three levels; the bottom, considerably more narrow than the upper two which are equal in height, serves as a podium or pedestal. The entire surface is rusticated stone and the two upper levels have superimposed orders with windows between the columns or pilasters as the case might be (the four in the center are columns). The windows are all rectangular but the lower of the two main rows have straight cornices. The entablatures are broken and project outward above each column and pilaster. The whole is topped by a simple balustrade. The interior is but one room, two stories high. A gallery encircles the room at the level of the second exterior order. The whole, exterior and interior, is severe, classical, and pure.

Two important historical events, which caused considerable alteration in English architectural development, occurred halfway through the seventeenth century. The English Civil War erupted and the king, Charles I, was tried and executed in 1649. The period immediately prior to this was a time of great destruction of both religious and private property. The ensuing Commonwealth under the stern leadership of Oliver Cromwell lasted for eleven years and was a time of Puritan austerity when anything that appealed to the senses was banned and no architecture of any consequence was built. In 1660, Charles II returned from exile in Holland and France to restore the monarchy in England. The king had spent considerable time with his cousin Louis XIV, and upon Charles' return to England attempted to create the luxury and lavishness that he had seen at the French court.

The second important event was the Great Fire of 1666, which burned a large section of London. This caused a flurry of building of homes, public buildings, and churches to restore those that were destroyed. Sir Christopher Wren (1632–1723) became the person who set new standards of design. Wren was a scholar with a strong background in mathematics and did not become an architect until he was in his thirties. He was greatly influenced by the French just as Inigo Jones had been by Palladio. Wren did not go to Italy but had been in Paris in 1665 and there had met Bernini (who was brought from Italy to design an addition for the Louvre), Mansart, and others who were responsible for the masterful palaces and châteaux.

Wren designed few residential structures—an exception is his large addition to Hampton Court Palace—but he was one of three royal commissioners who formulated standards for new houses in which wall thickness, floor heights, and materials (brick) were specified. These standards set precedents for many zoning and construction regulations that were later used in other cities and towns.

Wren's masterpiece is Saint Paul's Cathedral in London (1675–1710). Its plan is a Latin cross, 514 feet in length and 250 feet wide. The crossing is covered by a dome 112 feet in diameter sitting on a high drum. The total height is 366 feet. Wren, although more receptive to French Baroque than

10-22 *The majestic dome of Saint Paul's Cathedral by Sir Christopher Wren and based upon Michelangelo's design of the dome on Saint Peter's Basilica in the Vatican, has, in turn, inspired countless designers of domes since it was built. The cast-iron dome (finished 1865) on the Capitol in Washington, D.C., clearly reflects its heritage.* Photograph of Saint Paul's Cathedral courtesy of British Tourist Authority. Photograph of the Capitol dome courtesy of Architect of the Capitol.

10-23 *Based on the church steeples originated by Wren, St. Martin-in-the-Fields, London (1722–1726), by James Gibbs has a steeple of singular beauty.*

Italian, nevertheless, must have been influenced by Saint Peter's Basilica in Rome. The general plan is similar and although individual details and the facade are not the same, one cannot help but compare the two. Saint Paul's is smaller but its dome[21], more visible than Michelangelo's, is considered by many to be the finest in Europe. Another interesting comparison between Saint Paul's and Saint Peter's is that the former had only one architect and was constructed in 35 years, during the episcopate of one bishop; Saint Peter's had 13 successive architects, and took over 100 years to build, during the pontificates of 20 popes.

In addition to Saint Paul's, Wren was responsible for the design of 52 churches that replaced those destroyed by fire. These designs, perhaps even more than Saint Paul's have influenced subsequent church architecture. Each, fitted upon an irregular site, is a model of simplicity and restraint, and the first to be designed for Protestant worship rather than the Roman Catholic ritual. The plans, facades, and general mass of these churches are Renaissance in design but Wren added a new element, a steeple. Rising high above the roofs of the surrounding buildings, these spires, based upon Gothic prototypes, begin at ground level as a rectangular mass and are incorporated into the facade of the church, often in the center. Designed in ascending stages, each level is smaller in plan than the one below and often is polygonal or round in outline ending with a slender pyramid or conical spire at the top. Each stage is decorated with orders and other Renaissance ornament that increase in elegance in relation to the height. Wren's variations on this scheme produced some of the most beautiful church steeples ever designed and although many of these churches were destroyed during World War II, London still has one of the most interesting and distinctive skylines in the

10-24 *This church in New England is obviously patterned after the churches in London built after the Great Fire.*

[21]The dome and drum of Saint Paul's was the inspiration for the dome covering the rotunda of the United States Capitol Building in Washington, D.C. (finished 1865). Slightly smaller, 98 feet in diameter, it is constructed mostly of cast iron whereas that of Saint Paul's is made of brick and lead-covered wood.

world.[22] These churches set a precedent that, even today, is hard to improve upon, and the steeples have been copied and adapted both in England and in the United States since that time.

The end of the Commonwealth and the return of Charles II brought an increase in the construction of domestic architecture as it did that of the church. Houses developed throughout England with even better standards of comfort and convenience, and the most modest cottage became a solidly built form. Two types of residential structures emerged and by the Georgian period[23] were fairly well resolved. Both continued to use forms and details that were developed in the Renaissance but one was more cognate with Palladian concepts and the other was more Baroque. The grander houses tended to be Baroque and the greatest and most monumental mansion of this type is Blenheim Palace (1702–1720) by Sir John Vanbrugh, the home of the Duke of Marlborough. Although larger than others, its basic plan and orientation is typical. It is designed symmetrically in both plan and elevations. The plan is no longer a simple "E" and "H" but consists of a central block raised on a terrace with a broad flight of steps leading to it from a large courtyard (three acres). The entrance to the building is on the north and is centered under an imposing two-story "temple front." Extending from each side of the block and forward are *quadrants* and colonnades that connect this structure to wings housing kitchens and stables arranged around smaller courtyards. The main structure contains the great hall, salon or drawing room, gallery, internal courts, and numerous corridors and rooms. The whole is set in extensive formal gardens.

10-25 *The entrance court of Blenheim Palace showing the main block of the house, the curved quadrant, and a portion of the structure housing the Great Gallery.*

[22] In the last decade, several tall buildings have been constructed in London, and if the trend continues unabated this distinctive churchspire studded skyline will be obliterated.

[23] The term Georgian is applied to most of eighteenth-century English architecture and includes the reigns of Anne (1702–1714), George I (1714–1727), George II (1727–1760), and George III (1760–1820).

10-26 *The general outline of Blenheim Palace can only suggest its size. Between the two large service courts, the Kitchen Court on the left and the Stable Court on the right, is a distance of 350 feet.*

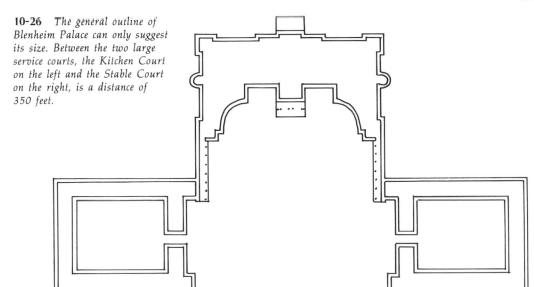

10-27 *The classicism of Palladio returned to England during the eighteenth century. Chiswick House (c. 1725) by William Kent and the Earl of Burlington has a square plan topped with a dome. However, the porticoes are only on two sides. The dome sits on an octagonal drum and the interior plan is different, but it is obviously based upon the Villa Rotunda.*

As early as 1630 in Holland there emerged an orderly, symmetrical residential structure that combined Palladian ideals of classical architecture with the late Gothic form of steep-roofed Netherlandish houses. This house form gained favor in England during the seventeenth century[24] and became the type that was generally used for less pretentious houses in both town and country in the eighteenth century.

Of rectangular plan, these houses are most often brick laid in Flemish bond and have symmetrically designed facades of two or three floors. The entrance is in the center and has a columned, or at least a pedimented, door frame of stone or wood. The stone or white painted wood contrasts pleasantly with the red brick. The windows are the double-hung sash type instead of the older casements and are arranged evenly on each side with little decoration around the openings except on the richest homes. Six or nine panes of glass are in each sash. Frequently, quoins of stone or brick are on the corners of the structural block and stringcourses sometimes are found indicating the floor levels inside. The walls are topped by a strong, well-designed cornice of brick, stone, or wood and the roof is hipped with dormers and large chimneys. This dignified exterior remained in favor for almost a century and reflects the refined and elegant interiors that are found inside.

The floorplans are as formal as the facades. A hall with a staircase occupies the center of the building and the principal rooms are arranged on each side

[24] Illustrated architectural books were very popular and were published by many of the leading architects. (A new edition of Palladio's *I quattro libri dell' Architettura* was published in 1715–1716.) During the sixteenth century architectural books were almost exclusively Italian or French, but by the seventeenth-century Dutch and English publications were available and these included many engravings of Dutch and English designs in addition to the usual ones of Italian and French origin. These books showing plans, elevations, and details such as doors, windows, and fireplaces were not only for the architectural connoisseur but were increasingly published for the builder and craftsman.

on the different floors. The basement contains the kitchen and storerooms and the servants' quarters are there or under the roof.

The interiors of both the larger Baroque mansions and the more modest, but no less elegant, Palladian homes are similar except in their size and proportions and in the wealth of decoration. The earlier interiors are paneled in natural oak with the panels measuring three or four feet wide and raised above the surface with the surrounding moldings of bold classical design. In sharp contrast to the quiet dignity of the walls are the white ceilings of elaborately molded plaster in broad classical designs. Garlands of strongly modeled fruit and leaves divide the white exapnse into areas—perhaps a large circle in the center with smaller shapes filling out the composition. The fireplace[25] and chimney piece above provide the most dominant center of interest. The mantel is usually a simple marble frame with a single panel or decorative painting above. Over and hanging on each side of this area is frequently found a rich, fully carved, and realistic garland of fruit, trophies, and foliage. A brilliant display of carved ornament holds the eye and provides the sparkle of full light and shade in an otherwise rather subdued room. The application of such high reliefs of realistic forms found in the ceiling and carved fireplace ornament was introduced by Sir Christopher Wren and his master carver Grinling Gibbons.[26] The rooms, although dark, are not gloomy and with the furniture upholstered in rich and colored fabrics, Oriental rugs, and the ever present bright Chinese porcelains, the feeling is one of vital masculine strength.

10-28 *A combination of brick and stone, and a formal Palladianism marked the English houses based on Dutch prototypes.*

---

[25] Coal came into use at this time, but about the only change was the addition of a basket grate in the fireplace.

[26] A native of Holland, Gibbons (1648–1720) and his Dutch assistants produced the most vigorous and brilliant wood carving of the period, and although it is open to criticism for its overrealism, these somber rooms owe much of their success to Gibbons's carving skill.

These strong, dark rooms became lighter and even more grand as the Georgian period progressed. This is primarily a period of interiors rather than exteriors just as it was in contemporary France. But the interiors in England have few curves and are far less feminine; the rectangle and the straight line were retained during the entire century. These rooms are often less intimate than in France and with larger proportions, especially the height of the ceilings. It is not unusual to find in the great homes halls with ceilings thirty or forty feet high.

The walls are not paneled in wood but are made of plaster, and the wall surface is broken with architectural details and moldings. Ceilings continue to be molded but are less heavy. Until the middle of the century the ceilings take on a Rococo attitude with cherubs and garlands but then return to classical designs. Everything is painted white and it becomes impossible to tell what is structure and what is applied. It is a different kind of interior —conscious of architecture and excellence in design.

Smaller homes reflect the trends found in the larger mansions. Yet even in the smallest house the walls might still be paneled in wood, but everything is white in the best dignified Georgian manner.

The second half of the century saw a change in Georgian architecture —what might be called Antiquarian in contrast to the earlier Anglo-Palladian. The devices and standards used by Palladio are based upon historical architecture, to be sure, but in England, as in France, a renewed interest in ancient Rome occurred. This was partly because of the recent archaeological discoveries and partly because of romantic inclinations. Architecture became more Roman than Renaissance, and even buildings of strong Palladian design began to have Roman elements added. Greek forms became very popular and heralded the beginning of the nineteenth-century style called Greek Revival.

The formal principles of Palladio were not only applied to individual

10-29 *Whole streets and squares were lined with shops and houses with formally designed neoclassical facades by the 1820s.*

buildings but to groups to town houses and whole urban designs. The most notable in England are those in Bath, the Circus, begun in 1754 by John Wood I, and the Royal Crescent (1767–1775) by John Wood II, his son. Both the Circus—a circle of town houses—and the Royal Crescent—a semicircle fronting on a park—present splendid unified facades of a single correctly proportioned order with windows and doors, placed between the columns.

It has been said that the Gothic spirit never died in England. It might well be true for structures that used Gothic forms, details, and elements were being built as early as midcentury. This was a deliberate return to more romantic areas and were attempts to recreate them architecturally. Many of the leading architects, including Wren and Vanburgh, had designed Gothic structures, usually to match older buildings, but the new interest was much stronger and was a design trend rather than just a group of isolated commissions. Built between 1747 and 1776, Strawberry Hill, the home of Horace Walpole, is an outstanding early example of "Gothick" and strangely, it has many Renaissance characteristics that have Gothic details—the reverse of 250 years before. The Gothic trend was first more apparent in interior and furniture design but it continued and developed in the next century into the full-blown Gothic revival or neo-Gothic style.

Whimsical and exotic sources provided inspiration for other buildings and there are examples of Chinese and Indian structures that are far from authentic. But these buildings indicate a searching for nonclassical and non-Renaissance forms. The Royal Pavilion in Brighton (1815–1821) is such a building. Remodeled by John Nash, the multiribbed, onion-domed exterior and fantastic interiors are now in the unlikely mixture of "Hindoo" and Chinese with some Gothic added for good measure.

No study of late Georgian architecture can omit the work of Robert Adam (1728–1792) and his brother James (1730–1794). Noted for their interiors more than for their complete structures, they have given their name to a style

that is delicate, refined, intimate, and freely based upon classical motifs.[27]
This is an extremely formal style with every object, ornament, detail, and
form within the room carefully selected to give complete unity to the total
composition.

The plan of an Adam interior is often elliptical or rectangular with
semicircular, segmental, or octagonal end walls or with apses as in the Roman
basilica. Regardless of what the plan might be, it is always strictly symmetrical.

The walls are decorated with classical architectural devices such as
columns, pilasters, entablatures, arched niches, and medallions enclosing
classical bas-reliefs. If there are panels, they are sunk into the wall and
frequently have delicate arabesques painted on them. Ceilings are no longer
heavily ornamented with strongly modeled figures and garlands but are
delicately decorated with arrangements of octagons, fans, and ellipses that
are reminiscent of Roman stucco decoration, and tinted and painted in a most
exquisite way. Color has returned to interiors; walls and ceilings are generally pale green or cream with panels of purple or faded rose.

Floors are polished wood, usually oak, but are covered with specially
designed carpets that have patterns that compliment the design of the ceiling.
Fireplaces are not always treated as the focal point of the room and are
smaller than they were previously. The mantels are made of marble or of
painted and carved wood. The Adam mantel is very beautiful and consists of
an entablature with a wide cornice that forms a shelf and usually on each side

[27] Robert Adam, a native of Scotland, lived in Rome for some time and did archaeological
work there and in Dalmatia (now part of Yugoslavia) where he measured the ruins of the
Palace of the Roman Emperor Diocletian. He and his brother were thoroughly familiar with
the true classic spirit of design and decoration in addition to Renaissance adaptations of
Roman forms. He was particularly knowledgeable about the stucco decoration used by the
Romans.

are decorative supports such as slender columns or pilasters. Fine carving and detail is judiciously used that enhances the delicate handsomeness of the mantel. The increased use of coal brought a refinement in the design of the fireplace grates and equipment. One is always aware in an Adam interior of the concern for exquisite detail; no detail is missed however small or seemingly insignificant. The decorative ornament is almost always inspired by Pompeii or by Greece and some of the most widely used ornaments are the rosette, honeysuckle, fret, classical urn forms, and fluted surfaces.

The neoclassical elegance attained by the brothers Adam has often been compared to that of the Louis XVI period in France. Both are called neoclassical and both freely interpret Roman and Greek forms rather than slavishly adhere to the standards set by Renaissance architecture critics. But it was in England that the first neoclassic interiors were developed and much of the credit for this development is given to Robert and James Adam.

11 Architecture: American to About 1800

The discovery of the New World was a product of the Renaissance; the insatiable quest for knowledge and scientific investigation promoted the exploration of the globe. The Renaissance developed in Italy and although several of the early explorers of North and South America, including Christopher Columbus, John Cabot (Giovanni Caboto), Giovanni da Verrazano, and Amerigo Vespucci, were born there, Italy did not play a major role in the development of the New World. Five other nations were most responsible for the explorations and discoveries that led to the settling of Europeans in North and South America. France, Spain, Portugal, Holland, and England sponsored the early navigators who braved the unknown waters of the Atlantic in search of riches and new routes to the Orient. These five nations were later to establish settlements on the shores of the newly discovered continents.

After the initial voyages for Spain made by Christopher Columbus in the final decade of the fifteenth century, adventurers from other countries investigated and claimed parts of the Americas for their sponsors. The Portuguese confined their exploration to South America, but the remaining four countries "shared" what is now the United States and Canada on the North American continent, each vying for supremacy during the sixteenth and seventeenth centuries.

The Spanish claimed the southeastern and south-central regions because of the expeditions of Juan Ponce de León and Hernando de Soto and the southwest because of Francisco Vásquez de Coronado. The French concentrated their activities in the north-central and northeastern portions after the discoveries of Jacques Cartier, Sieur de La Salle, Père Jacques Marquette, and Louis Jolliet, but although Giovanni da Verrazano had discovered New York Harbor in 1524 under the patronage of Francois I, the French did not claim the middle-Atlantic area. The Dutch settled the Hudson River valley and Manhattan Island after Henry Hudson (an English navigator who was sailing under the Dutch flag) had sailed up the river to where Albany is now located.

The English, after the voyages of John Cabot and his son Sebastian, the cartographer, settled most of the remaining eastern Atlantic seaboard. Yet it was England that made the most lasting impression on the land north of the Rio Grande River. The victory in the four-way struggle for domination was achieved through colonization. The English settled the land; out of the wilderness they created homes, farms, towns, and eventually cities. From no other country did colonists come in such numbers.[1]

The Dutch were the first to succumb to English domination. In 1664, 55 years after the voyage of Henry Hudson, their colony, New Netherlands, passed to the English. In this short time, however, the Dutch developed the Hudson River valley and along the banks were manor houses, farms, and towns. The architectural forms of the Dutch, steep-roofed houses with crow-stepped gables, decorative brickwork and ornamental tiles within, were to persist long after the colony and settlements were renamed—New Amsterdam on Manhattan Island at the mouth of the Hudson became New York and far up the river Beverwyck became Albany.

The French and Spanish did not attempt colonization to the degree that the English and Dutch did. The French established forts along the fur-trading routes and the major navigable rivers from Canada to the Gulf of Mexico. Some of these forts developed into permanent settlements but their inhabitants were mostly transitory, remaining only for a short period of time and then returning to France. The centers of French rule followed the social and cultural patterns of feudal times, and the *seigneur* and *curé* ruled their followers with a strong and disciplined hand. Always closely aware of current French fashion, the latest clothes, a few pieces of fine French furniture, and a new tune were often in evidence in even the most remote settlement.

11-1 *The famous "Five Flies" Restaurant in Amsterdam was once a private house. Built in 1627, it is similar to houses built during the seventeenth-century Dutch tenancy of the Hudson valley in America.*

---

[1] It is estimated that over 50 per cent of the inhabitants in the United States today can trace lineage to English immigrants settling in Virginia and New England prior to the nineteenth century.

11-2 *In the older section of New Orleans, wrought-iron balconies and railings
may still be seen, a holdover from the days
of French rule.*

11-3 *The Governor's Palace in Santa Fe,
New Mexico, was used as the official residence of Spanish, Mexican, and American
governors for 300 years, and since 1914
has been the Museum of New Mexico.*

However, in the vast area once ruled by France there is little to indicate, except in place names, the long French domination. The architectural influences left are extremely small except in New Orleans and Louisiana and elsewhere, to an even lesser degree, in eastern Canada. New Orleans was laid out in 1718 with a gridiron plan and had four houses at each street intersection. Within fifty years there were over 500 houses, their floors raised high above the ground and their roofs swinging out to make porches. Some had graceful wrought-iron balconies, fences, and decorations fabricated by imported French and local artisans. This use of delicate wrought iron has continued and today ornamental wrought iron is associated with old New Orleans. Otherwise, examples of architecture found in contemporary America that were based upon French prototypes, were influenced not by the design of indigenous buildings but by that of structures in France itself.

The French, after almost 250 years of exploration and rule, relinquished their lands east of the Mississippi River to England at the conclusion of the French and Indian War (1754–1763). And in 1803, with the Louisiana Purchase, French rule in North America came to an end.

The region held by Spain, although extensive and stretching at one time across the entire continent from Florida to California, also was absorbed by the stronger English-dominated culture. Not until after the American Revolution did the extent of Spanish rule began to diminish[2], with the result that native architectural forms based upon Spanish prototypes are more frequent and still are an important influence in building.

The Spanish architecture of Florida has long disappeared except for the outstanding Castillo de San Marcos in Saint Augustine (1672–1756), and

[2] Florida was purchased during the presidency of James Madison in 1819. Texas was annexed in 1845 and following the Mexican War the major portion of the remaining Spanish territory became part of the United States in 1848. The last portion that had once been Spanish was the Gadsden Purchase, a narrow strip on the southern edge of Arizona and New Mexico acquired in 1853.

though an excellent example of seventeenth-century defense construction, it is only of passing interest in this survey. The architecture of the Southwest and California is more relevant to this discussion.

Not until 1598, when ox-drawn wagons of 400 colonists arrived from Mexico, were permanent settlements to appear in the Southwest. In what is now New Mexico a unique type of building was developed in which imported Spanish forms are incorporated into native and ancient Pueblo techniques.[3] The Governor's Palace in Santa Fe (1609–1614) is a most impressive example and is probably the oldest surviving structure built for the use of white men in the United States. One story high, built of adobe bricks, and fronting on a large, open plaza, the palace has a long, covered porch supported by large round posts with smaller timbers (rafters) protruding through the surface of the wall above. The somber rhythm of the posts and the more insistent one of the timbers are foils for the large quiet expanses of sun-dried surface (walls and plaza) and the deep shadow under the porch.

The many missions founded and built during the seventeenth and eighteenth centuries in Texas, New Mexico, Arizona, and southern California[4] attest to the missionary zeal of the early Franciscan friars. Each mission structure is unique in itself but all exhibit the combining of Spanish and Mexican-Spanish forms with the Pueblo materials and techniques

11-4 *The late eighteenth-century Mission of Saint Francis of Assisi in Taos, New Mexico, combines the plan and general forms of Spanish churches with the materials and building techniques of the native Pueblo Indian builders.*

[3] Of the settlers from the major nations in the Americas, only the Spanish made use of native architectural techniques and material. This blend of native Indian and European architectural practices resulted in a distinct and new type of structure. The Dutch and English resisted native influences after their first months in the western hemisphere, and whatever changes from European architectural prototypes occurred were the result of climate and the availability of materials rather than the local Indian crafts. The few buildings constructed by the French show even less Indian influence.

[4] Between 1769 and 1823 twenty-two missions were founded by the Franciscan order in California alone.

—thick adobe walls, smooth surfaces contrasted with the heavy ornamentation on small important architectural units (doors, windows), tile roofs and floors, and courtyards and cloisters.

Very little remains of the early major nonreligious buildings in southern California but existing small farmhouses (mostly built in the early nineteenth century but echoing preceding structures) give clues to the forms of the larger buildings. These Spanish *ranchos* or *haciendas* have a low, one-story plan with a covered porch or veranda. With their central courtyard or patio, they are the ancestors of that popular house type found in suburbs across the country today—the *ranch house.*

Immigrants to the New World from two nations other than the four major ones were also instrumental in shaping the architecture of America. Coming in considerable numbers during the seventeenth century, the Swedes and Germans who settled in Pennsylvania, western New Jersey, and northern Maryland, are responsible for a contribution that proved to be important architecturally and, perhaps even more so, politically. This contribution was the *log cabin.*[5] No example exists of an early structure in which round logs were used, but there are extant more finished square-cut log houses dating from the seventeenth century. This method of house construction was unknown to early English settlers and was *not* used by the colonists of Virginia or of New England.

When the push westward over the Allegheny Mountains and into the great Midwest occurred, the knowledge of this method of wall construction, using notched logs laid one upon the other with the ends protruding, made it possible for one relatively unskilled man with only an ax to quickly build a snug home. Previously it had been a long and involved process for several

11-5

[5] The early Russian settlements along the west coast and in Alaska were almost entirely composed of log buildings, often more elaborate but using construction methods that were similar to the Swedes on the east coast.

men to construct a home with the traditional posts and beams tediously fitted together. The log cabin form continued to serve the pioneer as he progressed westward in all but the most treeless areas, and without this easy, quick, and albeit crude method of construction, it is doubtful if the continent could have been settled so rapidly.

Sir Walter Raleigh sent the first English colony to America in 1585. Landing on Roanoke Island, the 108 men ended their colonizing in failure, returning to England the next year. In 1587 a second colony of 91 men, 17 women, and 9 children left England for the New World, but this too ended in failure.[6] It was not until 1607 when Jamestown was settled that England at last gained its first permanent colony. Thirteen years later the Pilgrims landed at Plymouth Rock, and by 1660 there were six English colonies on the Atlantic coast. At the end of the century England could boast no less than 12 colonies stretching from New Hampshire to South Carolina.

From the beginning there were significant differences between the colonies of the South and those of the North. The first settlers who came to Virginia were, for the most part, gentlemen[7]—the second and third sons of nobility or of wealthy landowners—usually with no conception of what constituted manual labor; working with their hands was completely alien to them. Their reason for coming was to see the new land, get rich, and return home as soon as possible. Only when they realized that if they did not work they would perish did they begin to perform the necessary tasks, but with little skill, of course. The first shelters they erected were no more than huts made of

[6]This is the famous "Lost Colony," in which all members of the colony mysteriously disappeared before the supply ship returned in 1590. The first child born of English parents, Virginia Dare, was born here on August 18, 1587.

[7]The "First Supply," as Captain John Smith called the men who accompanied him on the *Susan Constant* and her two sister ships, included fifty-four gentlemen, four carpenters, and twelve laborers. The later southern colonies had slightly different settlers, sponsors, and leadership, but the type of economic society that developed was similar to that in Virginia.

crotched trees, bent together and covered with woven willow or other supple branches and mud. The roofs were thatched. As they became more established the colonists began to construct simple wooden, or even brick, buildings. These were clustered close together, as row houses, each about sixteen feet square, and surrounded by a palisade of logs for protection from the Indians. In a short time the settlers became more bold and the Indians less hostile, and small plantations were started along the many navigable rivers and streams of Virginia. Thus, towns did not develop and the plantation became the center of southern colonial life.

From the beginning the most important product of Virginia and the South was tobacco. John Rolfe, the husband of Pocahontas, in 1614 proved that tobacco could be grown profitably. Although the Indians had little difficulty growing the tobacco for their needs, the English settlers found that the extensive planting needed for the desired profits depleted the soil and after six or seven years the land had to lay fallow for several years to regain its strength. This constant need for land—in use, spent, and in reserve—made mandatory plantations of great size. The plantations were, therefore, isolated from each other.

The production of tobacco demanded a large labor force to plant, weed, and process the mature leaves as well as all of the other tasks that were necessary to maintain the increasingly complex plantations. The first Black slaves were brought to Virginia in 1619 by a Dutch ship, but during the seventeenth century most of the labor was performed by indentured white servants—men and women who bound themselves to work for a period of time (four to seven years usually) in payment for passage to the colony. Many of these bondmen were unskilled but some were already craftsmen. When they were eventually released from their indenture they proved to be an important addition to the economy. By this time they were all trained in farming or other skills and either became small farm owners developing new land farther inland or helped satisfy the ever-increasing demand for crafts-

11-6 *Bacon's Castle in Virginia reveals the Flemish and Dutch heritage of seventeenth-century English architecture in the gable ends of the structure.* Photograph by Wayne Andrews.

men. By the end of the Colonial period, however, it was the Black slave who was to supply most of the unskilled labor on the large plantation.

The lack of urban centers, whether cause or result, nevertheless expresses the economic practices that were to develop throughout most of the South. The ships loaded and unloaded at the docks of the plantations and almost all of the merchandise was obtained directly from England rather than from merchants in the few existing towns. This close contact with the mother country provided the plantation owner with a more intimate knowledge of the latest styles and fashions in clothing, furniture, and architecture. He thus created in his wild and uncivilized environment a small, relatively current, and often luxurious piece of England in which to live. Unfortunately, this importation of almost every needed article also caused very little manufacturing to develop in the South. This constantly re-enforced the dependence of the southern colonies upon the economy of England.

The only structures that survive from the seventeenth century in Virginia are constructed of brick although it is known that half-timbered houses were built. Virginia and most of the South had the raw materials, a good clay, and adequate lime (produced by burning oyster shells), and importantly, immigrants who had skills in brick-making and construction.

The early plantation house often had two floors and a plan adapted from medieval English plans and was usually in the shape of a "T" or a cross. The first floor consists of two nearly square rooms that form two arms of a cross with a center passageway between. This passageway extends the full width of the rooms and bisects the entire main structure. Protruding from one end of the passageway is an enclosed porch and from the other a stair tower, if the stairs are not in the passageway. This plan is very similar to that which developed in the northern colonies, except that the fireplaces in the southern house are on the outer end walls of the principal rooms, whereas, in New England the massive chimney and fireplaces are in the center of the house (for greater warmth) with only a small vestibule resulting. The second floor

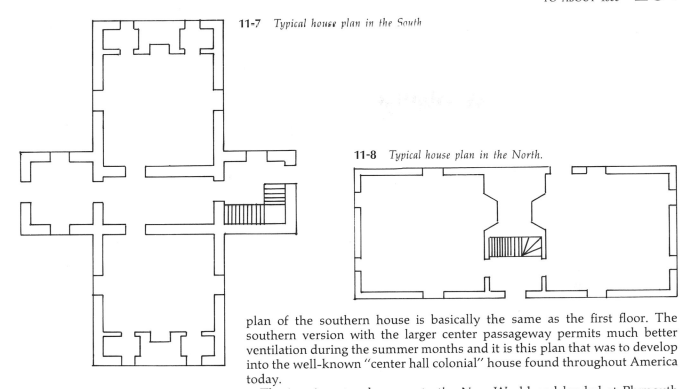

11-7 *Typical house plan in the South*

11-8 *Typical house plan in the North.*

plan of the southern house is basically the same as the first floor. The southern version with the larger center passageway permits much better ventilation during the summer months and it is this plan that was to develop into the well-known "center hall colonial" house found throughout America today.

The immigrants who came to the New World and landed at Plymouth Rock in 1620 were simple, industrious people, farmers and artisians. They knew the meaning of hard work and were prepared to more than meet the challenge of the forbidding land and climate of New England. Arriving in December the Pilgrims had little time to construct only the most primitive of shelters in which to live before the fierce New England winter was upon them. Not until the second year were simple wooden houses with thatched roofs built.

Also leaving England because of religious and economic reasons (although different than the Pilgrims), the Puritans arrived about ten years later and settled several miles north of Plymouth. Their colony, the Massachusetts Bay Company, and the Plymouth Colony, together, have influenced the later development of the United States more than any other group that was to settle here. The charter of the Massachusetts Bay Company was unique for it gave the leaders the right to regulate the type and number of immigrants and the nature of the government in the colony. It was also the first charter not to remain in London but to be carried to the New World.

Although given the right to dictate who the new settlers in the colony might be, not everyone was a Puritan. The virtual flood of immigrants who came to New England in the first twenty years was so numerous that by 1640 it is estimated that over 16,000 settlers were living in Massachusetts, Connecticut, and Rhode Island.

The resourcefulness and independence of the New England settlers is attested by their ability to turn the harsh world about them into a habitable and prosperous place. They were not so tied to England that they did not

11-9 *A reproduction of a primitive bark shelter used by the Pilgrims during their first desperate winter in New England.*

develop a commercial economy of their own, but rather, aware of the natural assets of the forest and sea and the advantages of local manufacturing and industry, they were soon able to enjoy far greater autonomy than the southern colonies ever experienced.

The plantation concept never developed in the North and towns and villages were laid out almost immediately. There were farms, of course, but they were never large as the rocky land found throughout most of New England did not easily lend itself to agrarian use.

Local industry flourished and the early development of shipbuilding, wood crafts[8], shipping, and fishing provided the means and products for great economic profit. The famous triangular trade route soon evolved with new barrels and dried fish being shipped to the West Indies. There molasses would be loaded and returned to New England where distilleries turned it into rum. The rum was then taken to Africa and exchanged for slaves who were brought to the West Indies or the southern agricultural colonies. In a short time, great financial gain was possible and many a New England fortune was made in this way.

The original simple wooden houses that the settlers first built have now all disappeared, but within twenty years after the arrival of the Pilgrims, more permanent and better constructed wooden houses[9] were being built.

[8] The plentiful forests of oak, maple, birch, and pine supplied material for many home industries—charcoal, shingles, and barrel staves and hoops. Barrels were in constant demand in the Colonies, the West Indies, and Europe and many New England farm families knew the skills of cooperage. The barrel is considered by many to be as important to the economic prosperity of New England as the codfish.

[9] The use of stone and brick as building materials was never extensive during the seventeenth century in New England, and, although the raw materials for each were readily available, the lack of a good mortar and the early colonists' unfamiliarity with masonry construction limited their use. Most of the settlers came from areas in England where wood construction was the major method of building and consequently were more comfortable using wood than they were using stone or brick.

11-10 *The Parson Capen House stands proud and tall. The overhanging second floor with its pendants and brackets owes much to the urban houses of England. Photograph by Wayne Andrews.*

Examples of these early homes may still be seen. The earliest surviving known one was built in 1636 at Denham, Massachusetts, but has been so altered by later additions that its present appearance is of little value. However, many of these houses built at a slightly later date have been carefully preserved and restored and it is now possible to see their early form clearly. Two of the finest are the Stanley-Whitman House in Farmington, Connecticut (c. 1660), and the Parson Capen House in Topsfield, Massachusetts (c. 1683). Both have plans based upon medieval examples that were still being built in England at the time. Their plans and general forms are similar although the Reverend Joseph Capen's house is larger and more pretentious, thanks to a prosperous father-in-law. Both houses are constructed of wood, are rectangular in form, and have split oak clapboards on the exterior.[10] Their steeply pitched roofs are covered with split shakes and a massive Tudor chimney protrudes at the center of the ridge. As in England their second floors extend over the lower floors on the front and this overhang is supported by brackets ending in pendants shaped like inverted tulips. The center doors are made of heavy planks studded with iron and hang on large hinges. Small diamond-paned casement windows pierce the exterior walls. A quasiformality is found in the arrangement of the elements in both houses but similar contemporary houses have often lost this symmetry through later additions.

The interior plan of both houses consists of two rooms on the first floor separated by a large chimney stack with massive brick fireplaces in each room. The central vestibule (*porch*) is very small and abuts the central

---

[10] In England, the spaces between the posts and beams of the half-timbered house were filled with various materials—*wattle and daub,* clay and straw or *nogging* (unfired bricks) —and then stuccoed. In New England, the lack of a good lime for mortar and stucco and the severity of the winters caused these materials to rapidly disintegrate; thus the use of protective clapboards, although not unknown but seldom used in England, became almost universal.

chimney on the front and is contained within the rectangle of the plan (there is no projecting enclosed porch as seen in the South). Against the chimney wall in the small vestibule is a narrow, twisting stairway leading to the second floor where two bedrooms are found.

The two principal rooms on the first floor are of approximately the same size, but their purposes were different. One (in both the Stanley-Whitman House and Parson Capen House it is on the right) was the *hall* or general living room. Here the family lived, food was prepared and eaten, candles were made, spinning and weaving were done, and all the other activities were performed necessary to the daily lives of the inhabitants. The room is dominated by the massive fireplace on the inner wall and the furnishings are sparse and utilitarian. The frequent comparison to the family room of today is not far amiss although the hall of the New England colonial house encompassed many more activities than does the modern family room.

The room opposite the hall, the *parlor*, was reserved for important occasions such as funerals, weddings, and the reception of important visitors. A large fireplace again dominates the room and the furnishings are much more dignified. If any piece of furniture was imported from Europe, it would be placed in the parlor as would the best bed for overnight guests.

The feeling of "wood" permeates the entire structure. All of the exterior surfaces are wood, left unfinished to weather, and within the house the structure is even more apparent than on the exterior. The oak frame of the house can be see, and between the exposed posts and beams of the outer-walls white plaster surfaces are found. The inner partitions, however, are made of a single layer of vertical boards. The wooden floor is composed of wide boards and frequently is double with a layer of sand between for insulation from the dampness of the basement below. The ceiling is low and the great *summer beam* that is on the longitudinal axis of the house supports the joists of the second floor. All the wood has no finish and is left to age naturally. With the simple wooden furniture the hall and somewhat more

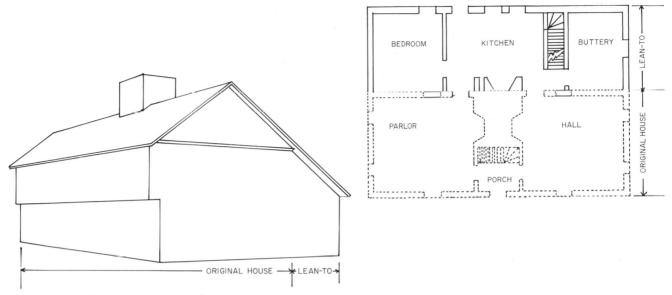

11-11 *Ground-level space was frequently added to the back of two-story houses in New England, which gave the basic shape of a saltbox to the house. The addition usually added a bedroom, kitchen, buttery, with a sloping loft above and a cellar below.*

elaborate parlor have the feeling of great warmth, comfort, and protection.

When time and finances permitted a lean-to was frequently added to the rear of the house and the roof slope was continued down over the addition. This, especially when included in the original plan of later houses, gave rise to the architectural term *saltbox* (so named because the resulting shape was similar to that of the wooden boxes used for salt).

Although most of the seventeenth-century houses in the colonies had simple single-pitched roofs with gable ends, a double-pitched roof was also used. Occasionally found in New England, New York, New Jersey, and even in Virginia, the *gambrel* roof is more likely to be seen in the middle colonies, but nowhere was it brought into such varied use as in Maryland. The gambrel roof is usually broken not quite halfway down from the ridgepole; the two sections may differ considerably in proportion and pitch. For example, some lower divisions are quite vertical, whereas others are almost the same pitch as the upper part. Regardless of the angles of the pitches, this kind of roof does not give as "clean-cut" gable[11] as does the single-pitched roof; however, it does provide more head room in the attic of the house and uses shorter rafters in its construction. The Swedes and the Dutch used the gambrel roof in their early settlements on the Delaware River. It is now also known, although incorrectly, as a Dutch Colonial roof.

After the initial rush of immigrants during the first half of the seventeenth century, relatively few settlers arrived until the first decade of the eighteenth century. From the time of Charles II's return to the throne of England in 1660 until 1720, only the founding of Pennsylvania by William Penn in 1681 is of great consequence. It was instead a period when the colonists took stock of their world, developed their native industry and commerce, and adjusted and

---

[11]The gambrel roof should not be confused with the mansard roof. Both have double pitches but the gambrel roof has gable ends whereas the mansard has no gables but is hipped, that is, the sides *and* ends are sloping.

blended their individual traditions and characteristics into the foundations of an American culture.

The beginning of the 1700s saw a fresh migration to the New World, but it was not now only the English who came in increasing numbers but West German Protestants, Scotch from Northern Ireland, Huguenots from France, and others, many of whom were expert craftsmen, carpenters, and cabinetmakers. The population was to multiply seven times by 1800[12] and the western limits of the colonies were pushed to the mountains and beyond as the new arrivals sought land on which to establish their homes.

The growing affluence and taste of the colonists demanded more elaborate homes and by the end of the first quarter of the eighteenth century, handsome dwellings, some rivaling those in England, could be found along the waterways of Virginia and Maryland, the countrysides of Pennsylvania and New Jersey, and in the seaports of New England. These new structures reflect a knowledge of the principles of Palladio and an interest in Renaissance and Baroque architecture. English translations of the numerous books on architecture that had been published throughout Europe during the previous 100 years became available in America.

It should be noted, however, that medieval building traditions continued far longer in America than they did in England[13], and few structures built prior to 1700 can be considered anything but medieval buildings. One exception, now called the Wren Building on the Campus of the College of William and Mary in Williamsburg, Virginia, was first built between 1695 and 1702. According to tradition, the building was designed by Sir Christopher Wren himself. Although the walls are still largely original, it has burned three times and subsequently has been rebuilt. The Wren Building

11-12 *The Wren Building in Williamsburg, Virginia, with its cupola, center pediment, and evenly spaced, small paned windows and dormers, presents a very formal facade. The quiet dignity of its design has inspired American architects for two centuries.*

[12] It has been estimated that even in 1763, two-thirds of the Americans were new men and not the sons and grandsons of earlier settlers.

[13] Inigo Jones designed his Banqueting Hall in 1619—almost sixty-five years *before* the Parson Capen House.

11-13 *The Georgian house can be almost austere on the exterior. Here, the garden facade of the Wythe House in Williamsburg has the requisite horizontality, water table, stringcourse, hip roof, and formal arrangement of the parts that were so admired in the eighteenth century.*

has now been restored to its second appearance (1708–1716). It was stylistically ahead of its time and has been the model for several later college buildings.

The new houses and public buildings that were being built along the length of the eastern seaboard were more of a single type than had been seen in the previous century. Those in Massachusetts, Pennsylavania, or Virginia had characteristics that were quite similar. Perhaps because of the Great Fire in London and the subsequent decree that all buildings must be made of brick, or because the designers and owners considered brick more impressive, the majority of the structures are made of brick although the affinity for wood continued to dominate the architecture of the North. Nevertheless, these buildings developed a clear form.

Their formal elegance at once establishes the classical heritage of the buildings. A feeling of the horizontal is accomplished with lower roofs, stringcourses indicating the level of the floors, and a projecting *water table* of molded brick above the ground level, capping the basement. This water table serves the same purpose as a pedestal, enhances the dignity of the building, and raises the principal floors above the ground level, which allows the introduction of windows to light the basement, The exteriors of these buildings are very similar to those first built in England 25 to 35 years earlier and both are called Georgian. The Dutch Palladian style, which had emerged about 1630 in secular architecture in The Hague and had come to England about the time that William, Prince of Orange, became William II of England was to become as popular in America as it was in England.

Many eighteenth-century American Georgian structures are extant from New Hampshire to South Carolina, and uncounted copies and adaptations of later date are found throughout the United States. Some of the finest of these houses, however, are located in Williamsburg, Virginia.

At the instigation of Dr. W. A. R. Goodwin, the rector of Bruton Parish Church, John D. Rockefeller, Jr., undertook the restoration of the Colonial area of Williamsburg in 1926. Between that time and 1935 when Colonial Williamsburg was considered basically completed in form, sixty-six colonial buildings were repaired and restored, eighty-four were reproduced and built on their original foundations, and the appearance of the colonial area was restored with lampposts, fences, brick walks, plantings, and gardens derived from authentic records. Since 1935 the refinement and elaboration of details, furnishings, and plantings has continued in addition to periodic restoration and reconstruction of more buildings. This vast undertaking has received much praise. Today it is possible to again see one the most beautiful Colonial cities with its architecturally significant buildings as it was at the time of the American Revolution.

Several intriguing questions must always be raised when considering restorations such as Williamsburg: What happens to structures that have been built at another time than that of the period of restoration? Are there no buildings of architectural importance at different dates? Are all of these buildings to be sacrificed (destroyed) because of their date or style? Does such a controlled restoration give a false impression of an area, town, or city? Does this make for a static, dead appearance instead of the more desirable living and growing picture that it could have? Is it the intention to create a "museum" city or one where life continues? Must buildings be authentic in design on the inside as well as outside or can they be adapted for contemporary living? Such questions must always be faced and answered in a most intelligent way, a most humanistic way. During the restoration of Williamsburg, 422 buildings were torn down and 18 moved outside the Colonial area.

The numerous articles and stories published about the restoration of Williamsburg, the Colonial capital of Virginia, have made almost everyone familiar with the houses and public buildings there. Familiarity, however, should not diminish the awareness of the importance of Williamsburg to American architecture and interiors.

Williamsburg, located on high ground between the York and James

11-14 *From the Palace Green, the Governor's Palace at Williamsburg is a study in symmetry. The whole arrangement of building mass and details, curving wall, general plan, and flanking structures are symmetrically balanced; yet the subtle spatial refinements in the Palace's facade, for example, raise the whole composition to aesthetic excellence.*

Rivers,[14] was first settled in 1633 and was then called Middle Plantation. Here, the College of William and Mary was established in 1693 near the old Bruton Parish Church (organized 1674). In 1699, in accordance with an act of the General Assembly, the city of Williamsburg was laid out in a modified gridiron plan and was designated the capital of the colony of Virginia. The capital had been in Jamestown prior to this time. In 1780, the capital was again moved, to Richmond. During the eighty years when Williamsburg was the capital, it was the "seat of empire"—the leading city in Virginia, a colony with few municipalities—and it was here that the latest fashions and wares from London were found. The buildings, interiors, furniture, clothes, and the way of life of Williamsburg served as models to be imitated throughout Virginia, the South, and, indeed, the entire thirteen colonies.

The plan of Williamsburg is an admirable one, well suited to the needs of the colonial capital. It covers about one square mile and includes about 300 houses. The major street, the Duke of Gloucester Street, is ninety-nine feet wide and extends seven-eighths of a mile bisecting the city. At the western end, where the street forks toward Jamestown or Richmond, is situated the college and at the eastern end the capitol stands. About halfway between the two is a tree-lined avenue, the Palace Green. At this junction is the Bruton Parish Church (1711–1715). At the termination of the Palace Green is the most important residence in Williamsburg and the first in Virginia to incorporate the characteristics of early Georgian architecture—the Governors Palace. It is one of the great houses in America.

Termed a "magnificent structure" even when built, the Governor's Palace was begun in 1706 and was repaired in 1751. The interior is believed to have been remodeled and the ballroom and supper room were added to the rear.

[14] The Colonial period of the United States began at Jamestown, reached its gracious peak at Williamsburg, ten miles away, and ended 174 years later at Yorktown—a total of only twenty-three miles.

The palace burned to the ground in 1781 while serving as an American
military hospital during the Yorktown siege.[15] The structure now standing in
Colonial Williamsburg is a reconstruction (1932–1933) and its design is
based upon three sources, the old foundations, a plan drawn by Thomas
Jefferson, and an engraving, the "Bodleian plate," c. 1737 (a copper engraving
found in the Bodleian Library at Oxford University in England). Although
the present palace is not the original building, its original importance and the
authenticity of the reproduction require that it be considered.

Approaching on the Palace Green from the Duke of Gloucester Street, the
formality of the arrangement and careful spacing of the separate parts of the
palace and its dependencies[16] is most apparent. The block of the building sits
back, centered on the axis of the green, and behind a slightly curved brick
wall that projects outward to an ornamental iron gate. Arranged on each side
of the resultant courtyard are identical buildings, their facades at right
angles to that of the palace and their gable ends and large chimneys forming
part of the enclosing wall. The palace facade is divided horizontally by a
brick stringcourse encircling the building on the second-floor level. The
simple double doors have a glazed transom and are centered with two
double-hung windows[17] on each side. The space between the door frame and
the first window is narrower than the space between the two windows, and
that space is narrower than between the second window and the outer corner

[15] More than 150 Revolutionary War soldiers are buried in the palace grounds.

[16] The arrangement of a central rectangular structure with identical flanking buildings on
either side had become popular in England several years before as a result of the Baroque
influence. Although the flanking buildings were often attached in some manner to the main
structure in England, in this country they are usually separate. Almost without exception
one of these dependent buildings was the kitchen, which was not included in the main
structure in the South until after the Civil War.

[17] Double-hung windows with small rectangular panes replaced the older casement
windows after 1700 in this country.

11-15 *The reserved magnificence of West-over reveals the high standard of living enjoyed by the owners of early eighteenth-century southern plantations.* Photograph by Wayne Andrews.

of the building. The openings on the second floor are arranged as on the first except for a wrought-iron balcony and large window replacing the double doors. The hip-roofed dormers above the simple cornice with Roman modillions (brackets) are arranged as the windows. This progressive scheme of window placement gives the feeling of strength and solidarity to the structure and provides a focus to the simple doorway. The hip roof above the cornice forms a truncated pyramid over the block of the building and is topped by a simple wooden balustrade. Rising above this is a double cupola or lantern that terminates in a weather vane. Large twin chimneys extend upward on the outer sides of the balustrade. The white wood trim contrasts pleasantly with the "salmon" pink color of the brick, and 250 years later this combination of white painted wood and mellow brick have become synonymous with "Colonial."

The Governor's Palace as the symbol of British imperial order was the gathering place of Colonial society and must have exerted much influence upon the landowners and planters who came to Williamsburg. Each great plantation house built after the palace reflects the architectural innovations first seen in the American colonies there. Fire and decay have claimed many of these houses, but of those that still survive few equal the elegance of Westover (c. 1730) in Charles City County, Virginia. Situated on the banks of the James River about twenty-five miles west of Williamsburg, Westover consists of a symmetrical brick mansion with steps leading up to a pedimented doorway and has two chimneys located at each end of the steeply hipped roof. On each side are lower buildings, each a smaller edition of the central block, but less ornamented. The three units are arranged on the longitudinal axis of the main building with all the facades parallel. Originally the three buildings were separate, but now they are joined by modern "hyphens" (connecting structures). The fineness of the detailing and the proportions of the two major facades of the center mansion attest to the skill and knowledge of the unidentified local designer. The entrance doors on both facades are of especial interest.[18]

Early Georgian architecture in the Middle Atlantic and New England colonies reflects the same Palladian characteristics as are found in Virginia, although the use of wood rather than brick as the major building material is more frequently seen.

Not every house built in the eighteenth century was as grand as those discussed and to imply this would, of course, distort the total picture. What then was the more modest home? The Brush-Everard House (c. 1717) in Williamsburg is typical of many found throughout the colonies. Only one story and of wooden construction with clapboard siding, it shows many characteristics that can be traced to the palace—the formal arrangement of the parts, a simple doorway in the center of the structure with steps leading to it, the progressive spacing of the windows, less pitch to the roof, the alignment of the dormers above the windows on the first floor, and the use of modillions on the cornice. It would be "at home" on almost any street in America today and it is frequently this type of house that is the "Colonial" house admired by many people rather than the larger and more pretentious eighteenth-century mansion.

The interiors of these houses, whether palace, plantation mansion, sea captain's residence, or modest home were strongly influenced by the current English interiors and this influence continued throughout most of the century. In the colonies the interiors are less ornate and elaborate than in England, and although their plan, detailing, and furniture are similar in both the North and the South, the size of the stairway and center hall is con-

[18]Other urban and plantation houses reflecting the early Georgian style are the Ludwell-Paradise House (c. 1717), Brafferton Hall (c. 1723), and the Wythe House (c. 1750) in Williamsburg; Stratford (c. 1725–1730) in Westmoreland County; and Carter's Grove (c. 1750–1753) in James City County.

11-16 *The classical details increase in size and importance in the Vassal-Longfellow house in Cambridge, Massachusetts. The New England choice of wood, instead of the southern brick as the building material, distinguishes the house from those in Virginia.*

siderably reduced, the ceilings are lower, and the carved decoration is less bold in northern houses. Plans are symmetrically arranged with a central entrance hall, usually with an open stairway. On either side of the hall are two rooms each with a fireplace. These fireplaces may be on the outside end walls of each room requiring four chimneys as at Westover or back to back on the walls between the rooms and using only two chimney stacks as in the Vassal-Longfellow mansion. The placement and number of chimneys is not dependent upon the geographical location of the structure as both plans are used in the North and in the South.

After 1750 an increasing interest in more classical architecture began to appear as it had in both France and England. The simple transomed doorway (Governor's Palace) and the broken pedimented entrance (Westover) tended to disappear and in their stead porticos with classical columns and triangular pediment, the "temple front," began to be used. Frequently, this portico was attached to a projecting bay that released the floor plan from the almost rigid rectangle it had been since the beginning of the century. Roofs were even less sloped and the balustrade at the tops took on added importance. Windows became larger and were almost without exception treated to exterior shutters. The Palladian window was in great favor and in its many variations is one of the dominant architectural devices of the latter half of the eighteenth century.

The new architecture was especially admired in the northern colonies and many examples are found in Massachusetts, Rhode Island, New Hampshire, and Connecticut. The Vassal-Longfellow mansion (1759) in Cambridge, Massachusetts, incorporates these classical details with the earlier Georgian form. This amply proportioned wooden house has a central projection that suggests a temple front with two slender Ionic pilasters supporting a triangular pediment. Additional pilasters at the outer ends of the facade support a narrow architrave and cornice decorated with modillions. The center doorway has curved brackets supporting a simple cornice above and the windows

11-18 *The exterior surface of Mount Vernon simulates rusticated stone although it is made of horizontal boards, a practice that was more common in New England than in Virginia. The lower photograph shows a corner of one of the flanking buildings.*

have shutters. The low, hipped roof is topped by a balustraded deck from which two large chimneys project.

The use of narrow clapboards on the exterior followed the traditional method of surfacing wooden houses. Another popular exterior wood surface was based upon precedents in Palladio, that is, wood planks were cut and finished to imitate blocks of stone. Admired in New England where wood was preferred, it is also occasionally found in the other colonies (Washington's Mount Vernon is the best known).

In the South, classical architectural motifs were similarly fused with the earlier Georgian, and one of Palladio's favorite devices, the double or two-story portico, can be seen on many structures in Virginia and the Carolinas. Thomas Jefferson is known to have used it at Monticello when he first erected his home between 1770 and 1775. Later he modified his design and his home now has a single, one-story portico.

The home of George Washington, Mount Vernon, in Fairfax County, Virginia, is historically important. Incorporated into its final design are several concepts and ideas that were favorites of the period. Washington was an inveterate remodeler and from 1757 until 1787, even during the period when he was commander-in-chief of the Continental Army, he was constantly changing his house. Mount Vernon was originally a small house built by his older half-brother Lawrence in about 1743. The house was enlarged several times until it now is an excellent example of the five-part plan with a courtyard surrounded by the main house, *flankers* (dependent buildings), and quadrant colonnades (hyphens). All of the buildings are made of wood, although they are surfaced with *chamfered* boards to appear as rusticated stone and painted with light buff-colored sand paint. Despite the frequent remodeling, the interior plan (six rooms and a central hallway on the first floor) forbade the desired perfect symmetry of the windows and doors. Nevertheless, the simple center door surrounded by two Doric columns, entablature, and triangular pediment; imitation stone surface; shuttered windows;

11-19 *Mount Vernon has not escaped the evils of being copied. This "gracious southern mansion" is a drugstore in a shopping center in northern Illinois.*

cornice with modillions; large triangular pediment breaking the lower line of the hip roof; small dormers and a stocky lantern on the roof, and the matching colonnaded hyphens and dependent buildings, together, create a very acceptable classical Palladian appearance on the "land" side. The "river" side has the familiar high piazza with eight square wooden columns supporting the entablature and cornice of a flat roof. A large Palladian window is on one end of the mansion.

The immediate sense of independency that permeated the whole of American life after the Revolution soon mellowed into a realization that not all of the cultural and economic ties with Europe could be cut. Nevertheless, distance and the American physical environment brought forces that changed even the most persistent forms and manners. The term Colonial cannot properly be used for this period; yet many of the architectural elements that had been used during the preceding years of the eighteenth century continued to be employed. The use of Georgian details, devices, forms, and floor plans persisted yet almost imperceptible changes had begun to take place, such as the introduction of more classicism, and in a short time a new style emerged. The Federal period, lasting until about 1825, is a time of delicate classical motifs applied with restraint and refinement. These motifs do not come via the Renaissance or from Palladio as had design during the past century but rather from the wall decorations discovered at Pompeii or Herculaeum and through the brothers Adam. The English Adam influence dominates all Federal architectural and decorative design, although there are French neoclassic persuasions that can also be found primarily as a result of the participation of France in the American War for Independence and the political missions to France by Benjamin Franklin and Thomas Jefferson.

Charles Bulfinch of Boston and Samuel McIntire of Salem were two of the most notable designers of the period. Bulfinch designed many buildings in and around Boston; the most important being the Massachusetts State House with its Corinthian columned porch and large smooth dome. He was later

11-20 *One of the finest Federal houses in America, the Peirce-Nichols house was designed and built by Samuel McIntire when he was in his middle twenties.* Photograph by Wayne Andrews.

(1817) to journey to Washington to direct the completion of the national Capitol.

Samuel McIntire was an excellent wood-carver and builder of houses, and if any person can be responsible for the appearance of a city, McIntire must be given credit for the transformation of Salem, Massachusetts. Settled in 1630, eighteenth-century Salem still retained the appearance of a seventeenth-century seaport, twisting streets, and steep-roofed gabled houses. But by the time of McIntire's death (1811) almost every street showed his hand. McIntire's clients, the prosperous merchants and shipowners, wanted to live in "fitting" surroundings that their "houses by the wharf" could not provide. New homes on new streets, away from the harbor were ordered. The three-story Pierce-Nichols house (1782) on Federal Street is made of wood, and is symmetrical and stolid. The clapboard surface is opened by the large, double-hung windows topped by strong entablatures and edged by dark shutters. The corners of the facade are accented by large fluted pilasters that support a wide cornice and surmounting balustrade. The central door is sheltered by a small Doric "temple" porch. The wooden fence enclosing the small front yard has posts with impressive carved wooden urns, flower garlanded and flame topped (suggested by the urns placed by the brothers Adam in niches in the interiors of English homes). Other homes designed and built by Samuel McIntire, his son, and his assistants are found on other Salem streets.

The symmetrical exteriors belied the interior arrangements. These houses are no longer so rigid in their formal plans but are composed of rooms of various sizes depending upon their function and needs. One of the most elegant of styles, the interiors are high ceilinged, with delicate-hued walls, damask draperies, chaste furniture, and with moldings and pilasters everywhere. The influence of Adam decorative ornament is most apparent with swags, delicate vines encircling columns and pilasters, frets, and classical figures, but upon close scrutiny these ornaments are often American

11-21 *Classically spare, rooms at the end of the eighteenth century became cleaner of line and purer in detail. This room from Newburyport, Massachusetts, was based upon the work of Robert Adam and Samuel McIntire.* Courtesy of the St. Louis Art Museum.

—American plant life, for example, a finely carved bouquet of native American flowers, a sheaf of American wheat, a classic bowl filled with American fruit or vegetables, and the American eagle. McIntire fireplaces are noted for their exquisite surface decoration and the excellent stairways curve gracefully upward and are frequently lighted by handsome Palladian windows. It is a linear, crisply carved, refined, and intimately elegant style.

Although the Federal movement was confined more to New England than elsewhere, another stylistic direction was developing in the Middle Atlantic area. This was to be more lasting and would be virtually unchallenged until about 1840. The Greek revival had its roots in Greece and Rome and although it is a continuation of the classical movement, which had been gaining momentum for over one hundred years, it is not a reworking of the neoclassical forms of late Georgian or of Federal decoration.

The citizens of the new nation, the United States, did not want to continue to copy British architecture when building their new public and governmental buildings. The feeling of national pride and independence was high, and many saw strong parallels between the democracy of ancient Greece and that which now was being attempted in their country. Greek architecture might also serve as the model for American architecture and consequently the shift was to classical prototypes, Greek and Roman, rather than those of the Renaissance. The respect for order, logic, and stability was readily apparent in classical buildings and these were the ideals to which the designers and builders turned.

Thomas Jefferson, one of America's most influential leaders, was known for his architectural interest and skill. Already thoroughly familiar with Palladio, his sojourn in France (1784–1789) as a commissioner and later as the minister gave him the opportunity to study at first hand the noted Roman ruins in the south of that country. Particularly taken with the Maison Carrée, Jefferson admitted that he spent hours "gazing . . . like a lover at his mistress." When he designed the new state capitol in Richmond, Virginia, it

11-22 *Jefferson, like Washington, constantly remodeled his home, but unlike Washington, Jefferson started with a new structure and achieved a more perfect Palladian result.*

11-23 *Designed by B. H. Latrobe for the Capitol building in Washington, D.C., at the request of Jefferson, this "Corinthian" capital uses the native tobacco leaf and flower instead of the more traditional Mediterranean acanthus leaf.*

11-24 *The porticoes of the classroom structures enclosing the rectangular lawn fronting the Library Rotunda at the University of Virginia are based upon purer classical architecture than were eighteenth-century Georgian buildings and must be included in the Greek revival style that was to dominate the early nineteenth century. In the photograph showing the corner of one of the porticoes, the frieze has relief sculpture only across the front. Jefferson was a practical man.*

was his favorite Roman temple that provided the inspiration for the design. Jefferson's first conception was more temple-like than the final version, but it is easily apparent from whence the design came. The elements are all there—the rectangular block sitting on a high pedestal fronted by a portico reached by broad stairs—however, the size is considerably larger than the original, the columns are Ionic rather than Corinthian, and the portico is one column less in depth. Between the pilasters (not the original half-columns) that encircle the architectural block are two rows of windows to light the two-story interior that has several rooms. Today wings extend from each side.

Near Charlottesville, Virginia, stands Jefferson's home, Monticello. Its final form also reflects his increasing interest in classical design and the arrangement of buildings and grounds, the central block with extended wings. The one-room-wide plan shows that it was inspired by Roman ideals. Jefferson originally had designed and built his home in a more Georgian style and, like Washington, he too was an inveterate remodeler and builder. The central section clearly is inspired by Palladio's Villa Rotunda yet the porticos on each side are more truly Roman.

Jefferson did not slavishly follow classical architectural forms but rather adapted them to fit new uses. It is his departure from the prototypes that is important. His final architectural triumph, late in life, shows how he adapted and modified the ancient classical architectural designs into a working synthesis. His design (1822–1826—the year of his death) for the new University of Virginia in Charlottesville is a masterly plan. The Rotunda, based upon the Pantheon, is not a temple or even a chapel, but perhaps even more appropriately, it is the library, the true center of learning. Circular, topped by a low-profile dome, and having the required portico, it sits at one end of a large rectangular lawn. This space is enclosed by a colonnade, reminiscent of the *stoas* of ancient Greece and Rome. Regularly spaced along this perimeter are double porticoed rectangular structures housing below the classrooms and above the homes of the professors. Each of these buildings is an example of a different classical order. A second set of buildings, student quarters, rim this arrangement. The famous serpentine walls (one brick thick) connect all of the buildings. The buildings are red brick trimmed with white-painted wood. As a total plan for resident education it combined the most comprehensive and searching solutions that had yet been devised. It has been called one of the greatest ideological masterpieces of American history.

12 Architecture: American and European After 1800

No review of architecture, particularly residential architecture, can disregard the society in which people live. The nineteenth century brought far more changes that affected man, his environment, and way of life than had any previous century in history. At the beginning of the century, the world, and especially the United States, was overwhelmingly an agrarian society. In 1790 it is estimated that in America only 3 per cent of the total four million population lived in cities of 8,000 or more. By 1820, however, the total population had swelled to over ten million and both New York and Philadelphia had passed the 150,000 population mark.

Until 1830 the number of new immigrants had been about 4,000 or 5,000 each year, but after that date the numbers rapidly increased until nine million arrived in one decade, 1880–1890. Large numbers continued to come to the United States until well into the twentieth century.

Almost every citizen was of English stock in 1800, but by midcentury peoples from northern and central Europe predominated. Later in the century the new immigrants were almost entirely from eastern and southern Europe. To illustrate the importance of these immigrants to the culture and economy, by 1890 fully 68 per cent of the population of the United States were foreign born with another 10 per cent being the children of parents born abroad.

The earlier newcomers headed west to settle and tame the wilderness, and although the cities along the coast maintained a steady growth rate, it was the development of the towns and cities on the frontier that was to be the most spectacular. Chicago, Cincinnati, Cleveland, Lexington, Louisville, and St. Louis became trade centers rivaling older cities in size and influence. Frequently the populations of whole communities were one nationality, some even from one area of a particular country. Vestiges of this imported culture of the mother country has often continued to the present time in many towns and cities.

Communication improved during the first half of the nineteenth century;

12-1 *Houses often reflect the ethnic and na-tional backgrounds of their owners. For exam-ple, many of Milwaukee's early settlers were of German origin and this house, one of many of the larger older homes there, is based upon German Baroque architecture.*

the isolated cities of the past century were linked by systems of roads, canals, railroads, even the telegraph, and the new towns of the west were not long separated from the rest of the world. Although existing regional differences in manners, speech, and culture were to continue, they were not as clear as in the past. Similarly, building styles and methods no longer remained unique to a particular geographical area but were found throughout the nation executed in various degrees of skill and accomplishments.

After the Civil War, both the North and the South were thrust into the modern industrial world. The primarily agrarian nation that had started the century became not just the producer of raw materials for the more advanced European countries but evolved into a major manufacturing power. The necessary labor force was supplied by the constant flow of arriving immi-grants and these, by now coming from eastern and southern Europe, settled in the cities near the growing complexes of factories and manufacturing plants. The hardships they experienced in the workshops and in the develop-ing slum squalor where they were forced to live caused much unrest and eventually brought about the formation of the labor unions.

The expanding economy after the Civil War also caused a marked increase in the numbers and wealth of the upper classes. In the eighteenth century a man was considered prosperous with a fortune of $100,000, but by 1890 over 3,000 "ordinary" millionaires were living in the United States and some men had personal fortunes as high as $300 million—untaxed.

The reader may ask what this has to do with architecture; a great deal. The technology that was developing, the new fortunes that were made, the lack of a settled upper class or pacesetting group, the variety of ethnic and nationalistic backgrounds, and the rapid geographical expansion of the nation required buildings to be constructed at a rate, in number, in concept, in materials, for uses, and often in places unheard of before.

Before an investigation of the architecture that developed during this

12-2 *During the late nineteenth century the expanding economy was often evidenced by the size and style of the homes of the more affluent citizens. These adjacent mansions in Milwaukee, Wisconsin, are in three different architectural styles, Gothic, French neoclassic, and Italian villa. The customary stylistic compatibility so prevalent in cities before the nineteenth century is no longer apparent.*

unusual century can proceed, a more definitive explanation of an architectural term must be given. The word *style* has been frequently used. It has been applied to recurring combinations of forms and shapes found in construction and decoration used for a period of time, for example, the Gothic style or the Louis XV style. If, however, after a period of disuse this combination is used again, it is known as a *revival.* The nineteenth century is a century of revivals. There is doubtlessly *no* style or period of architecture or decorative element that was not revived in some manner during this period. And repeatedly, these elements are combined in most "original" and unusual ways.

The acceptance of Greek and Roman buildings, invariably temples, as prototypes for nineteenth-century architectural designs was almost unanimous during the first quarter of the century. It was as if all the columns, entablatures, pediments, and decorative elements of the ancients had been transferred to the New World and compiled into a visual architectural mosaic. Churches, city halls, banks, state houses, railway stations, hotels, and waterworks—public buildings of every use and description acquired classical porticoes. Of course, it was necessary to adapt and change the structures and interiors behind the facades to accomodate the spatial and functional requirements of the buildings to be used for the purposes for which they were designed. Consequently, Greek porticoes are found with domes and blocky towers rising above them, windows are frequently incorporated into the surfaces behind the columns and even squeezed in the entablatures and pediments, and the size and proportions are sometimes stretched almost beyond limit. Nevertheless, the illusion remains, the recognizable ancestry of classical architecture.

The Greek revival was by no means confined to nonresidential structures. Homes also took on the appearance of the Parthenon or similar temples. Two homes that were strongly influenced by Greek architecture are the Lee

12-3 *Published in 1830, this engraving by A. J. Davis depicts the green in New Haven, Connecticut, and Yale College. Only the church on the left does not owe its design to classical architecture.*

12-4 *The classical spirit permeated everything and persisted until the midnineteenth century. This family register is divided by Corinthian columns and the four scenes at the top are framed by swirling acanthus leaves.*

12-5 *The stately portico of the Lee Mansion in Arlington, Virginia, is clearly based upon Greek architecture.* Photograph by Wayne Andrews.

12-6 *An imposing example of a Greek revival home in Marshall, Michigan (c. 1840). The uneven number of wood columns and lack of a central doorway indicate that the unknown designer was not thoroughly familiar with the style. The too high pediment has a window that was probably inspired by the Palladian window.*

12-7 *A small, wooden Greek revival house (c. 1840) in Ann Arbor, Michigan. The frieze of the entablature has been widened to provide space for window grills decorated with the honeysuckle motif for second-floor illumination. The square "Doric" columns are especially board-like.*

Mansion (1826)[1] in Arlington, Virginia, and Andalusia (1836) in Andalusia, Pennsylvania. Both have thick Doric columns (the Lee Mansion has columns that are not fluted), entablatures with triglyphs and metopes and plain pediments. The lower angle of the pediment and the fluted columns on Andalusia give it a more "authentic" Greek appearance[2]. Behind both of these impressive porticos, however, are boxes full of rooms that have little in common and contrast sharply with the classic front. The English domestic interior surrounded by walls that are still basically Georgian does not easily join with the design of an ancient religious temple. It must be said, however, that from a distance both homes impart the much admired and handsome beauty of the Greek temple.

Houses of less authenticity were also built. The plans of these houses often included extensions from the classic rectangle and "T" and "L" floor plans are not uncommon. The ingenuity of some of the builders in translating the Greek and Roman vernacular into the terms of the carpenter produced elements that were both strange and unusual, for example, four boards nailed into a long vertical box and with a molding or two around the top and bottom passed as a Doric column; a simple, wooden clapboard-covered house with a gable roof became "current" in design when a wide board was nailed vertically on each corner forming pilasters; a small cornice was extended from one eave to the other, across the gable, and a recognizable pediment was created; and a series of small blocks of wood nailed in an even row along the edge of the eaves produced the much admired dentils. But whether the buildings are made of wood, brick, or stone, their surfaces are generally

[1] Originally known as Arlington House, it was built by George Washinton Parke Custis, the only grandson of Martha Washington by her first marriage. The eldest Custis daughter, Mary, married Robert E. Lee, hence the present name. The mansion now stands within the Arlington National Cemetery.

[2] Andalusia was built for Nicholas Biddle and the portico is a copy of the Theseum (447–444 B.C.) in Athens, which Biddle had seen during a trip to the Aegean area.

12-8

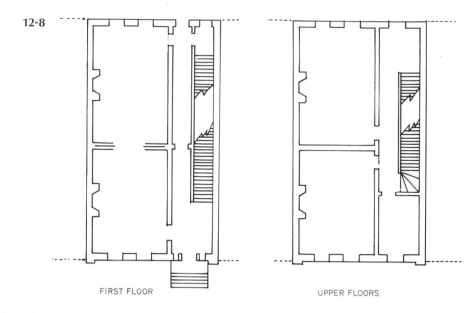

FIRST FLOOR   UPPER FLOORS

painted so that the distinct, natural qualities of the material are minimized.

The cities, towns, and countryside of the northern and central states were soon filled with Greek revival houses—from the largest mansions to the smallest cottages. And, it was also in the cities that the classical ideals met head-on with land values and the requirements of the American homeowner. With the rising cost of land, few men could afford a tract or lot that was large enough to permit the erection of a complete temple in which to live. Row houses had been previously built in England and the United States and were not unknown in the cities. But by the second decade of the century, a Greek revival type of row house was firmly established. These two-and-a-half or three-and-a-half story houses are narrow—just wide enough to permit one room and a hall—and are only two rooms deep with a small formal garden in the rear. The facade is not symmetrical, as the entrance is on one side, but the placement of the windows on each floor is orderly. A simple cornice tops the front. With the basement partially above the ground, the entrance is reached by a short flight of steps having a delicate iron railing. A small classical portico, or at least columns, decorate the door. Narrow side windows and a transom light the hall behind the simply paneled door with a polished but restrained brass knocker. The effect is clean, formal, and precise. An entire block of Greek revival row houses, each a slight variation of the classical mode, is a handsome addition to any city. The interior plan is vertical rather than horizontal. The first floor has a front and back parlor separated by sliding doors, which, when opened, allow the sun to flood both rooms with light filtered through the lace curtains. The hall and its narrow stairs lead to the floors above and to the kitchen in the basement. The second floor has two large bedrooms with a smaller one over the front entrance hall (this became a bathroom after 1830 when the primitive arrangement at the rear of the house was removed). Ceilings are high (14 feet) and ornamented with a richly molded rosette, the walls are delicately tinted and often divided by pilasters and moldings, and the fireplaces are made of marble. The furniture is heavy

12-9 *The nineteenth-century southern plantation house is based upon the earlier French house of the Mississippi valley. Of palisade construction (the logs were placed vertically) and surrounded by a wide, raised porch, it is only a small design step to transfer posts to columns and porches to verandas.*

and classically inspired. Bronze chandeliers hang in the center of the rooms.

In the South a different form developed. It too must be considered Greek revival but instead of the temple front it is the colonnade that is the dominant element. The fabled white pillared plantation houses that were built before the Civil War are an ideally resolved blend of classical elements and preferred regional residential architectural forms.[3] A block of rooms, which is usually bisected horizontally and vertically by a large center hall with a sweeping stairway, is frequently surrounded on all sides by colonnades of tall columns. This two-story colonnade supports a cornice that hides a low hip roof. The resultant structure satisfies the wishes for a shaded home, a cool veranda, and a monument to the owner's worth. The interiors were often as rich as the exterior was splendid. The high ceilinged, spacious rooms were filled with the results of the owner's and his agent's forays in Europe—the finest bronze and crystal chandeliers, colored marble mantels, French wallpaper, carved rosewood furniture, huge gilded mirrors, thick patterned carpets, and lavish draperies.

As in nature, while one blossom is developing to its fullest bloom another is a bud emerging. The Greek revival when in full flower was to be replaced by the Gothic revival. The symmetry and the carefully ordered arrangement of parts that is essentially in conflict with nature began to give way to the asymmetry and irregular arrangements that are more in harmony with nature.

The evolvement of architectural styles during the nineteenth century in the United States and in Europe is almost identical. To isolate each country, as was so easily done during past centuries, is now more difficult. A few years' delay may be evident with certain architectural developments from one

---

[3] The basic form of the Southern Greek or Plantation Greek house is not derived from ancient buildings but rather from the eighteenth-century French houses built in the Mississippi valley.

12-10 *The roof extends beyond the main structure of Oak Alley, Vacherie, Louisiana (c. 1836), and is supported by two-story high columns. There is, however, a second-floor balcony suspended from the columns.* Photograph by Wayne Andrews.

12-11 *Westminster Palace incorporates all of the design ornamentation associated with Gothic architecture, but is essentially a nineteenth-century building in plan and construction.* Courtesy of The British Tourist Authority.

country to another, or from one continent to another, but this is a minor consideration.

The development of Greek revival in the United States stylistically parallels the Empire period in France and the Regency period in England. Elsewhere in Europe the trends are approximately the same. Buildings, both public and private, are constructed for a wide variety of uses and are cloaked with Roman and Greek temple facades and colonnades, topped by domes and vaults, and are made to appear as classically monumental as possible.

In each country after the decade of 1820–1830, the revival of Gothic architectural design became increasingly apparent. The Gothic revival style was readily accepted for church architecture. It was considered morally pure since true Gothic had been developed by Christians for Christian churches and cathedrals. To rationalize the use of Gothic for secular construction was not so easy, although there never had been an extended period when some object or some building did not have elements that could be traced to the late medieval period. For example, the plans of Bacon's Castle and the Parson Capen house are both late medieval, the plan of Bruton Parish Church is modified Gothic, the home of Horace Walpole, Strawberry Hill (1747–1776), had Gothic detailing, and the noted Thomas Chippendale was but one eighteenth-century designer who designed furniture using Gothic elements.

One secular building that greatly influenced the acceptance of Gothic revival in England and in the United States is Westminster Palace (Houses of Parliament) (1840–1860), London, by Sir Charles Barry and A. W. N. Pugin. Built after the 1834 fire that destroyed the earlier Houses of Parliament, this elaborate neo-Tudor Gothic structure is 900 feet long fronting the Thames River. It is perhaps the largest Gothic revival structure ever built. Its plan is formally arranged but the elaborate tracery and other Gothic devices that make up the exterior and interior surfaces provide the prescribed look.

The initial resistance to Gothic revival as an architectural design for houses

12-12 *The board and batten siding and jigsawed bargeboards give the Delamater Cottage, Rhinebeck, New York, the "correct" Gothic look of the 1840s. Photograph by Wayne Andrews.*

rapidly dwindled in the United States as it did in England, and the style soon supplanted the classical idiom. The inherent freedom found in the Gothic revival style is in marked contrast to the rigid formality of most Greek revival designs. There are few restraints in its plan or facade; in fact, the less formal, more natural, and varied a design was, the more it was admired. Although Gothic revival church design copied more closely original Gothic churches in plan, structure, and detail, domestic architecture made no attempt to copy the homes of the Middle Ages. However, all the details, devices, and elements that are identified with Gothic architecture were used, but they were applied freely to informally arranged houses with more or less functional floor plans. Materials were again used in their natural state; stone was permitted to look like stone, wood like wood, and if painted, colors such as tans, ochers and slate gray merged the building with nature. Also, nature was allowed to grow to its own design and not be forced into man-made shapes.

As the buildings of the early nineteenth century were given classical porticoes to conform to the Greek revival ideal, houses now were remodeled to express the romance of the Gothic.[4] And romantic it was. The natural landscape provided the proper setting for the asymmetrically designed houses covered with turrets, buttresses, pointed arches, and lacy details. It was not unusual to even find a vine-covered "ruin" as a gatehouse, outbuilding, or hideaway. The formal garden was abandoned and in its stead was the garden that appeared unstudied and quaint. The rock garden with a pool and grotto was immensely popular.

[4]The Gothic revival style was largely an expression of the intellectual class and the avant garde. Among the early Gothic enthusiasts were James Fenimore Cooper, Washington Irving, and Samuel F. B. Morse, who all remodeled their homes into the favored style. It also appealed to the eccentric, romantic, and individualist, and as the English Horace Walpole, builder of Strawberry Hill, said a half century before, "One must have taste to be sensible to the beauties of Grecian architecture, whereas one only wants passions to feel the Gothic."

12-13 *Once fashionably in style, this house in the old mining town of Black Hawk, Colorado, drips with wooden icicles. The elaborate jigsawed bargeboards and board and batten siding make this house an excellent example of the "stick" school of architecture.*

The architect Alexander J. Davis[5] was noted for his Gothic revival houses. Two houses designed by Davis that illustrate the style are the Delamater Cottage (1844) in Rhinebeck, New York, and Lyndhurst (1836–1865), Tarrytown, New York. The Delamater Cottage, although symmetrically planned, shows many of the elements and details that were used throughout the East and Midwest: the emphasis on the vertical, the steep roof with wooden lace dripping from the edges, the board and batten exterior surface, the pointed arched windows with diamond panes, the medievally inspired double-diamond chimneys, the decorative wooden porch, and the projecting bay windows.

Wood became the most common material for these houses. The ease with which it could be shaped surpassed that of other materials and even though stone or brick might be used for basic structures, the ornament is almost always wood. The development of the jigsaw made possible the marvelous wooden lace that was fastened everywhere—*bargeboards* on the edges of the roofs, balustrades atop the porches and roofs, the surface of the house, the supports on the porch; in fact, it seems almost any place that the wooden lace would stick. The term Gingerbread Gothic is often applied to houses that have a wealth of this ornament.

Jigsaw Gothic is used when referring to ornament that is cut only with the

---

[5] A. J. Davis (1803–1892) was one of the founders of the American Institute of Architects. One of the leaders of the Gothic revival style, he with his contemporaries are unexpected godfathers of twentieth-century architecture because of their break with tradition in formally arranged floor plans and structure masses. Davis has also been compared with Frank Lloyd Wright and Mies van der Rohe in his conviction that the interior and its furnishing should be in harmony with the exterior. Davis often designed not only the floor plan and exterior but the interior detailing and most of the furniture; for example, records show that he made at least fifty separate designs for furniture for Lyndhurst between 1840–1847.

12-14 *A particularly fine example of a wooden Gothic revival church is the Calvary Presbyterian Church in Portland, Oregon (1882–1883). Flat boards have been ingeniously cut to produce the requisite effect of carving. Consequently, buildings ornamented in this way are often called "Carpenter Gothic."* Courtesy of Oregon Historical Society.

jigsaw and that has a rectangular cross-section—no shaping by plane or chisel. This less expensive decorative treatment was the aesthetic link between the affluent society and those of more modest means. The most untutored carpenter could express his artistic bent in the bargeboards, porch aprons, and roof finials that he attached to the houses of the ordinary homeowner. It was the architectural ornament of the people, all of the people. In its bold, self-confident exuberance and unlimited variety a harmony emerged that expressed the motto of the United States, "E pluribus unum." Extremely popular, even after the Gothic revival style had virtually disappeared, such ornament is found on houses built as late as 1910.

The use of vertical boards nailed to the exterior surface with narrow moldings covering the cracks between them (board and batten) reflected the vertical and linear qualities found in the original Gothic. It also expressed the interest in the "stick."[6] Houses with board and batten siding have been characterized as in the "stick style."

Lyndhurst began as a romantic country mansion designed by Davis and was later enlarged by him into an enormous Gothic castle. Made of gray Sing Sing marble, the final structure has all the familiar Gothic architectural devices: the high square tower of the English cathedral, the pointed arch, the large tracery lancet windows with stained glass, oriel (bay) windows, clusters of chimneys, crockets, pinnacles, and buttresses. The exterior has very little apparent symmetry, but upon inspection of the plan the rooms are arranged

---

[6]The use of the "stick" in design is found throughout history. Stick construction is especially evident in furniture and can be seen in Egyptian, Byzantine, medieval, Early American, and so-called "rustic" furniture design. The love of the quaint and picturesque, a Gothic revival trait, manifests itself not only in furniture made of sticks and the small limbs of trees, sometimes with the bark left on, but in cottages and cabins constructed of logs or surfaced with bark-covered slabs and having "gingerbread" decoration composed of naturally gnarled and forked branches instead of jigsawed wood.

in a most symmetrical way with a center axis traversing the length of the building.

Lyndhurst is now the property of the National Trust. Originally built in 1838 as a country retreat for William Paulding, a former New York congressman and New York City mayor, it was purchased in 1864 by a wealthy New York merchant, George Merritt. It was he who had it almost doubled in size by the original architect in 1865. In 1880 the mansion was purchased by Jay Gould, the railroad tycoon and financier. The exterior and interior have been preserved with only slight changes made by Gould and his heirs, Helen and Anna, his two daughters. It was Anna, Duchess of Tallyrand-Perigord, who bequeathed Lyndhurst to the National Trust in 1961 with all its furnishings and art collection as a memorial to her parents.

By the 1840s houses everywhere began to acquire jigsawed bargeboards, pointed arched moldings here and there, and other Gothic details that aided in the creation of the romantic look that was so desired. Within these Gothic revival homes, little light filters through the frosted and colored diamond paned windows. The entrance hall is narrow and the stair is no longer an important part of it, but is relegated to an obscure corner or to an adjoining tower. The many and irregularly shaped rooms with little nooks and crannies, asking to be explored, spread in all directions. Pattern is everywhere. The walls are covered with flowered or Gothic-design wallpaper; the floors are tiled, inlaid, and carpeted with an excess of flowers, tracery, and checkerboards; and the ceiling perhaps has pseudovaulting painted with appropriate designs. Even the woodwork is crenolated and painted with quatrefoils, rosettes, and other geometric designs. The effect is somewhat stifling.

The Gothic revival was but a preview of what would be revived after 1850. It was as if every form and style that had been previously built suddenly became favored, and it was not uncommon to see strange and wondrous

a

b

c

12-15 *These eight houses, all built after 1850 and before
1900, barely indicate the stylistic variety of homes that were
constructed in the United States during the last half of the
nineteenth century.*

d

e

f

g

h

combinations of disparate elements on one building. There was no longer the order and visual compatibility of adjacent houses in eighteenth- and early nineteenth-century towns and neighborhoods. Each house became the individual statement of its architect, builder, or owner. The jumble of revived styles and periods can be seen in A. J. Davis' 1867 repertoire of country and suburban houses: American Log Cabin, Farm House, English Cottage, Collegiate Gothic, Manor House, French Suburban, Switz Cottage, Lombard Italian, Tuscan from Pliny's Villa at Ostia, Ancient Etruscan, Suburban Greek, Oriental, Moorish, and Castellated. Later critics have disparagingly referred to the eclectic architecture of the latter half of the nineteenth century as Reign of Terror and General Grant. But whatever the name, it cannot be denied that the architecture did reflect the owner's (and architect's) need for personal expression, awareness of the past, and consciousness of "culture."

The Centennial Exhibition held during the summer of 1876 in Philadelphia caused two architectural styles to become popular. The historic occasion that was being celebrated spurred a renewed interest in pre-Revolutionary architecture, furniture, and artifacts (a "Colonial" kitchen on display was one of the most popular exhibits.) Houses began to be built in what is now known as the "Colonial style," some more faithful than others to the original designs. (The popularity of this style has not completely disappeared to this day and is still being built throughout the United States.)

The second stylistic development in domestic architecture was, for rather vague reasons, called Queen Anne. Again influenced by an exhibit at the Centennial Exhibition, this originally English style was eclectic and picturesque. An asymmetrical arrangement of the forms, spaces, and decorative elements was almost mandatory.

The Queen Anne style of architecture was a development within the Aesthetic movement in England, and was extremely popular there during the late 1870s and 1880s. English Queen Anne houses are invariably made of

12-16 *The woodworking machines of the nineteenth century were essential to create the wealth of ornamental detail that encrusted the Carson House in Eureka, California (1886).*

12-17 *The elaborate dormered mansard roof, the imaginative use of classical and Renaissance detail, and the sheer exuberance of the facade make the Mitchell Building in Milwaukee (1876) one of the best examples of Second Empire architecture in America.*

smooth, dark red brick with very narrow joints, and with brighter red brick and terra-cotta molded ornament and detailing. The sunflower motif (originally a Japanese decorative device) is almost always incorporated into the facade in a repeating border or in central panel as a symmetrical potted plant. The construction date is also prominently displayed. Many of the late nineteenth-century suburban middle-class developments of London and other English cities are almost completely Queen Anne style, and even today, have a remarkably unified, but in no way repetitious or monotonous, appearance.

American Queen Anne houses are perhaps best characterized by balloon framing, irregular outlines with several porches, balconies, sloping roofs, turrets, and balustrades. The exterior surfaces were often a combination of clapboard, board and batten, and diagonal and diamond patterned boards. Elaborately shaped shingles and jigsawed ornament were also incorporated into the exterior design. The interior plans were open, airy, and spacious. Large archways and fewer interior walls, especially on the first floor, created an openness that finally was practical in any climate because of the development of central heating.

By the 1880s elaborate houses of pretentious scale and eclectic ornament could be found throughout the United States, from the Victorian Mansion in Portland, Maine, to the Carson House in Eureka, California. No city, town, or village was without an example of these exaggerated houses, always grandiose, heavily encrusted with rather crude ornament, and obviously expensive to construct.

The mansard roof, so popular in France in the seventeenth and early eighteenth centuries, reappeared in the midnineteenth century with renewed vigor. Used on the new construction of the Louvre in Paris, it is believed to have been first used in the United States in New York City in about 1850. The fashionable mansions of the 1880s based upon the French château and the grandiose public, government, and commercial buildings in the "Flam-

12-18   *The massive and varied stonework of Trinity Church in Boston (1872–1877) is characteristic of H. H. Richardson. Although exhibiting many Romanesque details, the church is one of the landmarks of American architecture.* Photograph by Wayne Andrews.

boyant French," "General Grant," or "Second Empire" style are the direct result of the renewed popularity of the mansard roof.

An architect of considerable importance during the 1870s and 1880s was Henry Hobson Richardson (1838–1886). His buildings, commercial, religious, and residential, reflect a monumental ruggedness. Greatly admired during his lifetime, his mastery of stone and wood continued to influence lesser, and also younger, architects both in the United States and Europe long after his untimely death. On first inspection Richardson's buildings are strongly influenced by the Romanesque style but are, with careful analysis, remarkably innovative and he never hesitated to incorporate the latest mechanical convenience into his buildings.[7]

Perhaps the rugged massive stonework, laboriously constructed, best characterizes Richardson's buildings; there is no frivolity, ornament is extremely limited, and all parts have been hewn to exact taste. Possibly Richardson's best-known structure is the huge Trinity Church in Boston, Massachusetts, but his buildings also include a library, city hall and prison, train stations, lighthouse, warehouse, and private residences. In his houses Richardson developed a functionalism that was seldom achieved before. The Glessner House (1886) in Chicago, Illinois (the only surviving example of Richardson's Chicago buildings), has been cited by the Landmark Commission for "the fine planning for an urban site, which opens the family rooms to the quiet serenity of an inner yard; the effective ornament and decoration; and the impressive Romanesque masonry, expressing dignity and power." The interiors, however, are not as resolved as they might be because of Richardson's death prior to the completion of his work, but many of his interiors are beautifully arranged with fine woods, stone, and other dark materials used to perfection.

[7]In Richardson's Glessner House in Chicago, air conditioning was attempted by passing air over blocks of ice in the basement before it was circulated through the rooms above.

12-19 The exterior of the Glessner House in Chicago presents a rather formidable appearance and displeased many of the neighbors when it was built. (The French Renaissance home, photo 12–15f, is directly across the street.) However, the functional plan with its many light-filled rooms opening onto the sunlit inner court provides an excellent model for today's urban home.

Richardson was also instrumental in the development of a major wooden style of domestic architecture, the "shingle style" Richardson massed larger forms, pierced by strips of windows and bays, and then covered all with a rippling surface of wooden shingles. The effect was one of quiet, shimmering texture when compared to the quick linear rhythms of the "stick style." By the 1880s other major architects, especially the firm of McKim, Mead and White, were also designing in the "shingle style," but, unfortunately, the popularity of these innovative houses was short-lived.

The Great Fire in Chicago in 1871 induced a spurt of building that was seldom possible in other cities in the United States and, similar to the period after the Great Fire of London two hundred years before, there followed a development of new forms, new regularity, and new structural methods and materials. Architects throughout the United States were drawn to Chicago and, what became known as the Chicago School of Architecture then evolved.

The most notable development during this period was the skyscraper (a building of twelve or more stories high and of skeleton construction). The use of metal in architecture was not new, of course, as metal devices such as nails and clamps had been used for thousands of years. Cast-iron bridges had also been built in the late eighteenth century and the famous Crystal Palace was constructed of cast iron and glass in London for the Great Exhibition of 1851. During the 1850s and continuing for more than thirty years, many buildings with cast-iron facades were constructed in the United States and in Europe. It should be noted that during this period many men not trained as architects but as engineers were designing buildings. James Bogardus (1800–1874), a manufacturer of cast iron, began to produce component parts modeled from Gothic, classic, and Renaissance prototypes, which when combined could serve as facades for stores and other commercial buildings. Soon towns and cities throughout the eastern half of the nation had many of these often handsome and elegant structures. Today, they are still fairly

12-20 *Beautiful wood dominates the interior of the Glessner House.*

12-21 *Designed in 1887, the W. G. Low Residence in Bristol, Rhode Island, by McKim, Mead, and White is one of the finest houses in the "shingle style." Without ornamentation, it reflects the early houses of seventeenth-century America and forecasts the functionalism of the twentieth century.* Photograph by Wayne Andrews.

12-22 *The inherent strength of cast iron plus the ability to assume any form into which the molten metal is poured produced a building material of great flexibility. Portland, Oregon, until recently, had many buildings with cast-iron facades. The Kamm Building (1884), seen through the open corner of another cast-iron building (supported by a slender iron column) was one of them. The photograph on the right is a detail of the cornice and pediment that centered the entrance of the Kamm Building.* Courtesy of Oregon Historical Society. Photograph on the left is by Minor White.

12-23 *Primitive structures such as this wind house in Samoa may have suggested to William Le Baron Jenney the concept that made skyscraper construction possible.*

12-24 *The innovative skeleton construction of the Home Insurance Building in Chicago is easily discernible on the exterior despite the classically inspired detail. Unfortunately, it was destroyed in 1931.*

common in the older sections of the city but are increasingly becoming victims of urban renewal.

It was Chicago, however, where the first truly *skeleton structure* or *metal cage* was used. William Le Baron Jenney (1832–1907)[8] is usually credited as being the designer of the first skyscraper, the Home Insurance Building (1885). Almost immediately other buildings were designed with skeleton construction, as the next year the firm of Holabird and Roche built the Tacoma Building, an even more open and skeletal building. The era of tall structures had begun.[9]

At this time also in Chicago two more, yet opposing trends in architecture began, developing almost simultaneously, yet each pitted against the other. One was the outgrowth of the influence of the World's Columbian Exposition (1893), and the other, the architectural work of Louis Sullivan and the Chicago School of Architecture.

In 1889, almost twenty years after the devastating fire, a group of Chicago businessmen decided that the new, prospering metropolis should be shown to the world. Securing the approval of Congress, they planned an exposition to rival the previous world fairs of London, Paris, and Philadelphia. As first envisioned, the fair would be held along Lake Michigan in Jackson Park, a

[8]The son of a prosperous shipowner in Massachusetts, Jenney at the age of eighteen embarked on a voyage to California, the Philippines, and the South Seas. There he saw the flexible and durable, but light, bamboo skelton construction of the native huts. Although this may not be of major importance, only Jenney, among all the important nineteenth-century architects, came in contact with the building practices of primitive peoples. Upon his return home, Jenney decided to be a civil engineer and enrolled in the Ecole centrale in Paris, where his stay overlapped that of another pupil, Gustave Eiffel, designer of the Eiffel Tower.

[9]An invention requisite for skyscrapers had been perfected in 1852 by Elisha Graves Otis in New York—the passenger elevator with a safety device. The lower floors of buildings were no longer the most desirable; in fact, upper floors became the most in demand with their airiness, views, and distance from street noise; this was especially true in hotels.

12-25 *Viewed from the Court of Honor and toward Lake Michigan, the Central Lagoon of the World's Columbian Exposition was surrounded by gleaming white buildings encrusted with Roman and Renaissance detail. Despite the "approved" unified exteriors, the structures do not indicate what was within them. For example, on the right, surmounted by a dome topped by an almost nude Diana, is the Agriculture Building.*

windblown, underdeveloped area on the South Side, and was to be an amalgamation of architectural styles—mosques, pagodas, Romanesque towers, Russian onion domes, "barges, gondolas, flags and flutter." However, in January, 1891, during planning meetings, in deference to architects, mainly those from the east coast, the decision was made to limit building design to the classical tradition. What began as a colorful, vigorous architectural medley that possibly could have finally freed architectural design from the rigid dictates of the classical past, became instead a stupendous display of white Roman, Renaissance, and Beaux Arts of Paris "good taste." The forced symmetry, the monumental scale, and the sculptured multitudes, all made from a mixture of cement, fiber, and plaster, disappeared after the summer of 1893, but their classical influence lingered. It has been said that the development of functional architecture was set back at least fifty years and indeed, only during the past twenty years has architecture fully broken the stifling bonds of the past and begun to surge forward.

One architect who did not follow the dictum of the "White City" was Louis H. Sullivan (1856–1924). His original distinctive Transportation Building was the only major structure that did not resurrect the glories of the past. Sullivan, one of the most innovative architects that Chicago ever produced, had been a student of Richardson. Along with Dankmar Adler (1844–1900) Sullivan had built the magnificent Auditorium Building (1886–1889). Although it is reminiscent of Romanesque and is certainly influenced by the stonework of Richardson on the outside, the plan and inside decoration, in fact, the whole concept of the building is decidedly Sullivan. The civic and cultural center of Chicago for years, the building housed a hotel of four hundred rooms, 136 offices, restaurants, and a theater that has been considered to have the best acoustics of any in the world. After years of neglect and being closed, the theater has been restored to its original appearance and is now functioning again. The interior is a triumph of Sullivanesque decoration, gold, shimmering and exuberant. Based loosely upon nature and never

303

12-26 *Clearly influenced by the "White City" style of the World's Columbian Exposition of 1893, the Wrigley Building (1921–1924) in Chicago by Graham, Anderson, Probst, and White is sheathed in white terra-cotta embellished with Renaissance ornament. The whiteness was accented from the beginning by being floodlighted at night. Note the strong evidence of the underlying steel cage structure despite the surface detailing.*

12-27 *Sullivan and Adler's Auditorium Building, now housing Roosevelt University, in Chicago, despite its Romanesque stonework, is a masterpiece of functional design. Many innovations in construction and ornamental design were first used in the building.*

upon past styles, the decoration is applied; it is never part of the structure and one wonders can this be by the same person who coined the phrase "Form follows function?" Surely, Sullivan did not refer to only mechanical functions such as the traffic flow, heating, lighting and so on, but also to *human* function. Sullivan often repeated that a building was an act—an aesthetic act. To Sullivan, a building without ornament was lacking in life. He loved strong, bold, original structures but not without surface treatment. For only when a building expressed a "spirit" that reflected human satisfaction within its form did Sullivan consider it *architecture.*

Although the exterior of the Auditorium Building was derivative and did not express the inner structure, Sullivan's later buildings did. His masterpiece and America's greatest commercial building, the Schlesinger and Mayer Store (1899–1904, now Carson Pirie Scott and Company) in Chicago, clearly shows the metal cage on the exterior with a skin of large horizontal "Chicago windows"[10] stretched between the supporting structure. Although twelve stories high, there is an emphasis upon the horizontal that Sullivan believed bound the building to the human plane of man on earth. No heavy Renaissance cornice circles the top[11] but rather ornament is encrusted on the cylindrical corner entrance and stretched in two rich bands above the display windows and on the third-floor level. The exuberance of the luxuriant cast-iron ornament is without equal.

The Chicago School of Architecture, in spite of the magnetism of classical tradition, flourished over a half century until about 1925, and although many commercial and industrial structures were built during this time, the Chicago School influenced all types of architecture. It was an original, indigenous, and

[10] A window with a large, fixed central pane and narrow, movable sashes on each side.
[11] When first built there was a very narrow cornice that projected slightly, but this has now been replaced by a bald parapet.

12-28 *One of the most famous commercial buildings in the world, the Schlesinger and Mayer Store (now the Carson Pirie Scott and Company) designed by Louis Sullivan has a facade that is almost entirely of "Chicago windows." Only near the ground level, where the customer will be drawn to it, is there ornament.*

organic architecture that included skyscrapers, hotels, apartments, warehouses, schools, churches, and private residences.

Working in Sullivan's office as a draftsman was a young man from Wisconsin destined to become America's greatest architect. Frank Lloyd Wright (1869–1959) had arrived in Chicago in 1887 aged eighteen after two years at the University of Wisconsin and soon found work in the office of Adler and Sullivan. Staying with the firm five years, he then resigned and began an architectural career that lasted almost seventy years. It is difficult to conceive that one individual could be so productive, so creative, and yet remain always individualistic. His designs for almost one thousand homes, ranging in size from cottage to mansion, were products of his fertile mind and yet he was not limited to residential architecture. He also produced many major buildings—all architectural landmarks of prime importance. Wright's outstanding nonresidential structures include: Larkin Building, Buffalo, New York (1904); Imperial Hotel, Tokyo, Japan (1922); offices of the Johnson Wax Company, Racine, Wisconsin (1936–1939 and 1948–1950); Florida Southern College, Lakeland, Florida (1940–); H. C. Price Building, Bartlesville, Oklahoma (1955); and Solomon Guggenheim Museum, New York City (1959).

Space does not permit more than a cursory investigation of Wright's genius but he undoubtedly influenced more architectural design in the twentieth century than any other individual; however, he did not develop what could be called a "style." His was a *philosophy* of architecture—sensed and enjoyed by those experiencing his buildings and yet seldom fully understood. Wright was interested in the solution of problems developing from a structural system that was tempered by the nature of the site, materials, and the lives of those the building would serve. "Get the habit of analysis—analysis will in time enable synthesis to become your habit of mind." It was a philosophy that came directly from his *lieber Meister*, Louis Sullivan.

12-29 *The distinctively Sullivanesque reliefs above the curved entrance are richly and plastically modeled and yet, by their judicious placement, the total building seems very restrained.*

12-30 *Designed on a module of four feet, the plan of a house by Frank Lloyd Wright for an exhibition illustrates many of his ideas. Interior space flowing from one area to another, the carport, the lack of solid walls, the merging interior and exterior, large window areas, and wide protective eaves are but a few of his ideas.*

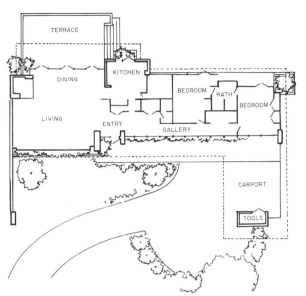

Early in his career, Wright discovered a truth that freed architecture and made modern architectural design possible. He discovered the vital difference *between* sculpture and architecture. It is not the exterior forms, as in sculpture, but the space within, the space enclosed, where man walks and lives that *is* architecture. Wright spent his life expanding upon this indisputable principle.

Wright's deep involvement with space repeatedly exposed one of the conflicting elements in the nature of man: the desire for free space versus the need for shelter and privacy. Wright's understanding satisfied both. He opened the interior of his buildings into great spaces and then divided, split, and partially hid portions so those within could experience and discover new distances. Wright gave architecture the *open plan.* He "exploded the box" and developed design devices that gave space a fluid and flexible vitality that was never rigid, lifeless, or apathetic. The following methods are some of the ways Wright developed spatial freedom. These are not hard and fast rules but rather illustrate some of the means he used.

1. Interior space should flow from one area to another. Half walls, cabinets not reaching the ceiling, and elongated sight lines provide ways of enhancing the feeling of continuous space. The eye is never stopped by a dead end.
2. Allow light to enter the building where structural planes meet rather than through holes cut into the walls. A hole (window) accents the presence and thickness of the barrier (wall) and does not minimize it.
3. The fewer right angles, the less defined the interior space appears. Instead of the square and rectangle, Wright used the circle, the triangle, the diamond, and the hexagon.
4. The overhead structure (ceiling or roof) should be interesting but should always be considered as shelter. Different heights and materials as well as unexpected light sources provide variety and excitement.

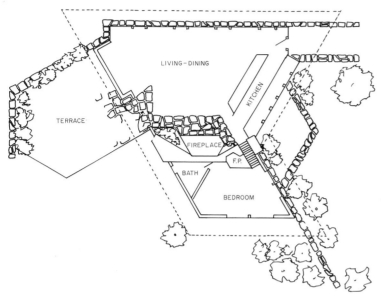

LIVING – DINING

KITCHEN

TERRACE

FIREPLACE

F.P.

BATH

BEDROOM

12-31 *Despite the small size (842 square feet) of this plan, Wright achieved a feeling of far more space. His use of 30-degree and 60-degree corners instead of the usual 90 degrees, many transparent walls, and the use of the same materials on the inside and outside make it difficult to define the actual enclosed space.*

Frank Lloyd Wright also destroyed the visual barrier between the indoors and the outdoors. He used the same materials inside and out and opened walls at their junctions rather than windows near the center with the corners solid, thereby enclosing the space without fully defining it—corners define boundaries and are reminders of the limits of a room. The use of large sheets of glass and corner windows in residential structures are two of his firsts. Wright also used electric lights in a straightforward manner, exposing the bulbs and treating them as a new type of light source, not masking them behind shades in traditional candelabrum and chandeliers. Wright also is credited with the first use of indirect lighting where the ceiling is brilliantly lit by bulbs hidden behind a deep molding. Wright introduced low, earth-hugging houses with wide protective eaves, cantilever construction[12] in houses, built-in radiant heating, the exterior and interior use of concrete blocks in residential construction, and carports. He also believed that all elements of the house were important. There could be no back or front, inside or outside. The kitchen was as important as the living and dining areas. Wright is also responsible for dispelling the Victorian house with the "Queen Anne front with the Mary Anne behind."

Wright first designed a pleasing, functional interior out of the materials and the structural system chosen. He then allowed the exterior to develop naturally (he did not neglect the exterior design, however.) Thus, as a seed (idea) is planted and grows so did his designs—"integral to the site, to environment, to the life of the inhabitants, integral with the nature of materials." It was an *organic* process, and Wright called his work *natural architecture.*

First there was Richardson, then Sullivan, and finally Wright; the triumvirate that changed architecture from the nineteenth century to the twentieth,

[12] Cantilever construction incorporates projecting horizontal beams or surfaces that are supported on only one side, the opposite side remains free.

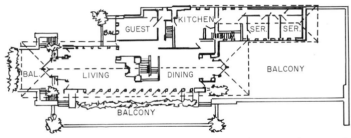

12-32 'The main floor plan of the Robie House shows Wright's use of open spaces and few right angles. The main longitudinal space for living and dining terminates on each end with windows at 45-degree angles to the axis and is punctuated near the center with a massive fireplace-stairs solid. The south wall is almost entirely glass.

12-33 The wide cantilevered eaves and an emphasis upon horizontal lines immediately identify the Robie House in Chicago as one of Wright's Prairie Houses. Note how the axis of the top floor cuts across that of the main floor.

12-34 The famous waterfall below the Kaufmann House, "Falling Water," is beneath the balconies in this photograph. Despite the rectangularity of the balconies, the house fits admirably into its setting. Photograph by Wayne Andrews.

from classical and medieval shams to buildings that are part of the landscape and compatible with the horizon wherever and whatever they are.

It is impossible to discuss even a fraction of Wright's structures, but one of his most famous and best houses is the Fredrick C. Robie House (1908–1909) in Chicago; indeed, it has frequently been called the "House of the Century." Earth-hugging with wide asymmetrical cantilevered eaves, the Robie House is the finest of Wright's "Prairie Houses." Echoing the flat prairies of the Midwest are the many horizontals, the planes of the roofs, the long, thin Roman bricks, and the bands of windows and terraces. It is also admirably suited to the narrow urban site. The interior spaces, anchored by a massive chimney, are arranged along a major longitudinal axis with a minor transverse axis on the upper floor. The rooms or living areas flow from one to another, ofttimes uninterrupted by walls and doors, yet they are defined. The spaciousness is further accented by the many high-placed windows circling the rooms, the mingling of exterior and interior walls, and the projecting window areas that thrust out onto the terraces allowing the interior and exterior to flow together. The wide roof, sheltering and shielding, seems to float above all. Recurring design motifs[13] are found throughout the house as Wright not only designed the building but also most of the furnishings. A complete harmony of site, structure, and interior is the result.

Noteworthy among Wright's other houses are the William H. Winslow House (1893) in River Forest, Illinois. This was Wright's first commission after resigning from Adler and Sullivan and it is remarkable for its forecasting of designs to come; the Avery Coonley House (1908) in Riverside, Illinois, a magnificent house with a variety of themes (fifteen in the windows alone)

---

[13] Wright was a master when giving variety to a motif. Often inspired by Japanese and Central American themes, Wright never copied but expanded upon them with great skill. Each variation was appropriate to the material from which it was made, wood, wrought iron, electro-plated glass, mosaic, bronze, or concrete.

12-35 *Wright's Taliesin West in Arizona is remarkably suited to its arid, sunny surroundings.* Photograph by Wayne Andrews.

interlocked like a symphony; Hollyhock House (1913) in Los Angeles, California, named because of its rich, abstract detailing based upon the hollyhock; the Charles Ennis House (1924) in Los Angeles, California, where concrete block has been used with such beauty and elegance; the Edgar J. Kaufmann House, "Falling Water" (1936) in Bear Run, Pennsylvania, so superbly tied to the site with the cantilevered concrete balconies echoing the natural rock ledges; the David Wright House (1951) in Scottsdale Arizona, the plan a series of arcs raised above the desert; and his own homes, Taliesin North, (1911–) in Spring Green, Wisconsin, hill and house merging into one, each enhancing the other, and Taliesin West (1938–) in Scottsdale, Arizona, a great tent, the ultimate frontier, an oasis of gardens, vast interior spaces, and massive stone forms in the desert.

The innovations of Frank Lloyd Wright far surpassed those of other architects of the twentieth century, but during this period other contributions were made to the humanism in architecture. The Prairie Houses developed in the Midwest and seem natural to it. In southern California the architectural firm of Charles S. Greene (1868–1957) and Henry M. Greene (1870–1954) were producing houses that are some of the finest examples of what became known as the California bungalow style. These homes are beautifully crafted and are masterpieces of the expert workmanship of the American Craftsman movement. Although somewhat influenced by Japanese architecture with Swiss undertones (a strange but successful combination), these houses are indigenous and are skillfully related to the social and regional environment. The Greene brothers had a deep love for wood and other natural materials and had the unique designing ability to produce a structure that became the decoration. No element or device was too small for their discriminating consideration. The interiors of their homes are a refined combination of rich materials, glass, metal, and wood (redwood, teak, mahogany, maple, and cedar) and each peg, beam, panel, tile, and molding has been designed into the whole. The furniture was also designed as part of the total. The exteriors

12-36 *The open porches, wide eaves, and projecting rafters are as carefully placed as is the precise construction and handling of materials in the Gamble House.* Photograph by Wayne Andrews.

are distinctive with broad overhanging eaves supported by exposed, hand-shaped beams and rafters, open sleeping porches and subtly stained soft green shingles that blend into the landscape. The general appearance is "rambling" and the popularity of the *patio,* an enclosed area, is largely the result of the early houses of the Greenes. One of the most complete and best preserved examples of their design is the David B. Gamble House (1909) in Pasadena, California.

Another visionary architect was Bernard Ralph Maybeck (1862–1957). Working almost exclusively in the San Francisco area, his influence shaped the architectural development of the entire west coast and is being felt elsewhere. He was a master in his combining of handcrafted materials and methods with the latest technological advances. His buildings enthrall the human spirit with their fantasy, romance, and poetry. Two of his most outstanding major buildings are the imaginative Palace of Fine Arts (1914), built as a temporary structure for the 1915 Panama-Pacific Exhibition in San Francisco and recently completely restored and rebuilt with permanent materials, and the First Church of Christ Scientist (1910), Berkeley, California, a rare and inventive combination of reinforced concrete, custom-forged fixtures, industrial window sash, carved wood, and hand-blocked ornament. However, later architects have been more influenced by his houses that are perhaps even more innovative, always stressing an individualism and respect for human scale, rare yet vital qualities, without neglecting modern technological advances. Maybeck's inventiveness was not confined to expensive designs; on the contrary, his more simple homes and community projects exhibit even greater originality. For example, he built several low-cost small homes with walls made of potato sacks dipped in concrete and then suspended over wires, an economic yet quite handsome solution.

An important stylistic development began almost simultaneously in several countries in Europe around the turn of the century. Lasting a little more than a decade, it is known in England and the United States by its

12-37 *Bernard Maybeck combined concrete, red-wood, and metal sashed windows, added a liberal dash of Gothic, and produced this window and facade detail of the First Church of Christ Scientist in Berkeley, California.*

French name, Art Nouveau. Mainly a style of decoration rather than structure, few buildings can be considered completely Art Nouveau in appearance. However, isolated architectural details, individual rooms, and, more importantly many pieces of furniture and accessories were designed in this style.

As the name implies, Art Nouveau, "new art," evolved when attempts were made to design without dependence upon the historical past. The most striking characteristics are the dominance of linear patterns—melodious, agitated, undulating, flowing, flaming, and sinuous—and the use of asymmetrical balance.

Although the major architectural developments in Art Nouveau were made in Europe,[14] three well-known American designers are closely identified with it. The decorative cast-iron and terra-cotta ornament of Louis Sullivan, much of Frank Lloyd Wright's early geometric decorative designs, and the interiors, glass and metal lighting fixtures and lamps, and exquisite stained-glass windows of Louis Comfort Tiffany (1848–1933) are all important features of Art Nouveau design.

The rejection of the past and an insistence upon originality was the aim of Art Nouveau, yet it did not continue as a major influence after about 1910. Why did such a vigorous artistic movement not continue? From the advantage of hindsight, the answer is clear; it failed to face the problems of modern, large-scale machine production.

World War I was a turning point in history.[15] In addition to its political

12-38 *The styles within the genus called Art Nouveau are varied—geometric or organic, flamboyant or austere—yet, there is a newness, creativeness about each. The Casa Milá in Barcelona, Spain, built by Antonio Gaudi between 1905 and 1907, is curved, organic, and assymetrical, and is full of motifs and details reminiscent of the sea.*

[14] Leading European architects were Charles Rennie Mackintosh (1868–1928) in Scotland; Antonio Gaudi (1852–1926) in Spain, considered the greatest Art Nouveau architect; Hector Guimard (1867–1942) in France; Joseph Hoffman (1870–1956) in Austria; and Victor Horta (1861–1947) in Belgium.

[15] There had not been such a cultural change since the Renaissance spirit replaced medieval thought, and future historians will probably mark 1914 as the end of the Renaissance period.

12-39 *The innovative use of a glass curtain wall on the Workshop Building of the Bauhaus set the precedent for the virtual elimination of the appearance of "structure" on most contemporary buildings.* Courtesy of The Museum of Modern Art.

implications, the war disrupted the social values and structures of a large part of the world, caused masses of people to be moved either as soldiers or victims of the conflict, and generated concentrated mechanical and technological developments. Following the war, the search for new original ideas intensified and several trends developed in Holland, Germany, and France. It was in Germany, however, where the most decisive and far-reaching architectural design philosophies developed. Wracked by disillusionment and poverty, Germany was ripe for change—the past had been beaten, and in 1919 a new school was opened under the leadership of Walter Gropius (1883–1969), an architect. Destined to be the most revolutionary design school of all time, the Bauhaus[16] brought together all of the arts, painting, architecture, graphics, and the crafts, and each focused upon industrialism and the potential beauty that could be possible when using machines. Gropius believed that the artist could give life to the machine and that the designer had to "become directly involved in mass production and the industrialist must be taught to accept the artist and his values." Soon Gropius had gathered around him some of the most experimental and original teachers[17] in Europe. Students were taught to search, probe, and experiment, and soon designs for all kinds of products and structures began to emerge from the school; designs that seemed exactly right for the time. The architectural designs that were produced expressed no national or historical heritage and were without precedent. Their influence was felt throughout the world and architects abroad began to design similar buildings; it was an International style.

Originally situated in Weimar, Germany, the Bauhaus moved to Dessau,

---

[16] *Bau-,* "structure," and *haus,* "house."
[17] The Bauhaus roster reads like a *Who's Who* of European painters, designers, and architects and included Paul Klee, Wassily Kandinsky, Josef Albers, Laszlo Moholy-Nagy, Marcel Breuer, and Ludwig Mies van der Rohe.

12-40   *The German Pavilion, International Exposition, Barcelona, Spain.*

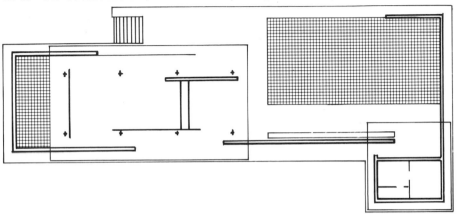

Germany, in 1925 and into a Gropius-designed group of three connected structures that housed studio-dormitories, dining hall, workshops, administration and social rooms, and classrooms. Straightforward, flat-topped, and structurally spare, these buildings were to become prototypes for uncounted future buildings. The horizontal bands of windows with cantilevered slab-like balconies on the living quarters can now be seen on many buildings, especially apartments, but the most dramatic innovation was the design of the workshop. Four stories high with the upper three stories cantilevered over the ground floor, it is enclosed with a continuous curtain wall of glass. This had been technically possible since the metal cage had been introduced almost 50 years before. Sullivan's Carson Pirie Scott building approaches the concept but the traditional idea that a window is a "hole in the wall" prevented him from accomplishing what Gropius did. Gropius in his Bauhaus Workshop Building states that in modern architecture the exterior is no more than a curtain or climate barrier, which may be made of glass, metal, or other material, and that the structure is entirely independent of the encircling walls. The United Nations Secretariat Building (1949–1951), Lever House (1952), and the Seagram Building (1958) in New York City are but three later buildings that owe their design heritage to the Bauhaus Workshop Building. A continuing development has been the use of mirror glass for curtain walls that often reflects the surrounding environment, buildings, sky, and the like. Frequently the whole form of a mirror glass-covered building is negated because the building becomes almost invisible. This visual phenomenon is a reversal of the past consideration that the form equaled the building. In the past the form of a building was visible and solid in appearance. This was followed by the organic concept of architecture, natural architecture, in which the building was blended into the landscape, but continued to be visible. The use of mirror glass, however, removes the building almost from sight; it becomes a "nonbuilding," and with the present trend of raising structures on stilts further erases all sense of weight and presence.

12-41 *Mies van der Rohe's apartment houses in Chicago revolutionized apartment house construction. The dark grid and glass exteriors, stark rectlinear forms, and elegant proportions were copied throughout the world.*

Ludwig Mies van der Rohe (1886–1969) designed the German Pavilion at the International Exposition at Barcelona, Spain,[18] in 1929. Still considered to have been one of the finest exhibition buildings ever built, this small, elegant, one-story shelter was made of onyx, green marble, travertine, gray transparent glass, and chromium-plated steel columns. Its immediate acceptance brought international recognition to Mies, and the next year he was commissioned to design a two-story version of the Barcelona Pavilion adapted for residential requirements. The result was the famed Tugendhat House built in Brno, Czechoslovakia. This house, sitting on a steep hill, is entered on the top level that contains the entrance hall, bedrooms, guest suite, and a garage. The lower floor, the main level, is partially divided by freestanding partitions into study, living, dining, and pantry areas. The interior is a remarkable composition of exquisite purity. Ebony, pale onyx, marble, chrome, bronze, and neutral colors are combined with immaculate taste and illustrates Mies's famous credo "Less is more."

In 1930, Mies van der Rohe was also appointed director of the Bauhaus School following Gropius' resignation. He continued in that post until 1933 when it was closed because of the political unrest in Germany.

The United States was the fortunate recipient of much of the talent and excitement that had permeated the Bauhaus. Many of the teachers eventually came to the United States to live. Gropius, after a few years in London, became head of the Department of Architecture at Harvard in 1938. Mies van der Rohe also arrived in this country in 1938 and continued to develop and refine his glass and steel theories. In the late 1940s Mies built four trailblazing, high-rise apartment buildings in Chicago, and in 1958 his 38-story glass and bronze Seagram Building was opened. These highly disciplined and exquisitely refined buildings cast a formula that, unfortunately, has been

[18] For this building Mies van der Rohe designed the famed chrome, steel, and leather Barcelona chair, the most beautiful modern chair.

12-42 *This facade of the Villa Stein is a study in precise spatial relationships.*

cheapened by the computerized, slick, boxy buildings that have been rapidly multiplying in every city.

In France the most noted and respected architect in the international style was the Swiss-born Le Corbusier (Charles Édouard Jeanneret, 1887–1965). Beginning as a painter and sculptor, "Corbu" has influenced modern architecture as much as has Sullivan, Wright, Gropius, or Mies van der Rohe. His book *Towards an Architecture*, published in 1923, helped shape and give direction to the movement, and his early houses are as important as the Prairie Houses but are *machines à habiter* ("machines to be lived in"). They draw a sharp line between man and nature and are *not* part of the landscape but remain separate and machine-like, a distinction of the International style.

One of Le Corbusier's most influential early houses was built for Michael Stein—the brother of Gertrude Stein. Located outside Paris, it was completed in 1928 and was the home of Stein and his wife for the next seven years.[19] When the Steins commissioned Le Corbusier to design their house he was still relatively unknown, but while he was designing this house he formulated his famous five points that became the creed of modern architecture. The Villa Stein was his first structure illustrating these points: 1) Columns rather than walls supporting concrete slabs. 2) Roof terraces—the south half of the top level is a terrace. 3) Open planning—with the structure not relying upon bearing walls, a more flexible plan could result. 4) Strip or ribbon windows. 5) A facade not dependent upon the structure, which permitted the design to be freely determined.

Le Corbusier's Villa Savoye (1929–1930), also outside Paris, is equally famous but is raised upon stilts (*pilotis*) and exhibits a geometry that is even purer.

After the early 1930s, Le Corbusier became more sculptural in contrast to

[19] The Steins sold the villa in 1935 to a Norwegian banker. In 1957 it was sold to the present owner who converted it into four apartments. It is hardly recognizable today.

12-43 *One of the more unusual and conceptually innovative recent structures, the Nakagin Capsule Tower Building (1971) by Kisho Noriaki Kurokawa and Associates, Ginza, Tokyo, Japan, is the result of the awareness of ecological necessities and contemporary life patterns. Designed for the businessman who must stay overnight in town, 140 one-room prefabricated steel apartments are hung from two towers that contain a cafeteria, elevators, and utilities. The apartment capsules were fabricated in a factory in Osaka in 3 hours and trucked to the construction site in Tokyo. Each filtered, air-conditioned capsule is 4 x 2.5 x 2.5 meters and contains a bath, bed, desk with calculator, color television set, and closet. The single round window on each unit easily suggests a large birdhouse—to which it might be compared. However, the efficient use of space in each capsule, prefabrication, and construction systems and unique design mark the building as an outstanding solution to a housing, pollution, and space problem. Photograph by Tomio Ohashi.*

the continued distillation of Mies. He also became involved with urban housing and his renowned Unite d'Habitation (1947–1952), an apartment house in Marseilles, shows a muscular strength that is not found in the work of Mies van der Rohe. This enormous block—200 feet long and eighteen stories high—is raised on massive *pilotis* and is ruggedly made of raw concrete (*breton brut*), the marks of the form boards have been left to give texture and a certain truthfulness to the material. More than a simple apartment complex, it is a complete community. The structure is bisected horizontally by a floor devoted to shops and services, an "internal street," and on the roof are play and sunbathing areas and a swimming facility. The 337 apartments are ingeniously arranged, interlocking in such a way that they occupy a floor and a half with the living room ceiling sixteen feet high. All apartments open onto terraces framed by concrete shields that control the sun's glare and provide privacy. The building's rugged handsomeness and innovative concept have been borrowed for major housing projects all over the world including those in Brasilia, Brazil, by Oscar Niemeyer (1960) and Le Corbusier's own Olympic Hill Apartment House in Berlin (1958).

Except for a few isolated examples, the International style was not accepted in the United States as readily as it had been in Europe and the rest of the world. It was not until the 1940s that "functional" architecture began to be admired and built in this country. (During the same period Wright also had few commissions, although Bear Run, the Kaufmann House, was built in 1936. This was no doubt in part a result of the financial climate during the 1930s and World War II, but it was also because of the pall of classicism that still hung over United States architecture.)

After World War II a decided shift occurred in architecture. The giants of contemporary architecture, Wright, Gropius, Mies van der Rohe, and Le Corbusier continued to produce outstanding buildings until their deaths. Their trailblazing opened the way for other architects to forge ahead, and

modern architecture has achieved complete acceptance, especially in non-residential buildings.

The proliferation of glass-walled structures has recently caused some architectural critics to voice concern about the sterile mediocrity of many new structures and, indeed, once the "formula" has been determined, it is often abused by lesser architects. However, it is heartening to find increasing numbers of exciting, innovative, functional, and significant nonresidential structures of all sizes being designed and built throughout the world. Optimistically, one can only hope that this trend will continue and grow, and that the number of banal and inferior buildings will decline.

Despite many significant technical and material developments in the last 25 years, residential architecture has lagged behind nonresidential architecture. There have been few truly innovative pacesetting houses, houses that have influenced the design of others. One house of especial merit that has proven to be of considerable importance since it was built in 1949 is the house that Philip C. Johnson designed for himself in New Canaan, Connecticut. Situated on a large, wooded tract of land, it rests with pristine purity on a carefully manicured lawn. The house is a clean, precise glass box, very simple in interior plan and clearly influenced by the International style of the 1920s.

There are no solid exterior walls, only large panels of clear glass. The entire interior is one large open rectangular space, about 1,600 square feet, floored with polished brick and pierced only once floor to ceiling by a brick cylinder ten feet in diameter that contains the bath and fireplace. The food preparation (kitchen) area is contained in and screened from the living and dining areas by a partial wall of walnut, $3\frac{1}{2}$ feet high. The sleeping area is divided from the rest of the interior by a six-feet-high walnut storage wall. The living area is defined by a white rug, five carefully placed pieces of elegant furniture, and a freestanding painting. The feeling of openness extends beyond the transparent walls and into the surrounding landscape

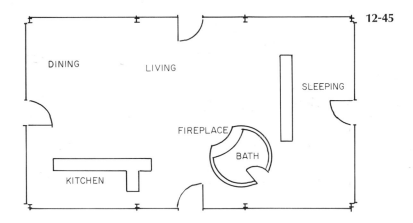

12-45

with the wide expanse of the high ceiling ($10\frac{1}{2}$ feet) serving as the only visible shelter from the elements.

Johnson's careful and thorough planning is evident throughout the house. The unique method of lighting is a case in point. At night, except for bed, bath, and kitchen lights, the interior is lighted by a complex system of exterior illumination. The trees are spotlighted and the lawn adjacent to the house is brightly lit from above, which creates the illusion that the interior brick floor is floating slightly above the ground. In addition, exterior flood-lights embedded in the ground project a diffused light onto the ceiling inside. With the light outside brighter than that inside, it is difficult to see into the house as the glass walls reflect the scenery, or else one sees completely through to the trees beyond just as during the day.

Philip Johnson's house was one of the first houses to consist of one room with the living areas marked off by furniture and storage units, and the kitchen open to the rest of the house. Such innovations, along with the sense of openness provided by the expanses of glass, have since been used again and again in domestic architecture. However, the Johnson house is no ordinary house and, although it has influenced many family houses, it was not meant for a family but to serve the needs of a bachelor. Johnson is the first to admit that the structure is not a complete, self-contained house and that any clutter or excess of objects would shatter the stark elegance he desires. His answer to the storage problem takes three forms. The first is an almost windowless brick guest house, which is basically the same rectangular form as the main house, and is the opaque counterpart of the transparent main house. Johnson then added in 1965 an underground gallery[20] for his extensive collection of paintings. The paintings are hung on huge screens that swing like pages in a book. Finally, in 1970, he built an underground

[20] This unique and thoroughly contemporary structure was surprisingly inspired by the Treasury of Atreus in Mycenae (c. 1325 B.C.).

12-46 *The Lustron House, the first real attempt to industrialize the whole house, was developed shortly after World War II. Steel framed with an exterior surface of enameled steel, it has weathered well the almost 30 years since it was first produced. Yet, despite its many attributes and rather traditional design, this house did not prove to be popular and without the large volume of production necessary to cut costs, the price remained relatively high, compounding its nonacceptance.*

sculpture gallery where his collection of contemporary sculpture is arranged on different levels around a central five-sided well.

Unlike most of the houses built in the International style of the 1920s and 1930s and that now frequently look dated, the Johnson House has survived the test of time extremely well and has become one of the classics of American architecture. It is probably the best known house built in the world in the past twenty-five years.

It must be remembered that the major responsibility for the construction of houses expressing new ideas rests upon the public's approval. Architects may design outstanding houses and manufacturers may produce new materials and develop new building techniques, but if they are not accepted and requested by homeowners and others responsible for building commissions, then architecture changes little and a stifling rigidity of design follows.

Several attempts have been made to produce good, innovative, relatively inexpensive houses on a large scale using industrial technology, but the public has preferred conventionally built smaller Mount Vernons or Williamsburg houses. Only recently are more houses being built incorporating new ideas and materials, and although their number is growing yearly, the proportion of these new houses is small when compared to the total number of houses built each year. These houses must be considered, for the most part, isolated examples hardly denoting any major shift in residential architectural design or construction. One noticeable trend, however, that started in the late 1960s and has unfortunately, been embraced by too many architects, builders, and clients searching for a contemporary idiom is the sculptural house type. Their clustered interpenetrating geometric solids (square and round), steeply angled shed and flat roofs, terraces, and flush exterior wall surfaces pierced with windows that make each facade an abstract composition often give these houses the appearance of contemporary, functionalized fortresses or castles. Yet, despite their "today" appearance, these houses are invariably constructed by traditional methods using conventional materials.

The somewhat pessimistic concluding paragraphs of this survey of architectural history are not meant to give the impression that all is hopeless. On the contrary, the increasing acceptance of recent developments in residential architectural design, materials, techniques, and concepts, although not as universal as one would wish, *does* suggest that at least domestic building may soon be released from many of the smothering bonds that architecture now has and permit more efficient, pleasant, positive, and humanistic environments to be built in the future.

Part Four

Furniture Design

The best and most picturesque
furniture of all ages has been
simple in general form.

Charles Lock Eastlake

13 Furniture: Prehistoric, Egyptian, Greek, Roman

Few objects in the environment reflect the psychological, moral, social, and political attitudes of a culture more than the furniture in the homes of the people. Architecture has historically revealed the grand design or a public consciousness. The exterior designs of buildings are changed less often than are the interiors and are many times monumental, removed from the human scale. But, it has been how man has filled his private places that more closely indicated what he wanted in life and how he went about getting it. From the beginning of time man has attempted to find suitable storage for his possessions, to increase his physical comfort, and to add aesthetic beauty to his domestic belongings by experimenting with various materials, construction methods, surface finishes, and forms of ornamentation. The evolvement of distinct furniture forms, from prehistory to the present, proves to be a fascinating record of the development of civilization. Much can be determined about a culture, the importance accorded to dignity, manners, elegance, and comfort—and even posture, by the kinds and numbers of chairs that were used. For example, the straight-backed, high-seated chair of eighteenth-century England gave way to the sloping, upholstered, and low-seated chair of the nineteenth century as more comfort and individuality were sought and social structures became less rigid.

A survey of furniture must begin with the realization that as an environmental factor, furniture represents the closest contact to man, save his clothing. Like architecture, furniture must be reviewed historically. How could a device for seating be evaluated without knowing what had previously been designed for this purpose? Furniture must also be placed in a social setting, placed in the context of its world, for as primitive man increased his degree of communication so did his amount of commercial trading and exploration. And with his increased travel, man began to borrow design ideas and materials from the peoples he contacted. Thus, a design development is often dependent upon man's cognizance of historical past, as well as the availability of contact and communication with contemporary influences.

327

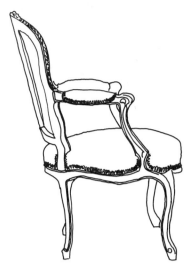

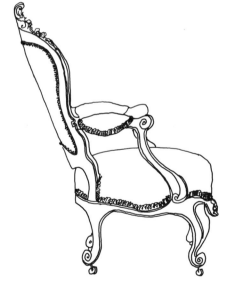

13-1 *The French armchair (c. 1750) on the left has a higher, padded seat and a more vertical back than the armchair (American, c. 1850) below. The second chair has a lower but thicker seat filled with springs and a more sloping and higher back. It allows the sitter to sit in a more relaxed position.*

Furniture making is often considered a craft but during some periods of history, it has been elevated to an art. It is then that furniture becomes more than a way to satisfy a utilitarian need but takes on forms that in their perfection rise above the ordinary and touch the spirit.

Furniture making also is dependent upon the manipulative skill, materials, and knowledge of construction techniques, as well as the imagination of the designer. Materials are also a factor of consequence. A shortage of good wood, for example, caused the Egyptians to develop sophisticated methods of joinery. The development of skilled craftsmen who could manipulate materials and design forms to their structural and aesthetic limits came only after generations practiced and perfected the tools and methods of previous generations.

All furniture, whether freestanding or built-in, is primarily utilitarian and can be divided into two functional classifications: 1) that in which objects are held or stored and 2) that on which objects are placed or displayed. Further, the basic physical forms of furniture reflect these classifications. Furniture is either a variation of the box (in) or the platform (on). Cabinets, chests, and wardrobes are boxes; beds, tables, stools, and chairs are platforms; and desks, buffets, and sideboards are combinations of the two.

Little furniture that is available today bears much resemblance to that first made by man; yet there *is* a direct line, the heritage remains. When the first man stuck a stick in a hole in another stick to make a backrest he formed the first cabinet-making joint and also started the long line of "stick chairs." The ubiquitous folding chair owes much to the first time two sticks were tied together to form an "X."

Does the furniture of early man exist? The answer must be, No, although it is not difficult to conjecture what it might have been. Undoubtedly, he first had nothing that might be identified as "furniture." He lived without tools, structures, or clothing, and without furniture. As he began to use natural

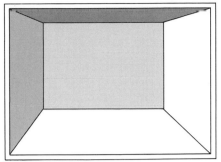

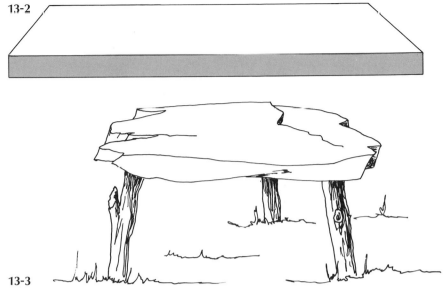

13-2

13-3

caves or depressions in the earth for shelter he probably rested or slept upon natural ledges or tree trunks. Eventually, a log or rock was moved nearer his shelter and he had taken the first step toward creating furniture.

Wood is presumed to be the first material used by man to make furniture. It is one of the most abundant and easily worked materials; however, because of its tendency to rot (except in the driest climates) and its vulnerability to insect attack, wood is not permanent. Stone and metal have also been used by primitive peoples but the tools, methods of construction, and technical skill necessary to shape these materials are far greater than early man possessed.

The most elementary seat is a solid block of wood or stone selected at random, succeeded by one that has been selected for its natural shape. Eventually, this monolithic mass was carved or ornamented to give it identity or to make it more comfortable. This is how it no doubt happened.

It can also be imagined that one day a block was not high enough so that two were used, one upon another, which led to two similar blocks with a larger flat stone or slab spanning the space between. It is a simple expansion of this idea to take two or more uprights (this time sticks), drive them into the ground, and place the slab on them. It becomes a permanent stool. But, what if the slab had the uprights in it rather than in the ground? The result is a movable stool. It may sound simple in the retelling, but what has taken a few sentences here took thousands of years to evolve.

The storage of objects also presented a problem for early man. The open stone outcroppings or holes in trees did not lend themselves to efficient storage. Perhaps it was not until the basket had been invented (considered to be one of the first arts known by prehistoric man) that an acceptable method of storage was found. With the addition of three or four legs, the basket became a container that was not subjected to the dampness of the shelter and it was also movable. Others may have discovered that a hollow log also proved to be a good container, but the addition of legs to raise the container and its contents away from the damp floor seems to be the important factor in the invention of furniture.

These first significant attempts at furniture-making by early man are overshadowed by the developments of the Egyptians. About four thousand years before the birth of Christ, the highly sophisticated artistic expression that evolved in the intellectually fertile climate of the Nile River valley matured. Eventually it became the dominant design influence during the early periods of furniture history in Greece, Mesopotamia, and Italy. Egypt developed an individualistic style of design that superbly exemplified the character of its culture, and displayed an excellence that exceeded the contemporary designs found in other cultures adjacent to the Mediterranean. The style developed independently from preceding stylistic movements now lost in the dimness of ancient history and served as a highly refined source of design inspiration for periods that succeeded it.[1]

The culture of ancient Egypt was so strongly developed that little foreign impact was made on the evolvement of Egyptian design. The invasions that did occur during Egypt's later years brought minor outside influences to the Egyptian culture, but the invader's artistic expressions were soon absorbed into the more dominant art forms of Egypt rather than supplanting the ancient designs.

The furniture forms of ancient Egypt were well established before 3000 B.C. and are not too different from those commonly found in the twentieth

13-4

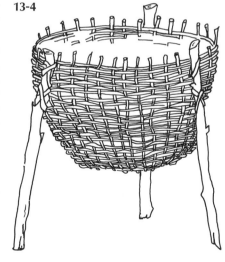

---

[1] Egyptian ornamental forms such as the *guilloche, palmette, wave pattern,* and *spiral* were used both in Greece and Italy, and the *solar disk, caryatid,* and *lotus plant* are found as ornamental motifs in Mesopotamia. The use of animal legs as supports for chairs, tables, couches, and beds originated in Egypt. Animal legs were used in Greek and Roman furniture, and still later during the Italian Renaissance and Baroque (1400–1750), French Directoire (1795–1799), French Empire (1804–1820), English Regency (1810–1820), American Federal (1790–1810), and Greek revival (1810–1860) periods.

13-5 *The legs and seat frame of an Egyptian chair dated about 1090–663 B.C. Made of wood, the legs are the legs of a lion and the cross and side rails of the seat are perforated for the insertion of leather thongs. This chair is more crudely constructed than many examples of Egyptian furniture. However, it is not primitive in its construction.* Courtesy of the Oriental Institute, University of Chicago.

century. Fragments of furniture made over five thousand years ago indicate that there was an advanced knowledge of the principles of joining, although it is believed that glue was yet to be discovered (individual parts were bound with leather thongs or secured with pegs).

Common pieces of Egyptian household furniture were chairs, stools, chests, beds, small tables, and couches. All of these pieces were usually soundly constructed, possessing such a delicate refinement of proportions that they might almost be called "modern" in form. Most of the early Egyptian furniture existing to this day was owned by members of the ruling aristocracy and presents a richness that is not typical of the furniture used by those with less economic and social status, although at least two hundred pieces have been found that are strictly utilitarian and simple in design. Many pieces were designed to be portable, indicating a rather high level of mobility among its owners, are light in weight, having either handles or bars for carrying, and are collapsible. The total design of Egyptian furniture was not left to chance; each part was individually considered in terms of the visual quality of the finished piece.

Although wood was not as plentiful in Egypt as in other areas, many native and imported kinds of woods were available. Acacia, sycamore-fig, sidder, tamarisk, and willow were some of the native trees and cedar, cypress, oak, pine, and ebony were imported. The Egyptian cabinetmaker thoroughly understood both furniture construction and the nature of his materials.

Many of the features that characterize Egyptian furniture design can be recognized by studying the chair and the stool. Both pieces usually have four legs, although stools are occasionally fashioned in a tripod manner with three legs. The most common type of chair leg duplicated that of a quadruped; chairs were designed using both the fore and the hind legs of an animal, with each leg being placed in its appropriate natural position on the chair. Consequently, many Egyptian chairs appear to be "facing forward" and seem ready to walk. All legs of this type are terminated by a naturalistic represen-

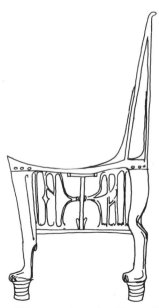

13-6 *When seen from the side, an Egyptian chair becomes even more animated with its legs of an animal, and front and back in proper relationship.*

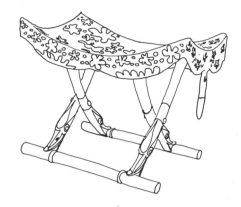

13-7 *Often designed to be folded, the stools and chairs of the "X" type were also rigid, as is this example made of ebony (c. 1366–1357 B.C.). The solid seat is inlaid with ivory and suggests the hide of a leopard, even to the wooden tail. The X-supports terminate in stylized duck heads also inlaid with ivory, a common decoration on this type of stool instead of animal legs.*

13-8 *The stool depicted in this detail from a wall painting in the Tomb of Nakht, Thebes, is elegantly simple. Only the most necessary components, pared to the limits of their material strength, have been combined to produce the stool.* Photograph by Egyptian Expedition, The Metropolitan Museum of Art.

tation of the animal's paw resting on a small cylinder or block of solid wood covered with a thin sheet of beaten gold, copper, or bronze to enhance the total richness of the chair. Between these four animal legs is a system of horizontal stretchers with vertical elements (often in hieroglyphic form).

Chairs and stools are either square or oblong in shape with the seat being either flat or concave in form. Such pieces were used by sitting flat on the seat with the legs facing forward or by crossing the legs and sitting in what is now referred to as the Hindu "lotus position." This position was probably not considered to be too uncomfortable because the Egyptians were also accustomed to squatting on the ground. Chairs and stools are, by today's standards, quite low, but it must be remembered that the early Egyptians were seldom over five feet tall.

Chairs and stools also are found to have supports that are in the form of an "X." Seldom in the shape of animal legs, the supports have square cross sections or are slender rods terminating in duck heads. The intersection of the "X" is fixed with a pin and may be either stationary or movable depending upon the material of the seat. The X-form method of construction is considered to have originated in Egypt, even though this form was used in the furniture of the contemporary Mediterranean and Near Eastern cultures. Since their invention, the X-chair and stool have been used in both stationary collapsible furniture designs in most periods in the history of furniture.[2]

The use of vertical and diagonal *struts,* or supports, is a common characteristic found repeatedly in Egyptian furniture design. Struts were used to reinforce the backs of chairs, usually taking the form of three vertical pieces of solid wood that are fastened at the top of the *raked* or slanting back and to a rear extension of the chair seat. Struts were also often placed between the

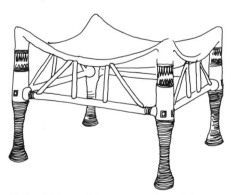

13-9 *This stool (c. 1500 B.C.), now in the British Museum, is characteristic of many pieces of Egyptian furniture. It has a low, shaped seat (originally covered with leather), has struts between the seat frame and the stretchers, employs sophisticated joinery, and is, above all, a furniture form that is easily recognized today. This stool has no doubt been the inspiration for many later pieces of furniture.*

[2]The familiar folding camp stool of today is but the descendant of such distinguished ancestors as the *diphros okladias* of ancient Greece, as well as the Dante and Savonarola chairs of Italy, the *faudesteuil* of France, and the faldstool of England, all of which were developed during the Renaissance.

13-10 *Without question derived from the Egyptian stool on page 332, this chair, designed by W. Holman Hunt and made in London by J. B. Grace in 1855, has a seat somewhat higher than the original stool. Cane, another material extensively used by the Egyptians, covers the seat instead of the original leather. The two side supports of the back repeat the general design of the legs, but an additional decorative device has been introduced, the lotus blossom.* Courtesy of the Museum and Art Gallery, Birmingham, England.

13-11 *Another interpretation of the stool, made of machine preshaped components, this wood stool (c. 1880) is American and has a seat of curved wooden slats screwed to the stool frame. The most notable construction adaptation, however, is at the point where the seat and legs join. Both the original stool and the chair above have a smooth transition between the legs and the seat frame achieved by complicated furniture joints. Here a wooden sphere is used, holes being drilled into it and the individual members doweled into it—exactly like the familiar children's toy, the Tinkertoy.*

bottom stretchers and the seat of stools and appear very similar to that of the truss system used in architectural construction.

Naturalistic animal legs are also found on Egyptian beds. Not much over twelve inches high, these beds consist of a rigid wooden frame on legs with a vertical panel at the foot. There is no headboard but rather the head of the sleeper was supported on a separate headrest.[3] The framework has a slight longitudinal curve, as if sagging in the center, and is filled with a closely woven mesh of linen cords. Soft blankets were then folded on top of the webbing for a greater sleeping comfort.

Beds used in traveling or in war were frequently made portable by dividing their lengths into three evenly spaced sections. Each section is hinged to the next, forming a three-tiered piece of furniture when it is folded. These beds are usually supported by eight animal paw legs; two pairs of these legs are under the two sets of bronze hinges and support and strengthen the piece when extended.

The item of Egyptian furniture that has survived in greatest number is the chest. Varying from large chests for storing bedding and clothing to small boxes for holding jewelry and cosmetics, the Egyptian chests are usually of panel construction and almost without exception are supported on legs that are extensions of the corner stiles and raise the chest above the floor. Stretchers a short distance below the chest brace those with longer legs and the space between the stretchers and the chest itself is filled with a design of struts or hieroglyphics[4] that is similar to that found on stools.

---

[3]Hundreds of Egyptian headrests have survived. They are usually made of wood and consist of a curved piece to fit the head supported by a vertical member attached to a base. It is interesting to conjecture why the Egyptians supported their heads on such contrivances. Similar supports have been used in cultures where elaborate hair arrangements were popular, but the Egyptians shaved their heads and wore wigs.

[4]The use of repeated hieroglyphic symbols was more than mere ornament. The symbols had religious significance, and were meant to guarantee an unthreatened afterlife.

13-12 *A small wooden Egyptian bed, mortised at the corners and having legs in the shape of bull legs. It does not have the usual footboard or headrest. The slots in the rectangular frame still have remnants of the leather thongs that formed the surface of the bed. This bed was constructed without glue and the individual parts were tied together (the present lacings are new). This bed probably dates back to the Old Kingdom (3000 B.C.– 2130 B.C.).* Courtesy of the Oriental Institute, University of Chicago.

There were no drawers in these chests but they were fitted with various kinds of compartments and dividers to better serve their specific function. Access to the chest interior was achieved by the removal of the tops that are flat, half-cylinder, or gabled. Although some tops were hinged as is done today, the majority of the chest tops were fitted on one end with a wooden joint of some kind. On the other end were two large knobs that could be tied with cord and then sealed with the owner's mark for security.

Most of the Egyptian furniture that has survived is in existence because of two factors: the dryness of the climate, and the Egyptian religious practice of interring household articles with the deceased in the tomb to ensure his immortality. Consequently, pieces of furniture, funerary accessories, food, clothing, and religious statuary were often placed in rooms adjacent to the burial chamber. Subsequent pillage of these tombs throughout the centuries has considerably reduced the quantity of furniture that has survived; however, thousands of well-preserved examples of Egyptian furniture still exist.

The oldest chair in existence anywhere is that of Queen Hetepheres, mother of Khufu, builder of the Great Pyramid. Discovered in 1925 and dated about 2580 B.C., it is not only the most ancient chair but is the only one to survive from the Old Kingdom. Built of wood[5] and covered with gold except for its back and seat panels, the chair is well constructed with fine joints and detailing. It is low and wide with seat sloping slightly toward the rear. The legs are those of lions, forelegs in front and the back legs behind. The high square arms are filled with a bold design of three papyrus flowers.

One tomb that remained relatively untouched until modern times was that

---

[5]When found, the original wood had become a fine powder but the exterior covering of gold and the inlays were intact, having their original shape and position. The wood forms have been painstakingly reconstructed to support the original gold sheathing and the parts have been rejoined, giving the chair its original appearance except for the patina of the surface.

of the XVIII Dynasty King Tutankhamen (c. 1350 B.C.). Discovered in 1922 by Howard Carter, an Englishman, this tomb astonished everyone by the richness and splendor of its contents. For example, besides quantities of jewelry, statues, furniture, textiles, and other objects, the inner coffin, which was made of solid gold, weighed 2,448 pounds! More than fifty pieces of furniture of all kinds were found in the tomb. What is amazing is that the tomb is small and belonged to a relatively unimportant ruler.[6] One wonders what riches were once stored in the larger and more elaborate Egyptian tombs.

The study of ancient Egyptian furniture only supports the premise stated earlier in the chapter that pointed out the significance of design based upon historical knowledge. The profound developments of this culture five thousand years ago led to a high caliber of furniture design and craftsmanship that is constantly evident in later eras. So incredible is the influence of this furniture that it is appropriate at this time to list and define a few of the major innovations of the Egyptian furniture craftsmen to serve as a foundation for further stylistic considerations.

1. TOOLS. Sometime prior to 3000 B.C. tools made of copper were developed. Although copper is a relatively soft metal and blunts easily, these copper tools were a distinct advancement over the older flint and shell tools, and they made possible the sophisticated joinery that is characteristic of ancient Egyptian furniture. After about 2000 B.C., copper was subsequently replaced by bronze, a hard alloy that required less maintenance and sharpen-

---

[6]Tutankhamen (or Tutenkhamon) was the son-in-law and successor of the remarkable Ikhnaton (c. 1375–1358 B.C.) who established the short-lived and only monotheistic religion in Egyptian history. The portrait bust of Ikhnaton's wife, the beautiful Nefretete (or Nefertiti), is one of the world's masterpieces. Tutankhamen was named king when he was very young, about twelve or thirteen, and died before he was twenty, the last male heir of the XVIII Dynasty.

13-13

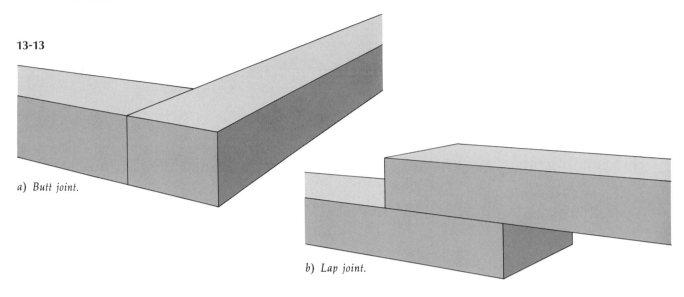

a) *Butt joint.*

b) *Lap joint.*

ing. Eventually iron replaced both of these metals as a more effective material for use in tools.

The ancient furniture makers used most of the woodworking hand tools that are now available. Examples of saws, bow drills, knives, scrapers, awls, mallets, chisels, and adzes have been found dating to the I Dynasty and are about the same form as twentieth-century tools. The adze, the most versatile tool, was used to shape the raw wood into the approximate desired form. With blades up to 11 inches wide, the adze in the hands of a skilled craftsman could be most efficient. The Egyptians had no planes but used the adze to smooth wooden surfaces.

The Egyptians also did not have the wood-turning lathe[7] until very late in their development. They did have, however, furniture legs and other components that appear to have been turned on a lathe, but it is believed these were shaped by hand.

2. M a t e r i a l s . Wood is the major material from which Egyptian furniture was fabricated, although small pins, fasteners, surface sheathings, and inlays were made of metals, principally bronze, gold, and silver. Straps, webbing, and flexible seats were made of linen, fiber, rush, and leather. The selection of woods for specific uses and qualities was highly developed. Although the extremely dry climate undoubtedly was instrumental in removing moisture from green lumber, the Egyptians were fully cognizant of proper drying and seasoning procedures, as well as methods to stabilize the tendency of wood to warp, check, and shrink. Veneering was also used and dates back to the I Dynasty, but the thin sheets of wood were pegged and not glued.[8] The Egyptians' thorough knowledge of the characteristics of wood is

---

[7] The lathe is now thought to have been invented by the Mesopotamians, although Pliny stated that Theodorus of Samos was the inventor in the seventh century B.C.

[8] A plywood coffin in which six $\frac{1}{4}$-inch-thick sheets of wood are pegged together (grain direction alternating) was discovered in the Step Pyramid at Sakkara.

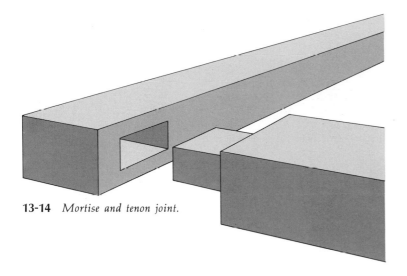

13-14 *Mortise and tenon joint.*

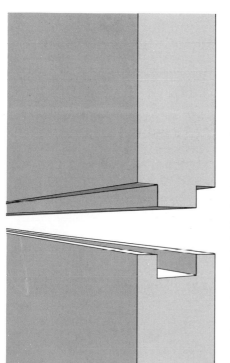

13-15 *Tongue and groove joint.*

indicated by the excellent furniture joints that are frequently almost as tight now as they were when first constructed.

3. J O I N E R Y . The Egyptians developed the major cabinetmaking joints and many of their variations that are now employed in the construction of furniture.[9] The *butt* and *lap joints* are so basic that one must assume that they existed from prehistory; however, the *mortise and tenon joint* was invented about 3100 B.C. The sturdiness of any joint is based not only upon fit but also upon the amount of glue surface,[10] and the mortise and tenon joint (the workhorse of woodworking joints) has a good glue surface. The joint is often further strengthened by the insertion of a dowel through the joint at right angles to the tenon. The narrowness of available lumber was solved by joining edges with the *tongue and groove joint.*

Wood, a cellular material that absorbs moisture, has a tendency to warp. This can be countered by having the width and thickness dimensions of individual pieces of wood similar. However, this often results in excessive thickness and heaviness and uses an unnecessary amount of wood for such "surface" applications as doors, tabletops, paneling, boxes, and chests. Aware of this, the Egyptians developed *panel construction.* As long ago as 3500 B.C., they fitted together lengths of wood to form a frame into which a panel of thinner wood was placed.

Even the complicated *dovetail joint,* joining two members, usually boards, at right angles was first used by the Egyptians in chest and coffin construction.

4. F I N I S H E S . The majority of Egyptian furniture had a painted surface; however, the paint was seldom applied directly to the bare wood, but rather,

[9]Many of these joints were "lost" during the Middle Ages and were subsequently rediscovered.

[10]The earliest Egyptian furniture joints were tied together with leather thongs but a good glue that differed little from the animal glue used today was later developed from gelatinous animal parts.

13-16 *Panel construction.*

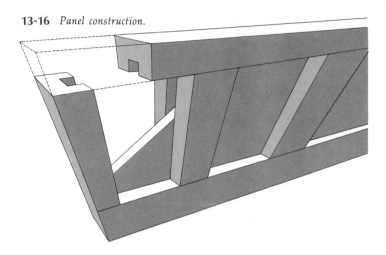

on a *gesso* surface.[11] It was the general practice to glue a layer of cloth to the bare wood prior to the application of the gesso. (This method is still practiced today.) When the surface is built up to its proper smoothness, it provides an excellent hard ground for any paint although the Egyptians only used *tempera*;[12] oil paint was not invented until the Renaissance.

The gesso surface was also an excellent ground for adhering gold leaf (as it still is) and much of the gold leaf that was applied by the Egyptians is still in excellent condition.

Varnish was also used as a finish for wood furniture and although its composition has not been determined, it is believed to have had a resin base. There were two types of varnish: a clear that was used over tempera painting and an opaque black used to simulate ebony.

The important territory contemporary with Egypt was Mesopotamia. This culture, which represented a far more aggressive and vigorous spirit with its citizenry preferring conquest and an interest in the immediate rather than the more contemplative concern of life after death, did not inter much domestic furniture with the dead. The moist climate of the Tigris-Euphrates valley and the subsequent disintegration of the mud-brick tombs during the heavy annual rains have prevented the survival of actual Mesopotamian furniture. Present knowledge of furniture designs of Mesopotamia is, therefore, limited to the use of secondary sources of information. Descriptions of architectural styles, furniture, and the ornamentation of the interior are found in contemp-

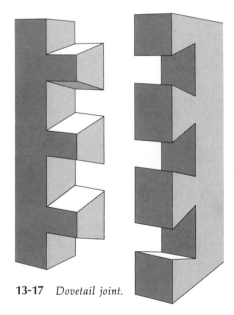

13-17 *Dovetail joint.*

[11] Gesso continues to be used as a surface for painting—furniture, paneling, and easel painting. It consists of whiting or a plaster mixed with a binding agent that is now generally an acrylic liquid but traditionally was an animal glue. This is applied in thin layers and sanded smooth between applications.

[12] Tempera is a very durable paint made of pigment mixed with egg yolk. It should not be confused with the inexpensive water soluble, opaque poster paint incorrectly called tempera that is available today.

13-18 *From the Treasury at Persepolis, Iran, this stone relief (522–486 B.C.) depicts King Darius I seated on his throne with Crown Prince Xerxes behind him. The rigid, squarish throne has disk turnings above lion feet that are raised above the floor level by tassel-like bases.* Courtesy of the Oriental Institute, University of Chicago.

orary cuneiform writings inscribed on clay tablets. Furniture is also depicted on seals and bas-reliefs.

Much of the furniture attributed to early Mesopotamia appears to have been loosely based on Egyptian furniture styles and ornamental motifs; however, the pieces are far from exact copies. The Egyptian precision of proportion and clearness of detail are missing and Mesopotamian furniture appears awkward and heavy by comparison.

Since no examples of Mesopotamian furniture have survived, little is known about the actual methods of construction, although wood was no doubt the primary material used. It appears also probable that tongue and groove and mortise and tenon joints were employed, as a result of the strong commercial contact and communication with the Egyptian culture.

Besides looking quite solidly constructed, the furniture seen in Mesopotamian bas-reliefs is heavily ornamented. Carving was extensively used on both the flat surfaces of pieces and also on structural supports. Ivory fragments have been found that indicate the widespread use of ivory inlay, and there is also evidence of individual parts, if not all, of some furniture's being made of ivory. In addition to adopted Egyptian decorative details, such as the lotus solar disk and lion paws, uniquely Mesopotamian motifs included carvings of wild animals, the ram, the bull, and the lion, which often formed the complete sides of throne chairs. The inverted pinecone form, a sacred Mesopotamian emblem, was frequently used as the terminal at the base of chair and table legs and is one of the dominant motifs. Considerably more furniture also appears to have been made on a lathe.

The influence of Mesopotamian furniture design and ornamentation spread to ancient Persia and large parts of Asia Minor, but since the Christian era, little if any furniture, except minor and isolated examples of exotica, exhibit any Mesopotamian influence.

The furniture of ancient Greece, however, has been the source of inspira-

339

13-19 *The massive, straight furniture of the Mesopotamians, although basically like that of the Egyptians, did not have the sophistication of the former and appears more crude. The heaviness of Mesopotamian furniture is emphasized by the excessive amount of textural ornament that almost covers it.*

13-20 *This relief, from the Palace of Sargon II in Iraq, has two courtiers carrying a lion-footed table. Included in the table's ornament are rams' heads, pinecones, lion feet, palmettes, and human figures. Courtesy of the Oriental Institute, University of Chicago.*

tion for centuries of furniture designers. Like Greek architecture, Greek furniture was adapted by the Romans. The Roman interpretations of Greek furniture design became the basis for the furniture forms and ornamentation made throughout the Roman Empire. Roman (and indirectly Greek) furniture thus served as the inspiration for centuries. When designers returned to more pure Greek forms in the early nineteenth century, a quickening of classical design occurred precipitating the Greek revival style.

Little of Greek furniture is of distinct design importance prior to the eighth century B.C. The furniture of the Aegean Islands and the Greek mainland was based largely upon Egyptian furniture and exhibits only minor differences. But around 750 B.C. there began to develop a defined style paralleling the emergence of the quest for beauty and the ideal in artistic expression that was to permeate all aspects of this highly gifted culture. Classical details coupled with a purity of design were to achieve a degree of sophistication surpassing even that of Egyptian furniture.

Most of the knowledge of the furniture used in ancient Greece is derived from secondary sources; only a few small fragments, metal pins, and some stone throne-like chairs have survived. Some references to furniture are found in Greek literature, but by far the most important sources of information come from scenes of domestic life painted on Greek vases and from reliefs that decorated Greek buildings.

The variety of scenes and the sensitivity of their execution afford a clear picture of Greek household furniture. One of the outstanding characteristics of this furniture is that it was movable. Each piece has the quality of spareness, a kind of tautness; the parts are pared down to the minimum with no excess weight, physical or visual. Moreover, the furniture is frequently depicted as being carried.

The Greek bed or couch (*klini*) was an important piece of furniture in the Greek house, for not only was it slept upon but it was also used while

13-21

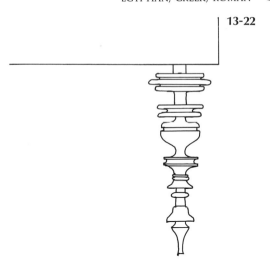

13-22

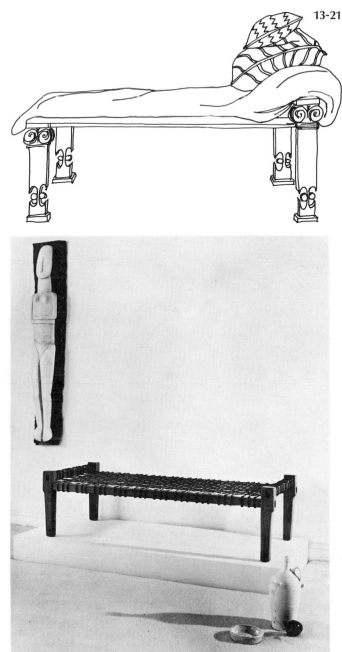

13-23 *Perfumed pillows supported by the interlaced leather thongs covered this simple Greek bed frame. Copied by T. H. Robsjohn-Gibbings from a bed dated about 1500 B.C., it is part of a major collection of authentic classical Greek furniture designs that have been manufactured by Saridis of Athens since 1960.* Courtesy of the Greek Trade Center.

13-24 *This three-legged marble-topped table was copied by Robsjohn-Gibbings from one depicted on a bell krater, third quarter of the fourth century, B.C., in the National Museum, Naples. The bronze legs are castings from an original Greek Bronze table leg that is now in the Palermo Museum, Sicily.* Courtesy of the Greek Trade Center.

eating.[13] The Greek beds were similar to those in Egypt, consisting of a horizontal frame, laced with cords or thongs, and having four legs and a raised end. Legs were turned on a lathe and appear to be a stack of disks or platters (*disk-turning*),[14] tapering to the floor, or were rectangular ending in an animal foot or having a deeply cut design about one-third of the way up the leg. A later leg type was a simple curve, somewhat like a saber. None of these legs had stretchers between them. However, the more distinct difference between Egyptian and Greek beds is the location of the raised end. Greek beds have no footboard but rather the opposite end is raised; the legs on that end project above the bed surface and often end in a capital. The raised portion serves as a support for the soft mattress or padding that continues up over it and upon which the user leans and rests his arm. A cushion was sometimes also added. Greek beds and couches were higher than the Egyptian and footstools were needed as in Mesopotamia.

At the side of the bed invariably stood a matching rectangular table (*trapeza*) with three legs, two at the corners of one end and one centered at the other. A "T"-shaped stretcher braced the legs. This table was placed under the bed when it was not in use. Other tables with round tops were also three-legged. Table legs were usually tapered, ornamented with simple grooves and subtle carving, or in the shape of animal legs. These animal legs are more often those of a deer than a lion, the common motif of Egypt and Mesopotamia, and are rather stylized.

Many stools were used in Greek houses and environs. The *diphros* was a four-legged stool with leather thongs supporting a loose cushion. The legs

13-25 *Depicted on the frieze above the east door of the Parthenon were the major Greek gods awaiting the Panathenaic Procession. Each god was sitting on a diphros. This walnut stool is copied from one on the Parthenon frieze. The subtle modeling of forms, especially at the corners, attest to the remarkable skill of the furniture craftsmen of the fifth century, B.C.* Courtesy of the Greek Trade Center.

13-26

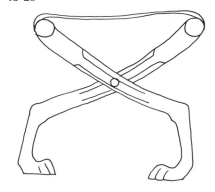

[13] Most citizens of the ancient world reclined when they ate, and not until well into the Byzantine era did people sit on chairs, stools, and benches during meals.
[14] The use of disk-turned legs is also found in the contemporary Roman furniture and in the later periods of the Spanish Renaissance and nineteenth-century America. The term *disk-turning* is also known as *clavated turning* and *spool turning,* when it is found in later periods in the history of furniture.

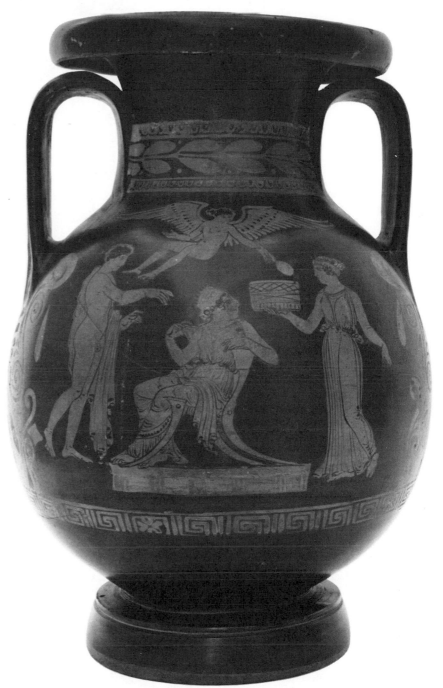

13-27 *This vase (c. 400–375 B.C.) shows a bride seated on a* klismos *receiving a gift from Eros. Also depicted on the vase are a fret border at the lower edge of the scene and around the neck is a wide band of ornament composed of two painted egg and dart moldings with a center of laurel leaves.* Courtesy of the St. Louis Art Museum.

13-28 *Although Homer said that this chair was fit only for goddesses, the* klismos *was in general use by the fifth century, B.C. and continued to be used well into the Roman era. With its outward-curving saber legs and sloping back, its distinct form has been the inspiration for chair designers for centuries. The sitter sat in the* klismos *in a relaxed position; not until almost A.D. 1800 was other sitting furniture designed in which the sitter could sit in the same attitude.* Courtesy of the Greek Trade Center.

were carved, turned, or rectangular. Almost without exception there is a thickening at the joining of the leg to the frame for strength. The *diphros okladias* folded and was in the familiar X-form. It had animal legs, deer or dog legs being the most popular, and generally these were bandy-legged. In other words, the legs bowed and not infrequently the feet faced inward. The similarity to the form of large pincers is very apparent.

Also in common use by the Greeks were chests, which were rather plain in shape but richly decorated.

All of the furniture just described had its roots in Egypt. One piece of Greek furniture was original, however, and its visual characteristics are of the greatest importance. This is the *klismos*,[15] a lightweight armless chair. The Greek ideal of beauty is immediately apparent in its refined rhythms, balance, and symmetry. The *klismos* was the favorite chair of classical artists and has been used in innumerable paintings and sculptures. No date can be affixed to its development, but it was pictured in a vase painting in the beginning of the fifth century B.C. After the defeat of the Persians by the Greeks (479 B.C.), the *klismos* became increasingly popular if the number of vase paintings depicting it can be a determinant.

This "perfect chair" was usually constructed of wood (probably walnut) and great attention was paid to the beauty and direction of the grain. Usually no ornamentation was added to its surface because its simplicity of form and elegance of line would have been destroyed by these disturbances. The curved tapered front and back legs are its most identifying feature.[16] There

---

[15] The term *klismos* refers to the concave or curved rail of the chair back and also to the name of the chair.

[16] The design of the *klismos* presented a problem in construction. The long saber-like legs and curved back, if made from a large straight-grained piece of wood, would have been weak where the cross-grain occurred. Consequently, the wood was probably bent with the aid of steam to the correct curve before final shaping.

13-29 *A slightly different version of the classical* klismos, *this design was taken from an earthenware plaque of the middle of the sixth century* B.C., *which is in the State Museum in Berlin.* Courtesy of the Greek Trade Center.

are no stretchers to brace these splayed legs, which must be perfectly constructed and balanced to support the downward weight placed on the seat. Each leg must also be carefully joined to the seat frame, and frequently the dowel that secured the tenon on the leg in the frame mortise became a decorative element. The back legs extend above the seat, reversing direction, and serve as a support for a curved horizontal back rail. A curved center *splat* was often placed between the seat and the concave back rail. This splat and the back rail followed the curve of the seated human body. The chair was made with two back heights. The higher backed version required the occupant to remain more upright than the lower back, which permitted a more relaxed position.[17] The back rail was also used as an arm rest when one sat in the chair sideways. The seat frame is laced with leather thongs and frequently supports a loose cushion.

As Roman influence increased in Greece, greater emphasis was placed upon applied ornament, often to the degree of sacrificing proportion for ornament. The *klismos* form continued to be used throughout the Roman period and well into the Middle Ages. The archeological excavations at Pompeii and Herculaneum in the mideighteenth century rekindled interest in classical architecture, furniture, and ornament, and the *klismos* form again became popular. It served as inspiration for chairs in France, England, and the United States and was later closely copied in the early nineteenth century, although these chairs are usually heavier in scale than the original Greek versions. Duncan Phyfe, the American cabinetmaker, is noted for his simplified adaptations of the *klismos*.

Surviving examples of Roman furniture are also rare compared to the number from Egypt, but individual pieces do exist. One of the major sources has been the buried cities of Pompeii and Herculaneum. The beautifully

[17] The *klismos* is practically the only chair until the nineteenth century that allowed the sitter to sit in a relaxed manner.

13-30 *The joining of an animal head and chest to a muscular leg produced a strong reverse curved leg. Legs, as this lion mono-podium, were sometimes placed back to back and were often joined by upward swirling wings into a single unit. They were also used in threes joined by a Y-shaped stretcher attached to the shoulder area of each animal.*

preserved frescoes and mosaics frequently depict furniture in extraordinary detail, and metal and stone furniture, protected by volcanic ash, have been uncovered in perfect condition. Other individual pieces and fragments have been found throughout the former Roman Empire.

The Romans contributed little new furniture, adopting instead the forms of Greece, Egypt, and Mesopotamia. The furniture, however, is usually more ornate, heavier in scale, and made of richer and more varied materials, for example, numerous woods and marble, bronze, and silver. Inlays of rare and unusual woods, mosaics, ivory, precious metals, and thin pieces of tortoise-shell were common.

The Romans adapted a Near Eastern table form to their needs and have become identified with it. This is a long rectangular table supported by two pedestals. Although wooden examples did exist, surviving stone pedestals are the most familiar. These pedestals are invariably the same basic out-line—a thick vertical slab with the sides cut in a strong "S" curve. This shape results from the subject matter of the vigorous carving. Under the tabletop (wood or stone) is an animal head resting on a bulging chest that flows into a single muscular leg terminating in a foot, the *monopodium*. The same com-posite animal is repeated on the other side. The modeling is boldly articu-lated and decidedly three-dimensional. Frequently the animal is a lion but the griffin and eagle were also sometimes used. Each is winged, indicating its Mesopotamian heritage. The space between the animals is filled with a classical honeysuckle motif or a similar decorative device. The table was used more as a sideboard than a dining table but during the Italian Renaissance became the prototype for many wooden dining tables (refectory tables).

The Romans also had a barrel-shaped chair. Developed from Etruscan models, this chair was made of bronze but a Roman relief in Germany shows a similar chair made of wicker.

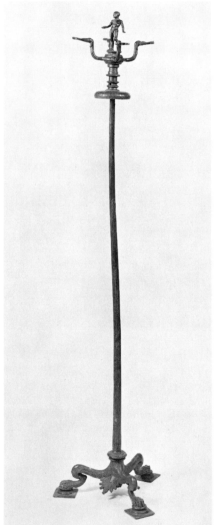

13-31 *A Roman bronze lamp stand (Lampadarium, c. 100 B.C.–A.D.) almost four feet tall, the four arms protruding from the top held small lamps.* Courtesy of the St. Louis Art Museum.

Although not always considered furniture, the Roman interior had many lamps and candelabra. These utilitarian accessories were beautifully crafted of terra-cotta or bronze. Frequently, the bronze candelabra supported several small lamps or candles that are attached to a shaft or column. The base invariably had three legs ending in animal feet.

14 Furniture: Early Christian, Byzantine, Romanesque, Gothic

By the first century after the birth of Christ, Roman culture and military influence had spread over most of Europe and the areas bordering the Mediterranean Sea. As the limits of the Roman Empire expanded so did the influence of its art forms. The design heritage that had been nurtured in Egypt, perfected in Greece, and matured in Rome was dominant from York in England to Alexandria in Egypt and from Gibraltar to the Euphrates. Yet, for all its seeming strength and influence, the Roman Empire with its accompanying culture was destined to collapse.

It was not a sudden fall, no instant breakdown. For three centuries the once powerful Roman Empire slowly disintegrated. The barbarians in the north, ever pressing southward, were but one factor that brought about its collapse. Internal corruption, waste, and civil strife were even more responsible.

During the reign of the first Christian emperor, Constantine I, early in the fourth century A.D., the center of the empire was shifted to Constantinople on the banks of the Bosporus (see Chapter 8, p. 178). The shifting of the capitol was a brilliant maneuver to save the empire but it also brought the destruction of Rome and precipitated the breakdown of civilization in the West.

In 395 the empire was divided into two administrative units; and almost immediately it became evident that the division was more than geographical. Religious thought and artistic expression, in fact, the total culture of each division assumed an identity of its own. The eastern portion of the empire was smaller, but it also was more urban, industrial, affluent and, above all, predominantly Greek. The Latin-speaking western part was larger, poorer, less populated, and rural.

The Byzantine Empire, as the eastern division became known, survived for another eleven hundred years. Although continuing the cultural traditions of the Roman Empire, the empire was significantly tempered by native Hellenistic taste and Oriental vigor. Coupled with the responsibility of representing the first Christian empire, adjustments were necessary, and within a short time the foundation of a Byzantine tradition was formed.

348

14-1 *The elaborately carved surface and precious material of the ivory throne of Maximian contrasts with its simple panel construction*

Rich surface ornament of brilliant hue became one of the dominant characteristics. The opulence of Byzantine design was never more evident than in the interiors. Rarely did a surface not have pattern, carving, or color, and furniture was no exception.

The furniture depicted on Byzantine manuscripts, ivories, and mosaics is not the furniture of the classical world. But rather, chairs, chests, tables, and beds are rigid, straight, and architectural. Gone are the subtle curves and careful articulation associated with classical furniture. From all evidence it must be surmised that many of the competencies of the cabinetmaker, the ability to make those skillfully executed joints that had been developed almost four thousand years before, were abandoned. What suited better the ideal environment of the new culture was imperial pomp and luxury, not subtleties. Magnificent thrones of strong architectural forms were more compatible with the lavish gold, mosaic, and marble interiors.

One of the most noted throne chairs is now located in the Museo Archivescovile in Ravenna, Italy. Belonging to Maximian, Archbishop of Ravenna (515–553), it is made of the precious material ivory rather than wood. The throne is panel construction with the rails and stiles profusely carved with vine, animal, and bird forms. The panels under the seat, on the sides, and in two rows across the concave arched back are in high relief and depict John the Baptist, the Apostles, and scenes from the life of Christ. The architectural character of the throne is very apparent, and despite the material and skilled carving could have been made by a carpenter. The quality of construction and joining does not necessarily require the proficiency of a cabinetmaker.

Other Byzantine furniture also indicates the abandonment of fine cabinetmaking. Tables, chests, and beds[1] are all constructed of heavy, straight

---

[1] Beds became magnificent structures with elaborate canopies supported by columns and posts. Heavy draperies hung from the canopies.

14-2 *Taken from a mosaic in Saint Mark's, Venice, this Byzantine bed is elaborately decorated and embellished with geometric, jewel-like ornament as well as with architectural details derived from those on classical buildings. Twisted columns capped with Corinthian-type capitals support the canopy.*

timbers with stretchers between the legs. Without the elaborate surface designs or the richness of the materials used, one would expect this kind of furniture construction to be used in only the most humble and utilitarian pieces.

Aside from the lamentable disintegration of cabinetmaking skills, the only furniture development that should be considered significant to twentieth-century furniture is the proliferation of complicated "stick" furniture. Stick construction must certainly be one of the oldest methods of making furniture and had been used in every period to this time. However, Byzantine joiners did develop stick furniture to a higher level than before. Using many rods and decoratively turned components, elaborate chairs and tables were made. These were especially popular in the monasteries.

The luxury that is so evident in the Byzantine Empire was far different from what became the norm in the West. The government gradually weakened and the economy in some areas was reduced to bartering. Large areas that had once been profitable farmland lay uncultivated. The tremendous task of defending the nearly 10,000 miles of frontier proved to be too difficult and costly; hence the borders were constantly being breached by the hordes sweeping out of the north and east.

The Rhine River, near what is now Mainz, Germany, froze during the winter of 406, and on the last night of the year an estimated 15,000 warriors, mostly Germanic barbarians, swarmed across. There was little resistance as the invaders headed south and westward leaving in their wake death and destruction. What is so extraordinary is that this handful of undisciplined barbarians, barely the population of an average town in the United States, could overrun the entire province of Gaul with its population of 20 million people. Within only four years the Visigoths under Alaric, their king, succeeded in capturing and sacking Rome. However, this was but the first of many destructive migrations of barbaric peoples across the once proud

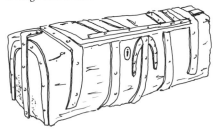

14-3 *Monolithic except for the heavy iron bands and the lid, this chest was made from a large tree trunk.*

Roman Empire, for during 150 nightmarish years (410–563), Rome was besieged at least eight times and conquered at least six.

Alaric's capture of Rome was more than a military triumph, for it marked the end of Roman domination of Western Europe. The old Roman civilization was gone; the final flickering light of classical culture was snuffed out. The period that followed has often been called the Dark Ages by men who were classically oriented and blind to anything that was not based upon the ideals of Greece and Rome. It was, to be sure, a period of strife, yet this age of great challenge produced noble achievements. Out of the dust and ashes of the destroyed Roman Empire rose a new culture, a life based on new elements, new sources, and new standards. The process was slow and painful and it took over five hundred years before skills, traditions, and living patterns again became firmly established so that a distinct and viable culture could exist.

The arts and designs of the late Roman periods that had been adapted to new Christian uses (the Early Christian style) absorbed barbaric details and developed as Romanesque. The architecture of the period is magnificent and dedicated to the glory of the church. The church was dominant; within its influence revolved the lives of all men and the wealth and luxury that did exist was centered in the church. However, even the most powerful rulers, both religious and political, lived in circumstances that appear primitive by twentieth-century standards, or even those of Byzantium or ancient Rome. The castles were cold and damp; there was little furniture and barely any general concern for body comfort.

The earliest furniture is by far the most primitive in construction.[2] Chests were frequently only logs that had been hollowed out, a lid attached, and

---

[2] As time passed more complicated methods were developed and yet it was not until the eighteenth century that all of the old skills of Egyptian and classical furniture making would again be used.

14-4 *A fifteenth-century rounded top marriage coffer with front panel detailing that suggests strong architectural influence. It could be the same tracery used in a church. Note the heavy lock.* Courtesy of the St. Louis Art Museum.

then bound in iron. Others were lidded boxes made of six thick boards. Structural and decorative wrought iron and complicated locking devices were extensively used to secure the chest's contents.

The need for new food supplies, war, and conquest caused the courts to constantly be on the move. This mobility and the need for storage was responsible for the development of the chest as the major furniture form. Chests of every size were required to carry the textile hangings, trappings, and assorted equipment that transformed an empty castle into some semblance of a comfortable residence. Often chests were combined to form display pieces, places to sit upon, or even to sleep on.

Chairs were rare; perhaps only one was found in an entire castle and it was reserved for the ruler or the person with the highest authority. This chair was throne-like, straight, stiff, and high, and almost always was accompanied by a footstool. Other ranking members of the household sat on folding[3] and nonfolding stools or backless benches.

Beds were also reserved for the lord and were often just fixed platforms with mattresses, quilted and padded covers, and furs. Others had complicated heavy frames of turned wood. All were surrounded by elaborate draperies and were placed in a corner of the great hall. The draperies afforded privacy[4] from the attendants who were also sleeping in the hall and warded off some of the ever present drafts.

All furniture was very architectural, suggesting that the craftsmen who created the buildings also made the furniture. And, indeed, this was the case.

---

[3] The folding stool had a special significance and was saved for distinguished guests. Apparently some of the import of the *sella curulis,* the Roman folding stool used by only the highest officials, continued.

[4] The importance of personal privacy to the medieval mind is, of course, hard to estimate, but it is known that people slept nude; nightgowns (or underwear) had not yet been devised.

14-5 *The interior depicted in this painting of* The Annunciation *by Hans Memling (active c. 1465–1494) is medieval despite its Biblical subject matter. The bed in the background with a canopy and curtains, but with no wood showing, is typical of the period. Later the bed frame becomes more important and more wood is shown. The curtains were often gathered within themselves to form the teardrop form hanging from the canopy. A chest-bench with tracery carving is beneath the window.* The Metropolitan Museum of Art, Gift of J. Pierpont Morgan, 1917.

14-6 *Of simple panel construction, this massive chest from England (c. thirteenth century) has three large, round chip-carved designs ornamenting the front. As the name implies, chip-carving is accomplished by removing small chips, usually triangular, from the surface. The result is a crisp design of rich texture.*

It is not uncommon to find the same details, decorative devices, and even construction methods of the building and furniture to be identical. Although examples of stone and metal pieces have been found, most of the furniture was wood and that wood was usually oak. Oak is the wood of the medieval period.

The harshness of the times and simple construction methods do not preclude ornament and decoration. On the contrary, much of the furniture was brightly painted in rich colors and with touches of gold. The surface itself was carved in abstract designs and architectural detail. Chip-carving was a favorite technique and numerous decorative designs were produced that, interestingly, resemble the familiar round "hex" symbols used on "Pennsylvania Dutch" furniture and barns today.

The rapid spread of Gothic architecture is echoed by the adoption of Gothic architecture details in furniture (the same basic methods of construction and forms continued to be used).

In about the middle of the thirteenth century a new craft was developed, that of the coffermaker (arkwright). Until this time the carpenter had continued to make the furniture; but now the chests and gradually other pieces were made by a specific guild. This led to a professional approach that increased the knowledge of joinery, a finer craftsmanship, and an increase in stylistic developments. The term *joined* became common and was used to describe better furniture, furniture in which joints were used (mortise and tenon, dowels, and hand-cut dovetails). Panel construction again became customary and new methods of sawing were developed to produce thinner panels and planks.

Considerable furniture of the Gothic period is still in existence. Much of it has been found in churches and monasteries, but it is generally late Gothic and of fairly recent date. Early examples are rarer. However, little difference is evident between the furniture of one country or area and another. Distinct national differences do not begin to occur until the Renaissance.

14-7

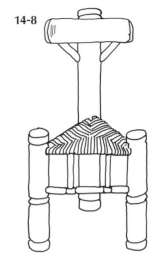

14-8

One piece of furniture that has been referred to but not discussed at any length is the stool. The Gothic period had many stools, but three kinds are important and have come down to the present almost intact. The origin of the first is lost in antiquity and examples are difficult to date or identify. It is the three-legged plank-topped stool. The seat is a thick circular piece of wood (in the more primitive versions this is a cross slice of a tree trunk). Three splayed legs are inserted in holes drilled through the seat. The ends of the legs were split before insertion and wedges were forced into them to tighten the legs in the holes. There is no decoration or ornament, and with their usual rough use appear aged and worn but of no specific period. The common utilitarian milk stools of 30 or 300 years ago are of this type. Three-legged stools were used throughout the Gothic castle in all manner of ways and by all kinds of people, from the highest rank to the lowest. Benches were also made in a similar manner. Both of these, the stool and bench, are seen in many genre paintings of the late Gothic period.

The second type of stool is also of stick construction and it too has three legs. These stools, however, were usually turned and connected to each other by stretchers and seat rails. The seat is woven rushes or cord. One leg sometimes was extended above the seat and a short horizontal piece was attached to it. It then became a *backstool.*

A third type was made of slabs of wood and consisted of three major pieces of wood or boards. Two boards serve as legs and are splayed out at the bottom. The third board is the seat. A stretcher is usually fastened between the slab-legs to strengthen the stool. These stools are easier to identify and date because they are frequently decorated. The slab-legs were often cut out at the bottom in trefoil or cusped arched shapes that create two short legs. Two lozenge-shaped holes are generally cut side by side in the seat center to permit the hand to use the wood between as a handle for easy carrying. The stretcher, sometimes directly under the seat and at other times nearer the floor, is often richly carved in the better and more elaborate versions. This

14-9 *A detail of a pulpit showing linen-fold ornament. The twisted molding on the left clearly shows the use of the wood-worker's chisel. Note the peg construction.*

14-10 *A sixteenth-century Italian chest that uses the linenfold decoration divided by panels of classical carving. Compare the design influences and placement on this chest with the chests illustrated on page 362.* Courtesy of the Virginia Museum of Fine Arts, Richmond.

type, too, was also a bench, the seat being extended to the desired length. Most of these slab-ended stools could be dismantled for easy packing (tenons on the stretcher extend completely through the ends and removable wooden wedge-shaped pegs secured them in the mortises).

Chests continued to be the most popular and necessary pieces of furniture. The nobles still traveled from one place to another even though times were more settled and it was possible to remain longer in one location. Chests became even more architectural in appearance with surface decoration influenced by decorative details of buildings, and especially stone buildings. Stiles were frequently carved to look like buttresses, and panels were covered with tracery. Carved tracery ornament and pointed arches in the form of blind arcading are two identifying features of Gothic furniture. Carving became more three dimensional as the Gothic period advanced and rich naturalistic carving of plant forms was very popular. Curled cabbage leaves, parsley, and watercress, maple leaves, and, perhaps the most popular, grapevines with leaves and fruit naturalistically represented were all used.

Another kind of Gothic surface decoration was *linenfold.* Panels covered with linenfold ornament appear to have symmetrically folded cloth on them. Developed in the fifteenth century, linenfold was especially preferred by English woodcarvers and was most compatible with oak.[5] Some of the other Gothic decorative motifs required small, fine detailing and do not seem particularly appropriate in oak because of its pronounced open grain.

The traditional chest form, a horizontal rectangular box with a lid, was adapted to different uses. The stiles were extended to form legs raising the chest above the floor. On long legs the top of the chest was fixed and the

[5] Although oak is the major wood of both the Romanesque and Gothic periods and was very abundant in north and central Europe, it was not as plentiful elsewhere. In other areas, Gothic furniture was made from walnut, fruitwoods, cypress, pine, and fir.

front panels became doors.[6] These cabinets were used for the storage of food and display of plate.[7] Called a *cupboard* ("borde" to set cups on) in England or a *dressoir* in France, these high chests are of many forms. Some lost the front panels completely and are sets of shelves. Others narrowed down and are almost tables with some storage in the apron and are called *credence* tables (which later during the Renaissance became the *credenza*). The credence or side serving table was used by the servant of the master of the house. Food intended for the master was first placed on the credence where it was then tasted by the servant before being given to the master and his honored guests. (During this period, members of the nobility lived in dread of being poisoned.) The servant acted as the "middleman" between the suspected food and the distinguished eater. Later examples of cupboards are fitted with drawers behind the door fronts.

The chest also acquired high side and back panels. This is the *box chair*. Frequently the seat could be raised to gain access to the storage space under it. Settles (benches with backs and arms) were also made in this way. The seats of settles sometimes had a long cushion or *banker* on them. As time went on the panels in the back were left off and it appeared to be a box only from the front. (The remaining panels and high back helped to keep drafts off the sitter.) However, chairs continued to be scarce although other pieces of furniture were more in evidence. The chair was also often placed on a *dais*, or elevated platform, to increase the distinction of its user and to allow him to

14-11 *The Campin Triptych (altarpiece, 1406–1444) depicts the Annunciation in the center panel with Joseph in his carpenter shop on the right and the donors of the altarpiece on the left. The center panel shows an early fifteenth century Flemish interior with the Virgin sitting by an open-backed settle that has tracery brackets between the legs. The table has a polygonal top with a carved base. The fireplace is typical of the period with its large opening, supporting brackets, and fire screen. With the settle backed against the fireplace and the window shutters open, one must assume that it is a warm day. The right panel is also of considerable interest. On the simple workbench before him, Joseph has a number of woodworking tools, a hammer, chisel, knife, pincers, and drill. He sits on a high-backed bench of simple panel construction. Again, the window shutters are open and through the windows can be seen a Flemish town with buildings similar to those in the left panel. The Metropolitan Museum of Art, The Cloisters Collection, Purchase.*

---

[6]One early method of hinging doors and lids employed the *pin hinge*. This hinge was integral with the lid (or door) and the frame; a pin was inserted through the frame on each end into the edges of the lid permitting it to pivot. These were not too strong and easily split out. More substantial and decorative hinges were later made of wrought iron.

[7]The term *plate* originally referred to articles made of silver and gold, and not to the dish used for eating. Because both of these metals were expensive, a lavish display of plate was one major way used by individuals to indicate their material wealth and, therefore, their importance.

14-12 *Pin hinge.*

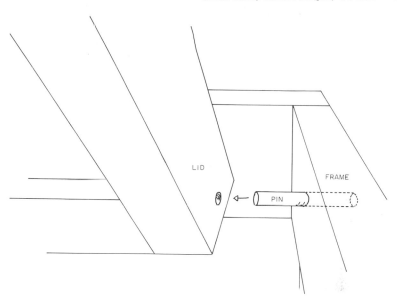

LID

FRAME

PIN

see everyone easily,[8] as had been done during the Early Christian and Byzantine periods.

Chairs themselves were also treasured and protected; again, because of their scarcity. Castles furnished by the wealthier nobles rarely had more than two or three chairs present in them. Although many of the larger chairs remained permanently fixed, when an elaborately carved chair was used when traveling it was sometimes carried in its own trunk or *bourge*. This was more common in France than in the rest of Europe, but it indicates the prestige the chair had.[9]

During the Gothic period the ability to write became more common and was no longer centered only in the monasteries and churches. The need for a smooth surface upon which to write and convenient storage for writing equipment resulted in the desk and book cupboard, a small, portable chest with a smooth hinged and slanted top or lid. Writing materials and books could be easily stored under the lid and the top of the lid provided a good surface upon which to write. This small portable desk was the ancestor of all slant-top school desks, drafting tables, and lecterns.

Tables of the Gothic period remained similar to those used previously. Some small fixed tables were evident but the majority of the tables were trestle tables that could be taken apart and stored when not needed. Near the end of the period a new table form developed. The *table dormant*, or permanent table, has four legs that are usually large and sturdy (later resulting

14-13 *This French "Bishop's chair" (c. 1500) has linenfold paneling and open tracery across the top of the back. Beneath the modern cushion is a hinged seat secured by a lock. This chair is really a small chest with a back and arms extended above the lid.* Courtesy of the St. Louis Art Museum.

[8] The significance of the Gothic chair has passed down through the ages. Our contemporary usage of the term *chairman* refers to the person who "chairs" or leads a meeting. The importance of this term originally developed during the Gothic period when the "leader" or most important person, would be seated while his subordinates stood during the meeting or interview.

[9] During the medieval period the special seat or throne-chair used by a bishop was called a *cathedra*, accordingly, the bishop's church in which his cathedra was situated was called the *cathedral*.

14-14

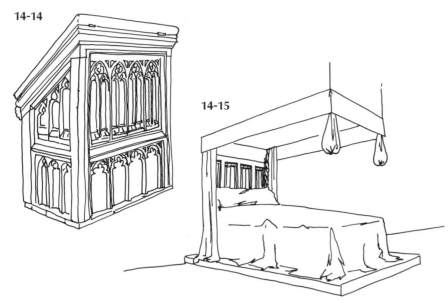

14-15

in the *melon-bulb* form in England). Stretchers, resting directly on the floor,[10] and rails, or the *apron* as they are collectively called, under the thick tabletop brace the legs. In essence, this is a support that is very box-like, a chest with all the panels removed.

The beds of the Gothic period were the most expensive single pieces of furniture and were often of great size. Heavy draperies hung from a suspended canopy and enclosed the occupants at night, similar to that of the late Romanesque period. The bed has a high and richly carved headboard but no footboard. As the period continued, beds became even more elaborate and costly. The headboards were made ever higher and frequently had half-testers, projections at the top of the headboard. A *trundle bed* (or "truckle bed") was often stored under the main bed to be pulled out at night for the use of servants or children.

The close affinity of Gothic furniture to the architecture of the period cannot be overemphasized. Its detailing and ornament were drawn directly from the churches and major secular buildings, and its construction was, except in later and rare examples, akin to carpentry. This produced a ruggedly handsome, vital furniture that is much admired today. It should not, however, be confused with the furniture of the midnineteenth century called Gothic revival. This furniture, which applied Gothic ornament to eighteenth and early nineteenth-century furniture forms, is a contrived hybrid. This is not to say that some of it is not desirable, elegant, or skillfully made; it is, but it does not have the vitality and robust exuberance of the original Gothic furniture.

---

[10] The location and use of stretchers is a good indication of the approximate date and the joining skills of the time. Over time stretchers will be raised until the apron and the stretchers are one (eighteenth century).

15 Furniture: Italian Renaissance, Spanish

The early years of the fifteenth century were a period of change. The old forms, ornaments, and decorations were being refined and adapted toward new uses, and as the climate became less desperate, the "human" desire for luxury and comfort grew. Veterans of the Crusades had returned with an acquired taste for Byzantine, Venetian, and Muslim elegance and were disposed to furnish the cold and bare interiors of the Gothic and Romanesque castles, monasteries, and churches with sumptuous textiles and better constructed and more elaborate furniture. The developing merchant class in the growing cities were demanding comforts and furnishings that would indicate their new status and wealth.

North of the Alps existed the culture of the medieval world in its brightest and most enlightened form. The strife-filled years of the barbaric conquests were far behind and the scattered grains of culture that had survived had taken root and were now ripening into the elaborate and viable Gothic system. The political and social structures were as unique as the architecture and the furniture.

Ironically, despite this high level of Gothic culture existing to the North, it was in Italy that the next development in furniture design occurred. Italy had never accepted the Gothic style as wholeheartedly as had other areas of Europe and the Near East; it had clung steadfastly to Romanesque. Conceivably, the predilection for the round arch was supported by the existence of the many ancient Roman ruins still standing.

An important aspect of the Renaissance, when comparing it to the medieval period, is the shift from a religious to a secular emphasis. The whole medieval world was closely tied to the Church. It was the most influential factor that governed all thoughts and actions. Renaissance man, on the other hand, was much more temporal. Although the Church retained a place in his life and continued to receive his financial support, he had broadened his horizons to include other worldly matters. As a result, he was not a recluse

with a single purpose, but rather an outward oriented person with many interests.

One of the chief interests was in the life and the arts of ancient Rome, which permeates the whole Renaissance and subsequent periods to the present day. Furniture was as affected by this interest in ancient Rome as was architecture and literature. New style or details frequently meant not an original development but rather a design that was copied from Roman models.

The interiors of the early Italian Renaissance palace or *pallazzo* (the word *castle* with its defense structure implication is no longer appropriate) became increasingly opulent. It was a richness relying on the interior architecture rather than the furnishings. Inventories taken early in the fifteenth century sometimes list no more than three or four beds, eight to ten chairs, a table or two, various stools and benches, and a large number of chests as the furniture of an entire pallazzo of many rooms. Much of this furniture is movable and could be taken from one room to another.

Despite the small number of pieces, the visitor from the medieval North was undoubtedly struck by the history and elegance of the interiors and furnishings of Renaissance Italy. The flat surfaces and panels vibrated and glowed with sumptuousness, covered with brilliantly painted designs and inlays of ivory, lapis lazuli, marble, onyx, and other semiprecious stones. Furniture was also gilded to further increase its richness.

Early in the Renaissance a concern for strongly contrasting light and shadow produced by very three-dimensional moldings and paneling appeared in the design of furniture as well as in architecture forms. The rectangular masses and flat planes of early furniture were broken up. Panels that were formerly placed slightly below the surrounding framing began to project above it and are thus more dominant elements. Undulating moldings and carvings were also used to increase the three-dimensional qualities of the furniture surfaces. A strong visual movement generated by both simple and

15-1 *A fifteenth-century Italian chest that shows the influence of the repeated round arch in its decoration, and yet on the stiles are carved small Gothic lancet window forms.* Courtesy of the Virginia Museum of Fine Arts, Richmond.

15-2 *A fifteenth-century Italian cassone with richly carved inlaid panels demonstrating the concern for architecture.* Courtesy of the Virginia Museum of Fine Arts, Richmond.

complex curved structural supports for chairs and tables and curvilinear applied ornamentation became increasingly evident. In addition, the utilization of elaborate turnings for both structural supports and applied ornamentation increased considerably.

Furniture of the High Baroque period or late seventeenth century often appears to be overly enthusiastic in its plasticity, especially when it is seen apart from the interior for which it was created. The furniture of this period was designed to complement the interior, and when seen in such an interior, the forms and applied ornament appear more appropriate, designed solely to increase the viewer's joy of movement through space and time. Each individual piece was always seen as one part of a completely developed whole and never as a thing completely unto itself.

As it had been for centuries, the most common piece of furniture in the Renaissance palace was the chest or *cassone*. Early fifteenth-century chests were generally rectangular in shape, gaining their richness from the large painted or inlaid panels[1] surrounded by classical orders and moldings. These chests sat directly on the floor, and the exterior elevations were usually divided in the three major "temple front" divisions—pedestal, column, and entablature. The surface of the early cassoni are covered with gesso and except for the painted center panel were frequently covered with gold leaf.

During the fifteenth century, the cassoni changed from simple rectangular shapes to the forms of ancient sarcophagi, which were supported on animal feet. The surfaces were richly carved[2] with scenes of ancient Rome and were no longer gessoed. Instead, they remained natural and polished, for the wood

---

[1] Many of the painted panels were done by the major artists of the period. Consequently, many of these chests have been destroyed so that the painting could be framed, presumably increasing its value.

[2] The wood-carvers who decorated these elaborate chests were considered equal, if not superior, to the sculptors who worked in stone or bronze.

15-3 *The painted panel, executed about 1470, probably by a skilled painter working with others in a guild shop, shows the increased interest in illusionary painting. The surface of the panel virtually disappears. Note the family crests on each side of the painting and the use of classical moldings. Courtesy of the Virginia Museum of Fine Arts, Richmond.*

15-4 *The rich carving seen on this walnut Florentine chest (c. 1560) almost completely obliterates the rectangular chest form. Courtesy of the Virginia Museum of Fine Arts, Richmond.*

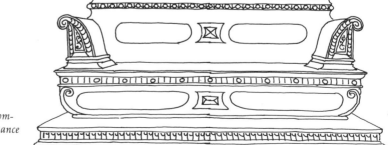

15-5 *Made of walnut and without doubt horribly uncomfortable by today's standards, the cassapanca of Renaissance Italy was the forerunner of the modern sofa.*

used in the Italian Renaissance was walnut.[3] The oleaginous walnut takes on a warm sheen when rubbed, similar to the highly esteemed look of old bronze; an additional reason for its popularity with antique-minded Renaissance patrons.

Cassoni were often made in pairs and were used to hold the trousseau of a bride, with one chest displaying the coat of arms of the bride and the other the groom. Naturally not all Renaissance chests had such significance, but this precursory use has interestingly continued on into the twentieth century.

The *cassapanca*[4] was developed from the cassone although it was more popular in Florence than elsewhere. Arms and a back were added and the lid was often covered with cushions. The result became the ancestor of today's sofa and yet harked back to Roman high-backed couches that were popular in the first century. The cassapanca is very often richly carved with architectural details and frequently has the appearance of being integral with the wall.

The *credenza* in the early years of the Renaissance was a plainly constructed table covered with a rich cloth. As the desire for more decorative pieces grew, credenze became more elaborate and were no longer covered. Used mainly for the storage of table articles such as dishes and linens, credenze were designed with architectural details such as columns and cornices surrounding a series of doors. Behind the doors are drawers and divided storage spaces.

Two kinds of Renaissance beds were used. One type is massive and box-like with paneled head and footboards. The panels are richly decorated with carving, paintings, or inlaid designs. The understructure that raises the

[3] As the Renaissance spirit developed throughout Europe, walnut replaced the Medieval oak. Being native to the Mediterranean area, walnut was first imported by the northern countries, but later locally planted walnut trees were used.

[4] Derived from *cassone* ("chest" or "box") and *banca* ("table" or "bench").

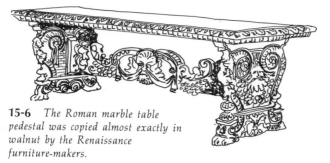

15-6 *The Roman marble table pedestal was copied almost exactly in walnut by the Renaissance furniture-makers.*

15-7 *This sixteenth-century Florentine table also reflects its Roman heritage.*

bed above the floor and serves as a dais consists of cassoni (a good way to protect one's belongings is to sleep on them).

The second type of bed also has head and footboards and incorporates the cassoni in its design, but is more delicate in feeling even though it has a canopy or tester that is supported by four posts and furnished with draperies. Few examples of this type of bed have survived; however, it was depicted in many paintings indicating its popularity.

By far the most common tables of the Renaissance were the nonpermanent trestle type, which were easily set up and removed as needed. However, two other tables are identified with the Italian Renaissance, and both are based upon Roman prototypes.

The largest table is rectangular and is supported on two heavy and elaborately carved pedestals, sometimes connected by a carved stretcher. Usually made of walnut with a solid plank for a top, it is very similar to the Roman table described in Chapter 13. Called a *refectory* table, it was placed in the center of large reception rooms and could be used for dining. Frequently this type of table is a *draw table;* that is, extensions can be pulled out at each end to lengthen the top.

A second and smaller type of table is called the Florentine. The wood or stone tops are hexagonal or octagonal and edged with ornamental moldings (always based upon Roman models). The top surfaces are frequently decorated with detailed and complicated inlays. The bases are tripedal; sometimes with three volutes ending in lion feet or with three dolphins, tail high, joined to form one central pedestal. These tables were copied in later periods such as French Empire and English Regency.

Chairs during the Renaissance became more popular and were represented by several different styles. The straight box-like armchair or *sedia* continued to be used. It was no longer reserved for the head of the household, but was found throughout the palazzo. The straight, rectangular legs are attached to

15-8 *An Italian sedia with elaborate gilt finials. Note the sled-like appearance of the floor stretchers that end with lion paws.* Courtesy of the Virginia Museum of Fine Arts, Richmond.

15-9 *Derived from the three-legged plank stool of the Middle Ages, the simply designed sgabello of the fifteenth century developed into the ornate version on the right a century later.*

floor stretchers on each side, which suggests the appearance of a sled. The rear legs are carried up past the seat and form the back stiles. These invariably end in a carved finial. Turned *baluster* or vase-like forms support the front of the arms and are often the only turned elements on the very plain chair frame. The back and seat are upholstered in velvet, tapestry, or ornamented leather and decorated with nailheads and fringe. Armless versions were also made, but generally these are not as ornate and the upholstery is not as fine.

The *sgabello* is a very versatile, lightweight chair that has many of the characteristics of a stool with a back. The small octagonal or rectangular seat is supported by three legs in the early versions and by two scroll-cut slabs or planks braced with a stretcher in later models. A narrow, high, and richly decorated back almost soars above the seat and give the sgabello its distinctive appearance. Used as a dining and all-purpose chair, its style continues, especially in native and peasant furniture in all European countries.

The old favorite, the X-chair, which had never been forgotten, became even more popular during the Italian Renaissance and assumed three distinct identities. The Dante or Dantesque chair has reversed-curved members forming an "X" in the front and in the back. These two sets of crossed members are separated by floor stretchers and the arms. The point of intersection is frequently decorated with a *boss*[5] or a mask that is able to conceal a movable joint. The front "X" curves upward past the seat to form a support for the arms. The rear "X" is higher; in addition to having the arms attached it becomes the side posts of the back panel. If the chair can be folded, the back and seat are usually made of leather. Wooden backs and seats are found in nonfolding Dante chairs. A loose fringed and tasseled

[5] A boss is a projecting round or oval decorative ornament that is often placed where two structural elements meet.

15-10 *A pair of heavy, plain Dante chairs. Aside from their almost too fine fringe and velvet pads, there is little decoration or subtlety of form.* Courtesy of the Virginia Museum of Fine Arts, Richmond.

cushion is often placed on the seat. The frame is frequently carved or decorated with *certosina* inlay.[6]

The Savonarola chair is similar to the Dante chair but instead of having only two crossed units, it has several closely spaced and parallel "X's." These make up the entire space of the chair from front to back. The Savonarola chair, although having more "X's" than the Dante chair, is usually lighter and more delicate in appearance.

The third type of X-chair is the Monastery chair, which is constructed like the Savonarola chair, but is less ornamented and has straight interlacing slats. The Monastery chair is the least elegant of the X-chairs and was usually found in more humble surroundings.

Chairs as well as tables and chests were sometimes covered with fabric rather than being carved or painted. When covered with fabric, which was usually velvet, each edge was outlined with ornamented nailheads, a practice that continues to this day.

The influence of Italian Renaissance furniture was considerable; Spanish and French furniture styles were especially affected. In the sixteenth and early seventeenth century, Italian furniture forms were highly favored and it is often difficult to immediately determine if an isolated piece of furniture is Italian, Spanish, or French. Craftsmen from Italy were in great demand throughout Europe, and even England, the last country to accept the Renaissance, had Italian craftsmen in the early 1500s. Yet, it is not Italian Renaissance furniture that directly affects design today, but rather the furniture styles of the countries that *it* influenced. The sixteenth through eighteenth-century styles of Spain, France, and England, and in a lesser way of the Low

15-11 *An Italian sixteenth-century writing cabinet decorated with certosina inlay.* Courtesy of the Virginia Museum of Fine Arts, Richmond.

[6]A type of inlay in which small geometric elements of bone, ivory, or light wood are embedded into a dark ground. Probably Muslim in origin, certosina inlay is found not only on Italian Renaissance furniture but is also a very popular method of ornamenting the surface of Spanish furniture.

15-12 *The seat and back of this Savonarola chair can be removed allowing the chair to fold.* Courtesy of the Virginia Museum of Fine Arts, Richmond.

15-13 *Sixteenth-century door from Seville.*

Countries and Germany, are more clearly the inspiration for much of today's furniture.[7]

The development of the Italian Renaissance was but one factor that affected the furniture of sixteenth-century Spain.[8] It was, in fact, far less important to the total than the cultural, political, and economic changes that were taking place during Spain's finest period. The final expulsion of the Moors from Spain in 1492 laid the way for a period of relative peace. Furthermore, the dramatic discovery of the New World with all its wealth in the same year stimulated Spain's economic growth. The resulting prosperity provided the stimulus for new palace and upper-middle-class house construction. These houses are a combination of Moorish, Christian medieval, and Italian Renaissance elements melded into one synthesis of design.

The ethnological and economic character of sixteenth-century Spain is also apparent in the furniture. The forms and decorative elements are freely mixed and together produce a style as distinctive as the architecture. Spanish

[7] Interestingly, pseudo-Italian design has greatly influenced the furniture of the 1960s and 70s. Italian provincial furniture, a term coined by the American furniture industry, refers to straight legged, fruitwood surfaced furniture having a few classical details. Although it has some of the characteristics of French neoclassic furniture of the late eighteenth century, it is a concoction of the furniture manufacturers and has no historic design base. One questions the reasons for its sizable popularity.

A second but authentic Italian influence, and by far the more preferred, is the exciting developments in furniture design that have originated in Italy during the last two decades. These new designs, materials, and construction techniques have profoundly influenced current furniture design and may over time affect the direction of design thought as much as did the designs of the Renaissance.

[8] The furniture of the sixteenth century is the most distinctively "Spanish" and it is upon this style of furniture that later adaptations have been based. It is not the province of this book to give detailed and involved aesthetic backgrounds of each national style or period but rather to give identifying characteristics that can be traced, either directly or indirectly, to the furniture available today. Therefore, furniture that is influenced unduly by other nationalistic styles is not discussed in this section or in subsequent sections.

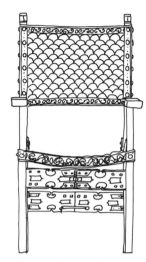

15-14 *The rigid rectangularity of the sillón de fraileros was offset by the elaborate surface design of the tooled leather seat and back. The pierced front and back stretchers below the seat were hinged, which permitted the chair to fold compactly.*

furniture was sparingly used (a Moorish tendency) as each piece stood alone, isolated from the others, almost as a valued piece of freestanding sculpture.

The fundamental characteristic of all Spanish furniture is its simplicity and boldness. It is not delicate. Proportions are generally heavy and the carving is not as fine as that found in Italy. Curves are more generous when used, but are in the minority; most individual pieces appear far more rectangular than curvilinear. Panels are geometric—squares, diamonds, or circles—and are repeated over an entire surface to give an overall pattern.

Walnut was the most commonly used wood, but chestnut, poplar, oak, orange, and pine were also popular. Imported woods such as mahogany and ebony were employed, and mahogany became increasingly preferred for Spanish furniture when English and French influences became strong in the eighteenth century. The wealth of the New World also affected the materials used in furniture and with the discovery of the silver mountain Potosí in Peru in 1545, furniture began to be decorated with, and later fabricated of, silver.

Spanish chairs are adaptations of other chairs but are in themselves important additions to the vocabulary of furniture designers. The *hip-joint* chair (*sillón de cadera*) was introduced from Italy and resembles the Dante chair except that the upper portion is almost always larger and the chair appears to be top-heavy. Exposed surfaces are usually carved or inlaid with a flat decorative pattern. Inlaid designs are often geometric and when ivory or a light wood are used, the ornamented surface is very similar to the Italian certosina. The back and seat, and sometimes the frame, are upholstered in rich embroidery and are further decorated with fringe and nailheads.

About 1650 a new chair began to be developed in Spain. This chair form came from Flanders[9] but is reminiscent of the sedia chair of Italy. This

[9] Spain ruled the Low Countries at this time and there is a strong aesthetic interrelationship between the Netherlands, Flanders, and Spain. Spain also had political interests in Italy, so it was natural that such an interchange occurred.

15-15 *The combination of heavy wood construction, large-scale decorative elements, wrought-iron braces, and splayed legs characterize many Spanish tables.*

15-16 *The Moorish table, which originally held a brazier, could easily be adapted to hold plants. Consequently, during the 1920s when Spanish furniture styles were popular, small side tables such as this simply constructed example were frequently found in average midwestern American homes. Inlaid and carved versions of this table were often called Damascus tables.*

armchair, known as *sillón de fraileros,* or monk's chair, is now considered to be the most "Spanish" type of chair. It has the squarish frame and floor stretchers of the sedia but there is a wide, carved, and sometimes pierced front stretcher just below the seat. (This is a distinct and identifying feature.) This armchair is made to fold, permitting it to be carried easily from one place to another. The decorated front stretcher and the two plain ones in back are hinged. The seat and back are flexible leather, plain or tooled, and on some more elegant models the leather is covered with decorative fabric.

Spanish tables are also distinctive in design. The splay-legged table is the most characteristic.[10] These tables have a plain slab or a top with carved-front drawers in the apron. The supports or legs, however, are the most distinguishing features. They slant outward and are steadied by decorative, curved wrought-iron[11] underbraces. (The tables can also be taken apart.) There are two types of supports both of which have similar trapezoidal shapes. The first has an outline composed of curves (a shape somewhat like a lyre) and appears to have been sawed from a large plank or planks. The flat outer and inner surfaces of each support are parallel and only the edges are curved. The second type of support, also trapezoidal in shape, is made of turned components. There are often *clavated* (spool or disk shaped) or baluster shaped.[12]

Small versions of the larger tables are also found in Spanish interiors. A

---

[10] Dismountable trestle tables covered with floor-length cloths were also common.

[11] Decorative wrought-iron stretchers, handles, hinges, and locks are characteristically Spanish and reflect the craft heritage of the Moors.

[12] A marked absence of classical architectural details is found in Spanish furniture. Where tables, chairs, and chests in Italy would have had columns, pilasters, and decorative moldings derived from ancient Greek or Roman temples incorporated in their designs, in Spain the supports and decorative elements are combinations of spirals, spools, knobs, disks, or vase shapes and the edges are almost always plain without the traditional classical molding cross-section.

15-17 *A fantasy concoction of disks, spools, and swirls, the ornate, high headboard on many Spanish beds often rivals the decorative ironwork that is typical of Spanish crafts.*

holdover from Moorish days, these small tables are usually less than two feet high and serve many uses. One type is the *brazier*, a small table with a metal pan in the top that was filled with charcoal and supplied additional heat to the room. These were essential in the large and high-ceilinged rooms found in sixteenth-century Spanish houses.

The highly developed Spanish skill of turning wood on the lathe is no more apparent than on the beds. These masterpieces of spirals, disks, and spindles resemble in their complexity the wrought-iron railings and grills found in the houses and churches of the period. The ornate and high headboard of dark colored wood is sharply delineated against the light colored wall behind. There is usually no footboard. Four elaborately turned posts support a canopy from which hang rich colored draperies.

The most unique piece of furniture and the only one considered to be of original Spanish design is the *vargueño*. This is essentially a chest resting upon a support or table. The exterior is generally rather plain and unadorned with perhaps nicely designed wrought-iron handles on each end, hinges, and an elaborate lock. The support is similar to one of the previously described tables, or it may be a stand with vertical legs connected by an arcaded stretcher (one of the few architectural elements in Spanish furniture). Directly under the top section are pulls that can be extended to support the drop lid front[13], of the *vargueño* when opened and form a writing desk. What is so distinctive and unrivaled about the *vargueño* is the superb cabinetmaking and decorative detail on the interior. It is divided into small drawers and cabinets of exquisite design with rich and exuberant inlay, carving, and fabrics covering every surface. The dissimilarity between the plain exterior and the remarkable and lavish ornamentation inside parallels the severity of the exterior and the interior luxury found in the Spanish house itself.

15-18 *Behind the front lid, the vargueño is a masterful arrangement of compartmented storage. This example has a severely plain exterior relieved only by the wrought-iron handles and the large lock, but once opened the full beauty of Spanish woodworking is revealed.*

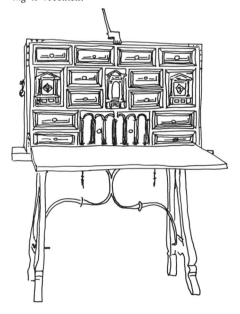

---

[13] Another chest on a stand is called the *papelera* and although it resembles the *vargueño* it does not have a drop-lid front.

16 Furniture: French

The French did not succumb to Renaissance influence until just before the beginning of the sixteenth century. (See Chapter 10.) The splendid glory of the flamboyant Gothic style, that last flowering medieval design, was too vital and tenacious. It was, after all, in France that the Gothic style burst upon the Western world. However, the orderly, rational, and humanistic spirit of the Renaissance proved stronger and the energy of the Gothic diminished.

The reign of Francois I (1515–1547) gave its name to the early Renaissance in France. From about 1495–1547 the Francois I style of furniture is almost entirely medieval in form. The square, rugged designs lost most of the tracery and linenfold ornament that were so dear to the Gothic carvers, but traces of Gothic lingered on the sides and backs, tucked here and there amid the shallow but lively decorative elements of the Renaissance. French Renaissance furniture exhibits more carved surface than does the Italian. Seldom is there any surface bereft of some form of high or low relief or three-dimensional elements. This characteristic can be attributed to a continuation of the late Gothic wood-carving tradition. However, gradually more Renaissance surface decoration, such as gilding, painting, and inlay, was employed.

The Francois I style is noted for the decorative use of many elongated nude and partially nude figures. These appear in panels and medallions surrounded by moldings or plant forms and as caryatids and terms. The salamander, the kings' personal symbol, is also a recurring motif. Walnut was used, and although oak and other woods were often utilized, walnut made possible the requisite subtleties of carving found in early French Renaissance furniture and that marks it "French."

Gradually, more sophisticated joinery was used as the miter was combined with the mortise and tenon resulting in hidden joints. Hidden joints and larger panels allowed the wood carvers to decorate the entire surface.

Following the style of Francois I is a period in which even more Italian influence is apparent. Called the Henri II style (1547–1589), there is a certain

371

16-1 *A French, sixteenth-century carved walnut two-part cabinet that has the form of the medieval period but is almost smothered with the motifs associated with the Renaissance— garlands, partially nude figures, griffins, goats, and eagles. The medieval spirit is not totally missing from the ornament, however; the large panels and some of the carving on the friezes hark back to medieval combat.* Courtesy of the Virginia Museum of Fine Arts, Richmond.

degree of plainness when contrasted with the earlier furniture but much vigorous ornament was still used. Classical and Italian Renaissance details —lion heads, dolphins, chimerae, human figures (caryatids and terms), garlands, masks, and pilasters and columns—were interpreted rather than copied and eventually became more French than Italian.

Furniture lost some of its medieval forms. Chairs, which had remained quite box-like during the first half of the century, lost their lower side panels. Stretchers, however, remained low and near the floor. It was not until the late seventeenth century that they were placed closer to the seat or tabletop than to the floor. This is probably because of the fact that many floors were not level and furniture legs could not withstand the stresses of an uneven floor without additional bracing.

The early French Renaissance chairs were straight, rectangular, and imposing. Backs were gradually lowered from the throne-like forms of medieval times but remained simple in construction. Chairs with upholstery increased in number (the search for comfort again), and following the Italian precedent, some were completely covered with fabric as well as just the padded seat and back. Silks, velvets, and tapestry weaves were popular.

One chair type did evolve during this period, the *chaise caquetoire* or "chair for cackling" (gossiping). The seat shape is what gives this chair its distinction. It is trapezoidal, the front being wider than the back. This allows two such chairs to be placed in such a way that two women with the wide-hooped skirts of the period could sit close enough to speak in hushed tones. The high and decorated back and outwardly curving arms[1] are in contrast to the almost plain, straight legs and low stretchers, as if the skirts should always hide them.

Tables, like chairs, were Italianate in form. Often called tables à italienne,

16-2 *Strongly influenced by similar chairs in Italy, this simply constructed French chair of the latter half of the sixteenth century has columnar legs in front and fabric covered back and seat. Note that the chair frame between the seat and the back is also covered with fabric.* Courtesy of the Art Institute of Chicago.

---

[1] The term *chaise à bras* or "armchair" began to be used to designate a chair with side supports, or arms as they are known today.

16-3 *The distinctive seat shape of the chaise caquetoire easily identifies these two sixteenth-century armchairs. The construction and details of the trapezoidal area below the seats are almost identical. Above the seat there is less similarity. The chair on the left is plainer and probably was made by a less skilled craftsman than the one on the right. The carving, the more carefully hidden joints, and the abundance of classically derived motifs identify the latter as being made later or in the more fully developed style of the French Renaissance. Both chairs would have been used with a cushion similar to the one on the left. The cushion on the right chair has been removed to show the recessed seat panel, which, with the cords, held the cushion in place. Courtesy of the St. Louis Art Museum.*

16-4 *A walnut draw-leaf table made in the late sixteenth or early seventeenth century. This table is very Italianate in design with small Doric-like columns as the supports. Note the turned pendant ornaments under each corner of the tabletop and the dark-stained walnut and fruitwood insets with arabesques. This table is also seen in the interior on page 378. Courtesy of the Toledo Museum of Art, Toledo, Ohio. Gift of Mr. & Mrs. Marvin S. Kobacker.*

16-5 *A* dressoir *made of walnut in the sixteenth century in France. The carving is especially varied and rich on this piece.* Courtesy of the St. Louis Art Museum.

they frequently have architectural supports and differ little from the Italian prototypes except for the turned pendant ornament that is often found under each corner of the tabletop. Invariably, these tables are draw tables and can be extended. However, the old style trestle and plank table was commonly used for dining. Many small tables with tops of inlaid marble were also constructed during this period.

The French beds of the sixteenth century continued the heritage of the canopy supported on four posts and hung with curtains. However, the structure of the bed itself rather than the draperies took on importance during the latter half of the century. The posts, no longer simple, are elaborately carved with caryatids or terms, garland-entwined columns, and urns, and the bed itself has a carved and exposed frame with the legs frequently taking the form of lions, griffins, or other fanciful animals. The headboard is embellished with rich carving and a pediment or some other architectural device tops if off.

The *lit de repos* or daybed became a popular resting place and was richly decorated but did not have the canopy, posts, or draperies that are identified with the larger bed.

Chests continued to be used and were decorated with carved, inlaid, and painted designs. The *dressoir* or dresser, similar to the earlier sideboard, became an increasingly important form within the French Renaissance interiro. In two sections, which could be separated, the upper part of these large decorative cabinets consists of two or more carved doors adorned with a medallion in low relief and surrounded by an architectural framework. A cornice projects from the top of the piece and what would be the podium of the "temple front" is filled with two drawers. The whole is supported upon an open arrangement of columns or a solid cabinet base again fitted with doors. The top invariably is not as wide as the bottom.

Ebony partially supplanted the use of walnut and is responsible for the term *ébéniste,* applied to those furniture-makers of cabinets and other case

16-6 *A sixteenth-century armchair with each arm terminating with the head of a ram and supported by a volute. The base is still box-like with a low stretcher arrangement. Compare this chair with the* chaise caquetoire *of similar date on page 373 (right) and also with the somewhat later chairs on page 376. Courtesy of the Virginia Museum of Fine Arts, Richmond.*

pieces. The *dressoir* gradually became the *armoire.* This tall, double-doored cabinet with a projecting cornice at the top is the ancestor of the closet. It served as a storage piece (originally as the name suggests, for armor but later for clothing).

During the late sixteenth century and the first half of the seventeenth century, French furniture developed a complexity and ornateness, but only at the expense of losing a sense of orderliness. In 1608, Henri IV, the first Bourbon king (r. 1589–1610), established workshops and apartments for artisans in the Louvre. Here painters, sculptors, goldsmiths, cabinetmakers, and other craftsmen could work under royal patronage. Most of these craftsmen were Flemish or Italian, and not French, but this attempt to increase the importance of the decorative arts in France was established and of seminal significance.

The king was assassinated in 1610 and was succeeded by his son, Louis XIII, a child of nine. Marie de'Medici, the mother of the young king, became regent and with Cardinal Richelieu firmly established the political and aesthetic design direction of the court. These two strong and willful individuals brought all the components together and set the process in motion. Spanish, Flemish, Italian, and native French decorative elements and their requisite skills (available in the Louvre workshops) were used, sometimes in strange combinations, but by the time Versailles was built by Louis XIV the synthesis of these elements was completed and a truly French Baroque style existed.

Although a Florentine, Marie was enraptured by the Flemish painter Rubens, and his profound influence left a deep impression upon French design. For example, the inlaid ornament of tortoiseshell[2] and pewter, which

[2] The shell of the tropical turtle, *Carotta imbricata,* can be split into thin semitransparent sheets. These sheets can be flattened when heated and used as a veneering material. When applied to furniture, this rare and costly veneer has a rich and mottled surface that is easily polished to a high sheen. The individual pieces of tortoiseshell are seldom large and must

16-7 *A pair of turned and tapestry-covered sidechairs (early seventeenth century). There is an H-stretcher, raised from the floor, between the legs, and an additional front stretcher closer to the seat frame. The upholstery is secured by closely spaced round-headed nails that give the effect of a bead molding.* Courtesy of the Virginia Museum of Fine Arts, Richmond.

was to become highly developed later in the century, and the elaborate and overly decorated cabinets, which were so prized were both Flemish favorites.

Louis XIII furniture embodies the rectangular forms of the past, but basically differs in the use of richer fabrics, surface ornament, and materials, chairs are squarish, tables are covered with fabrics, cabinets and armoires are richly ornamented, and the furniture in the interior remains generally sparse. Upholstered furniture was, however, in greater evidence.

The square, low-backed chair is either completely covered with fabrics attached with gilded or silvered nails or the frame is exposed with only the seat and back upholstered. If exposed, the wooden frame components are usually turned on the lathe. The most frequent and characteristically Louis XIII form is the spiral (*piliers tors*), but knobbed (*en chapelet*) and baluster (*en balustre*) forms were also used. The legs are braced with an H-stretcher near the floor and a front stretcher just below the seat. There are both arm and armless versions of this chair. The arms of the armchair (*fauteuil*) terminate in the head of an animal (lion or ram) or the bust of a woman.

The bed was still located in the major room of the house and is the most elaborate single furniture item, the masterpiece of the upholsterer. The ornately carved bed frame that was popular in the latter part of the sixteenth century is no longer evident. Rather, the beds of the early seventeenth century are again elaborately draped with none of the framework showing. The canopy is covered with fringed textiles and on each corner is a vase of ostrich feathers (*panaches*). The hangings and covers, whether of the most splendid silk brocade or less costly wool serge, are fringed, tasseled, and embroidered. Frequently, the bed was in an alcove and the space around the

16-8 *Made about 1650, this large ebony veneered cabinet is 89 inches high. One of its large exterior doors has been removed as has a smaller interior door to allow the viewer to see the carefully fitted and carved drawers and the center architectural setting for the display of objects d'art.* Courtesy of the St. Louis Art Museum.

be fitted together if surfaces are extensive. Tortoiseshell is, however, often combined with other materials and the rather obvious joints are then less noticeable. Tortoiseshell was first used in ancient China but its use on furniture is usually associated with seventeenth century Europe.

377

16-9 *An early seventeenth-century room from the Château de Chenailles. Carved, painted, and gilded woodwork surrounds 18 oil paintings on panels and five oil paintings on canvas. The draw-leaf table with matching chairs is somewhat earlier than the more Baroque upholstered chair by the fireplace.* Courtesy of the Toledo Museum of Art, Toledo, Ohio. Gift of Mr. & Mrs. Marvin S. Kobacker.

16-10 *A detail from a carved door in Versailles made about 1685. The background is painted white and all the carved ornament is gilded. Incorporated in the design of interlaced "L's" enclosed in the elliptical molding is the doorknob.*

bed (*la ruelle*) had stools and cushions that were used by guest. (It was common to receive visitors while the host was still in bed.) The ruelle was often the most decorated area in the room, if not in the entire house. It was also the most intimate and personal.

The large ebony cabinets that were used to both hold and display *objets d'art* are also of interest. These cabinets are similar in form to the dressoirs of the previous century, although the upper portions are the same width as the base. The exteriors are richly carved with shallow ornamentation.[3] The interiors are fitted with shelves and drawers and embellished with inlay, marquetry, mirrors, and architectural details to provide suitable settings for the display of treasured objects.

Louis XIII was not a strong and particularly enlightened king with regard to stylistic development. However, it was during his reign (1610–1643) that the foundations for the rich and almost unbelievable French Baroque of Louis XIV were established.

The Baroque style had originated in Italy but was brought to its fullest development during the reign of Louis XIV. Characterized by the use of curved and visually moving forms, theatrical effects, and a richness of materials heretofore never achieved, Baroque exemplifies the new movement in which man's awareness of himself and the world is uppermost.

The development of the architectural style of the Palace of Versailles, still the epitome of French Baroque architecture, is credited to Louis Le Vau and later to Jules-Hardouin Mansart. But it is Charles Le Brun, more than any other individual, who set the French Baroque style. It was he who was responsible for the interiors and furnishings of Fouquet's château and those in Versailles. His concepts and ideas shaped, adjusted, and combined classical and Italian, Spanish, Flemish, and French Renaissance decorative

[3] The basic structure of these cabinets is often not solid ebony but is overlaid with sheets about $\frac{1}{3}$-inch thick of this precious wood—sufficient to allow for the surface reliefs

16-11 *The strong, vigorous design of French Baroque furniture is evident in this carved and gilded wooden table (c. 1680).*

elements; the skills of weavers, painters, stucco-craftsmen, cabinetmakers, sculptors, metalworkers, and all the other artisans; and the materials of the known world into the richest aesthetic environment the world had ever known, or perhaps will ever know.

The public and private rooms in the Palace of Versailles were created to provide spaces for the entertainment and assemblage of the king and the large number of attendant courtiers. The entire interior was regarded as a vast background for the activities that took place in it. The walls, floors, and ceilings were like a large, fresh canvas to be lavishly filled with mirrors, paneling, carvings, murals, and decorative ornament. The furniture was always stylistically compatible with the interior architecture and was usually grouped along the walls, leaving the center of the rooms empty for human activities.

Nicolas Fouquet, *surintendant des Finances,* established a centralized workshop devoted to the decorative arts at Maincy with the young Charles Le Brun in charge. It was to be the model for the *Manufacture Royale des Meubles de la Couronne des Gobelins* started by Louis XIV's *Surintendant des Bâtiments* or minister of the arts, Colbert, in 1662 when he purchased the high warp and low warp tapestry workshops of the Gobelin brothers outside Paris. By 1667, the Gobelins' workshops with over 800 craftsmen had been expanded into a complete source for all the decorative and furniture arts needed to furnish the royal residences. Charles Le Brun was also in charge and although Flemish and Italian craftsmen were there, alongside the French, Le Brun soon evolved a mature national style.

The long reign of Louis XIV can be divided stylistically into three periods. The first period (1643–c. 1661) (during the minority of the king) is strongly influenced by Italian design. The second period (c. 1661–c. 1690) is the golden age of French Baroque, and the one of importance in this furniture survey. This is the period when Charles Le Brun was in charge of the *Manufacture Royale des Meubles de la Couronne des Gobelins* and when the major work and furnishing of Versailles was accomplished. Despite monetary worries and military setbacks the work on Versailles continued until it reached its mature peak in the late 1680s. The third and last period (c. 1690–1715) echoes the spirit of the aging king. It is a period of transition as the king's strong will and rigid court etiquette decayed and a new way of life matured. The formality of French Baroque was replaced with the more personal and informal French Rococo.

The furniture of Louis XIV is monumental, befitting the architecture. It is formal, grand, and absolute, clearly reflecting the glory of the Sun King. (Louis XIV, having the sun as his emblem, was frequently depicted as Apollo, the Roman god of the sun.) Dimensions are greater than before, the richness of ornament is increased, and a certain stateliness permeates all of the furniture.

The richness of surface, so evident in all French Baroque furniture, is no better expressed than in the work of André Charles Boulle, 1642–1732. Boulle was a master of marquetry and is most noted for his use of tortoiseshell, metal, and ebony—a technique orginating in Italy, developed in the Low Countries but now bearing Boulle's name. Boulle work[4] is seen on cabinets, armoires, desks, tables, and almost every piece of furniture that had a hard, relatively flat surface. Its rich, sober splendor was a perfect foil for the rather severe forms of Le Brun's furniture designs.

Boulle work is marquetry at its finest, combining metal, usually brass or silver, and tortoiseshell. The technique is relatively simple in explanation but because the beauty of the surface relies on the complexity of the design as well as on the materials used, the actual execution calls for the finest of

[4] Boulle work, or buhlwork, continued in popularity long after Boulle himself died or the supremacy of the French Baroque style passed. Boulle work techniques were used for surface ornamentation during the entire eighteenth century and through most of the nineteenth century.

16-12

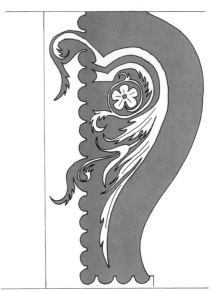

a) De première partie.

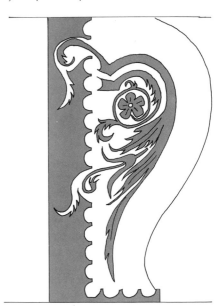

b) De contra-partie.

workmanship. A thin sheet of brass and one of tortoiseshell of equal thickness are fastened together with the cartoon of the design glued on the top. The design, customarily a symmetrical arrangement of foliage, architectural detail, and figures, is carefully cut out with fine saws. The two sheets are then separated and intermixed. A tortoiseshell ground and brass design, called *de première partie,* is the preferred mix but the reverse (brass ground and tortoiseshell design), or *de contra-partie,* is also used. Frequently, identical furniture forms were made utilizing both combinations. The brass elements are engraved to enhance their design whereas the support beneath the semitransparent tortoiseshell is usually colored, red or green being the most popular, adding an extra dimension to the surface.

Boulle work is extremely vulnerable to atmospheric changes and modern dry and overheated interiors can play havoc with the glues. Extreme care must be exercised to preserve Boulle work surfaces as many excellent examples have been irretrievably lost, not by neglect, but by steam heat.

The panels of doors and drawers are frequently Boulle work with the frames of regular veneer (ebony or other precious wood). Incorporated into the total design are chased and gilt bronze mounts that provide protection to the edges while adding some three-dimensional quality to the surface.

Boulle work was but one method of enhancing the surface of furniture. Marquetry employing various colored woods, stained or scorched to give variety and shading, was equally popular for case pieces. Cabinets on stands with realistic bouquets of flowers or still-life arrangements, all in intricate marquetry, were highly prized. These cabinets were often the work of Dutch craftsmen and display the influence of Dutch still-life painting. Paint (red or green) and gold and silver leaf enriched furniture frames and other pieces without flat surfaces. The use of upholstery also increased; damask, velvet, tapestry, gold brocade, and embroidered fabrics were all used with the additional elaboration of braids and fringes. Prior to 1650, such surface

16-13 *Covered with large-scale patterned silk damask, the high-backed chairs of the late seventeenth century provide a luxurious appearance if not comfort.*

16-14 *The French bergère, or fully upholstered armchair, provided comfort that was not previously available in the history of furniture. This example is from the first half of the seventeenth century.* Courtesy of the Virginia Museum of Fine Arts, Richmond.

16-15 *Chaise à capucine.*

treatments were rare but became quite common and continued through the eighteenth century.

All manner of stuffs from China and Japan were treasured during Louis XIV's reign. Porcelain figures and vases, lacquer work, silken fabrics, screens, and cabinets were incorporated into the interiors. The workshops at the Gobelins perfected a substitute for oriental lacquer work, *Vernis Martin,* and the secret of oriental porcelain was discovered in Germany and subsequently made in France. Chinese motifs (*chinoiseries*) were freely mingled with Baroque, and later with Rococo, elements.

The chairs of the French Baroque illustrate well the magnificence and monumentality of furniture of the period. They have a sense of "greatness." The chairs are high-backed and provide dignity to the sitter and a fitting background to the high headdresses of the period. Both men and women wore complicated and elaborately curled hair, often towering high above the brow. The back of the chairs slant slightly and is completely upholstered. The upholstered seat is large by today's standards and appears to be wide enough for more than a single person but by necessity had to be that wide—skirts and coats required such width.

More familiar seating furniture forms began to be developed at this time. The *canapé* or sofa was first created just before the time of Louis XIV and the *bergère,* or fully upholstered armchair, made its debut at this time. One chair that was very popular with all classes and is used to this day in almost the same form is the *chaise à capucine.* This small, straight, ladder-back chair with simply turned frame and rush seat was found in all levels of society. The more humble home had it as well as the richest where silk-covered cushions added elegance. The ladder-back chair, provided the French with seating that was flexible, convenient, and lightweight, similar to what the sgabello did in Italy two hundred years before.

Baroque beds are even more elaborately draped than those of Louis XIII.

16-16 *Bureau plat.*

The canopy is still supported by posts, but the complicated drapery often in seeming disarray and tied with artfully contrived cords and tassels engulfed everything.

The richest and most magnificent bed is the *lit de parade.* Found in the *chambre de parade* or reception room, its importance can be traced to medieval times when the best bed was in the great hall. This bed, and every household of consequence had one, is hung with the most sumptuous fabrics, covered by tassels, and adorned with fringe. The canopy is topped by four vases filled with scores of ostrich and aigrette feathers. Full draperies hang behind the shaped headboard, which is either fully upholstered or partially so with carved and gilded wood scrolls.

Tables of many designs were used during the Baroque period. *Consoles,* attached to the wall beneath large mirrors, were part of every interior. These half-circular or rectangular topped tables usually have one or two legs that are carved to form a scroll. Some appear to be molded rather than carved, so rich and plastic is the surface.

Tables almost always possess marble tops. They are not inlaid, as was previously fashionable, but are highly figured and colorful. One of the most remarkable furniture creations of this period is the *bureau plat* or desk, which became one of the grand pieces of Baroque and subsequent styles. At first a rectangular table with drawers in the wide apron, it soon developed into the kneehole form with a tier of drawers on each side beneath the top. The exquisite workmanship and the superb detailing of the decorative elements evident on this important piece of furniture indicates the value placed upon the *bureau plat.*

Tables for special uses were constantly being made. Small serving tables with trays to serve chocolate and coffee were additions to many rooms. Gaming tables of different sizes and with top shades determined by the requirements and number of players of the games were also common.

16-17 *A Louis XV side table with diaper patterned marquetry on the apron.* Courtesy of the Virginia Museum of Fine Arts, Richmond.

Ornately carved tables in the shape of a Moorish boy were used to hold lamps or candles (*guéridon*).

The fashions of the day demanded elaborate preparations. The *toilette*, the diminutive of *toile* (French for cloth), was originally a piece of linen upon which the medieval lady placed her cosmetics. When finished, she wrapped them in the cloth and placed all the items in a chest. The term *toilette* eventually was used for the cosmetic articles themselves and later was given to the container in which they were placed. By the time of Louis XIV, elaborate and costly compartmented tables and small chests with mirrors, matched jars, bowls, and candlesticks were made. Some of the finest craftsmanship and materials went into the toilette furniture.

The chest of drawers, the most common piece of current case furniture, made its initial appearance in about 1690. It replaced the chest, which until this time was still the major storage piece. (Only the humblest homes continued to display the chest, others put them away, out of sight.) The first chests of drawers or *commodes*[5] had two or three drawers, their form was based primarily on the Italian cassoni or ancient sarcophagi. They were often used beneath a mirror or *trumeau*. As the eighteenth century developed, the commode became a highly decorative piece with lavish marquetry surfaces embellished with finely chased bronze mounts.

One other well-known furniture form, the bookcase, was developed during the reign of Louis XIV. Boulle is credited with its development as he is with the commode, and each had similar early shapes. Bookcases did not become too common until standard book sizes were reduced. The earliest bookcases have doors that are either glazed or filled with wire grills.

Handsome armoires with two vertical doors and a horizontal projecting

[5] The term *bureau* was used for a chest of drawers until about 1710 and then commode became common.

cornice at the top were common to all types of interiors. The complexity of the ornament and the nature of the materials differed greatly but the imposing presence of an armoire frequently dominated any room in which it was placed.

The furniture of the French Baroque period is the furniture of the court. Little is known of the furniture of lesser citizens, but it can be assumed that it was far simpler and probably retained much of the qualities of the earlier periods, especially that of Louis XIII. Baroque furniture was not scaled or even conceived to fit in humble surroundings.

The later years of the reign of Louis XIV had less formality and ostentation than the middle period. The king did not stay at Versailles as much as before and a more personal and intimate way of life began to emerge. Furniture styles became less monumental and took on the new spirit, that is, smaller scale, increased mobility, and a touch of frivolity.

The first twenty years of the eighteenth century are referred to as the Régence. It does not exactly correspond to the period following the death of Louis XIV when the Duc d'Orléans was regent for the new king, Louis XV, from 1715–1723. However, it is an important transitional period stylistically. During the Régence, furniture lost some of its symmetry and became lighter and more curvilinear. The simple curves used during the Baroque period became longer and more sensuous, frequently combining into a languid reverse curve.

The transition from the large, high-backed armchair of the late seventeenth century into the armchair of the early eighteenth century illustrates well the change of attitude and way of life, and links the style of Louis XIV to that of Louis XV. The Régence armchair has a lower, less rectangular back (hardly a straight line can be seen in later versions), a lower seat, smaller dimensions, and legs that are not braced with stretchers. The frame of the chair is more exposed, encircling the upholstered back, for instance, and is delicately carved. The carved arms still swing out from the back but have

16-18 *A pair of eighteenth century fauteuils with painted frames. The line of the cabriole legs flows smoothly into the seat frame. The plump cushions provided softness, as there are no springs in these chairs.* Courtesy of the Virginia Museum of Fine Arts, Richmond.

padded surfaces on the tops and end short of the seat. The arm supports are not an extension of the legs but are set back from the front (again, the dictates of dress fashion caused a change in furniture design. With the arms set back, it was easier for a lady to sit in the chair when she wore *panniers* (literally "breadbaskets"), the wide, puffed arrangements that distended her skirt at the sides. In addition to being without a stretcher, legs took on the reverse curve of the *cabriole* ending in a volute of an acanthus leaf rather than a flattened ball or animal hoof. The leg also flowed smoothly into the exposed, shaped wood apron below the upholstered seat.

The mature style of Louis XV continued the trends that were started during the Régence. Intimate, small, comfortable interiors became the rule rather than the exception as the old houses were constantly being remodeled to provide the type of living spaces that were required for the new and more relaxed way of life. This occurred throughout France and the rest of Europe. (France had secured its role as pacesetter and was without doubt the cultural and artistic leader of most of the world; England and her American colonies are perhaps the only exceptions.) Even the majestic spaces of Louis XIV's Versailles were redesigned and made smaller. Often several rooms were clustered together to form an *appartement*—a more private environment than was heretofore possible. These rooms might include a bedroom(s), a living room (one did not receive visitors in the bedroom anymore), an anteroom, a boudoir, a dressing room, and if very grand and "current," a dining room (*une salle à manger*).

Specific rooms reserved for dining appeared about 1750 and most were furnished much like they are today. However, the ultimate and by far the most private dining room had a table *volante,* or "flying" table. The center of the room was without a table, but, upon a given signal, a section of the floor disappeared and a food-laden table ascended through this opening. As a result, the diners could be completely alone and were not bothered or overheard by the servants. (Although Louis XV is credited with having the first table *volante*, his was by no means the only one; the tables became quite popular throughout Europe.)

To furnish these new rooms, new furniture was needed. Aside from the court furniture's being too large and ill-suited for these more intimate rooms, there was just not enough of it. Fashion "suggested" that the furniture should not only be matched or *en suite* but should also be upholstered with appropriate fabrics for each season. To conserve wood, as well as money, removable covers were designed—the omnipresent slipcover.

No other style of furniture echoes and enhances the interior architecture, the clothing, manners, conversation, and indeed, the whole culture as does the style of Louis XV, or Rococo as it is now known. The period exhibits a total harmony of design seldom before attempted, and rarely achieved with such success. Yet, who was responsible for such a remarkable synthesis? It is difficult to say, because unlike the furniture and decorative ornament of England of the same period, French furniture was the creation of a team, a group of craftsmen belonging to separate and very distinct guilds. A member of one guild was forbidden to do the work of another.

For example, the *carcase* (carcass) or basic structure of an individual piece of furniture, would be designed and made by a *maître* of the Corporation des Menuisiers, or after 1743, the Menuisier-Ebénistes.[6] It was his workshop that would shape and join solid wood to construct the piece and apply the veneer or marquetry, if needed. Any detailed carving would have to be done by a *sculpteur.* If the piece was to have gilded bronze mounts or *ormolu,* they would be designed, cast, and chased by the *fondeurs-ciseleurs,* but the gold leaf would be applied to them by the *ciseleurs-doreurs.* (These mounts had to be delivered to the cabinetmaker by a member of the founders guild although, surprisingly, the *ébéniste* could attach them.) The required marble tops on all case

---

[6]The ébénistes took their name from *ébène,* although by this time ebony was not a popular veneering material.

16-19   *Flowers, one of the dominant motifs of the French Rococo period, cover this elegant cabriole-legged table and matching jewel casket. Executed in marquetry, the rich wood surface is accented by the bronze mounts.* Courtesy of the Virginia Museum of Fine Arts, Richmond.

16-20 *An example of a canapé or sofa. The upholstry is Beauvais tapestry and the carved wooden frame is gilded. Although not as ornately carved as some pieces of furniture of the Rococo period, this canapé is especially interesting in the fluid sweep of the arm supports.* Courtesy of the Virginia Museum of Fine Arts, Richmond.

pieces and tables were supplied by the *marbrier*. Should there be upholstery, it was the responsibility of the *tapissier* to select the fabrics and decide how they would be used. Finally, the piece would be waxed and polished by the *ébéniste*. Each of these separate processes was done by members of different guilds. (There was even a guild for the *plumassier* who attached the ostrich feathers to the tops of beds.) Consequently, it is common to find identical ormolu mounts on furniture stamped by different ébénistes.

The guilds required the *maître-ébéniste* to mark with an iron stamp his name, initials, or other symbol on each piece of furniture. The stamp was usually put on the carcass under the marble top of case pieces or on the underside of chair or table frames. Although these marks have proved invaluable when attempting to identify the maker of an individual piece of furniture, a *maître* stamp should not be considered a prideful signature. It is there merely in compliance with a guild regulation and in no way identifies the other craftsmen who were also responsible for the final appearance of the piece.

The finished piece of furniture was usually placed in the hands of the *marchand-merciers*, or furniture dealers, who sold it.

The question still remains, who decided upon the style? Who instigated the marvelous extravagance, the evolving forms, and the ever-changing decoration known as Rococo? Except for a few distinguished *maîtres* such as Boulle, Charles Cressent (1685–1768), the master of Régence furniture and ébéniste to the Duc d'Orléans; or Jean-Henri Riesener (1734–1806), the finest ébéniste of the Louis XVI style, most of the more than 1,000 master ébénistes were humble men with limited stylistic training and preferred to repeat models rather than creatively design new ones.

The average eighteenth century client was, as are many of his twentieth-century counterparts, as conservative as the craftsmen and exerted little influence on the design of furniture. On the other hand, some clients did; Louis XIV was very much involved with every detail of the construction and furnishing of Versailles. Madame de Pompadour and especially her brother,

the Marquis de Marigny, *Directeur des Bâtiments,* are believed to have exercised considerable influence upon furniture design. Louis XV was particularly receptive to the Rococo style but was reluctant to accept anything new or different. Certainly other clients, known and unknown today, were responsible for some development of furniture design, as there are small and full-scale plaster and clay models of projected furniture still extant.

Pattern books were very popular and influential. They were probably the nearest and best source of design for the average ébéniste. One of the most prolific ornamental designers and a principal proponent of the Rococo style was the goldsmith Juste Aurèle Meissonnier (1693–1750). Appointed *dessinateur de la chambre et du cabinet du roi* in 1726, a position he held until his death, Meissonnier could be called the high priest of the Rococo. His book, *Oeuvre,* published in Paris in 1750 shortly before his death, was an immediate international success and was prized by craftsmen and connoisseurs alike. It contained 118 engravings illustrating designs for silverware, interior and decorative ornament, furniture and accessories, sculpture, and festival architecture. The diverse subjects are all remarkably within the style of Rococo, although some critics find Meissonnier's fluid, swirling, and asymmetrical designs excessively restless. Yet, it must be acknowledged that despite the substantial influence of pattern books, regardless of their quality, they were usually published *after* a style had been established and were used by those who wished to emulate a style but did not set it.

These influences, notwithstanding, there is more evidence to support the role of the *marchands,* the merchants, as the prime motivators of style development. Their influence on style and taste throughout the eighteenth century is inestimable. The *marchands* were perhaps the richest guild in France at this time and were in the position to coordinate the production of the hidebound craft guilds. Originally importers of stuffs from around the world, they had developed into dealers of every kind of object, device, and accessory needed to furnish an interior. They cannot be considered just interior designers, but

16-21 *A detail from the painting* L'Enseigne de Gersaint (The Signboard of Gersaint) *painted in 1720 by Antoine Watteau. The artist has suggested the important relationship of the* merchands (merchants) *and the customer in this painting.* Courtesy of the Schloss Charlottenburg, Berlin, Germany.

16-22 *The excessive manipulation of the material offers minimal identification that this eighteenth-century console is wood. The marble top is typical. The painting by Antoine Watteau is framed in a frame representative of the period and this type of frame continues to enjoy considerable popularity to this day.* Courtesy of the Virginia Museum of Fine Arts, Richmond.

more the arbiters of taste and *chic.* Although they have no exact equivalent today, the *marchands* decreed what was new, *avant,* and, therefore, the thing to possess in much the same way that "Madison Avenue" is now accused of doing.

During the eighteenth century, the life and activities of the average citizen in France, more than in any previous age, was remarkably like that of today, and the furniture forms that were then used in the smaller interiors fit very well into twentieth-century homes. There have been changes of materials, construction, and ornament, of course, but, by and large, all of the basic furniture forms used today were in existence by 1750.

Throughout this investigation of historical furniture development, in addition to a cursory description of identifying characteristics, an attempt has been made to stress the changes to and creation of furniture forms and types that are familiar to the reader. The lack of furniture in past periods—both in surviving examples and variety of types—posed problems of description that at this point in the survey suddenly are no longer relevant. The proliferation of furniture that occurred in the eighteenth century presents a new and more contemporary enigma. There are so many variations within one type of furniture and so many types that specific descriptions are impossible. More general style characteristics that identify a period or style must now be given. The accompanying photographs can do more to show the wide range of possibilities than can words, but are only a small sampling.

French Rococo furniture can best be described as small, curvilinear, adapted to the human body, luxurious, sinuous, sensuous, intimate, comfortable, delicate, exceedingly feminine, sometimes exotic (chinoiserie, turquerie, and singerie), light, sumptuous, frivolous, ornamented with flowers and shells, extravagant, and made with consummate skill.

One comment that can be readily applied to this style of furniture is that the design criteria of "truth to materials" can certainly not be justified by these forms. Wood and metal were manipulated with an ease that suggested their inherent characteristics to be the same as clay or some other plastic substance. Craftsmen were so proficient in handling their raw materials that they could easily translate any design that was usually delineated on a flat surface into three-dimensional reality. Many of the individual pieces are so lacking in straight lines that they appear disturbing and unstable to twentieth-century eyes. Planes and edges bulge, curve, slant, and billow as if filled by an unseen source of air. There is also a lack of "surface"; that is, the marquetry, lacquer, and painted decorative elements along with the carving and applied ornament are exceedingly three-dimensional in appearance. For example, the decoration of a commode may visually appear three-dimensional, utilizing shading and other visual devices to indicate depth, yet the design is actually two-dimensional. In addition, the strongly modeled ormolu mounts are lavishly applied to the surface and are frequently "lifted" free of the commode to become handles for the drawers.

One must not construe these comments as being a negative reaction to the furniture of mid-eighteenth-century France. On the contrary, the forms are sensitively designed, carefully made, deliberately adapted to the life-style, and completely compatible with the interiors of the period. The positive qualities are far more numerous than those that are negative. The furniture is scaled to fit the size and contour of the human body; consequently, most of the furniture appears modest and unpretentious in scale and proportion but gains its elegance through the materials, ornament, and workmanship. Dominant in the design of this furniture is the almost exclusive use of the curvilinear form with the cabriole legs flowing from the body of the piece without any noticeable break in form or motion. Rich ornamentation is applied in an aesthetically selective manner enhancing the overall visual impression of the piece; yet, the form is not subordinated by the ornamentation. To visually retain the desired intimate scale, and minimize the actual size, the surfaces of many larger pieces of furniture are broken into smaller panels and have planes that are curved (*bombé* or *serpentine* fronts). Thus, a

16-23 *An example of a Louis XV carved bergère. Note the small, delicate proportions, the plump, loose cushion, and the continuous flow of the back and arms, all contributing to the comfort of this chair.* Courtesy of the Virginia Museum of Fine Arts, Richmond.

marvelous continuity is achieved in the individual pieces and throughout the entire style.

The placement of furniture within the interior space changed during this period. Prior to this time, chairs, tables, and other furniture were almost always placed around the perimeter of the room with the center left free. During the Rococo period, furniture was placed throughout the room, and, being light, smaller, and more easily moved, it could be shifted as the occasion warranted. For example, small tables with bronze handles were often brought out for use when serving food, chocolate, coffee, or tea.[7]

Of all the furniture made during the period of Louis XV, the *bergère* and *commode* are the most characteristic. Literally scores of table variations were made, each exquisite and often with complicated mechanical devices to lift, open, or otherwise permit the table to serve one or more purposes. Beds lost their canopies and became less important. Bureaus and desks were notably prominent, but none are as exemplary Rococo as the bergère and the commode.

The bergère is a wide, low armchair that has a deep seat. Despite an exposed frame, it is fully upholstered[8] and the back and arms flow together; there is no break, only a gentle curve from one to the other. The seat is covered with a plump, loose cushion. The back slopes gently so that the occupant does not sit upright, but at a comfortable angle clearly expressing the more informal and relaxed attitudes that prevailed. Other seating was the fauteuil (the open-armed chair), canapes of various sizes *tête-à-tête, à corbeille, marquise*), and, of course, daybeds of different kinds (*duchesse, sultane, chaise-longue*).

The commode is the foremost case piece and, because of the workmanship

---

[7] It became fashionable to have *thé à l'anglaise* after 1750.
[8] Lighter versions of the bergère have cane rather than upholstery on the back, arms, and seat.

16-24 *The furniture of the mid-eighteenth-century French court was adapted to the smaller interiors of the provinces. The excessive ornamentation and the more fragile qualities were stripped away leaving a handsome, yet graceful, decorative, yet honest, style that is easily adjusted to twentieth-century American homes. This dining room filled with furniture in the French provincial style by a well-known manufacturer seems admirably suited to today's living.* Courtesy of Henredon Furniture Industries.

lavished upon it, rich materials used, and its welcomed place (usually under a tall mirror in the major rooms of the period), it rivals the bergère as *the* singular Rococo piece of furniture. The Louis XV commode has two drawers that are virtually hidden[9] by the elaborate ormolu swirling over it. The veneer and marquetry surface[10] echoes the design of the bronze mounts, and with the slender cabriole legs, intensifies the weightlessness and feeling of movement suggested by the ormolu.

The country furniture that developed in eighteenth-century France displays many of the same qualities of line and form as did the court furniture. In the provincial châteaux and farm manor houses, as well as in the homes of the growing number of bourgeoisie in Paris and other cities, there was a demand for more comfortable and better furniture. The luxurious, expensive, and indeed, fragile furniture of the court was not suitable or within the financial means of most of the pople of France. Consequently, adaptations were made by craftsmen whose skill varied from the high standards set by the guilds of Paris.[11]

Although there are some differences evident between one district and another (bordering provinces tend to have more foreign influences, for example), the major characteristics of this more simple furniture are similar. French provincial furniture is Louis XV furniture—free, unaffected, and almost innocent. There is much charm in these honest and graceful pieces. Instead of the gaily painted and gilded furniture of the court, the country furniture has the warm natural glow of polished wood. It is usually made of solid wood such as walnut, chestnut, or the fruitwoods (cherry, plum, or

[9] The Régence commode usually has three drawers that are quite visible, less ormolu, and shorter legs.

[10] Because of the undulating, complex-curved surfaces of these commodes, the technique of veneering and marquetry was extremely difficult.

[11] It should not be forgotten that the French were in North America at this time, and there is a considerable amount of excellent, locally made French furniture still extant in Canada.

16-25 *An example of a late Louis XV mahogany marquetry commode. The flatter surface forms, the trophy and military equipment depicted in the marquetry, and the bronze mounts in a more classical design forecast the coming of the neoclassic style.* Courtesy of the Virginia Museum of Fine Arts, Richmond.

pear) and is seldom veneered. The curves are less pronounced but are there nevertheless, the carving is not as ornate or as complicated but just as expressive, and the upholstery fabrics tend to be printed cottons or linen rather than damasks or tapestries. However, the style remains intact. The analogy can easily be made: eighteenth-century French provincial furniture is as a farm girl in the provinces—a little thicker, a little plainer, a little more vigorous, a little warmer, but utterly charming.

The rush-seated *chaise à capucine* is a favorite provincial chair; bergères are a little more casual, not as common, often displaying turned supports. The linen-filled armoires are sturdier, still dominant, and assume the role of the prize possession in the farmhouse. The furniture had a further quality that identifies it with the land. Because the kitchen was the center of the household in many of the country and smaller houses, more furniture was identified with the storage, preparation, and serving of food. Hanging shelves and cupboards (*étagères and panetières*), kneading troughs (*pétrin*), and other household objects are common.

In the colder provinces the *lit clos* ("built-in bed") is a typical piece. Often appearing as a large built-in armoire when the paneled doors are closed, the *lit clos* afforded privacy and a modicum of warmth. Some versions are built in a corner rather than centered within the wall; others may consist of two levels and may have curtains instead of doors (*lit demi-clos*).

Hardly had the style of Louis XV matured when the beginnings of *neoclassic* tendencies commenced.[12] The excavations at Herculaneum and Pompeii gave, for the first time, a look at the interiors, furniture, and household articles of the ancient Romans and several books were soon published that were filled with copperprints illustrating the newly discovered Roman

---

[12] The French classical movement is divided into three major divisions: the period of Louis XVI (1765–1789), the Directoire period (1789–1804), and the period of the Empire (1804–1820).

decorative motifs. A wealth of ornamental designs that were new to the designers of the period was suddenly at hand.

The design possibilities were welcomed as the eighteenth-century arbiters of taste were certainly not opposed to trying new ideas. Had they not embraced the new forms of Régence and Rococo not long before? Had they not rejected the massive grandeur of Baroque with its heavy classical detail for the light and colorful interiors of the Louis XV style? But, it *was* time for a new look; the aesthetic and commercial prospects were excellent. Furthermore, it was not just a return to classical ornamentation, but a direct resurgence from ancient Rome deliberately disregarding the attitudes of the Renaissance. The tastemakers were weary of all the plasticity and excessive movement. The flowers and shells were beginning to look jaded and the sinuous foliage tiresome. The time was ripe for a little more purity of line, a little more sedateness and order, and since this attitude expressed the new enthusiasm for archeology and Rome, so much the better.

The transition from the freely drawn Rococo curves to the more mechanical and geometric straight lines and circles was not instant, however. A classical molding or detail crept into a Rococo design, then perhaps more, and gradually ornament began to assume a marked classical look. The straightening of the forms took somewhat longer. By 1770–71 the process was almost complete and, almost five years before Louis XV was dead, a style that was to bear the name of his successor was in vogue.

Louis XVI or *French neo-classical* style furniture is considered by many to be the highpoint in furniture design. It has the exquisite proportions, workmanship, materials, and elegance of Rococo but is more reserved, quiet, and subdued. Louis XVI furniture is a synthesis. It is not an attempt to re-create the furniture of the ancient Romans, far from it, but it is, rather, an excellent example of the adaptation of styles. The manners and customs that had developed in the eighteenth century did not appreciably change with the incoming new style, but continued until terminated by the French Revolu-

16-26 *A small console table in the style of Louis XVI. The straight tapered legs are braced by a low stretcher arrangement supporting a classical urn. All the ornament is of classical derivation.*

tion. The same furniture needs, types, and arrangements were retained, but the concepts of the fashionable classicism were applied to them. The result was the new style.

The construction skills that had developed during the Rococo period were called upon for even greater precision in the Louis XVI style, as the dependence upon carved ornament, fundamental to Rococo, gave way to a reliance upon meticulous construction, materials, and proportions necessary to the current taste. Furthermore, the essential rectangularity was far easier to achieve on case pieces and tables than it was on seating furniture. Therefore, the distinction between the two major styles of eighteenth-century French furniture is more marked on commodes, cabinets, and bureaus than on chairs, *canapés,* and daybeds.

The leg form of the furniture is the most distinguishing characteristic of this new style. The cabriole leg became straighter and thicker and was soon replaced by a straight square or round tapered leg.[13] This leg is usually fluted, sometimes spirally, and if long is often called a *pied en carquois* (quiver leg).[14] Moreover, the legs on any Louis XVI piece can be recognized because, unlike the gentle flow from frame to leg on Louis XV furniture, there is an abrupt break in direction, which is repeatedly emphasized by a square, rosette-decorated block at the joining.

The short legs on cabinets and commodes rapidly taper and frequently have a wide projecting and carved molding at the top just below their junction with the body of the piece. The commodes of the Louis XVI style are severely rectangular in form and without bombé and serpentine fronts. The gilt bronze mounts that had twined so abundantly over the surface of Rococo

[13] During this period, more turned elements were used, such as *toupie* feet (top-shaped), balusters, and columns.

[14] The shape and fluting suggests a quiver of arrows, sometimes intensified by carved feathers at the top.

commodes are less exuberant[15] and are applied with much more restraint. Of exceptional fineness and more like the work of a goldsmith rather than a bronze worker, Neoclassic ormolu is generally restricted to narrow decorative moldings of classical design (bead, egg and dart, leaf and dart, oak and laurel leaf bands, and dentils), bows and ribbons, wreaths with ring handles, and trophies. As well as being flat and smooth, the surface on commodes is often divided into large symmetrical panels of rectangular shape bordered by the bronze moldings. The panel surfaces are sometimes Oriental lacquer, but more often are veneer or marquetry. If marquetry, it is probably a repeating pattern of lozenge or diamond shapes studded with bronze rosettes (rose, narcissus, or cornflower, Queen Marie Antoinette's favorites).

The dignified *secrétaire à abattant* is one of the most striking pieces of Louis XVI furniture. The fall-front desk is almost architectural in character and was a favorite of the ébénistes. The upper part is either supported on tall legs or a cabinet, and the large flat panels are excellent surfaces for architectural scenes in marquetry or a richly patterned veneer. Around the top, almost like an entablature, a band of richly patterned ormolu or boulle work contrasted with the restrained moldings surrounding the panels.[16] On each side the corners are angled or canted and the space is filled with slender supports in the form of finely detailed caryatids (a favorite decorative element of this period).

The tables and bureaus are similar in form and scale to earlier ones; however, the legs are no longer cabriole and stretchers are again introduced.

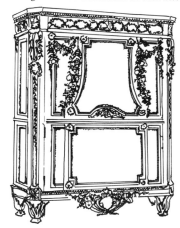

16-27 *The* secrétaire à abattant *reveals the return to a more severe furniture style. Although this example is ornamented with bronze garlands of flowers and plant forms, it has regained an architectural character.*

[15] A feeling of movement permeates the whole of Rococo ornament. Each element seems to quiver, shift, billow, or be capable of doing so. Classical ornament, on the other hand, is static; there is no feeling of movement, and although the ornament subject matter may be similar, for example, the same kind of flower, this difference in movement is most apparent.

[16] This frieze is decorated with a repeating pattern of classical inspiration: *guilloches,* dentils, frets, *entrelacs* (interlacing ribbons), or, most often, short rows of fluting. Similar bands decorate the aprons of tables and desks.

These stretchers, often decorative "X's" and "H's," are more for ornament than support and frequently at the crossing of the elements of the stretcher a classical vase or a woven basket of bronze rests. On many of the side tables, desks, and commodes a *fret gallery*, a miniature railing of pierced brass or bronze, is attached on three sides of the top (uniquely Louis XVI even though it was originally a Chinese invention). Many of the tables are mahogany, an increasingly important wood in the Louis XVI period.[17]

The major chair of the period shifts from the comfortable bergère to the open armed fauteuil. The legs, of course, are straight and invariably are joined to the exposed seat frame at a distinct right angle with a square block at the corner that is decorated with a rosette on the exposed surfaces. The upholstered back is square, oval, or rectangular with a repeating band carved into the frame rather than the rich sculptured ornament of the Rococo chair. The arms swing down in a simple curve from the side stiles of the back, often beginning almost at the top rail, and continuing forward to a distance of about two-thirds the depth of the seat and ending in an acanthus leaf volute. The support in another single curve comes up from the top of the front leg to meet the arm just back of the volute. This is different from the Louis XV chair, which had a vertical support from the seat rail to the arm. Both arms served the same purpose: they permitted the women to sit while wearing the still fashionable *panniers*. The total appearance of the chair is one of straight lines suggesting a little less comfort. The bergère remained almost the same as the previous style with the exception of the legs.

Little mention has been made of painted furniture. The furniture of Louis XIV was often gilded and some pieces were painted in strong reds and

[17] The use of mahogany was but one indication of the interest in things English during the last 25 years of the eighteenth century. For example, side chairs made with carved and pierced splats using motifs such as the lyre, wheat sheaf, or urn were very popular; even Chippendale's designs were used as inspiration for furniture.

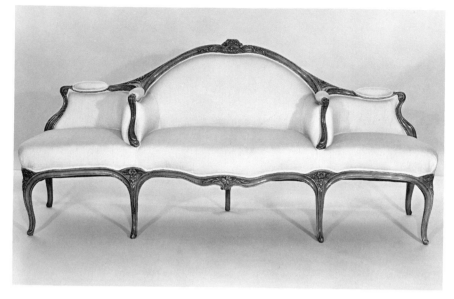

16-28 *The confident was a popular furniture form during the neoclassical Louis XVI period. This example from northern Europe, however, is in the earlier Rococo Louis XV style and dates slightly before 1750.* Courtesy of the Art Institute of Chicago.

greens. However, the decisive change in character of the Louis XV furniture indicated a change in color choice. The furniture was painted in lighter, but no less bright colors—jonquil yellow, cream, sea green, and light blue, with little of it gilded. With the return to classical elements, even more painted furniture was used. Chairs and small tables, especially, were often painted pale grays, white, and ivory, and gold furniture also returned to favor. During the later years of the period, more and more furniture was either veneered in ebony or stained black, both of which brilliantly contrasted with the bronze mounts and established a precedent for the dark woods of the Empire period. If the furniture was painted, it invariably was gessoed first and then painted,[18] a practice that was established by the Egyptians almost 3,500 years before.

Canapés, sofas, and daybeds are even more in evidence and are basically the same as before, except for the legs, which are like the chairs to which they usually are matched. One type of *canapé* that did develop was the *confident,* a large canapé with an additional seat extending beyond each side arm. Appearing almost like an attached chair on each side, it seems to tie the piece into the wall. These larger pieces of furniture were often designed for a specific place and matched the wall panels in carving, design, and color.

The beds of the period took on a new significance. The four-post bed, or *lit à colonnes,* disregarded during the Rococo period, was again used, but it was not as popular as the *lit à la polonnaise.* Even with its classical and sometimes military ornament, this fabulous concoction belies the restraint normally shown in Louis XVI furniture. The bed itself has both a head- and footboard, upholstered and elegantly carved. It is the canopy that makes it distinct. The four posts on the corners go up only part way and end in a decorative finial.

---

[18] Much of the painted furniture and paneling of this period has since been stripped of its paint and gesso, and the wood is whitened with the remants of the gesso in the surface pores—a not unattractive look, and one frequently achieved today by rubbing paint into raw wood and wiping off the excess.

16-29 *A late eighteenth-century French secretary of the Directoire period. The rigid rectangularity is relieved somewhat by the delicate classical inlaid designs. The larger ornamental elements are based upon Roman and Egyptian architectural and sculptural prototypes.* Courtesy of the St. Louis Art Museum.

From these posts, curved supports swing up and, in turn, carry a round and often domed confection of moldings, draperies, emblems, and ostrich plumes with a pair of doves (beak to beak) surmounting it all. Long draperies of luxurious fabric and embroidery cover the curved supports completely and give the whole a somewhat magical appearance.

Simpler beds with head- and footboards of equal height were frequently placed against the wall lengthwise. Half canopies and draperies were sometimes used over these beds; when not covered in this manner, the beds were set in an alcove.

The period that developed after the French Revolution of 1789 serves as a design link between the earlier French neoclassic period and the later period of the Empire. The only stable government between the reign of Louis XVI and the empire of Napoleon, the Directoire (1795–1799), gives the period its name. During this period an attempt was made to re-establish the crafts, business, and a general semblance of order. The furniture and interiors of the period exhibit a stronger tendency to imitate the antique styles than had existed before. When the furniture is based upon the Louis XVI style, it displays simpler forms and is generally less refined. The destructive elements that were present during the Revolution took their toll.

Furniture-making practically came to a halt for several years as artists, craftsmen, designers, and textile manufacturers were forced to flee Paris during the Reign of Terror (1793–1794) and because of the sudden lack of wealthy clients (almost all of the old fortunes were lost). Consequently, the furniture of the Directoire is a spontaneous mix and often appears clumsy with the various stylistic elements being poorly combined.

As the quality of life improved, a demand for furniture again developed but it was no longer possible to produce the quantity and quality of previous years. This was due in no small part to the absence of skilled cabinetmakers: the guilds had been abolished in 1791. Of course, master cabinetmakers who were trained prior to the Revolution were still living and continued to produce furniture. Men such as Riesener,[19] Georges Jacob (1739–1814) and his two sons, the new luminaries, Charles Percier (1764–1838) and Pierre-Francois-Léonard Fontaine (1762–1853), are especially noteworthy—but there were fewer of these masters working. The new clients and style setters were often not as knowledgeable as those before the Reign of Terror and naturally there was a resistance to styles representing the Ancien Régime.

Directoire furniture designers borrowed extensively from the ancient Greeks. The Greek *klismos* chair was adapted in form and line, and many chairs of this period feature rear legs that curve back in a saber shape. The front legs either curve outward like the *klismos* or remain straight and grooved similar to those of the Louis XVI period. Chairs have backs that curve away from the main plane of the piece with the top rolling back. If the chair is not upholstered, the back has a splat that is ornamented with carved classical designs.

Color schemes became stronger and more striking in value and intensity. One of the most popular color schemes was based upon the colors found in the new flag of the French Republic: white, red, and blue. Large areas of white were frequently bordered with scarlet and contrasted with blue molding and trim. Further indications of an increase in patriotism was the rampant use of revolutionary and military emblems such as the liberty caps of the army, drums, spears, armor, clasped hands (fraternity), triangles, and laurel wreaths. There were even "patriotic beds," that is, beds with motifs of the Revolution rather than of the monarchy. The use of classical motifs was continued, however, as these forms were considered to be not opposed to the cause of the Revolution.

---

[19] Riesener survived the Revolution and Reign of Terror by supplying rifle butts to the Revolutionists' cause. He was later employed to remove royal emblems from the furniture of the court, and replacing them with panels and symbols of a more acceptable nature.

The wood of the Directoire period is almost exclusively native. Fruitwoods, walnut, and oak dominate because foreign trade had not been extensively resumed, although mahogany was still highly prized and saved for only the finest pieces.

The last style of French furniture to significantly influence design throughout Europe and the world was developed during the reign of Napoleon. The Empire style spread rapidly and continued long after the political downfall of Napoleon (1814). It is hard and cold, and exudes an austere grandeur. The intimacy associated with the eighteenth century is completely gone and is replaced by the antique severity of the Napoleonic court.

The neoclassic painter Jacques Louis David (1748–1825), who had spent several years in Rome and became devoted to the classical cause, designed some pieces of mahogany furniture based upon classical models in about 1788 and had Jacob make them. These are considered to be the first forms that are direct copies of Roman furniture, and this commission establishes the date for the first display of the characteristics of the Empire style. David often used them as models for his paintings, as well as for use in his studio. Consequently, his paintings are excellent sources for classical design information as the clothes and interiors, in addition to the furniture, are, for the most part, authentic.

David was politically active during the Revolution and his star rose with that of Napoleon, achieving the position of being virtually the dictator of art during the years of the Revolution and the Empire. He is credited with introducing Percier and Fontaine to Georges Jacob and, more importantly, to Napoleon.

Percier and Fontaine had seriously studied architecture in Italy and were thoroughly familiar with the interiors and furniture of the ancient Romans. They, even more than David, were responsible for the immediate acceptance of the Empire style. Commissioned to redecorate the Château de la Mal-

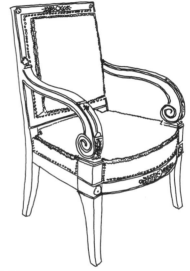

16-30 *The heaviness of the individual parts of this Empire chair is emphasized by the dark rich color of the mahogany and the small-scale bronze applied ornament.*

maison, the residence of Madame Bonapart, later the Empress Josephine[20], they created imperial opulence by combining freestanding columns, smooth surfaces of mahogany, glittering bronze ornament against dark wood and rich marble, heavy draperies, and copies and adaptations of Greek and Roman furniture.

To complete this commission at Malmaison as rapidly as possible, Percier and Fontaine resorted to a time-conserving design strategy. They draped the walls, windows, and furniture with rich and opulent fabrics (an easy way to increase the luxuriousness of any room). And, Jacob, who made the furniture from their designs, used standardized forms[21], utilized little carved ornament, and covered large surfaces with plain veneer rather than with the more time-consuming marquetry. (These all became distinct features of the Empire style.) Despite these shortcuts, the result is not meager; on the contrary, it is luxurious, masculine, and imposing and was an immediate artistic success. Thus established as the official style of the Empire, this severe classical style ushered in the nineteenth century.

The success of the Malmaison interiors spawned a virtual epidemic of furniture in the Empire style. No longer was the clientele for furniture limited only to royalty, but the emerging middle class, people of position and wealth, also demanded fine furniture. The best examples of the Empire style are those pieces made with only superior materials and by the most accomplished craftsmen, as the inherent severity of form and ornament, which can be extremely handsome when controlled by the knowledgeable designer, becomes clumsy and unwieldy in lesser hands.

[20] It was at Malmaison that she stayed following her divorce from Napoleon.
[21] Because he standardized forms by using the same carcases over and over again, and varying only the surfaces and ornamentation, Georges Jacob must not only be considered one of the last great eighteenth-century furniture-makers but also one of the first to use production-line methods.

The desired Empire furniture forms were those of Rome, Greece, and, following Napoleon's victories on the Nile, Egypt. However, life during the early nineteenth century was far different from that experienced in Greece, Rome, or Egypt since the ancients spent most of their time outside the home, using it primarily for sleeping. The ancients had need of very little furniture and what pieces they did have, did not always fit the uses that were demanded of it by the nineteenth-century French. Consequently, it was necessary to adapt the ancient forms or create new furniture that would better serve the needs of the people and fit into the living spaces available, and yet still appear to be classical.

Aside from the classicism, the severe rectangularity of Empire furniture is by far the most pronounced characteristic. Panels with moldings or with the rails and stiles evident lost favor and are seldom seen. Instead, the framing members and the panels are of the same thickness and the whole is invariably covered with one sheet of veneer, which gives the panel the appearance of a smooth, solid piece. This spare rectangularity is emphasized by the sharp edges that can, and often do dominate the whole design of many pieces. There are very few curves or even moldings to break up the planes of the furniture. There is also very little carving, and if a detail is carved it is done in a shallow bas-relief. The preponderance of 90-degree angles produced a visual stability that was not evident in furniture design since the Middle Ages.

Mahogany was by far the favorite wood of the Empire period. Its rich, dark-red coloring and beautiful grain was highly valued and served exceedingly well to cover the plain surfaces that were considered absolutely essential. Rosewood and ebony were also esteemed. For lesser pieces, walnut, oak, maple, and elm were used but were often stained to imitate mahogany.

There are glints of brass and bronze on the dark patterned wood surfaces, but this metal ornamentation is not the richly chased and modeled ormolu of the Rococo or even that of the neoclassic style. It is, rather, almost entirely flat, with stiffly modeled appliqués nailed on. Repeated indiscriminately on various pieces, one design may be found on a commode, desk, or chair —sometimes with little regard to proportions or appropriateness. This ornament often has an isolated appearance where it seems to be "stuck on" rather than seeming to be integral with the total design, and tends to accent the flatness of the larger veneered surfaces and heighten the massiveness.

The "appliqué" ornaments are almost all taken from Greek, Roman, or Egyptian sources. The formalized designs are stiff and seldom have any feeling of movement. The imagery describes shields, quivers and arrows, wreaths, flattened palm fronds, laurel and oak leaf sprays, honeysuckle, winged figures in flowing robes, torches, lyres, and the symbols of Napoleon, the bee and the letter "N." The use of animal forms is everywhere. The winged lion, the winged sphinx, and the eagle were especially popular. Classical caryatids and terms, and that strange monster, the monopodium (the animal head, chest, one leg and paw), supports tables, chairs commodes, and desks. Another curious decorative and structural motif that was also used, consists of a human head and chest (usually female) emerging from a square tapered column (similar to an inverted obelisk), and at the bottom a pair of human feet. Many times these geometric figures have bronze heads and feet with a shaft of solid wood.

Swans became a favorite device and are seen carved in the round and used as the entire arm of chairs or even as the front leg and arm support. They also are frequently found on the ends of beds as large decorative elements.

Handles and pulls are reduced to the simplest forms and are seldom more than a knob or ring. In many examples the key in the lock must be used as the knob to open a door of a cabinet.

Chairs are for the most part stiff and uncomfortable. The bergère and fauteuil continue to be chair types, but are straighter and are no longer the inviting seating they once appeared to be. The interest in classical and Egyptian ornamental motifs creates other variations. Chairs that were in-

16-31 *A French* guéridon *made of burl grain walnut and bronze. The legs are figurative—bronze heads and sandled feet with a square, tapered wood column between. Around the top is a bronze egg and dart molding and classical scenes in bronze illustrating the arts are applied to the apron.* Courtesy of the St. Louis Art Museum.

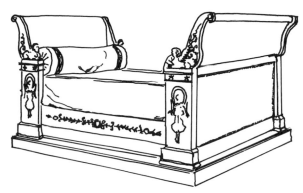

16-32 *The massive architectural forms of the* lit en bateau *are clearly derived from the classical, but also owe much to the Italian Renaissance cassapanca.*

spired by the Greek *klismos* and the Roman sella curulis were popular in many versions. The support for the arms of most of the chairs is a continuation of the front leg as the dress fashions had ceased to be full-skirted.[22]

Not having ancient models upon which to base their designs, the furniture designers of the Empire period created "classical" commodes, drop-front desks, and cabinets from simple box shapes. Their flat front surfaces are split horizontally into the drawers or vertically into the doors. At each side a plain round or square column supports a narrow cornice or overhanging drawer. Frequently, in place of the classical capitol there is a human or animal head, which often has an Egyptian cast to its design.

One of the most popular pieces of furniture was the daybed that was copied from antique sources. A raised end permitted the user to rest in a semiprone position and allowed the lady of fashion to arrange her Greek inspired, semiopaque clothing and herself into accepted and stylish poses that were based upon classical sculpture.

The *lit en bateau*, or boat bed, was without question the bed of the Empire period. Sitting on a platform, the bed had the head and footboards of equal height and was placed with the side of the bed parallel to the wall. Very architectural in design with a heavy wood frame sitting directly on the

[22]The clothing of the Empire period is considered by many to be one of the most beautiful styles in the history of costume. Men's clothing, with the high-collared fitted coats, tight trousers, boots, elaborate vests and knotted stocks, flowing cloaks, and high hats, is extremely elegant, refined, and handsome.

The high-waisted dresses of the women were based upon classical prototypes and are still known as the Empire style. Made of sheer, fine cotton or silk with low-cut bodices, small puffed sleeves, and long straight skirts, they are feminine, sensuous, and suggestive of nightgowns.

The simple elegance and grace of the clothing of both the men and women is in marked contrast and is almost incongruous with the severity of the dark massive furniture. The difference is even more apparent when compared to the marvelous compatibility of seventeenth and eighteenth century clothing, furniture, and interiors.

16-33 *Supported by bronze winged sphinxes with arabesque tails, this cheval mirror of mahogany was designed by Charles Percier. The candle brackets on each side are attached to uprights somewhat in the form of quivers of arrows.*

platform, it is not difficult to see the inspiration for its name. The ends of the bed, or the head-and footboards, curve away from the center as the mattress level and are often carved or ornamentated with cornucopias, dolphins, winged sphinxes, or swans. A round bolster at each end fills the space where the mattress meets the bed ends. A small domed canopy is sometimes centered on the wall above and complicated, heavy, fringed, and braid ornamented draperies are suspended from it. These are draped over the ends of the bed and tied back with tasseled rope in a studied arrangement.

Heavy marble-topped tables of every size, often round with pedestal or tripod supports, were in abundance in the interiors. The winged monopodium leg was everywhere, but saber and animal legs were also numerous. The toilet tables of the eighteenth century with all of their grace and feminine charm were replaced with a new type. Masculine in appearance, an important characteristic of Empire furniture, it is a medium-sized rectangular table with a marble top and concealed in the apron are drawers holding the toilet articles. The legs are generally in the form of crossed sabers.

Sitting on the top of the toilet table is a framed mirror called a dressing mirror, which is supported by two uprights or columns. The mirror can be tilted and candelabra are attached to the supports. The dressing mirror is usually separate and freestanding and can be placed on any table or commode. Its usefulness was not ignored by designers in other countires as it is frequently a part of English and American furniture as well as French. Large, tilting, full-length mirrors, called *psyche* or *cheval glasses,* were also popular and were found in many interiors.

17 *Furniture: English*

The disparity in furniture development between two contemporary cultures or regions is seldom as defined as was the difference between the furniture of England and continental Europe in the sixteenth century. England clung to the medieval world longer than any other country and continued to employ forms, construction techniques, materials, and even ornament that were associated with the Middle Ages far past the time that such elements had been discarded in Italy, Spain, France, Germany, and the Low Countries.

The Tudor political period encompasses the entire sixteenth century and ends with the reign of Elizabeth I. Throughout this period[1] the interiors gained much of their richness through the use of fabrics rather than with an abundance of furniture. This medieval holdover is indicative of the whole attitude toward the older systems. In fact, even when the Renaissance was fairly bursting with energy in Italy and changing France into the stylistic leader of the world, England was having a resurgence of the Gothic spirit.

The first evidence of Renaissance influence in England is the tomb of Henry VII constructed between 1512 and 1518. This tomb, however, considered architecture or sculpture rather than furniture, is an exception to a rule rather than the strong beginning of a trend. Henry VIII is often referred to as the first Renaissance king in England, and, indeed, he did bring in many craftsmen from Italy. However, his quarrel with the Pope and the subsequent change in religion (1534) kindled a negativism in England toward things Italian. The Italian craftsmen, who but a few years before had been welcomed in England, returned home leaving little or no influence on English furniture as compared to that exhibited in France at the same time. During the entire sixteenth century, the construction of English furniture continued to be like that used centuries before. The box-like chairs, chests, settles, beds, and

---

[1] Traditionally, furniture and interior design historians have divided the sixteenth century into two parts—Tudor (1500–1558) and Elizabethan (1558–1608).

17-1 *The ornamental detail of the Renaissance decorated medieval furniture forms during the sixteenth century, but that was about the only indication that the Renaissance existed beyond the boundaries of England.*

trestle tables described in the chapter on medieval furniture were still being used. The only clear evidence that the Renaissance existed is in the substitution of Renaissance and "Romayne"[2] ornament for the Gothic linenfold and tracery designs. The new decorative elements are certainly Renaissance, but are not Italian; they arrived in England by a circuitous route through Germany and the Low Countries and are more liberally interpreted. As early as the 1550s large amounts of Flemish cabinets and chairs were imported into England. The extensive use of strapwork designs, male and female figures with strapwork panels substituted for clothes faceted ornament, deep moldings, split turnings, glued-on buttons, and oval ornaments are all traced to Flemish origins. The influence of Flanders cannot be discounted in the Elizabethan period and continued as a source well into the seventeenth century.

Another indication of the Renaissance spirit in England was the increased awareness of comfort. The chair, for example, was no longer reserved for the master of the household or his honored guest, but was provided more commonly, although certainly a plentitude of chairs did not exist. Furniture was still sparse and would remain so until the latter half of the seventeenth century. Near the end of Elizabeth I's reign, the use of upholstered furniture increased and frequently the simple frames of chairs were completely covered with fabrics as noted in Italy and France. Much of the seating, however, was on "joyned" stools and benches.

The temporary trestle table continued to be used, but by midcentury the permanent table or *table dormant* became more common and was an important piece in the halls. This large rectangular table was placed on a raised platform and used for dining. Many of these tables are draw tables and can be extended almost double their length. The thick wooden tops are supported

2"Romayne" ornaments are medallions centered with carved portrait heads done in a pseudoclassical manner.

17-2 *An oak armchair of large proportions with very primitive carved ornament. Made about 1535, the carved designs reflect an awareness of Renaissance motifs but not a real knowledge of them.*

17-3 *This Dutch oak draw-leaf table has the same basic forms as contemporary English tables; however, its melon-bulb legs are plain. English tables invariably had the lower portion of the melon-bulb carved to resemble acanthus leaves (although they look more like cabbage) and the upper portion with a variation of egg and dart molding.* Courtesy of the St. Louis Art Museum.

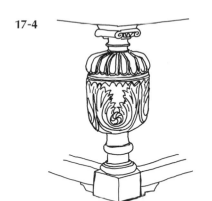

17-4

on four turned and carved legs of a distinct form braced by heavy floor stretchers.

The legs of the tables which are similar to those on cupboards, beds, and other pieces, are peculiar to the Elizabethan period. They have a strong outline and are easily identified, for the dominant form is a bulbous shape called a *melon-bulb*. It has also been compared to a bowl with a lid since there is usually a sharp division around the widest part, generally above the center, with the top section frequently being more ornately decorated than the lower. The carving on these bulbs, although usually based upon classical models, for example, variations of egg and dart and acanthus leaves, displays a wide variety of skill and amount. Quite often a small and somewhat naïve representation of an Ionic capital is placed above the melon-bulb.

In use also were permanent tables of smaller size and shape with rectangular and octagonal tops that were appropriate for games; drawers in the apron held cards and dice. There were also *faldyn* tables with hinged tops and gate legs.

The cupboards of the period are basically shelves for the display of plate but some incorporated doors. During this time the cupboard form of today developed, that is, a series of enclosed shelves with doors on the front. The *court cupboard* was so designated in the late sixteenth century and is seldom over four feet high (*court* means "short" in French). Used for display, the court cupboard is, in fact, three shelves, one resting directly on the floor or on short legs and the other two being supported by melon-bulbs. The richly decorated sides or friezes of the shelves contain drawers.

The large and draped four-posted bed of the late Middle Ages evolved into a well-defined style during Elizabeth's reign. Draperies are still important, but the bed itself takes on a massive grandeur that was not previously evident. The headboard is enlarged and elaborately decorated, functioning as a support for the canopy. The headposts are vestigial and eventually disappear into the overhall design of the architectural headboard. The front

17-5 *The massive proportions of the court cupboard betray its rather small dimensions. This walnut example dated about 1590 is about four feet tall.*

17-7 *Although Flemish, this small oak desk is similar to English examples of the mid-seventeenth century having drop leaves, baluster-turned legs and floor stretchers. The drawer or till is ornamented by fanciful strap carving.*

17-6 *Sixteenth and seventeenth-century English and French design elements were frequently incorporated into late nineteenth-century furniture. Hidden behind the decorative excesses of this American 1890 dining room is a veritable gold mine of furniture design elements of 300 years before. The table is supported on melon-bulb legs and winged griffins are below the buffet, to name only two.*

17-8 *Two Flemish armchairs reflecting the style established by the French court. This type of chair was just beginning to be used in England in the second quarter of the seventeenth century.* Courtesy of the Virginia Museum of Fine Arts, Richmond.

posts, which are highly decorative concoctions of melon-bulbs and clavated turnings, stand free of the bed platform and take on a new significance. There is no footboard. The canopy is frequently divided into a semblance of the classical entablature with the frieze carved in guilloches or strapwork designs.

The chest remained as the important storage piece, and in about 1650, drawers (*tills* or *drawing boxes* as they were called) emerged as an integral part of the form.

Oak continued as the important material for furniture in England until it was replaced by walnut near the end of the seventeenth century. The furniture in the earlier years was painted and gilded, presumably to preserve the wood and to add color to the interiors. Later it was varnished and allowed to be natural in color.

With the death of Elizabeth I in 1603, the Stuarts moved into a position of leadership. Although this period is called Jacobean,[3] and includes the reigns of James I (1603–1625) and his son, Charles I (1625–1649), the furniture of the period is a continuation of the Elizabethan style. Details are less heavy, melon-bulbs are slimmed down, and ornamentation is more simple, otherwise, there are few innovations or major changes in the design. Nevertheless, it was an important period in architecture as Inigo Jones introduced the Palladian style to England. Perhaps if the status quo had prevailed and the natural sequence of design change had taken place, significant stylistic developments in furniture would have come to pass.[4] However, history

[3] From Jacobus, Latin for James.
[4] The Palladian architectural style was revived a century later in the 1720s and furniture appropriate to the Palladian code was designed by William Kent and others. Taking architectural elements such as mantels and doorways, Kent interpreted and adapted them to serve as the fronts of cabinets and bookcases. The results are massive, monumental, and seemingly more suitable for stone than for wood. Nevertheless, they are indicative of what might have developed under more ideal conditions in the early Seventeenth century.

intervened, and the political, civil, and religious strife that rent England inhibited any important development. Indeed, during the austere period that followed the beheading of Charles I (1649), most of the furnishings of the royal houses were either sold or destroyed and very little authentic furniture remains that existed prior to that time.

To Americans, however, it is a significant design period because during the Jacobean period, the first permanent English settlements in America were established. It is this style of furniture that was used by the early settlers of Jamestown (1607) and Plymouth (1620). The late Elizabethan and Jacobean furniture forms, ornament and methods of construction were adapted and used in America, especially in New England, until the end of the seventeenth century.

The death of Charles I marked the beginning of a period during which furniture production in England was insignificant. The Puritans decreed their furniture and interiors to be plain and unadorned and no luxury or excessive ornamentation was permitted. Table and chair legs, however, were usually elaborately turned, because, being primarily functional components, any added decorative qualities were secondary and not considered objectionable.

Furniture that served two purposes was especially admired and high-backed chairs and settles that could be converted into tables were popular. The *table-chairwise* had a hinged back that dropped over to form the tabletop. These functional pieces were used for the next two hundred years in England and America.

The monarchy was restored in 1660 and Charles II (r. 1660–1685) returned from exile. He had spent the 11 years during the Commonwealth in France and Holland, and with his return the austerity of the Puritans was swept away and replaced with the exuberance of the Baroque. It is often difficult to arrange in one's mind episodes that happen simultaneously but are discussed

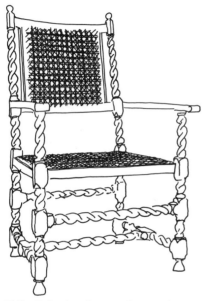

17-9 *Reflecting the turned supports permitted during the time of Cromwell, this walnut armchair (c. 1660) is made almost entirely of spiral turnings. The seat and back are large-meshed cane. During the reign of Charles II, spiral turnings and caning increased in popularity.*

at different times or appear out of sequence. This period in history, the beginning of the third quarter of the seventeenth century, is full of contrasts and there is no greater contrast than between the life-styles of the rulers of France and England. The luxurious grandeur enjoyed by Mazarin, Fouquet, and the young Louis XIV is the diametrical opposite to the severe surroundings demanded by Oliver Cromwell and the Puritans. The immediate change from one life-style to another has seldom been so rapid. The mantle of depressive gloom that clothed everything and everyone in Puritan England was lifted and manners, morals, architecture, clothing, and furniture, the whole structure of life, became flamboyant to the point of being excessive.

The returning Royalists, who were thoroughly familiar with the Continental way of life, brought with them furniture and furnishings to help establish "a politer way of living" as John Evelyn stated in his diary, and which was soon to pass "to luxury and intolerable expense." The old solid furniture forms were discarded and the newly built or remodeled great houses of England were filled with the grandiose curves and volutes of the Baroque.

The furniture of the Restoration period was influenced by Flemish and Dutch designs. It is known that the king encouraged craftsmen to come to England, not only to supply furniture but also to train English furniture-makers.

The choice of walnut as the preferred wood for use in furniture has always accompanied the shift from medieval furniture construction practices; yet, it is more than merely a change of wood species. "Oak" furniture is generally solid construction and more simply made. "Walnut" furniture, on the other hand, employs veneers (solid walnut is used only for legs, moldings, and other difficult-to-veneer components). The veneers are glued to a carcass of another wood, which, incidentally, is often oak, but in this case is always

17-10 *Made about 1680, this walnut and cane chair is almost entirely composed of scrolls embellished with crisply carved acanthus leaves and rosettes. A chair of this type and complexity required considerably more skill and knowledge of materials than was needed to make chairs of the earlier straight-lined styles.* Courtesy of Spink, London.

17-11 *The almost excessive use of Baroque scrolls during the reign of Charles II was somewhat abated during the later years of the seventeenth century. The basic chair form and material is still used in this chair (c. 1690) and scrolls are still in evidence, but the arms and back vertical supports and the stretchers are straight baluster turnings.* Courtesy of the Art Institute of Chicago.

considered secondary wood. The complicated veneer and marquetry surfaces throughout the period are in sharp contrast to the previous periods.[5]

Walnut wood was first imported and used by the English as early as the late sixteenth century. However, sometime about 1650 the first walnut trees were planted in England and after these and other trees matured, most of the wood used in English furniture is of this native variety (*Juglans regina*). It is significant, however, that this walnut along with that used in European furniture, is not the familiar American black walnut (*Juglans Nigra*), but is the species originally native to Persia and is lighter and more distinctively patterned.

Shortly after 1660 a new chair design was introduced from Flanders. Its acceptance was immediate and it is now called the Restoration chair. It remained popular past the end of the century, and during that time many variations were made with different legs and ornament. However, the basic form of the chair remained and it is easily recognizable. The high back, intricately carved with pierced parts, scrolled arms, wide front stretcher, spiral turnings, and cane seat and back panel make it unique. The chair has a stately appearance and its extraordinarily rich ornament expresses the completeness with which the Baroque spirit penetrated English design.

Spiral turning, so favored during the Louis XIII period in France, also belongs to the Restoration period in England, and exists not only on the Restoration chairs but on all kinds of legs and supports. Only near the end of the Restoration period does its popularity wane and the scroll leg supplants it.

The short reign of James II (1685–1688) was followed by the period of William and Mary (1689–1702). The Baroque lavishness of the Restoration

[5] A new designation for a furniture craftsman also began to be used in about the 1680s. Heretofore, a *joiner* and/or a *turner* made furniture; however, with the introduction of veneering, marquetry, drawer construction, and more sophisticated joints, the term *cabinetmaker* was increasingly employed and implied skill in the new techniques.

period is somewhat abated near the end of the century and the furniture is more disciplined in design; the scrolls and elaborate ornaments are still much in evidence but there is a restraint not seen before.

The most notable design change, and one observed throughout the reign of William and Mary, is the straight baluster turned leg. The details vary from piece to piece, but the William and Mary leg has a long tapered cone, small end down, topped by a slightly wider hemispherical form. This combination occurs immediately above the low, horizontal X-stretcher. This stretcher appears to be cut from a single board and the four legs penetrate its ends rather than the stretcher's being inserted into the legs. Ball feet are below the stretcher.

During the second half of the seventeenth century, the development of defined furniture types in England paralleled those in France. The Revocation of the Edict of Nantes[6] in 1685 by Louis XIV caused the flight of many French furniture craftsmen to England, thereby completing the assimilation of the continental style. The cabinets, bureaus or desks, toilet tables, chairs, and other household furniture that were being used in France were also finding their way into English homes; a comprehensive view of French and English furniture and interiors of this period displays a striking resemblance. English furniture is less complicated or lavish and has a solidness about it that is not evident in the furniture of Louis XIV. This is largely due to the adoption of the style in the homes of lesser persons, which caused simplified and less expensive designs in oak and the more fashionable walnut to be produced. These pieces have the general outlines of Baroque furniture, but instead of the extraordinary detailing of the elaborate furniture of France and the greatest houses in England, the majority of this furniture relies on veneered

---

[6]The Edict of Nantes, proclaimed by Henry IV of France in 1598, granted considerable religious and civil liberty to the Huguenots (French Protestants).

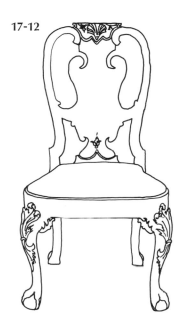

17-12

surfaces and restrained carving to give it character and, consequently, it becomes truly English in the process.

Just 42 years elapsed between the return of Charles II and the beginning of the reign of Anne, but during those four decades, English furniture design underwent a complete metamorphosis. England, formerly so completely dependent upon foreign design and craftsmen, had by 1702 attained a proficiency in design and furniture-making skills that launched an illustrious course that would establish her as a major creator of furniture design. Consequently, the glorious eighteenth century had not one mode to follow, but two; though there were some common details and decorative elements, English furniture and interior design is distinct from French and neither is measurably influenced by the other.[7]

One of the most notable designs in the history of furniture is the Queen Anne[8] chair with its distinctive back and leg shape. This armless chair is almost without peer in its elegant simplicity and has been used throughout

[7] The collectors of fine antique furniture usually prefer French or English eighteenth-century furniture to other periods if they plan to live with and use their collections and concentrate on one or the other. It would seem, however, that the furniture in the more formal interiors is French whereas that in somewhat informal interiors is English, although exceptions always exist. One reason for this is that the English furniture appear to be, and often is, less fragile and can withstand strenuous usage—the surfaces are not as vulnerable and the forms are less delicate. The English heritage that permeates American history is far stronger than the French and undoubtedly this influences today's consumers. The "Early American syndrome" is very evident in the selection on antique reproductions and adaptions. English styles are much more popular today in the United States than French styles regardless of the degree of design authenticity, price range, or quality.

[8] Queen Anne (reigned 1702–1714) apparently had no interest in the design of furniture or architecture. Nevertheless her name is associated with the lighter and more graceful furniture made in England and the American colonies during the first part of the eighteenth century and later with a fashionable residential architectural style developed around the 1870s.

17-13 *Two Dutch chairs in the English Queen Anne Style, from the early part of the eighteenth century. The surface is made of marquetry flowers and birds with the primary wood being French walnut. Despite their elaborate and rich surface and Dutch origin, the distinctive Queen Anne form is easily recognized.* Courtesy of the St. Louis Art Museum.

the world. Rather than depending upon carved or applied ornamentation for interest, it displays the beauty of wood. The refined proportions and general outline of this chair are believed to have come to England from the Orient.[9] The well-defined form of the top rail has been traced to the yoke of a Chinese milkmaid. The graceful curvilinear form of the slanted back requires exquisite craftsmanship and is both more comfortable and pleasing to the eye than previous chairs. The center splat—usually devoid of decoration—is curved in plane and runs from the bottom of the shaped top rail to the back of the chair seat. The solid splat's contour is either vase or violin shaped and with the curved outline formed by the uprights creates negative shapes that resemble a pair of parrots. This feature is most characteristic of Queen Anne chairs. The chair seat is wider in the front than in the back and almost always is padded.

The front legs of the Queen Anne chair, and most other furniture of the first half of the century, for that matter, are always cabriole. Significant of the cabriole leg is the elongated "S" curve, which is the major line of the eighteenth century and is a dominant line in French as well as English furniture. Not only is it found in the legs of the furniture but in chair backs, table aprons, bureau fronts, and all manner of interior architectural detail.

The form of the cabriole leg has also been traced to foreign sources. It resembles the animal leg used on ancient furniture and a short-curved leg of similar form is found on some Chinese furniture. The French incorporated the cabriole leg into their furniture design shortly before it appeared in England. The leg may be modeled after a goat's leg because in French the word *cabriole* means "leap of a goat." The similarity to an animal leg is further acknowledged by calling the thickened and strongly articulated curved area at the top, the *knee*. There are many variations of the cabriole leg but each has

[9]Chinese chairs called *abbot's chairs* were imported by the Dutch prior to 1700 and have a curved back splat and top rail similar to those on the Queen Anne chair, although the rest of the chair is quite box-like and does not resemble the Queen Anne chair.

17-14 *The reverse curve, the curve of the cabriole leg, is very evident in this early eighteenth-century interior. The tapestry upholstered sofa has cabriole legs with a minimum of carving—a single shell at the knee. Two ornate Queen Anne chairs with carved backs and low stretchers flank the secretary-desk, whereas the desk chair is without stretchers. All are composed of many "S" curves. The imposing secretary-desk with beveled mirror doors in the upper section has a top outline of the same reverse curves. The large dimensions of the individual wall panels and the height of the ceiling (17 feet, 4 inches) are both typical of the period.* Courtesy of the St. Louis Art Museum.

17-15 *The wing chair remained in virtually the same form except for the legs from the time it was first introduced. This walnut example, dated from the second quarter of the eighteenth century, has straight, square legs and stretchers. Other chairs might have cabriole legs, scroll legs, or animal legs depending upon the designer or the period.* Courtesy of the Virginia Museum of Fine Arts, Richmond.

a distinct knee[10], a thinner, slightly curved shaft, and a rounded form (foot) at the floor.

The cabriole legs on early Queen Anne chairs are usually slender and plain and are braced with an H-stretcher. The use of a stretcher, however, does not enhance the graceful curves of the legs and is dispensed with in most later models. Retrospectively, the earlier plain legs are now admired as the more perfect forms, but they are less common because after the second quarter of the century carved versions largely replaced them. However, the carving is restricted to the knee and is invariably a scallop shell or acanthus leaf (the preferred ornament by 1750).

The foot of the cabriole leg can be pad shaped, scrolled, or even a cloven foot of a deer or goat, but one of the most popular foot is the *ball and claw*. Derived from the Chinese, the ball and claw was originally a dragon's claw holding a pearl. However, the design has been interpreted by Western craftsmen as any clawed foot and around the middle of the century the eagle claw was widely used. When terminated with a ball and claw, the cabriole leg is frequently less slender and is more ornately carved at the knee.

Other Queen Anne seat furniture is also important. The *wing chair*, or "easy" chair as it was called, became fully developed during this period first appearing during Charles II's reign, and has remained relatively unchanged for virtually 250 years. This all-upholstered chair has curved panels or wings attached to each side of the back. These wings are vertical continuations of the arms flowing up in an unbroken line from the curved or rolled front portion of the arms. The chair seat is covered with a matching plump cushion. This comfortable chair was also called a *draught chair* as the wings protected the sitter from drafts and permitted him to sit next to the fire in sheltered warmth.

[10]The knee is less pronounced on French furniture and is often no more than a slight bulge.

Small upholstered sofas and settees were also popular. The concept of the individual chair was incorporated in the design of the settee. For example, two or three individual chair backs were structurally joined together to form the larger piece known as the *chair-back settee.* This form was to continue until the end of the century.

The piece of furniture that rivaled the plain splat-back chair as the most typical furniture form of the Queen Anne period is the card table. The passion for gambling during the eighteenth century was intense, and interiors seldom existed that did not have at least one table for playing cards or other games of chance. A representative card table has elongated cabriole legs with elaborately ornamented knees, but without stretchers. The top could be folded in half, permitting the table to be placed next to the wall when it was not in use; however, when open, the top is square and surfaced with plain or embroidered cloth. At each corner is a round depression in which a candlestick could be placed and in the center of each side is an oval depression for money or counters. Card tables of similar design continued to be made until the nineteenth century.

Previous comments have alluded to the Chinese source of the back of the Queen Anne chair and the ball and claw foot, but it is worthwhile now to expand upon the influence of English trade with China. The interest in anything Chinese developed to almost a frenzy by the beginning of the eighteenth century. Original Chinese furniture, as well as imitation, was very popular and lacquer work was highly prized. Collecting Chinese porcelain was such a craze that no horizontal surface was safe from being loaded with Oriental bowls and vases. The corner display cabinet with glazed doors was designed at this time to display these imported ceramics. The English habit of drinking tea developed in the seventeenth century, and by the time of Queen Anne had become universal. Special small *tea tables* were in use for preparing and serving tea, and many of these had tops that could be tilted so that they took up little room when not needed.

Large chests of drawers were designed with a scroll or broken pediment at the top. Such treatment was also given to the tops of bookcases and secretaries. Many chests of drawers were lacquered in the Chinese manner as well as being smoothly veneered. Beautiful veneered surfaces are peculiar to all Queen Anne furniture, and only when mahogany began to replace it about 1725 was this veneer not walnut.

Although the introduction of mahogany changed construction techniques but scarcely affected design, it should, nevertheless, be noted. The mahogany imported from Cuba and Santo Domingo (the only source in the early years of the century) has properties that are even more superior for the making of fine furniture than does walnut. Mahogany is firmer and has less difference in grain and is thus easier to work and to carve. It also takes a polish more easily. An even more important difference is that mahogany was available in wider boards; less joining meant it could be used without veneering and was subsequently less expensive to use. Solid wood construction began to dominate again. Despite these obvious advantages, mahogany did not entirely replace walnut, or the old favorite, oak, but the middle years of the eighteenth century are known as the Age of Mahogany.

About the time the German, George I, Elector of Hanover, was named king (1714) there was not one but several furniture styles existing simultaneously in England. The furniture that is now called Queen Anne, and just discussed, continued to be made until the midcentury, but was often constructed of the more fashionable mahogany.

The renewed interest in Palladian concepts produced some architectural designs of superb magnificence. The noble proportions on the exteriors are restrained and sober, but they are foils for the more elaborate interiors. The dramatic use of classical architectural elements in the interior architecture was matched by the majestic furniture. Much of this furniture can best be described as grand, massive, and definitely Baroque in feeling. English Baroque furniture is extremely well-made and adorned with swags of fruits

and flowers, masks, scallop shells, acanthus leaves, animal (usually lion) legs and heads, volutes, and even more in evidence, the moldings, details, and elements of classical architecture. The furniture was often gilded, which added to its opulence.

The prime proponent of the style was a young painter-architect-designer by the name of William Kent. Having spent ten years in Italy, he had sketched innumerable details of buildings of particular interest when, in 1719, he returned to England with Lord Burlington, an extremely rich and active young man. The combination of Lord Burlington, who became an influential amateur architect, and Kent[11] produced some of the master examples of the eighteenth-century Palladian exteriors, interiors, and furniture. Following their leadership, others also followed suit and a plethora of English Baroque designs were made.

The English preoccupation with Baroque design seems at first to be somewhat anachronistic when, at the same time in France, Rococo was already maturing. However, the French Rococo soon also influenced English styles. The bold asymmetrical and swirling forms that were so typical of Juste Aurèle Meissonier caught the fancy of some of the more liberal and experimental leaders of English society.[12]

English Rococo furniture was popular during the middle years of the eighteenth century and tends to fall into three categories. The first is very near the Rococo of France and, except for a sense of formal symmetry with a bit more reserve to it, it is basically the same and need not be discussed.

The second category is more unique; it is exceedingly fanciful and has a touch of whimsy about it. It is much more distinctly English than the first

[11]Kent was the first English architect to design furniture for specific interiors. The compatible forms and details thus established a continuity that is unprecedented in England.

[12]Meissonnier, himself, was commissioned to design Rococo silver tureens and a table-center for the Duke of Kingston in 1735.

17-17 *A candlestand of carved and painted wood from a design by Thomas Johnson.*

group of furniture although it exhibits most of the Rococo elements. This furniture does not include seating or storage pieces but it is *carvers' pieces,* as it was called at the time. That is, it is furniture that is decorative and displays the skill of the wood-carver rather than of the cabinetmaker. One of the most important designers of such furniture was Thomas Johnson (1714–c. 1778), a wood-carver. Between 1755–1758 and in 1760 and 1762, Johnson published sets of copper engravings for girandoles[13], console tables, mirror and picture frames, candelabra, and the like. His designs are very asymmetrical and are so restlessly nervous they seem to quiver and have a life of their own. Composed of "C" and "double-C" curves that oppose each other rather than flow together smoothly, pierced and freely designed shells, rocks, foliage, buildings, animals, and people[14], there is a surrealistic fantasy about each design. Not restricted to Johnson's designs but a characteristic that is evident in all fanciful English Rococo furniture is the jaggedness of the outlines. Primarily as a result of the incorporation of water and waterfalls in the design, the water form, frozen as it were in wood, drips and flows out of crevices and off the ends of the curves everywhere. Another recurring motif is the "C" curves, which are decorated with closely spaced repeating balls or similar shapes giving the curves somewhat the appearance of pea or bean pods. Neither of these motifs is seen in French furniture.

Whereas the first two categories owe much of their character to French forms, the third kind is unmistakably English. The interpretation of Rococo ornamental details and forms, the stylistic character expressed, the visual weight of the pieces, the materials used, indeed, the very essence of the furniture is unique. It could not be French.

Today this furniture style, in all its many variations and adaptations, is

[13] A girandole is a mirrored wall bracket or sconce for candles.
[14] Many of Johnson's designs depict scenes from Aesop's *Fables,* which were illustrated by the English artist Francis Barlow in 1687.

identified with the English designer, Thomas Chippendale.[15] Chippendale's name has long been connected with the fine furniture of the eighteenth century. Nevertheless, his reputation has not been based upon the furniture he made, although he was a successful cabinetmaker and had a large shop, but upon the books of furniture designs he published. Important design books had been published on the Continent and in England for years (Palladio's books were first brought out in Italy in 1573), and many had included furniture as well as architectural designs. However, Chippendale's *The Gentleman and Cabinet-Maker's Director* published in 1754 had 160 engraved plates and was the largest book devoted exclusively to furniture designs. Its success can be measured by the fact that a second and identical edition was published the following year. A third and even more comprehensive book of furniture design (200 plates) was published in 1762.

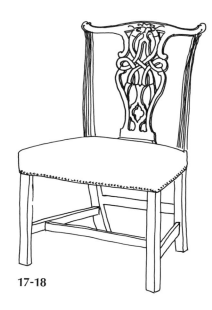

17-18

The first two editions illustrate practically every piece of furniture that might be found in the well-furnished house. These are in all of the favorite styles of the period but the curvilinear Rococo is the principal style and there are exotic and romantic wanderings into Oriental (chinoiserie) and medieval (Gothic revival) decorative designs. As most of the designs were neither original or new, and were in such a wide range of styles, an interesting question can be raised, "Who designed the furniture in Chippendale's *Director?*" It is not known for sure, but most experts believe that Thomas Chippendale could not have designed them all, if in fact he actually designed any. The designs are simply too diverse and there are just too many for one man to have done them all. Some of the designs are obviously copies of Johnson's designs and many of the others can be traced to different contemporaries of Chippendale.

[15] Thomas Chippendale was born in Yorkshire in 1718, the son of a joiner and the grandson of a carpenter. By 1748 he was established in London and in 1753 he moved to St. Martin's Lane, the center of the furniture business. He died in 1779. His son also named Thomas Chippendale, continued in the furniture business until his death in 1822.

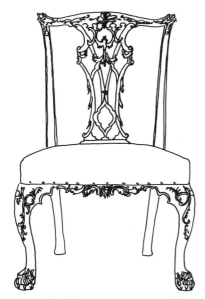

17-19 *The "Chippendale" chair. This chair is more ornate than the chair on page 426 but both are unmistakably "Chippendale." The back splat is pierced and the back uprights and top rail meet in projects or ears. This chair has cabriole legs that end in lion feet, whereas the former chair has plain, straight legs.*

The authorship of the designs is of little consequence now and the importance of the *Director* or of Chippendale as a leading maker of fine furniture certainly should not be minimized. The original purpose behind the publication seems to have been to promote and publicize Chippendale's firm. This it certainly did as some of his best and more important furniture was made after 1754. The book, therefore, was not meant to be a book of original ideas for cabinetmakers as were Johnson's books, but rather to aid Chippendale's clients.[16] Even though it was published as a catalog of designs that could be made by Chippendale's shop, the *Director* was widely distributed and influenced cabinetmakers around the world. The designs of innumerable pieces of furniture made after the publication of the *Director* can be traced directly to this very important book. It is interesting, though, that there exists little furniture similar to the designs in Chippendale's books that can be ascribed to his firm. The majority of the pieces attributed to Chippendale are in the Neoclassic style of the brothers Adam rather than Rococo.

If Chippendale did not design any of the furniture in the *Director* or did not make furniture similar to that illustrated in it, what then is the famous "Chippendale style?" This is a difficult question to answer because it is more a school of furniture than a single look. The generic term *"Chippendale"* refers to furniture of several design persuasions made from about 1740–1770 during the Middle Georgian period,[17] and had very little to do with Thomas Chippendale, the cabinetmaker.

There is the Chippendale chair, for example. This chair evolved several years before the publication of the *Director*, and vestiges of the style can be seen as early as 1725, about the time of the introduction of mahogany. In many ways it is similar to the Queen Anne chair, and the two styles are the

---

[16]The 310 subscribers listed in the first edition include five dukes.

[17]The Georgian period (c. 1714–c. 1810) includes the reigns of George I (1714–1727), George II (1727–1760), and George III (1760–1820). The term is more often used when referring to the architecture of England and the United States than to the furniture.

most important and distinctively eighteenth-century English chairs. They both have backs with center splats, they both can have cabriole legs, they both are not fully upholstered but only have the seat padded, and they are obviously "wooden" chairs. Despite this parallelism, they are different and should not be confused.

The splat, for example, on the majority of Queen Anne chairs is solid; on Chippendale chairs it is pierced and often carved in a fanciful design. The most elaborate Chippendale chair is the *"ribband-back,"* which has a center splat that is carved and pierced to look like ribbon bows with flying ends. Chippendale chairs might also have the splat pierced to resemble Chinese frets, Gothic tracery[18], or several other designs.

The legs of the Queen Anne chair are always cabriole, and stretchers brace the earlier and unadorned examples. Cabriole legs are also found on Chippendale chairs, but they have a more pronounced reverse curve, are heavier, and are more elaborately carved with shells, acanthus leaves, or volutes at the knee. Both may have ball and claw or scroll feet. Chippendale legs might, however, be straight, square, and solid with a smooth or simple reeded surface, or covered with Chinese frets or Gothic tracery. They may also be pierced and carved to resemble bamboo clusters, open fretwork, or tracery. Stretchers are often added on the straight-legged chairs.

The seats of the Queen Anne chairs were of several trapezoidal shapes, straight or curved, and the upholstery was a *slip seat*[19] let into the exposed framing. Chippendale chair seats are wider and either rectangular or trapezoidal; they are never curved. They may be slip seated but are often padded with the seat frame or rails covered with the fabric.

---

[18] The use of Gothic decorative elements on fundamentally Rococo furniture forms at this time is peculiarly English.

[19] A slip seat is a loose or easily removed padded panel or frame. The fabric covering was not attached to the chair frame itself.

17-20 *Believed to have been made by Thomas Chippendale in about 1750, this red, black, and gold bed, now in the Victoria and Albert Museum in London, has a canopy in the shape of a pagoda roof and with flying dragons on the corners, and a headboard with a fret design.*

The most easily recognized difference between Queen Anne and Chippendale chairs is the outline of the back. The upper portion of the former is rounded; there is no break in line from the upright to the top rail. Chippendale chairs, on the other hand, have a definite break at the junction of the top rail and the uprights. This is often accented with carving or decorative ornament on the ear (the projection). The top rail is invariably shaped with a high center section, then it drops down slightly and swings up again at the corners (ears). This traditional "yoke" shape is sometimes adapted to a pagoda roof on the Chinese Chippendale[20] chairs.

There are Chippendale chairs other than those with splat backs. Ladder-back chairs with parallel horizontal "rungs" echoing the top rail were also popular. The identifying back outline is unchanged from the splat backs.

The Chippendale sofa developed in England at this time but found its greatest expression in the American Colonies. This graceful upholstered sofa has a gently arched back that gives a beautiful undulating line to the whole piece. The high rolled arms are the same height as the back. The seat is padded and does not have a loose cushion. The only exposed wooden parts are the short legs (cabriole or square), and the frame is not exposed as was usual in French *canapés* at the time. The Chippendale sofa is far more sculptural than sculptured in appearance and is a suitable companion to the commendable wing chair of the period.

Chests, cabinets, desks, and tables of many sizes and descriptions were also designed in the Chippendale style. The small pedestal tilt-top tea table

[20] In Chippendale's *Director* and Sir William Chambers' *Designs of Chinese Buildings, Furniture, Dresses, Machines and Utensiles,* published in 1757, as well as in other design books, furniture and ornamental details are shown that are more closely based upon actual Chinese prototypes and are less freely interpreted than in other countries. Chinese pagodas, dragons (ball and claw feet and the whole animal), figures, bamboo, and above all the fret appear in many guises on all manner of furniture. The alliterative term Chinese Chippendale is used today to identify all of the English furniture that was so fashionably Chinese.

with three cabriole legs is especially significant. This table form developed earlier in the century, but had a plain, flat top. During the Chippendale period, however, the tops took on the ornamental detailing found on silver trays. The tops were given *"pie crust"* and *scalloped* edges.

The free transposition of designs originating with different cultures is very evident in Chippendale furniture. A piece may be quite classical or Rococo in general form, but have Chinese or Gothic detail. For example, a secretary-bookcase might have a rectangular carcass with pilasters on the sides and the top shaped like a simple or broken pediment of clear classical or Renaissance heritage; yet, the divisions or mullions of the class doors are definitely based upon Gothic tracery with pointed arches.

The remarkable popularity of the Chippendale style was soon challenged by an increased interest in classically inspired ornament. Like the tides, the ebb and flow of fashion brings design elements that were discarded in one period to the fore in another, seemingly fresh and new. In 1754, the same year that the *Director* was published, a young Scotsman, Robert Adam[21] went to Italy to study architecture. Four years later he returned and settled in London. He soon had an important architectural practice and in 1761 was appointed Architect of the King's Works with Sir William Chambers.

Adam's large number of commissions included some of the most fashionable houses in England. He was often responsible for the design of the furniture and interiors as well as the exterior. It is impossible to separate his designs for the furniture from his designs for the interiors, as there is a complete integration of all elements. Adam believed that the architect should design *all* decorative components, the interior architecture, furniture, and

[21] There were four Adam brothers, John (1721–1792), Robert (1728–1792), James (1730–1794), and William (1738–1822), sons of a successful architect and writer. The eldest was not actually engaged in London, but James was the principal draftsman and William was the bookkeeper. Robert, however, was the designer and was responsible for most of the innovations credited to the brothers Adam.

17-21 *A small girandole in the style of Robert Adam. The flower swags are held in place by hidden wires. The whole object is gilded, unifying the different materials from which it is made.* Courtesy of the Art Institute of Chicago.

accessories in a room and that the same motifs be used throughout thereby attaining the required harmony. For example, there are houses with ceiling stucco ornament of the same design as the carpet on the floor. Although an excellent concept, there was a serious flaw in Adam's particular approach to design; his disregard for the inherent qualities of different materials. His patterns might be for wood, stone, brick, metal, stucco, fabric, or any other material used in an interior or on furniture; yet, regardless what the true properties of a material might be, the designs were the same. A slender swag of delicate flowers would be identical whether in limestone, silver, or damask. To add to this transgression, Adam loved to fake materials and often used composition and imitation marble[22] in his work.

The designs of Robert Adam fall into two distinct phases. The first phase, from about 1756–1770, is bold, masculine, and large in scale. The furniture was often based upon earlier Georgian forms embellished with classical rather than Rococo decoration.

The second phase of his work, dating from about 1770–1792, is far more delicate and feminine. It is this style for which he is best known and which most influenced subsequent furniture and interior design. Adam used fine, linear arabesques and grotesques to decorate his furniture and interiors. They have no architectural significance as he believed that the heaviness of the past designs should be replaced by delicacy, grace, and beauty. Basing his designs upon ancient Roman stucco ornament and wall paintings, and on the early Renaissance designs of Raphael, he set an English style, which is known as Adam.

Robert Adam was one of the first to champion the neoclassic idiom. Except

[22] Adam was especially taken with *scagliola* tabletops. This imitation stone, first used by the ancient Romans and revived during the Renaissance, could be produced with complicated designs and colors on it and was often used as a substitute for the very expensive *pietre dure* (inlaid stone). Most *scagliola* tabletops were made in Italy but the designs were often English.

17-22 *A small, three-legged console table purchased in the 1920s. It is an interesting combination of styles. The front leg, ornamented by a large, stylized acanthus leaf, is an elongated cabriole terminating in a rather large ball and claw. The two back legs are slender, fluted columnar supports, obviously classical in derivation. Although the table is of American manufacture, it illustrates the almost universal popularity of eighteenth-century English furniture during the present century.*

for a few early elementary examples executed in Paris, Adam produced accomplished neoclassic designs for architecture and furniture in England a decade before they were popular in France. In fact, many of his furniture designs are quite similar to later French designs and are believed to have influenced French designers at the end of the Louis XVI period.

No discussion of Robert Adam can omit his designs for mirrors. They are, along with the stucco ornamented ceilings and wall reliefs, and his side tables, some of the most individualistic of all his designs. The favorite shape during the greater part of his career was the oval mirror in a rather flat, reeded molding. However, what makes it so "Adam" is the open, linear, and delicate design of festoons and swags of husks or bellflowers extending beyond the mirror frame with a dainty urn or finial topping the whole arrangement. These extremely fragile looking decorations are often metal or are metal supported composition and then painted to match the frame.

Adam is also credited with the innovation of the sideboard. The spacious dining rooms being built during the latter half of the eighteenth century required large furniture. Consequently, Adam, insisting upon small and delicate ornament, needed pieces that appeared suitably scaled, yet not overpoweringly majestic. He devised the sideboard, a long rectangular table, at first without drawers of any kind, and at each end he placed a pedestal topped with a large urn.[23] These three matching pieces gave the desired grand effect. In a few years the separate pieces were structurally joined and a distinctive sideboard form was achieved.

Painted surfaces and designs were favorites of Adam and often substituted for the more complicated marquetry. Frequently the surface was either painted a light color or was simply veneered with light, golden satinwood or

[23]The pedestal bases provided storage for dishes or wine and the urns held knives or water for rinsing glasses and silverware between courses, a practice continued until the early nineteenth century.

17-23 *A side table with matching pedestals and urns designed by Robert Adam. Painted and partially gilded, these pieces combined in this manner are the beginnings of the sideboard.*

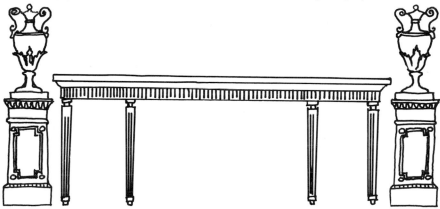

harewood.[24] Over this toned ground are placed delicate designs of repeating festoons of husks, bellflowers, or little leaves held in place by medallions or animal heads, winged griffins, honeysuckle, shells, *rinceau,* and small rectangular or oval panels of classical figures[25]. These same decorative motifs are used throughout Adam's work and are identified most closely with the style.

Adam was not a cabinetmaker and, despite the masterful and prolific designer that he was, many of his designs were impractical. Much credit must be given to the cabinetmakers whom he commissioned and who translated his ideas into reality. All of the leading furniture-makers executed Adam's designs including Chippendale, and it is in the Adam's style that the finest Chippendale furniture was made.

One cabinetmaker who was to add his own name to furniture was George Hepplewhite. Little is known of Hepplewhite except that he died in 1786 and that his wife's name was Alice. Strangely, it is Alice who was responsible for Hepplewhite's fame. Apparently, he was a moderately successful cabinetmaker, but two years after he died his wife published the *Cabinet Maker and Upholsterer's Guide,* a furniture design book of nearly 300 designs. It was the first major book of this type to be published since the *Director* and was a remarkable success. A second edition came out the following year and a third edition was published in 1794.

Several comparisons can be made between the *Director* and the *Guide* and their authors. The most interesting and relevant is that it is quite possible that Hepplewhite could have designed the furniture in the *Guide,* although in the preface he admits that not all of the designs are original. Whereas Chippendale's book illustrated furniture that, if followed exactly, would

---

[24] Harewood is sycamore wood stained light gray.
[25] These figures are painted in *grisaille,* various shades of gray or neutral tints, imitating the look of carved reliefs.

17-24 *The straight, tapered, square legs with spade feet and the shield back with garlands identify this chair as a Hepplewhite design.*

often have been impractical if not impossible to construct, Hepplewhite's designs are extremely practical and show that whoever did design them understood cabinetmaking and materials well. Further, each piece of furniture in the *Guide* is usable and the general thrust of design throughout the book is not toward titled or rich clients but for the average person, something that neither Chippendale or Adam attempted to do. Hepplewhite brought the neoclassic style of Adam to the masses, and after almost 200 years Hepplewhite furniture designs are still being adapted to today's furniture needs.

Hepplewhite chairs often have straight, slender, and slightly tapered legs, usually ending in a smaller tapered block, called a *spade foot.* (This tapered leg is original with Hepplewhite.) There can be stretchers. The backs are oval-, shield-, or heart-shaped and exhibit a wide range of back splats and pierced designs. Urns, vases, festoons, slender balusters, lyres, and the new decorative device, the Prince of Wales feathers (three feathers) are all used. His chairs also have upholstered backs.

Sofas are light in scale and often display a very shallow curved back or later straight top rails. The ends flow smoothly to form the arms and the whole body rests lightly on slender, straight legs. The distance from front to back is slightly greater than earlier sofas allowing the sitter to sit in a more comfortable position.

There is some question as to who first combined the table and two pedestals to form the sideboard, but Hepplewhite is often credited with this design. It is thought that he designed the single piece to fit into more modest rooms and in so doing adapted Adam's idea of 20 years before. The Hepplewhite sideboard often has numerous legs; seldom does it have merely four, but often six or more tapered legs are found. In the breaking up of the surfaces, the legs often extend up to form the stiles between the panels (doors) and reveal the heritage of the piece.

Although he did not design it, Hepplewhite was the first to illustrate the Pembroke table, a small dropleaf table with slender, tapering legs with a

17-25 *The Pembroke table.*

17-26 *Hepplewhite introduced the use of wire mesh in bookcase doors, which replaced glass.*

drawer in the ends. Other innovations that are credited to Hepplewhite are the pull-out *secrétaire* ("desk") drawer, the pouch work table, and the washstand. The latter was a modest affair but was one of the first instances of a design concerned with cleanliness.

Beds during the eighteenth century continued to have four posts. By the end of the century, these posts are slender and fluted, and near the bottom there is a vase or baluster shape covered with acanthus leaves. The cornice supported by the posts is delicate and often topped by an urn. Many of these cornices have disappeared and the posts now support a light frame that is hidden by gathered fabric. More designs for bedroom furniture appeared in Hepplewhite's *Guide* than in any other published design books. His designs for chests of drawers, chests on chests or tallboys, dressing tables, and other necessary furniture set examples for many later craftsmen who were interested in producing furniture for the bedroom.

The lightness of Hepplewhite furniture is perhaps the most noticeable quality. There is a refined elegance that is never heavy or overdone. The ornament that is used is restrained and judiciously applied but it always consists of the common neoclassic devices, husk and bellflower garlands, urns, reeding and fluting, *rinceaux,* and similar forms.

Hepplewhite furniture is largely made of light toned woods, such as satinwood (the most popular), harewood, and mahogany. Marquetry was revived but the imagery described fans, scrolls, swags, and urns, rather than the Rococo and Baroque designs of the past. Surfaces were also painted, with touches of gold or brass making their appearance. This is very evident in the doors of bookcases and tall desks or secretary cabinets. Instead of glass in the doors, a gilded mesh or grill backed with stretched fabric was used.

Additionally, a change in the handling of veneered surfaces developed during the last twenty-five years of the century. Panels that had been bordered with moldings and carved ornament gave way to smoothly veneered surfaces. Frequently, a center panel or area (rectangular or oval) was of one veneer, perhaps mahogany, surrounded by a border of a lighter veneer, such as satinwood. The total surface was smooth and on one plane. However, between the panel and border was invariably a thin line of holly or some other contrasting wood. The use of banding, or a thin line of veneer, is very typical of the Hepplewhite style.

Between 1791–1794 another influential furniture design book appeared and a new style name was added to the vocabulary of designers. Thomas Sheraton (1751–1806) published his book, *The Cabinet-Maker and Upholsterer's Drawing Book,* in four parts. It contained 111 plates of furniture and ornament designs (two more editions were printed—1793 with 119 plates and 1802 with 122 plates.)[26] Not an accomplished cabinetmaker, although he did have some experience in the craft, he was primarily a not–too–successful drawing teacher, preacher, and author (as well as several other attempted occupations). He died as he had often lived, in destitute circumstances; yet, he designed and offered to a wide audience some of the most elegant and refined furniture ever conceived.

Sheraton came to London in 1790 when he was about 40 years old. He must have already had considerable work done on his *Drawing Book* prior to his arrival because within a year the first part was issued. In addition, the 522 names on his list of advanced subscribers were scattered across England, suggesting that he had gained important contacts prior to his arrival in London. These names include cabinetmakers, joiners, and upholsterers, all of whom were professionals who were in a position to increase the success and widespread influence of his publishing and designing efforts.

Sheraton, was by far the most original designer along with Chippendale

---

[26] Sheraton's *Drawing Book* gave more designing and technical information than did either of the other design books. It included a section on the methods of making perspective drawings, a comprehensive description of the classical orders, a section with the furniture designs, and a fourth part devoted to moldings and ornaments. It was more than 440 pages in length and was more a "teaching" book than merely an "idea" book.

The furniture, walls, and accessories of this midseventeenth century French interior, gathered from different sources, all seem to "belong." The paneling (c. 1735), taken from a house in Paris, still reflects some of the rigidity of French Baroque but the decoration is lighter and more linear. The folding stools dating from about 1738 and the lacquered writing table (1759) were in Versailles; the table was in the apartment of Louis XV. Courtesy of the Metropolitan Museum of Art.

This elegant room, finished about 1748, with its rich, fully modeled plasterwork on the walls and ceiling, is from Oxford, England. The lofty spaciousness of the room is further accented by the furniture being placed around the perimeter of the room. The library desk dates from about 1725. Courtesy of the Metropolitan Museum of Art.

The delicate plaster relief ornament that encircles the walls and enriches the ceiling of this dining room is typical of Robert Adam. Designed for Lord Lansdowne in the 1760's, it displays the elegant classicism for which Adam is best known. Courtesy of the Metropolitan Museum of Art.

Although the term Duncan Phyfe furniture usually brings to mind the style popular at the turn of the Nineteenth Century, however, during Phyfe's long career other styles came from his shop. This set of parlor furniture, made by him in 1837, still shows classical precedents, but the smooth mahogany surfaces and heavy scrolls identify the style as French Restauration. Courtesy of the Metropolitan Museum of Art.

17-27 *Requiring great technical skill to make, chairs following the designs of Thomas Sheraton are very delicate in appearance. This black and gold reproduction of a parlor chair illustrates well the design concepts of Sheraton—the graceful upward sweep of the arms, the slender, tapering legs, the cane seat, and the square back with a linear design.*

and Hepplewhite. His designs were often influenced by French neoclassic styles, but he infused them with a freshness and precision of proportion that was his alone. Sheraton's drawings are also far more skillfully executed than those of other designers and, in addition, show many construction details indicating his thorough understanding of each piece.

Sheraton's name is today almost synonymous with satinwood furniture. He was not the first or the last designer to design furniture of satinwood, but his designs display the beauty of the wood perhaps better than any other. His furniture is very rectangular, spare, and precise; seldom is a complicated curve seen. Only the most crisp, geometric forms are used and the ornament is restricted to inlay, marquetry, or painted designs.

There is an overlapping of furniture forms and types between Hepplewhite and Sheraton, although Sheraton usually eliminated the curves that recur in Hepplewhite's furniture. Sheraton chairs, for example, have square backs. (The legs and seats are very similar.) The two side uprights are connected by a low plain rail near the seat and by a more ornate one at the top. Within this defined square or rectangular space are splats and designs of extreme delicacy, usually lyre, vase, oval, or diamond forms. Invariably, there is a drapery festoon or two incorporated in the arrangement. The drapery festoon, which was a favorite of Sheraton, is found throughout all of his designs.

A design characteristic of many Sheraton pieces is the slender column at the chamfered corners of chests of drawers and secretary cabinets. These columnar forms extend from the floor to the top surface and often break through any horizontal moldings or planes. Used in France in Louis XVI furniture, in England this column is identified entirely with Sheraton as it was never used by Hepplewhite. The same idea was adapted by Sheraton for use on tables and chairs, the legs breaking the plane of the aprons and seat rails.

Although most of Sheraton's furniture is very rectangular, he did produce

17-28 *A Sheraton design for a "Grecian squab."*

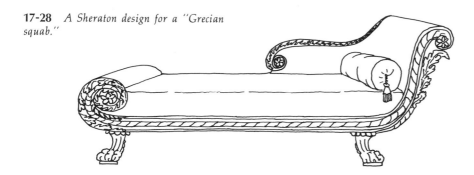

some simple curvilinear furniture. He designed "an Elliptic Bed for a Single Lady," a sofa shaped like a sausage or banana, and his most popular design —the "kidney-shaped" pedestal desk.

Many of Sheraton's sideboards are similar to Hepplewhite's, but Sheraton frequently added a framework of brass rods the length of the piece at the back. Candleholders were often attached to the framework, and when lighted, gave a sparkling effect to the large dishes resting against the brass rods.

Sheraton's inventiveness included folding furniture and furniture that could serve two purposes, such as washing and toilet facilities hidden within the carcass of a chest of drawers, or library steps folding out of a small table. Sheraton also designed "a summer bed in two compartments" prior to 1792. This elegant affair was really the bane of the twentieth century, twin beds, united with a single headboard and under a single canopy.

The conflict across the English Channel had almost as much effect upon English style as it had on the French style of furniture. The large influx to England of French furniture craftsmen and refugees with other skills and persuasions, as well as the importation of fine furniture by these refugees (a result of the sale of the contents of the French royal palaces) increased the French influence upon English design. Consequently, a large amount of furniture made in England in the last decade of the eighteenth century is almost identical to the late Louis XVI style.

The conquests of Napoleon were not ignored in England, and despite the existing enmity between France and England, the Empire style was increasingly to dominate the thinking of designers. By the beginning of the nineteenth century, the delicate elegance found in Hepplewhite's *Guide* and Sheraton's *Drawing Book* was losing favor to the more archaeologically correct furniture. The change is nowhere more apparent than in Sheraton's second book, the *Cabinet Dictionary.* Published in 1803 and containing 88 fine copper engravings, this book included, for the first time, furniture that is identified

17-29 The stylistic shift from delicately scaled furniture to heavier forms is evident in this table designed by Thomas Hope (c. 1810). Instead of having the narrow square or round legs tapering to a small dimension near the floor, which are characteristic of Hepplewhite and early Sheraton, this table has a solid pedestal supported by great animal feet and decorated with large-scale bronze classical ornament. Courtesy of the Art Institute of Chicago.

as Regency.[27] Sheraton illustrated furniture with lion paws, chairs adapted from the Greek *klismos* and the Roman *cella curulis* along with other classically derived details. He was first to show the "Grecian" couch with lion-paw feet, scrolled ends (one higher than the other), and a scrolled backrest that extended only half the length.

The trend toward pedantic correctness (and archaeological discomfort) was clearly stated by Thomas Hope (1769–1831) in his *Household Furniture and Interior Decoration* in 1807. Although Hope has been described as a dilettante, one must not discredit his influence. Said to be one of the wealthiest men in Europe, he was well traveled, an expert on ancient (Greek, Roman, and Egyptian) archaeology, and a prolific author and designer. Along with the architect Henry Holland (1751–1805), who also was thoroughly familiar with ancient styles, Hope set the style of the Regency. Unfortunately, the clearly stated ideals of their austere classicism were often misused. The increasing popularity of this furniture style caused a degeneration to the point of clumsiness of form and proportion and an indiscriminate application of classical and Egyptian ornament.

Although many excellent examples of Regency furniture have survived, it is clearly evident that the introduction of industrialization and the geometrically simple forms of Regency caused large amounts of furniture of questionable significance to be produced. Aside from some notable examples, a preponderance of furniture of this period lacks refinement of design, workmanship, or both. The best Regency furniture is extremely well constructed, and though some of the pieces appear almost exotic in their incorporation of ancient designs and symbols, their "presence" cannot be dismissed as meager.

[27] Historically, the English Regency period lasts from 1811–1820 and technically covers only the period when the Prince of Wales (later George IV) was regent during the final days of the incapacitated George III. Stylistically, English Regency extends from 1800 to about 1835.

Darker woods, especially mahogany and rosewood, are more prevalent at this time and the rich grain is fully exploited in the smooth surfaces of the cabinets and commodes. Seating furniture is often painted black or dark rich green. Gilt bronze ornament and a revival of brass marquetry (Boulle work) give a resplendent glow to the pieces. More realism is found in the images used for the structural and decorative components. Lion feet are carved with exact detail of claw and hair; human and animal heads, sphinxes, dolphins and sea serpents, swans, sinewy animal legs, monopodia, and lion heads are all vigorously fashioned of wood and metal.

The inclusion of Egyptian motifs in furniture and interior design assumed the proportion of a craze in England after 1798, the year Lord Nelson stopped Napoleon's Egyptian campaign. The popularity of Nelson also caused naval and marine elements to be freely interspersed with the more usual classical details. Furniture was seldom free of dolphins, fish, rope and cable moldings, and the whole gamut of Egyptian designs that were illustrated in D. V. Denon's *Voyage dans la basse et la haute Egypte,* published in Paris and London in 1802, the archaeological report of Napoleon's campaign. Hope was especially taken with Denon's book and used it as a prime source of design information.

Indirectly, Nelson figured in the development of a popular English chair form that was copied in France and the United States. The reintroduction of the saber leg from the *klismos* established a new character to chairs. The former rigidity observed in the legs of neoclassic chairs is replaced by a fluidity of line. The Trafalgar chair[28], fully developed by 1805, has a rolled back with either a turned or shaped top rail. The curved line of the back

17-30 *Reminiscent of the Greek* klismos, *this mahogany chair (c. 1820) combines classical, Egyptian, and Assyrian ornament.*

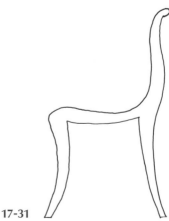

17-31

---

[28] Although Trafalgar and Nelson are closely identified, the Trafalgar chair is named after the firm that first made it, the Trafalgar workshops. Previously, however, these workshops had been called Morgan and Saunders, but were renamed in honor of the great naval hero.

17-32 *Four gilded dolphins support this rosewood sofa table (c. 1813). This table, although placed in front of a sofa, is about 28 inches high.*

splits at the seat flowing in a single uninterrupted sweep to the floor and swinging forward to form the side seat rail. The curved line then turns abruptly, but without a defined break, into the front saber leg. The seat and back panel is often caned, a favorite of the Regency period.

Other Regency innovations are the convex, *circular mirror* and the *sofa table.* Circular mirrors with elaborate frames, often with marine and naval details or topped with an eagle, are distinctly Regency and are found in many interiors of the period. The sofa table, which developed from the Pembroke table, has a long rectangular top with two small drop leaves at the ends. There are two or more drawers in the apron beneath the tabletop that can be withdrawn from either side. The support vary from "X" shape, monopodia, lyre, or simple uprights with splayed feet. The sofa table should not be confused with the modern "coffee" table, although it was placed in front of the sofa. The sofa table is much higher—the top is about 28 inches from the floor—and was used when writing or doing needlework.

During the first 30 to 35 years of the nineteenth century, English furniture changed significantly. The basic types of furniture remained almost the same, but the methods of construction, perfection of materials, and purity of design, which in the beginning were supreme, began a steep decline in quality. The elegant furniture craftsmanship of the late eighteenth century dwindled rapidly as the industrial revolution gained momentum and mass-produced, stamped out, machine-modified cheap copies became available to all. The spawning of the affluent middle-class whose tastes were less cultivated minimized the need for *fine* furniture. The need was only for *more* furniture, which was easily satisfied by the machine.

The furniture of England, and of the world, had arrived at a point of paramount importance. Previously, furniture had been handmade by master craftsmen for the cultured and affluent few. Seldom has any of the furniture designs in these chapters been for the ordinary citizen whose furniture requirements were usually met by his own crude adaptations or by the castoffs of the rich. Sociocultural conditions were rapidly changing in Europe and coincidental with the ascendancy of Queen Victoria (r. 1837–1901) a demand for adequate and comfortable living spaces and furniture began to develop. The exciting, vulgar, expensive, grand, shoddy, cheap, eclectic, superb, inventive, and regressive styles of the nineteenth century, a most wonderful mix, were to mingle, mature, and become the foundation for twentieth-century design.

18 Furniture: American to About 1800

18-1 *A small oak table (c. 1690–1720) with low stretchers and simply turned legs. A drawer is fitted between the legs in the apron. The initialed box is somewhat earlier, about 1660–1690. The design of the flat relief carved in the front panel is based upon the acanthus leaf.* Courtesy of the Art Institute of Chicago.

American furniture made in the seventeenth and eighteenth centuries is almost exclusively English in derivation. This is primarily the result of the predominance of *settled* English colonists. Although the English were relative latecomers to the Western Hemisphere, they were responsible for more permanent towns and villages, and even more importantly, for a more permanent citizenry. The men and women of other nationalities who had colonized America (especially the French) did not come to permanently settle but rather to make their fortunes, serve their king, or perform some other duty, and then return to the mother country. The majority of English arrivals came to stay. They put down roots, created permanent homes, and raised their families, generation after generation. Eventually the English government, language, and loyalties supplanted the other national sympathies and influences.

This permanency of tenure also influenced the direction of artistic expression. The French had isolated outposts that were usually more "current" than their English counterparts and there are known instances of actual French furniture's being transported and used in the most distant forts. However, when the time came for the French personnel to leave, their furnishings did also, and, consequently, few examples of French furniture remained to establish a design heritage. In Canada, however, there is a stronger French heritage as more people remained permanently in the French colonies and their furnishings later served as models for the local craftsmen. Below the Saint Lawrence River, the English colonists stayed and their furniture was subsequently copied serving as prototypes long after the style had ceased to be favored in England.

The English, who first settled Jamestown in 1607 and Plymouth in 1620, brought little furniture with them. The small ships and large number of passengers (102 on the *Mayflower*) permitted little household equipment or furnishings to be carried. But judging from the number of pieces currently claimed to have been "brought over on the *Mayflower*," Oliver Wendell

443

18-2 *The most impressive pieces of furniture in late seventeenth-century American homes were the court cupboards. Not as elaborately ornamented, but having cabinets on the upper level, they are made of oak. Split turnings, painted black to simulate ebony, were a common method of decoration.*

Holmes' estimate, voiced in his poem, "On Lending a Punch-Bowl," even falls short:

"With those that on the Mayflower came, a hundred souls or more,
Along with all the furniture to fill their abodes,
To judge by what is still on hand, at least a hundred loads."

The known primitive conditions under which the colonists first lived corroborates there being little "real" furniture at hand.[1] What few authentic pieces of early furniture that do exist come from the latter part of the seventeenth century. This furniture is based primarily upon Jacobean forms, the popular furniture style in England, and, consequently, the style the colonists continued to construct in America. The return of the monarchy in England in 1660 caused few stylistic changes in America and the older Jacobean forms remained until almost the eighteenth century. There is, however, a marked difference between English and American Jacobean furniture. American furniture, comprised of native woods, can be distinguished by carving that is less sculptural, less skilled, and less evident. The whole piece has a vigorousness, boldness, and primitiveness that are not apparent in English examples. There is a refreshing simplicity about the furniture of the period that is especially appealing today.

Additional differences can be identified between the colonies. New England retained the Jacobean forms longer than did the middle or southern colonies, and even within Massachusetts there are variations. For example, the Pilgrims (only those settled at Plymouth) had much simpler furniture

[1] John Alden, better known as the husband of the beautiful Priscilla Mullins, was a cooper and has often been considered the first furniture-maker in America. During his lifetime he prospered and was twice assistant governor of the colony. Yet when he died in 1687 the contents of his house were inventoried and consisted of only one table, one bench, one cupboard, two chairs, bedsteads, chests, and boxes. The total value was 33 shillings.

18-3 *An early twentieth-century machine-made adaptation of the seventeenth-century press cupboard. This cupboard is used in a dining room, however, functioning more like the similar court cupboard. The enclosed storage areas have been enlarged, the proportions have been changed, the applied ornament and melon bulb supports have become less heavy, and the whole design appears rather clumsy. The decoration on the large door panels is derived from classical arabesques and appears too delicate for the piece.*

than did the Puritans (Boston, Ipswich, and other Massachusetts Bay Colony communities). The furniture of the William Penn settlement was more elaborate and closely followed the contemporary English style with a tendency toward ornamentation, which was to continue until after the Revolutionary War. The furniture used in the southern colonies frequently was imported. What was not imported was made locally and is somewhat simpler than that of Philadelphia but more elaborate than that of New England.

The amount of furniture owned by the early colonists was even more sparse than that found in English houses a half century before. The most important piece in the homes of the more affluent was the *court cupboard*.[2] This piece, however, is not the court cupboard of England. English court cupboards described in the preceding chapter were basically three shelves separated by large melon-bulb supports. American court cupboards have a cabinet between the two upper shelves. The cabinet is usually not the full depth of the piece, but is recessed, often at an angle. The ornamentation consists of large, simple, bulb-turnings, applied split turnings, and bosses (all ebonized), and complicated moldings and strapwork carving. They are truly majestic pieces for the display and storage of pewter, silver, or Delftware. A variation of the court cupboard is the press cupboard of similar form, ornamentation, and size. The press cupboard has cabinets below as well as above and frequently drawers are inserted in the center frieze. The two cupboards have different functions, however. The court cupboard was used to store and display plate and cooking utensils; the press cupboard was used, on the other hand, to store clothing. Together, they are the most elaborately ornamented furniture in the seventeenth-century American colonies.

In addition to court and press cupboards, chests were also used for essential storage. They continued to be prominent in the interiors until after

[2]The court cupboard was more common to the coastal area of Massachusetts than to other American colonies, but it was certainly not restricted to that area.

18-4 *Two small chests from New England
of simple plank construction. Both have top
lids but there are also drawers in the bottom.
The chest on the right, dated 1692, is decorated with gouge carving, a type of relief reflecting the carving tool. The design on the
three largest half circles is based upon the
classical egg and dart motif.* Courtesy of
the Art Institute of Chicago.

18-5 *The Hadley and the sunflower and
tulip chests are similar in construction but
their surface decorations are quite different.
These two details show the Hadley (above)
and the sunflower and tulip (right). The
Hadley chest has very flat carving of abstract tulips and leaves. The design is repeated with a minimum of variation over
the whole chest. The sunflower and tulip
chest has a similar carving technique only
on the panels and the center panel is different (the sunflower) from the end panels (the
tulip). The stiles have black split turnings
attached to them, whereas rails have lines
cut into the length of the individual pieces.
The Hadley appears to be somewhat primitive and plainer when compared to the sunflower and tulip chest.*

18-6 *This Carver chair from Massachusetts is dated 1690–1710.* Courtesy of the Art Institute of Chicago.

the beginning of the eighteenth century, long after they were relegated to the attic in England. Of simple to complex construction, the simplest was the "borded chest" made of 6 large planks pegged or nailed together, whereas others are paneled. Two distinct types warrant consideration. The Hadley chests, named after the town of Hadley, Massachusetts, were made between 1675 and 1740 and over 120 have been recorded. They are distinguished by a top-opening chest with one or two drawers below. It is the surface decoration, however, that makes the Hadley chest unique. The entire front surface, including panels, drawers, rails, and stiles are covered with very flat carving of leaves, vines, and tulips painted red, black, shades of brown, or, infrequently, green. Incorporated in the design are the initials of the girls for whom they were made.

The *sunflower and tulip chests* (sometimes called tulip and aster) are more typically from Connecticut. These chests are constructed basically like the Hadley chest, but the surface decoration is different. The three panels are invariably carved in a flat, formally balanced design of tulips and sunflowers. The framing and drawer fronts are not carved but have ebonized split turnings and bosses that have been glued to the surface. The result is less flatness to the chest front and a more lively contrast of value with the grouped dark ebonized elements against the lighter background of oak.

The most common seating was provided by joined stools, similar to those found for several centuries in England. Their thick baluster legs are raked and joined by low stretchers and are 20 to 22 inches high, almost the height of today's small tables.

Armchairs were rare; seldom more than two or three were found even in the wealthiest seventeenth-century homes, but several types were in use. The turned chairs are the old familiar "stick" chair forms. There are two types, the Brewster and the Carver chairs. The Brewster chair is named for Elder William Brewster (1567–1644) and in addition to the heavy turned simple frame, has rows of spindles across the back *and* under the arms and seat. The

Carver chair, named after Governor John Carver (1576–1621), also has a heavy turned frame and spindles across the back but does *not* have spindles under the arms or seat. The back and front vertical supports or posts (sometimes as large as $2\frac{1}{2}$ inches in diameter) originally were topped by round balls that are now frequently missing. The seat is slightly sunken to hold a loose cushion.

Wainscot chairs are also found and differed little from earlier English versions, although there was less carved ornament and the individual components are slightly thicker in the American versions. The joiner was usually responsible for making these chairs, and, of course, the turner made the Brewster and Carver chairs.

Another chair that was popular in the colonies was the ladder-back or slat-back. Similar in basic form and construction to the other turned chairs, this chair had horizontal, slightly outwardly curved slats across the back instead of rows of spindles. Although the uprights are vertical, the slight curve of the slats permitted a little more comfort. These American slat-back chairs, despite their heavier appearance, are not far removed from the *chaise à capucine* of eighteenth-century France or the Shaker slat-back of the nineteenth century. This simple chair form has remained popular and may still be seen in many unfinished furniture and "country furniture" establishments.

Seventeenth-century tables were trestle, gateleg, or draw table types. Their heavy bases are constructed like the English types, but are less ornamented and their charm lies in their simple strength. The draw table with its heavy turned legs and floor stretchers was sometimes called a stretcher table; it was also listed in old records as a *long joined table*.

A new form of table, which appeared near the end of the century, is an American invention, believed to have originated in Connecticut. The top has two drop leaves and almost invariably is round or elliptical in shape when open (rectangular tops are known, however). Within the frame below the top is a single drawer. The baluster or vase turned legs are canted and braced by

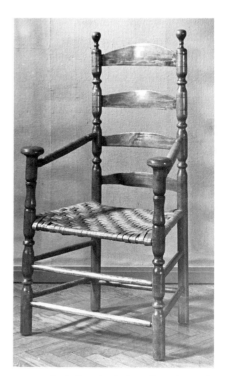

18-7 *The ladder-back chair has changed little through the ages. This 1690–1710 chair has more elaborately turned uprights than later versions, but its basic construction is the same.* Courtesy of the Art Institute of Chicago.

18-8 *Made of maple, pine, and oak, this small butterfly table is only 23 inches high and dates from the first half of the eighteenth century.* Courtesy of the Art Institute of Chicago.

matching low stretchers. The characteristic supports for the leaves give the table its name and grace. These are solid wood triangles with a decoratively shaped outer edge and pivot from the center of the side stretchers and the table top. They have somewhat the appearance of wings; thus, the *butterfly table.*

The inventories of the period indicate that almost every room had a large draped bed, but because bed frames at that time were crude and largely dependent upon the fabric for character, few beds have survived. The high-post bed no doubt existed, but there are only some low–post beds dating from the late seventeenth century extant. These are, as was the rule of American furniture at this time, more simply ornamented than the English models.

In the eighty years or so between the time the first Englishmen established permanent settlements on the coast of North America and the beginning of the eighteenth century, the level of comfort and sophistication experienced by the colonists had been raised to equal if not surpass that of England. The cities and towns had grown and prospered, and an affluent merchant class had emerged. Their elegant homes were furnished with the finest furniture, fabrics, and accessories that were available locally and abroad. The favored styles in England were being adopted sooner and were more closely copied than had previously been the rule. Oak was replaced by walnut and other more decorative woods. The Dutch-Anglo style that dominated English furniture design in the last years of the seventeenth century during the reign of William and Mary was freely blended with the older Jacobean style.

At the time the Hadley and sunflower chests were being made, chests of drawers were coming into more common usage, revealing the trend toward the William and Mary style of England. These three- or four-drawer chests resting upon flattened ball feet had small bronze drop handles instead of the earlier wrought-iron handles, and depended upon veneered surfaces and decorative moldings for interest. Chests of drawers were sometimes com-

18-9 *The William and Mary high chest, a chest of drawers supported on a framework of turned legs braced with curved, flat stretchers, is an important furniture form. Dating as early as 1660, this example was made about 1700.*

bined with a desk or bookcase top to create another important and architectural piece of furniture.

The innovation that was primarily responsible for the replacement of the chest was the William and Mary *highboy,* although that name has only been used since the nineteenth century. A more descriptive name is the *high chest,* for it is a chest of drawers resting on a multilegged high base. First appearing in England after 1660 and based somewhat upon Oriental prototypes, the high chest remained popular for over 125 years. The top section is a flat-topped chest of drawers, usually with four or five drawers, and a simple narrow cornice projects around the top edge. Although a rarity today, a pyramid-shaped set of shelves was often placed on top of the high chest to serve as a display stand for Oriental and Dutch ceramics. The base section, slightly wider than the top section, is equipped with one or two drawers and has a shaped skirt and usually six turned legs (five or even four are sometimes seen). These legs are distinctively shaped, a series of knobs and small disks above a large mushroom or inverted cup shape topping a long cone (trumpet) extending down to a knob. The foot is ball-shaped. Bracing the legs, just above the ball foot is a flat, but shaped, stretcher.

The construction of the high chest is the work of the cabinetmaker, not of the turner or joiner; the carcass and drawers are well made and, if veneered, it is well done. Strangely, the stand is less skillfully executed than the drawers and is an excellent illustration of how fashion can supplant or counter rational construction practices. The legs are in two parts, the bottom ball foot is a separate piece and has a dowel on the top that is inserted through a hole in the connecting stretcher board and into the end of the larger portion of the leg. The legs are attached and are not integral with the carcass of the base. The legs are simply inserted into holes of the relatively thin skirting. The instability resulting from this method of attachment is considerable and a high chest, if not retightened, may move two or three inches off center. Later, construction caught up with fashion and in Queen

18-10 *The six-legged support of the William and Mary high chest was replaced with cabriole legs early in the eighteenth century. Dating from 1725–1730, this walnut high chest reflects the Queen Anne style. The legs are no longer inserted into the skirting but are integral with the structure.* Courtesy of the St. Louis Art Museum.

Anne high chests a top extension of the leg is incorporated into the frame of the stand adding substantially to the structural sturdiness.

The eighteenth century was well into its second decade and the queen, Anne, was dead before the furniture style bearing her name reached the American colonies. The curve of the cabriole leg slowly replaced the vertical line of the turned supports found on William and Mary furniture, and the eighteenth-century Rococo spirit of England did not replace the Renaissance-Baroque style of the seventeenth century much before 1720–1725.

The furniture styles were welcomed because they were expressive of the striking socioeconomic changes taking place in the American colonies. The once almost forgotten outposts of civilization were fairly bursting with wealth and prestige by this time, and the commercial and shipping centers of Boston, Newport, New York, Philadelphia, and Charleston provided some of the richest and most comfortable surroundings available within the English sphere of influence. Communication and travel between these centers, which a few years before had been difficult if not impossible except by sea, was now fairly easy and swift. The Indians were slowly being pushed farther to the west and the whole eastern seaboard had been completely tamed into a civilized world, an English world.

The American Queen Anne chairs, sofas, settees, and tables are very similar to the Queen Anne styles of England, yet some differences do exist and should be noted. For example, the major material used remains walnut wood, but it is American black walnut and not English walnut. Santo Domingan mahogany was also an early favorite in Rhode Island and was used later in the rest of the Colonies, having been first imported around 1700. Other woods, white walnut or butternut, maple, and cherry were also frequently used. There were very few chair-back settees made in America, despite their popularity in England, although upholstered sofas were fairly common.

England had one main center of furniture production, London. Con-

18-11 *Made in Salem, Massachusetts, between 1750 and 1769, this superb example of a Queen Anne walnut high chest has an elegant simplicity. The slender cabriole legs, small pendants on the shaped skirt, the simple scallop shells, the sweeping broken pediment of the bonnet, the flame finials, the pierced brasses, and the figured walnut enhance rather than detract from the basic form of the piece.* Courtesy of Israel Sack, Inc., N.Y.C.

sequently, furniture that was made in outlying districts was almost always of less quality, skill, or style. Similar circumstances existed in France; Paris was the major center. In the American colonies this was not the case; there were several centers of furniture manufacture and each, although often exhibiting distinct regional characteristics as noted later, produced excellent and well-designed furniture. In fact, some of the finest eighteenth-century furniture extant was made in the colonies.[3] The quality of the craftsmanship, selection and integrity of the materials, and the total design concept was superb.

Of all the modifications in design that can be observed in the Queen Anne American style, none are as noteworthy as those affecting the high chest. The design of the American William and Mary high chest was essentially English, but during the first quarter of the eighteenth century the high chest assumed a distinctively American character and remained essentially in this form, except for minor variations, throughout the Queen Anne and following Chippendale style.

The Queen Anne high chest of drawers is one of the most distinguished individual pieces of American furniture and the striking elegance of its form in addition to the precision of its ornament, has seldom, if ever, been matched. The upper section has taken on more vertical movement despite the horizontal drawers. This is primarily the result of the important *scrolled broken pediment*, or *bonnet* and the one, two, or three skillfully executed finials that replaced the older horizontal cornice. The reverse curves of the bonnet superbly echo the four slender cabriole legs. An additional identifying feature and one that further marks the Rococo tendencies is the introduction of the "scalup" shell. There are two such shells, usually large and carved, applied to the center of the top and bottom drawers. No English style

[3] Up to the time of the American Revolution, several of the major cities of the British colonies exported furniture to other parts of North America and even to England. To give some idea of the extent of this trade, in 1769, according to shipping reports, 1,288 chairs, 27 bureau desks, and 102 tables were exported from Massachusetts alone.

18-12 *Matching the high chest in photograph 18-11, this lowboy is also of walnut.* Courtesy of Israel Sack, Inc., N.Y.C.

development is comparable to the American Queen Anne high chest and it must be considered uniquely American. Similar bonnets, finials, and applied shell ornaments were also added to chest-on-chests, and secretary desks creating, with the high chests, a family of furniture forms of matchless magnificence.

The differences that distinguish the furniture of one region from another can be easily discerned in a comparison of several Queen Anne high chests of drawers. The following listing of differences is not exhaustive, but is typical, and frequently can be applied to other types of furniture. The legs on Pennsylvania high chests are rather short and have a strong, clear curve, whereas those of New England are taller, thinner, and are noticeably straighter. The bonnets on Massachusetts high chests are higher and more curved in appearance than those of other regions, and on the skirts are pendants, a continuation of a decorative element once found on medieval and early New England architecture, but not ordinarily used on furniture at this time. The shells on Connecticut high chests are almost flat or merely an inlaid design, yet those from neighboring Rhode Island, especially Newport, are formed very sculpturally. In Boston, more than elsewhere, the art of Japanning reached its highest level and high chests and other pieces were decorated in this imitation of Oriental lacquer.

The base section of the high chest was often duplicated and used as a separate and matching bedroom piece. The *low boy* served as a *dressing table* when a standing mirror was placed upon it.

The influence of Chippendale's *Director* had little effect upon American cabinetmakers until after 1760, but shortly thereafter almost all furniture design "shifted" to Chippendale, and it is American Chippendale furniture rather than English that best illustrates Chippendale's designs. This is probably because the style that is now considered Chippendale was already in existence in England when the *Director* was published and most cabinet-makers were thoroughly familiar with its characteristics. It should also be noted again that Chippendale's primary purpose in publishing the *Director* was not as an aid for cabinetmakers. However, cabinetmakers in America were not familiar with the style and the *Director* was their principal source of ideas. Thus, excellent and almost exact three-dimensional translations of some of Chippendale's two-dimensional designs were made in America.

Mahogany was almost always the wood of the Chippendale style and it was usually solid wood rather than veneer, necessitated by the increase in carved ornament. Many of the forms that had been so wholeheartedly accepted during the Queen Anne period continued to be employed in the Chippendale period. The two distinctively American case pieces, the high chest and the dressing table (high boy and low boy), gained in ornamentation and elaborateness but their basic structure and outline are almost identical to the earlier examples. The splat-back chair of Queen Anne lost some of its height and took on the identifying yoke-shaped top rail of Chippendale before it acquired the pierced and carved splat. (The curved horseshoe seat of many Queen Anne chairs was retained and used on Chippendale chairs of New York.) The regional differences are as clear as before; as with Queen Anne furniture, it is often a relatively simple matter to identify the origin of Chippendale furniture.

Philadelphia, by the mideighteenth century the second-largest city in the English-speaking world, had a thriving furniture trade. Its importance as a trade and cultural center was reflected by the fact that a greater number of craftsmen lived there than in any other American city at the time. The period just prior to the American Revolution was one of political and economic tensions, but it was also one of tremendous craft and artistic activity throughout the colonies, particularly in Philadelphia, where some of the most renowned silversmiths, furniture-makers, and builders plied their crafts.[4]

[4] No fewer than 100 furniture craftsmen paraded in Philadelphia at the ratification of the Constitution in 1788.

18-13 *Philadelphia furniture is usually more vigorous in detail and ornament. These two matching pieces were made in Philadelphia at the same time the previous high chest and lowboy were made in Salem, Massachusetts. Although the Philadelphia pieces are considered "Chippendale" and the others "Queen Anne," the regional differences are very apparent. This high chest is 8 feet, 4½ inches high, perfectly scaled for the high ceilinged rooms of the eighteenth century.* Courtesy of the Art Institute of Chicago.

18-14 *Two Chippendale side chairs from Philadelphia (c. 1775). Courtesy of the Art Institute of Chicago.*

18-15 *A mahogany Chippendale chair probably from New England. Compare this chair with the two side chairs on page 455. Courtesy of the Art Institute of Chicago.*

The most striking characteristics of Philadelphia Chippendale furniture are the ample proportions; the scale is grander. There is a "gusto" about much of the furniture made in Philadelphia; that is, the curves are somewhat more generous, the ornament is richer, and the carving is particularly crisp and very Rococo in feeling. Naturalistic forms were favorites along with Gothic and Chinese elements as delineated in the *Director*. The exuberance of Philadelphia furniture is seen in the finely sculptured ball and claw feet, acanthus "grasses"[5] swirling across surfaces, and the free use of the shell motif. The straight-legged furniture seen in the *Director* was also used and is said to have been introduced to Philadelphia by Thomas Affleck (1740–1795), an English master cabinetmaker who emigrated to the New World about 1763. The leg, called Marlborough or Marlboro (the reason for the name is no longer known), is essentially a stocky square shaft terminating with a block at the floor.

Philadelphia case furniture has fluted quarter Doric columns at the angles, whereas Ionic and Corinthian capitals were preferred by Boston cabinetmakers. From the center shells on high chests and dressing tables are scrolls of acanthus grasses often filling the whole area surrounding the shell. Naturalistic vases of flowers and latticework below the scrolled pediments are frequently used and are carved with exquisite delicacy contrasting with the generous proportions of the forms.

Chippendale tables of Philadelphia are of many shapes and sizes, and serve many uses. There are rectangular card tables with folding tops, long narrow side tables, round or elliptical drop-leaf dining tables, square drop-leaf or "handkerchief" tables, small and tall kettle stands, and the ever present tea table. The tables are often carved so plastically that frequently the ornament might appear to be molded rather than carved if it were not for the crispness

---

[5]"Grasses" are very linear interpretations of the classical acanthus.

18-16 *A piecrust tea table dated 1760–1775. Made in Philadelphia, its pedestal support does not have the usual acanthus leaf carving, but the robust cabriole legs ending in ball and claw feet are typical.* Courtesy of the St. Louis Art Museum.

of execution. Whether cabriole or Marlborough, the leg surfaces are enriched with acanthus grasses, fretwork, or garlands. The piecrust tilt-top tea table made in Philadelphia is especially bold. The round top is edged with a raised and rippled molding of sensitive invention similar to the edges of trays made by the master silversmiths of the city. The "bird cage" below the top permits the top to tilt and seemingly releases the top from the pedestal. The design of the pedestal is indigenous to Philadelphia; the upper part is a short, squat, fluted Doric column below which is a rounded vase form often covered with acanthus carving. Three vigorous and robustly ornamented cabriole legs that end in superb ball and claw feet support the pedestal. The blending of styles and influences that is evident in this table is essential to Philadelphia Chippendale; the Rococo edge of the top and cabriole leg form, the classical Doric column and acanthus leaf ornament, and the Oriental vase form and ball and claw foot.

New York furniture has a heaviness that is not evident in Philadelphia furniture despite the latter's ample proportions, a heaviness that is reflected in the awkwardness of the larger ball and claw feet. The "freedom" expressed in Pennsylvania furniture is not apparent in New York furniture and the ornament is rather dated and uninspired. Many of the New York chairs have the tassel splat of English George II chairs (about 1740) and the carving is flatter and less vigorous.

Massachusetts Chippendale is light in scale and visual weight. It has a linear quality not found in either Philadelphia or New York furniture and is also smaller proportioned. Chairs were often upholstered to the frame rather than having a slipseat that was common elsewhere. Preferred case pieces were not the high chest and dressing table of the other Colonies, but rather were chest-on-chests and a new development, the *kneehole desk.* Blockfront construction, which is further discussed shortly, was also used. The pediments topping many of the chest-on-chests and secretaries are not scrolled

but are broken triangular pediments reflecting the Palladian influence in architecture.

Newport, Rhode Island, was one of America's most flourishing ports by 1750 and home for some of the wealthiest citizens in the colonies. The rich shipowners demanded the finest furniture for their homes and it was in Newport that some of the most original and accomplished furniture was produced. Moreover, in addition to the embellished furniture of the townsmen, a great deal of furniture of more simple design was made for export to the southern colonies and the islands of the Caribbean. Newport furniture was almost exclusively dark Santo Domingan mahogany, a natural choice because of the extensive trade with the West Indies.

The Newport Chippendale style originated and was brought to its magnificent fruition by the renowned Townsend-Goddard families. There were twenty-one members of these interrelated families associated with fine furniture and their work spans over a century. The most outstanding, however, was John Goddard (1723–1785), who was born in Massachusetts, the son of a "housewright." When he was about seventeen, his family moved to Newport and he and his younger brother James were apprenticed to Job Townsend (1699–1766), a Quaker cabinetmaker. The two brothers later married two of Job Townsend's daughters. By the 1760s, John Goddard was recognized as the leading cabinetmaker in Newport and together with his relatives had established the "Newport School" of furniture.

The Townsends and the Goddards made all manner of furniture but they are most noted for their case pieces and are credited with the development of the *blockfront.* Blockfront chest-on-chests, dressing tables, chests of drawers, kneehole desks, and clock cases have the characteristic two raised and one (center) lowered vertical panels that comprise the whole front of the piece. Although the projecting blocks can either be cut from a solid piece of wood or applied to the drawer fronts, it is their strong vertical visual movement

18-17 *The handsome detailing of this mahogany blockfront secretary bookcase attributed to John Goddard makes it a truly magnificent piece of American eighteenth-century furniture.* Courtesy, Museum of Fine Arts, Boston, M. and M. Karolik Collection.

that is the most pronounced design element. The secondary undulating cross movement is a beautiful counterpoint to this. The "swelled front" furniture, as Goddard called it, was not invented in Newport, but was adapted from Dutch forms derived from designs by André Charles Boulle. The blockfront was never popular in England, and, as developed in Newport, must be considered an American innovation of the latter half of the eighteenth century. Subsequently used in the other furniture-making centers, the blockfront never achieved the handsomely effective form that it did in Rhode Island.

The blockfronts are often embellished with large carved shells on each of the panels, (the two outer ones are convex and the center is concave). Reminiscent of Chippendale style, it is a marked change from the single concave shell seen on Queen Anne case pieces. These blockfront shells are stylized, almost to the point of abstraction, but are exceedingly rich in ornamental value and clearly enhance the three-dimensional quality of the front surface.

Goddard's ball and claw foot designs are singular because the talons are undercut and slightly separated from the ball. He also used bracket feet with a distinctive superimposed small scroll on many of his chests and secretaries. These short, stubby legs that have somewhat the appearance of cabriole legs are not exclusively Goddard's, however, as other family members used them too, but they do indicate a Newport origin.

The bonnets on Rhode Island case pieces are closed and are not just across the front but extend to the back. Having no cornice across the front that would create a division between the pediment and the chest portion, the verticality of the front plane is emphasized.

The masterful furniture of the Queen Anne and Chippendale styles was not the only furniture made in the colonies during the eighteenth century. Some of the most famous stick chairs ever devised were also made during

this period and their basic characteristics have been retained for more than three centuries. The Windsor chair[6] developed in England, although there are German chairs of similar style and date; nevertheless, some of the finest were produced in America.

The Windsor chair is a "turner's" chair; there is no true joining employed, for example, mortise and tenon. The chair is of the simplest construction; sticks are merely inserted in holes of the same diameter. Windsor construction has been used not only in chairs but also in settees, cradles, and beds.

Windsor chairs are identified by their thick saddle-shaped seats, splayed baluster and vase turned legs with H-stretchers, and slender spindle filled backs. There are several types and many variations of the Windsor chairs, but the *comb-back* and *hoop-* or *bow-back* are the most common. The comb-back is identified by a top rail supported by the spindles (not unlike a hair comb.) The bentwood hoop or bow into which are inserted the spindles represents the other type. The two types are sometimes combined.

The English Windsors have a central back splat that is often pierced in a wheel design. The seat and legs are thinner than in American models but the back spindles are usually somewhat thicker.

American Windsors were first made as early as 1725 in Philadelphia and by the 1760s were being made and exported (even to England) in large numbers.[7] They were also made in the other colonies and most of the surviving eighteenth-century Windsors date from the last quarter of the century.

The American Windsor is an admirable exercise in wood technology. It is

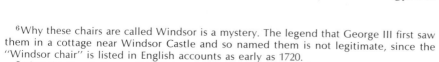

18-18   *A continuous bow-back Windsor armchair made in New York state about 1785. The vigorously turned legs and arm supports contrast with the slender spindles of the back.* Courtesy of the Art Institute of Chicago.

18-19   *The heavy construction and pierced back splat identify this armchair as an English Windsor.*

[6]Why these chairs are called Windsor is a mystery. The legend that George III first saw them in a cottage near Windsor Castle and so named them is not legitimate, since the "Windsor chair" is listed in English accounts as early as 1720.
[7]After the Revolutionary War the manufacture of Windsor chairs continued and in the 1790s, seventeen men specialized in Windsors in Philadelphia alone.

made of not one wood but of many, and the qualities of each are fully understood and exploited. For example, the legs and stretchers are usually maple because maple turns beautifully on the lathe and is extremely hard and strong. The seat is made of a softer wood, such as chestnut, pine, or tulip poplar, as it shapes easily into the thick saddle form. The spindles and bows are hickory or ash because these woods are wiry and can be easily bent. The chairs are made of green wood (with the exception of the spindles, which are seasoned), and as the wood dried the natural shrinkage tightened the many joints. Wood is strongest along its grain and the bending of the wood by steaming or soaking in water rather than by cutting a curve from a straight board provided additional strength to the chairs.

Windsor chairs are always painted; green was the most popular color although red and black were also used. The chairs were found in all kinds of places, from the humblest to the most elaborate homes,[8] in inns and taverns, and were the chairs used by the delegates to the Continental Congress, which met in 1778 in the State House of Pennsylvania (now Independence Hall) in Philadelphia.[9] Windsors were also used outside as garden chairs and because of their excellent construction and painted surfaces were able to withstand the weather quite well.

The furniture of settlers who were not of English origin is seldom of universal interest today, although it did exert regional influences for varying periods of time and, of course, is important locally. However, the German and Dutch immigrants who settled in south-central Pennsylvania did not assimilate the English styles, but continued to produce furniture that was reminiscent of their homeland. The influence upon later decoration, espe-

18-20 *Made in Rhode Island in about 1750, this comb-back Windsor armchair has been stripped of its original paint showing the maple, pine, and hickory wood from which the chair is fabricated. From the high comb-back a shawl was often hung to protect the sitter from drafts.* Courtesy of the Art Institute of Chicago.

[8] President Thomas Jefferson bought "3 dozen stick (Windsor) chairs, painted black with a yellow ring" for the president's house.
[9] One of these chairs survives (they were sold about 1814 after the capitol of Pennsylvania was moved to Harrisburg). It is a bowback Windsor made by Francis Trumble between 1775 and 1778.

18-21 *The Windsor chair, despite its distinctive form, did reflect changes in styles. This rod-back settee and bow-back side chair are both dated about 1800–1815 and, instead of baluster turned legs, they have legs, stretchers, and spindles turned to imitate bamboo, a design device that was popular about 1800 in England and America.* Left, Courtesy of the Art Institute of Chicago.

cially during the first half of the twentieth century, and its uniqueness does not allow this furniture to be ignored or merely labeled quaint. Some of the finest Pennsylvania-German furniture (incorrectly called Pennsylvania-Dutch) was made during the last half of the eighteenth century.

The forms of Pennsylvania-German furniture are not eighteenth century but are older and can be traced to an earlier age. Consequently, the exact date of construction is difficult to identify by form alone, but fortunately, dates are often incorporated into the decoration. The furniture is usually simple in construction and consists of chests, chairs, tables, beds, and *shranken* (wardrobes). The surface decoration rather than elaborate shapes gives distinction and interest to these pieces. What little carving was done is often shallow and seldom of artistic importance; it is, however, the brightly colored painted surfaces that are the most characteristic type of decorative embellishment. Flat surfaces are often marbled[10] or divided into panels. The panels have fanciful and decorative designs that are invariably quite stylized. Tulips and hearts were the favorites, and vases of vines, paired birds (distlefinks), unicorns (symbols of virginity), and pomegranates are everywhere, painted, carved, pierced, embroidered, cast, and molded. The widespread use of these designs is evident on furniture, cast iron, linens, pottery, wedding certificates, barns and other architecture, farm implements, household accessories, and even food.

The *dower* or *marriage* chest is a top-opening chest and one of the most common Pennsylvania-German pieces. It often consisted of simple plank construction, but in more elaborate examples, panel construction was used. It is almost invariably painted in formal, bright, stylized designs. The *shrank*, or *wardrobe*, is similar to the *kas* of the seventeenth-century Dutch settlements of New York. It is a large two-doored wardrobe of architectural proportions,

---

[10] A frequent method was to roll or twist a corncob over fresh paint of a color different from that underneath.

18-22 *Using plank construction of an earlier
time, the maker of this dower chest of the early
nineteenth century from Berks County, Pennsylvania, painted it to resemble panel construction.
The entire surface is stippled and grained to imitate
a decorative wood grain and the panels have unicorns, tulips, vases, and vines in their designs.*
Courtesy of the Art Institute of Chicago.

often with two or more drawers in the lower base, and a wide projecting cornice at the top. In addition to painted surfaces, the *shranken* are sometimes left with a natural surface but designs are inscribed into the wood and filled with wax inlay (beeswax and white lead). The result has the appearance of fine ivory inlay and is reminiscent of the certosina inlay of the Italian Renaissance.

The tables are chiefly massive trestle types and hold little additional interest. Chairs are wainscot and banister back types or a peasant form that is reminiscent of the back stools of late medieval times and the sgabello chairs of Italy. They are made of walnut and have simple square or octagonal plank seats and elaborately shaped slab backs, each with a small heart cutout. The legs are straight "sticks" inserted and wedged through the seat plank at a strong slant. There are no stretchers. This chair is the only chair in eighteenth-century America that is not of English origin.

The period following the American Revolution was not fraught with the strife that accompanied the French Revolution a few years later. It was instead a period of great energy; the new nation was busy establishing itself and the pride that permeated the whole country is reflected in its furniture. The first forty years of its existence are frequently referred to as the Federal period, ending about the time of the administration of President John Quincy Adams (1825–1829). The political climate of the new republic was constantly being compared to that of the ancient Roman and Greek governments, and it was inevitable that designers and craftsmen should begin to seek out classical motifs and detail to strengthen the similarity.

Few new stylistic influences came to America during the Revolutionary War, and the taste for classical elements developing in France and England was not displayed in the furniture. It was not until the war's end that the neoclassic furniture designs of the Louis XVI, Adam, Hepplewhite, and Sheraton styles were evident in America. The change was swift and throughout the major cities of the eastern seaboard, the furniture craftsmen began to discard the Rococo tendencies of Chippendale. The proportion of furniture became more slender and delicate and smoother surfaces began to appear again.

The Federal period can be divided into two parts for purposes of discussion. Early Federal design (1790–1815) shows influences from French and English neoclassical styles. Whereas Late Federal (1815–1825) is more akin to the Empire and Regency styles, the latter is discussed in the next chapter. The furniture of the French court was admired and freely adopted by American craftsmen. Jefferson, while ambassador to France (1784–1789), bought a large assortment of furniture, fabrics, and accessories and returned home with 86 crates of purchases. Most of these were shipped to Monticello, his home in Virginia, but some were sent to Philadelphia where he served for four years as secretary of state under President Washington. The effect of this and other imported French furniture upon Philadelphia furniture cannot be ignored. In contrast to furniture designers in the other Colonial cities, those in Philadelphia had always been strongly influenced by French design, having used the French volute and shell motifs more during the Rococo styles, and now during the Federal period preferred painted furniture in the French manner. However, English designs, the recent hostilities notwithstanding, dominated the Early Federal period.

Despite the fact that the influence of the brothers Adam had waned by this time in England and was never strong in America, Adamesque ornament was beautifully conceived and executed by the Salem, Massachusetts, woodcarver Samuel McIntire. The son of a joiner, McIntire is noted more for his buildings than his furniture, but he did produce some pieces and is known to have also executed the carving on the work of others. His mantels and interior architectural detail, although not exactly furniture, do exhibit his clear concept of the delicate linear qualities of Adam. McIntire did not slavishly copy Adam design, however, as he did not use solely classical elements. What is so American and unique about McIntire's detail and crisp

18-23 *Samuel McIntire, noted for his fine houses, designed and executed some of the finest carved furniture and architectural accessories in the Federal period. This pine mantle from Peabody, Massachusetts (1813), has the typical McIntire delicate detail. The overmantle mirror frame is gilded with painted medallions and is based upon Sheraton designs introduced shortly after 1800.* Courtesy of the Art Institute of Chicago.

18-24 *The exposed frame and straight lines of this sofa reflect the influence of Hepplewhite and Sheraton. Made just before 1800 by Duncan Phyfe, America's leading Federal cabinetmaker, in New York, it shows many of the neoclassic characteristics that were also being incorporated in furniture in France and England.* Courtesy of the St. Louis Art Museum.

carving is that the subjects are native American plants rather than European.

It is principally the influence of Hepplewhite and Sheraton, rather than Adam, that can be seen throughout the Early Federal period. Hepplewhite's influence occurred a little sooner than Sheraton's but many times designs by both men were combined in a single piece. The straight legs, tapered and square in section; veneered surfaces with inlay; shield, heart, and oval chair backs; and flared bracket leg on case pieces are all typical Hepplewhite. Sheraton furniture is characterized by the turned, reeded straight leg; chairs and sofas with rectangular backs; and lighter woods.

Centers of manufacture for Federal furniture remained approximately the same as those earlier in the century, but the leadership and the style setting emphasis changed. New York became the major producer of furniture after 1800 and a new center developed in Baltimore, Maryland. A newcomer to the furniture scene, Baltimore craftsmen produced some of the finest Federal furniture. The city doubled in population shortly after the war because of its burgeoning shipping industry. Traditionally, Philadelphia had served to satisfy Baltimore's furniture needs, but at this time, Baltimore craftsmen began to develop superb Hepplewhite- and Sheraton-inspired designs of their own. This furniture is noted for its elegant veneers[11] ornamented with marquetry and inlay and with oval-shaped glass panels. Seldom used elsewhere, these panels were decorated with a technique known as *verre églomisé*, reverse glass painting depicting classical figures against a black background. Baltimore furniture has an elegance and restraint that was unrivaled in the Federal period.

Aside from the style change Early Federal exhibits several innovations. The major one, of course, was the sideboard, which was not known in the United

[11] The veneered surfaces of many Baltimore case pieces are almost always divided into areas defined by fine inlaid lines, within which are large ovals surrounded by mitered veneer of contrasting color or value.

18-25 *This superb example of a Baltimore sideboard in the Hepplewhite style (1795) combines mahogany and satinwood veneers. The delicate lines, marquetry designs in ellipitical shapes, and slender tapering legs are characteristic of these smooth-surfaced masterpieces. The heritage of the side table and two separate end pedestals is still evident in the design.* Courtesy of the Virginia Museum of Fine Arts.

18-26 *A detail of an American Hepplewhite sideboard. The grain pattern of the veneers is subtly used to enhance the surface rather than carved ornament.*

States until this period and is essentially the English sideboard as developed by Hepplewhite. Dining tables also assumed a new form. They are sectional, composed of two or three separate units, each with a central supporting pedestal. A three-part table contains a center section with a rectangular drop-leaf top, and the top of each end section has one semicircular leaf and the other rectangular. (If the table consists of two parts, the center section is omitted.) These end sections were often used as side tables when not needed but could be combined with the center section in several ways to provide the required amount of table surface.

The imposing chest-on-chest, high chest, and dressing table lost favor in the Federal period and were soon replaced by a lower chest of drawers with a fixed mirror above. This design originated with Sheraton and remained a favorite throughout the nineteenth and early twentieth centuries. It is the predecessor of the bureau of the Victorian period.

Early Federal furniture, as did contemporary furniture in England, relied upon the veneered surface for its decorative emphasis. Satinwood, mahogany, and bird's-eye maple were the principal woods used in America. Carving was at a minimum and except for that of McIntire is seldom of consequence. Chair backs were elaborately cut out and these designs were augmented by painted or inlaid detail rather than by sculptural carving.

The regional differences that were so evident before the Revolution were almost negligible by the beginning of the nineteenth century. The improved communication systems between cities eliminated the development of isolated characteristics. What does mark one piece from another are the design and decorative preferences of individual furniture craftsmen and these are invariably more subtle than regional differences. The curve of a line or the shape of a small detail may be all that identifies a particular piece as to its origin or maker.

The last years of the eighteenth century ushered in the phenomena of industrialization. The time-honored method of the master craftsman and his group of skilled assistants working on each object to completion, gently and subtly adjusting the design concept to best fit the materials and form, was soon to be replaced by the machine and accompanying mass-production methods. Even at this time, early in the age of mechanization, some parts were beginning to be mass-produced for later assembly. Only a few years would elapse before furniture would no longer be the product of the crafts-man-designer, but of the machine. Furniture design would be critically affected by this profound development.

Admirably sited, these clus-
tered houses were designed by
Wilmsen, Endicott, Greene,
Bernhard, and Associates.
Their shingled shed roofs re-
peat the sawtooth forms of the
trees. Courtesy of Olympic
Stain, A division of Comerco,
Inc.

The house at Philipsburg Manor in
North Tarrytown, New York (c.
1683), has two kitchens, one above
the other. This room, "The Upper
Kitchen" as it was called in a 1750
inventory, was used for dining as
well as preparing some food because there was no separate dining
room in the house. The cupboard on
the left (c. 1690) is still painted
gray-blue, a favorite color in the
Hudson valley. The chandelier is
dated 1722 and probably came
from Holland.

Reflecting the more informal life styles
prevalent today, carpeted platforms and several long, loose and colorful tubes filled with
polyurethane foam are the only "furniture"
in the entrance lounge of the University
Center, Indiana State University in Evans-
ville, Indiana. IDS, Incorporated, the interior
designers of the space, has relied on strong
color, graphics and recurring shapes to
furnish and set the mood of the room.
Photograph courtesy of IDS, Incorporated.

This mahogany side table was made in Philadelphia
about 1760-1775 and is especially rich in its decoration.
The gadrooning along the lower edge of the apron
and the cabriole legs with carved acanthus leaves
extending from the knees almost to the ball and claw
feet are unusual features. The top is gray King of
Prussia Marble. The table measures 35 inches high,
51¾ inches wide and 19¼ inches deep. Photograph
courtesy of Harry F. Breen.

19 Furniture: American and European After 1800

American furniture was starting to reflect the trend toward more pure classical forms as had the furniture in France and England by the time the nineteenth century began. By 1800, the stylistic center of furniture design was New York City, which had replaced Philadelphia. Two of the finest furniture-makers of the period established shops in New York City; Duncan Phyfe who arrived there in 1792 and Charles-Honoré Lannuier who arrived in 1803.

Duncan Phyfe, probably the best-known name of any American cabinet-maker in the Late Federal period or in any period, for that matter, was a Scotsman.[1] First setting up shop on Broad Street, in 1795 he moved to Partition Street where his shop prospered—eventually employing over one hundred craftsmen—until he retired in 1847. He was not only an excellent craftsman but evidently an astute businessman since at the time of his death in 1854, he was worth almost $500,000. Phyfe's long career spanned several styles; he started with fairly accurate interpretations of Hepplewhite and Sheraton, but soon became the leader in Directoire, Empire, and Regency styles. Later, his shop produced furniture of increased opulence, and before he retired, still keeping abreast of fashion, Duncan Phyfe was making Rococo revival and the other ornate styles of the midcentury. Nevertheless, the style for which he is best remembered is the Regency-Empire.

Duncan Phyfe is not considered to be a master innovator; his designs are not especially new or different, but he did evolve a highly personal style during the first years of the nineteenth century. His craftsmanship was superb; his handsome furniture is extremely well constructed, beautifully veneered, and skillfully carved, and the ornamental fittings (he is noted for

---

[1] Duncan Fife was born in 1768 and came to America in 1783–1784 with his family (his father was also a cabinetmaker) settling in Albany, New York. By 1792, he was living in New York City and had changed the spelling of his name from Fife to Phyfe, apparently to imply a French heritage.

19-1 *The trend toward more classical forms was reflected not only in early nineteenth-century architecture and furniture, but wearing apparel as well. This simple, high-waisted, white cotton dress was worn in Rhode Island in about 1810 and copies the classically inspired clothing styles of Napoleon's court.*

19-2 *Mirrors became increasingly important accessories after 1800 and this girandole, topped by the popular American eagle, is carved and gilded wood. The table beneath is mahogany with a white marble top. The four legs, modified cabriole, end in bronze feet and are lifted from the floor by small metal casters.* Courtesy of the St. Louis Art Museum.

19-3 *Chairs were often based upon the Greek* klismos *form. This painted chair from New York state is obviously such a chair.* Courtesy of the St. Louis Art Museum.

the fineness of the metal claw foot-tips on table legs) are superior. His furniture stands well beside the work of French and English master furniture craftsmen of the period.

The shop of Phyfe produced a large amount of furniture, far more than any of his contemporaries, and it is Phyfe who must be acknowledged as one of the founders of the American industrial tradition. He made fine furniture not only for the select few but for the public in general.

Charles-Honoré Lannuier (1779–1819) was French and brought the Empire style to the New World. By the time of his arrival in New York in 1803, Lannuier was thoroughly familiar with the French Empire style and it is believed that he had seen the work of Percier and Fontaine before he left France. His shop was soon engaged in making furniture for some of the most influential and wealthiest clients in the United States. His furniture is more elaborate and exhibits an originality that Phyfe's sometimes lacked. Lannuier's furniture is more closely allied to French styles than to English and his pieces often have imported metal mounts applied to their surfaces (a continuation of French Rococo and neoclassic tradition). Unfortunately, few examples of Lannuier's superior furniture are available today, principally because of the original limited quantity (he died when he was 40 years old and had only been in New York about sixteen years).

The other master craftsmen in New York and other major cities of the eastern seaboard were all producing furniture of excellent quality and style. The continuing improvement in communication had diminished the stylistic time lag between Europe and America. Where once there had been ten or twenty years, now there was only a matter of months before similar styles and decorative elements were being utilized on both sides of the Atlantic.

The furniture of the first twenty or thirty years of the nineteenth century is similar to that already discussed under French Empire and English Regency. The chairs were often versions of the Greek *klismos* and the Roman *curule*. Duncan Phyfe and other craftsmen produced chairs with saber legs and

19-4 *A splendid sofa table (c. 1827–1829) of rosewood veneer on white pine, marble, and gilt. The classically inspired designs are painted rather than marquetry or applied bronze mounts. Note how little carving is found on this table.* Courtesy of the St. Louis Art Museum.

rolled backs that are very similar to the popular Trafalgar chair in England. (Phyfe used the saber leg as early as 1807.)

The feet of tables, sofas, chests, chairs, and all manner of furniture that was not too large usually ended with cast bronze animal feet to which small casters were attached. The casters raise the heavy furniture off the floor slightly and give it a strange and incongruous appearance.

All forms and details were becoming increasingly heavy and massive as the years passed. Sofas possessed rolled ends, often transformed by carved detail into cornucopiae or dolphins. The asymmetrical couch form with rolled ends of unequal height and a scrolled half-back was also popular; its design is based both upon the "grecian squab"[2] illustrated in Sheraton's *Cabinet Dictionary* of 1803 and upon the Roman banquet couch. These couches are sometimes elaborately carved and ornamented with bronze mounts or with stenciled designs in their imitation.

The bases of dining tables are heavier and are often a single pedestal or column supported by four animal legs ("pillar and claw"). *Pier tables*[3] of elaborate design often have mirrored back surfaces beneath the tabletop and were very popular. They were often made in pairs with matching veneers and bronze mounts.

Sideboards, bookcases, and desks became almost ponderous in appearance as the long, slender legs of Hepplewhite and Sheraton were replaced by cabinets with short animal feet. The large veneered surfaces exhibited beautifully matched veneers that were chosen for their rich markings; however, the delicate inlay and stringing that were favored only a few

[2] These couches had a loose padded mattress or "squab" placed on them to increase their comfort.
[3] The pier table was originally placed between windows or against a "pier," the structural support of the building. A *pier glass* (a long mirror) was usually hung above the pier table, similarly to the manner in which console tables were used in France. Later, the pier table and glass were placed elsewhere.

19-5 *An original Hitchcock chair with an elaborate center horizontal back slat in the shape of two cornucopiae, vegetables, fruit, and acanthus leaves.* Courtesy of the Virginia Museum of Fine Arts, Richmond.

years before were no longer utilized to separate one panel of veneer from another, but rather small, smooth columns or narrow reeded panels were used.

Beds were sleigh-or boat-shaped and placed against the wall with handings suspended from a round tester in the manner of the French. These beds were often decorated like the sofas and couches, but because of their placement were only ornamented on one side.

During the Late Federal period painted furniture increased in popularity. Echoing the Empire style, colors were usually black or "grained" in a dark color and then enriched with gold paint. By far, the favorite individual furniture type was the painted "fancy chair." Based upon late Sheraton designs, these slender chairs are presently identified as Hitchcock. True Hitchcock chairs were made by Lambert Hitchcock (1795–1852) in Connecticut,[4] although similar chairs were made in New York, Ohio, and other states.

Hitchcock chairs are constructed of both turned and flat shaped parts with some of the turned components being partially reshaped after their initial forming on the lathe. The seats are usually made of woven cane or rush. These chairs are made of maple and hickory and are either painted black or a dark reddish brown and then lightly "grained" to simulate tortoiseshell or rosewood. The turned portions are frequently banded with gold paint, but what is perhaps the most distinctive characteristic of the Hitchcock is the stenciled designs of fruit and leaves, cornucopiae, arrows, flowers and eagles in gold and bronze powders on the flat surfaces of the top rail, horizontal back splat, back uprights, and chair seat front.

Hitchcock's production methods are as important as the form of his chairs. He was one of the first to employ production-line methods in the construc-

[4]Lambert Hitchcock established a factory first in Barkhamsted (1818), then in Hitchcockville (1823), (now Riverton), and finally in Unionville (1841).

19-6 *The Hitchcock chair is based upon an earlier Sheraton "fancy" chair form. The chair on the right is an authentic reproduction of a popular Hitchcock model. With the exception of the shaped back slat, note how similar all the component parts of this chair are to those forming the chair in illustration 19-5. The chair on the left (c. 1830), however, is an unknown chairmaker's attempt to copy the Hitchcock chair. Not having a lathe or jigsaw, he shaped each part by hand to approximate the desired effect. The solid slab seat is reminiscent of the earlier Windsor chair. The chair is made of several woods and was painted at one time.*

tion of these fancy chairs.[5] The individual parts were mass-produced and being identical could be either assembled at the factory or shipped knocked down and put together by the purchaser. The painting and stenciling were done by nearby craftsmen as a "cottage industry."

Stenciled designs shaded with bronze powders were often utilized in the United States to enrich the surface of many kinds of painted and veneered furniture.[6] Even the more expensive and elaborately conceived American pieces often had complicated stencil decoration incorporating several shades of powders. These were freely intermixed with attached three-dimensional bronze mounts. The visual interplay between the flat shaded designs and the fully modeled mounts added variety and interest to the massive and often box-like forms.

Although Hitchcock mass-produced chairs of good quality, he was by no means the first indication of industrialized manufacturing processes. What had started in France a century before when waterpowered textile looms were introduced was now a full-fledged revolution, an industrial revolution. The first changes were in textile production,[7] but by the latter half of the

19-7 *The rich stenciled and painted designs that decorate the surfaces of most Hitchcock chairs are usually based upon classical motifs. This back detail of the chair in photograph 19-6 (right) clearly shows how the different bronze powders were shaded as they were rubbed through stencils, a relatively simple technique, but especially compatible with the general forms of the chair.*

[5] At peak production, Hitchcock made about 15,000 chairs a year or about fifty a day. A bill dated October 9, 1829, lists nine chairs @ $1.50 each or $13.50.

[6] One of New York's finest furniture painters was William Marcy Tweed (1823–1878). An apprentice in his father's shop when he was eleven years old, he later inherited his father's thriving business, which made furniture, mostly chairs, in the late Empire style. The Tweed firm had a large export business and sent furniture as far away as Egypt and Brazil with thousands of Tweed's Boston rockers being sent to Turkey. Tweed was noted for his fine use of gold leaf and mother of pearl decorations. However in 1857, at the age of thirty-four, he gave up his furniture business and entered politics, and eventually he became the infamous "Boss" Tweed of New York City's Tammany Hall.

[7] The *flying shuttle* was invented by John Kay in 1733; the *spinning jenny* by James Hargreaves in 1770; *water operated roller spinning frame* by Sir Richard Arkwright in 1769–1775; the *power loom* by Edmund Cartwright in 1785 (all Englishmen); and, of course, the American invention of the *cotton gin* by Eli Whitney in 1793.

19-8 *A large sofa based upon the popular
Empire lines. The flat wood surfaces are
covered with veneer and the carved decoration appears applied rather than integral to
the frame. A patriotic shield nestles beneath
the rose and "C" curve on the back crest.*

eighteenth century new methods of smelting iron were being widely used.
James Watt's invention of the steam engine (1769) made waterpower no
longer necessary and factories were no longer tied to rapid or falling water, or
even to rivers.

The shift from farm to city and the rapid increase in population in Europe
and the United States in the early nineteenth century as discussed in Chapter
4 caused more than congestion and deplorable conditions; there was also an
increased demand for furniture. The newly rich were insistent upon furniture
that would reflect their newly attained status in life. The less fortunate
needed the cheapest furniture they could find, and consequently by 1830,
with the aid of machine production, few pieces of furniture were being
completely handmade. Products that had once been produced slowly by the
inch or by the single object by master craftsmen were now being spewed
forth by the yard or by the hundred by unskilled labor tending machines.

The furniture resulting from the merging of the social revolution with the
industrial revolution sometimes defies description, but several generalities
can be made.

1. The differences and peculiarities of the individual pieces of raw materials
    naturally could not be considered by the machine when making identical
    components. Consequently, knots, crossgrains, flaws, and the like in
    wood, for example, were shaped without difficulty, but the machine often
    produced parts that were inferior.
2. To overshadow competition, manufacturers produced objects of unbeliev-
    able proportions, details, and embellishments. There seemed to be little
    that machines could *not* do, quicker, easier, and, of course, cheaper, than
    the craftsmen of past times. However, elaborate ornament often hid poor
    construction.
3. The new middle class demanded symbols of success and body comfort
    was their primary goal. This search for comfort resulted in *overstuffed*

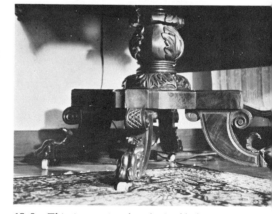

19-9 *This impressive drop-leaf table has crisp leaf carving on its vase-shaped pedestal. The four curved legs end in lion feet topped by an acanthus leaf that curls back—a distinctive feature seen on some furniture dating about 1825–1830.*

furniture of fantastic design and opulence. The eighteenth century has often been called *magnificent* but the word that best describes the nineteenth century is *comfortable*.

4. The machine, for all of its bad connotations, did encourage development of experimental techniques, forms, and materials; that is, new furniture. Although much of the furniture of the nineteenth century appears to be based upon past styles, the furniture does incorporate many new and inventive ideas and methods of manufacture.

5. Until the nineteenth century, furniture styles were fairly consistent, either developing out of a former style or being influenced by an individual or event. But, more importantly, furniture styles were almost always singular, and except for transitional periods, only one style existed at a time. During the nineteenth century, the variety of furniture styles were overwhelming and not only did many styles exist concurrently but elements from different styles were frequently combined in one piece of furniture.

Before becoming too involved in the many ornate and historically derivative styles of machine-made furniture of the nineteenth century, attention is directed toward a parallel development of furniture design that is significant. Sir Thomas More coined the word "utopia" (Greek *ou* and *topos*, or "no place") in the early 1500s. America, or what had been the British Colonies, became the Utopia or "promised land" after the American Revolution. Over 100,000 people—men, women, and children—immigrated, seeking political and religious freedom, cheap land, the prospect of riches through hard work, and certainly, a new life. Of these immigrants, no group was more unique or remained as steadfast and constant to their beliefs than the Shakers.

The official name for the Shakers was The United Society of Believers in Christ's Second Appearing. However, they are usually referred to as Shakers, a name attributed to their frenzied dancing during their religious services. The Shakers developed in Manchester, England, in the mideighteenth

19-10 *A Shaker rocking chair with a seat of woven webbing (c. 1850).*

century. Anne Lee joined the group in 1758 and became its head in 1770. Teaching a gospel of singleness and celibacy, Mother Anne, as she was called, came to New York in 1774 with eight followers. Two years later she settled near Albany, New York, and by 1780 hundreds were being converted and the sect prospered. By the time of the Civil War, 6,000 Shakers were living in nineteen communities throughout the eastern part of the United States.

The architecture of the Shakers[8] is of considerable interest, although it has not appreciably influenced twentieth-century architecture. Since the Shakers lived in a communal setting, strict discipline was necessary for celibacy and communism. The buildings had two entrances, stairways, sleeping quarters, dining tables, in fact, almost two of everything, one for the men and one for the women. The interiors were sparse, clean, and extremely well ordered.

The Shakers displayed great ingenuity when designing architecture, furniture, and products of all descriptions. Being economical, they developed designs of elegant simplicity, and always of superb craftsmanship. In 1824, a Shaker said, "That is best which works best" (a concept very similar to that expressed a hundred years later at the Bauhaus in Germany). The high standard of excellence of all the Shaker products generated a ready market outside the Shaker community.

No Shaker craft exhibits better the truthful simplicity that is inherent in all Shaker designs than does the cast-iron stove. This almost pure form expresses the material, processes, and function so well that after 150 years it is still considered to be one of the best designed functional objects ever made. And it was a product of an industrialized society; the Shakers were among the first to use mass-production techniques in the United States.

[8] The round barns of the Shakers were their most notable architectural design. Built in the side of a hill, these barns could be entered at different levels. Hay was stored at the top and could be dropped down, through a center shaft, where it was easily available to feed the animals on the lower levels.

19-11 *The success of the design of this massive French Restauration chest of drawers (c. 1840) depends on the use of large sheets of figured veneers on flat and bandsawed surfaces.*

Shaker furniture is characterized by its functional design; each piece reflects its use and a fine sense of materials. There are no superficial ornaments or embellishments. Several of the colonies were more engaged in furniture production than others, but Shakers wherever they lived all produced pieces of exceptional purity of design that is much admired today. Their slim chairs, for example, were lightweight ladder-backs with rush seats. Some were low enough to slide under the tables when not in use and others were hung from the rows of pegs that encircled every room about 6 feet above the floor. Walnut and cherry were used for the best pieces, but butternut (white walnut), maple ash, pine, poplar, and oak were also used. Walnut and cherry were usually left natural, but the other woods were sometimes painted or stained red or blue or "Shaker mustard."

The major portion of the nineteenth century is within the reign of Queen Victoria of Great Britain (1837–1901). Many authorities and laymen justly call this the Victorian period, and, of course, it is the Age of Victoria in England; her impact on the United States was also considerable. However, so many styles and influences are found in the furniture produced during this time that it is unwise and meaningless to label all of the furniture of this period "Victorian." No specific period name is therefore, used; instead, the various styles, technical and material developments, and designer innovations are discussed separately. It must be remembered, however, that many of these styles were used concurrently, often with reckless abandon, and if one modifier must be applied to the period coinciding with the reign of Queen Victoria, it would have to be *eclectic.*

The development of new machines during this period was often reflected in the design of the furniture. For example, the *circular saw* existed in the latter part of the eighteenth century, but came into increasing use between 1830 and 1850. (The Shakers were known to have been using such a saw by 1821.) The circular saw not only cuts lumber easier but also permits the production of larger and thinner sheets of veneer. Secondly, the *band saw* was

19-12 *The flat surfaces of the scrolled supports, pedestal, apron, and top of this center table are all covered with beautiful veneer.*

19-13 *Many times furniture is not just one style. This secretary bookcase (c. 1840) is such a transitional piece. The bottom is French Restauration with its large scrolled veneered supports, but the upper part has pointed arches that herald the coming Gothic revival style.*

patented in England in 1808, and although not really perfected until about 1850, the earlier band saw did make curved cuts in planks and boards with less difficulty than the previous methods of shaping wood. These two inventions coupled with the strong classical tradition existing in the early nineteenth century caused furniture to assume another form after 1830.

The new style, called French Restauration after the period in France when the monarchy was briefly restored, has lost none of the massiveness of the Empire style from which it developed. However, practically all ornamentation has been removed. The carcasses of the case pieces are invariably made of softwood surfaced entirely with smooth, flat sheets of figured mahogany veneer. Simple "C" and "S" shapes serve as supports. Continuing in popularity until the 1850s, the whole style of French Restauration furniture in America appears to have been cut from thick lumber with a band saw into massive and rather clumsy "C" and "S" scrolls and panels, smoothly veneered on all sides, and then assembled into the required piece. If not designed by a master designer, the furniture is often awkward in appearance, and, although still definitely classical in derivation, it is far from the delicate French neoclassic and English Hepplewhite and early Sheraton designs made forty or fifty years before.

The ability of machines to reproduce carvings in unlimited amounts permitted more ornate designs to be manufactured. Not required on the massive and simple forms of French Restauration furniture, elaborate ornamentation was desirable for the other "revival styles."

Shortly after 1830 there began the period of "revivals." Seldom was a furniture style of the past not resurrected during the nineteenth century and then used in strange and wondrous ways, sometimes stretching the original design almost beyond recognition. The exceptional variety of architectural styles discussed in Chapter 12 was also reflected in the furniture, and with the remarkable and expanding ability of machines to carve, shape, stamp,

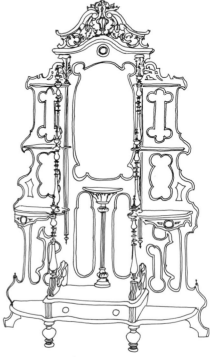

and emboss, as well as to make mortise and tenon and other furniture-making joints, an abundance of furniture of diverse quality was produced with acres of ornament derived from whatever influence or inspiration the pattern maker desired.

The first of the "revival" styles was based upon Gothic architecture. The Gothic revival furniture had little in common with actual medieval furniture just as much of the Gothic revival architecture had little in common with medieval architecture. The furniture was more akin to the forms that were popular during the immediately preceding fifty years.[9] Much of this furniture is delicate and reminiscent of neoclassic furniture forms except all decorative elements are based upon Gothic rather than classical architectural details. A support that might be derived from a classical column is instead a Gothic clustered pier. Chair backs and cabinet fronts are ornamented with tracery designs. Crockets, finials, trefoil and quatrefoil forms, rose window shapes, and, above all, pointed arches are everywhere. Turned components and jigsawed fretwork were often incorporated into the designs of Gothic revival furniture.

Perhaps no furniture form was as "natural" to the Gothic revival style as was the *whatnot*. This set of display shelves was first introduced near the turn of the century and was rather small. As the century progressed so did the size and ornateness of the whatnot. The name, first coined about 1810, was partially replaced by the French term *étagère* after 1850. The delicate structure and many shelves of the whatnot or étagère were an ideal place to develop fanciful Gothic Revival designs.

So many stylistic and technical developments originated during the nine-

19-14 *A combination of Gothic, Rococo, and classical decorative elements are combined in this grand étagère made during the last half of the nineteenth century.*

---

[9]The medieval spirit was never quite dead in England and "Gothic" furniture was designed by Chippendale and published in his *Director.* His designs were forerunners of the nineteenth-century Gothic revival style of England and America.

19-15 *The scroll saw provided the ornament of this Gothic revival chair. Of walnut, the back is a single plank.*

teenth century that it is no longer possible to follow a single design direction. Yet there is an essence, a quality, a "thread" or continuity that does bring the design of the period together. Perhaps this analogy is appropriate. If each style, each technical innovation, each new material were considered to be a yarn or filament of a different texture or color, it follows that the fabric woven with these yarns would be the *design climate* of the nineteenth century. The periodic introduction of new yarns (that is, new inventions) or the dropping of old ones (style derivations) increases the variety and interest of the textile being woven. Furthermore, a good textile, as any good design, should become an entity in itself, and not remain just a collection of separate yarns or elements. So it is with the furniture of the nineteenth century. Even though the isolation of the styles and new methods of construction of this furniture are considered necessary for purposes of this discussion, all the furniture styles, techniques, and so forth did interweave into a rich and exciting whole of great vitality, and today, almost a hundred years later, critics are becoming increasingly aware of this vigor exhibited in nineteenth-century design and are no longer considering it to be a deplorable hodge-podge of little import.

One invention that profoundly influenced seating furniture design was the coil spring, patented by Samuel Pratt of London in 1828. It revolutionized seating and, in turn, physical attitudes. Prior to this time, chairs were padded with various materials, such as wool, cotton, feathers, and curled horsehair, to give a modicum of comfort. The coil spring provided a softness that was almost beyond imagination and its acceptance was immediate. Chair designs had to be altered to accept the coil springs. Proportions were changed as legs became shorter, seats thicker and also deeper, and the back less vertical. The "lounge chair" evolved. The high seated, vertical backed chair that had been universal since antiquity and in which the sitter sat upright was replaced by a chair of more comfort in which the occupant sat at a slant and in an attitude

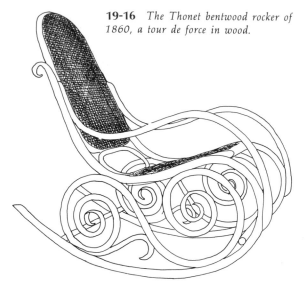

19-16 *The Thonet bentwood rocker of 1860, a tour de force in wood.*

19-17 *The Viennese café chair, the most famous bentwood chair.*

of less formality. Later in the century, these lounge chairs developed into large, tufted affairs called Grandfather chairs.[10]

Curved forms had always been a problem in furniture making. It was discovered in ancient times that wood could be bent with the aid of heat and moisture. The Greeks are believed to have used bentwood in the *klismos*, for example. However, it was not until the 1850s that techniques for bending wooden rods were perfected. Michael Thonet (1796–1871), an Austrian and the son of a cabinetmaker, began experimenting with steam and pressure to bend laminated wood into furniture components as early as 1830. His furniture proved to be strong and economical. By using bentwood for curved forms, the grain runs the length of the piece, and lacking any crossgrain, is extremely strong. Being a completely machine-made, mass-produced product, there was little need for highly skilled craftsmen, so that bentwood furniture could be produced with less cost. Despite these advantages, Thonet was bankrupt by the time he was in his midforties, when he left his hometown of Boppard-am-Rhein for Vienna. Starting again, Thonet developed a method of bending beech[11] rods into simple and complex forms. Although his chairs have somewhat Rococo forms, they consist of few individual parts; for example, his famous Viennese Café chair (1860) has but seven parts.

Thonet shipped his chairs in pieces and they were assembled at their destinations with glue and screws. Factories were soon established in Poland, England, Germany, and in the United States (a New York retail store opened

[10] The term *grandfather* was first applied to tall clocks after 1878 when a poem "My Grandfather's Clock" was published. Later it was applied to chairs.

[11] Beechwood is extremely elastic, has a close, parallel grain, and does not tend to split. Thonet, in partnership with his five sons, established a factory at Koritschan in 1853 because of its proximity to large beech forests. The Thonet Company later planted large stands of beech trees in the area to guarantee a good supply of the necessary wood. Some of these matured forests were partially destroyed during World War II.

19-18 *Several versions of this sofa (c. 1850) by John Belter exist. An elaborate confection of roses, cornucopiae, leaves, vines, acorns, and fruit, this one is gilded rosewood, although others were left the natural color of the wood. Called the "arabasket" (a combination of arabesque and basket), it originally cost about $175.* Courtesy of the Virginia Museum of Fine Arts, Richmond.

in 1876), and just prior to World War I, these factories were producing about 15,000 chairs a *day.*

The Thonet firm made many different types of bentwood furniture, some of amazing complexity and sinuous charm. However, the extremely simple Viennese café chair has continued to be the most popular. It has become almost standard seating in bistros and "atmospheric beer joints" and, of course, it is the "lion tamer's chair." Still being produced, over 50 million copies of this small, light, strong, straight chair have been made. The café chair is now considered to be one of the "great" chairs of all times and exhibits an integrity of materials and techniques that is seldom observed in chairs today.

New York retained its leadership in the furniture industry well past 1850, but several important changes had taken place since the city assumed that position. Shortly after the turn of the century, many French cabinetmakers immigrated to the United States, which caused a gradual shift from English to French design sources. Although the tendency toward French furniture styles continued in this country for several decades, by the 1840s and 1850s, the dominant nationality of the major furniture craftsmen had become German.

Despite the predominance of German craftsmen, the overwhelming preference was for "French modern," a nineteenth-century version of "Louis Quinze" (Louis XV). Based upon French Rococo design, if anything, it "out-Rococoed" Rococo. The carving is generally extremely representational and covers almost every surface (roses and bunches of grapes and leaves were the preferred subject matter), and the requisite "S" curves are almost snakes in their sinuous plasticity. American black walnut proved to be an excellent material for the machine- and hand-carving and when combined with richly patterned fabrics and strongly colored marbles, the furniture is singularly opulent.

The most renowned name connected with some of the most extraordinary and luxurious furniture of this style and whose name is often used to identify

it was John Henry Belter (1804–1863). Born and trained in Württemberg,   **19-19**
Germany, he was producing furniture in New York by 1844. It was he who
devised and patented the technique of laminating thin layers of rosewood,
each layer turned 90 degrees from the adjacent layer, and $\frac{1}{16}$ inch thick. Glued
together, the layers were placed in a form or "caul" and steamed into the
desired curve. These panels, composed of as many as 16 layers, were then
pierced and carved into the elaborate and realistic forms that are closely
identified with Belter. The resulting furniture was very strong despite its
fragile appearance. Furniture of this type, even during Belter's lifetime, was
designated "Belter Furniture" no matter who actually made it. Unfortunately,
many copies of his furniture were made despite the existence of his patents.
Slight variations of technique or material allowed other craftsmen to escape
the protection granted by the patent laws, and not all furniture constructed in
this manner can be attributed to Belter.

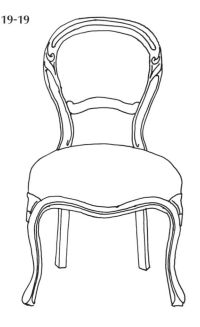

Two innovations in furniture forms became popular about this time. A side
chair was developed with a back that was similar in outline to that of an
old-fashioned balloon. Sometimes upholstered and sometimes left open, it
has become one of the most familiar forms found in midnineteenth-century
chairs. When three of these backs were placed together (a continuation or
reinterpretation of the double and triple chair-back settees of the latter half
of the eighteenth century) and then upholstered as one unit, they formed the
triple-backed sofas form that enjoyed a popularity for over a decade.

The developments of the machine age during the first half of the nineteenth century affected all manner of industry. However some critics were
not convinced that all products produced by the fabulous machines were as
good as they might be. On both sides of the Atlantic, voices were being
raised questioning the validity of the designs of machine-made products.
John Hall published the *Cabinet Maker's Assistant* in 1840 with the hope that
his suggested designs might aid the manufacturers of furniture. Henry Cole
in England was the leading proponent of excellence in design. Cole who was

19-20 *The Crystal Palace depicted in a contemporary engraving.*

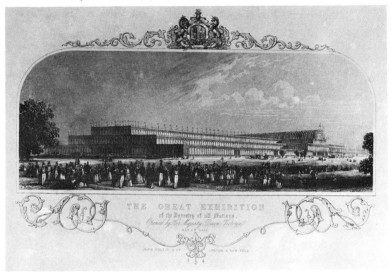

THE GREAT EXHIBITION

instrumental in getting Prince Albert, consort of Queen Victoria, interested in such matters, in 1849 proposed the idea of holding an international exhibition of manufactured products. Queen Victoria was not especially artistic nor interested in the arts, but she gave her approval and financial support to the idea.

A competition for an exhibition building was held and although 233 plans were submitted, none was found suitable. Sir Joseph Paxton, the former gardener for the Duke of Devonshire and at that time a director of the Midland Railroad, then proposed a "notion" he had. Paxton proposed a giant greenhouse, 1848 feet long (as near to 1851 as eight-foot units would permit) and 408 feet wide (51 eight-foot units) at the lowest level. The intentional numerical symbolism did not go unnoticed. The technical prowess of British industry was evident in the construction of the building. Nearly 300,000 panes of glass, almost eight feet square, and the largest made up to that time, were used. A total of 5,000 columns and girders of iron were required and many had been cast within 18 hours of installation. The whole structure was prefabricated and shipped by rail to the site. The Crystal Palace was to be the first of many such exhibition buildings and must be considered the forerunner of modern metal and glass construction. It was immediately accepted, and nine months after the contracts were let, the Great Exhibition at the Crystal Palace opened in Hyde Park on May 1, 1851, with much pomp and pageantry.

The queen, dressed in pink and silver and covered with diamond jewelry, following the opening ceremonies inspected the whole exhibition, walking the entire length of the Crystal Palace. The industrial marvels from around the world on display demonstrated beyond doubt the wondrous accomplishments wrought by the industrial revolution.

The furniture displays were filled with gargantuan pieces, each more grand, more elaborate, and more extravagant than the last. Some were so huge that they seemed more suitable to live *in* than to live with. Few of the

19-21 *The small davenport desk in veneered and solid walnut was introduced for ladies after the Civil War. Elaborate scrolls support the sloping desk top. The pedestal is filled with drawers.*

pieces exhibited were proportioned for general use, and each exhibited piece was completely smothered with very realistic carving, and if nothing else, displayed the virtuosity of the furniture manufacturer's machines.

The effect upon design and furniture design in particular was immediate. Furniture became even more eclectic than had been observed prior to the Crystal Palace Exhibition[12], and in the United States and in England, furniture of almost unbelievable ornateness, large proportions, and complicated design was favored. Although the large case pieces were vaguely based upon historical precedents, seating furniture acquired new and more original forms. The use of coil springs and the even stronger search for comfort caused chairs to assume rounded, billowing forms with no apparent inner structure. Of course, chairs did have a supporting frame and the Turkish frame chair became an important addition to furniture construction. The Turkish frame is metal from which the coil springs are supported. The entire chair is voluptuously upholstered with botton-filled tufts and full curves. Frequently, short wooden legs support the chair, but often these wooden legs are exchanged for metal legs when heavy fringe surrounds the bottom.

Other metal furniture was also made such as cast-iron furniture. It was popular, especially as garden furniture, and has a wide range of styles, although it tends to be Rococo in general form. Often the entire piece, chair, table, or bench, is composed of very representational vines and bunches of grapes, broken twigs, or fern fronds. These effects flaunt the integrity of the material, yet often create such amusement that what should be considered undesirable becomes accepted because the piece is so badly designed. Other furniture is designed with architectural elements taken from Renaissance and Baroque buildings; the fact that it is cast iron does not detract unduly from its value. Garden furniture was also constructed of twisted wire, and despite the

[12] A similar structure was built and an exhibition was held in New York in 1853.

19-22 *Turkish frame furniture continued to be made until the end of the nineteenth century. In this 1890 interior, the two upholstered pieces probably have Turkish frames.*

19-23 A cast-iron garden bench (c. 1868). The design limits to which cast iron could be molded was only limited by the knowledge and imagination of the modeler. Courtesy of the St. Louis Art Museum.

19-24 *An English armchair of pâpier-mâché in a modified Rococo style. Painted black, naturalistic flowers and fine linear designs in gold decorate it.* Courtesy of the Art Institute of Chicago.

spidery appearance, the furniture is strong, truthful, and exhibits an original use of material and technique.

Spring steel and steel tubing were both incorporated into furniture of cast iron and the more traditional wood construction. Spring steel chairs provided flexible comfort and became the ancestor of the typist chair. An example made by the American Chair Company of Troy, New York, was exhibited at the Crystal Palace in London. A rocker of steel tubing was also shown at that time.[13]

Furniture of *papier-mâché* enjoyed considerable popularity during the 1850s and 1860s. Constructed of paper pulp or strips of paper, this furniture was very durable when properly made and kept dry. Using the more "fluid" styles of the period as inspiration, papier-mâché chairs, settees, and tables often appear as if they are about to melt. They invariably have painted surfaces that are almost always black and have much of the surface texture of Oriental lacquer. Delicate colored floral patterns, stenciled and freely painted gold decorations, and inlaid bits of mother-of-pearl sparkling in the painted surfaces are added embellishments.

Furniture of rattan and cane were also found on porches and inside homes.

19-25 *Originally, mother of pearl was inlaid into the top of this tilt-top papier-mâché table, and then the designs and picture were painted over it allowing only glowing touches to show through. However, age and wear have removed most of the covering paint. The design on the pedestal in gold, green, and red is faintly Egyptian.*

[13]The rocking chair or rocker was still considered a novelty at the Crystal Palace Exhibition although it had been in existence for almost a hundred years. Benjamin Franklin is believed to have invented it in around 1760, but this theory has not been proved conclusively. The rocker is apparently more American than European, however, and was extremely popular here. (It has been called the only habit-forming piece of furniture.) The Boston rocker, a variation of the Windsor chair, and the ladder-back with rush seats were on porches and in bedrooms throughout the United States until recent times. The *bentwood rocker* by Thonet has proved to be as popular today as it was in 1860 when it was first designed. The original rocking chair had curved "bends" attached to the legs and this continues to be the more common variety. Near the end of the nineteenth century the *platform rocker* was developed. It has a stationary base upon which the upper part rocks with the aid of springs. One made entirely of turned elements, reminiscent of the old stick chairs, was very popular around 1890–1900.

19-26 *This black mantle clock with marble inserts on the sides is covered with gold incised linear designs, a favorite decorative device of Renaissance Revival designers. Rams heads protrude from the ends.*

19-27 *The rectangular back with the upholstered center panel tufted and the turned front legs identify this side chair as Renaissance revival.*

These flexible materials allowed the craftsmen to develop the most whimsical designs and as the years neared the end of the century, rattan and cane furniture acquired a frivolity that completely matched the spirit of the "Gay Nineties."

The introduction of new furniture styles was incessant after 1850, and regardless of the name or derivation, the styles were all welcomed enthusiastically. One of the major styles was the Renaissance revival style, somewhat faithful at first to the French Renaissance furniture style of the sixteenth century, but it soon succumbed to the predilection for ornateness and often became a massive example of the woodcarver's skill. Its heavy and architectural appearance, strengthened by the black walnut and rosewood coloration, is in contrast to the lighter Rococo revival style. Both were, however, used interchangeably in interiors. Furniture of essential French neoclassical design was also made, but a tendency toward heaviness, thicker seats (to hold the coil springs), complicated tufting, and less delicate bronze mounts distinguish it from the original Louis XVI style.

In England, many of the stylistic influences displayed at the Crystal Palace Exhibition in 1851 continued as furniture manufacturers produced ever more complicated and massive furniture for an eager public. On the whole, most of it echoes the styles already discussed, but as so often happens, dissident voices were heard decrying the atrocities produced by machines. No voice was stronger in England, and to a somewhat lesser extent in America, than that of William Morris (1834–1896), the artist-craftsman, designer, poet, author, medievalist, and social reformer.

Morris, born of comfortably rich parents[14], became interested in architec-

[14]Although William Morris' father was a London bill and discount broker, it was a chance happening that made possible Morris' career. When William was still a boy, his father reluctantly accepted 272 shares of copper stock in lieu of payment for a bad debt. Some time later, the "worthless" stock rose almost overnight from $5 to $4,000 a share, thereby creating a fortune and releasing William Morris from any future financial worries.

ture, painting, and the allied arts while at Oxford and after reading John Ruskin's *Stones of Venice*. Morris apprenticed in the architectural firm of George Edmund Street, known for Gothic revival buildings, but stayed only a year. Nevertheless, he formed a lifelong friendship with another young man in the firm, Philip Webb (1831–1915). Morris then went on a trip with some of his Oxford friends, Sir Edward Burne-Jones, William Holman Hunt, and Dante Gabriel Rossetti, all to become well-known painters in the Pre-Raphaelite school of art.[15] Morris was persuaded to be a painter rather than an architect by Rossetti and set upon this course.

After he married in 1859, Morris had a house designed by his friend Philip Webb, who had just set up his own architectural practice. This house was in red brick (a material not common around Oxford, stone being most often used). It was, however, a forerunner of the English Queen Anne style of the 1880s.

The importance of the "Red House" cannot be discounted. It was for this house that Morris, with his friends, designed the furniture and other furnishings. This endeavor resulted in the founding of the firm Morris, Marshall, Faulkner and Company[16] in 1861 for the purpose of designing, manufacturing, and selling home furnishings (murals, stained glass, embroideries, furniture, wallpaper, chintzes, and carpets). Morris was named general manager of the firm (primarily because he was the only one with financial stability). At the Exhibition of 1862 in London, Morris's firm first exhibited

19-28 *Drawing taken from "Tulip" chintz designed by William Morris in 1875.*

---

[15]Believing that the mechanicalism and eclecticism found in the arts of the midnineteenth century and the general decline in craftsmanship were unfortunate, this group of young men took inspiration from the painters and craftsmen before the Italian Renaissance master Raphael (1483–1520) and espoused a return to simplicity and sincerity.

[16]The firm included Ford Madox Brown, a painter; Rossetti, poet and painter; Burne-Jones, painter; Webb, architect; Charles Faulkner, business manager; and Peter Paul Marshall, surveyor and engineer. In 1875, the firm was reorganized and became simply Morris and Company.

19-29 *The Morris chair enjoyed tremendous popularity for years. This example with its adjustable back and loose cushions is in the Mission style and was probably purchased early in the twentieth century.*

their painted furniture and textiles. At first, the designers were closely allied to Gothic and Gothic revival sources, but as time passed, they became more original and must be considered the transitional link from past styles to Art Nouveau.

The greatest contribution that Morris made to interior and furniture design was his insistence that art and design are, or should be, a part of everyone's normal life. Morris and his firm gave impetus and direction to the Aesthetic Movement of England and America during the 1870s and 1880s, a period in which it seemed that everyone "taught, thought, wrote and spent . . . money and hours of time cultivating and indulging their taste."

Considered to be one of the first interior designers,[17] Morris is credited with the all-white sitting room (favored during the 1870s), the use of painted woodwork (often dark green), the use of stronger color (pure white is considered strong as opposed to pale hues and off-whites), and he developed a system of ornament. The first original design system since Rococo, Morris' system considered materials and processes and the flatness of the surface to be ornamented (he resisted illusionistic designs). The latter development by Morris provided the direction that made possible well-designed machine-made furniture for the ordinary consumer. Although he abhorred machine-made products, Morris was strongly socialistic and the availability of good furniture for the common man was certainly not opposed to his ideals. He did concede in later years that men should master machines so that the machine would become an "instrument for forcing on us better conditions of life."

Perhaps the most important single innovation with which Morris' name is associated is the Morris chair. With an exposed wooden frame and loose

[17] Morris, who was concerned with the entire interior and exterior of buildings, is also one of the first total environmentalists. In addition, he formed a society in 1877 for the protection of ancient buildings. He believed that the architectural heritage should be preserved for future generations.

19-30 *Despite Charles Lock Eastlake's admonitions about too much ornament, his ideas were often freely interpreted. This organ, made about 1880, is embellished with many small turned, jigsawed, or incised designs, all of which are now associated with Eastlake's name.*

cushions in the seat and against the adjustable back, the Morris chair was such a popular design that almost every house in England and the United States had one during the later years of the 1800s and the early 1900s. Morris discounted comfort as being important saying, "If you want comfort, go to bed!;" yet, his adjustable chair is rather comfortable and is notably a chair in which the occupant does not sit upright.

Seldom does an individual piece of furniture influence later furniture design and designers. However, a cabinet of ebonized wood designed by T. E. Collcutt and exhibited in 1871 in England became the prototype for similar "art furniture" made during the next 10 to 15 years. Its influence was as strong in America as it was in England (it had been exhibited in Philadelphia in the Centennial Exhibition of 1876) and can be seen not only in cabinets but in tables, bookcases, and fireplace overmantels. The design of this cabinet combines paneled doors, beveled mirrors, open shelves, and turned supports. The ebonized wood is the background for brightly painted designs. The cabinet was expressly made for the display and storage of art objects that were considered absolutely necessary in an "artistic" home.

An English "tastemaker" with even more influence in the United States than Morris was Charles Lock Eastlake (1836–1906), whose book, *Hints on Household Taste,* published in England in 1868 and subsequently published in eight editions in the United States from 1872 to 1890, is considered to have affected American interior and furniture design as profoundly as did the design books of Hepplewhite and Sheraton at the beginning of the century. Eastlake's book was not a design book as their books had been, but expressed his theories and ideas, and provided furniture manufacturers in America with design concepts that were easily produced on machines.

Eastlake objected to excessive curves and ornamentation. His written design suggestions (there are only a few sketches of his ideas in the book) called for rectangular, plain furniture exhibiting excellent, but simple, con-

BROOKLYN FURNITURE CO.
The Furnishing of Country Homes a Specialty.

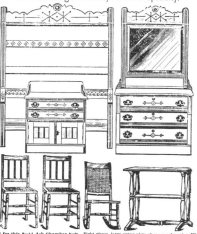

$18 for this Solid Ash Chamber Suit. Eight pieces, large swing plate glass; regular price, $30.

SEND FOR ILLUSTRATED CATALOGUE, MAILED FREE.

BROOKLYN FURNITURE COMPANY,
The Largest Retail Furniture Manufacturers in the World,
559 to 571 Fulton Street, Brooklyn, N. Y.

19-31 *From an advertisement in* Frank Leslie's Illustrated Weekly Newspaper *in 1887, this eight-piece set of bedroom furniture, sale price $18., clearly reflects the Eastlake concepts as interpreted by mass-producers of inexpensive furniture. The three pieces at the top are all constructed of "boards" with no attempt to hide joints; the carved decoration is minimal and machine-made.*

19-32 *Panel and border designs frequently
found incised on Eastlake style furniture.
The use of the drill press and router is particularly evident on this machine-made furniture.*

struction. His basic premise was to return to the simplicity of medieval times
and to use materials with truth and integrity. He disliked artificial and
applied finishes, but preferred natural wood, and oak, the traditional medieval material, was his favorite. Eastlake's ideas were immediately translated
into inexpensive machine-made furniture, although no actual pieces made
from his designs have been found. Eastlake, however, did not condone the
use of machines.

This mass-produced furniture is easily identified by the uncomplicated
rectangular forms, shallow linear surface carving, jigsawed fretwork, simple
turned elements,[18] and unfinished surfaces. It is assigned today, as it was a
hundred years ago, the name "Eastlake." The numerous examples of Eastlake
furniture still in existence attest to the tremendous popularity it then enjoyed. Eastlake furniture is one of the most prevalent styles found in the
smaller "antique" shops throughout the country.

The influence of Eastlake was not restricted to only the makers of mass-
produced furniture. Some of the finest and most skilled furniture designers
and craftsmen incorporated his concepts in their furniture. The linear carving, rectangular forms, and general detailing are easily identified with the
Eastlake style, but the superior proportions, materials, and overall elegance
are additionally discerned without difficulty.

Eastlake's ideas concerning interior design were also based upon simplicity. He did not advocate the cluttered, overfilled rooms that were then
popular. He did, however, suggest that examples of handmade objects,
". . . anything which illustrates good design and skillful workmanship"
should be collected and admired as each "sincere" object would strengthen
the aesthetic knowledge and enjoyment of the owner. Despite Eastlake's
dislike for clutter, his idea of collecting "art" objects brought *more* clutter to

[18] The forms of most of the turned components used in Eastlake furniture appear to have
been derived from mechanical sources, such as engine cylinders, pistons, and valves.

the interiors of the United States and England. To display these collected objects, all manner of shelves and cabinets were made, but all owe their design heritage to Collcutt's cabinet of 1871. A favorite display piece was the hanging "art cabinet," a combination of shelves, beveled mirrors, jigsawed shapes, shallow carving, and a myriad of small turned elements.

Many of Eastlake's design concepts ring remarkably true today. The following selection bears thoughtful consideration:

1. Every material used in art manufacture is obviously restricted by the nature of its substance to certain conditions of form.
2. The best and most picturesque furniture of all ages has been simple in general forms. It may have been enriched by complex details of carved work or inlay, but its main outline was always chaste and sober in design, never running into extravagant contour or unnecessary curves.
3. Public taste is often very perverse and inconsistent as to choice and appliance of material and ornament.
4. The most formidable obstacle which lies in the way of any attempt to reform the arts of design in this country is perhaps the indifference with which people of even reputed taste are accustomed to regard the products of common industry.
5. The real secret of success in decorative colour is quite as much dependent on contrast as on similarity of tint; nor can real artistic affect be expected without the employment of both.
6. When did people first adopt the monstrous notion that the "last pattern out" must be the best?

19-33 *Not even the smallest, least expensive accessory escaped the Eastlake influence in the 1870s and 1880s. This crudely made folding wall bracket, only 11 inches high, has the requisite jigsawed shape, routed lines, and drilled dots.*

Eastlake's ideas were seeds that bore worthy fruits—the collections that formed the nuclei of many of the major museums in the United States that were started in the 1870s and 1880s. The world of art and design owes much to Charles Lock Eastlake.

19-34 *Magnificent examples of the furniture manufacturing skills extant in 1876, these walnut and walnut burl bedroom pieces were exhibited at the Centennial Exhibition in Philadelphia. Made by Berkey and Gay Furniture Company of Grand Rapids, Michigan, and called the "Centennial Suite," they are in the American Renaissance style. Ornate exhibition furniture such as these pieces guaranteed Grand Rapids the leadership of American furniture production. The bed headboard is 99 inches high.* Courtesy of the Grand Rapids Public Museum.

Out of the concepts expressed by Morris, Eastlake, and their associates came the Arts and Crafts Movement (late 1880s and 1890s), an attempt to promote handcrafted objects. Several exhibitions were held, and guilds and other organizations dedicated to the renewal of the craftsmen's skill were formed. The basic goals of this movement were similar to those of the earlier Aesthetic Movement. However, the later movement was given direction by craftsmen and designers who were interested in hand-manufacture, whereas the aesthetic movement was a general awakening, and an attempt to incorporate art and design in the daily lives of all.

Following the opening of the Crystal Palace in 1851, other international exhibitions of manufactured products were held in New York, Paris, and London, to name but three. At all of these exhibitions, new designs, technical developments, and materials were displayed to a responsive public, and were soon reflected in the products being manufactured. The Philadelphia Centennial Exhibition of 1876 was no exception. Housed in several buildings of extremely varied architecture, the main exhibition building nevertheless continued the architectural trend set 25 years before and was made primarily of glass and iron (its length even echoed its year of erection—1876 feet long).

Although the extravagances displayed at the Philadelphia Exposition were nothing short of phenomenal, they were relatively unimportant stylistically. For example, a $6,250 cabinet of ebony and lapis lazuli in the style of Henri II, a ruby-colored Bohemian glass vase 3½ feet high, another vase 4½ feet high of sterling silver and valued at $25,000 (it took 5 years, 38 weeks, and 22 days to make), a Sleeping Iolanthe modeled in Arkansas butter displayed in a tin frame filled with cracked ice, a majestic armchair made from a limb of the elm tree under which Washington took command of the Continental Army in 1775 (the upholstery pictured the "Father of the Country" in needlepoint), an immense ceramic sculpture of America riding a bison, or a huge George Washington astride an eagle rising toward the heavens. Regardless of what they were, most displayed objects—sculpture, painting, furniture, or "every-

19-35 *Although purchased at the beginning of the twentieth century, this Hepplewhite style sideboard exhibits excellent workmanship and is fairly authentic in design. Furniture of this type continues the trend established at the Philadelphia Centennial Exhibition for furniture styles and forms used in the eighteenth century.*

day" objects—were perversions of truth; materials were tortured almost beyond their structural and often well beyond their aesthetic limits.

One exception was a "1776" kitchen, which, although not architecturally or archaeologically accurate, did exhibit former American furniture forms that had been all but forgotten. The sentiment of the centennial of the country, that sudden awareness of the historical heritage of the United States, made the kitchen one of the most popular exhibits.

Almost immediately a resurgence of interest in "Colonial" objects occurred[19]. People began to collect everything that was associated with the early years and some of the finest surviving examples of seventeenth and eighteenth-century furniture were "rescued" from total destruction at this time. Large amounts of new furniture, especially Queen Anne and Chippendale styles, were also manufactured. Many of these reproductions are extremely well-made and faithful in design. Today, a hundred years later, it is often initially difficult to distinguish these reproductions from the originals, but there are almost always differences in proportions, details, and construction that, upon close examination, identify the copies. Although this nineteenth-century furniture was based upon eighteenth-century styles, it was popularly called "Centennial," rather than the correct stylistic names.

The last twenty-five years of the nineteenth century are marked by furniture of an almost unbelievable variety. During each decade since the 1830s, new styles and influences were introduced and continued to be made in many versions, qualities and materials. In addition to the European and American styles that were used as sources of inspiration, exotic and Oriental designs were also popular. Oriental designs fitted very well into the ideals expressed by Eastlake and Morris. The whole Aesthetic Movement was closely tied to Japanese design, such as the use of sunflower, fret, bamboo,

---

[19] Many houses were designed then and have continued to the present day to be designed in "Colonial" styles.

19-36 *The sunflower in an asymmetrical design was one of the most popular motifs of the Aesthetic movement.*

19-37 *Furniture of bamboo and pseudo-bamboo was the rage in the United States in the 1880s. This table of maple turned to imitate bamboo is characteristic of the many rectangular, spindled, and knobbed pieces manufactured in New York. Bedroom bamboo furniture was especially popular.*

19-38 *This small, square-topped table with turned legs is typical of cottage furniture.*

and stork forms; asymmetrical balance; two-dimensional design; and "Oriental" colors (jade green, golden yellow, "ceramic" blue, and white—all taken from Japanese prints). Furniture made of bamboo or with turned wooden parts simulating bamboo was very popular.

The dominance of New York furniture manufacturers was challenged by newly built furniture factories in the Midwest. Mostly German craftsmen, these producers made large quantities of machine-made furniture that were shipped throughout the country. Grand Rapids, Michigan, Cincinnati, Ohio, and Muscatine, Iowa, were three of the largest centers and only recently have their leadership been supplanted by southern centers, notably the area around High Point, North Carolina. The furniture manufactured in these factories did not have the stamp of one designer or firm, but was of all types and grades. (Some of the most fantastic examples of furniture making displayed at the Centennial Exhibition were products of these firms, and "Grand Rapids" was a term often applied to mass-produced furniture during the early years of the twentieth century.)

A group of mass-produced furniture that originated in the 1840s and continued to be very popular for the rest of the century was a type called *cottage furniture*. This furniture was made of softwood and then painted a flat color (often white) and was frequently decorated with floral motifs. Simple and inexpensive, it was nevertheless quite handsome. Split turnings were used to decorate flat surfaces, and legs, stretchers, and the frames of beds and chairs were usually turned in repeating *bobbin, spool, or ball shapes*. The very popular *spool bed* or "*Jenny Lind*"[20] *bed* is a cottage type.

The last decade of the nineteenth century was one of the most extraordinary in social and design history. In America, the World's Columbian Exhibition was held in Chicago in 1893 and although it affected architecture

19-39 *The pride of every middle-class parlor of the 1890s was the base burner heating stove. A masterpiece of cast iron, nickle plate, and isinglass, its surface bulged with ornament of vague historical heritage.*

[20] Jenny Lind (1820–1887), "the Swedish Nightingale," was a very popular soprano who toured the United States in 1850–1852 under the management of P. T. Barnum.

19-40 *The interiors at the turn of the century were still rich in furniture and accessories of many nationalities and periods. This room has a back stool of medieval design (no doubt because of the Centennial in Philadelphia), a Japanese fire screen behind a "French" table, Islamic pillows and pictures, a German beer mug, and the new miracle—electric lights.*

considerably, it proved to be of little importance to furniture design. However, in Paris and the rest of Europe, the "Gay Nineties" was under the influence of a new style, now generally called Art Nouveau.[21]

The Art Nouveau style was an international movement and was *the* style of fashion and the avant garde. It developed almost simultaneously in Scotland, Belgium, France, and Austria and to a lesser extent in the United States. Art Nouveau reflects, in many ways, the love of the exotic, erotic, unusual, and sensual pleasure associated with this remarkable period. The style is not based upon historical precedents but rather upon natural forms, although it is possible to trace individual elements of Art Nouveau back to Rococo, Celtic, Japanese, and Gothic art, and it is certainly linked to the Arts and Crafts movement in England. But, it was a new style and one that affected furniture and accessory design more than it did architecture. (Some excellent Art Nouveau buildings were designed, however.)

For all of its importance, the Art Nouveau style developed very quickly, matured, and then began to decline in a short time; the whole period lasting no more than thirty years and the most important Art Nouveau designs being developed in less than ten. (A revival of many motifs associated with Art Nouveau has been observed during the 1960s and early 1970s, although the interest is more in the original designs or reproductions than in developing new designs in the Art Nouveau style.)

If Art Nouveau is to be characterized by a single term, it would have to be

[21]Although it was not called Art Nouveau until 1895 when Samuel Bing opened his shop called *L'Art Nouveau* in Paris, the stylistic movement that started several years earlier was referred to as the *Schnorkelstil* ("flourish-style"), *Bandwurmstil* ("tapeworm-style"), and *Jugendstil* ("youth-style," named after the popular magazine *Jugendl* of Munich), all used by German-speaking peoples. It was called the "Glasgow School" in Scotland, "Stile Liberty" in Italy, "Modernismo" in Spain, and *Paling Stijl* (*paling* is Flemish for "eel") in Belgium. As these names, that is, tapeworm, flourish, and eel imply, curvilinear motifs abound.

19-41 *The swirling leaves and nodding tulips in electroplated silver on dark green glass exemplify the linear quality of Art Nouveau design.*

linear. Line is all important, as important as during the Rococo style, but it is less abstract, being based more upon natural plant forms than was found in Rococo. In Art Nouveau interiors and on furniture and accessories, lines are everywhere and, regardless of the materials—wood, iron, plaster, or stone —suggest vines, climbing stalks, and clinging tendrils of exotic hot-house plants.

Certain motifs occur again and again, the lily, the peacock, the sunflower (a holdover from the Aesthetic Movement and Japanese influence), the lizard, and the snake. The peacock feather is used more than the whole bird, and the lily pad and stem are used more than the flower. (Buds of flowers are more common than the open blooms.) The female figure, although frequently seen, is not as prevalent as a decorative motif as is just the head and the long flowing hair. (Male figures were seldom used.)

Art Nouveau is an ornamental style, but often the ornament grows out of the structure and is so much a part of it that it is often difficult to separate one from the other. One aspect of Art Nouveau that contrasts with other "new" styles of the nineteenth century is its acknowledgment of machine and industrial technology. Although the designs often appear nonmechanical, they are made with the latest methods of technology and materials. For example, the sinuous forms that are so characteristic of Art Nouveau are often cast in iron and form the structure as well as the decoration of an interior. Further, designers in this style were the first to develop electrical lighting fixtures and lamps that were not based upon historical prototypes but ones using the electric light bulb, and even the wires, as part of the total design rather than something to hide or disguise.

The general description and characteristics of Art Nouveau design just given can be applied to most furniture. However, there are some distinct differences in the work of the various Art Nouveau designers and countries. By far, the most "different" designs were those done in Glasgow, Scotland; yet, they are definitely within the sphere of Art Nouveau and, in turn,

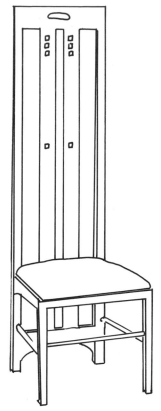

19-42 *Charles Rennie Mackintosh designed a number of elegant chairs with extremely tall rectangular backs.*

influenced the furniture designs of such Americans as Louis Sullivan and Frank Lloyd Wright.

The leader of the Glasgow School was Charles Rennie Mackintosh (1868–1928), an architect. Not only his architecture but his furniture as well has a "sense of fitness." His furniture is simple, rectilinear, and squarish, and incorporates many straight, parallel, and narrow elements in the designs. There is a quality of "brittleness" in his interior and furniture designs that is often heightened by his frequent use of smooth, white painted surfaces. The ornament, applied only to key structural points, is unique. The decorative elements were almost always the work of the Macdonald sisters.[22] Most of their designs incorporated thin, enigmatic human figures as a dominant motif. There is a subtle glittering, suggesting precious gems, throughout the ornament, but upon close examination it turns out to be made of gesso inlaid with string, jet beads, and glass and them subtly tinted in soft grays, pinks, pale apple and olive green, blue, and rose. The ornament, delicate though it may be, is in perfect harmony with the severly architectural furniture.

On the Continent, Henry van de Velde (1863–1957), perhaps more than any other single individual, was responsible for the theory and spread of the Art Nouveau style. Following the example of Morris, van de Velde believed that unity of design was all important,[23] but he differed with Morris in his belief that machines were acceptable tools for the designers. Van de Velde's importance is not restricted to furniture design (he designed little furniture) but to his wide influence on other furniture designers. In addition to his

---

[22] Mackintosh met these two extraordinary designers while attending classes at the Glasgow School of Art. He married Margaret and his good friend and associate Herbert McNair married Francis. Together they became known as The Four and are almost singularly responsible for the Glasgow School of the Art Nouveau style.

[23] At a well-known luncheon at which Henri de Toulouse-Lautrec, the French painter, was a guest, the table setting, furniture, curtains—the entire interior—choice of food, and even van de Velde's wife's gown harmonized in color and design.

19-43 *Although not characteristically high-backed, the rectangularity of form and the delicate, linear inlaid designs of wood, brass, and ivory on the side panels of this American chair echo the designs of Mackintosh.*

501

19-44 *Upholstered in green-gold embroidered velvet, the design of this mahogany armchair (c. 1900) by Louis Majorelle is reminiscent of Rococo furniture, but upon close examination the recurring iris motif and the sinuous curves of Art Nouveau identify it.*

native Belgium, van de Velde also worked in France, Germany, Switzerland, and Holland. His work is more abstract than many Art Nouveau designers and he was able to develop beyond the narrow confines of the style. Shortly after the turn of the century, van de Velde was invited to teach at the Weimar School of Applied Art in Germany, where he reorganized the methods of instruction. Highly regarded, he was dismissed as an enemy alien at the eruption of World War I when he moved to Switzerland. His post in Germany was filled by the young Walter Gropius, who after the war, reorganized the school into the Bauhaus. Van de Velde remained active and in 1938 helped design the Belgian Pavilion at the New York World's Fair.

Along with the name, some of the more definitive Art Nouveau designers developed in France. The most notable and one of the earliest to use the strong linear qualities and motifs associated with the style was Emile Gallé. Born in Nancy, France, and trained in his father's ceramic and glass workshop, Gallé, while in London, explored the techniques used in Chinese and Japanese glass snuff boxes. He later developed overlay glass in which the top layer of colored glass is cut away to form the raised decoration on the bottom layer. At first concerned with the production of glass and ceramic objects in his huge shop (over 300 craftsmen), Gallé turned to furniture design in 1884. Gallé's furniture exhibits strong linear qualities and is very delicate in appearance, and, as an early example of the Art Nouveau style, his designs influenced many other designers. Gallé was one of the first to develop designs for electrical lighting fixtures, probably a natural outgrowth of his glassmaking skills.

Other important French designers of Art Nouveau furniture were Louis Majorelle, also of Nancy, and Hector Guimard. Majorelle's furniture is often distinguished by his use of bronze mounts. Seemingly made of pulled taffy, these mounts are ingeniously attached to his furniture and do not have the "applied" look that even those on Rococo furniture had. Guimard was an

19-45 *A detail of one of the supports holding the sign of the Paris Métro. Of cast
iron, these forms by Hector Guimard have
the organic quality of plants or pulled taffy.*

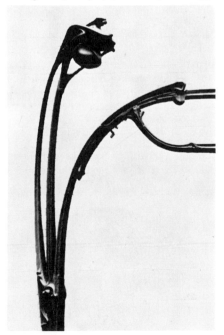

architect[24] as well as a designer, and is considered to be one of the most
original Art Nouveau designers. He too believed that one designer should be
responsible for every element and detail in an interior, if not the entire
building, and it was Guimard who achieved, better than anyone else, the
ideal Art Nouveau interior. His work is now considered to be the high point
of French Art Nouveau design. He was largely responsible for the Art
Nouveau decorations at the Paris Exhibition of 1900. Interestingly, Guimard
continued to design in his own style, which he called the "Style Guimard"
and which became increasingly geometric. It developed into the style called
Art Moderne or Art Deco of the 1920s. He eventually came to the United
States in 1938 and died in New York in 1942, a forgotten man.

Art Nouveau was never as clear or as popular in the United States as it was
in Europe, but one of the most famous and influential designers in the style
was Louis Comfort Tiffany (1848–1933). Tiffany was born in New York City,
the son of the owner of Tiffany Jewelers. Showing a strong inclination toward
art and design at an early age, he was educated in Paris and spent five years
in Europe and the Orient. Being primarily interested in glass, in 1878 he
founded a company to promote the decorative arts in the United States and
especially develop colored glass windows. His firm was called Louis C.
Tiffany and Associate Artists.

Commissions for his windows and mosaics led to the manufacture of other
accessories and, in time, to the production of all the components of interiors.
To have one's home "done" by Tiffany became an indication of superior
taste.[25] His furniture is well-made and often has an Oriental cast. Tiffany is

---

[24] The famous Art Nouveau entrances to the Paris Métro system are his design.
[25] During the presidency of Chester A. Arthur (1881–1885), Tiffany was charged with the
redecoration of the White House. History records that twenty wagonloads of furniture were
sold at public auction to make way for the new Tiffany designed furniture. Ironically, only a
few years later, Theodore Roosevelt had the White House completely redecorated in a
more "current" style and Tiffany's imprint was removed.

credited with the design of the glass ball held in a brass claw foot. This design was later used by many other furniture-makers and is probably most familiar on the circular piano stool, c. 1900.

Tiffany's name is almost synonymous with his glass-shaded hanging and standing lamps. In 1885, he was responsible for the decoration of the first theater to be completely illuminated by electricity and he continued to develop designs for lighting fixtures. Often the bases of his floor and table lamps are bronze cast in forms based upon the stems, tendrils, or roots of plants. The shades are the most outstanding component of the lamps, however. Fabricated from lead, glass, and bronze, they are vibrantly colorful concoctions that evoke an elegance and richness seldom found in the work of later imitators. The subtle variations of hues[26] within the strong coloration limits is phenomenal and is accomplished by fusing layers of glass together. The best known example of his lamp-making is the *wisteria table lamp* designed about 1900. As so often happens, other craftsmen in glass attempted to duplicate Tiffany's achievements, and although they spread the popularity of stained-glass lamp shades and windows, they were seldom successful in equaling his exquisite designs and colors. Today, "Tiffany" has become almost a generic term for any colored glass lamp shade regardless of make or period. Perhaps, this does credit to the man who did more to develop the decorative arts in America than anyone else has until recently.

An independent furniture designer-maker developed a style that was to be even more popular in America than the Art Nouveau had been in France. Gustav Stickley[27] of Eastwood, New York, was designing and manufacturing

19-46 *The familiar piano stool. Louis Comfort Tiffany must be given the credit for the design of the brass claw foot holding the glass ball although the stool is not Art Nouveau in design.*

19-47 *The wisteria lamp shade of vibrant blue and green leaded glass is supported on a cast bronze base in the form of a rooted trunk.*

[26] In 1898 it was estimated that Tiffany had over 5,000 colors of glass on hand to use in his workrooms.
[27] Born in Osceola, Wisconsin, in 1857, (d. 1942) Gustav Stickley was brought up on a farm although his father turned to furniture-making while Gustav was still a boy. This may account for the sturdiness and excellent consideration of materials that are so very evident in his furniture.

19-48 *The bronze base of this glass
shaded lamp of the 1920s is similar to
Tiffany's organically designed bases. The
shade, however, is farther from the original.
It has a decorated cast metal frame that is
faintly reminiscent of French eighteenth-
century ornament. Single curved sheets of
marbleized glass are clipped behind each section of the frame.*

19-49 *The "Mission Oak buffet," the
overwhelming choice for dining room storage
in the first quarter of the twentieth century,
is fairly small in scale despite its rather
large rectangular appearance. This example
is less than five feet high.*

his excellent, handmade Craftsman furniture by 1900. Constructed of
squared components of oak and joined by very visible mortise and tenon
joints, Stickley's furniture has a quality of primitiveness, but can certainly
not be called crude. It was truly functional and has survived decades of hard
usage in libraries, schools, lodges, offices, and homes.

The sturdy chairs, tables, bookcases, and couches with their vertical slat
backs, square legs, leather padding, squared copper pulls and handles, and
exposed joints clearly indicate, as Stickley insisted, that each piece has a
"mission." Indeed, the mission was to be used. The terms *mission furniture* and
mission oak furniture came to be the more common name when countless
imitators adapted Stickley's designs and massed-produced them. The popularity of the mission style was enhanced by the coincident renewed interest in
the Franciscan missions of California and the publication of books such as
Ramona, by Helen Hunt Jackson, a popular novel about the early days
of California. Many homes across the country were built in pseudomission
style and Stickley's simple and machine-made furniture fitted them
perfectly.

From 1901 until 1916, Stickley published a magazine-catalog, *The Craftsman*, in which he expounded his ideas of furniture, craftsmanship, materials,
and taste. When he had perfected a design he seldom changed it because, as
he rightly wrote in the 1913 edition of his publication, "Most of my furniture
was so carefully designed and well proportioned in the first place, that even
with my advanced experience I cannot improve upon it." Unfortunately, the
cheaper and less skillfully made adaptations of Stickley's designs eventually
forced him into bankruptcy in 1916. The mission style remained popular
until the 1920s, however, and today is being sought by collectors who
appreciate its sturdy, functional, and rather monastic qualities.

The term *modern* is used frequently today when describing furniture, yet it
is difficult to state when the modern period began. Two dictionary definitions
of this term may be of some assistance.

19-50 *This oak armchair, devoid of excessive ornamentation, is obviously a piece of
furniture to be sat in. The Morris chair on
page 491 is also Mission style.*

1) of or pertaining to present and recent time; not ancient or remote. 2) of, pertaining to, or characteristic of contemporary styles of art, literature, music, etc., that reject traditionally accepted or sanctioned forms and emphasized individual experimentation and sensibility.

No definitive date marks the beginning of the modern period, but the social, political, and technological upheaval that accompanied World War I spawned a search for new forms and a rejection of old ones. In such a climate of experimentation, the first contributions to modern design were made.

Holland, which had not suffered too greatly during the war, was the center of one modern movement called de Stijl.[28]

Gerrit Rietveld (1888–1964) designed some of the most original furniture ever conceived. His pieces are so original that they appear to have been based upon no historical models; in fact, they are as if his chairs and sideboard are the first seating and storage pieces ever designed. This is a very remarkable designing accomplishment. Rietveld's 1917–1919 painted chairs and sideboard are all constructed of rectangular elements and appear to be temporarily placed together to form the individual pieces of furniture. There is a sense of impermanency in their design, almost as if they were meant to be dismantled and joined again in another arrangement. The smooth planes of the structural elements are painted in flat, primary colors that give movement, weight, and direction to the various parts. Each piece of furniture is almost a nonobjective piece of sculpture and should be so considered (every chair should be for that matter), and although Rietveld's work appears

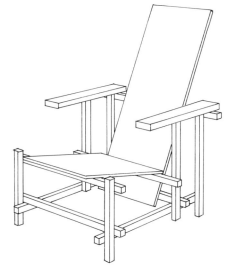

19-51 *The "Red-Blue" chair (1917) by Gerrit Rietveld has a red back and blue seat with all of the horizontal and vertical components of the frame painted black.*

[28] Named after a magazine published by a group of artists to air their aesthetic theories, the de Stijl principles of design were based upon the complete nonobjectivity of form (the reduction of everything to rectangular elements), the use of flat planes of only black and white and the three primary colors, and asymmetrical arrangements judged by visual weight and movement. Well-known leaders of the de Stijl movement were Theo van Doesburg, Gerrit Rietveld, and Piet Mondrian.

19-52 *A lady's desk of modified kidney form (c. 1925). The Art Deco geometric interpretations of eighteenth-century French styles are easily discernible in the legs.* Courtesy of the Art Institute of Chicago.

19-53 *Designed in 1926 by Emile-Jacques Ruhlmann, this side chair is of Makassar ebony.* Courtesy of the Art Institute of Chicago.

somewhat "archaic" today, more clearly than any other furniture it marks the beginning of modern furniture design.

In France, furniture design was developing along another path. As early as 1910, some of the most experimental designers were shunning the sinuous curves of Art Nouveau and returning to more geometric forms. The war halted further development, but shortly after peace was restored the trends that started earlier became stronger and by 1925 were a distinct style. In that year, the French government underwrote the Paris *Exposition Internationale des Arts Décoratifs et Industriels Modernes* for the distinct purpose of re-establishing the leadership in design that the country had during the eighteenth century. The exhibition was very successful and until the Depression, French design was again the pacesetter. The design style came to be known as Art Deco, a name derived from the title of the exhibition.

The Art Deco furniture style was fully developed by 1925 and the best pieces display the fine cabinetmaking skills that were inherent in eighteenth-century French furniture. The beautifully executed joinery, the superb veneer and marquetry, and the choice gilt-bronze mounts are there. Indeed, even some of the basic forms are retained, but these forms are "streamlined," stylized, and tuned to a severe sophistication. Ornament, when employed, is often derivative of the cubism associated with Pablo Picasso and Georges Braque. The glint of steel and eggshell white add even more crisp elegance to the usually black lacquer or dark natural wood forms (ebony and palisander wood, a brownish wood with a purple cast, were especially admired by Art Deco designers). Some of the first pieces of furniture that were expressly designed for the radio and phonograph were in this style.

Art Deco is closely identified with the late 1920s and early 1930s and might have survived longer as a leading style but for the Depression. Despite its excellent design possibilities and strong beginning, it was probably doomed from the start, for like Art Nouveau, it was primarily a style that was more compatible with handmade products than with those made by the machine.

19-54 *Geometric simplicity combined with rich veneers are characteristic of Art Deco furniture, and this 1930 "D-end" vanity table is no exception.* Courtesy of the Art Institute of Chicago.

The finest workmanship and best Art Deco designs could be incorporated only in furniture for wealthy clients. When the Art Deco style was translated into less expensive and even cheap products, it lost much of its distinctive quality. The Depression of the early 1930s dealt the final blow to the Art Deco movement and it soon disappeared. (The Art Deco style has been resurrected in the past few years and has been especially influential in textile and wallcovering design.)

The country that was to influence midtwentieth century furniture design (and architectural design) more than any other was Germany. Germany, most affected by World War I and the period following the conflict, was frought with disillusionment, defeat, and poverty. It was a period when the past was no more; a time for a new beginning. In 1919, the Weimar School of Applied Art was reorganized by Walter Gropius and renamed the Bauhaus.

The impact of the Bauhaus upon design was immediate. Furniture, architecture, textile, costume, and industrial design around the world were all affected and some of the early experiments in design, especially for the machine and machine-made products, resulted in outstanding contributions to the world of furniture. The first revolutionary chair design to come out of the Bauhaus was the armchair designed by Marcel Breuer. Called the Wassily chair,[29] it was designed in 1925 when Breuer was only twenty-three years old—he got his idea from the handlebars of his bicycle. It is the first chair made of metal tubing, an industrial product. Called the "most influential furniture invention of the century," it is, like Rietveld's, a totally new approach and relies upon its vertical and horizontal parallel gleaming chrome lines (tubing) and machine-made precision for elegance rather than extraneous ornamentation. The seat, back, and arms are canvas slings instead of upholstery or padding (it is now possible to have leather rather than canvas).

[29] Breuer named it after his friend and mentor Wassily Kandinsky, the nonobjective painter.

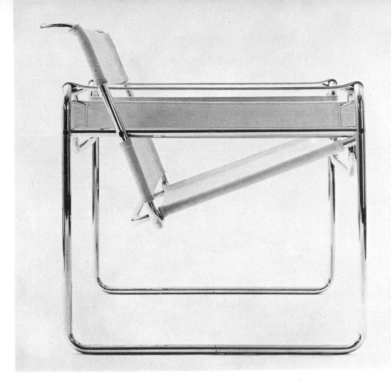

19-55 *Remarkably spare, yet surprisingly comfortable, the Wassily chair has seldom been equaled in its purity of design during the past fifty years.* Courtesy Knoll International.

19-56 *The elegant simplicity of Breuer's cantilevered chair was translated into the chrome dinette chair of the 1940s. This inexpensive chair once had a padded plastic-covered seat and back, which has now been prelaced by a more textural contrasting corduroy.*

Shortly after his Wassily chair, Breuer designed an end table-stool that is best described as a chrome tubing "square-U" placed upside down. The continuous tubing creates runners instead of legs and is a perfect partner to his armchair. Turning the table stool on its side, the basic principle of Breuer's next innovation becomes evident. In 1928, he designed the *cantilevered side chair*, which unfortunately was to be copied in many bastardized versions, filling uncounted kitchenettes and lunchrooms during the 1940s and 1950s. His chair, however, is an elegant example of the tensile strength of chrome steel tubing and the purity of design that is possible with machine production. It is truly a functional design using but one piece of tubing and requiring no expensive joints or complicated forming. Its design integrity has held up well for over four decades, despite the cheap copies, and is still being manufactured in its original form. Interestingly, the seat and back are wooden frames stretched with woven cane and, although they add a beautiful contrast of texture and color and increase the visual lightness of the chair, the caning must be done by hand and can be traced back to the Egyptians. Breuer continued to design tubular steel furniture, tables, beds, and cabinets as well as chairs, and when sensitively placed in a simple architectural environment, they are exceedingly serene and elegant.

About the same time that Breuer was developing his squared version of a cantilevered chair, Mies van der Rohe designed a curvilinear lounge chair (1926) using the same cantilever principle. Considered to slightly predate Breuer's, the two chairs make an excellent comparison duo. Mies's chair has a sweeping curved front that gives it a languid air when contrasted with Breuer's more rigid rectangularity.

Without doubt, the most celebrated chair designed in the twentieth century is Mies van der Rohe's Barcelona chair.[30] The beauty of line,

---

[30] The Barcelona chair was initially designed for use in the interior of the German Pavilion at the International Exposition at Barcelona, Spain, in 1929. Since its appearance, this chair has been the first choice of architects and designers whenever they need a modern chair.

19-57 *The visual elegance of the Barcelona chair by Mies van der Rohe is matched by its exquisite craftsmanship. Many copies, adaptations, and interpretations of this chair have been produced since it was first designed in 1929, but none approach its pristine purity of form and craftsmanship.*

proportion, and perfection of materials mark it as a chair form without equal. The chrome flat steel bars that are the frame, when viewed from the side, form an "X." This old and familiar "X" chair type is subtly changed into a matchless linear pattern. One bar is a simple curve that rapidly sweeps up from the floor and becomes the back support. The other is an elongated reverse curve starting at the seat front and slowly swinging down to the floor at the rear. The tufted rectangular leather cushions are supported by parallel leather straps attached to the almost hidden cross braces. The graceful cantilevering of the seat produces a kind of "alertness" to the chair and gives it a sense of movement. Mies also designed a table and a stool to go with the Barcelona chair.

The importance of the Bauhaus and the furniture designs emanating from it cannot be minimized. The furniture of Rietveld and the whole Art Deco style made scarcely an impression upon subsequent furniture design. The Bauhaus contributions have been so lasting that many of the original designs have continued to be produced through the years and are currently on the market and in substantial demand. In addition, the design of almost all of the "functional" furniture being produced today can be traced to the Bauhaus designs of the late 1920s.

While the Bauhaus was producing furniture designs that reflected the industrialized methods of machine production, the Scandinavian countries were developing another concept of furniture design. This furniture coming from Denmark, Sweden, Norway, and Finland echoes the tradition of hand-crafted furniture and is often inspired by historical forms, but by and large appears new and original. Its impact upon the furniture of America in the 1950s and 1960s was as great as was the influence of the Bauhaus. Most importantly, Scandinavian design tempers the functional forms of industrialization with warmth and tradition.

As early as 1917 in Denmark, an architect and designer Kaare Klint (1888–1954) began to study the interrelationship of people to furniture. His studies developed into a set of basic dimensions that revolutionized compartmented and modular storage. His original research predated similar studies done at the Bauhaus.

Diametrically opposed to the Bauhaus philosophy of getting ideas from only contemporary sources, Klint believed that to do so narrowed one's vision and consequently adversely affected one's designs. Yet his work does not superficially reflect the styles of the past, although he was particularly fond of eighteenth-century English furniture, because his designs evolved out of functional considerations. Klint's furniture designs have a timeless quality about them, seldom indicating by style or material when they were made, and all of his pieces have a sensitivity toward material and detail that could come from a craft tradition.

Industrialization came late to the northern countries of Europe and the continuation of the craft tradition is a major reason for the distinctiveness of Scandinavian furniture. During the early years of the twentieth century, the traditionally skilled Scandinavian furniture craftsmen were being employed less and less with the increasing dominance of machine production. The guilds were concerned and apprehensive as to their future, but being a stubborn lot and taking fate into their own hands, they were determined to remain an important part of Scandinavian life.

In 1927, the Cabinetmaker's Guild of Copenhagen held an exhibition of furniture, that has since become an annual event. The first exhibition was severely criticized for its lack of current styles, and immediately a concentrated effort was made to develop designs that were not so traditionally imitative. The exceptional result was that the handcraftsmen developed the spare, elegant, beautifully crafted furniture that is now called Scandinavian. The new designs developed for the next exhibition were too expensive for the average purchaser, but because of their simplicity and forthrightness, it was possible to adapt them to mass-production and this excellent furniture was soon available to the average consumer. This marriage of mass-production and handcrafts was responsible for the subsequent growth of both the mass-produced and handcrafted furniture industries and has marked this furniture since then. Many of the forms are sculptural and exhibit detailing seldom produced by machines. The use of natural woods, notably teak, follows the craft orientation and intensifies the feeling of warmth and a certain closeness to nature that permeates most Scandinavian furniture.

Similar stylistic developments also occurred almost simultaneously in the other Scandinavian countries and new furniture of outstanding originality and merit began to be designed. The significant changes taking place in the furniture industry had their effect upon the other crafts and before long there was a complete renaissance in the Scandinavian applied arts.

Leading Danish designers who contributed to the world of furniture during the midtwentieth century were Børge Mogensen, Hans J. Wegner, Finn Juhl, and Arne Jacobsen. Mogensen (b. 1914), who is especially noted for furniture that emphasizes usefulness, designed (1954) some sturdy yet small scale, simple, low-backed chairs with rather thick, slightly tapered round legs and rush seats. These chairs have become almost a standard design today for "rugged" furniture used in lounges and libraries.

Hans J. Wegner (b. 1914) is Denmark's outstanding chair designer. His chairs have an unassuming elegance derived from traditional craftsmanship and design mingled with fine contemporary thinking. A handsome chair in ash and teak that he designed in 1947 is reminiscent of the Windsor chair but definitely expresses the midtwentieth century. The high arched bow-back is in sophisticated contrast to the wide, low seat. The slender radiating spindles have a flattened portion that suggests the tail feathers of a peacock.

Two years later, Wegner designed another chair of exceptional refinement which has become one of the best known Danish chairs. A combination of teak, oak, and cane, this chair is skillfully molded into subtle flowing curves not unlike modern sculpture and is an excellent combination of function and

19-58 *The subtle beauty of this great chair clearly reflects the long heritage of Scandinavian chair craftsmen, yet it is also strikingly comtemporary. The "peacock" chair by Hans Wegner melds the past and the present in a most elegant manner.*

19-59 *The Ægget (Egg), on the left, and the Svanan (Swan) chairs by Denmark's Arne Jacobsen are both thinly padded sculptural shells. Handsome and remarkably comfortable without the usual thick upholstery, both chairs reflect the Scandinavian tendency toward deceptively simple, pure design, but are carefully structured for strength and comfort.* Courtesy of Fritz Hansen, Inc.

grace. For example, the top rail, which is both the arms and the back, is one smoothly sculptured form shifting direction and planes as the function demands. It is made of three pieces of wood joined with finesse, permitting the wood's grain to continue to be essentially parallel to the direction of the curving forms.

Striking out in new forms, that resemble sculpture more than even the designs of the others, is Finn Juhl (b. 1912). Juhl's chairs are flowing, linear, tapered forms, joined ever so lightly. The seats, backs, and other upholstered surfaces are like chips or slightly curved planes that practically float within the space defined by the exposed wood frame.

Some of the best uses of laminated beechwood can be seen in the inexpensive, small, pressure-molded, stacking plywood chairs by Arne Jacobsen (1902–1971). The first, a three-legged version, was designed in 1952 and was a departure from the craft-oriented production of Danish furniture. This chair is an industrial product completely, but has none of the impersonal qualities that are often associated with such objects. The thin, curved, fanciful shell somewhat resembles a falling leaf, but its fragile look contradicts its elastic strength. It has proved through the years to be one of the most popular chairs made in Denmark.

Jacobsen also designed the *Ægget* ("egg") and *Svanan* ("swan") chairs in 1958 for installation in two Copenhagen hotels. These chairs of sculptured simplicity resting lightly on chrome pedestals have greatly influenced subsequent chair designs. The smoothness of their thinly padded upholstered surfaces is devoid of any extraneous detail that would mar their pure forms.

Denmark was not the only Scandinavian country to develop furniture of beautiful form. Sweden, too, began to produce furniture early in the 1920s and by the 1930s had a rational approach to design, which has had remarkable durability. The Swedish Exhibition at the New World's Fair of 1939 showed interiors and furniture that were called Swedish Modern. Photographs of these rooms look extraordinarily "contemporary," appearing to be of much more recent vintage than they are. This furniture proves most convincingly that well-designed objects seldom appear "dated."

Bruno Mathsson (b. 1907) is Sweden's most noted designer and furniture-maker and has consistently produced furniture of technical and aesthetic brilliance. For over four decades he has refined and perfected the use of laminated-wood chair and table frames. He uses thin layers of wood with parallel direction of grain, which are glued, bent, and shaped into the desired slender forms. The resulting thin, ribbon-like forms belie their strength. Mathson originated the use of webbing rather than padded upholstery as the seating surface. Consequently, Mathsson's chairs are light in weight and appearance, but are still remarkably comfortable because of his careful attention to *human* forms and postures.

The furniture designed in Finland, the most eastern of the Scandinavian countries, tends to be less rational and less prone to common-sense stolidness than does furniture designed in the other Scandinavian countries. This does not imply that Finnish furniture lacks design sense or functional attributes, but there is something light and gay about most Finnish furniture that is missing in other Scandinavian furniture. There is a little extra twist or detail that sets most Finnish furniture apart.

The most distinguished architect and furniture designer in Finland is Alvar Aalto. It is primarily his work that first gave impetus to the modern movement in Finland. Born in 1898, Aalto's innovative and original treatment of living spaces is matched by his original furniture designs. Since the early 1930s, he has been exploring the possibilities of using bent laminated wood in furniture. His early curvilinear chair made of bent plywood translated some of the existing designs of steel tubing into wood, but the billowing sheet of plywood that forms the seat and back is his own. The silky grain and natural spring that is inherent in the native birch wood is exploited with almost unequaled skill in this chair. Birch is used for most of Aalto's other designs.

19-60 *The structural and technical possibilities of curving sheets of birch plywood were admirably realized in Aalto's lounge chair, 1935.*

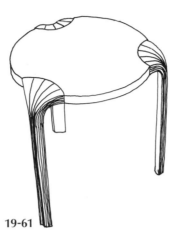

19-61

Through the years Aalto has developed other chairs and furniture forms using laminated wood, and in 1954 he evolved a stool of extraordinary pleasing design. Aalto did not follow the traditional concept of legs being "attached" to a top but was more "organic" in his design approach. From the circular ash or leather covered seat "grow" three laminated legs. These legs are not only constructed of thin sheets of wood glued together, one upon another, but are also composed of five sections glued side to side. The result is a refined interpretation of the living tree.

Aalto lived in the United States from 1940 to 1949 as a professor at the Massachusetts Institute of Technology and was one of the leading teachers of architecture and design in the eastern United States. Aalto is considered by many critics of twentieth-century architecture to be as important as Wright, le Corbusier, and Mies, and his influence is still evident in the work of many of his students.

Most of these Scandinavian designers have not limited their talents to the field of furniture. None, however, has been as versatile as Finland's Ilmari Tapiovaara (b. 1914), who has not only designed some interesting and functional furniture but also toys, glass, lighting fixtures, ceramics, and houses.[31] He first became known in 1941 when he designed a wooden stacking chair called the *Domus*. With a solid wood frame and molded plywood seat and back, it became the prototype for a later version with metal legs. The method of construction is easily seen by the exposed screws that attach the seat and back to the frame.

None of the Scandinavian furniture that has been discussed was designed within the last decade. It is furniture, however, that is still being produced and has been most influential in setting a style. The furniture being designed and made today in northern Europe shows a great deal of influence from the

19-62 *The 1941 Domus Stacking chair by Ilmari Tapiovaara, despite the truncated appearance of the arms, is a sturdy, comfortable wooden chair.*

[31] Tapiovaara lives in Tapiola, Finland in a four-family row house that he and his three architect neighbors designed and which sits upon a single foundation.

19-63 *Throughout the history of design, styles often linger after they have been replaced in the leading fashion centers. This light standard outside a 1935 elementary school in Illinois reflects the eventual commercialization of Art Deco.*

19-64 *An armchair of molded fiberglass
(1950) by Charles Eames. This chair resulted from design experiments based upon
the entry that Eames and Saarinen submitted for the "Organic Design in Home
Furnishings" competition. Its one-piece body
and metal legs have been interpreted and
copied countless times by other designers.*

Italian designers who have recently come to dominate the field of furniture.
The patina of hand-rubbed natural wood has given way, in part, to the look
of metal and plastics. The designs of the Scandinavians are, however, more
disciplined than the Italians and retain the "classic" look. Wood is still a
popular material, along with the newer molded plastics and metals, but
instead of having a natural finish, much of the wood is now painted or
stained in brilliant colors or bleached almost white.

Practically all of the furniture produced in the United States before World
War II was based upon past styles. Machine-made residential furniture
showed little indication of any of the outstanding inventive and original
designs that were currently being developed at the Bauhaus or evolving in
Scandinavia. And yet, there were evidences of the awareness of the newer
stylistic developments. In 1929, the Metropolitan Museum of Art in New
York had an exhibition called The Architect and the Industrial Arts
addressed primarily to the Art Deco style. In the next Metropolitan exhibition five years later, the emphasis was more toward the Bauhaus approach to
design. As a result of these two exhibitions, commercial establishments and
kitchens in this country began to gleam with chrome tubing. Based upon the
chrome tubing furniture of the Bauhaus, but with the restrained elegance of
the original designs frequently missing, restaurants, lunch counters, and
stores of all kinds went "modern," and the ubiquitous chrome "dinette set"
filled the corners of many American kitchens during the 1930s and 1940s.
The dinette chairs, influenced by Breuer's original design, clearly showed
that exact proportions and workmanship were as necessary in machine-made
furniture as they were in handcrafted furniture.

The Museum of Modern Art in New York held a competition in 1940 for
"Organic Design in Home Furnishings." The winners were two young
architects, Eero Saarinen (1910–1961) and Charles Eames (b. 1907). Their
revolutionary design for a chair is one of the most significant innovations in
the history of seating furniture. The chair consists of the back, seat, and arms

19-65 *Two versions of the famous "petal" chair (1946). The lounge version on the left has a lower and wider seat. The chair is still available; however, the bent plywood legs have been replaced by tubular steel.*

molded into a single multicurved shell, made of laminated veneer and glue, and formed in a cast-iron mold. (The shell is padded with a thin layer of foam rubber and covered with fabric.) In the original design, the legs were to be aluminum rods, but the war had caused a shortage of that metal, so that the first interpretations of the chair had wooden legs. The significance of this chair is compound: a) the basic form and construction methods that predict plastic furniture fabrication, b) the use of thin foam padding on curved shells instead of thick padding on flat surfaces, c) the use of attached metal rods for legs instead of integral wooden legs, and d) a minimum number of individual components required to form the chair.

Eames introduced his famous molded plywood side chair in 1946. An outgrowth of the original 1940 design, the chair has two thin plywood multicurved planes that served as the seat and back (the similarity to flower petals or potato chips was not ignored by admirers and critics). The support can be either a frame of thin metal rods or curved plywood and the curved plywood seat and back are attached by electronically welded rubber disks. The basic chair design has been adjusted by Eames to different heights and widths and is available in lounge and dining versions.

The long period of experimentation required to produce this aesthetically pleasing and surprisingly comfortable unpadded wooden chair was far from wasted. In addition to the "petal" (Eames prefers this term to "potato chip") chair, he introduced, in 1950, a new interpretation of his 1940 armchair in polyester plastic reinforced with fiberglass, again available in different heights, widths, bases, and colors. Not content, Eames again, in 1960, designed his upholstered lounge chair and ottoman. This chair of separate elements backed with molded laminated rosewood and lushly padded with down-filled soft leather cushions is supported on a swivel pedestal base. Its elegant and luxurious richness has endeared it to interior designers and architects since its introduction and is one of the most frequently used modern lounge chairs ever designed.

19-66 A lounge chair of great comfort and beauty. Owning this chair by Saarinen and the "petal" chair by Eames was the dream of virtually all young married couples after World War II.

19-67 The pedestal chair is the first chair to completely break with the design tradition started by the Egyptians before 3000 B.C. The one-piece molded seat, back, and arms are supported by one superbly proportioned pedestal. The cast aluminum base joins the fiberglass top portion without a break in the smooth, upward movement of the pedestal form.

Eames has also designed several chairs of steel wire mesh that utilizes the tensile strength of metal to its fullest potential (1951). Light, and almost invisible without the seat covering; one version has a one piece cover that leaves the back wire frame exposed, but an even more minimal and unusual style has the cover in two pieces joined with a buttoned loop in a strong "V" shape.

Eames has continued to be one of America's most prolific furniture designers. Each of his designs, whether chairs, modular storage pieces, or office components, clearly shows his appreciation and complete understanding of mass-production methods and techniques, and the inherent possibilities of materials, *plus* his fertile and imaginative mind, not hampered by hidebound traditional concepts. His furniture is engineered to exact specifications governed by human proportions, materials, and function.

Eero Saarinen was one of America's outstanding architects before his untimely death, but in the twenty years after his joint prize-winning chair design with Charles Eames, he also designed some outstanding furniture. An upholstered side chair of fabric covered foam rubber and plastic with metal legs was Saarinen's first success, followed shortly by a lounge chair. The graceful ribbons of laminated birch forming the arm-legs lightly support the angled frame between. Available in both a webbed or an upholstered version, the one-piece seat back breaks direction exactly at the points required for body comfort. The subtle variations of width and direction evidenced upon examination in this chair prove the early design skill of Saarinen.

His 1948 *Womb* chair surpassed even the ingenious lounge chair and guaranteed his fame as an exceptional designer. An expanded interpretation of the chair design of eight years earlier the "Womb," however, is even more comfortable and includes within its wide, undulating, thin sculptured form two loose cushions. The molded plastic shell, lightly padded with foam and smoothly upholstered, rests gently upon a framework of metal rods.

Saarinen achieved his greatest triumph when he designed the single pedestal chair and table (1957). The elimination of all but one slender support emerging smoothly from a thin disk on the floor gave a purity that is seldom equaled in any furniture design. The chairs are more akin to delicate goblets or chalices than to the chairs of the past. The bases are made of weighted cast aluminum and the upper seat and back units are one-piece molded fiberglass reinforced plastic. The upper units are similar to Eames' fiberglass reinforced plastic. The upper units are similar to Eames' fiberglass chairs but take on a new significance when combined with the pristine bases. The tables, like the chairs, have no break between the base and the top, but seem to flow effortlessly up and out to their rim. Like most of the furniture of Eames and Saarinen, they are available in large and small, high and low versions.

Needless to say, the furniture of these two ingenious and creative designer-architects has been copied countless times, and translations of their designs have been made in all grades and faithfulness. A cursory examination, however, will quickly identify the original furniture by its exquisite craftsmanship and skillful handling of materials.

Of chairs designed by others, the famous Hardoy chair (1938) must not be overlooked, although it does not fall within a specific category. Designed by three Argentinians, Jorge Ferrari-Hardoy, Antonio Bonet, and Juan Kurchan, it is based upon a wooden folding chair used by Italian soldiers in North Africa. Relying on the principle of a suspended sling in a frame, the Hardoy chair is a rigid cradle of welded steel rods from which a leather cover is hung by its four corners. Being one of the least costly chairs to produce, the proliferation of inexpensive versions of this chair with canvas slings is known to everyone. However, the integrity of the original design has been preserved in almost every version and attests to the excellence of the original concept.

Little reference has been made to twentieth-century furniture other than chairs. The omission was not intended to indicate a lack of design development but rather reflects the greater changes that were made in the design of

19-68 *The Hardoy chair.*

chairs in this century than were made in tables, beds, and chests. The introduction of modular components to construct storage walls, which took place mainly since World War II, has altered many of the storage habits of the past, and many designers have developed new storage systems. Adequate storage is a serious problem today because of the increased amount of objects that are "required" and must be stored from one season or time to the next, and because houses are generally smaller and often without attics, basements, and "storerooms." Modular storage units, whether freestanding and movable, or built-in, can provide more efficient storage in a given space than most other solutions. The building-in of furniture has also increased in recent years and, with the exception of the chair, every type of furniture now used can be built-in.

Beds have remained practically the same since the beginning of the twentieth century. A headboard usually accompanies a matching lower footboard, and bed sizes have been standardized (double bed size (75 inches by 54 inches), and twin size (75 inches by 38 inches). However, what was slept *upon* has drastically changed. Prior to the 1920s, the most common bed support was a cotton-felt mattress resting on coil springs. Large feather beds (like huge pillows) were also used. In 1921, the first innerspring mattress accompanied by a box spring (a set of springs enclosed in a slightly padded cloth cover) was introduced and afforded much greater comfort than was previously possible. The innerspring remained the standard mattress until the introduction of foam rubber and later urethane foam mattresses.[32] Beds have also increased in size. In addition to the twin and double sizes, queen size (80 inches by 60 inches) and king size (80 inches by 78 inches) beds are

[32] The use of foam (rubber or plastic) has revolutionized upholstery methods. Regardless of the style of padded and upholstered furniture, today one or more of the foam padding materials are used almost invariably. In many pieces foam materials have completely replaced coil spring construction. Several newer examples of seating furniture have no rigid frame, relying upon varying densities of foam to give substance to the furniture.

now available. In the late 1960s, *water beds,* large plastic bags filled with water usually set in a wooden framework, were introduced and have been enthusiastically received by the "young adult" consumers. Prime considerations in water bed selection is the necessity for exceptional waterproof construction and the adequate structural support for the inherent weight of the bed.

It is interesting to note how many architects have designed furniture. Practically every architect of note since the Renaissance has attempted the design of a chair, for example. Disregarding successes and failures, the rationale for this fact is a provoking and intriguing question. The need for compatible furniture for the architect's structure may be important, or perhaps the simple desire to create a functional, intimate object is significant.

The leadership in furniture design has changed in the past ten years. The exciting and original designs of the United States and Scandinavia during the 1940s and 1950s have relinquished their foremost place to the developments in Italy. The Italian influence in furniture design and manufacture has been overwhelming and some of the most original and aesthetically satisfying designs in plastics and synthetic materials have been employed, challenging for the first time in history the dominance of wood furniture.

Gio Ponti (b. 1891) has been one of the major innovators in Italian architecture, furniture, and product design for the past several decades. His exceptional Chiavari chair is clearly a descendant of the ladder-back peasant chairs found throughout Europe, for example, the *chaise à capucine* in France. However, the Chiavari is the epitome of exquisite refinement. The delicate crisply but subtly sculptured elements are pared to their extreme limits. The high standards of design and craftsmanship of this chair have seldom been challenged and have been universally admired since the chair was introduced in 1950. Ponti has been extremely instrumental in developing and promoting Italian design and is largely responsible for the new renaissance in Italian furniture.

The furniture developed in Europe and the United States within the past

19-69 *The exceptional grace and delicate precision of Gio Ponti's version of the traditional ladder-back chair must be seen to be fully appreciated. The careful shaping and reduction to the barest visual and structural essentials has produced a wooden chair of sculptural beauty.*

19-70 *The Soriana Series designed by Italy's Afra and Tobia Scarpa (1970) reflect the return to "soft" furniture. Having a wooden base and chromium-plated steel exterior frame, the main body of these comfortable pieces is different densities of polyurethane foam.* **Courtesy of Atelier International, Ltd.**

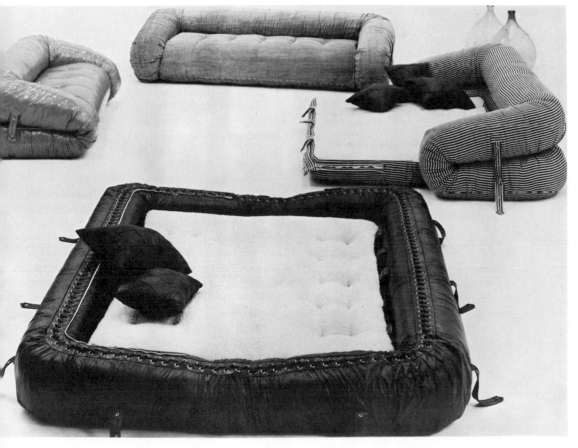

19-71 *Versatile and comfortable, this Italian sofabed called Anfibio was designed by Alessandro Becchi. Zippers, buckles and lacing hold the polyurethane and dacron filled components together in a variety of ways. This design clearly expresses today's multi-functional life style.*

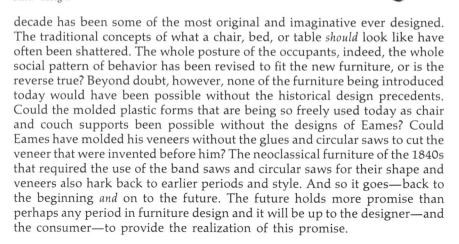

19-72 *These three side chairs clearly illustrate the historical development and the ultimate perfection of a chair design. The unique wooden chair at right was designed in 1934 by the Dutch designer Gerrit Reitveld. The center chair is of molded plastic and echoes the "Z" form of Reitveld's chair, however, it was designed by Verner Panton, the Danish designer, in 1968. The chair at bottom was also designed by Panton and was introduced in 1974. It has a tubular metal frame that is spanned with a fiberglass surface, padded with polyurethane foam, and covered with a removable cover of stretch fabric all gently poised on a polished chrome disk. Although the design of each chair is elegantly simple, the third chair exhibits a sophistication of design seldom achieved in contemporary chair design.*

decade has been some of the most original and imaginative ever designed. The traditional concepts of what a chair, bed, or table *should* look like have often been shattered. The whole posture of the occupants, indeed, the whole social pattern of behavior has been revised to fit the new furniture, or is the reverse true? Beyond doubt, however, none of the furniture being introduced today would have been possible without the historical design precedents. Could the molded plastic forms that are being so freely used today as chair and couch supports been possible without the designs of Eames? Could Eames have molded his veneers without the glues and circular saws to cut the veneer that were invented before him? The neoclassical furniture of the 1840s that required the use of the band saws and circular saws for their shape and veneers also hark back to earlier periods and style. And so it goes—back to the beginning *and* on to the future. The future holds more promise than perhaps any period in furniture design and it will be up to the designer—and the consumer—to provide the realization of this promise.

Afterword

*If one advances confidently in
the direction of his dreams and
endeavors to live the life which he
has imagined, he will meet with
success unexpected in common hours.*

Henry David Thoreau

Through the three and a half centuries of European civilization in the Western Hemisphere, the right of the individual has been paramount in the minds of most men. Perhaps more than any other country, the United States has exemplified the freedom of individual expression and has often set an example for the rest of the world. Each American citizen has steadfastly believed that he has the right to decide his own actions. Recently, this tradition of American ideology has been challenged by scholars and commentators of the current scene who contend that this is no longer a valid premise. Seldom can anyone now wholly decide what constitutes his way of life, his social contacts, or his environmental components. As stated in Chapter 6, decisions pertaining to almost every aspect of our lives are determined by some one or some agency, often removed from our own immediate presence, and only within the walls of his own home can the twentieth-century American citizen enjoy relative self-expression. It is there that he is less controlled by others and his actions and decisions can be more freely his own. Elsewhere, it is well nigh impossible today to be completely free of the influence of others. The fabled "desert island" retreat is not available to many of us. However, it is vitally important for individuals to be able to make or at least participate in making decisions and especially those that concern our environment. For without this feeling of participation, human beings tend to "turn off" and seemingly do not care. But we *must* care! We must be a part and contribute to the betterment of our surroundings. No longer can any individual afford nor can society allow the nonparticipating and unconcerned citizen this alternative.

This brings us to a second consideration. Since we in the United States have always championed the right of the individual to his freedom of expression, it follows that he has the right of property. In other words, he has the right to do anything he desires to or with his property. In the past, if this "basic right" was repeatedly challenged, the individual frequently either pulled up stakes and moved farther west, or fought back, often violently. Today, circumstances forbid such actions and we must now alter our thinking on this right of property. We do not condone violence (although, sadly, there is much in our world), and there are few places left where we can go to start anew.

We all must acknowledge the right of *all* property, not just our own. Gestalt-like in theory, we must all admit that in the contemporary world we live in, what one person does to his property affects the properties around it. There can be no isolationism. The Gestaltists expound that the whole is greater than the sum of its parts and that we must consider the whole as more important than an individual part. Past philosophers and ordinary citizens often believed that the individual parts became the whole, and by concentrating on the parts, the problems of the whole would be solved. The present condition of our near and far environment proves that this attitude is far from reality. Therefore, everyone *must* concentrate his efforts upon the *whole* environment and *then* and only then make decisions concerning the smaller components.

There is no conflict between the need for individual expression and the concern for the whole environment. The expression of an individual's ideals concerning his environment when planning is being done is healthy and an indication of good involvement. Decisions should be made only after an abundance of individual input and thoughtful and thorough consideration by knowledgeable persons who are concerned for the betterment of the whole environment and not motivated by personal gain. After the decisions have been made, however, it is then the responsibility of everyone to act in accordance with the decisions. There is no other way to retain a semblance of individuality and still maintain and improve the environment in which we must live.

In thinking of many people, experts and nonexperts alike, one of the greatest determinants that affects all of our lives is the "commercial interests." Undoubtedly, our world would not be as it is if manufacturers, salesmen, and their outlets—the stores and shops of America—did not produce the merchandise that is available today. Right or wrong, good or bad, it is primarily the consumer who causes the continual dispersal of a certain product, for if it is not commercially profitable, there are few firms that will continue to make it. It is, therefore, up to the consumer to select and choose with care and discrimination.

Almost every product now being made becomes in some degree a component of our environment. However, in this book we have been primarily

A-1 *The omnipresent "mansard" roof at its worst, appearing as if it had sunk below the sidewalk, this restaurant building is actually an extension of the house behind it. Must we be subjected to such visual and functional atrocities as this?*

concerned with the design of exterior and interior spaces and the major objects that fill them. The difference between what is now technically, materially, and conceptually possible and the vast majority of current urban planning, furniture and architectural design and construction now being developed for the people of the United States is, unfortunately, great. As we have discussed, some of the more "human" urban developments have been built in Scandinavia, yet in America, with too few exceptions, our urban renewal projects and regional "improvements" have tended to compound the errors and problems rather than alleviate them. Some of the major non-residential architecture in the United States is increasingly exciting and innovative. New materials and techniques are being used and developed with insight and experimentation, but on the other hand, buildings of lesser commercial importance and design are mushrooming at such a prolific rate that it is rare in most urban areas to see a truly well-designed structure. Burlesques of materials and stylistic forms far surpass the excellent buildings. The major portion of residential construction, too, is almost devoid of merit. The gulf between the outstanding and the ordinary grows wider each year.

The preponderance of residential architecture built in the United States since World War II, disregarding most of what has been built in the entire twentieth century, has not been experimental and innovative, but unfortunately, has been based upon pseudohistoric styles. It is the rare street in America that cannot offer the observer a short, but often very inaccurate, history of domestic architecture. The split-level house with the classical columned portico sits next to the fake Tudor-cottage ranch house, and on the corner or in the next block stands a Spanish hacienda duplex with attached garages. Sadly, this is true even in the most recently developed areas, regardless of the quality and price of the houses.

To enhance the "authenticity," the house designs and the subdivision areas are invariably labeled with such historical names as "Colonial Dutch,"

A-2 *The failure to comprehend basic design and historical architectural styles often results in structures that are devoid of aesthetic merit. Although design insensibilities are not confined to any one architectural style, geographic region, or economic level, this house is a case in point. Obviously inspired by French châteaux and carefully maintained, even a cursory analysis of the facade reveals that the two wings that extend at obtuse angles have corner pilasters that do not reach the "minicornice" (one of the wings contains the garage, incidentally). The windows also appear to be too low and to compensate, the builder (I hesitate to use the term designer) has applied what appears to be permanent flat window shades above. The mansard roof is pierced by two small arched dormer windows that give the central block of the house the surprised look of a jack-o-lantern.*

Williamsburg West," Cape Cod Acres," "Hillside Manor," "Crestwood Abbey," "Heathcliff Drive," or "Tudor Arms Condominium" (and it usually seems the more aristocratic the name the lower is the price range). And yet, despite the obvious attempt to "traditionalize" these homes, they are not without twentieth-century innovations, that is, glass-walled extensions or at least a "patio door" or two, central heating and cooling, inside bathrooms, a kitchen equipped with the latest electrical and gas appliances, split-level floor plans, and living areas instead of isolated rooms. The important point is that responding to this type of salesmanship must indicate the consumers' need for a "heritage." Yet, they do not actually want to live as their forefathers did, but are eager to accept "improvements."

The interior furnishings are no better and are attempts to express the times and materials of another era, because the furniture forms seldom reflect the more advanced thinking of the late or even the entire twentieth-century designers. It would seem much less of a tragic parody if original period furniture or even faithful reproductions were selected, but usually the houses are filled with feeble attempts to disguise machine-made mass-produced furniture with traditional fakery.

The tragedy of it all is that the excellent and worthy original architectural and furniture styles have been so abused as to site, materials[1], scale, and time

---

[1] The current availability of traditionally designed furniture and architectural details and devices made of nontraditional materials raises the specter of the integrity of design. For example, it is now possible to obtain columns, capitals, bricks, clapboard siding, beams, moldings, carved panels, shingles, rough stucco surfaces, and even entire pieces of furniture made of various metals, plastics, and other synthetic materials. The appearance of these materials is often quite true to the originals, and their installation, maintenance, and lasting qualities are frequently as good or better than the original. However, can such rationalization justify this inane copying of traditional design and this flagrant disregard of the time honored designer's creed of "Truth to Materials?" No, it should not! Other more truthful designs should be evolved for these excellent materials.

A-3 *The design of this house discloses the designer's knowledge of historical styles, awareness of environmental setting, and understanding of design considerations. The house has a totality of concept and, although it reproduced a house type of the past and undoubtedly had to be adapted for today's living, the results are aesthetically pleasing.*

that we must question what really is the purpose of such deceit. Are those who live in these travesties and with these impostors under the illusion that their homes signify taste, wealth, or heritage? We must assume they are, but the true connotation is more likely the reverse.

The reader is undoubtedly asking, "If houses built today and the furniture that fills them are based upon historical models and are given names reflecting an historical heritage and yet are both considered wrong, then *why* has there been such emphasis upon historical styles in this book?" Original design, like almost every other creative act, must be based upon experience. The designer must know what has been done, what ideas have failed as well as succeeded, so that he may avoid or profit from past decisions and then innovatively proceed toward his goal. "Without a foundation there is no stability" is a truth that is particularly applicable to design, the design of the most simple object or the most complex structure. It has never been the intention of this book to emphasize historical design for itself, but to provide the historical background for decisions affecting today, and yes, tomorrow. We must always plan, design, and steadily look toward the future. Santayana has stated, "Those who forget the past are condemned to repeat it"; William Butler Yeats put it this way, "How but in custom and in ceremony are innocence and beauty born?" And Frank Lloyd Wright said, "I believe that out of the past comes the best of the present and that out of the present comes the future."

The fault of much recent architectural and furniture design has been that the integrity of historical design has been lost or ignored, because rather than *developing* from the past (and only yesterday must here be considered the past), the past has only been superficially *copied*. The past thus becomes a shell, rigid and unyielding, whereas it should provide concepts and qualities that can serve as inspiration. Man, as far as is known, is the only animal capable of looking forward by the force of looking backward, an accomplishment that, if successful, can enhance life as little else can.

A-4 *Old buildings of considerable architectural merit survive in many of our cities. This reserved, cast-iron example remains, yet its first floor now suffers from the thoughtless indignity common to the midtwentieth century—lack of design unity.*

Ironically, the very structures that could provide the background for new designs are frequently ignored and allowed to be destroyed. Some of America's finest buildings, both commercial and residential, have been wantonly demolished when they were still structurally sound and could have been profitably utilized. In their stead, we have, almost without exception, been forced to tolerate mediocre, poorly designed structures or, the bane of all citizens, parking lots. Of course, not every old building is constructionally sound or stylistically valuable, but those that are outstanding should be preserved at all cost for they can never be replaced. The current neglect of our architectural heritage by "responsible" city officials and citizens alike must stop. It is far better to preserve excellent buildings of all ages than to subject the people of today, *and of the future,* to commonplace and banal structures that ofttimes are currently being built.

Despite this seemingly pessimistic attitude, I am repeatedly thrilled with design developments that are new, humanized, and innovative. Some of the most original concepts in the fields of urban, architectural, and furniture design have evolved within the last twenty-five years. Of course, some of these designs may prove to be in need of revisions, but they strike out in new directions and open wide the essential doors of experimentation. I am particularly impressed with the often amazing developments in furniture design wherein new materials, processes, and construction techniques have been combined with original thinking. This creative approach to all environmental design, even if too minimal, is most heartening.

Even though I am impressed and excited with the innovative, contemporary furniture and architecture currently being produced, and distressed with the tragic and abhorrent misrepresentation of traditional styles, I find nothing remiss when furniture and architectural design of different periods are combined in a total design consideration, but they must be authentic in style and used with taste and discretion. The inclusion of individual pieces of furniture and accessories of another period enhances any interior and when,

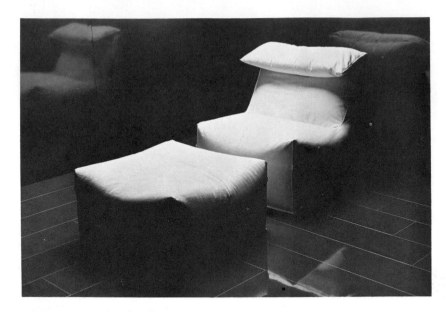

A-5 *The deceptively simple pillow-like forms in this lounge are only possible because of the different densities of synthetic foams combined with a rigid under structure.* Courtesy of Atelier International, Ltd.

for example, period furniture is combined with more contemporary pieces (one style dominating, of course) their contrasting detail, structure, materials, or forms can be stunningly effective. However, again, it takes stylistic and design knowledge and consummate skill to combine furniture and architectural styles in this eclectic manner; yet I would prefer a somewhat successful attempt to do so, than no attempt at all. The most dreary of interiors are the "safe, all-one-style" interiors, and this is true regardless of whether they are "traditional," "period," "modern," or "contemporary."

The frequent question of whether a particular style is "right" for a certain effect has no basis. The elegance, warmth, formality, friendliness, comfort, or design characteristics associated with a particular time can be achieved without strictly adhering to the dominant style of the period. It is entirely false to assume that a traditional interior or house design is the only one that exudes warmth and comfort, for example. It is just as incorrect to think that modern or contemporary design indicates the "last word." Any desired feeling or quality can be achieved in an interior, an entire house, or even a neighborhood by the judicious selection of forms, elements, and details and not just by strict stylistic adherence. This, by the way, is not a contradiction to my previous statements. It is rather a *caveat* against poor, ignorant, and misrepresented design.

I finished the Foreword of this book with my personal maxim—"If you have two loaves, sell one and buy hyacinths." Since writing that last sentence and throughout the preparation of the manuscript, my awareness of the deep insight and truthfulness of this Persian proverb has been repeatedly confirmed. During each stylistic period reviewed, there are many evidences that the individual's need for food for the soul is almost as demanding as the need for food for the body. It was true generations ago and it is true today. We have only to go to the nearest market or store to see the infinite variety of articles for sale that purportedly visually enhances our environment. Seldom do we find a person who does not in some way react or who is unaware of

A-6 *Contemporary consumers are exceedingly fortunate; beauty is not limited to past ages. This group of chairs, illustrating a variety of periods and national origins, designers, and materials, is a representative sampling of currently available designs from European and American chair manufacturers.*

A-7 *The smooth, flowing surfaces of this innovative fiberglass rocking chair by Larry Bell express the inherent beauty of the material and are the synthesis of the designer's considerable technical knowledge, complete understanding of the qualities of the material, and cognizance of historical furniture styles tempered by a sound design background.* Courtesy of Larry Bell.

beauty. In recent years the word *beauty* has not enjoyed the reputation and usage it once had in critical discussions, but despite this seemingly omission or slight, most individuals still ascribe to aesthetic modifiers, that is, "pleasant" surroundings, "attractive" designs, "lovely" colors, "harmonious" forms, and so forth. Each of us has developed a different level of taste and appreciation that has been acquired through our education, background, and inclination, and unless we are completely dehumanized by the negative forces in our contemporary culture, we instinctively react in some manner to the aesthetic qualities that we perceive.

My stated purpose in writing this book was to broaden the foundations of critical awareness, that is, to augment the affective as well as the cognitive knowledge of the reader—the student of environmental design and the interested layman. I have pointed out that basic design considerations are the underlying structure of all consumer products and that each object, man-made or natural, in our environment can be critically analyzed by using the elements and principles of design. Whether we are consciously aware of such criteria or not, each of us does use them. We consider the color, we consider the form, and we consider the function of each item in each choice that we make.

However fundamental design considerations may be, they are not, of course, the only criteria that we encounter. There are also the qualities of individual materials, techniques, and processes, the previously cited historical design heritage, and the inherent concept of beauty. Each material available to the designer and craftsman has inherent characteristics that are unique to it alone. Some materials can assume the qualities of others, and the designer, and indeed the consumer too, must be incessantly cognizant of this and make evaluative judgments accordingly. The number and scope of the technological developments experienced during the past quarter century have been legion and together nearly overshadow *all* the developments of the past. The rapid changes wrought by today's expanding technology must also be carefully considered if we are to maintain the credible quality of our environmental components and of the environment itself.

The first responsibility of every designer of the environment, regardless of his scope, area, or field of concentration, must be to design and develop ideas, concepts, and philosophies that will aid those who are not as conversant with environmental concerns. He must take an active part in environmental decision-making and fight with persuasive evidence that the apathy and ignorance toward design that permeates much of the public's thinking today must not be condoned. He must help to develop and intensify a conscientious public design awareness as it is the responsibility of *everyone* to take an active part in the aesthetic as well as the functional planning of *our* environment. For, if we are thinking individuals and are knowledgeable as we must be, we then can better judge the potential outcomes from which we shall all benefit.

ndex

535